Gloria Grahame,
Bad Girl of Film Noir

Gloria Grahame,
Bad Girl of Film Noir

The Complete Career

Robert J. Lentz

McFarland & Company, Inc., Publishers

Jefferson, North Carolina, and London

ALSO BY ROBERT J. LENTZ AND FROM MCFARLAND

*Korean War Filmography: 91 English Language
Features through 2000* (2003; paperback 2008)

Lee Marvin: His Films and Career
(2000; paperback 2006)

Frontispiece: Gloria Grahame, as she appears in the 1950 drama *In a Lonely Place*, at that point the largest, and finest, role of her career. Gloria was directed by her second husband, Nicholas Ray, and the film echoes the disintegration of their relationship.

LIBRARY OF CONGRESS CATALOGUING-IN-PUBLICATION DATA

Lentz, Robert J., 1960–
Gloria Grahame, bad girl of film noir :
the complete career / Robert J. Lentz.
p.   cm.
Includes bibliographical references and index.
Includes filmography.

ISBN 978-0-7864-3483-1
softcover : 50# alkaline paper ∞

1. Grahame, Gloria.
2. Actors— United States— Biography.
I. Title.
PN2287.G665L46 2011   791.4302'8092—dc23   [B]   2011031681

BRITISH LIBRARY CATALOGUING DATA ARE AVAILABLE

Front cover: Gloria Grahame in *The Cobweb*, 1955 (Photofest)

Manufactured in the United States of America

*McFarland & Company, Inc., Publishers
Box 611, Jefferson, North Carolina 28640
www.mcfarlandpub.com*

For my wife Barbara,
who has patiently remained
by my side through everything

and for Gloria Grahame,
a beautiful lady whose career choices
sometimes obscured her remarkable talent

Table of Contents

Preface and Acknowledgments

This book is a comprehensive analysis of the film and television work of the beautiful and talented actress Gloria Grahame. The book explores her motion picture jobs from her earliest days in "Soundies" (1943–44) until her final film, *The Nesting*, which was released the year of her death, 1981. During her rise to stardom in the late 1940s, Gloria graduated from small, sexy parts to co-starring status with some of filmdom's finest actors. The 1950s were her heyday, when she fashioned a memorable *film noir* persona, co-starred in some of the decade's biggest films and won an Academy Award. Her tempestuous personal life led her out of stardom by the end of the 1950s but she returned to supporting roles in major films and made-for-television productions in the early 1970s, then successfully battled cancer into remission. A second bout with breast cancer finally felled Gloria, but not before she had fulfilled her lifetime ambition to play Shakespeare on the stage, and created a legacy of outstanding performances in many classic movies and stage plays.

This book is not intended to be Gloria Grahame's biography. It is, rather, an examination of her working life, based on the thesis that a performer's career can (and perhaps should) be evaluated on her performances and films rather than on the personal details of her life (her family and friends and lovers, the famous people with whom she became acquainted), however entertaining those details may be. Too many biographies focus on a performer's private life while ignoring what made that person famous in the first place. Even Vincent Curcio's valuable and incisive 1989 biography of Gloria, the unfortunately titled *Suicide Blonde*, contains factual errors and misstatements regarding her film work, and doesn't devote nearly as much attention to her movies as Gloria's fans would have liked. Gloria appeared in some absolutely wonderful movies (as well as a few deplorable turkeys) and they all deserve critical attention.

As I did with my earlier Lee Marvin book (*Lee Marvin: His Films and Career*), I have constructed this movie reference book as a documentation of Gloria's work on screen and television. Her thirty-nine feature films are discussed chronologically, with full casts and credits, followed by detailed synopses and thorough commentary regarding the film itself and its place in history. Gloria's performances are discussed in detail, with attention given to her personal life during production and how each project moved her career forward (or, in a few cases, backward). Following the feature film chapters are similar entries for Gloria's eight made-for-television movies, miniseries and television specials. A brief listing of Gloria's television series appearances concludes the book's text. I have also included appendices regarding Gloria's films and stage appearances, and the brief film career of her older sister, Joy Hallward.

It is my intent and hope that this exploration of Gloria's career is viewed as worthwhile by her fervent fans (of which there remain many), to people who have encountered her performances and want to know more about her, and to purely casual movie fans as well. Gloria Grahame was a terrific actress and a fascinating person. I hope this book does justice to her memory.

I would like to thank everyone who helped make this book a reality. Madeline F. Matz, Zoran Sinobad and the staff of the Library of

Congress; Kristine Krueger and the staff of the Margaret Herrick Library; Emma Smart and Victoria Crabbe of the British Film Institute; and the staff of the New York Public Library of the Performing Arts at Lincoln Center were all very helpful guiding and furthering my research.

Many thanks to the people and organizations who helped find obscure Gloria Grahame titles: Jim Berrien, George Johnson, R. D. Mitchell, Dave Sindelar, Brian Rake, Sidney P. Bloomberg, Paul Nelson, the Library of Congress Film and Television Archive and the UCLA Film and Television Archive. Without their guidance, this book could not have been completed.

Jerry Ohlinger and the staff of Jerry Ohlinger's Movie Material Store (New York), Jim Shepard of Collector's Book Store (Hollywood), Tom Boyle and the staff of Yesterday (Chicago) and Art Harvey (New Jersey) were especially helpful in procuring stills, pressbooks and movie artwork to document Gloria's career. The *Macbeth* photo is courtesy of the Regional History Center, Northern Illinois University, DeKalb.

Studios and production companies represented by photographs and artwork include ABC-TV; American International Pictures; Andrew J. Fenady Productions; Anglia Television; the ATV Network; Bard Productions, Ltd.; Bryna Productions; the Carlin Company; CBS-TV; Charles Band Productions; Columbia Pictures; Comptoir Française du Films Productions; Contemporary Filmmakers; Dagonet Productions; David Gerber Productions, Inc.; Desilu Productions; Eric Biedermann; Fanfare Films; Fenady Associates; Four-Leaf Productions; Group 1 International Distribution Organization, Ltd.; HarBel Productions; Harve Bennett Productions; Howco International Pictures; Independent Film Distributors, Ltd.; ITC Entertainment Group; Joseph Kaufman Productions; the Katzman Corporation; Liberty Films; Liberty Mutual Insurance Company; Magna Corporation; Mark Goodson-Bill Todman Productions; MGM; National General Pictures; NBC-TV; the Nesting Company; Northern Illinois University; Orfeo Film Productions; Paramount Pictures; Paramount Television; Premiere Releasing Organization; Remus; RKO Radio Pictures; Rodgers and Hammerstein Productions; Romulus Films; Santana Productions; S. Benjamin Fisz Productions; Screen Gems Television; Sentinel Productions; the Soundies Corporation of America; Stanley Kramer Pictures Corporation; Sumar Productions; the Tiger Company; Triple Play Productions; 20th Century–Fox; United Artists; Universal Pictures; Universal Television; Vagar Films; and William Mishkin Pictures. Photographs and advertising materials are used only to illustrate the properties that are discussed and reviewed in this reference book.

Appreciation also goes to the handful of people who talked to me or responded to my queries about working with Gloria, or on projects in which she appeared. Their comments helped shape the narrative, offering views of Gloria in perspectives other than my own. As always, my friend Michael Ferguson was there for support and expertise, while my wife Barbara served as muse and proofreader, correcting my grammatical errors. Any mistakes (and most of the opinions) that appear in this book are my own.

Introduction

Some people seem fated for Hollywood stardom, and one of those was Gloria Grahame (*née* Gloria Hallward). Born on November 28, 1923, to architect Michael Hallward and his wife Jean McDougall, a Scottish actress, young Gloria spent her youth in Pasadena, California, and turned to acting while enrolled at Hollywood High School. Her mother taught acting at the Pasadena Playhouse and Gloria appeared in several stage productions before and during her prep school years. Gloria also had an older sister, Joy Hallward, who eventually made a few appearances in front of movie cameras as well (see Appendix C). Coaxed into a touring production of *Good Night, Ladies*, and chaperoned by her mother and older sister, Gloria left high school a semester early and finished by completing correspondence courses on the road. Gloria and her mother spent a year in Chicago with the show and then moved on to New York City, lured by the bright lights of Broadway.

Hard work and coaching by her mother ensured that Gloria found parts quickly; within a year, Gloria was a veteran of the Broadway stage. Spotted by an MGM talent scout in the comedy *A Highland Fling* in early 1944, young, vivacious and beautiful Gloria Hallward was signed to a standard seven-year contract by MGM's boss, Louis B. Mayer. She was all of twenty years old. It was Mayer who changed her surname from Hallward to Grahame, as he felt Hallward was too theatrical for such an All-American beauty. He settled on Grahame after he learned that Grahame was Gloria's grandmother's maiden name, and that her mother had acted under the name Jean Grahame. MGM quickly rushed her into a comedy, *Blonde Fever* (1944), in which she and Marshall Thompson were both officially "introduced" to film audiences. Despite the usual marketing ballyhoo, the movie did nothing. Gloria then spent the next two years marking time at the studio, spending most of her time being photographed in swimsuits and short shorts and the odd dress, along with the rest of the young fillies in MGM's stable of starlets.

To help pass the time, she and other MGM girls made brief USO tours to stateside armed forces bases and their environs. On one of these war bond tours, Gloria met a young Army soldier named Stanley Clements. They fell in love quickly and violently, and in one of the truly rebellious acts of her youth, Gloria didn't bother to consult her mother about him. Gloria didn't even know Stanley was an actor until they were married and he exited the Army to return to Hollywood (he had featured roles in *Going My Way* and *Salty O'Rourke* before he enlisted). Although her career was at about the same point as Stanley's at the beginning of their relationship, they soon learned that as a couple they were neither compatible nor complementary. Stanley had a gambling problem and when he drank, which became more frequent as his career stalled and hers picked up speed, he became violent. The marriage lasted from August 29, 1945, until December 16, 1947, and encompassed at least one separation along the way. After two years at MGM, Gloria's career was also in limbo, so when Frank Capra asked to borrow her for his first feature film after returning from the war, MGM agreed. The movie, *It's a Wonderful Life*, was her big breakthrough.

MGM still didn't know how to properly capitalize upon her beauty or talent, so after a few minor movies MGM sold Gloria's contract to RKO Radio Pictures. RKO had also "bor-

This mid–1940s publicity photograph of Gloria Grahame is typical of those that MGM asked their starlets to make. The setting is completely artificial and the pose is elegant, sweet and sexy without being prurient. Gloria was just 21 or 22 at the time.

rowed" Gloria for *Crossfire* in 1947, and she had netted an Academy Award nomination as a sympathetic taxi dancer. Soon after joining RKO she became romantically involved with her new director, Nicholas Ray, for whom she was making *A Woman's Secret*. The very day that Gloria divorced Stanley Clements, she married Ray. Gloria was pregnant with Nick's child, a son they named Timothy (born November 12, 1948, just five and a half months later), which was another reason for the speedy nuptials. It was Ray who directed Gloria in the acclaimed melodrama *In a Lonely Place* (yet another loan-out, this time to Columbia), which marked her first prestigious part, but which also seemed to chronicle their rapidly deteriorating marital relationship. Gloria remained married to Ray for another two years (from June 1, 1948, until August 14, 1952) but they were already living separately by the time shooting started on *In a Lonely Place*. A rising star at RKO, Ray was a temperamental personality except while he was filming; that was the only time he focused his formidable energies. If not for the pregnancy, Ray probably wouldn't have married Gloria (he later said as much), despite his attraction to her. The night they were married, Nick famously gambled away all the money he had — some $40,000 — so that she wouldn't be able to get her hands on it. He said later about Gloria, "I was infatuated with her but I didn't like her very much." Ray never fully recovered from his collision with Gloria; her actions, especially later, always haunted him and affected his relationships with his children.

In 1951, separated from Ray and released from her RKO contract, Gloria was finally on her own both personally and professionally, and she threw herself into freelance work. She co-starred in four very popular 1952 releases, including *Sudden Fear* and *The Greatest Show on Earth*. The icing on the cake was winning an Academy Award for her softly comedic role in *The Bad and the Beautiful*. Her seemingly sudden success catapulted her into stardom, which was also meteorically brief. She signed a multi-picture deal with 20th Century–Fox in late 1952 but then made only two films for them over the next four years. She fit best at Columbia, where she made more films than anywhere else during her heyday, yet even there she was something of an outsider.

Gloria married a third time in 1954, to comedy writer Cy Howard, but that marriage was just as bumpy as her others had been, lasting just three years (from August 15, 1954, until October 31, 1957). This marriage produced a daughter, Marianna (born October 1, 1956, and better known as Paulette). Howard was, like Clements and Ray before him, a volatile personality and a gambler as well. Gloria's fights with Howard, and the resulting bruises on both

of them, were legendary among their circle of acquaintances. Even so, she loved his quick wit and showmanship. Howard had created the radio shows "Life with Luigi" and "My Friend Irma" and was considered a *raconteur* on the Hollywood party circuit. However, he was unable to handle Gloria's insecurities or to prevent her from undergoing the plastic surgeries that eventually led to the numbing of her upper lip. He also tried to control aspects of her career, which resulted in clashes with executives on sets (especially on *Oklahoma!*) and hard feelings about Gloria.

By 1955 Gloria's screen persona had evolved into that with which modern audiences are familiar: the good bad girl. She is the gorgeous dame who wants some of the action and isn't above murder to get it; the mobster's moll who just wants to be ensconced in mink; the bored woman too busy enjoying nightlife to pay any attention to her husband; the other woman. A handful of these roles enabled Gloria to make her mark in post-war Hollywood *film noir*, and it is for these roles that she is most fondly remembered. Gloria had one splashy, final chance to break away from the slattern roles: the musical *Oklahoma!* Chosen for the role of Ado Annie by Richard Rodgers, Gloria (at last!) sings her own songs, quite adorably, and is delightful in the part. But Gloria (and husband Howard) became such a headache for the cast and crew for various reasons that she was tagged with the appellation "difficult," and she rarely worked in a truly major motion picture again. Although Gloria appeared in a number of popular and acclaimed films during the mid–1950s — *The Big Heat, Not as a Stranger, Oklahoma!, The Man Who Never Was* — her turbulent personal life, penchant for plastic surgery on her upper lip (she was never satisfied with it), increasingly erratic behavior and perceived eccentricities led to her rapid withdrawal from Hollywood.

Gloria's film career was winding down precipitously as her marriage to Howard ended. She spent the next several years in domestic duties, taking care of her two children and only acting on occasion. Gloria would have acted more often during this period, but after the word had spread about her problems on the *Oklahoma!* set, offers were simply not forthcoming. She wasn't lonely, for in 1958 she began

By the time Gloria made *The Big Heat* in 1953, her publicity shots were far more risqué. No longer was she a pretty but innocent young woman; now she was a mink-coated sex kitten, immodestly wearing nothing beneath the luxurious coat.

seeing the man who would become her fourth husband. They had met in 1948, when Tony Ray was only ten, and reportedly spent an afternoon of bliss together just three years later. It was this episode that caused Nicholas Ray so much pain and which abruptly ended his marriage to Gloria, as Tony Ray was Nick's son by his first wife, Jean Evans (Gloria was Nick's sec-

ond wife). After the ruckus that their afternoon rendezvous caused, Gloria didn't see Tony again until 1958, but their friendship blossomed into love and they were married in 1960. Perhaps surprisingly, Gloria's union with Tony Ray lasted more than four times longer than any of her other marriages, from May 13, 1960, until May 4, 1974.

Nicholas Ray never really recovered from Gloria romancing and marrying her stepson, Tony. Father and son were estranged for the rest of their lives. But Tony had fallen in love with Gloria that 1951 afternoon, and later, when he was old enough to learn if he could share a life with her, he returned. Their marriage produced two boys, Anthony, Jr. (born April 30, 1963), and James (born September 21, 1965). Tony, like his famous father and all of Gloria's other husbands, was also intense and temperamental, sometimes violent. He and Gloria separated a few times over the years and had a lot of financial trouble, since she wasn't working very often and he was struggling to earn a living as an actor and assistant director, yet they were still devoted to each other.

There was, of course, a public uproar when news that Gloria married Tony was finally released in 1962. Few people had known about it because the wedding was performed in Tijuana, Mexico, and because the immediate family felt it was best to keep the news private for as long as possible. The Hollywood tabloid press had a field day, insinuating that, by marrying the son of her second husband (her own stepson), Gloria was casually breaking taboos held sacred by every moral person in America. Because of the close family ties, Cy Howard repeatedly took Gloria to court claiming that she was unfit to care for their daughter Paulette, and the ensuing custody battles raged for years. The early years of the Gloria-Tony marriage were so contentious and stressful that Gloria endured a brief mental breakdown and eventually underwent shock treatments in 1964 to help clear her mind of her troubles. Naturally, movie work was out of the question; no one would hire her during this period.

However, Gloria was never far away from acting; it was in her blood. She agreed to quick guest shots on television series (usually arranged by old friends) when the itch to act could no longer be ignored, or when she needed some cash. As her children grew older, Gloria gradually forged a second career on the stage, where she had begun. As early as 1960 she began making forays into regional theater, in plays like *The Marriage-Go-Round* and *The Country Girl*. Gloria eventually fulfilled her dreams of interpreting Shakespeare on stage; and touring with a national company, as she did in *The*

Time of Your Life in 1972 with Henry Fonda. She loved the stage even more than movie work, yet she befuddled her directors because she rarely played a scene the same way twice. Each time a line of dialogue was spoken with different emphases or the timing was somehow altered. She had done the same thing on movie sets, but that simply gave directors and editors more choices (although the practice was time-consuming, costly and sometimes enraging for the directors). But on stage, her little alterations were sometimes major challenges for the other actors.

After sporadic television guest appearances and one small movie role in the 1960s (*Ride Beyond Vengeance*, 1966), Gloria returned to movies—and made-for-television movies and miniseries—in the early 1970s. About half of these were horror projects, which she abhorred but did because they were currently popular. A few of these—*Blood and Lace, Mama's Dirty Girls, Mansion of the Doomed*—are pretty dreadful. But there was also *Rich Man, Poor Man, Chilly Scenes of Winter* (aka *Head Over Heels*) and *Melvin and Howard*. She worked incessantly throughout the 1970s, whenever she could. What few people realized was why she was working so often and so strenuously.

Gloria had been diagnosed with breast cancer in 1974; through strict dieting and homeopathic remedies it had gone into remission within a year. The cancer returned with a vengeance in 1980 but this time Gloria refused to acknowledge it, or take time for treatment. Gloria simply continued to work, as much to take her mind off of her rapidly deteriorating body as to provide a monetary legacy for her children. She worked right up to the end, preparing for a stage role in *The Glass Menagerie* in London, when she finally collapsed from peritonitis (inflammation and infection of the abdominal wall). After a few days of care in London, Gloria was flown back to New York and lasted a few hours before dying at St. Vincent's Hospital, surrounded by her two oldest grown children, on October 5, 1981. She was just 57 years old.

While in some ways the film career of Gloria Grahame serves as the archetype of the path of a typical Hollywood starlet — young beauty discovered on stage, whisked to Hollywood and molded into a studio's conception of a sexy movie star rather than an accomplished actress—Gloria achieved notoriety and fame well beyond that of most of the women who flock to Hollywood looking to prosper in the limelight. Gloria's career was certainly founded upon her beauty, yet she strove diligently (under the constant tutelage of her mother, an expert acting coach) to act as well as she possibly could, and she succeeded spectacularly. Rex Reed wrote of Gloria, "When she was good she was great, but when she was bad she was even better." At the height of her career, Gloria fully assumed the cinematic persona of the notorious yet bewitching "bad girl." Whether she portrayed a gangster's moll, a sluttish neighbor, an ambitious woman on the make or merely a nice girl forced by circumstance into moral compromise, Gloria became Hollywood's most fascinating and believable woman in trouble. She is enshrined in *film noir* legend despite only appearing in a handful of films that fit that description, simply because she is so effective in them. Mention *The Big Heat, Crossfire, Sudden Fear* or *In a Lonely Place* to any fan of movie classics and those titles will spark instant memories of Gloria in action.

Had she been born a few years earlier, Gloria might have found her calling as a femme fatale in the 1940s crime dramas that RKO and Warner Bros. were churning out month after month. As it was, Gloria found fame as the *film noir* cycle was beginning to wind down. It is no accident, however, that Gloria succeeded in the genre of dark shadow and moral morass because she was so well suited to its parameters. Not by background or personal situation, of course, but because Gloria, with the help of her ever-present, stage-veteran mother, instinctively knew what her troubled characters were feeling and could relate to them. Gloria was young and beautiful when she made *Crossfire, A Woman's Secret, In a Lonely Place, Macao, The Glass Wall, Human Desire, Sudden Fear, Naked Alibi, The Big Heat* and *The Good Die Young,* yet she also conveyed a timeworn, jaded, cynical, burnt-out quality that was absolutely essential to all of them. Her remarkable mix of beauty, worldliness, sensuality and inescapable air of doomed destiny was perfectly suited to the style of the time. Try to imagine sunny Debbie Reynolds as Halloran's girl in *Macao,*

or bubbly Betty Hutton as the troubled singer in *A Woman's Secret,* or glamourous Lana Turner as the penniless woman in *The Glass Wall.* Not that these fine actresses couldn't perform the roles, but they simply wouldn't be well suited to them. They were especially well suited to Gloria.

Her facial features—the gorgeous green eyes, arched eyebrows, painted mouth—were enhanced by the way she spoke, with a gentle lisp that gave each word its own unique quality. She had a quick, sharp tongue and could ramble off long soliloquies when called upon, yet often said just as much with a single look. Her body, while rarely voluptuous, was very attractive; in particular, she had great legs. Fans of *film noir* love Gloria because of her (relatively) unbridled sexuality, which, in that genre, is so often mixed with violence and dark deeds. In *Sudden Fear* she just about dares Jack Palance to brutalize her. She uses the promise of sex to lure men in at least three separate movies to try to kill other people. Even when murder isn't the ultimate goal, she sometimes uses sex to punish or destroy the men with whom she is unhappy, as in *The Good Die Young.* At a time when movies had fairly strong restrictions on what could not be shown, Gloria's come-hither appeal allowed filmmakers to imply a great deal more than they could actually present.

Kris Kristofferson once said of Gloria, "She's sexy in a strange way. Like a woman who's begging you to wallop her in the mouth 'cause she'd just love it. I used to see her in movies and escape into a world of freaky fantasies." Author David Ragan wrote, "In her youth Gloria Grahame was easily—without nudity or vulgarity—the most blatantly sensual girl on the screen." Author Barry Monush concurred: "With her pouting upper lip and an arched brow that could speak volumes, Gloria Grahame was just about the sexiest thing to come along in the 1940s. She also happened to be a terrific actress who could play sweet, cunning, dumb, brash, or pathetic with equal aplomb." Working with her on stage in *The Time of Your Life,* a young Richard Dreyfuss said, "It's impossible for her to believe that anyone admires her. She can't relate to the movie star bit. I can't tell her that I had wet dreams over her in *The Bad and the Beautiful.* She's re-

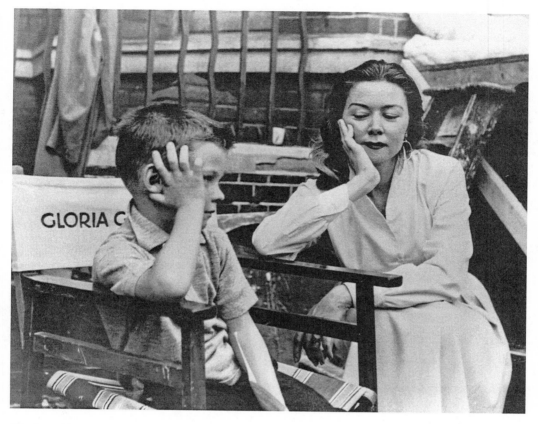

Gloria and her son Timmy relax on a movie set, circa 1955. Gloria seems to be playfully mimicking her boy, although it could be the other way around.

ally a fine actress and cares about doing a good job and worries about what she's doing. She projects a goodness on and off stage that's exciting and sexy. When you get to know her, she's one of the warmest people you're ever likely to meet. Everyone in the cast loves her."

Gloria's apotheosis is in *The Big Heat*. Within its compact ninety minute running time Debby Marsh evolves from a perky gangster's moll (Gloria has rarely been more animated than when she is teasing Lee Marvin) to a woman whose life has been utterly destroyed by violence (the infamous hot coffee scalding sequence). Finding compassion with cop Dave Bannion (Glenn Ford), Debby sets in motion the only plan she can imagine, one that mixes her need for revenge with a bit of redemption for Bannion, whose wife was killed by Debby's mobster friends. It is a brilliant performance that incorporates all the aspects of Gloria's talent and persona into one dazzling, unfor-

gettable character. Gloria is sexy, funny, complex, surprising and achingly sincere. She should have won her second Academy Award for her work in *The Big Heat*, but the film was not taken very seriously at the time.

But *The Big Heat* was the pinnacle of her *film noir* aggregate. Fritz Lang's follow-up with Gloria, *Human Desire*, was a disappointment. *Naked Alibi* was worse. *The Good Die Young* was just fair, and Gloria was underused. With the advent of mammoth widescreen color releases the *film noir* era came to a close very rapidly. It is just providential that Gloria appeared in what might be one of the last, if not the final, big studio effort in the genre, *Odds Against Tomorrow* (1959). Her appearance in the film is more blatantly sexual than those of her past, so much so that she threatened to sue the studio if they followed through with plans to release press photos of her in just her undergarments, as she appears in the film, to publicize it. Hers is also a very minor role, serving as a seamy diversion from the main business of three men robbing a bank.

All in all Gloria appeared in about a dozen movies that can be considered *film noir* projects. A few of these are, like many of the lower-end products that filled the genre on the bottom ends of double features of the era, quite routine and eminently forgettable. But *The Big Heat, In a Lonely Place, Sudden Fear* and *Crossfire* are classics of their kind — and they owe much of their considerable success to Gloria Grahame.

Yet the *film noir* aspect is only a facet of Gloria's career. She is quite memorable portraying singers in several films and television episodes, despite the fact that she could not carry a tune. Gloria is dubbed in *Song of the Thin Man, A Woman's Secret* and *Naked Alibi*, yet she seems perfectly cast anyway, since she fits so well into the *film noir* oeuvre. It *is* Gloria's voice in *Oklahoma!*, unforgettably crooning "I Cain't Say No" and "All 'er Nothin'," but those songs were painstakingly recorded phrase by phrase, sometimes note by note, in recording sessions that took weeks to complete and drove the recording artists crazy. It is Gloria's acting ability that makes her so believable as a singer, whether she is pretending to croon a torch song in *A Woman's Secret* or mischievously poking fun at her character's lack of propriety in *Oklahoma!*

She loved playing comedy, but producers were reticent to cast her in comic films, putting perhaps too much belief in the old bromide that beautiful women aren't funny. Gloria found greater freedom to play comedy on stage than she ever did on film, and that is a loss for moviegoers. Yet watch *Oklahoma!, Merton of the Movies, It's a Wonderful Life, Chilly Scenes of Winter* or even her first feature, *Blonde Fever*, to see evidence that Gloria could deliver laughs with ease. Her best dramatic performances, in films like *The Greatest Show on Earth, The Bad and the Beautiful, In a Lonely Place* and *The Big Heat*, are all shaded with humor. This humor usually takes the form of insolent, often sexually charged remarks she casually tosses off as if she has a million more in her purse just waiting for their turns. She wasn't Lucille Ball (whom she replaced in *The Greatest Show on Earth* when Lucy became pregnant) in terms of

physical comedy, but she wasn't above rescuing Betty Hutton from Cornel Wilde's romantic clutches by leading an elephant to Betty's rescue. And her reaction shots to the mugging of Red Skelton (in *Merton of the Movies*), James Stewart (in *It's a Wonderful Life*) and Eddie Albert (in *Oklahoma!*) are priceless.

Had Howard Hughes loaned Gloria, as she and Columbia's boss Harry Cohn had requested, to Columbia to make *Born Yesterday* (1950), her career might have turned in a whole different direction. But then movie audiences would not have had the pleasure of watching Judy Holliday repeat her Broadway triumph. Gloria attempted to play Billie Dawn on stage years later, but could never secure the rights, as its author, Garson Kanin, felt that she was then too old for the role. Even as late as 1980 Gloria was heard to recite lines from the play, forever keeping it alive in her memory in case she ever had the opportunity to perform it.

Gloria's greatest talent, however, was her ability to convey exactly what she was thinking. Writer Michael Buckley referred to this ability as "The Thought Behind the Look," based upon a famous quote (to Rex Reed again) in which Gloria remarked, "It wasn't the way I looked at a man, but the thought behind it." It sounds deceptively simple, but it isn't simple at all, because one's thoughts are always more complex and confused and sometimes contradictory. Many actors focus on transmitting one emotion or feeling or thought at a time, often because that's what they are told to do. The best performers are those who can convey the complexities of human thought and emotion in the fullest senses of those terms. Gloria was masterful at allowing the other characters — and the audience — to witness the whole spectrum of her character's thoughts in brief but spectacularly radiant moments. It is in these moments when Gloria's acting becomes transcendent.

Gloria's first great moment is her introduction in *It's a Wonderful Life*, as she flounces along a sidewalk in a flimsy, form-fitting, frilly dress, catching the attentions of James Stewart, Frank Faylen and Ward Bond. Their eyes widen at the sight of this gorgeous young woman, but Gloria plays it coy when Stewart compliments her dress. "What, this old thing? I only wear it when I don't care how I look." With that, she smiles, casually flips her golden hair and undulates down the sidewalk, perfectly aware that their eyes are following her. In that moment, Gloria has introduced the town sexpot, given her some unexpected class, piqued the interest of every man in the scene (and in the audience) and sparked the notion that she and Stewart will be colliding, probably in a romantic way, in the very near future.

Another example is Gloria's seduction of Jack Palance in *Sudden Fear*. Jack has already warned her that if she ruins his set-up with new wife Joan Crawford, she will need a new face (an interesting precursor to *The Big Heat*). Gloria lies on the sofa where he has roughly thrown her, looks up at him with limpid eyes and purrs, "Thanks for still loving me." In that moment, she is offering herself to his virulent advances, she is daring him to take advantage of the opportunity, she is setting the hook to reel him into her own sphere of action (involving Joan Crawford) and she is letting the audience know that he will be under her control for the rest of the picture. There is nothing he can do but close the door and move toward her (with just the tiniest bit of reluctance) as the screen fades to black.

Another moment occurs late in *The Big Heat* when Gloria, half of her face hidden beneath a bandage, visits Jeanette Nolan, the widow of a cop who commits suicide at the beginning of the movie. Both happen to be wearing mink stoles, and Nolan insists on being very formal, addressing Gloria by her character's last name. "Debby," Gloria corrects, in a very gentle voice. "We should use first names, Bertha. We're sisters under the mink." At that moment Gloria is conveying that she understands exactly how Nolan "earned" her mink stole, she is acknowledging that accepting such gifts in return for cooperating with their criminal partners makes them equal, she is using the minks to create a bond between them and she is imploring the other woman to help her, or else. The audience, well aware of Debby's doomed destiny ever since the coffee scalding, is being told that Nolan's future may be short as well. Sure enough, a few moments later as Nolan tries to call the mob boss, Debby calmly fires three bullets into Nolan and her beautiful mink coat, an action that also foreshadows her own violent demise.

Yet another moment takes place at the conclusion of *In a Lonely Place*, as Humphrey Bogart staggers away from Gloria after being interrupted by a telephone call while beginning to strangle her. Gloria watches him leave through the doorway, happy to still be alive but devastated by the ruin of the man she loved. "I lived a few weeks while you loved me," she whispers as the tears begin to flow. "Goodbye, Dix." In that moment, the dashed promise of a relationship gone wrong is visible in her face. Regret, fear, resentment, grief; it's all there. Such moments occur in many, if not most, of Gloria's movies, and they are her greatest legacy as an actress. Those moments are what bond her to receptive audiences, both then and now, and are why her performances are so effective.

The other reason why Gloria Grahame became a successful actress has nothing to do with her looks, or her considerable talent. It was simply that she worked hard at her job. She learned her lines, worked out the emotions behind the actions with her mother (who was her lifelong acting coach), and tried to make each take vivid and fresh. Gloria used various accents throughout her career, some more successfully than others, but she always located a real person upon whom she could model each new accent. She often preferred to stay home and run lines than frequent the Hollywood party scene. If a role called for her to know a particular action, such as filling Charlton Heston's pipe during *The Greatest Show on Earth*, then she learned how to do it and practiced it so that filling it would appear natural on screen. She had a difficult time repeating movements, specific blocking and reactions to dialogue because that wasn't learning; it was simply repetition. But as long as something creative was involved and the acting process fed upon itself to reveal something fresh and interesting, Gloria was wonderfully enthusiastic.

Besides her beauty, talent and humor, it is Gloria's guilelessness that makes her so memorable on screen and so personable in real life. Men in particular were taken with this beautiful woman who loved to laugh and tried to find joy in every aspect of her life. According to many of the men who she bewitched over the years, Gloria had a special talent for "remaining in the moment" with whatever man she happened to be with at the time, for making that man feel that he not only had her full attention and appreciation but her devotion as well. It was easy to fall in love with Gloria; lots of men did. It never seemed to last very long, and Gloria found that she liked her husbands more *after* she had divorced them, but she loved being in love. She always related well to men and loved being the center of male attention. Gloria didn't have many close female friends, though there were a few. Mostly, however, she surrounded herself with men. She was a "guy's gal," a pal who just happened to be gorgeous, flirty and fun.

Gloria was an eternal optimist. She refrained from speaking ill of others and avoided reading material that discussed her (she didn't want them to upset her with lies, distortions of the truth or inaccuracies). She had no interest in her own movies, though she did enjoy watching those of others. She hated interviews because she didn't feel worthy of the attention, and she could never understand why people thought of her in the ways they told her they did. She loved the acting process but didn't care at all for the celebrity that accompanied it, especially during her fourth marriage, when so much of the attention focused on her was neg-

ative. She believed in what she did, although she didn't seem to take its importance very seriously at times. Gloria was surprisingly naïve in certain regards and had to be informed by her friends of things they were astonished she didn't already know. When she had children she constantly read books on how to rear them properly, and when she needed to tackle plumbing repairs or such, she read about those subjects, too. She looked upon life as a constant process of learning, and she was forever the student.

Gloria was one of a kind in Hollywood. She had a combination of looks, talent and personality that was, and remains, unique. Gloria never became a major star, but even as a "major minor" star, her career is perhaps more fascinating than many of the rather homogenous stars that Hollywood produced during the same era. Watching Gloria on screen is always interesting and occasionally revelatory. She was an underused and underrated actress even during her prime, and is a treasure waiting to be discovered by future generations. She was wrong when she so often claimed that she was unworthy of attention from the media or from fervent fans; Gloria Grahame was, is and always will be a Hollywood legend.

Short Films: Soundies (1943–1944)

Entering the realm of feature films is usually a time-consuming, difficult process for a performer. There are many paths which can lead to being hired for a feature film: establishing one's name via stage work, sports championships, singing and dancing, appearances in commercials, daredevil feats in various professions, radio, short films, comedy clubs, modeling, playing in a band, reality television, as an Internet video sensation or even just making the local news in some way (either favorably or unfavorably). All of these paths and more have been employed by future Hollywood stars. In the 1940s, there was yet another method — appearing in a Soundie.

Soundies were a new form of visual entertainment, the precursor to the music videos that came on the scene in the 1980s. Each Soundie was approximately three minutes long, filmed in black and white with an optical soundtrack, featuring mostly musical and dance acts, with an occasional comedy act thrown in for variety. Jazz and swing music dominated the Soundie musical terrain, yet gospel, blues, Latin American, country and western, Irish, Hawaiian, big band and even hillbilly music were featured as well. Most of the songs were popular hits or novelty items; some classical, patriotic, dance-only, sing-along and comedy numbers were filmed, too. The occasional non-musical Soundies offered vaudeville routines, ice-skaters, swimmers, knife-throwers, gymnasts, jugglers and even strippers!

Greater than eighteen hundred Soundies were produced and released between 1940 and 1947, with the most popular titles reissued every couple of years. Each week, a reel of eight Soundies (roughly 25 minutes worth of programming) was distributed to the specialized jukebox-like video projection machines in nightclubs, bars, restaurants, hotel lobbies, bus stations, arcade centers and other public places. Each individual Soundie cost a dime to play, and they had to be played in order because they were mounted on a continuous 16mm loop inside the projection machines. Thus, if one particular Soundie was very popular, the other seven had to be played (at a dime each) before the desired subject would come around again. The format was intended to be self-sufficient, with the only maintenance involved being switching of the reels, cleaning of the outer case and screen and collection of its coins.

The largest company to market the projection machines was RCM Productions, headed by President Franklin Delano Roosevelt's son James Roosevelt, songwriter Sam Coslow and Herbert Mills, the brains behind the design. Their machine was known as a Mills "Panoram"; more than forty-five hundred Panorams were in operation in North America during 1943. Customers fed coins into the Panoram and the 16mm projector inside projected the image across a series of mirrors to a 18" × 22" ground glass viewing screen on top while the soundtrack played through the machine's audio speakers. Other companies (Vis-o-graph, Phonovision, Nickel Talkies, etc.) developed their own projection formats but RCM was indisputably the industry's foremost manufacturing firm.

Soundies were popular from 1941 to 1943, and then their popularity began to wane. This was due to wartime restrictions on raw materials for the machines, which severely constrained the manufacturers' ability to expand; a musician's union ban on musicians appearing in Soundies from August 1942 until late 1943, which severely curtailed Soundie production during that year; and public interest in the war, which simply dominated everything else. The musician's union was not the only group opposed to Soundies (it feared that "canned" entertainment would supplant "live" performers; thus, the ban on appearing in the mini-movies); movie theater owners and operators disliked them for similar reasons. In actuality, they had little to fear. For every public Panoram machine it is estimated that there were one hundred standard audio-only jukeboxes, so Soundie saturation clearly never occurred, even in the biggest cities. By war's end the Soundie fad had passed. Although new Soundies were produced into 1946 there were fewer locations where they could be seen. Panoram service was discontinued in 1947, which sounded the death knell for the niche industry.

Yet for a niche industry, some of the acts filmed for the series featured big names such as Stan Kenton, Duke Ellington, Gene Krupa, Nat King Cole, Tommy and Jimmy Dorsey, Count Basie, Louis Armstrong and Cab Calloway. Others were not so well known, but found their fifteen minutes of fame when their one hit novelty song was chosen for inclusion in the series. And some of the people hired as singers, dancers or extras in these short films graduated to greater success in show business. Dorothy Dandridge, Alan Ladd, Doris Day, Ricardo Montalban, Evelyn Keyes, Gale Storm, Liberace, Yvonne de Carlo, Spike Jones, Mary Healy, Morton Downey, Marilyn Maxwell, Ozzie Nelson, Lena Horne, Lawrence Welk, Lucille Bremer and Cyd Charisse all appeared in Soundies.

So did young Gloria Hallward (she was yet to be dubbed Gloria Grahame by MGM chief Louis B. Mayer). In fact, Gloria appeared in five Soundies before she made her feature film debut in 1944. They are, in order of copyright date, *Pin-Ups on Parade* (1943), *My Heart Tells Me* (1944), *Polka Dot Polka* (1944), *Oh! Please Tell Me Darling* (1944) and *Loads of Pretty Women* (1944).

Pin-Ups on Parade
(copyrighted December 31, 1943)

Lee Sullivan croons "Pin-Ups on Parade" while the "Dream Dolls" illustrate the beauty he is singing about. One of those Dream Dolls is young Gloria. No copy of this Soundie could be found to view for this book.

My Heart Tells Me
(copyrighted April 3, 1944)

The musical trio The Three Suns plays "My Heart Tells Me" spotlighted in a darkened studio corner. Interspersed with the musicians playing and singing are shots of three romantic couples; Gloria is half of the first couple. She does a full twenty seconds of gazing, eyes roaming all over the man's face (the man has his back to the camera).

Polka Dot Polka
(copyrighted April 24, 1944)

Carroll Hood, backed by his orchestra, plays "Polka Dot Polka" in a nightclub-like setting with several appreciative women in black evening gowns comprising the audience. One of those women is Gloria, then just twenty years old. Four of the women are shown individually; Gloria is the third. Late in the song, a group of six female dancers join the song and do a few dance steps.

Oh! Please Tell Me Darling
(copyrighted May 8, 1944)

Al Trace and His Silly Symphonists play "Oh! Please Tell Me Darling" with a bevy of beauties modeling behind them; Gloria is one of the models. No copy of this Soundie could be found to view for this book.

Loads of Pretty Women
(copyrighted October 2, 1944)

Red River Dave McEnery sings "Loads of Pretty Women" as a parade of lovelies passes before him on stage. He doesn't have to look far for Gloria, who is one of two girls swaying and dancing next to him throughout most of the song. She has a light-colored dress, and most fetchingly watches Red River Dave croon.

It is possible that Gloria appears in more than these five Soundies. There is no record of her making Soundies, even in Vincent Curcio's biography of Gloria, but it seems safe to assume that she made them while appearing on Broadway in *The World's Full of Girls* and *A Highland Fling* in 1943 and 1944, before she travelled to Hollywood for *Blonde Fever*. New York was a center for Soundie production; many were filmed at the Fox Movietone studio. Most Soundies were made in California, but quite a few of them were shot on tight schedules and with minimal production values in New York City. One company, Minoco Productions, boasted a stock company of young performers who sang and/or danced in many Soundies, or sometimes just appeared in crowd scenes. It is logical that, seeking cash and experience before film cameras, Gloria found her way into this group or one similar to it. Or she may have been approached to appear in Soundies by a talent scout looking to populate the short films with pretty faces (she wouldn't have to sing or dance, just be attractive and attentive to the featured act). Either way, making these short movies provided Gloria with a taste of the film business, enough experience to familiarize herself with how film cameras worked, and something she could put on a résumé (not that she ever did, at least later in her career).

When she returned to California to meet with Louis B. Mayer about accepting a movie contract, Gloria was no babe in the woods; she had legitimate stage experience in New York and other cities, plus, thanks to the Soundies, she knew that she looked very appealing on camera. It would not be long before her newfound experience was put to use, in a large part in a feature film at the famed MGM studios in Hollywood.

Feature Films

Blonde Fever (1944)

CREDITS MGM. *Directed by* Richard Whorf. *Produced by* William H. Wright. *Screenplay by* Patricia Coleman. *Based on a play* (*Delila*, also known as *The Blue Danube*) by Ferenc Molnár. *Director of Photography*: Lester White. *Film Editor*: George Hively. *Musical Score*: Nathaniel Shilkret. *Recording Director*: Douglas Shearer. *Art Direction*: Cedric Gibbons and Preston Ames. *Set Decorations*: Edwin B. Willis. *Set Decorations Associate*: Richard Pefferle. *Costume Supervision*: Irene. *Costume Supervision Associate*: Kay Dean. *Assistant Director*: Raleigh Asher. *Sound*: John F. Dullam. *Orchestrators*: Robert Franklyn and Joseph Nussbaum. Black and White. Flat (1.37:1). Monaural Sound. 69 minutes. Released on December 5, 1944. Not currently available on commercial home video.

CAST *Peter Donay*, Philip Dorn; *Delilah Donay*, Mary Astor; *Johnny*, Felix Bressart; *Sally Murfin*, Gloria Grahame; *Freddie Bilson*, Marshall Thompson; *Brillon*, Curt Bois; *Mrs. Talford*, Elisabeth Risdon; *Willie*, Arthur Walsh; *Mr. Alexander*, Paul Scott; *Cab Driver*, John Phipps; *String Quartette Leader*, Carlyle Blackwell, Jr.; *First Waiter*, Edward Kilroy; *Second Waiter*, Sherry Hall; *Diners*, Hume Cronyn and Jessica Tandy; with Ava Gardner, Dagmar Oakland, Tom Quinn and Celia Travers.

Three months after signing a standard seven-year MGM contract (for $250 a week), Gloria Grahame (*née* Hallward; Louis B. Mayer formally changed her surname in July) began work on a real motion picture. It was a comedy titled *Blonde Fever*, freely adapted from the play *Delila* (also known as *The Blue Danube*) by Ferenc Molnár, and it began filming on August 1, 1944. Gloria was not the star of the show, yet she was undeniably the picture's most colorful attraction. Colorful posters and lobby cards featured Philip Dorn and Mary Astor as the stars, but Gloria's picture was just as prominent as Mary Astor's—and the film's titillating title was certainly not referring to Miss Astor. All advertising used the phrase "and Introducing Gloria Grahame and Marshall Thompson" when referring to its new stars, and the marketing department even created a poster spotlighting Gloria in a skimpy outfit. The movie itself was not considered a major release by the studio, but they put a great deal of money and effort into promoting their new starlet, Gloria Grahame.

Blonde Fever takes place south of Reno, Nevada, at the Café Donay. It's a swank and sophisticated restaurant in the middle of nowhere operated by Peter Donay (Philip Dorn) and his wife Delilah (Mary Astor), and it is very successful. Young Freddie Bilson (Marshall Thompson) arrives on his loud motorcycle with Mrs. Talford (Elisabeth Risdon), who's visiting Reno for yet another divorce. A local lad with no appreciable ambition, Freddie is there to pick up his girlfriend, waitress Sally Murfin (Gloria Grahame). Sally is supposed to be quitting because Freddie doesn't like the attention Donay lavishes upon her, but Donay refuses to allow her to quit, and Sally isn't inclined to do so anyway. Even though his marriage seems happy, Donay wants Sally for himself.

The Donays are unhappy. Donay is being driven crazy by flirtatious Sally, and his wife knows something is wrong; she talks to her close friend Johnny the bartender (Felix Bressart) about it. The Donays argue about the café's financial success and its staffing. When Delilah suggests hiring Freddie, her husband reluctantly agrees, knowing that Freddie is in love with Sally, too. The state lottery numbers are announced on the radio, crushing Freddie's hopes; he was counting on winning enough money to be able to marry Sally. Instead, Peter Donay wins $40,000.

A few days later, Sally flirts outrageously with Donay as he browses through catalogs trying to pick something especially for her. She tells Freddie she isn't in any rush to marry him, then purposely flirts with her lovelorn employer, finally going so far as to kiss him. She daydreams about spending his newfound lottery money.

Freddie tries waiting tables at the café and is terrible at the job. Donay fires him. Down in the wine cellar, Donay finally succumbs to Sally's charms and kisses her. She frightens him when she talks about marriage but he eventually agrees to marry her once he divorces Delilah. Freddie enters with a gun and threatens Donay, but they appeal to Freddie's love for Sally, explaining that he should want her to be happy. Distraught, Freddie leaves without harming anyone. Later that night, Donay admits to his wife that he is going to leave her. She agrees to file for divorce and goads him into signing the lottery check over to her, just to prove to him that Sally isn't out for his money. And then she sends him to the guest room for the night while she hatches a plan with Johnny.

The next morning, Donay admits to Johnny that he has made a mistake; he does not want to divorce his wife, nor to marry Sally. Delilah, however, is all dressed up and raring to leave. Their breakfast is interrupted by Sally, whom Delilah invites to join them. Delilah tells her that Donay no longer has the lottery winnings, which upsets Sally. Freddie arrives on a sleek new motorcycle, announcing that he is "going away to forget." Donay, finally seeing that Sally wanted his money, calls her a gold-digger and she dumps him, apologizing to Freddie. She agrees to be his and his alone, and Freddie takes her back. They ride off together (with a healthy chunk of the lottery money, given to Freddie as "compensation" by Delilah). Delilah still acts as though she is going to leave, but Johnny returns the rest of the lottery money not taken by Freddie to Delilah and carries her luggage back into the café.

Blonde Fever is pretty slim for a romantic comedy, and there's not very much romance involved anyway. It's all about desire, usually the desire for relationships that one cannot consummate. Donay and his wife are successful and content, but he grows bored and then becomes infatuated with the young and vital Sally. The catalyst of the story, Sally enjoys the adoration of Freddie Bilson but desires to see the world with money and class, persuading herself that Donay and his lottery winnings constitute a wiser choice than honorable but perennially broke Freddie — so long as her reputation is preserved by marriage. Donay's and Sally's desire for what each other represents (not necessarily for each other) almost ruins his current marriage and nearly traps her in a bad marriage with him. Sally's desire for wealth colors her choice of men; despite being married, Donay is fair game until he gives the lottery winnings to his wife, while Freddie is considered less than suitable until he gets some money — and a new motorcycle — at the story's conclusion.

In terms of its views on marriage, fidelity and divorce, *Blonde Fever* attempts to seem cosmopolitan, but it is in fact rather old-fashioned. The adopted setting near Reno, the divorce capital of the world, is not accidental. For many years, people who wanted divorces traveled to Reno, stayed in the city's vicinity for six weeks to establish Nevada residence and then filed for divorces, which were usually granted very quickly by the state. Mrs. Talford is a perfect example. She is in the area for yet another divorce; it seems almost a seasonal journey for the rich lady, and much of the café's clientele appears to consist of Easterners making the journey westward for the same purpose.

When Donay finally admits to his wife that he wants to run away with Sally, Delilah accepts the news matter-of-factly. After seeing it happen to so many other people, Delilah is not very surprised that it is now happening to her, especially after watching her husband pine after Sally for weeks. Yet Delilah doesn't simply concede the divorce; she believes she can save her husband from a mistake, and devises a plan to stop the divorce before it begins. And Donay never comes close to consummating his infatuation with Sally. Sally doesn't want to have anything to do with him without the guarantee of marriage supporting her claim to his money and name. For the main characters, marriage is the safe ground, from which occasional flirtations and forays may be ventured.

Blonde Fever. This inconsequential MGM comedy introduced both Gloria and Marshall Thompson, but only Gloria — "She's gorgeous! She's dangerous!" — was visually featured in the movie's advertising with stars Philip Dorn and Mary Astor.

This conservative viewpoint is constructed by Ferenc Molnár, the Hungarian playwright and author whose play *Delila* (translated into English as *The Blue Danube*) is the source of this film. Molnár specialized in domestic triangles involving romantic and sexual distress as his characters learned that happiness was often elusive and fleeting. Yet Molnár's hopeless romantics were drawn with a clever hand, imparting their travails with a humor and liveliness that made their author quite popular in Budapest. *Delila*'s characters are typical Molnár inventions: the men are somewhat confused and easily driven mad by romantic lust, while the women are lovely, intelligent, rapacious and fully aware of the power of their charms. And in Molnár's battle of the sexes, the women rarely lose.

Screenwriter Patricia Coleman adapted *Delila* with care, retaining its central characters, situation and themes while expanding its setting, dialogue and playfulness. Molnár is more pointed in his description of the Sally character as a greedy temptress, while Delilah admits that she captured her husband using the same tactics as her younger rival. The film version softens the characters, and thus their emotional pain, because MGM wished to create a more pleasing product. *Blonde Fever* then fulfills its title, as Peter Donay acquires what amounts to a seasonal craving for Sally which passes when she receives what she really desires — a share of his lottery winnings (through Freddie, who has received it from Delilah).

The marital relationship between Donay and Delilah is the most cosmopolitan element of the film (and the play). Delilah takes Donay's infatuation in stride, noting in the play that after ten years of marriage, it's "true to form" that the husband will stray. In the play, Delilah isn't concerned about her husband having an affair; in fact, she reprimands the bartender for contending that her husband could not have one. But the specter of divorce — of losing her husband to a younger, greedier version of herself — is simply not to be tolerated. She conceives a plan to save their marriage and rid themselves of the ill-begotten money (an inheritance from America in the play). For his part, Donay is torn between the woman he truly loves and the woman who inflames his desires. Because he acts respectably, if not responsibly, he is to be pitied, not reviled.

Delila was the last play to be written by Molnár before he emigrated to the United States in 1938. While he never found the fame in America that he had achieved in Hungary — he continued to write until he died in 1952 following depression and illness — Molnár was a consistent source for Hollywood to plumb. Films from Molnár's works had been made in Hollywood as early as 1915 and would continue well beyond his death, encompassing various versions of his most famous play *Liliom* (including the 1956 musical *Carousel*), as well as multiple versions of his plays *Olympia*, *The Devil*, *The Swan* and *The Guardsman*. Billy Wilder's frenetic Cold War comedy *One, Two, Three* (1961) also springs from the Molnár imagination. *Blonde Fever* is among the least of these works.

Just sixty-nine minutes long, *Blonde Fever* was not one of MGM's major productions of 1944. It was filmed in twenty-three days, cost $313,000 to make and grossed more than $550,000, making it a profitable, if not blockbuster, project for the studio. It has never been released on the commercial home video market and today relatively few people have ever seen it. It is now known mostly for introducing Gloria Grahame to the big screen and providing early roles for Marshall Thompson (also "introduced," although this was his third film role), and in bit roles, Ava Gardner, Hume Cronyn and Jessica Tandy.

The dramatics of the story are handled by Philip Dorn and Mary Astor, who, most unfortunately, have absolutely no chemistry together. Astor brings dignity to the role of a woman being thrown over for a younger rival and has some nice moments throughout, but Dorn is ineffectual as the lovelorn cad. He's rather expressionless anyway but too many of his scenes conclude with him slapping his hands to his face in frustration. Dorn seems physically suited to the elegant, aristocratic role, yet he fails to convey the troubled essence beneath his fancy exterior. His scenes with Astor are stale. On the other hand, Grahame and Thompson are fresh and lively as the younger couple. Their parts are undoubtedly sillier but their enthusiasm and charm makes them far more interesting than the Dorn-Astor pairing.

It is Gloria Grahame who best takes advantage of her role. While the striped café dress she usually wears is disconcerting, there is no camouflaging her youthful beauty. Gloria twinkles with vitality even in the opening credits, where she playfully crinkles her nose. Her flirty nature drives all of the film's men to distraction while she seems barely aware of her impact upon them. This is mostly due to Molnár's original conception of the character, but Gloria knows exactly how to balance her persona between innocence and lasciviousness. Gloria's Sally Murfin plays at being bad, much as her Violet Bick would two years later in *It's a Wonderful Life*. Her trampier characters would follow in short order.

Gloria in *Blonde Fever* is wonderfully winsome. One of the joys of the film is watching Sally seem completely at a loss when the men come sniffing around like bloodhounds on the trail. She has lines like, "What is it about me makes everybody tell me all the time 'Life is calling?'" and, "Is it my fault if men have to be so silly?" that belie her own self-awareness but endear her to the audience. Sally is determined to remain respectable no matter what, and she makes that clear early in the film: "There are two kinds of women, Mr. Donay. Nice girls and, and the other kind. Mr. Donay, I certainly hope you don't think that I'm the other kind." Yet her desire for money and nice things is apparent, even to Donay. When Sally sniffles, "I never meant to destroy anybody. I just try to go on my way, minding my own business, doing the best I, I can," he replies brusquely, "Like a panzer division."

The one incongruous aspect regarding Sally is her lack of regard for Delilah. Sally always acts civilly to Mrs. Donay, yet seemingly has no regrets about stealing her husband.

Considering how nice the Donays are to Sally and the staff, feeding them and even arranging for temporary housing for Freddie, Sally's disregard for Delilah is not very plausible. This is the fault of the script, which tries to create conflict out of thin air. In the original play, the relationship between the two women is cattier, and Sally's greed is much more apparent (although not to herself).

While the film is neither very deep nor very entertaining, it does provide Gloria with a nice showcase in her feature film debut. She looks fabulous, especially when she is playing with her hair. It's impossible to divine a great acting talent from a role this thin, but Gloria presents a naturally inviting personality that indicates a bright future. The same can be said for Marshall Thompson, who plays his comedic scenes broadly but with conviction. In fact, both Gloria and Thompson fashioned long, enduring Hollywood careers. In a letter to his parents on August 8, 1944, Thompson tells them

he's having fun on the set and that "the work isn't half as hard as Universal" (where he made *Reckless Age* earlier in the year. He also tells them, "I took Gloria to dinner last night. She's very nice and really talented." Gloria returned the favor at the end of the letter where she wrote, "Marshall is doing a wonderful job — you'll be very proud of him," and signed her name. Director Richard Whorf, Mary Astor and Curt Bois also signed the letter or wrote brief notes about Thompson to his parents as well.

Despite doing moderately brisk business during its short theatrical run, *Blonde Fever* was largely ignored by critics of the era. National magazines such as *Time* and *Newsweek* declined to review it, as did the *New York Times*. *Variety* termed it "a placid comedy," and questioned the Sally Murfin role: "Gloria Grahame, as the blonde waitress, shows possibilities, but [is] given a conflicting, indefinite role in this opus." Neither was the *London Times* im-

Blonde Fever. Freddie Bilson (Marshall Thompson) reiterates his love for Sally Murfin (Gloria), but Sally is thinking about things promised to her by her boss, Peter Donay (Philip Dorn, not pictured). *Blonde Fever* is a comedy based upon the play *Delila* by Ferenc Molnár.

pressed with the film: "The restaurant's kitchen is immaculate, but the *soufflé* fails to rise."

For Gloria, however, it was a good start. She had not had to struggle along in bit parts for years before getting her big break; here it was, a co-starring role in an MGM comedy after just three months on the lot. Moreover, Gloria was the focal point of all the advertising, for she embodied the "blonde fever" that the movie was hawking. Her mother was present to guarantee her well-being, and to facilitate her performance. In this part, however, Gloria did not need much coaching. Despite her character's naiveté, Gloria was well aware of the effect she had on men. She used that knowledge to bolster Sally's sexuality in subtle ways yet was able to project a disarming innocence that was completely charming. The project itself held no great fascination for Gloria but the process of making it did. She watched and learned, asked questions and patiently listened to the answers. When someone made a suggestion about her performance, she carefully considered whether the tip would improve it. She kept to herself on the set, as would become her custom, but she was not reclusive. Gloria strived for understanding regarding the making of movies because she was positive that making them was what she wanted to do. She had come to Hollywood and accepted the MGM contract because she had set her mind to making a name for herself, and there seemed to be no better place to do so than on the mammoth MGM lot.

That was Gloria's one miscalculation, as she would discover while awaiting her next assignment at the studio.

Without Love (1945)

CREDITS MGM. *Directed by* Harold S. Bucquet. *Produced by* Lawrence Weingarten. *Screenplay by* Donald Ogden Stewart. *Based on the play by* Philip Barry, *as produced by the* Theatre Guild, Inc. *Director of Photography*: Karl Freund. *Film Editor*: Frank Sullivan. *Musical Score*: Bronislau Kaper. *Additional Music by* Eric Zeisl and Mario Castelnuovo-Tedesco. *Recording Director*: Douglas Shearer. *Art Direction*: Cedric Gibbons and Harry McAfee. *Set Decorations*: Edwin B. Willis. *Associate Set Decorator*: McLean Nisbet. *Special Effects*: A. Arnold Gillespie and Danny Hall. *Costume Supervisor*: Irene. *Associate Costume Supervisor*: Marion Herwood Keyes. *Montage Effects*:

Peter Ballbusch. *Makeup Artist*: Jack Dawn. *Assistant Director*: Earl McEvoy. *Hair Stylist*: Irma Kusely. *Orchestrators*: Robert Franklyn and Wally Heglin. Black and White. Flat (1.37:1). Monaural sound. 111 minutes. Released on March 22, 1945. Currently available on DVD. Previously available on VHS and laserdisc.

CAST *Pat Jamieson*, Spencer Tracy; *Jamie Rowan*, Katharine Hepburn; *Kitty Trimble*, Lucille Ball; *Quentin Ladd*, Keenan Wynn; *Paul Carrell*, Carl Esmond; *Edwina Collins*, Patricia Morison; *Professor Grinza*, Felix Bressart; *Anna*, Emily Massey; *Flower Girl*, Gloria Grahame; *Caretaker*, George Davis; *Elevator Boy*, George Chandler; *Sergeant*, Clancy Cooper; *Taxi Driver*, Eddie Acuff; *Colonel Braden*, Charles Arnt; *Professor Thompson*, Wallis Clark; *Professor Ellis*, Donald Curtis; *Officer on Elevator*, Brooks Benedict; *Girl on Elevator*, Hazel Brooks; *Pageboy*, Ralph Brooks; *Headwaiter*, Franco Corsaro; *Sergeant*, James Flavin; *Doctor*, William Forrest; *Porter*, Clarence Muse; *Man in Corridor*, Heinie Conklin; *Man in Elevator*, Sayre Dearing; *Soldiers*, Joe Devlin, William Newell and Garry Owen; *The Dog*, Dizzy.

Following her large role in *Blonde Fever*, Gloria's second film was a letdown, even considering that she shared the screen with Spencer Tracy. Gloria has one scene as a flower girl and just a few lines, crying through them because the flowers give her character hay fever. It was clear that MGM didn't know just what to do with her; it's a decorative part, but nothing more, lasting less than thirty seconds late in the story. Still, it was a part in a major MGM comedy, and Gloria had been selected over dozens of other young and beautiful starlets to play it.

Without Love casts Spencer Tracy as Pat Jamieson, a scientist who arrives in Washington, D.C., during wartime, unable to find lodgings for himself and his small dog Dizzy. Pat shares a cab with drunken Quentin Ladd (Keenan Wynn), and wrangles an invitation to stay with him for the night at Quentin's cousin's home. In the morning, Pat surveys the basement, finds it to his liking and attempts to persuade the cousin, widow Jamie Rowan (Katharine Hepburn), to allow him to stay there while she is away. Jamie doesn't like Pat's blunt demeanor but changes her mind when she discovers his identity; her father held his father in high regard, and she feels she must do the same for him.

Pat establishes a laboratory in Jamie's basement to perfect his invention, a high-altitude oxygen helmet. Jamie tries to stay away but soon offers herself as his assistant. Jamie proposes a platonic marriage of convenience, devoid of love; she tells him, "You don't want [love] because you've had all the worst of it. I don't want it because I've had all the best." Pat accepts after learning that his old flame Lila — the girl who destroyed all of his romantic illusions — is in town and wants to hear from him. The wedding between Pat and Jamie takes place (but isn't shown) and the Jamiesons set to work on his oxygen helmet. They take turns in a decompression chamber, testing the device under pressure. Time and again the helmet fails due to equipment problems.

Meanwhile, Quentin's on-again, off-again relationship with haughty Edwina Collins (Patricia Morison) is interrupted by his flirtations with realtor Kitty Trimble (Lucille Ball). Kitty warns Jamie about getting too close to one of Pat's friends, Paul Carrell (Carl Esmond), and sure enough, Paul makes a move on Jamie during a buggy ride. She rejects him, but glories in her rediscovered femininity.

The helmet is finally finished and Pat takes it to Chicago for presentation and a final test. Jamie joins him on the train, displacing an Air Force colonel. She mentions Paul's pass at her to Pat, but he doesn't say anything. In Chicago, Pat impulsively buys Jamie some flowers from a pretty flower girl (Gloria Grahame). Jamie turns on her charm to seduce Pat, but he pulls back, reminded of his terrible experience with Lila. When he walks out, she goes back home. The helmet is tested in a centrifuge with Pat whirling around and around. It passes the test, and Pat is given a medal for his work.

Pat returns home with a birthday cake for Jamie, but she is out dancing with Paul. Kitty tells Pat that Jamie has met Lila, and they have been discussing him. Quentin arrives in a sailor's uniform; he has joined the Navy. Edwina tries to drag Quentin away, but he rejects her and asks Kitty to marry him. Pat visits Paul's apartment to learn if Jamie has joined him. Evidence of a woman is apparent, but no one is to be found. Back at home, Jamie pretends to be like Lila, trying to provoke some response from Pat. It doesn't work, and they agree to divorce. But then they perform a role-playing routine, allowing them to see each other's perspectives, which changes Jamie's

mind. Pat gives her the medal he received for the oxygen helmet. They are finally happy together as man and wife, complete with love.

Without Love is the film version of a Philip Barry play, one which Katharine Hepburn had played on Broadway opposite Elliott Nugent. Hepburn had found great success starring in Barry's earlier play *The Philadelphia Story* and its film version; she hoped for a repeat of that success by casting Spencer Tracy as her co-star. It was their third movie together (they eventually appeared together in nine between 1942 and 1967, when Tracy died). However, this Barry play is not nearly as resonant, witty or interesting as his previous hit. The play ran on Broadway for 113 performances, as opposed to *The Philadelphia Story*'s 417.

Without Love suffers from slightness. The central theme — that two people share the same disdain for love for completely different reasons, yet are destined to fall in love anyway, with each other — is stated unequivocally early in the story, but it still takes nearly two hours for these people to realize it. That theme is hardly fresh and certainly not imperative in any way. The secondary themes in Barry's original play involving international diplomacy and Irish neutrality during World War II have been excised in favor of Pat Jamieson's (now an inventor rather than a diplomat) development of an oxygen helmet for pilots at high altitudes. Thus, the rather serious subjects and themes of the play have been eliminated in favor of purely comedic moments, such as scenes of Jamie sneezing inside the oxygen helmet and being unable to blow her nose, and, later, becoming lightheaded and turning a weightless somersault in Pat's decompression chamber.

Not only do these changes result in lighter fare, but scriptwriter Donald Ogden Stewart and director Harold S. Bucquet also choose to emphasize character peculiarities rather than story structure or content. For instance, Pat sleepwalks. Or he tries to, but his dog Dizzy prevents him from doing so. It's a cute bit, but it's as phony as can be. More amusing is Pat's bluntness, which ought to result in him being slapped or slugged by most people he meets. But Jamie simply turns the other cheek when Pat insults her lifestyle or her clothing style (at one point he remarks that her paisley dressing gown looks like "fish eyes in mucilage"). Such remarks are entertaining, but they're made theatrically, adding to the artificiality of the entire enterprise.

The supporting characters are also amusing, but they serve little purpose in the story other than to provide romantic complications for each other. Quentin Ladd (Keenan Wynn) seems to spend his days constantly schnockered and has no real reason to be hanging around. The same can be said for Kitty Trimble (Lucille Ball), the pretty real estate lady whose desire to rent Jamie's house is thwarted by Pat, who finagles it for himself. There's no logical reason for Kitty to return, yet she does. Edwina Collins (Patricia Morison) is a haughty society dame who, for no discernable reason, has her hooks in Quentin. Edwina is a caricature rather than a character, and an unpleasant one at that. Finally there's Paul Carrell (Carl Esmond), the skirt-chasing friend of Pat's whose pursuit of Kitty and Jamie is as artificial as Pat's sleepwalking. As Pat is a scientist trying to develop a secret government project, there is simply no realistic reason for these people to be constantly barging in and out. The play needs such interaction; the film suffers from it.

Barry's dialogue is, for the most part, excellent. The relationship between Pat and Jamie develops with charm, and their arguments erupt from personality conflicts, just as in real life. Pat's deadpan comments are funny and usually on target. Jamie tends to talk too much, but it suits her character. The most artificial dialogue occurs in the final scene, after Pat and Jamie decide to divorce. They fall into a role-playing charade, allowing them to pretend to be other people, yet still be commenting about themselves. It is an intrinsically hollow exercise, straight from the play. Clever it may be, but it distances the characters from each other, and from the audience.

Tracy and Hepburn work well together; the developing feelings of their characters toward each other are handled subtly, yet with conviction. Critics raved about Keenan Wynn's supporting work as Quentin, with James Agee of *The Nation* hinting that Wynn was becoming the best actor in Hollywood. Lucille Ball also received kudos as Kitty, a change-of-pace role. Wynn and Ball are solid in their roles, providing more punch than was originally written. It also indicates the slimness of the lead roles

when two such unsubstantial supporting roles receive so much attention.

Critics generally liked *Without Love*. Agee wrote, "I like it all right and have very little to say for it or against it.... [A] good deal of the dialogue is happy to hear and happier in its skill; Katharine Hepburn and Spencer Tracy are exactly right for their jobs." According to Philip T. Hartung of *The Commonweal*, "*Without Love* dallies with a single theme, too, but manages to seem very amusing because of its bright performances and snappy repartee." *Time*'s critic called the picture "a completely successful projection of the Philip Barry play." Walcott Gibbs of *The New Yorker* opined, "I think you can go to *Without Love* with a reasonable assurance of having a very pleasant time," while Manny Farber of *The New Republic* termed it "worthlessly pleasant." It was not a huge hit, but it did brisk business in the spring of 1945.

Without Love is a minor entry on the résumés of everyone involved. Of the nine Hepburn and Tracy vehicles, it rivals *Keeper of the Flame* (1942) and *The Sea of Grass* (1947) as the least known. It is certainly the flimsiest of their movies together, though it is amusing, and offers movie fans an opportunity to see the two legendary stars in a romantic comedy, where their true feelings for each other seem evident.

Gloria Grahame had also found someone to swoon over, while on a USO tour that went to Texas. Actor Stanley Clements had appeared in nineteen films before entering the Army in 1945, including small roles in *The More the Merrier* (1943) and *Going My Way* (1944). He had a studio contract waiting for him when he finished his tour of duty, which ended in a Texas hospital when he came down with pneumonia during training. He met Gloria while recuperating in the summer of 1945 and within weeks they were secretly engaged. They married on August 29, 1945, and it was not until after the wedding that Gloria introduced him to her mother. Jean Grahame was furious, but there was nothing she could do about her daughter's impetuous marriage.

For her part, Gloria didn't even know Stanley was an actor until after the wedding occurred. "I'd never seen him in Hollywood. Then one day he was saying he would be able

Without Love. A pretty Flower Girl (Gloria) with allergies to her wares sells some to scientist Pat Jamieson (Spencer Tracy). This comedy was based on a Philip Barry play that Katharine Hepburn had insisted on bringing to the screen after starring in the Broadway production.

to take care of me after the war because he had a contract waiting for him. Imagine an actor not telling you right away that he was one, can you? Suddenly it dawned on me: He was the young fellow in *Going My Way*!" The marriage was stable for a few months but could not be easily sustained; by May of 1946 Gloria and Stanley separated for the first time, though they reconciled a couple of months later. This, un-

fortunately, was to set a pattern for the rest of Gloria's personal life.

As for *Without Love*, the film is just a blip on the radar of Gloria's career. Almost a year after filming *Blonde Fever* she spent a couple of days on an MGM set shooting this microscopic role. It was the only movie work she completed for the studio in two years there. Gloria spent a few rewarding moments with Spencer Tracy, who encouraged her to stick with acting. She did. But it was almost another year before she made another movie. Luckily for Gloria, it was a doozy.

It's a Wonderful Life (1946)

CREDITS Liberty Films. *Distributed by* RKO Radio Pictures. *Produced and Directed by* Frank Capra. *Screenplay by* Frances Goodrich, Albert Hackett and Frank Capra. *Additional Scenes by* Jo Swerling. *Uncredited Revisions by* Michael Wilson and Dorothy Parker. *Based on a Story by* Philip Van Doren Stern. *Directors of Photography:* Joseph Walker, Joseph Biroc and Victor Milner. *Film Editor:* William Hornbeck. *Musical Score Written and Directed by* Dimitri Tiomkin. *Special Photographic Effects:* Russell A. Cully. *Art Director:* Jack Okey. *Set Decorations:* Emile Kuri. *Makeup Supervision:* Gordon Bau. *Sound by* Richard Van Hessen, Clem Portman and John Aalberg. *Costumes by* Edward Stevenson. *Assistant Director:* Arthur S. Black. *Special Effects by* Daniel Hays and Russell Shearman. *Gaffer:* Homer Plannette. *Stock Music Composed by* Leigh Harline, Alfred Newman, Leith Stevens, Dave Torbett, Edward Ward and Roy Webb. *Music Orchestrators:* Herschel Burke Gilbert, Paul Marquardt, Nathan Scott and David Tamkin. *Still Photographer:* Gaston Longet. Black and White. Flat (1.37:1). Monaural Sound. 130 minutes. Released on December 20, 1946. Currently available on DVD (also available in a colorized version). Previously available on VHS and laserdisc.

CAST *George Bailey*, James Stewart; *Mary Hatch*, Donna Reed; *Mr. Potter*, Lionel Barrymore; *Uncle Billy*, Thomas Mitchell; *Clarence Oddbody, Angel Second Class*, Henry Travers; *Mrs. Bailey*, Beulah Bondi; *Ernie Bishop*, Frank Faylen; *Bert*, Ward Bond; *Violet Bick*, Gloria Grahame; *Mr. Gower*, H.B. Warner; *Harry Bailey*, Todd Karns; *Peter (Pa) Bailey*, Samuel S. Hinds; *Cousin Tilly*, Mary Treen; *Sam Wainwright*, Frank Albertson; *Ruth Dakin*, Virginia Patton; *Cousin Eustace*, Charles Williams; *Mrs. Hatch*, Sarah Edwards; *Mr. Martini*, Bill Edmunds; *Annie*, Lillian Randolph; *Mrs. Martini*, Argentina Brunetti; *Little George Bailey*, Bobbie Anderson; *Little Sam Wainwright*, Ronnie Ralph; *Little Mary Hatch*, Jean Gale; *Little Violet Bick*, Jeanine Ann Roose; *Little Marty Hatch*, Danny Mummert; *Little Harry Bailey*, Georgie Nokes; *Nick*, Sheldon Leonard; *Potter's Bodyguard*, Frank Hagney; *Joe (Man in Luggage Shop)*, Ray Walker; *Reineman (Potter's Rent Collector)*, Charles Lane; *Tom*, Edward Keane; *Janie Bailey*, Carol Coombs; *Zuzu Bailey*, Karolyn Grimes; *Pete Bailey*, Larry Simms; *Tommy Bailey*, Jimmy Hawkins; *Ed*, Ernie Adams; *Mr. Welch*, Stanley Andrews; *Sheriff*, Al Bridge; *Jane Wainwright*, Marian Carr; *Dr. Cavanaugh*, Henry Cheshire; *Miss Davis*, Ellen Corby; *Horace (Bank Teller)*, Eddie Featherston; *Mr. Carter (Bank Examiner)*, Charles Halton; *Mr. Partridge (High School Principal)*, Henry Holman; *Mr. Randall*, Arthur Stuart Hull; *Marty Hatch*, Harold Landon; *Mickey*, Mark Roberts; *Freddie Othello*, Carl "Alfalfa" Switzer; *Charlie*, Charles C. Wilson; *Nervous Banker*, Sam Ash; *Singer at Martini's*, Adriana Caselotti; *Man on Porch*, Dick Elliott; *Tollhouse Keeper*, Tom Fadden; *Violet's Boyfriend*, Frank Fenton; *Relieved Banker*, Sam Flint; *Piano Player at Nick's*, Meade "Lux" Lewis; *House Owner*, J. Farrell MacDonald; *Bill Poster*, Garry Owen; *Nick's Bouncer*, Cy Schindell; *Potter's Secretary*, Almira Sessions; *Bartender at Nick's*, Charles Sullivan; *Cashier at Nick's*, Max Wagner; *One of Violet's Suitors*, Jack Bailey; *Military Officers in Montage*, Brooks Benedict and Frank O'Connor; *People at Graduation Dance*, Lew Davis, Helen Dickson, Priscilla Montgomery and George Noisom; *Men with Sheriff*, Dick Gordon and Bert Moorhouse; *Building and Loan Depositors*, Herbert Heywood, Eddie Kane and Mike Lally; *Reporters and Photographers*, Milton Kibbee and Franklin Parker; *Voices of Angels*, Joseph Granby and Moroni Olsen; *Donna Reed's Stunt Double*, Lila Finn; with Jean Acker, Monya Andre, Mary Bayless, Beth Belden, Joseph E. Bernard, Buz Buckley, Lane Chandler, Michael Chapin, Tom Chatterton, Edward Clark, Tom Coleman, Bryn Davis, Harry Denny, Lee Frederick, Herschel Graham, Carl Eric Hansen, Art Howard, Bert Howard, John Indrisano, Carl Kent, Effie Laird, Irene Mack, Wilbur Mack, Charles Meakin, Philip Morris, Netta Packer and Cedric Stevens.

For her third feature film, Gloria Grahame had the good luck to be cast in the first postwar effort from Frank Capra, a movie that was a major production at the time and one that — following a long period of lethargy — would eventually resound throughout cinema history. And unlike her tiny role in *Without Love*, Gloria snagged a juicy, memorable part in *It's a Wonderful Life*, essentially jump-starting her film career with a casual toss of her beautiful blonde hair. It is telling that she didn't make the film at MGM; they were trying to fit Gloria into the Margaret O'Brien drama *Tenth Avenue Angel* when she was requested by Liberty Films for this project.

Many of *It's a Wonderful Life*'s moments, scenes and dialogue have embedded themselves in America's cultural memory; this film is among the most beloved ever produced by Hollywood. That Gloria's presence and performance is not lost among them is a credit to the way she delightfully plays the role, and to Frank

Capra, who worked very hard to ensure that so many characters were spotlighted with genuine care and empathy. That, perhaps more than anything else, is what makes *It's a Wonderful Life* the enduring classic that it is.

It's a Wonderful Life begins with titles written in a Christmas card-like format, which refers obliquely to the origin of the story that inspired it. It is snowing in the town of Bedford Falls and voices from various homes are ascending skyward to ask the heavens to help someone named George Bailey. Two angels (voices of Moroni Olsen and Joseph Granby and pictured as blinking stars in the night sky) discuss the situation and agree to send angel Clarence Oddbody down to Earth to help George in his time of need. It is Clarence's turn to be sent on assignment and if he does a good job he will finally win his angel's wings. To help Clarence understand his assignment, the other angels show him — and the audience — much of George's life leading up to his current situation.

Several boys take turns sliding down a snowy hill on shovels in 1919. Young Harry Bailey slides too far and falls into icy water. Clarence is told that Harry's brother George jumped in and saved him, but lost the hearing in his left ear by doing so. Later, young George is working as a druggist's helper when the druggist, Mr. Gower (H. B. Warner), distraught at the news that his son has died from influenza, drinks heavily and mistakenly fills a prescription with poison tablets. George takes the prescription but does not deliver it; Mr. Gower boxes his ears when he returns until George explains about the poison, whereupon Mr. Gower cries with remorse. George vows never to tell anyone about the mix-up, and as the angels affirm to Clarence, he never does.

Older now and ready to leave Bedford Falls for a life of adventure, George (James Stewart) is given a suitcase by Mr. Gower. George sees beauty Violet Bick (Gloria Grahame) and admiringly tells her she looks good in the new dress she is wearing. "Oh, this old thing?" she replies. "I only wear it when I don't care how I look." With a flip of her blonde curls she perambulates down the street, distracting everyone who looks in her direction. At home, George is dismayed when his father asks him if he would stay and help run the family business, the Bailey Building and Loan. George wants to be an architect and build things — in places other than Bedford Falls. His father understands and doesn't press the issue.

George reluctantly agrees to accompany his younger brother Harry (Todd Karns) to Harry's graduation party at the local high school. George is welcomed back by many and asked to dance by Violet, but he only has eyes for Mary Hatch (Donna Reed), who is now a beautiful eighteen. They dance the Charleston, annoying the boy who was going to dance with Mary (Carl "Alfalfa" Switzer). In retaliation, he and a friend open the dance floor to reveal a swimming pool beneath it. George and Mary dance toward the opening and eventually fall in, to the delight of everyone watching. They continue to dance in the water, prompting everyone else to jump in and join them. Walking home in borrowed clothes, George romances Mary but is too shy to kiss her. Their evening is cut short when George's Uncle Billy (Thomas Mitchell) arrives with the news that George's father has suffered a stroke.

After Pa Bailey's death, the Building and Loan is up for grabs. Ready to leave town, George pauses to plead for the Building and Loan to remain open, if only to give people an alternative to groveling before the town's dominating businessman Mr. Potter (Lionel Barrymore). George's speech wins the day and the Building and Loan will stay open — if George stays to run it. So George gives his travel money to Harry so that he can go to college, where Harry becomes a big football star while George tends to the family business. Harry graduates and comes home, but with a wife and a firm job offer, meaning that George's dreams of roaming around the world are frustrated yet again.

In a grumpy mood, George wanders around town, finding himself at Mary Hatch's home. She is back from college but is dating Sam Wainwright (Frank Albertson). Sam calls and offers George the opportunity to invest in his new venture in plastics, but George isn't interested. He tries, quite roughly, to declare his personal independence once and for all, but finds himself embracing Mary with all the passion in his being. They marry. On the way to the train station for their honeymoon around the world, George pauses when he sees a crowd milling outside the Building and Loan. There's a run on it, and Uncle Billy has closed the doors. George talks to Billy, then lets everyone in and tries to explain the situation. Panic is averted when Mary brings in the honeymoon money and George doles it out to his customers. At closing time just $2 is left, but the Building and Loan has survived. George finds Mary at a broken-down old house that Mary and two friends have fixed as best they can, and his home life as a married man officially begins.

Years later, George and Mary introduce the Martini family to their new home in Bailey Park, a subdivision of nice little houses. Sam Wainwright and his new wife stop by on their way to Florida for vacation and ask the Baileys to join them. But they cannot get away, there's too much to do. Mr. Potter calls in George and offers him a job, at $20,000 per year. George is tempted, but then realizes that Potter is still after total control of the town and refuses. George calls him "a scurvy little spider." Mary becomes pregnant and has a boy. Then a girl. She has two more children before World War II begins. George is ineligible to serve because of his hearing loss. Harry Bailey becomes an air ace, shooting down 15 planes and winning a Medal of Honor for downing a plane that would have destroyed a transport full of American troops. Harry is on his way back to Bedford Falls and a big party is in the works.

Uncle Billy gloats to Mr. Potter about Harry's heroics and accidentally hands him $8000 of Building and Loan deposit money. It's terrible timing, as a bank examiner is waiting to check the Building and Loan's records before the Christmas holiday. When the money can't be found, Billy cracks under the strain, and George turns nasty, yelling at his family and losing most of his reason. Facing ruin, George goes to Potter to ask for help. Potter responds by calling the police to issue an arrest warrant. Panicking, George goes to Martini's bar and drinks himself into trouble, getting into a fight with a man whose wife he insulted on the phone a few minutes earlier. George drives drunkenly, crashes into a tree and wanders to the bridge overlooking the river. He's thinking of jumping in when Clarence the angel (Henry Travers) beats him to it. George jumps into the river and saves Clarence. Drying out in the

bridge tollkeeper's office, Clarence explains who he is to George, who doesn't believe a word of it. It's only when George states that he should never have been born that Clarence gets his inspiration, and takes action.

Clarence arranges for history to be rewritten. George has never been born. Then they walk around the town, with George completely confused by the town's abrupt changes and decided lack of hospitality. Nobody knows him. Martini's is now Nick's, and Nick throws them out after listening to Clarence call himself an angel. The town is full of seedy nightclubs and bars. George sees Violet Bick, now a streetwalker, being hauled off to jail. His own mother (Beulah Bondi), now running a boarding house, doesn't recognize him. Mary is an old maid librarian and screams when George accosts her. Running for his life, George goes back to the bridge and pleads for his old life back.

The angels listen and order is restored. George is ecstatic to find that people again recognize him. He runs through the streets yelling "Merry Christmas" to friends and familiar buildings. He gets home, ignores the sheriff with an arrest warrant and hugs his kids. Mary comes in and they embrace passionately. Then people start arriving with money for George. Mary has spread the word and everyone in town is coming over with whatever cash they can find. Word comes from Sam Wainwright that he will advance George whatever money he needs. Then Harry comes in, having flown through a blizzard to get home. Harry sees how well-supported George is by his friends and offers a toast: "To my brother George, the richest man in town." Joy floods through the house as the crowd sings "Auld Lang Syne." And a bell rings, indicating that Clarence has, at long last, won his angel's wings.

It all started in a bathroom. Writer Philip Van Doren Stern had an epiphany while shaving on February 12, 1938, regarding a man who wishes he had never been born and then is given the opportunity to see what the world would have been like without him. A two-page outline was produced that day but it would be years before anything more came of it. Stern revised his story several times but it never satisfied him and it failed to sell. Finally, in 1943, Stern rewrote it one more time with a Christmas background, titled his story "The

It's a Wonderful Life. Lonesome George Bailey (James Stewart) has just propositioned Violet Bick (Gloria) to walk through grass barefoot, then scale Mt. Bedford, swim by a waterfall and stay out all night, sure to cause a public scandal. Violet is having none of it.

Greatest Gift," and printed 200 copies of what was now a 24-page pamphlet. That year he sent them, in place of traditional Christmas cards, to friends and family. Upon receiving a copy, Stern's Hollywood agent sold the movie rights to it to RKO Radio Pictures for $10,000, with an eye toward casting Cary Grant as the man who discovers that life is indeed the greatest gift. The story itself, retitled, "The Man Who

Never Was," appeared in *Good Housekeeping*, and in 1945 was also published as a small book under its original "Greatest Gift" title. Meanwhile, three screenplays were produced attempting to translate the story to the big screen for RKO, but none of those scripts were deemed suitable. This, despite the fact that the scriptwriters were Marc Connelly, Clifford Odets and Dalton Trumbo!

It wasn't until Frank Capra, just back from serving in the Office of War Information in World War II, read Stern's pamphlet that film history began to be made. Once he read "The Greatest Gift," he knew that he had found the vehicle that would serve as his comeback project, and he was determined to do everything possible to make it successful. Capra loved the concept, exclaiming later in his autobiography, "It was the story I had been looking for all my life!" The RKO studio chief was eager to unload the story that he was convinced could never be properly filmed, and so sold it to Capra for $50,000 (claiming, says Capra in his autobiography, that he had paid that much for it originally; other sources hold with the $10,000 figure). The three rejected scripts were thrown into the deal for free. After five years of Hollywood inactivity due to wartime service, Capra was nervously raring to get back to work. He had to see for himself if he still had the talent that had won him three Academy Awards for directing, and if the public would still appreciate his optimistic, sentimental viewpoint on life. Capra was no longer working for a studio; he had formed Liberty Films (with two other major directors and a producer to oversee them) to independently produce the kind of features he wanted to make.

Realizing the difficulty in producing a workable script, Capra decided to start from scratch, basing the screen story firmly upon Stern's central idea. He hired the married writing team of Frances Goodrich and Albert Hackett to get back to the story's basic premise of a desperate man who must literally be shown what an impact his life has had on others. Goodrich and Hackett recycled ideas from all three earlier scripts but were the only writers who were able to integrate all the elements together into a cohesive whole. But Capra still wasn't satisfied, and had writer Jo Swerling rewriting the Goodrich-Hackett script — even before they were finished! The married writers were so upset to discover this that they finished it immediately and refused to do any further work on it. Following Swerling's rewrite, Capra called in Michael Wilson and Dorothy Parker for "polishes" and contributed a few changes himself. Ultimately, Goodrich, Hackett and Capra were credited with the script, with Jo Swerling receiving credit for "additional scenes."

All this turmoil involving the writers indicates that Capra wanted as much control over the final product as possible, as well as all the credit for it. Years later, even Mrs. Philip Van Doren Stern complained that Capra was always referring to her husband's original 24-page story as "a little Christmas card," and Capra replied that the story had merely served as inspiration. This, despite the fact that the story clearly delineates the central concept of what would become the film. Capra went right on referring to the story as "a little Christmas card" until his death in 1991, relentlessly reinforcing the notion that he was solely responsible for the film's enduring greatness. Prior to *Mr. Smith Goes to Washington*, Capra's biggest hits had been written by Robert Riskin, from whom Capra had ultimately disengaged, feeling that Riskin was receiving too much credit for their success. Riskin had gone his own way and Capra went his — but the director still needed someone to write scripts that conveyed his sense of morality and love of life. Hence, he tended to tinker with scripts in his post-war career more so than he had during his glory years. Capra felt, as the driving force behind his movies, that he deserved to have his name before their titles — and it is in front of *It's a Wonderful Life* — so much so that he named his autobiography *The Name Above the Title*. The result of Capra's selfish attitude was that writers became wary of working with him and his career suffered. He only directed five feature films in the years following *It's a Wonderful Life*.

Another explanation for Capra's career decline in the 1950s is that his movies went out of style. Capra's last four films are light entertainments, three of them musicals — two with Bing Crosby, one with Frank Sinatra — with his final effort being *Pocketful of Miracles* (1961), a big-budget, all-star remake of his own *Lady for a Day* (1933). Those films seem more attuned to the 1930s than the '50s and '60s. Even *It's a Wonderful Life* and *State of the Union* (1948) were viewed in some quarters as retreads of Capra's pre-war successes *Mr. Deeds Goes to Town* (1936), *Meet John Doe* (1941) and *Mr. Smith Goes to Washington* (1939). As public tastes evolved, the director's trademark virtues — occasionally mocked as "Capra-corn" — simply faded from the spotlight. Capra's inherent optimism, belief in the common man and unwavering faith in the American way of life became an increasingly tough sell to people who had lost family and friends and suffered during the war, or, conversely, those traits seemed sadly simplistic and out of fashion to those who considered themselves sophisticated. While Capra's 1950s films were relatively popular, they didn't have the same high status as his earlier productions, and the director gradually faded into obscurity.

Perhaps the essence of Capra's gradual career decline is that, following *It's a Wonderful Life* in 1946 and the excellent *State of the Union* in 1948, the director had little else of substance to say about America, having made his ultimate statement in *It's a Wonderful Life*. Except for the sharp political commentary and defense of humanism present in *State of the Union* (a more pessimistic film), it can be argued that Capra summarized his feelings about American society, the dehumanizing effects of poverty and moral lassitude, the importance of love and the sacred trust of life in *It's a Wonderful Life*. Not only is this film the pinnacle of Capra's artistic career, it also encapsulates all of his most cherished beliefs and feelings about life. What more could he have to say?

It's a Wonderful Life was the first production for Liberty Films, Capra's new company, and he spared no expense in bringing it to the screen. Originally budgeted at $2,362,427 — which was very expensive for that time — it finally totaled $3,180,000, more than $800,000 over budget, and finished four days later than scheduled. Those cost overruns eventually made the difference between the film breaking even and showing a modest profit. Capra ensured, however, that most of the money was visible on the screen. Although the film takes place in the Northeast, reportedly based on a small New York town (Seneca Falls) that caught Capra's fancy, Liberty Films built a four-acre, three-block-long set on RKO's Encino Ranch. The set featured some seventy-five separate stores and features, built in four separate sections that were eventually combined. Asphalt was laid for the streets and twenty large oak trees were transplanted along the main parkway thoroughfare through the town set. Animals that would be indigenous to the area — dogs, cats, squirrels, pigeons— were brought to the set and let loose to make themselves at home.

And the whole set had to be decorated for not only all four seasons but almost a dozen specific time periods between 1919 and 1945 as well. In addition the set had to be converted from the homey Bedford Falls into the disreputable Pottersville for the dramatics of the final act.

One of Capra's pet peeves was the manner in which traditional Hollywood snowstorms, which usually consisted of cornflakes bleached white, completely ruined recording tracks because their crunching underfoot was often audible and sometimes even drowned dialogue, necessitating dubbing in post-production. For *It's a Wonderful Life*, he was determined to find a different method, and under his guidance, RKO's staff did. Instead of noisy cornflakes for falling snow and gypsum for snow already on the ground, RKO's special effects team, led by Russell Shearman, mixed foamite, the chemical compound found in fire extinguishers, with ordinary soap and water. The mixture, when sprayed under various pressures, was found to effectively mimic snow, both in the air and on the ground. It could be manipulated for various effects, it didn't stain clothing or sets, and best of all, it was silent. Gypsum and the old standby, plaster, were still used, as was shaved ice on the roadways, but the new mixture cut the traditional plaster and gypsum costs by a considerable amount and looked completely real. "Tastes swell, too," joked James Stewart about the new method. "The only trouble is, you have to work fast with it. If I take too long, what with the soap and the water, I'm apt to find myself frothing at the mouth." The snow method was so successful that it was honored with a technical citation at the Academy Awards. The RKO Special Effects Department received a Class III Certificate of Honorable Mention "for the development of a new method of simulating falling snow on motion picture sets." For years to follow, the new technique became the industry standard for winter and blizzard effects.

The switch from Bedford Falls to Pottersville was very involved, since it meant changing the entire look of the town, plus the snowstorm effects, for just a few minutes of screen time. Nevertheless, it was absolutely necessary, as it provides George with the visual proof that his existence matters very much, that things would have changed drastically without his influence. Another edifice that undergoes a thorough transformation is the old Granville house at 320 Sycamore. It is seen in utter disrepair early in the film, serves as the dubious "Waldorf Hotel" for George and Mary Bailey's honeymoon, and ultimately becomes the homey Bailey residence. This dwelling best visually represents Capra's tenet that tender loving care can benefit anything or anybody ... except perhaps Mr. Potter. One effect that was not specially designed for the film is the retractable gym floor covering a swimming pool, into which Stewart and Donna Reed unexpectedly fall. Although many viewers believed that the device was fabricated for the film and was not realistic, the retractable floor was for many years in use at the Beverly Hills High School, where Capra filmed the graduation party. It provides the comic highlight of the movie, turning a routine Charleston dance into a number more suited for Esther Williams!

One area where Capra eventually economized was his depiction of Heaven in the opening sequence. He had balked at filming scenes of the angels in Heaven discussing George's predicament because, he said, so many people had so many different ideas about what the hereafter would look like. He was also afraid that whatever approach he used would elicit unwanted laughter. So, after many brainstorming sessions with his production staff, he settled on the visual of a clear, starry night, with three stars that moved and twinkled as angel dialogue was heard on the soundtrack. Any audience laughter would take place at the very beginning of the scene, and would be intentionally coaxed because of the unusual presentation. Symbolizing Heaven in this way was cute, it was designed not offend anyone, and it was cheap to produce. It was a bright, innovative and fiscally responsible way for Capra to overcome a production difficulty with originality, artistry and finesse.

Capra cast the film with care. He was a big believer that good casting was more imperative than good acting; that matching performers with roles specifically suited for them was the key to success. James Stewart was his only choice for the role of George Bailey. Stewart, also fresh from the war, and having just forced his release from a long-term contract at MGM, was very apprehensive about a return to the big screen, but he figured that his best bet would be with Capra. "I don't pick a story, I pick a director," he said. Stewart was unimpressed with Capra's story pitch but signed on anyway. To play Mary, Capra approached Jean Arthur, who turned him down because she was in rehearsals for the play *Born Yesterday*, from which she would eventually retreat, opening the door for Judy Holliday. Capra rethought the role and offered it to Donna Reed, a fresh-faced Iowa farm girl currently biding time in MGM's stable of starlets. Casting Reed set a proper small-town tone for the film, encouraging Capra to forego more urbane actors like Claude Rains and Vincent Price in the Potter role in favor of Lionel Barrymore, who was rather more folksy. With the major roles filled, Capra turned to two more troublesome parts. On his casting sheet Capra had no ideas for Clarence, the bumbling angel who helps George. He finally settled on Henry Travers, whom he had also considered for the roles of Mr. Gower, Pa Bailey and Uncle Billy. Travers is an inspired choice, mischievous and sweetly guileless in the role.

The other part that Capra had trouble filling was that of Violet Bick. Among the names on Capra's casting sheet were Ann Doran, Iris Adrian, Claire Carleton, Veda Ann Borg, Bernadene Hayes, Doris Merrick, Betty Lawford, Isabel Jewell, Jean Porter and Myrna Dell. But none seemed quite right to Capra, who wanted something very specific. (Ann Sothern fit the bill but she was unavailable.) He told Stewart, "She has to be sultry! She must be beautiful, too, because she'll be vying with Donna Reed for your love. But she can't be a big-town siren. She's got to have a small-town goodness about her." With shooting ready to commence, Capra was still searching for the right actress. He met with MGM's casting director, Bill Grady, who showed him screen tests of the studio's starlets. When he saw Gloria Grahame's test, he stopped in his tracks. Capra describes the moment in *The Name Above the Title*: "The second test was that of a sultry, surly young blonde that seemed undecided whether to kiss you or knock you down. 'Hey, Bill! Who's *that* dame?' 'Who is she? She's a star! But do you think I can get any of our jerk directors to listen? Two years she's been around her snapping her garters. You can have her for a cuppa coffee. Her name's Gloria Grahame.'" A few days later a deal was struck and Gloria was borrowed by Liberty Films for the duration of the shoot.

With Gloria in tow, the cast settled in at RKO's Encino Ranch for the summer of 1946 to make the film. Although much of *It's a Wonderful Life* takes place in winter, the cast was sweltering in the summer heat while filming those pseudo-snowy scenes. James Stewart spent some seventy days in front of the cameras; he's in almost every scene, and despite the rust he feared from five years away from moviemaking, he delivers one of his finest performances. Stewart is the perfect everyman in Capra's idyllic small town, friendly to all and exceptionally faithful to his friends, yet haunted by the notion that the opportunity to live a better, more exciting life is passing him by. Even though he doesn't age — Capra decided against using makeup to visibly age either Stewart or Donna Reed — Stewart captures the essence of George Bailey from his first scene. He's at his absolute best in the scene at Martini's bar, desperate for the first time in his life and reluctantly asking for divine assistance, only to be humiliated further by a punch to the jaw. *It's a Wonderful Life* marked an altogether triumphant return to the screen for the lanky Stewart, who had spent World War II in the Army Air Corps as an instructor and bomber pilot and emerged as a colonel (he was later promoted to a brigadier general in the Air Force Reserve). Stewart received an Academy Award nomination as Best Actor and he was the favorite to win, but the film lacked the support necessary to secure it for him.

None of the other cast members was singled out for acting honors, though several could have been. Donna Reed is well nigh perfect as Mary. Mary is a great match for George, and Reed is wholesomely sexy and splendidly resolute as Mary. The courtship scene after the dance is a highlight for Reed, not least of which because she (not a stunt double) accurately throws the rock that breaks the window in the Granville house. Capra noted many years later that his biggest regret regarding the movie (other than its tepid reception, over which he had no control) was his handling of Mary during the Pottersville sequence. He wished he had shown Mary (seen as a spinsterish librarian) to be a stronger, more independent character.

Thematically, the most effective motif would have been to have Mary marry Sam Wainwright, who would not have been a big success because George would never have told him about soybeans (Sam made a fortune turning soybeans into plastic aircraft hoods during the war). Showing the Wainwrights poor and unhappy would have made more sense than showing a timid, spinsterish Mary closing up the public library at 11:00 P.M. on Christmas Eve!

Lionel Barrymore is just right as the greedy Herbert F. Potter, who, contrary to the Production Code in force at the time, never receives any comeuppance for forcing George Bailey to the edge of insanity. Capra commented that he received more mail regarding the absence of punishment for Potter than any other aspect of the film. Barrymore's gruffness and relentlessly condescending demeanor balances the whole of Capra's more optimistic tone, and the fact that Potter gets away with larceny and *still* cannot close the Bailey Building and Loan is proof positive of Capra's belief that good will find a way to overcome adversity. It was also Barrymore, incidentally, who prodded Stewart into positive thinking. Upon his return to acting, Stewart was nervous and even dismayed, thinking that the profession was perhaps an unworthy one. Barrymore talked to him about it. "Don't you realize," he said, "that you're moving millions of people, shaping their lives, giving them a sense of exaltation? What other profession has that power or can be so important?" Barrymore helped persuade Stewart that acting was not only honorable but also valuable, and from that moment Stewart felt comfortable again as an actor.

In supporting roles Thomas Mitchell (as forgetful Uncle Billy), Samuel S. Hinds (gentle Pa Bailey), Beulah Bondi (kindly Ma Bailey), Ward Bond (boisterous Bert the cop), Frank Faylen (mischievous Ernie the taxi driver), Bill Edmunds (humble Mr. Martini), Sheldon Leonard (wise guy bartender Nick) and H. B. Warner (cast against type as troubled druggist Mr. Gower) are all superb, providing Capra with exactly the kind of characters — wise and foolish, eccentric and mundane, kind and cruel — with which he wanted to surround George Bailey. Even the smallest roles, such as Mrs. Davis (Ellen Corby), the woman who asks George for just $17.50 during the bank run sequence, are written, cast and enacted for maximum effect.

Balance is important to this story, and Capra needed a character to rival Mary for George's affections, a dynamic counterpoint to offset the wholesome purity represented by Mary. Enter Violet Bick. Violet is first seen as a youngster (Jeanine Ann Roose) in Mr. Gower's drug store with young Mary (Jean Gale). Both girls are interested in young George Bailey (Bobbie Anderson), who is employed running errands and delivering prescriptions for Mr. Gower. George knows what Violet wants for her sweet tooth, ringing up a sale for 2¢ worth of shoelaces (a bagful of licorice vines) without her even asking. "I like him," Violet confides to Mary, who is still thinking about what she wants to order. "You like every boy!" Mary replies. "What's wrong with that?" asks Violet, flirty even as a schoolgirl. She calls him "Georgie" and asks him to help her down off the stool. But young George doesn't fall for that ploy. It's obvious that he likes Mary when he fills her order and casually calls her "brainless" for not liking coconut, and for not knowing that coconuts come from Tahiti, the Fiji Islands and the Coral Sea. Mary confirms their true love by whispering in his deaf ear, "George Bailey, I'll love you till the day I die."

George (now played by Stewart) grows up and is ready to explore the world. And Violet has grown, too. In the lovely form of Gloria Grahame, Violet is a beautiful blonde traffic hazard. In Violet's most famous scene, she stops in front of Ernie's cab, where George, Ernie and Bert are talking. They all stop and stare at the luminous young woman who pauses to say hello to George, and George compliments her dress, a frilly, rather form-fitting frock that looks decidedly fresh. "What, this old thing? Why, I only wear it when I don't care how I look." With a sexy smile and a casual flip of her blonde hair, she continues strolling down the street. Capra stages a visual metaphor as the heads of George and Bert are seen rising above the roof of the cab to watch Violet walk away. And they're not the only spectators; as Violet crosses a street behind the parked cab, a middle-aged man pauses to turn and watch her pass as well. His reverie is broken by the horn of a car that nearly runs him over. Bert, George and Ernie turn to each other and Ernie asks,

"How would you like to..." "Yes," interrupts George, finishing their lusty thoughts and keeping the censors at bay.

Violet appears again at the high school graduation dance, asking Harry Bailey to dance and being surprised to find George there. Her efforts to get George to dance are thwarted by Marty Hatch, who implores George to dance with his sister Mary. Violet finds herself dancing the Charleston with Sam Wainwright — a character with whom she would seem to fit quite naturally — and is gently admonished by the school principal for showing a bit too much leg during the dance. She laughs and hugs him. Interestingly, Violet is not seen plunging into the pool like most of the other people. That doesn't seem to be her kind of thing.

On the night that Harry returns to town (with a new wife and prospective job), George decides to roam Bedford Falls. Just closing up her beauty shop, Violet sees him and leaves two men waiting for her. "I think I've got a date," she tells them, spotting George, "but stick around, just in case." Violet, still frilly and flirty, meets George in the parkway in the center of the town's main street, calling him "Georgie Porgie" and taking his arm as they walk. When she asks, "Don't you get tired of just reading about things?" he takes her question as an invitation to adventure. Unfortunately for George, the prospect of walking ten miles up to Mount Bedford, running barefoot through the grass, swimming in the green pool by the waterfall without any clothes, staying up to watch the sunset and creating a town scandal is not the sort of adventure that Violet had in mind. George's mood is soured even further by having a score of people listen to Violet's astonished reaction to George's proposal and getting a good laugh out of it. Embarrassed, George tells her to forget about the whole thing, adding to the bystanders' merriment, and soon finds himself at Mary's house.

That would seem to be it for Violet, but that's not the case. She is present at George and Mary's wedding; in fact, Violet catches the bouquet thrown by Mary, and she couldn't be happier. Perhaps Violet finally realized that George just wasn't for her. In fact, perhaps Bedford Falls just isn't for her. The next time Violet appears is on George's "crucial day," as the head angel calls it. When Violet visits George at the

Building and Loan, he gives her an envelope of money and then some more out of his own pocket, since she's broke and about to go to New York City to start over again. George clasps her hands and wishes her the best. "I'm glad I know you, George Bailey," she says in a voice full of emotion before kissing him on the cheek, leaving some lipstick. What could be viewed as a compromising situation — and is by Potter later — is diffused because the people seeing it, except for the visiting bank examiner, know that George would never cheat on Mary. And at the grand conclusion, after Mary has issued a call for help for her stricken husband, Violet arrives and returns the money George has lent her. "I'm not gonna go, George," she proclaims happily. "I've changed my mind." Violet is singing along with everybody else at the end of the movie.

Violet also appears in the Pottersville sequence, and she isn't as fortunate. The police are manhandling her into a paddy wagon from a dime-a-dance joint called Dreamland, and she's kicking and screaming all the way. "He's a liar," she screams. "I know every big shot in this town! I know Potter and I'll have you kicked off the force...." Violet's alleged crime isn't depicted but the clear implication is that she is a prostitute, and that this isn't her first collision with law enforcement. Just how Violet is turned from the town flirt into the town floozy without the presence of George Bailey is never explained. Since George never paid much attention to her, how did his presence manage to keep her respectable? Perhaps Violet needed her own guardian angel.

Gloria was a fresh-faced twenty-three when the call came from Capra to borrow her from MGM for *It's a Wonderful Life*. A deal was struck and Audrey Totter was assigned the small role in MGM's *Tenth Avenue Angel* that Gloria had been expected to play. Gloria recalled, "For a year and a half I hadn't done a thing but wait around." That wasn't strictly true; there were studio classes to take, lots of photo opportunities— usually in swimsuits— and USO tours to make to relieve the boredom of not acting. She was making decent money ($500 a week) by then, which also offset some of the frustration she was feeling. Her marriage was also in deep trouble. Before filming had commenced in the summer of 1946, Gloria had

already filed for divorce from Stanley Clements, then changed her mind. It would be another year and two more divorce filings before she would finally leave her immature, sometimes violent first husband behind. Yet in front of the cameras, Gloria was blonde dynamite.

Capra knew from the moment he laid eyes on Gloria that she was perfect for Violet Bick. He needed a woman whom audiences would understand was alluring to George but who would have ruined him had they gotten serious about each other. Gloria was sexy enough to entice any man in town, flirty enough to make physical temptation seem irresistible, and an actress secure enough to handle her scenes with pros such as James Stewart. Gloria had spent months hanging around the MGM lot and was familiar with just about everybody. She was impressed with the director and star but not cowed by them, and she was confident in her ability.

Gloria is excellent as Violet, commanding the screen in her first scene just as Lana Turner had in *They Won't Forget* (1937). She hits just the right notes of warmth, flirtatiousness and sexual promise in her street scenes. And later in George's office, confiding in him before leaving town, Gloria is dramatically solid. Then there's the Pottersville sequence, where Violet is being arrested and hauled away. It's just a quick vignette but it is absolutely believable thanks to Gloria's angry refusal to submit to the arresting police. Violet is well on her way to becoming a harridan in that scene and Gloria plays it to perfection. All in all, hers is a very impressive performance, the more so for being surrounded by such talented veterans of the silver screen.

Because her part was large, Gloria felt that she belonged with the company, and she did her best to fit in and do whatever the director wanted. Capra was very pleased with the result, often claiming later in life (and not without cause) that it was he who had made her a star. Gloria's beauty also gave Liberty Films and RKO, not to mention her home studio MGM, a solid publicity angle and those companies were quick to capitalize. Gloria found herself on the October 21, 1946, cover of *Life* magazine (she was shown "dancing in a swirl of tulle"), and briefly profiled as an up-and-coming MGM starlet inside. It wasn't either of her first two films that put her there; it was the buzz surrounding Capra's return to Hollywood and resulting film, still two months from being released.

RKO and Liberty Films had planned a late January release for *It's a Wonderful Life*, ignoring the built-in holiday appeal of the movie.

But when RKO could not secure Technicolor prints for their planned Christmas release *Sinbad the Sailor* in time for the holidays, they asked Capra if his movie could take its slot. So on December 20, 1946, just one week after film labs began producing prints, *It's a Wonderful Life* received its first premiere in New York City,

It's a Wonderful Life. Violet Bick (Gloria) tenderly thanks her friend George Bailey (James Stewart) for providing the funds to start all over again somewhere else after her Bedford Falls beauty shop closes.

and it opened for regular business the following day. It opened in Los Angeles on Christmas Eve, thus fulfilling the requirement to play in both cities for a week to qualify for the Academy Awards, and by the first of the year was playing in about forty theaters around America. Its general release was rescheduled for January 7, 1947, but by having it out in time for the holiday, RKO hoped that it would build word of mouth, it would fill a gap in their schedule and it would qualify for the Academy Awards. It was a gamble that should have worked, but seems to have backfired.

The weather was awful that Christmas season on the East Coast and the reviews of the film weren't as warm as expected. The movie did business, eventually finishing as the twenty-seventh highest grossing film of 1946-47, but did not achieve the spectacular business expected for it.

Reviews were surprisingly mixed for Capra's return to the screen. On the positive side, *The Hollywood Reporter* claimed that the film "is just a wonderful picture.... The Capra show is fine and clean, heart-wringing in spots, and in others, hilariously funny.... It's the greatest of all Capra pictures, and in saying that, one must mean one of the greatest pictures of this or any other year." *Newsweek*'s critic stated, "*Wonderful Life* is sentimental, but so expertly written, directed and acted that you want to believe it." *Time* concurred, calling it "a pretty wonderful movie. It has only one formidable rival (Goldwyn's *The Best Years of Our Lives*) as Hollywood's best picture of the year." Philip T. Hartung of *Commonweal* challenged his readers: "I defy you not to be moved by *It's a Wonderful Life.*"

Other critics liked it, but found faults. Bosley Crowther of the *New York Times* seemed to enjoy the "moralistic fable" but ended his review thusly: "Mr. Capra's nice people are charming, his small town is a quite beguiling place and his pattern for solving problems is most optimistic and facile. But somehow they all resemble theatrical attitudes rather than average realities. And Mr. Capra's 'turkey dinners' philosophy, while emotionally gratifying, doesn't fill the hungry paunch." Richard Griffiths in the *National Board of Review Magazine* praised Capra's directorial mastery yet castigated its premise "that kindness of heart is in

itself enough to banish injustice and cruelty in the world." And a few simply derided it. John McCarten of *The New Yorker* summarized his synopsis of the film's story this way: "As you have possibly gathered by now, *It's a Wonderful Life* is chock-full of whimsey (*sic*), and in his direction Mr. Capra has seen to it that practically all the actors involved behave as cutely as pixies." Manny Farber of *The New Republic* wrote that the film, "the latest example of Capracorn, shows his art at a hysterical pitch."

Audiences attended the film but did not flood the theaters that had booked it. This was due partly to the extremely cold weather, traditional last-minute holiday shopping and a general lack of interest in the film. RKO's advertising totally ignored the holiday angle that should have been exploited; its ads of the time make the film seem like a simple but sincere romance. Despite the powerhouse talents involved, and the fresh faces of Donna Reed and Gloria Grahame, the marketing department did not capitalize on those names and faces whatsoever. Rushing to get the movie into theaters before Christmas had caught the marketers unprepared. That rush also spoiled the film's Oscar chances. It received five nominations, a healthy quantity, but Liberty Films and RKO expected more. And then at the ceremony, the film was snubbed in all categories, while its chief rival, *The Best Years of Our Lives*, earned seven Academy Awards. Had the film been released as planned in late January, it might have fared better in terms of both immediate popularity and opportunity at 1947's Academy Awards, which, in historical hindsight, was considered to be a fairly weak field. The film did not go completely unrewarded; it was listed on several "best of the year" lists around the country, including that of the National Board of Review, and Capra won a Golden Globe award for his direction.

Still, Capra and Stewart were both very disappointed by the lukewarm reaction. Capra admitted later that perhaps the Christmas of 1946 was not the right time to release *It's a Wonderful Life*. Stewart commented, in an interview with Leonard Maltin, "It has always been amazing to me that after the war, people didn't want this story. They had been through too much. They wanted wild slapstick comedy, they wanted westerns, stuff like that. It just took a while for the country to sort of quiet down. Then we could start to think about family and community and responsibility to family and work and so on."

Regardless of its reception, both Capra and Stewart loved the movie, with each claiming it as his personal favorite of all their careers. In his autobiography, Capra is even more emphatic: "I didn't give a film-clip whether critics hailed or hooted *Wonderful Life*. I thought it was the greatest film I had ever made. Better yet, I thought it was the greatest film *anybody* ever made. It wasn't made for the oh-so-bored critics, or the oh-so-jaded literati. It was my kind of film for my kind of people; the motion picture I had wanted to make since I peered into a movie camera's eyepiece in that San Francisco Jewish gymnasium."

Yet while *It's a Wonderful Life* disappeared after a few months the way films did in those days, seemingly forever, it kept Capra busy for the next decade in another way. He was busy answering the letters from people writing about the movie. The letters came in the dozens, then in the hundreds. It was the kind of movie that made people reach out to others, especially around the holidays. Letters just kept coming, and Capra spent much of the rest of his life answering as many as humanly possible, thanking people for liking his favorite movie, and answering questions about it. For years he was genuinely astonished that so many people remembered his movie and took the time to write to him about it, for it wasn't very widely known. That is, until 1974.

Having sold Liberty Films and its properties, Capra was not involved in the rather complicated fate of his favorite film. It passed through several companies and somehow passed its copyright renewal date without a renewal. Thus, it passed into the public domain, meaning that anyone who possessed a print could exhibit it without having to pay for the privilege. Gradually television stations across the country began to broadcast the film, sometimes several times a year. Within a few years its exhibition during the Christmas holidays became so prevalent — with rival stations within the same regional markets playing it repeatedly, sometimes even in the same time slots — that its repetition became a national running joke. Even so, the strategy worked. Au-

diences watched in droves, year after year. Its television exposure, more than any other factor, led to *It's a Wonderful Life* being embraced as a national cinematic treasure.

The constant broadcasts finally came to an end in 1994 when Republic Pictures purchased the rights to the film's music from various sources, then used those rights to assert a claim upon the film itself. Republic was granted a new copyright and determined to show the film only once each holiday season on network television, hoping that a single showing would turn into "event viewing" for families around the country. But the impact of the film doesn't end there. In 1977, the made-for-television remake *It Happened One Christmas* starred Marlo Thomas in the role of Mary, whose life it is that needs to be saved. The cast includes Wayne Rogers as George, Cloris Leachman as the angel Clara and Orson Welles as Mr. Potter. Capra was in the process of writing a sequel to the original story in 1985 and approached Universal regarding its production. Its plotline is astonishing (read it in the *It's a Wonderful Life Fiftieth Anniversary Scrapbook* by Jimmy Hawkins [young Tommy Bailey]) and it is just as surprising that Capra even *considered* spoiling his masterpiece by besmirching it with a needless, ridiculous follow-up. Fortunately, the idea of a sequel has never seriously taken root.

At least three separate musical theatrical versions of the story have been staged at college and regional theaters. It seems probable that other versions — prequels, sequels or what have you — are inevitable, given the original's incredible popularity. For when Capra fashioned Philip Van Doren Stern's story about a man who wishes he had never been born into a film now beloved around the world, he, like Mary Shelley with her *Frankenstein*, created something that in time acquired a life of its own, with effects far beyond what its creator ever thought possible. *It's a Wonderful Life* is an American classic that, perhaps surprisingly, contains different meanings for different people. Its philosophies and politics can actually be interpreted in several ways, and not all of them as optimistically as Capra would have wanted. Yet its basic tenets, that each person is valuable, that no one is a failure who matters to others, that life itself is sacred, continue to resonate with each new audience that views the film.

It's a Wonderful Life is not a perfect film. It has clumsy moments, various gaffes and continuity issues and it is too sentimental for some tastes. At one point, George Bailey actually refers to Violet Bick as Gloria! That said, it remains one of the greatest of American films, not so much because of what it says (George Bailey, after all, is just one man) but because of what audiences receive from it. Few films have ever affected audiences as this one has. It was the summation of Frank Capra's career, and provided the springboard that catapulted Gloria Grahame into the public eye. She, along with James Stewart and the rest of the cast and crew, were perennially grateful to Capra for providing it to them.

It Happened in Brooklyn (1947)

CREDITS MGM. *Directed by* Richard Whorf. *Produced by* Jack Cummings. *Screenplay by* Isobel Lennart. *Original story by* John (J. P.) McGowan. *Director of Photography*: Robert Planck. *Film Editor*: Blanche Sewell. *Musical Supervision, Direction and Incidental Score by* Johnny Green. *Orchestrations*: Ted Duncan and Robert Franklyn. *Frank Sinatra's Vocal Orchestrations*: Axel Stordahl. *Piano Solos Played by* André Previn. *Musical Numbers Staged and Directed by* Jack Donohue. *Songs by* Sammy Cahn and Jule Styne. *Art Direction*: Cedric Gibbons and Leonid Vasian. *Recording Director*: Douglas Shearer. *Set Decorations*: Edwin B. Willis. *Set Decorations Associate*: Alfred E. Spencer. *Makeup Created by* Jack Dawn. *Assistant Director*: Earl McEvoy. *Additional Music Composed by* André Previn and Lennie Hayton. *Non-Original Music by* Léo Delibes (*Lakmé*) and Wolfgang Amadeus Mozart (*Don Giovanni*). Black and White. Flat (1.37:1). Monaural Sound. 104 minutes. Released on March 13, 1947. Currently available on DVD. Previously available on VHS and laserdisc.

CAST *Danny Webson Miller*, Frank Sinatra; *Anne Fielding*, Kathryn Grayson; *Jamie Shellgrove*, Peter Lawford; *Nick Lombardi*, Jimmy Durante; *Nurse*, Gloria Grahame; *Rae Jakobi*, Marcy McGuire; *Digby John*, Aubrey Mather; *Mrs. Kardos*, Tamara Shayne; *Leo Kardos*, Billy (William) Roy; *Johnny O'Brien*, Bobby Long; *Police Sergeant*, William Haade; *Corporal*, Leonard Bremen; *Canon Green*, Lumsden Hare; *Bus Driver*, Al Hill; *Mr. Dobson*, Raymond Largay; *Printer*, Mitchell Lewis; *Captain*, William Tannen; *Cop*, Dick Wessel; *Fodderwing*, Wilson Wood; *Soldier*, Bruce Cowling; with Harry Burns, Freddie Chapman, Antonio D'Amore, Boyd Davis, Phil Dunham, Bertha Feducha, Vincent Graeff, Jane Green, Mahlon Hamilton, Dell Henderson, Ralph Hodges, William Leicester, Frank Marlowe, Al Masiello, Angi O. Poulos, Carmela Restivo, Mickey Roth, Bob Stebbins, Richard Terry, George Travell, Leon Tyler, William Wagner, Joe S. Weber, Constance Weiler.

Gloria's third film at MGM gave her a slightly larger role than her second, though just barely. *It Happened in Brooklyn* is a musical vehicle for the talents of Frank Sinatra, Kathryn Grayson, Jimmy Durante and Peter Lawford. Billed fifth in the cast, Gloria only appears in the opening sequence and does no singing or dancing. Nevertheless, her character is the catalyst for what occurs in the story, and is referenced at the conclusion with fondness. A rare opportunity to see Gloria play comedy, the film provides her with perhaps her finest MGM role of the 1940s. That may be a stretch, considering its brevity, but Gloria could not have been better suited to a part at this point in her career. If the studio had found other such sharply delineated roles for her, Gloria would undoubtedly have meant more to the studio and found it much more to her liking than she did.

It Happened in Brooklyn begins "Somewhere in England," where a large contingent of American G.I.s are dancing and partying prior to being shipped back to the States at the end of World War II — all except for Danny Miller (Frank Sinatra), who watches the proceedings wistfully from an empty upstairs room. A comely nurse (Gloria Grahame) enters and chastises Danny for not celebrating with the other soldiers. She unwraps a silly-looking bandage from around his head (he had the mumps) and asks why he doesn't chase girls, including herself. When he shows her a picture of his girl — the Brooklyn Bridge! — she gasps. "You're not from Brooklyn! A Brooklyn guy is a friendly guy!" She's also from Brooklyn, and doesn't believe his claim. Danny goes downstairs and tries to mingle, with no success, as the nurse notes. "Brooklyn!" she huffs dismissively. He sees Jamie Shellgrove (Peter Lawford) playing the piano and shows Jamie how to play "Whose Baby Are You?" As the nurse hovers nearby, Danny makes an effort to befriend Jamie and an older man, who is introduced as Jamie's grandfather, Digby John (Aubrey Mather). Jamie is painfully shy, more so than Danny, and his grandfather wants to bring him out of his shell. After Jamie leaves, Danny suggests sending him to Brooklyn, but the conversation is cut short when Danny and the other soldiers are called away to return to America.

Back in the States, Danny visits the Brooklyn Bridge and sings a song about it. He needs to re-enlist for the draft and asks a cop for directions. The cop stops a woman driving by and pressures her into driving Danny to an armory. The armory sends him to a high school recruiting office, and there, leading a high school chorus, is the woman who gave him a ride, Anne Fielding (Kathryn Grayson). She thinks he's stalking her, but accepts his explanation for their second meeting. In the hallway, they are interrupted by custodian Nick Lombardi (Jimmy Durante), who remembers Danny from his high school days and invites him to stay in his schoolhouse apartment while Danny finds a job. Danny wants to work at a music store, but is only offered a shipping clerk's position. He wants to sing and sell records, and with Nick's encouragement, evidenced by their duet on "The Song's Gotta Come from the Heart," he is hired in that capacity. One of the songs Danny sings is "Time After Time," with music that Danny heard Jamie Shellgrove play. Nick tries to bring Danny and Anne together, but their dinner is a disaster. It is interrupted by the arrival of Jamie from England, sent by his grandfather to learn about life and girls from the Brooklyn expert, Danny.

At a celebration dinner, Danny and Anne sing a duet from *Don Giovanni* in a restaurant, but it becomes clear that Jamie is highly attracted to Anne, even though she is now seeing Danny. The teenagers who flock to the music store love to listen to Danny sing and play piano; he's a hit. He comes home one night to announce that the "Time After Time" song will be published; Anne sings it to Jamie, who was unaware of its creation. One of Anne's students, Leo Kardos (Billy Roy), is a piano prodigy who isn't old enough to be eligible for a scholarship. So Danny, Anne, Nick and Jamie arrange for a community concert featuring Leo at the music store and invite the scholarship committee. Jamie asks Anne what she would sing at a concert; she chooses "The Bell Song" from *Lakmé* and sings it in a fantasy production number.

As Leo's concert nears, it becomes evident to Nick that Jamie has deep feelings for Anne, while Danny, who is seeing her socially, does not. Nick tries to convey this to Danny, but he doesn't believe it. Danny finally realizes that Nick is right when Jamie talks about Anne in ways that Danny cannot. The concert is a big success and Leo is awarded the prestigious scholarship. Danny relinquishes his hold on Anne to Jamie just as Jamie's grandfather arrives from England. They have another celebration dinner, at which time Danny realizes that the woman with a hold on his heart is the Brooklyn nurse he met in England. He determines to find her.

It Happened in Brooklyn, as should be evident, is gossamer-thin in terms of story, character development and theme. It is quite entertaining, however, thanks to the talents of its lead performers, a solid song score and a few in-jokes along the way (Nick tells Jamie, "We got a tree here in Brooklyn," just two years after the release of *A Tree Grows in Brooklyn*). Yet there is no disguising the slenderness of its central idea: that Brooklyn is a great place to live. Whether or not this concept is true — and the movie itself seems unsure of that answer — the fact remains that it is a pretty flimsy idea upon which to construct a movie. One indicator of this is that only one song in this musical, "The Brooklyn Bridge," actually refers in any way to life or love in Brooklyn.

Danny Miller's fondness for Brooklyn is shared only by the nurse who chastises him at the beginning of the story — which may explain why she remains in his mind. The residents of Brooklyn have their own opinions of the borough. The cop who helps Danny get a ride is spending his last day there; he's to be transferred to Manhattan the following day. His first words to Danny are sarcastic: "Happy? Sonny, you're in Brooklyn," and "Brooklyn is where they send the bad policemen." Anne Fielding is even more deprecating, telling Danny, "There aren't any nice days in Brooklyn," "No one is friendly here; everything is horrible," and "Everybody in Brooklyn is miserable," all of which reflect her own unhappiness at not becoming an opera singer. Ultimately, of course, Anne discovers that Danny is right, that Brooklyn is a wonderful place to live and work, particularly as evidenced by the people who support Leo Kardos when he gives his first public concert.

The exteriors were shot in Brooklyn and much of the story takes place at New Utrecht High School, a real school which educated future show business folks Gene Barry, Jack Carter, Buddy Hackett, Harvey Lembeck, John Saxon and Patty McCormack, among many others. Stanley Ralph Ross, who co-authored *The Motion Picture Guide*, attended New Utrecht High School and mentions in his review of *It Happened in Brooklyn* that "none of the female teachers looked one bit like [Kathryn] Grayson. The prettier ones were more like [Jimmy] Durante."

Casting the beautiful and talented Grayson as a high school music teacher struggling to become an opera singer is just one indication of the film's preference for fantasy elements, yet such an approach is a hallmark of the MGM musicals of the time. Other instances include the singing and tap dancing of high school student Billy Long in the "I Believe" sequence set in the school gymnasium, Grayson's fantasy production number of "The Bell Song" from *Lakmé*, her restaurant duet with Sinatra from *Don Giovanni*, the notion that Peter Lawford could be painfully shy and insecure, and the somewhat elderly bobby-soxers who crowd the music store to hear Sinatra sing. This type of MGM musical, of which *It Happened in Brooklyn* is a perfect example, stresses entertainment value over other considerations—and are much beloved for that emphasis. The only question, which was asked by film critics of the time, is why MGM didn't present this film in color. But this was a minor musical for MGM, only the second to feature Sinatra in a leading role, and the second to team him with Kathryn Grayson. (*Anchors Aweigh* [1945] was the first on both counts, and, like this film, was also written by Isobel Lennart.)

It Happened in Brooklyn is unusual in that it features *two* separate production numbers featuring classical music. This is a rare opportunity to hear Sinatra singing opera, as he does

It Happened in Brooklyn. Stationed in England at the end of World War II, an Army nurse (Gloria) is dubious when Private Danny Miller (Frank Sinatra) insists that he is a Brooklyn boy. "A Brooklyn guy is a friendly guy," she exclaims.

in his restaurant duet with Grayson on "La ci darem la mano" from Mozart's *Don Giovanni.* And Grayson has her own fantasy number with Delibes' "Bell Song" from *Lakmé.* Including classical music in such a popular entertainment vehicle is uncommon, yet it provides the movie with an extra boost of class (perhaps emphasizing that Brooklyn has more to offer than one might imagine). However, critics have also noted that there is a strong reason why popular entertainers so rarely perform classical music in movies. Clive Hirschhorn in his book *The Hollywood Musical* termed Sinatra's duet with Grayson "charmingly ill-conceived"; he also called it "the comic highspot — albeit unintentionally." John McManus of *PM* noted, "Miss Grayson being the niftiest Lakmé in the business, if not the most bell-like...." This type of classical production number allows its popular performers an opportunity to stretch their talents and exposes audiences to historically significant music, yet also presents that music in less than optimum circumstances, unless its performers are at the top of their talents.

One performer at the top of his talent is Jimmy Durante. He was stuck in supporting roles for most of his career, but this is one time he was able to steal the spotlight. He is perfectly cast as a working-class guy, a janitor, with a heart of gold. He is the comic relief of the film, waxing about his hero, Mr. Chips, even while lamenting the fact he never got a girl. His voice threatens to screech several times and his malapropisms are quite amusing. He and Sinatra cut loose on "The Song's Gotta Come from the Heart," with Sinatra even mimicking the Schnozzola for a few verses. That song is reminiscent of Durante's old vaudeville routines; it is even interrupted for a chorus from an old Russian song, "Otchichornya." And Durante is endearingly tender in the film's best scene, when Nick asks Danny if he really loves Anne. He is stuck with some truly corny dialogue ("You don't have to help me. I like dirty dishes," he says just before "Time After Time"), but he brings an endearing style and welcome burst of energy to the proceedings.

Sinatra was beginning to make the jump to movie stardom here. Still thin and reedy, he sometimes seems intimidated by the task of carrying a movie's dramatics, yet he projects enough maturity to carry it off most of the time. He does a nice job with the songs, whether crooning his "Brooklyn Bridge" song on location or joining Durante for "The Song's Gotta Come from the Heart." Best of all is "Time After Time," a genuine classic love song sung without ostentation. If Sinatra isn't particularly impressive singing opera, he can be forgiven; it was not his strong suit. Grayson had more experience with opera and her voice is excellent, but neither is she up to the rigors of her specialty numbers. In fact, Grayson is not shown to advantage in this musical, which is unfortunate. On the other hand, she is perfectly believable as a music teacher and romantic foil for either Sinatra or Peter Lawford. The British Lawford does what he can with his silly role, pretending to be shy and then blossoming before the eyes of the bobby-soxers by rocking the house with "Whose Baby Are You."

Gloria Grahame plays her small but important role early in the film. In her crisp military uniform she is sharp, smart and stylish. Her unnamed nurse moves purposefully, gracefully in and out of scenes, keeping a critical eye on Danny Miller, unwilling to accept that he is really from Brooklyn. Gloria provides a tension to this sequence that is dramatically sound and darned funny at the same time. A simple quizzical raise of an eyebrow is all it takes to convey her disbelief — and yet it is also obvious that she sort of likes this guy. It's no wonder that when the story concludes, he remembers the color of her eyes. Gloria nails the part with seemingly effortless skill; it's a shame the script did not continue so that Danny could find her and prove once and for all that he really was a Brooklyn boy. At least the audience sees that he is going to try. This is the type of role that Gloria loved playing and should have essayed more often. *Variety* noted, "There's one excellent bit by Gloria Grahame as the nurse, which rates her further spotlighting. A real looker, the gal's also a fine comedienne."

Despite the film's superficiality, most critics liked it and endorsed it. Shirley O'Hara of *The New Republic* admitted that she "had a remarkably good time," and called the film "a professional job of popular entertainment." *Newsweek*'s critic outlined the film's appeal quite nicely: "The whole thing is consciously cute and blandly inconsequential, but if you're killing time, you could go a lot farther than

Brooklyn and do worse." The film industry trade publication *Estimates* labeled the film a "delightfully entertaining romantic comedy with music."

It Happened in Brooklyn, while not a prestigious project, was quite popular and made a surprising amount of money for MGM. It boosted or cemented the appeal of its stars in the eyes of the public and provided an all-too-brief showcase for Gloria Grahame at its beginning. Had Gloria been around at the end of the picture, she might have shared some of that popularity, but the film ends with Danny's determination to find the nurse instead of actually depicting that interaction. Still, for Gloria, this was a step forward in her career, and the next step would be a jump forward. A big jump.

Crossfire (1947)

CREDITS RKO Radio Pictures. *Directed by* Edward Dmytryk. *Produced by* Adrian Scott. *Executive Producer*: Dore Schary. *Screenplay by* John Paxton. *Adapted from the novel The Brick Foxhole by* Richard Brooks. *Director of Photography*: J. Roy Hunt. *Film Editor*: Harry Gerstad. *Art Directors*: Albert S. D'Agostino and Alfred Herman. *Special Effects by* Russell A. Cully. *Set Decorations*: Darrell Silvera and John Sturtevant. *Makeup Supervision*: Gordon Bau. *Music by* Roy Webb. *Musical Director*: C. Bakaleinikoff. *Sound by* John E. Tribby and Clem Portman. *Assistant Director*: Nate Levinson. *Dialogue Director*: William E. Watts. Black and White. Flat (1.37:1). Monaural Sound. 86 minutes. Released on July 22, 1947. Currently available on DVD. Previously available on VHS and laserdisc.

CAST *Captain Finlay*, Robert Young; *Sergeant Peter Keeley*, Robert Mitchum; *Montgomery*, Robert Ryan; *Ginny Tremaine*, Gloria Grahame; *The Man*, Paul Kelly; *Joseph Samuels*, Sam Levene; *Mary Mitchell*, Jacqueline White; *Floyd Bowers*, Steve Brodie; *Corporal Arthur Mitchell*, George Cooper; *Bill Williams*, Richard Benedict; *Detective Dick*, Richard Powers [Tom Keene]; *Leroy*, William Phipps; *Harry*, Lex Barker; *Miss Lewis*, Marlo Dwyer; *Military Policemen*, Robert Bray, Don Cadell, Jay Norris and George Turner; *Deputy*, Carl Faulkner; *Tenant*, Harry Harvey; *Major*, Kenneth MacDonald; *Police Surgeon*, George Meader; *Police Sergeant*, Philip Morris; *Waiter*, Bill Nind; *Soldier*, Allan Ray.

Crossfire is one of the two Hollywood treatises on anti–Semitism to appear in 1947. Both were huge hits and both were nominated for the Best Picture Oscar; the other one, *Gentle-*

man's Agreement, took the prize. Over the past six decades, however, *Crossfire* seems to have maintained the better reputation, perhaps because it presents its message within the parameters of its *film noir* setting, while *Gentleman's Agreement* is perceived as an obvious social diatribe. That either movie, let alone both, were made in Hollywood at that time was viewed by studio heads as a major risk; this serves as the perfect example of the studios being completely wrong in their evaluation of what audiences were interested in and willing to see — provided, of course, that controversial material was handled with a high standard of quality. It was Gloria Grahame's luck that MGM (one of the studios that warned RKO against making *Crossfire*) was nonetheless willing to loan her to the production, for it marked a milestone in her career.

Crossfire begins with a murder on a Saturday night in Washington, D.C., and the quick investigation into the crime by pipe-smoking police detective Finlay (Robert Young). The murdered man, Joseph Samuels (Sam Levene), was found in his apartment by his dinner date (Marlo Dwyer), who tells Finlay that he was last seen with a trio of Army servicemen in a nearby hotel bar. Finlay finds one of those servicemen, Montgomery (Robert Ryan), loitering outside Samuels' apartment door. Finlay also sends for Sergeant Keeley (Robert Mitchum), the superior officer of a corporal named Mitchell, whose wallet was found in Samuels' apartment. Mitchell himself is missing.

Montgomery, who has been out of the Army for two weeks but is visiting a few of his buddies stationed at the Stewart Hotel, tells Finlay and Keeley how he and servicemen Mitchell (George Cooper), Leroy (William Phipps) and Floyd Bowers (Steve Brodie)— who, like Montgomery, is newly discharged — were at a bar, met and befriended Samuels and followed Samuels to his apartment. He claims that they left Samuels alone and in good health. Knowing only that Mitchell is in trouble, Keeley sends men looking for him, and they are able to prevent the police from apprehending him. Hiding out in a movie theater balcony, Mitchell tells Keeley that Montgomery's story is basically true. Samuels befriended Mitchell and took him to his apartment, and the others followed a few minutes later. But then Mitchell

Crossfire. **This lobby card offers two Glorias for one: as Ginny Tremaine, hustling Corporal Arthur Mitchell (George Cooper) for drinks during an actual scene; and sexing up the movie's artwork behind Robert Young.**

left before the others because he felt sick. After wandering the streets, Mitchell found himself in another bar, talking to a hostess named Ginny (Gloria Grahame), who took pity on him and gave him the key to her apartment to get some sleep until she finished work. At Ginny's apartment, Mitchell was awakened by a mysterious man (Paul Kelly) who made himself at home, claiming at one point to be her husband. Uncomfortable with the strange man, Mitchell left and was almost caught by the police, finding refuge in the theater balcony, bringing the story back to the present.

Montgomery visits Bowers in a dark apartment and pressures him to keep to the story to which they have agreed. Leroy is persuaded by his friends to tell Keeley where Bowers is hiding. When Keeley arrives, Bowers asks him for some money and says he wants to leave town. Keeley agrees to help him, leaves and tries to tell Finlay where Bowers is, but is forced

to wait. Montgomery learns that Bowers talked to Keeley and is furious. When Keeley finally sees Finlay, the detective berates him for not telling him sooner; Bowers has been found dead, hung by his own necktie. Mitchell's wife Mary (Jacqueline White) arrives from out of town, determined to help her husband. She and Finlay visit Ginny to verify Mitchell's story. Ginny is reluctant to help but eventually admits meeting Mitchell and giving him the key. She cannot provide any details regarding time, however. But then the mysterious man appears from behind a curtain and authenticates Mitchell's story. Finlay and Mary leave as Ginny tells the man to get out of her apartment and leave her alone.

Finlay questions Montgomery and Mitchell again, then asks Keeley for help to prove that the anti–Semitic Montgomery killed Samuels. Leroy is asked to deliver a message to Montgomery, ostensibly from the dead man Bowers.

Finlay persuades Leroy to help by appealing to his basic sense of dignity. Leroy tells Montgomery that Bowers said, "The necktie wasn't any good." Not finding any proof of Bowers' death in the papers, Montgomery broodingly accepts that he is alive and goes to meet him. Finlay is waiting and tries to arrest him for murder; Leroy has provided Montgomery with the wrong address, but he arrived at the right place anyway, proving that he knew where Bowers was killed. Montgomery flees and is shot by the detective in the street. Keeley and Leroy watch him die. Finlay says, "He was dead for a long time. He just didn't know it," to assuage Leroy's guilt in the matter — and then go for coffee, as a new day is dawning.

Crossfire was the second film made about anti–Semitism in 1947, but it was the first one released to theaters, because executive producer Dore Schary, producer Adrian Scott and director Edward Dmytryk put the film on a fast track, with a shooting schedule of just twenty-two days and 140 camera setups. Schary delayed other films for a couple of weeks to allow Dmytryk to film on their already constructed sets, and the director was so economical that the filming wrapped two days early and under budget. While 20th Century–Fox was making a huge — and very public — display of adapting Laura Z. Hobson's best-selling book *Gentleman's Agreement* to the screen, RKO quietly and quickly made *Crossfire*, shooting almost entirely at night with the only leading cast in memory consisting of three Roberts: Young, Mitchum and Ryan.

RKO was able to release *Crossfire* in late July, while *Gentleman's Agreement* bowed in December and didn't receive a full release until February of 1948. Ultimately, *Gentleman's Agreement* was the bigger winner; it earned four times as much money as *Crossfire* and won three Oscars to *Crossfire*'s none. But in the summer of 1947 the public at large was either unaware of or didn't care that a big social message movie with the same central theme was just months away; millions of moviegoers plunked down their 40 cents to enjoy a hard-edged, *noirish* thriller that just happened to have a social conscience.

Relatively few people realized that the film they were seeing had a completely different central conceit than its literary origin. *Crossfire* is

based on future Hollywood writer-director Richard Brooks' debut novel *The Brick Foxhole*, in which a man is killed by because he is believed to be homosexual. While gay characters and themes are all the rage these days, no studio would openly handle the subject at the time. In fact, homosexuality was closeted on the big screen into the 1960s, and didn't become faddish as a story element until the 1990s. Producer Scott had the idea to downplay the homosexual element in favor of the character's already present racial hatred and pitched the idea to Schary, who had recently become production head of RKO. Though hesitant at first, Schary was persuaded by the power of John Paxton's treatment, and felt it was high time for Hollywood to tackle the subject of anti–Semitism. He put his reputation on the line for the film to be made, overriding studio concerns about the subject's "limited appeal" and objections from other studio heads (many of them, ironically, Jewish) about "stirring things up."

The film takes a completely different approach to the subject than *Gentleman's Agreement*. Where the 20th Century–Fox film centers on a writer who pretends to be Jewish in order to experience discrimination first-hand, *Crossfire* is a dark murder investigation that utilizes a character's hatred of Jews for his motivation to kill. This motivation is hinted early but not fully developed until two-thirds through the story. Most critics lauded such an approach then, and still do today: Otto Penzler notes in *101 Greatest Films of Mystery and Suspense*, "*Crossfire* is the first of the pure *noir* films to raise a serious social issue and as a result achieved the kind of critical acclaim that was never accorded equally good films that lacked a serious message." The brutal killing of a man because of his heritage is dramatically more powerful than whether such a man (as in *Gentleman's Agreement*) will be allowed to check into a fancy hotel or be accepted into a country club. That simple fact helps explain why *Crossfire*'s reputation has remained high while *Gentleman's Agreement* has undeniably slipped over time.

There are many terrific elements in *Crossfire*. It is a true *noir* adventure; the story takes place over the course of two days but is shot almost exclusively at night in Washington (although as photographed, it could be anywhere), a town filled with cheap gin joints, crowded dance halls, dark apartments and shadowy characters. It is just after World War II, yet the peacetime air is filled with foreboding. It is precisely this feeling—an anticipation of conflict—which is intended, and which is explained by Joseph Samuels (Sam Levene) to obviously troubled soldier Arthur Mitchell (George Cooper) in the bar during the second flashback sequence:

> I think maybe it's suddenly not having a lot of enemies to hate any more. Maybe it's because for four years now we've been focusing our mind on ... [Samuels lifts a peanut from a tray at the bar] ... on one little peanut. The "Win the War" peanut. That was all. Get it over. Eat that peanut [Samuels pops the peanut into his mouth and eats it]. Now we start looking at each other again. We don't know what we're supposed to do, we don't know what's supposed to happen. We're too used to fighting. But we just don't know what to fight. You can feel the tension in the air. A whole lot of fight and hate that doesn't know where to go. A guy like you maybe starts hating himself. Well, one of these days maybe we'll all learn to shift gears. Maybe we'll stop hating and start liking things again, eh?

Samuels' dialogue summarizes the story's dramatic conflict on a personal level, while trying to communicate with Mitchell, and also provides a larger psychological basis, almost direct reasoning, for his own impending murder. It is the single most important piece of dialogue in the film, yet Mitchell, in a voice-over, downplays it, calling Samuels "screwy," thereby shifting the dramatic emphasis away. But gradually Mitchell, with the audience tagging along with him, begins to see the sense in Samuels' words. He gleans enough wisdom from the man that he agrees to go to dinner with Samuels and his date. Mitchell doesn't know or care that Samuels is Jewish (he is told later, by Finlay), and it wouldn't make any difference at all if he had known. He is an innocent, confused soldier, lonely for his wife and unsure of his future. He is easily led by more powerful personalities; Montgomery (Robert Ryan) leads him into vice, while Samuels begins to lead him back to rationality. Unfortunately, Samuels, who observes that Montgomery is a troublesome influence, is not powerful enough to defend himself when attacked.

Samuels is shown to be a nice, caring person; a bit nosy, perhaps, but someone who clearly doesn't deserve his fate. His killer, Montgomery, is aggressive and abrasive, a disgruntled chatterbox with little regard for the feelings of others. Montgomery casually derides his servicemen companions, unconcerned that he embarrasses them in public. As portrayed by Robert Ryan, Montgomery is a belligerent bully, outwardly vivacious but inwardly hostile. Utterly self-centered, he cares only about his own immediate world, and if in his mind that world is invaded by a "Jewboy," a member of a race that he tells Finlay is filled with "guys who played it safe during the war, scrounged around, keeping themselves in civvies, got swell apartments, swell dames, you know the kind," then he feels required to take some action about it. Ryan's dynamic portrayal resulted in an Academy Award nomination for Best Supporting Actor, the only such nod in Ryan's long and prolific career (he lost to Edmund Gwenn in *Miracle on 34th Street*).

Montgomery is a difficult character. He's been out of the service for two weeks, but doesn't have anywhere to go. He is ostensibly visiting "some buddies" still in the Signal Corps, stationed at the Stewart Hotel (although Bowers, like himself, has left the service), but it's hard to accept that any of these guys would like Montgomery enough to hang around with him, especially with his constant insults. Would the Army condone his ongoing presence or tell him to get lost? Montgomery states that he is a former St. Louis cop and "knows the score." Yet he regularly reveals clues about his own participation in the murder and personal hatreds. He and Bowers are the perpetrators of the murder, and he eventually murders Bowers when Bowers seems ready to crack and confess. Why wouldn't he go after Mitchell, and do so early after Samuels' murder? Mitchell is the prime suspect, having left his wallet at the scene of the crime because he was drunk and sick. When Mitchell is eventually found by the police he might be able, despite his drunken condition, to prove his innocence. Why wouldn't Montgomery find and eliminate Mitchell, making Mitchell's death look like suicide, brought about by guilt over the murder? Finally, knowing that the police are closing in, why wouldn't he just leave town, as Bowers thinks to do? If Montgomery is as sharp as he is supposed to be, he would see, as the audience does, that Finlay and Keeley consider him to be the killer. Yet he remains oblivious because he is so self-centered.

And that leads directly to the film's greatest weakness, which is that there's no real mystery in this murder mystery. That's why earlier in this review, the film is termed a "murder investigation." From the middle of Mitchell's recalled flashback of events, it is perfectly clear that Montgomery is the killer, as well as why he kills Samuels. The fact that it takes Finlay another half-hour of running time to figure it out is exasperating, although Finlay's explanation for his own shortsightedness is satisfactory. Paxton's screenplay should have maintained the illusion that Mitchell could have killed Samuels for a longer period of time, and toned down Montgomery's sudden outbreaks of anger, while making him smarter.

There is yet another character even more bizarre than Montgomery, one listed in the end credits as simply "The Man," played by Paul Kelly. When Mitchell meets at Ginny Tremaine's apartment, he claims to be her husband, then refutes his own statement. As he makes himself at home in Ginny's apartment, waiting for her to come home, he gives Mitchell, and the audience, the creeps. If he really is her husband, why is he acting so weirdly? If he's not her husband, then who is he? Later, when Ginny is visited by Finlay and Mrs. Mitchell, he appears again, verifies Mitchell's story and offers to testify on his behalf. At that point he truly does seem to be her husband, yet Ginny hisses, "I hate you! I hate your guts!" and threatens to throw him out. His purpose in the story is unclear, and detracts from its clarity of purpose, although Kelly tries to make the most of his character's mystery. The character is quite faithful to its origin in Brooks' original story, and it seems out of place there as well.

Ginny Tremaine, however, is another story. In the novel, she is a prostitute who sleeps with Mitchell to relieve his loneliness. In the movie, she is a bitter, unfortunate B-girl, forced to court drunks at gin joints for a living. Ginny (Gloria Grahame) can perhaps be viewed as the distaff side of Montgomery. She, also, is completely self-absorbed and hostile toward others. Both have jeering attitudes and are tart-tongued. Montgomery's favorite adjective is "stinking," which he uses at least half a dozen times to indicate offensiveness; the only other person to say it even once is Ginny. Yet Ginny still retains a basic decency and compassion, traits which have died in Montgomery. At first wary of Mitchell's attempts to talk to her, she finally recognizes that he doesn't wish to take advantage of her and she gives him the key to her apartment so he can rest until she comes home, when she can cook him a good meal. She reluctantly responds to a person who needs her, thereby demonstrating that faith in the good of humanity still survives even in the dark, dangerous world this movie depicts.

Gloria is quite good as Ginny, the second of her soon-to-be-trademark floozy characters. There's a great moment when Mitchell quite innocently asks, "You know what I'd like to do?" and Ginny murmurs knowingly, "Um-hum." At the Red Dragon, she is dressed in a lacy black gown, very low cut in front and behind, and black high-heeled shoes, the epitome of the relatively cheap promise of sex. She readily kisses Mitchell, and takes offense when he says she reminds him of his wife. Screen restrictions of the time prohibit the character from being played as originally written by Brooks, but Gloria leaves no doubt as to Ginny's easy virtue.

Yet when Finlay and Mrs. Mitchell come calling later, Ginny is almost dowdy in a housecoat with circular patterns all over it. Ginny's appearance, however, doesn't change her character. She refuses to answer most questions and takes verbal jabs at Mrs. Mitchell, demanding why she wasn't with her husband: "Okay, where were you when he needed you? Maybe you were some place having beautiful thoughts. Well I wasn't. I was in a stinkin' gin mill, where all he had to do to see me was walk in, sit down at the table and buy me a drink." Just as with Mitchell, however, Ginny eventually recognizes that no one is trying to take advantage of her, and tells Finlay what she can. It isn't enough to clear Mitchell, but then the strange man steps out from behind a curtain and confirms that Mitchell was indeed sleeping in the apartment when he arrived, thus eliminating the soldier as a murder suspect.

Gloria regarded her *Crossfire* role as the best of her career. She worked for just two days but created an indelible portrait of an embittered, down-on-her-luck, yet still vulnerable woman forced by circumstance to survive by any means necessary. Director Dmytryk met her in a casting session and felt that she was "confused and insecure, and kind of kooky, but a serious kind of kooky. She had psychological problems that were on the verge of being serious, but weren't really, not at that time." Dmytryk used Gloria's smoldering sexuality in her scene at the Red Dragon to offset the preponderance of testosterone throughout the rest of the film, further offsetting the male bias with the primness of Jacqueline White in the role of Mitchell's caring, selfless wife.

Crossfire also represented Gloria's coming-of-age as an actress. In an interview with the magazine *Time Out* in 1978, she credited dialogue director Bill Watts with introducing her to the psychological side of acting. "It's *thinking*," she said. "I was doing my hair for a scene and he said, 'Forget the hair.' And he started talking and I forgot the hair, the makeup and everything. All he did was talk to me about *who* the character was, *where* she was, *what* she was until I was so immersed in what it was all about. After that, maybe I just did it for myself." For her efforts, Gloria was also nominated for an Academy Award, in the Best Supporting Actress category. She lost to Celeste Holm from the rival *Gentleman's Agreement.*

Gloria excels in presenting the defensive side of Ginny's personality. Ginny resists the approaches of Mitchell, Mrs. Mitchell and Finlay, reacting to each of them with disdain and a trace of fear. But eventually, reluctantly, she allows them to penetrate her antisocial armor and meet the compassionate woman underneath. And that melting away of her armor may be the key to Gloria's performance. Dmytryk writes in his autobiography *It's a Hell of a Life but Not a Bad Living,* "Transition is what acting is all about," and Gloria illustrates this truism quite beautifully. Sensing the vulnerability beneath her viperous attacks allows the other characters, and the audience,

to appreciate Ginny as a real person, to empathize with her. Ginny is only tangentially involved in the murder investigation, yet she provides more than her share of the movie's drama.

Although the mystery surrounding the murder is weak, the investigation itself is quite strong. Except for Finlay's one brief bungle when he keeps Keeley waiting for two hours (and then unfairly blames Keeley for Bowers' death), Finlay's methodology and intellect are superior. Robert Young plays Finlay as a tired professional no longer captivated by his work; he just wants to find the killer and do it quickly. In the space of a day he understands the case inside and out and he sets an ingenious trap to catch the killer, who really should have known better. Finlay takes his time, collects the facts, and then tries to make sense of them. Young is very good in the intellectual role.

And Finlay is the movie's moral con-

Crossfire. One of the most famous images of Gloria is this publicity shot of the blonde beauty lounging on a chaise, although she seems tense rather than relaxed. She wears this provocative dress in her first *Crossfire* appearance (later donning a conservative polka-dot housecoat).

science. It is he who must determine the truth and he who eventually dispenses justice to the killer. Finlay has the most dramatic dialogue in the film, describing to Keeley how "the motive had to be in the killer himself," and commenting to Leroy, "Hating is always the same. Always senseless. One day it kills Irish Catholics, the next day Jews, the next day Protestants, the next day Quakers. It's hard to stop. It can end up killing men who wear striped neckties. Or people from Tennessee [Leroy is from Tennessee]." He summarizes Montgomery's level of racism quite succinctly: "This business of hating Jews comes in a lot of different sizes. There's the 'you can't join our country club' kind. And 'you can't live around here' kind. Yes, and the 'you can't work here' kind. And because we stand for all of these, we get Monty's kind."

It works dramatically to have Finlay a one-man judge, jury and executioner, but it isn't particularly realistic in police procedural terms. Other policemen are present, but serve little purpose. Finlay is at his best bouncing his ideas off of Sergeant Keeley, a former newspaperman, who is at least as sharp as the detective. Keeley knows instinctively that Mitchell is innocent and works to solve the case without having to surrender Mitchell to Finlay, whom he suspects is looking for the easiest solution to the murder. He tells Finlay several times that Mitchell could not have killed Samuels, or anyone else. "How do you know?" asks Finlay. "Could you?" "I have," replies Keeley, referring, of course, to his wartime exploits.

Robert Mitchum seems his usual laconic self in the role of Keeley, yet it is Keeley who continually moves the action forward: He sends men to find Mitchell, hides him from the police, calls in Mitchell's wife, unwittingly hurries Bowers' death and helps persuade Leroy to try to set up Montgomery. It is Keeley who first throws suspicion on Montgomery's version of the evening in question and repeatedly reminds Finlay that Montgomery is not to be trusted. He doesn't beef when Finlay locks him away for interference, and he's ready to help catch the real killer when given the opportunity. (In the novel, it is Keeley, not Finlay, who settles the score with Montgomery.)

Dmytryk was so taken with Mitchum's understanding of the character and seemingly effortless charisma that wherever possible he padded Mitchum's role, which was reduced in the screenplay from the novel. In terms of the three major roles, Keeley is the least significant (despite his penchant for moving the action forward); in terms of the three stars, Mitchum may be the most memorable. Mitchum plays Keeley as a no-nonsense guy who allows the men under his command to live their own lives but who cares enough to aid them when they need it. This role helped Mitchum receive bigger, though perhaps less rewarding, roles in other pictures, and solidified his reputation as a box office draw.

Robert Ryan also found that *Crossfire* affected his career. While he appreciated the acclaim he received and never regretted taking the role that he had told author Richard Brooks he wanted to play as early as 1945, Ryan disliked the typecasting that followed him in subsequent years. One of the most liberal men in Hollywood, and a man who fervently believed in civil rights for all, Ryan was constantly offered villainous roles in the same temperament as that of Montgomery. Occasionally, as in *Odds Against Tomorrow* (1959, also with Gloria), he would play them, and he couldn't help but extend his bigoted screen persona because he was so convincing an actor.

When *Crossfire* debuted in July 1947, it was greeted with praise. *Newsweek* began its review by saying, "*Crossfire* is an example of what Hollywood can do (and on a fairly modest budget) if it wants. Or if it has the courage more than once in a blue moon. [It's] the sort of film that the critics and a critical public have come to expect only from abroad." It was listed by *Newsweek* as one of the year's best films. It also landed on the "best of the year" lists of *Time* and the *New York Times*. *Time*'s critic claimed, "Much of the movie is as brutally effective as a series of kicks in the solar plexus," and praised everyone in the cast, including Grahame: "Gloria Grahame is one of the very few well-baked tarts in any recent movie." Bosley Crowther of the *New York Times* awarded the film an "unqualified A for effort," and termed it "a thematically articulate film," while also noting, "Gloria Grahame is believably brazen and pathetic as a girl of the streets."

Shirley O'Hara of the *New Republic* loved it: "*Crossfire* deserves superlatives and RKO, congratulations. The picture is made with a straightforward, intense simplicity, a surety and lack of pretension, an almost taken-for-granted assumption of the reality of decency." Otis L. Guernsey of the *New York Herald-Tribune* seconded that theme: "*Crossfire* is a savage melodrama which keys the problem of race hatred into an unusual murder story."

Even those critics who didn't love the film admitted its importance. Philip T. Hartung of *Commonweal* objected to Montgomery's second killing, which he felt vitiated the social impact of the first. Yet, "Assets like Dmytryk's thoughtful direction and the good cast in which Robert Ryan, Gloria Grahame and Paul Kelly excel, outweigh its faults. And its point that murder grows out of minor hatreds (for which we may all be to blame) is something to be considered seriously."

In 1948 *Crossfire* was nominated for five Academy Awards (Picture, Director, Screenplay, Supporting Actor and Supporting Actress) but failed to win any. It won the Best Social Film prize at the Cannes Film Festival, the Edgar Allan Poe award for Best Picture from the Mystery Writers of America, and was nominated for the Best Picture award from the British Academy of Film and Television Arts. It was selected as one of the ten best films of the year by the National Board of Review, and won quite a few social humanitarian awards.

The success of *Gentleman's Agreement* (currently in theaters at Oscar time) overwhelmed *Crossfire* at the Oscars, but there was another factor that worked against *Crossfire's* chances. In October 1947, after the film had already made its money but before the Academy Award nominees were chosen, producer Scott and director Dmytryk were subpoenaed by the House Un-American Activities Committee (HUAC). In very public Congressional hearings, the two men were among ten Hollywood writers and directors who were found to be in contempt of Congress, and were subsequently jailed (almost three years later, after a series of appeals had been denied). The Hollywood Ten were national news by the time the 1947 Oscars were awarded and many historians believe that the film industry was turning away from any perceived association with Communists, no matter the merit of the work created by those accused. On Oscar night, according to Gloria's

biographer Vincent Curcio, the *Crossfire* honorees were rather pointedly ignored; despite a big box office hit and five nominations; they were pariahs in the suddenly changing political climate.

Scott and Dmytryk were fired from RKO despite their success with *Crossfire*; Scott never produced another movie. Dmytryk ultimately testified before another Congressional committee, named names (all of whom were already known to the committee) and slowly re-established his directing career. Having lost two prime talents of his studio, Dore Schary was forced to retrench in the face of a changing social landscape. His preferred program of gritty, realistic social dramas was scrapped in favor of lightweight entertainments. Less than a year later, Howard Hughes purchased a majority interest in RKO and Schary, forced to abandon his pet projects, stepped down, eventually landing at MGM. Under Hughes' tenure, RKO quickly lost the prominence for which Schary and his staff had fought long and hard. But for the short while that Schary was in charge, RKO became, for the first and only time, an industry leader mixing social commentary with entertainment to create some remarkable movies.

MGM didn't know what to do with Gloria, and she was having serious trouble remaining married to Stanley Clements, who was gambling harder than ever. The loan-out to RKO changed the course of her career. Gloria was making $500 a week at the time, but MGM made $3750 for loaning her to RKO for just two days of work in *Crossfire*. She was perfectly cast and, thanks to the coaching of Bill Watts, able for the first time to truly understand what she was doing. Further, her symbiosis with the part quickly made the rounds of Hollywood's casting directors and "typed" Gloria's persona as a "bad girl," a situation that solidified when she received the Oscar nomination. Gloria's first foray into *film noir* opened a range of projects to her and opened the eyes of others who suddenly wanted to cast her in their dark dream projects. Finally, *Crossfire* proved that her performance in *It's a Wonderful Life* had been no flash in the pan, and that she was an actress of some accomplishment.

Edward Dmytryk relates this anecdote in his autobiography: "After our rough-cut showing to the sound and music department, one of the young assistant sound cutters, an Argentine, complimented me on the picture. 'It's such a fine suspense story,' he said. 'Why did you have to bring in that stuff about anti–Semitism?' 'That was our chief reason for making the film,' I answered. 'But there is no anti–Semitism in the United States,' he protested. 'If there were, why is all the money in America controlled by Jewish bankers?' I stared at him in astonishment. 'That's why we made the film' was all I could think of to say."

Song of the Thin Man (1947)

CREDITS MGM. *Directed by* Edward Buzzell. *Produced by* Nat Perrin. *Screenplay by* Steve Fisher and Nat Perrin. *Additional Dialogue by* James O'Hanlon and Harry Crane. *Story by* Stanley Roberts. *Based on the Characters Created by* Dashiell Hammett. *Director of Photography*: Charles Rosher. *Film Editor*: Gene Ruggiero. *Art Direction*: Cedric Gibbons and Randall Duell. *Musical Score*: David Snell. *Song "You're Not So Easy to Forget" by* Herb Magidson and Ben Oakland. *Recording Director*: Douglas Shearer. *Set Decorations*: Edwin B. Willis. *Set Decorations Associate*: Alfred E. Spencer. *Costume Supervision*: Irene. *Costume Associate*: Shirley Barker. *Hair Styles Designed by* Sydney Guilaroff. *Makeup Created by* Jack Dawn. *Unit Production Manager*: Robert E. Barnes. *Assistant Director*: Jerome Bergman. *Additional Music by* George Bassman, Robert Franklyn, Lennie Hayton, Bronislau Kaper, Nathaniel Shilkret, Edward Ward and Roy Webb. *Orchestrator*: Wally Heglin. Black and White. Flat (1.37:1). Monaural Sound. 86 minutes. Released on August 28, 1947. Currently available on DVD. Previously available on VHS and laserdisc.

CAST *Nick Charles*, William Powell; *Nora Charles*, Myrna Loy; *Clarence "Clinker" Krause*, Keenan Wynn; *Nick Charles, Jr.*, Dean Stockwell; *Tommy Edlon Drake*, Phillip Reed; *Phyllis Talbin*, Patricia Morison; *Fran Ledue Page*, Gloria Grahame; *Janet Thayar*, Jayne Meadows; *Buddy Hollis*, Don Taylor; *Mitchell Talbin*, Leon Ames; *David I. Thayar*, Ralph Morgan; *Dr. Monolaw*, Warner Anderson; *Jessica Thayar*, Bess Flowers; *Phil Orval Brant*, Bruce Cowling; *Bertha*, Connie Gilchrist; *The Neem*, Henry Nemo; *Al Amboy*, William Bishop; *Helen Amboy*, Marie Windsor; *Dunne*, George Anderson; *Police Inspector*, Morris Ankrum; *Male Nurse*, Gregg Barton; *First Mug*, Leonard Bremen; *Officer Nagle*, Al Bridge; *Officer Michael Callahan*, James Burke; *Italian Boatman*, Harry Burns; *Young Chinese Man*, George Chan; *Stickman*, Sayre Dearing; *Officer Davis*, Tom Dugan; *Gambler*, Herbert Evans; *Officer Reardon*, James Flavin; *Nick Charles, Jr. — age 5*, Jerry Fragnol; *Whitley*, Bill Harbach; *Bert*, Clarke Hardwicke; *Baggage Man*, Earle Hodgins; *Sadie*, Esther Howard; *News Photographer*, Donald Kerr; *Second Mug*, Lyle Latell; *Jailkeeper*, Mitchell Lewis; *Oriental Girl*, Marya Marco; *Taxi Driver*, Matt McHugh; *Officer Kramer*, Howard Negley; *Amboy's Hoods*, Jimmy O'Gatty, Eddie Lou Simms; *Pete*, William Roberts; *Croupier*, Jeffrey Sayre; *Stage Manager*, John Sheehan; *Albert*, George Sorel; *Police Sergeant as Waiter*, Charles Sullivan; *Mr. Purdy*, Clinton Sundberg; *John the Butler*, Henry Sylvester; *Lewie the Shiv*, Tom Trout; *Asta the Dog*, Asta Jr.; with James Conaty, Franklyn Farnum, Harold Miller, Henry Norton, Larry Steers, Bert Stevens, and Robert E. Strickland.

Crossfire was still going strong in theaters when Gloria's sixth movie appeared, although it had been lensed prior to *Crossfire* (as was her seventh, *Merton of the Movies*, which was actually filmed right after *It Happened in Brooklyn*). *Song of the Thin Man* became, in fact, the last movie she would make at MGM under her current studio contract. It was also the last entry in the enormously popular *Thin Man* series, one of MGM's most distinguished and polished franchises. This final go-round, with its convoluted story, jazzy subtext and necessary assortment of human decoys, provided roles to future familiar names such as Keenan Wynn, Jayne Meadows, Don Taylor, Patricia Morison, Marie Windsor and, of course, Gloria Grahame.

Song of the Thin Man opens with Fran Ledue Page (Gloria Grahame) singing "You're Not So Easy to Forget" on board the gambling ship *S.S. Fortune*. Among the gamblers are Nick and Nora Charles (William Powell, Myrna Loy), enjoying an evening away from home. They're not paying attention to the bandstand, but that's where the action is. The saxophone player, Buddy Hollis (Don Taylor), is loaded and not playing well. The bandleader, Tommy Drake (Philip Reed), follows Fran off the stage and taunts her about Buddy, who is still blue after being dumped by Fran. Fran regrets leaving Buddy for Tommy and says so. Fed up with her attitude, Tommy dumps her for good. Back on the bandstand, he stops Buddy from getting another drink and slugs him to make his point. The ship's operator, Phil Brant (Bruce Cowling), breaks it up but Tommy later tells him he wants out. He's got a better offer involving a tour, and he just wants Phil to pay him off.

Tommy owes $12,000 to gangster Al Amboy and needs the cash immediately. But Phil doesn't want to pay. Tommy asks Mitch Talbin (Leon Ames) for an advance, as Mitch will be sponsoring his tour, but Mitch also declines. Meanwhile, Phil tries to dance with Janet Thayar (Jayne Meadows) despite her father's obvious disapproval. They have a romantic clinch and Janet agrees to elope with Phil later that night. Phil takes some money from his office for their rendezvous. Tommy watches Phil leave the office and then searches for money himself. He is shot and killed by a gunshot through the open office door (the killer remains unseen).

Nick and Nora know nothing about the murder the next morning back at home, as they insist Nick Jr. (Dean Stockwell) practice piano before playing baseball. When he tries to sneak away, Nora catches him and forces Nick to spank him (a quick series of flashbacks showing Nick Jr. misbehaving provide Nick with the necessary fortitude). Phil and Janet Thayar arrive and announce that they are married. They ask for the Charleses' help, but after hearing about the murder, Nick sends them away. A gunshot outside the Charleses' apartment forces everyone back inside. When the police arrive, Nick turns the couple in — for their own protection, since one of them seems to have been the target of the gunshot.

Coerced into the case by Nora, Nick prowls around the waterfront, ostensibly walking his dog Asta, and pays a man $25 to row them out to the *S.S. Fortune*. There, he prowls around Phil's office and Asta discovers a thin razor blade. The dog also finds one of Al Amboy's hoods, who wants a receipt for $12,000 that Tommy had when he died. Asta grabs the receipt, written on the back of some sheet music, and speeds away with the goon in hot pursuit, but Asta jumps overboard and swims to shore. Still on board the ship, Nick discovers the jazz band members, who had returned for their instruments. The clarinetist, Clarence "Clinker" Krause (Keenan Wynn), identifies the razor blade as the one Buddy Hollis used on his saxophone reed. Under pressure from Nick, Clinker agrees to help find Buddy, who seems to be the key to the mystery.

Clinker leads Nick and Nora on a jazz tour across New York City. At one club they are intercepted by Al Amboy (William Bishop), who wants the $12,000 receipt to prove to the police that he didn't kill Tommy. Nick rebuffs him. The trio travels to Mitch Talbin's apartment, where a hot jazz session is beginning. Clinker inadvertently burns the receipt to ashes while Nick is talking to Mitch, who states that he did not lend the money to Tommy, figuring he was a bad risk. Nora notices that Mrs. Talbin (Patricia Morison) is missing the expensive necklace she had been wearing on the boat. Clinker leads the Charleses from hot spot to hot spot, but nobody has seen Buddy since the shooting.

The next evening involves more of the same. Finally, they stop at a place where Fran Page is singing Buddy's song "You're Not So Easy to Forget." The Talbins are also there. Clinker reveals that the Charleses are detectives, something he neglected to mention the previous evening. Clinker and Nick corner Fran in her dressing room but she denies knowing Buddy's whereabouts and refuses to cooperate with them. Arriving back at home at 3 A.M., Nick and Nora discover that their apartment has been burgled; Nick suspects Al Amboy, looking for the receipt. Nick Jr. and Asta are fine, undisturbed by the visit. Nick notices his son's toy gun in the bedroom and gets a revelation. He and Nora visit the Thayars at 4 A.M. and Nick proves that one of Mr. Thayar's (Ralph Morgan) antique guns is missing, and is probably the murder weapon. Janet Thayar receives a phone call and rushes away. Nick and Nora follow her by cab and are led to Fran Page's apartment. They enter and find Fran on the floor with a knife in her back. Moments later, Janet enters and expresses shock at the scene.

Janet confesses that Fran had asked for $2500 for Buddy Hollis, who was staying somewhere in Poughkeepsie, New York. Nick, Nora and Clinker eventually find Buddy at the Valley Rest Home, where he is so disturbed that he is not allowed visitors. Nora sneaks back anyway and talks to him about Fran; Buddy catches her in a lie and threatens to kill her. He has the antique gun and fires it, missing Nora, who is saved when Nick and Clinker arrive with medical staff. Even though Buddy confessed to killing Tommy and had the murder weapon, Nick believes he is innocent. On the way back

Song of the Thin Man. All of the key characters are present in this magazine ad, including slinky Gloria, the only personage not looking toward whatever everybody else, including the dog Asta, is facing.

to Manhattan, Nora discovers that Nick Jr. is missing from home; he was being babysat by Janet Thayar. He is still missing when they arrive, but Janet appears with him some time later. It seems that Al Amboy's hoods had

stopped by and Janet snuck him outside for a walk, just in case.

Faced with dead ends, Nick devises a plan. The S.S. *Fortune* is to be reopened with a gala celebration, capped by an announcement from

Buddy as to what really occurred that evening. With police cooperation, Nick arranges everything, including the guests' seating. But it is Nora who recognizes that Al Amboy's wife (Marie Windsor) is wearing the necklace that matches Mrs. Talbin's earrings. A bit later, while dancing, Nora notices that Mrs. Talbin is suddenly wearing the necklace again. Nick confronts Mitch Talbin but it is his wife who confesses that she traded the necklace to the Amboys for the money to pay Tommy. Mitch is clearly not happy about his wife's actions.

Buddy comes onstage and plays a bit before Nick interrupts him. Nick publicly asks Buddy to tell everybody what happened that night, and specifically who killed Tommy. Before the still shell-shocked Buddy can protest the question, Mitch Talbin rises and confesses to the killing of Tommy and Fran Page. He then points a revolver at Nick and threatens to kill him. Before he can, his wife shoots him. "I swore I would kill whoever killed Tommy," she defiantly states and pumps three more bullets into her husband. She is led away by the police. Back at home after another late night out, Nick announces that he's going to retire. "You through with crime?" Nora asks. "No," he replies. "I'm going to bed."

The sixth and final go-round for the *Thin Man* series came thirteen years after the first entry. By scheduling a new mystery every two or three years, MGM was able to keep the series fresh and keep their stars content (and busy) with an assortment of projects, yet maintain public interest in the franchise. It helped that stars William Powell and Myrna Loy enjoyed making the series—and working with each other. Together they starred in fourteen films in fourteen years, beginning with *Manhattan Melodrama* (1934) and ending with *The Senator Was Indiscreet* (1947). Powell and Loy usually portrayed modern married couples, and their teaming in the *Thin Man* series served as the common thread for their continued popularity, with their other movies providing comedic and dramatic variations.

Much has been written regarding the social impact that Powell and Loy made as Nick and Nora Charles. Other than the constant boozing that seems terribly out of place today, the Charleses function beautifully as a complementary couple. When Nick and Nora are not deftly solving mysteries or enjoying posh New York society bashes, they enjoy a relatively happy home life. They tease each other, finish the other's sentences, flirt a great deal and generally display a witty, romantic idealistic life to which viewers could only hope to aspire. Nick and Nora rarely seem to tire of each other, which may be why viewers never tire of watching them. Seeing a new *Thin Man* movie every few years became like visiting favorite relatives who live too far away to see regularly.

Nick and Nora became the movie model for generally happy couples. It seems odd today, but prior to the *Thin Man* series, the institution of marriage had not really received a fair shake in American cinema. There were plenty of movies in which the result was a happy couple tying the knot, yet those inevitably climaxed with the promise of a passionate honeymoon. There were also plenty of movies with disintegrating partnerships; these situations evolved into murder stories, histrionic weepies and a few high quality dramas. But happy married couples? Hollywood didn't get the concept. When *The Thin Man* struck a chord with audiences, critics were astonished. Gilbert Seldes, in *Photoplay*, wondered why Nick would want to make love to his own wife, and said that Nora was wasting her time being in love with her own husband. And yet, that is exactly the element that made the series such a resounding success.

In addition to their abundant wit and flirtatious sexual chemistry, Nick and Nora are also very wise. It is this wisdom, this knack of thinking their way out of trouble, that sets them above most other movie couples of the era, as well as most detectives and detective teams throughout cinema history. Hundreds of private eyes, detective couples, investigators both male and female, policemen and special agents have come and gone over the years, but few have had the staying power of Nick and Nora Charles. To be sure, it isn't the criminal cases, nor the manner in which they are solved, that bring viewers back to watch them year after year. The cases are secondary to the films' entertainment value. The key to their success is the fun and adventure that they find while solving the riddles. To Nick and Nora, a new case means new adventure. There's always a hint of danger, but Nick can take care of him-

Song of the Thin Man. Singer Fran Ledue Page (Gloria) waits, cigarette in hand, while her backing band plays a song's introduction. This was the sixth and final film in MGM's popular *Thin Man* series.

self, and Nora can always talk her way out of trouble. Together they are an unbeatable team.

With the immense popularity of the first *Thin Man* (1934), MGM's bosses realized they had opened a gold mine. They were very careful with their treasure, being sure to craft each new story carefully, paying special attention to tone and supporting cast. And in each new episode, the Nick and Nora relationship would develop further. They added Nick Jr. to the family in the third installment, *Another Thin Man* (1939), and he grew quite a bit between each new adventure. Nick's parents join the fun in the fifth film, *The Thin Man Goes Home* (1944), and in *Song of the Thin Man* Nick Jr. comes into his own as a character, just as sassy and smart as his father, and only eight years old!

But six adventures over fourteen years was enough. The first three were based on Dashiell Hammett stories; the last three were original scripts. Many viewers know that the series title is a misnomer. The "Thin Man" was actually a character (Edward Ellis) in the first film, an in-

ventor whose disappearance spurs that film's mystery. The titles of the second and third films also refer to the inventor, though much of the film-going public was unaware of it. Grammatically, however, the third film's title applies to both the inventor and the current criminal, while the fourth film's title, *Shadow of the Thin Man* (1931), applies solely to the criminal suspect. For the fifth and sixth films, the titles are referring to Nick Charles as the "Thin Man," as MGM simply stopped trying to be precise and used the appellation that had become familiar. And "Song" indicates the musical background that becomes important in the final adventure. In their book *The Great Detective Pictures*, James Robert Parish and Michael R. Pitts suggest that the film should have been entitled "*Swan Song of the Thin Man.*"

The music is important, and it helps cover some of the thinness of the plot. MGM was trying to exploit the post-war jazz craze and tailored the story toward young viewers, figuring the series' regular fans would come no matter what. In 1947 stars Powell and Loy were in their fifties and forties, respectively. The studio believed that while they were still very appealing, the series needed a new slant and that jazz would provide it. Thus, the film was populated with smoky gin joints, hepcat musicians, all-night jams and relentless jive dialogue that develops into a running joke throughout the story. It seems, however, that MGM either did not want to or could not commit itself to presenting the real stuff, with the result that *Song of the Thin Man*'s jazz is less than top notch. Had the studio really wanted to swing, it might have imported some recognizable names and faces and mixed them into the story, thereby upping the musical contribution and adding some interest to music aficionados. But they didn't and an opportunity was lost.

One major recurring character hasn't yet been discussed — Asta. Actually, Asta was portrayed by Asta Jr. in this film. The original Asta, a wire-haired fox terrier named Skippy, had cavorted through the first five Nick and Nora tales, as well as a few other movies, but had died in 1946. The dog's death was widely publicized, and there was much interest in his replacement Asta Jr. New dog, same role. The new Asta is just as lovable, helping Nick outwit the villain on the ship, snuggling up to Nick Jr. in bed and generally stealing the show whenever he is on-screen.

The supporting cast is a who's who of familiar 1940s faces. Keenan Wynn drives the comedy with his relentless patter and bursts of energy. As "Clinker" the clarinetist, Wynn utilizes his easy charm to the fullest, and his jive talking is unimpeachable. Don Taylor is less fortunate as clarinetist Buddy Hollis; his mental breakdown is not at all convincing, especially at the climactic concert where he is totally befuddled. Phillip Reed, Leon Ames, William Bishop, Bruce Cowling and Ralph Morgan round out the men; Patricia Morison, Jayne Meadows, Marie Windsor and Gloria Grahame round out the women.

It was certainly a step up at the studio for Gloria from her previous decorative roles in *Without Love* and *It Happened in Brooklyn*. As a singer with a romantic penchant for bad boys, Gloria provides a luscious presence, a sultry sexuality and her soon to be familiar aura of inevitable tragedy. The one element she does not provide is a beautiful singing voice; this is supplied by Carol Arden. In fact, Gloria isn't very convincing when lip-synching to "You're Not So Easy to Forget," a title that unfortunately does not adequately describe the song itself. Fortunately the song is but a minor facet of the role, and although Gloria is obviously not singing, she looks fabulous while thus not singing. Gloria portrayed a few singers throughout her career despite being tone-deaf, but she always looked great all dolled up and pretending to warble.

In her second *film noir* appearance, Gloria is perfectly comfortable and at home portraying a singer, bouncing romantically from one musician to another, and inevitably doomed because of it. This characterization of tragedy — resplendent upon first sight, the epitome of glamour; later found on the floor with a knife in her back — would earmark her career and establish one glittering facet of Gloria's screen persona. Other actresses played this type of part more often, but no one did it better. Even while Fran is singing (or rather pretending to sing), there's an air of preordained trouble surrounding her, a restless ennui that telegraphs her fate, invoking the audience's understanding.

And yet, Fran is never a submissive victim. It is her antagonism that drives Tommy Drake away. After Buddy's breakdown, Fran gets him to a rest home and protects his secret location, eventually with her life. She continues to work, to sing, wherever she can find a job and to visit Buddy when she can because she feels that he is her responsibility. She loves him and even resorts to asking Janet Thayar for money to help him get away and recover. Beneath Fran's cool, glamourous public poise is a woman who really cares about someone in trouble, and Gloria is very convincing in both aspects of Fran's character. Finding, and displaying, a character's reality beneath the skin was one of Gloria's greatest assets, one which proved invaluable in the shadowy world of *film noir*, where she made her greatest impact as an actress.

This sixth Nick and Nora escapade was profitable for MGM but critical reaction was mixed and, to the studio, surprisingly negative. Myrna Loy herself chirped with displeasure in her autobiography *Being and Becoming*: "*Song of the Thin Man* was a lackluster finish to a

Song of the Thin Man. Sleuth Nick Charles (William Powell) questions singer Fran Ledue Page (Gloria) about the disappearance of a murder suspect.

great series. I hated it. The characters had lost their sparkle for Bill and me, and the people who knew what it was all about were no longer involved." John McNulty of *The New Yorker* questioned the climax: "The latest of the *Thin Man* series is, like the others, slick, smooth and some fun for about seven-eighths of its length. Then it comes to the most ridiculous windup I've seen lately." And in two film books, one about William Powell, the other about Myrna

Loy, author Lawrence J. Quirk slams their final teaming as Nick and Nora: "The sixth and last of their *Thin Man* sojourns represented a dismal item that sent them out with the proverbial whimper rather than a bang."

But a few critics actually enjoyed the festivities. *Variety*'s critic called it "one of the better [*Thin Man*s]. It's likely to get top box-office." Thomas M. Pryor of the *New York Times* gushed, "While *Song of the Thin Man* is no world beater, it still is a mighty pleasant picture to have around.... The blind alleys that Nick and Nora run into in their quest of the slayer are all used to good advantage, and whatever the script lacks in the way of logic is more than compensated for by the lighthearted manner in which the incidental scenes are worked out."

Gloria was happy to be back at work, and suddenly she was busier than ever. She had already wrapped a comedic role in *Merton of the Movies* and as soon as she was killed off in this film she was lent to RKO for *Crossfire*, which was rushed into release as quickly as possible, beating both of Gloria's MGM projects to theaters. Personally, she was in a cycle of separating from, and then reuniting with, husband Stanley Clements, although the separations were becoming ever more serious. Gloria filed for divorce over the summer of 1946 but later withdrew the petition. She and Stanley kept trying to keep their marriage together, but she was working all the time and he was having a difficult time finding acting jobs.

Song of the Thin Man marked a couple of firsts for Gloria. She first portrayed a singer, which she was quite self-conscious about because she could not sing well at all. That fact is unfortunately apparent on movie screens, mainly because she never seems to take enough breath to convince anyone she is singing. Even so, she looks great. This is also the first time Gloria's character is killed on screen. Soon Gloria would become expert at death scenes, having several in her *film noir* adventures. And technically, this was her first *film noir* role, although *Crossfire* beat it to the screen by a couple of months. If MGM had continued to furnish roles such as this one for Gloria, the studio might not have been so eager to give her away.

There's no question that this final Nick and Nora episode is their least significant. The original writers and director are nowhere in sight, and the new, jazzy direction of the action just doesn't suit the style of the mature leads. That said, there should also be little doubt that even the least *Thin Man* movie is as good or better than most other movies of that time period. It isn't the stinker to which Quirk refers. *Song of the Thin Man* is fun, amusing and witty. It provides Gloria with a glamourous role and Keenan Wynn with a jaunty one. If it becomes a little tiresome among the jazz joints and more than a bit ridiculous during the shipboard climax, it can be forgiven for having brought Nick, Nora, Nick Jr., and Asta back together once again, and allowing them to exit the scene as gracefully as they had entered some thirteen years earlier.

Merton of the Movies (1947)

CREDITS MGM. *Directed by* Robert Alton. *Produced by* Albert Lewis. *Screenplay by* George Wells and Lou Breslow. *Based on the novel by* Harry Leon Wilson *and the play by* George S. Kaufman and Marc Connelly. *Director of Photography*: Paul C. Vogel. *Film Editor*: Frank E. Hull. *Art Direction*: Cedric Gibbons and Howard Campbell. *Musical Score*: David Snell. *Recording Director*: Douglas Shearer. *Set Decorations*: Edwin B. Willis. *Set Decorations Associate*: Joseph W. Holland. *Costume Supervision*: Irene. *Costumes Designed by* Helen Rose. *Men's Costumes by* Valles. *Makeup Created by* Jack Dawn. *Hair Styles Created by* Sydney Guilaroff. *Assistant Director*: Alfred Raboch. *Stunts*: Gil Perkins. *Additional Music by* Robert Franklyn. *Orchestrator*: Wally Heglin. Black and White. Flat (1.37:1). Monaural Sound. 82 minutes. Released on October 11, 1947. Currently available on DVD. Previously available on VHS.

CAST *Merton Gill*, Red Skelton; *Phyllis Montague*, Virginia O'Brien; *Beulah Baxter*, Gloria Grahame; *Lawrence Rupert*, Leon Ames; *Frank Mulvaney*, Alan Mowbray; *Jeff Baird*, Charles D. Brown; *Von Strutt*, Hugo Haas; *Mr. Gashwiler*, Harry Hayden; *Marty*, Tom Trout; *Phil*, Douglas Fowley; *Chick*, Dick Wessel; *Goodfellow's Club Manager*, Morris Ankrum; *Baird's Assistant*, Phil Arnold; *Mother in Theater*, Polly Bailey; *Boy in Theater*, Charles Bates; *Man in Casting Office Line*, Hank Bell; *Assistant Directors*, William "Billy" Benedict, Jim Davis, Frank Eldredge; *Mr. Purdie*, Oliver Blake; *Club Members*, George Bunny, Elmer Jerome, Tom Leffingwell, Paul Scardon, Pietro Sosso, Wyndham Standing; *Keystone Kops*, Chester Conklin, Heinie Conklin, Vernon

Dent, Clarence Hennecke; *Photographer*, Bill Conselman; *Little Man*, Billy Curtis; *Man on Couch*, Antonio D'Amore; *Mr. Hubank*, Frank Darien; *Girl*, Gail Davis; *Gus Blanchard*, Hal K. Dawson; *Photographer*, Drew Demarest; *Goodfellow's Club Clerk*, Eddie Dunn; *Officer*, Ralph Dunn; *Mrs. Effie Gashwiler*, Helen Eby-Rock; *Man Raising Theater Curtain*, Franklyn Farnum; *Thug*, Duke Green; *Evvy*, Gloria Gunther; *Writer*, Bert Hanlon; *Script Girl*, Eloise Hardt; *Laughing Stagehand*, Kenner G. Kemp; *Writer*, Donald Kerr; *Set Guard*, Mitchell Lewis; *Gateman*, George Magrill; *Ernie*, Frank Marlowe; *Von Strutt's Cameraman*, Walter Merrill; *Big Man*, Robert Milasch; *Heavy*, King Mojave; *Thug*, Ben Moselle; *Mac*, Robert Emmett O'Connor; *Butler*, Vesey O'Davoren; *Jarvis (Casting Director)*, Steve Olsen; *Electrician*, Frank Pharr; *Landlady*, Constance Purdy; *Butler*, Gordon Richards; *Actor (Union Officer)*, Dick Rich; *Mammoth Studios Night Guard*, Tim Ryan; *Photographer*, Fred Santley; *Mammoth Studios Nurse*, Almira Sessions; *Heavy*, Jack Sterling; *Secretary*, Celia Travers; *Gladys (Casting Director)*, Mary Treen; *Employment Man*, Charles Wagenheim; *Club Waiter*, Larry Wheat; *Bit Roles*: Sam Ash, Joan Blair, Helen Boyce, George M. Carleton, Roger Cole, Bert Davidson, Helen Dickson, Mike Donovan, Phil Dunham, Budd Fine, William Frambes, Louise Franklin, Bobby Johnson, Ben Lessy, May McAvoy, Frank O'Connor, John Phipps, Tom Pilkington, Victor Potel, Carl Saxe, Cedric Stevens, Eddy Waller and Britt Wood; *Sam Montague*, Tom Dugan (scenes deleted).

The third cinematic rendition of Harry Leon Wilson's novel *Merton of the Movies*— which became better known as a Broadway play, adapted by George S. Kaufman and Marc Connelly — is homogenized in the effort to tailor it to Red Skelton's personality, yet at least some of the story's appeal survives intact. Its foundation is the concept that a mild-mannered store clerk (or in this version, a movie theater usher) who dreams of Hollywood celebrity could actually attain it. Such a story appeals to everyone who has ever dreamed of movie stardom and of experiencing the respect that usually accompanies movie stars. Its irony lies in the fact that moviemaking is shown to be rather degrading, soulless and fickle — yet its aura of magic persists anyway.

Merton of the Movies begins in 1915 in Tickerton, Kansas, where movie usher Merton Gill (Red Skelton) is so engrossed in the movie playing on the screen — featuring silent stars Lawrence Rupert (Leon Ames) and Beulah Baxter (Gloria Grahame) — that he inadver-

tently sits on and wrestles with one of the patrons, ruining the man's suit. Merton is fired by the theater owner, Mr. Gashwiler (Harry Hayden), only to stumblingly foil a robbery of the theater as he is leaving. Feted as a hero, Merton is awarded with a fancy walking cane and a trip to Hollywood to meet his idol, Lawrence Rupert. But Merton has larger plans; he has graduated from a correspondence school on acting and plans to be a movie star himself. At the Tickerton train station, as he is given a big send-off by the townsfolk, Merton loses the cane.

At Mammoth Studios in Hollywood, Merton meets Rupert, albeit briefly. He is photographed with the silent star in several locations, designed to give Rupert some badly needed publicity. Rupert presents Merton with a cane, which he promptly loses. When the pictures are done, Merton is given enough money to afford the trip back to Kansas and told in no uncertain terms by Rupert's aides to go home. After a month of searching for acting jobs and hanging around the Mammoth Studios casting office, Merton lands a job as night porter at a club for elderly gentlemen. He tries to keep everything quiet in the "Over 70" room, even squeezing the lips shut on the cuckoo clock's cuckoo on the hour, but a handful of light bulbs and a tall ladder prove to be his undoing.

Actress Phyllis Montague (Virginia O'Brien) befriends Merton, who is now reduced to sleeping in a local park. When Merton talks of Beulah Baxter admiringly, she invites him to see Beulah attempt a dangerous stunt at the studio at night, hoping to prove to him that Beulah is not the heroine he believes her to be (Phyllis will be doing the stunt in Beulah's place). Merton sneaks onto the lot but doesn't see Phyllis taking Beulah's place on a tall ship's mast. When she falls into the water, Merton goes in after her to rescue her (even though he can't swim), and is astonished to find that it isn't Beulah but Phyllis. While having coffee afterward, Phyllis learns from her agent that she has been hired for the female lead in Lawrence Rupert's next detective drama, to be called *Souls on Fire*.

On the studio lot, Merton persists in trying to talk to Rupert, but is knocked unconscious by the front gate for his trouble. In bandages, Merton is mistaken for an extra for a war

Merton of the Movies. Mammoth Studios' glamourous movie star Beulah Baxter (Gloria) is treated like a queen by everyone, including director Frank Mulvaney (Alan Mowbray, with the beret), in this version of the oft-told Hollywood tale.

drama and given two lines, which he recites so poorly that he is fired by German director Von Strutt (Hugo Haas). Phyllis is watching, however, and she sees that Merton has natural comic timing. When Rupert disappears, again, from the set of his movie to go on a bender, Phyllis suggests that director Jeff Baird (Charles D. Brown) turn the war drama into a satire, with Merton impersonating his idol Rupert. The trick is to keep the ploy a secret from Merton, who believes himself to be a good serious actor and has taken the stage name of Clifford Armytage. Faced with closing down an expensive production, the studio decides to take the risk.

Merton is so excited by his stroke of luck that he doesn't suspect anything for a while. When he does begin to notice things, Beulah is convinced to distract him by lavishing her attentions on him. This almost works, until Phyl-

lis arrives to save him from Beulah. Then Rupert shows up and is dumbfounded to learn that he has been replaced by an unknown. Rupert's assistants are sent after Merton to end his brief career. Merton arrives at the preview of his movie, still unaware of the deception. When he is dismayed at the laughs the movie is receiving, Phyllis pulls him into the lobby and tells him the truth, that he's a natural comic, and that the audience loves him. She convinces him to accept his newfound success, but Rupert's assistants arrive with guns drawn and chase him around the theater until Rupert joins Merton in front of the screen. By introducing Merton as his protégé, Rupert saves his own career and launches Merton's at the same time. Jeff Baird and Phyllis join them on stage and Rupert presents Merton with yet another cane, which pulls Merton and Phyllis up into the rafters when it catches on the rising curtain.

Merton of the Movies is an affectionate, if rather superficial, glimpse at moviemaking in the silent era. One quick sequence shows how movies were churned out under less than ideal conditions, when Merton walks to film his first big scene and passes three separate and wildly different movies being filmed on adjacent sets, in apparent haste. Merton's own movie — eventually titled *Soles on Fire* instead of the original *Souls on Fire* — is lensed almost on the run, partly to keep Merton in the dark about its reality, and partly because that's how Mammoth Studios seems to film *everything*. The portrait of this fictitious film studio is not very flattering, and this extends to its personnel, from its gullible studio guard (Tim Ryan) to its maniacal Germanic director Von Strutt (Hugo Haas); from its rather spoiled and pampered ingénue, Beulah Baxter (Gloria Grahame), to its often soused star, Lawrence Rupert (Leon Ames). It's kind of odd that an MGM-produced film which pertains to the making of movies would be so negative about the process, even if it is a comedy.

Yet it's not an unbalanced approach. Despite troublesome characteristics of the temperamental moviemakers and an undeniable commercially oriented rush to put products in theaters, the studio's movies are shown to be quite popular and worthwhile. *Merton of the Movies* begins with an audience fully enjoying a Rupert-Baxter drama and ends with an audience fully enjoying a Civil War spoof with Clifford Armytage (Merton) impersonating Rupert to a tee. The film — and the play and book as well — admit, albeit reluctantly, that moviemaking can be artistically rewarding, for the audience anyway, if not so much for the participants in its creation.

Ultimately, *Merton of the Movies* attempts to play both sides of the fence, with disappointing results. Its irony is not structured or conveyed deeply enough to merit audience consideration. The basic situation is ripe for ridicule, what with the studio desperate to finish its film, star Rupert disappearing on yet another drinking binge, and the unthinkable gamble of turning drama into comedy on the strength of a brief and pathetic screen sample of an unknown actor who can't even get his lines right (in a silent film, no less). This should lead to frantic activity, ever-increasing deception,

heartless but funny amorality and a wickedly cruel but fully understandable climax in which the Merton character accepts his fate. Alas, this film softens the already gentle flavor of the play, offering Skelton's Merton more pathos than is occasioned or required.

At 36 Red Skelton seems too old for the role of a movie usher determined to become a star in Hollywood, yet the argument can also be made that Skelton's age serves to make Merton even more pathetic. MGM hired Buster Keaton to tutor Skelton in silent screen acting for the part. Yet it's the pathos of the role that prevents the film's comedy from fully succeeding. Skelton is bumblingly hapless when Merton should be cluelessly confident. When he finds nothing but failure in Hollywood, Merton's sad eyes beg the audience for sympathy even while he fakes a brave front. In a drama this would be effective, but *Merton* is intended to be comedic. Later, in the drunk scene he shares with Gloria, Skelton is allowed to animate his rubbery face, but even pie-eyed, Skelton cannot help but play for sympathy. Such sentiment prevents a natural flow of comedy. To be fair, both earlier film versions of the story emphasize pathos, as does the Kaufman-Connelly play. Styles have changed a great deal, of course, but this film remains too heavy on the schmaltz and too light on the laughs.

Two extra sequences are included to provide comedy yet have virtually nothing to do with the story. At the Goodfellows Club, night porter Merton is assigned to the "Over 70" room, where he is instructed to keep everything perfectly quiet. When his shoes squeak, Merton walks bow-legged. After he prevents the cuckoo clock from cuckooing, he walks around with a small sign indicating the time. Of course, a chandelier needing new light bulbs and a tall ladder with a protruding nail bring Merton's night porter career to a very loud halt. The second sequence involves Merton's first day on the movie set, when he obliquely asks Phyllis for kissing lessons. This overlong sequence has its moments, but Merton's innocent act is more tiresome than funny.

Much is made, once Phyllis recognizes it, of Merton's innate comic timing and impeccable impersonation of dramatic star Lawrence Rupert. In the lobby scene, when Phyllis tells Merton the truth, she refers to him as "a

Watch out, Merton... that Hollywood vamp has designs on you!

Merton of the Movies. Merton Gill (Red Skelton) is rather uncomfortable as the object of the affections of movie queen Beulah Baxter (Gloria). She is under studio orders to keep Merton distracted, because the dramatic movie he thinks he is making is really a comedy.

satirist, a *farceur*, a *raconteur*." Unfortunately, audiences pretty much have to take Phyllis' word for it, because such talent is not evidenced in the brief scenes Merton makes either as the clumsy wounded soldier in Von Strutt's film or as the Rupert-esque hero of *Soles on Fire*. These are key scenes that should establish and then reinforce the idea that Merton has latent comic talent (if not dramatic skill), but actor Skelton doesn't demonstrate that. He simply looks foolish. And while allowing oneself to appear foolish is an old comedic tradition, it isn't what is necessary in this situation. Since Merton does not display any real talent, his successful reception at the preview is artificial and unsatisfying.

Far more successful are the lead actresses in the picture. Virginia O'Brien is charming as Phyllis Montague, who remembers all too well her humble origins in the business and takes Merton under her protective wing. She is the

one person who seems at ease in the studio system; she takes advantage of breaks when she receives them, but she also doesn't fret when things don't go her way. She warns Merton about the pitfalls of the business, but she also helps him up the ladder when she recognizes an opportunity for him. This was O'Brien's last major film. A popular singer and stage actress, she only made two more film appearances while turning to stage and recording work for the rest of her career.

Gloria landed the plum role of silent film queen Beulah Baxter right after making *It Happened in Brooklyn*. Or rather, it should have been a plum role. Besides Beulah's two very brief movie appearances which bookend the picture, she only has a few other scenes, with the longest being Merton's seduction scene. As she plies Merton with champagne and cigarettes (both for his first time), there is no doubt what she wants in return. Beulah was asked by the producer to seduce Merton because he was becoming suspicious on the set, but she is only too happy to play along. "He's cute" is enough reason for her to turn on the charm, thus giving the impression that she may have been down this road a few times in the past. Such trampy behavior, of course, would become common for Gloria's future characters, but here it is presented with a bare minimum of sexual desire. For Beulah Baxter, it's just another romp.

This is certainly the most glamourous of Gloria's early roles. Beulah is always dressed in elegant gowns and elaborate makeup, and presented as if she were a true movie queen. As she is being lifted to the ship's mast by crane, there is a very nice shot of Gloria's legs; hers were becoming known as some of the best gams in Hollywood. Yet Gloria's glamour and looks are not enough to create a memorable part; there simply isn't much here with which to work. Gloria looks the part of a coddled movie star, but she never really registers as a character. Nor is she funny; she plays her dumb blonde role straight while Red Skelton does his wide-eyed, guileless act. The result is artificial and unconvincing, and not particularly entertaining.

Critical response was lukewarm. Thomas M. Pryor of the *New York Times* judged that *Merton* "is a brutishly slapstick prank, and so help us it's not the least bit funny." *Newsweek's* critic liked it more: "If you subscribe to the Skelton school of comedy, *Merton of the Movies* is an entertaining film." Otis L. Guernsey Jr. of the *New York Herald Tribune* concurred: "Some of it is corny and none of it is inspired, but a lot of it is mildly funny." *Variety's* critic also liked it, noting that Gloria "has herself a time as an old-time screen vamp," and predicted that the movie "should register heftily at the ticket windows." Alas, this was not to be. After being shelved for a time by MGM, allowing both *Crossfire* and *Song of the Thin Man* to precede it into theaters, it flopped upon its release and became Skelton's first starring feature to lose money.

Hollywood had filmed Harry Leon Wilson's story in 1924 with Glenn Hunter as the starstruck youth, and again in 1932 (titled *Make Me a Star*) with an older Stuart Erwin as the erstwhile actor. Other variations also appeared, such as *Mary of the Movies* (1923) and *Polly of*

the Movies (1927), which changed the protagonist's gender but kept the same basic themes. The play adaptation by George S. Kaufman and Marc Connelly was a big success, probably even more popular than the original story. But by 1947, the formula was wearing thin. The Skelton film was not commercially successful, disappointing its studio and its stars. For Gloria it represented great costuming and welcome publicity, but that didn't last very long, and the film's commercial failure helped convince producers that comedy was not her strong suit. This was the last outright comedy Gloria would make for a long, long time.

Though *Merton of the Movies* was filmed in late 1946, it was not released until October of 1947. It would be the fourth and final film of hers to appear that year, which certainly raised her visibility — and the chances for awards recognition. But late 1947 was not a happy time for Gloria. *Merton* would be the last the public would see of Gloria for almost a year and a half, and it also marked the end of her first marriage. The cycle of separating from and reuniting with Stanley Clements finally came to an end in November, just one month after *Merton of the Movies* was released. Gloria had finally had enough of his gambling, his temper tantrums and his jealousy. Not that she was innocent; Gloria had a temper too, and she had a tendency to fan the flames of his jealousy whenever she met someone new, inadvertently or not. At the time, Gloria said of Stanley, "He became jealous if I would talk to a man. When I was working on a picture he was jealous of any man who was connected with the picture. Finally, it got to the point where he refused to allow me to shake hands if I was introduced to a man." The divorce she requested in November was finalized on June 1, 1948.

Divorcing Stanley did not prevent Gloria from continuing to see him from time to time, however. She could not live with him, but she never quite stopped loving him. They kept in touch into the mid–1950s, sometimes going to movies together and sitting in the back row like a couple of teenagers. Occasionally, according to Vincent Curcio, their attachment resumed its physical aspects. But their lives eventually took separate paths, and the bonds between them loosened. By the late 1950s they were no longer keeping track of each other. When Gloria died in 1981, Clements was in a hospital with emphysema. News of her death dispirited Stanley, and he passed away just eleven days after the death of Gloria.

A Woman's Secret (1949)

CREDITS RKO Radio Pictures. *Directed by* Nicholas Ray. *Produced and Written by* Herman J. Mankiewicz. *Based on the novel Mortgage on Life by* Vicki Baum. *Director of Photography*: George Diskant. *Film Editor*: Sherman Todd. *Art Directors*: Albert D'Agostino and Carroll Clark. *Special Effects by* Russell A. Cully. *Set Decorations*: Darrell Silvera and Harley Miller. *Makeup Supervision*: Gordon Bau. *Music by* Frederick Hollander. *Musical Director*: C. Bakaleinikoff. *Sound by* Frank Sarver and Clem Portman. *Gowns by* Edward Stevenson. *Assistant Director*: Doran Cox. *Production Design*: Clark Burke. *Makeup Artists*: James R. Barker and Jack Barron. *Hair Stylists*: Hazel Rogers and Fae M. Smith. *Production Manager*: William Dorfman. *Sound Recorder*: Earl A. Wolcott. *Gaffer*: S. H. Barton. *Grip*: Jim Kurley. *Still Photographers*: Oliver Sigurdson and Ernest Bachrach. *Camera Operator*: Charles Burke. *Additional Cinematographer*: Harry J. Wild. *Continuity*: Mercy Weireter. *Singing Double*: Kaye Lorraine. Black and White. Flat (1.37:1). Monaural Sound. 84 minutes. Released on March 5, 1949. Not currently available on DVD. Previously available on VHS.

CAST *Marian Washburn*, Maureen O'Hara; *Luke Jordan*, Melvyn Douglas; *Susan Caldwell/Estrellita*, Gloria Grahame; *Lee Crenshaw*, Bill Williams; *Brook Matthews*, Victor Jory; *Mrs. Mary Fowler*, Mary Philips; *Inspector Jim Fowler*, Jay C. Flippen; *Assistant District Attorney Roberts*, Robert Warwick; *Doctor*, Curt Conway; *Mrs. Matthews*, Ann Shoemaker; *Mollie*, Virginia Farmer; *Nurse*, Ellen Corby; *Desk Sergeant*, Emory Parnell; *Conductor*, C. Bakaleinikoff; *Tommy the Messenger Boy*, Conrad Binyon; *Mr. Pierson*, Oliver Blake; *Dr. Ferris*, Raymond Bond; *Ship's Waiter*, Eddie Borden; *Radio Director*, Bert Davidson; *French Baker*, Marcel De la Brosse; *Stage Manager*, Dan Foster; *Harold the Butler*, John Goldsworthy; *Radio Program Moderator*, Paul Guilfoyle; *Fred*, Alvin Hammer; *WLR Radio Announcer*, John Laing; *Lieutenant Benson*, Rory Mallinson; *Reporter*, Frank Marlowe; *Algerian Waiter*, Alphonse Martell; *News Photographer*, Ralph Montgomery; *Mr. Emory*, Forbes Murray; *Ship's Emcee*, Frederic Nay; *Professor Paul Carnelli*, John Parrish; *Police Clerk*, Lee Phelps; *Intern*, Bill Purington; *Mr. Harris*, Ralph Stein; *Waitress*, Loreli Vitek; *Algerian Piano Player*, Charles Wagenheim; *Actress*, Lynn Whitney; *Nurse*, Bernice Young; *Policemen*, Guy Beach, Tom Coleman, George Douglas and Mickey Simpson; *Announcers*, Norman Nesbitt and Jack Rourke; *Girls*, Donna Gibson and Evelyn Underwood; *Ship Dance Extras*, James Conaty and Suzanne Ridgeway; *Bit Part*, Robert Malcolm.

For the second time in three movies Gloria portrayed a singer, although in real life she couldn't carry a tune at all. Of her movie appearances as a singer this one presents her in the best light, a remarkable fact considering that her dubbing — by singer Kaye Lorraine — is rather obvious. Lorraine's voice is noticeably lower than Gloria's, yet it was well chosen, nicely complementing Gloria's persona. Not only did director Nicholas Ray match the non-singing Gloria with a reciprocal voice, he also provided her with a second husband — himself. Ray was so taken by Gloria during filming that as soon as shooting was completed, the couple headed to Nevada, where Gloria spent six weeks in Las Vegas waiting for her divorce from Stanley Clements to finalize. She married Ray the same day it was finalized. The marriage wouldn't last very long but it would have repercussions on the rest of Gloria's life.

A Woman's Secret begins with an announcer for New York City radio station WLR gently purring "Hear Estrellita tonight ... and go to sleep with love in your heart." Estrellita (Gloria Grahame) sings her signature tune "Estrellita" while her business partner, Marian Washburn (Maureen O'Hara) listens to the radio at their Park Avenue apartment. When Estrellita arrives home, she and Marian argue because Estrellita wants to quit; her real name is Susan Caldwell and she doesn't want to be "Estrellita" any longer. The women also argue about a man named Luke Jordan; Marian claims that she means nothing to him. Susan storms up to her room and Marian follows a few moments later; the argument continues in Susan's room behind a closed door. Downstairs a maid hears a gunshot; Susan has been shot. Marian calls a doctor and Susan is carried away to a hospital. The police arrive and Marian confesses that she shot Susan.

Luke Jordan (Melvyn Douglas) is a musician and music expert whose radio appearance is interrupted by a call from Marian, in jail. Jordan doesn't believe that Marian shot Susan, partly because he is deeply in love with Marian. He visits socialite lawyer Brook Matthews (Victor Jory), Susan's former fiancé, asking him to

A Woman's Secret. Passengers aboard a luxury liner crossing the Atlantic are about to enjoy a performance by singer "Estrellita" (Gloria). It was during this film that Gloria fell for her director, Nicholas Ray, who became her second husband.

help Marian, but Matthews is unsure of what he should do. Jordan pressures Matthews into taking the case; he is certain that Marian didn't try to kill Susan, despite her confession. Back at the police station, Marian tells her story to the district attorney, with Matthews, Inspector Fowler and Luke Jordan in attendance.

A flashback presents what happened in Susan's room. Marian refuses to let Susan quit and walk away. Susan is determined; she wants to live her own life. Marian refuses, saying it would be suicide for both of them, and threatens her. Marian finally shoots Susan with a German Luger pistol which she claims she received in Germany in 1944 from a soldier.

The lead investigator, Inspector Fowler (Jay C. Flippen), is bewildered by the case. Jordan buys him lunch and attempts to gain the inspector's confidence by supplying the backstory. In brief flashbacks, Jordan describes how he met singer Marian in a small club and quickly became her favorite piano player. They were always chummy, but never romantic, despite Jordan's hints that he would like to become so. Marian had a beautiful voice but somehow lost it to a rare type of laryngitis. After months of recovery, Marian tries singing again, but with bitter results. By chance the pair meets Susan Caldwell, a free-spirited but flighty girl who just happens to have a sensuous way of singing. Marian becomes her mentor, teaching her how to properly present songs.

Back in the present, a man wants to visit Susan in the hospital. It is Lee Crenshaw (Bill Williams), the soldier who gave Susan the Luger, and whom she saw recently in New Orleans. As Susan is still unconscious, he is turned away. Jordan and Crenshaw meet and instantly dislike each other. Jordan continues to tell Inspector Fowler about Marian's past, and the inspector's wife (Mary Philips) takes an interest as well. Jordan describes how Marian mentored Susan, taking her to Paris for lessons. A lengthy flashback shows that while in Paris, Susan leaves Marian to go to Algiers for six weeks on a romantic whim. Jordan joins Marian in Paris, then journeys to Algiers to bring Susan back. He teaches her the song "Estrellita" in Algiers, and when she sings it on the transatlantic crossing back to America, a star is born. They meet a lawyer with prominent show-biz connections, Brook Matthews, on that return trip, and he agrees to help make Susan a star. Matthews' mother worries that her son might be getting serious about Susan, so Jordan tells her he will be marrying Susan, which causes Marian to feel jealous. But the plan works; soon "Estrellita" is singing on the Broadway stage and in major concerts.

Back in the present, the inspector isn't convinced that Marian is innocent. The inspector's wife does some of her own investigating and uncovers a key of Susan's from New Orleans. Susan awakens briefly and confirms Marian's story, which sends Jordan into mild shock. He still cannot believe Marian would attempt murder. Then the inspector's wife produces the key, which inspires the inspector and Jordan to simultaneously discover that Susan married Crenshaw in Louisiana, but didn't tell anybody. Back at the hospital, the inspector's wife proves that a nurse read Susan the local newspapers, which is how Susan knew what explanation she would be expected to provide for her shooting. But Susan finally confesses the truth.

Another flashback to the night of the shooting shows that Susan is upset about being impetuously married, and burns a telegram from Crenshaw stating that he will arrive the following morning. She holds the Luger, considering using it on herself, when Marian enters. Susan quickly hides the gun. Marian tries to be helpful but Susan is in a wicked temper and refuses to listen. Marian suddenly sees the gun and tries to wrestle it from Susan's grasp. They fiercely struggle with it and it fires, accidentally wounding Susan.

Back in the present again, an extremely penitent Susan is mortified by her actions and apologizes to Brook Matthews for betraying him. He stays with Susan after the others leave. To Jordan's relief, Marian is released from custody and they patch their relationship permanently, cementing it with a passionate kiss in the back of a cab.

A Woman's Secret is an uneven mix of mystery, music, mirth, muddled motivation

and old-fashioned moral value that is far more entertaining than it has any right to be. Based upon Vicki Baum's novel *Mortgage on Life*, which had been serialized in *Colliers* as "The Long Denial" (the film's title while in production), the story is alternately flimsy, melodramatic, absurd and cute. If not for the occasionally witty dialogue and interesting performances by most of the cast, this would be a waste of time. It was director Nicholas Ray's second film, one that he was pressured to helm by studio head Dore Schary. It contains little of Ray's signature style; most analysts consider it his most anonymous film. It is lensed almost entirely indoors, without any particular ambience, and builds little suspense or atmosphere. None of the leading performers wanted to make it, either, yet once signed, everyone contributed something of value and the result is pleasantly entertaining, and a movie that improves on repeat viewings.

As with most adaptations, the movie is much different than the book. Baum's book is an engaging read with much deeper characterization, additional supporting characters and situations, plus a divergent climax and motivations for it. What is similar is the tone of the piece, which Ray and scriptwriter Herman J. Mankiewicz consistently duplicate, and the characters of Luke Jordan, Susan Caldwell (named Marylynn in the novel) and Marian Washburn (named Bess Poker in the novel). Working with that triangle, Mankiewicz shaped a similar but slightly incongruous story that Ray augmented with ambivalence at its conclusion. The most telling differences are the omission of the inspector's wife in the book, the novel's frank discussion of suicide and a wildly different picture of the husband, Lee Crenshaw. Ray's film treats Crenshaw with some contempt; it may be that Ray saw something of himself in the character and the folly of an unwise, rushed marriage, though he wouldn't marry Gloria until after the film was completed, so that observation may not be quite fair.

Although the ladies are the dramatic centerpieces (it is, after all, *A Woman's Secret*), the character of Luke Jordan carries the day. Described by a radio announcer as a "celebrated composer, concert pianist, wit — and all-around gadfly," Jordan is a good guy at heart and a rascal by nature. He is also the audience's window into the private world of Marian's star-making efforts. He is the only person who believes in Marian, forcing viewers to scrutinize the mystery — and Marian's confession — with greater care. Jordan is an adept guide, for he tickles the ivories with the best of them, and can also throw a solid punch when appropriate. He's a no-nonsense guy with a friendly, laid-back manner who has seen it all and done it all, and is superbly realized by Melvyn Douglas.

The film's perspective shifts from one character to the next — and famously contains two flashbacks among its six which seem to contradict each other (because they are from different viewpoints) — yet most of the story is told from Jordan's level-headed perspective, or centers on his recreations of the past for Inspector Fowler. His belief in Marian's innocence flies in the face of all logic, especially once she confesses to attempted murder, but it creates the drama and reinforces the story structure established by Mankiewicz. Jordan's one-sided crusade to uncover the truth and save the woman he loves is in the best tradition of romantic fiction, made even sweeter by the fact that he never declares his love for her; it's just taken for granted by the audience.

Less successfully realized are the ladies. Maureen O'Hara works hard as Marian Washburn, the singer who loses her voice and copes by discovering and mentoring a similar young woman, driving her toward a stardom Marian was unable to achieve. Marian is an interesting role with a fatal flaw, one that demonstrably weakens the drama. Her Svengali-like control of Susan is transparent, finally resulting in her decision to assume blame for Susan's shooting. The real reason for the shooting, according to the script, is that Susan's quickie marriage to Crenshaw so depresses her that she attempts to kill herself. Marian tries to prevent her suicide and Susan is shot accidentally. Then Marian takes the blame publicly, going to jail, so that Susan's (Estrellita's) reputation would not be ruined. Granted, there was far more importance attached to reputations at the time this movie was made, but even then this explanation was weak. It was also a radical departure from the motivation as stated in the book. Such self-sacrifice on Marian's part seems foolish at best and quite stupid to most modern audi-

ences. And the situation is not helped by Ray's direction, which does not clearly delineate Marian's motivation until Susan's confession in the hospital — a scene that was shot after primary filming had completed and a preview had indicated that audiences remained confused. The movie's pressbook asserts that "Matthews assures Susan that he will wait for her until her marriage to Crenshaw is annulled" but the movie itself never really spells things out, a fact that many of its initial reviewers noted.

Perhaps Ray felt that too much explanation lessened the story's impact, that real life often hid true motivation and obscured larger, symbolic meaning. But it is more likely that he just didn't bother trying to persuade audiences to accept a story that he was not keen on telling in the first place. Ray's only interest was in the characters and their conflicts; he didn't really care about the story resolution. There was one character he found especially interesting: Susan Caldwell, aka Estrellita.

Gloria was cast as Susan before anybody else; producer Dore Schary had borrowed her from MGM to make *Crossfire* and brought her back to RKO afterward, purchasing her contract from MGM on June 9, 1947. He hoped to make her a star where MGM had failed. According to Maureen O'Hara in her memoir *'Tis Herself*, gossip on the set said that Schary was in love with Gloria, which is why the film was made despite a script that wasn't quite polished. That may have been true, although Schary doesn't even mention Gloria in his autobiography *Heyday*. Whatever Schary's feelings, they became subordinate to those of director Ray, who found himself irresistibly attracted to his twenty-two-year-old second lead. Ray later famously admitted, "I was infatuated with her but I didn't like her very much." Any ideas Schary might have had regarding his ingénue dissolved when, shortly after filming completed, Ray and Gloria traveled to Nevada to finalize her divorce from Stanley Clements. (California divorce laws required a minimum six month waiting period before the divorce was finalized, so Gloria established a residence in Nevada for six weeks to get one there.) So, on June 1, 1948, Gloria officially divorced Stanley in Nevada and later that day married Nicholas Ray.

It is obvious that Ray is fascinated with

Gloria, as evidenced by the way in which she is filmed. Nonchalantly putting on stockings by the fireplace; singing "Paradise" in beautifully composed close-ups with rivers of rain flowing down the window behind her; languidly singing "Estrellita" in the black dress with the criss-cross collar on the ship going back to America; lying on the hospital bed completely covered in white sheets except for that beautiful, expressive face — Gloria is obviously the focal point of the film. Compare how she is constantly seen singing in close-ups while Maureen O'Hara's Irish song contains almost none. Gloria is marvelous in the part, even while just pretending to sing. Her breathing during the songs is too soft to be convincing, but she manipulates her eyebrows, particularly during "Paradise," to convey the emotion of the song in spectacular fashion. Her modest re-action after the song is just perfect for the moment.

Atypical for Ray is the high level of comedy mixed into the proceedings. From the joc-ular desk sergeant to Susan's explanation of her home town, Azusa, California, the script provides moments of mirth and wit. The tone of the piece changes drastically once Jordan visits the inspector and his wife at home; most of their dialogue together is playful bantering. As the inspector's wife begins to investigate on her own, the film ventures into the territory of silly fun. Susan is often the subject of the joke, as when she talks about saving her money to see a fortune teller at $100 a visit: "How was I to know he really can't tell much in less than three visits?" Or when she says she wants a little water before she sings, and then guzzles an entire glass as Jordan and Marian watch, mesmerized. Her best moment occurs after she explains the first two letters of her hometown's name of Azusa: "Everything from A to Z." Jordan says, "I still don't get it. What does the U-S-A stand for?" Susan is perplexed, finding it difficult to believe he's that stupid. "United States of America," she says gently. "Everybody knows that."

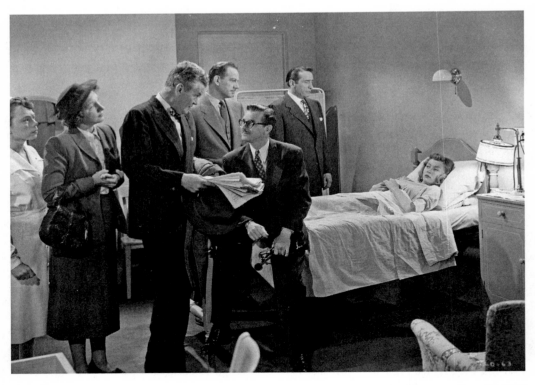

A Woman's Secret. Susan Caldwell (Gloria), known to the world as "Estrellita," recovers in a hospital bed. Discussing her and her case are, left to right, Ellen Corby, Mary Phillips, Jay C. Flippen, Melvyn Douglas, Curt Conway and Victor Jory.

Gloria's personality and talent grabbed Ray's attention, and their shared desire to raise a family bonded them together. He was infatuated enough to impregnate Gloria during filming, and they were married on June 1, 1948. Five and a half months later on November 12, 1948, their son Timothy Ray was born. Described by RKO's publicity department as a premature baby, Tim was fully nine pounds when born. Ray attempted to bring his various personal problems under control for the marriage and for a time was at least partially successful. Gloria was thrilled to become a mother and abstained from acting for the whole of Tim's first year to properly raise him.

Despite Schary's enthusiasm, the studio didn't know quite what to do with the film (which was photographed in early 1948) and didn't even release it until 1949, long after he had left RKO to head the operation of MGM, the studio that Gloria had left. *A Woman's Secret* lost a great deal of money and gathered terrible reviews, although several noted Gloria's effective acting. According to *Time*'s review, "This indigestible lump of melodrama is leavened now and again by a stretch of slapstick which is equally unreal. The only real moments, in fact, are provided by Gloria Grahame, who proves once again, as she did by her performance as the sullen taxi dancer in *Crossfire*, that she can be one of Hollywood's most convincing chippies." *Newsweek* noted the film's basic script problem: "It is somewhat difficult to understand why Marian stubbornly insists she put a Luger bullet into her reluctant protégé when she really didn't," and also praises Gloria: "But Miss Grahame, who unfortunately gets shot in the first reel, is the only member of the cast who makes it worth a second glance." Philip T. Hartung of *Commonweal* called it "a very flat melodrama."

The film faded away quickly in 1949 but has regained some fraction of its reputation over the years as Nicholas Ray's stature gradually increased, especially in Europe. It is not one of his better films, but it is unexpectedly, charmingly entertaining. *A Woman's Secret* doesn't hold up well as a mystery but it is a durable vehicle for watching Melvyn Douglas, Jay C. Flippen, Mary Philips and especially Gloria at the top of their talent. It's an inconsistent and sometimes disappointing film, but it's certainly worth watching, especially to see Gloria still youthful, vibrant and fresh. It is, of course, better known now as the film that brought Gloria and Nicholas Ray together. And while their marriage was volatile and occasionally violent, it did, during the time this movie was in postproduction, produce a son to Gloria and Nick, and for that blessing they were always grateful.

Roughshod (1949)

CREDITS RKO Radio Pictures. *Directed by* Mark Robson. *Produced by* Richard A. Berger. *Executive Producer*: Jack J. Gross. *Screenplay by* Geoffrey Homes [Daniel Mainwaring] and Hugo Butler. *Story by* Peter Viertel. *Director of Photography*: Joseph F. Biroc. *Film Editor*: Marston Fay. *Art Directors*: Albert S. D'Agostino and Lucius O. Croxton. *Special Effects by* Russell A. Cully. *Set Decorators*: Darrell Silvera and John Sturtevant. *Makeup Supervision*: Gordon Bau. *Music by* Roy Webb. *Additional Music* by Paul Sawtell. *Orchestrator*: Gil Grau. *Musical Director*: C. Bakaleinikoff. *Sound by* Jack Grubb and Clem Portman. *Gowns by* Renié. *Assistant Director*: Nate Levinson. *Makeup Artists*: Karl Herlinger and Roland Ray. *Hair Stylists*: Mabel Carey and Florence Guernsey. *Production Manager*: Sam Ruman. *Camera Operator*: James Daly. *Gaffer*: Homer Plannette. *Grips*: Mike Fitzgerald and Mike Graves. *Script Supervisor*: Bill Shanks. *Still Photographers*: Alexander Kahle and Art Say. Black and White. Flat (1.37:1). Monaural Sound. 88 minutes. Released on May 11, 1949. Not currently available on commercial home video.

CAST *Clay Phillips*, Robert Sterling; *Mary Wells*, Gloria Grahame; *Steve Phillips*, Claude Jarman, Jr.; *Lednov*, John Ireland; *Elaine Wyatt*, Jeff Donnell; *Helen Carter*, Myrna Dell; *Marcia*, Martha Hyer; *Jim Clayton*, George Cooper; *Jed Graham*, Jeff Corey; *Ma Wyatt*, Sara Haden; *Pa (Ed) Wyatt*, James Bell; *Jed Fowler*, Shawn McGlory [Sean McClory]; *McCall*, Robert B. Williams; *Peters*, Steve Savage; *Sheriff Gardner*, Edward Cassidy; *Sam Ellis*, Stanley Andrews; *Mr. Hayes*, Paul E. Burns; with Michael Wallace.

Roughshod is a modest western in the *Stagecoach* mold, though with fewer characters and a stronger emphasis on women and morality in the burgeoning West. It was actually filmed on location in Northern California in 1947, shortly after Gloria signed her RKO contract (June 9), but was withheld from release for nearly two years. The film was completed just as the studio changed hands, with Dore Schary resigning and Howard Hughes taking command; it was withheld from release until the studio stabilized and created a window for it. It was one of the few Westerns Gloria was to make, despite being seen to great advantage in the great outdoors. It was also one of the few films that Gloria just loved making. Away from the studio, the cast and crew bonded like family and, according to all reports, had an uproarious time on location. Had her other movies progressed as smoothly as this one, Gloria would have been a very happy actress. But this was to be the exception rather than the rule.

Prior to *Roughshod*'s opening credits, three men in prison uniforms creep toward a campfire at dawn, kill the three men around it and steal their clothing, food and horses. Following the credits, Jed Graham (Jeff Corey) finds the dead men and half-burned prison uniforms at the campfire site. On the trail to town with the bodies, he stops a wagon carrying four women heading for Sonora, California, from the nearby town of Aspen. The four fancy fillies—dance hall hostesses led by Mary Wells (Gloria Grahame)—have been evicted from Aspen by the wives of the men they had been entertaining. Graham sympathizes with Mary and her girls. "I knew it would happen when they started puttin' up fences and passin' laws," he drawls.

In Aspen, Clay Phillips (Robert Sterling) and his teenage brother Steve (Claude Jarman, Jr.) see Graham and the bodies arrive and hear the sheriff says he believes that one of the killers is a man named Lednov. The sheriff advises Clay that Lednov and his two henchmen recently escaped from prison. Clay refuses to join the sheriff's posse; he's got to move ten horses over the Sonora Pass to his ranch. After much badgering, Clay finally tells Steve that he had been instrumental in sending Lednov to prison, and that the outlaw had vowed revenge. For protection along the trail, Clay buys Steve a rifle and some ammunition.

On the trail toward Sonora with their ten horses, Clay and Steve happen across the four women, whose wagon has broken a wheel. Clay agrees to transport the women to the nearest ranch, but no farther. That night, lone rider Jim Clayton (George Cooper) spies their campfire and comes in to claim one of the women for his own. He was too late to stop the girls in Aspen, so he's followed them. He asks Marcia

(Martha Hyer) to marry him and she agrees, over the objections of Mary, who is taking her friends to work with her in a gambling house. Marcia and Jim ride off together. Another girl, troubled Elaine (Jeff Donnell), runs away but Steve finds her and brings her back with the help of the posse.

Lednov and his pals visit the Wyatt ranch, helping themselves to Wyatt's guns and ammunition and forcing him to shoe a lame horse. They ride away at night, anxious to reach Clay's ranch. Soon after they leave, Clay, Steve and the women arrive at the Wyatt ranch and discover that Elaine is the Wyatts' daughter. Clay tries to leave all three women at the ranch but the third girl, cynical but pragmatic Helen Carter (Myrna Dell), pressures Elaine into begging Clay to take them further toward Sonora. He reluctantly agrees. The following day Clay, Steve, Mary and Helen push forward, almost catching up to Lednov. Not wanting to meet the villains on the open road, Clay finds a different trail to use, one that leads to a one-man mining camp run by a man named Fowler (Sean McClory). Helen discovers that Fowler has found gold and decides to stay with him rather than travel to Sonora.

Meanwhile, Clay and Mary are drawn to each other, but their backgrounds and opposite social stations prevent them from doing anything other than kissing and fighting with each other, and upsetting Steve in the process. In a pique of anger, Mary drives away in Clay's wagon but loses control and crashes into a river. Clay saves her from drowning but determines to send her on her way as soon as possible. Clay, Steve and Mary continue toward Clay's ranch. When Lednov finds Helen and Fowler at the mine, he kills Fowler and seemingly has his way with Helen before resuming his search for Clay.

As Lednov and his henchmen close in for the kill at the base of a rocky area, Clay notes their approach, abruptly puts Mary on a passing stagecoach and angrily sends Steve away for his own good. Steve returns, having also spotted the trio and discerned that his brother was simply trying to protect him, and they prepare to fight the outlaws. The two henchmen are dispatched fairly quickly near a stream, but Lednov shoots Steve as he tries to protect their horses. Clay circles around in the

Roughshod. Though Robert Sterling and John Ireland are the primary stars in *Roughshod*, it is Gloria who is spotlighted in the movie's advertising. RKO Radio Pictures knew how to market its movies and wasn't afraid to exploit its female stars while doing so.

rocks and blasts the varmint Lednov to end the battle. Steve is taken into town where a doctor patches his flesh wound and Mary joins them. Clay finally professes his love for her and they kiss as Steve watches and smiles, wondering what took his brother so long to come to his senses.

Although it ends on a very predictable — and satisfying — note, *Roughshod* is an unusual western in that its themes regarding morality and the loss of innocence are highly developed. The women are dance hall hostesses and perhaps of worse reputation, at least enough so that they have been forcibly evicted from Aspen. Elaine's parents have been shamed by their daughter's choice of profession and her father does not allow Mary and Helen to stay at their ranch when Elaine returns. Steve mentions that when he and Clay passed Mary's place in Aspen, Clay and he would cross to the other side of the street, although Steve didn't

understand why. And while Clay is civil and helpful to the women, it is clear that he does not approve of them in a social context. Yet he cannot help being attracted to Mary, and he eventually sees past her reputation.

Mary states that her desire is to open a gambling house in Sonora, and Clay believes her. Yet he also sees that she takes the time to teach Steve how to read, that she looks after the other girls with genuine fondness, that she understands the importance of his establishing a working ranch, and that she isn't afraid of people's opinions of her. Clay's feelings and admiration for Mary — even as he struggles with accepting her poor reputation and materialistic nature — gradually convince the audience as well as himself that she is a special woman, one worthy of his conservative attentions. Even though he kisses her, he will not tell her that he loves her just to justify those kisses, and he quickly retreats from the situation when it becomes clear he has offended her. In fact, all of the men — except for Lednov and Elaine's father — treat the women cordially. It seems natural that the women should have little trouble finding respectable futures. Indeed, the film's stance is spoken by Jed Graham when he meets the women on the road and blames society for "puttin' up fences and passin' laws." The film posits that it is "progress" which leads to puritanical standards and, ultimately, driving decent women (in admittedly tawdry jobs) out of town.

Clay's own feelings for women have been subordinated to mentoring his brother and establishing his ranch. He hasn't had time to teach his younger brother how to read, hasn't had time to spend time and money on females. In fact, Clay never really discusses his feelings for or preferences regarding women, but Mary intimates those feelings for him when she mentions "the girl in the spotted gingham." "The who?" Clay asks. "You should know, she's in your dream. Ever since you've looked after Steve, you've had the dream. The ranch on the river, good grass, good water, barn, corral, house. That part you've shared with Steve. The girl in gingham you planned to sneak in when he isn't looking. She wears this gingham dress, cooks popovers, makes jam in season, makes her own soap out of pig fat and wood ashes and has cheeks the color of red apples." "I'll make the soap myself. Will she be dark or fair?" Clay asks. "Blonde as a new mop and beautiful as the girl on the feed store calendar. I hope you find her," she earnestly replies.

Mary is, of course, describing herself, but the movie has a long way to go before Clay realizes it. The audience realizes it, however, which is why their tortured romance is so resonant. She keeps hoping that he will rise above his self-centered, puritanical thinking and treat her like a real woman, but he refuses to acknowledge his growing attachment to her until the danger represented by Lednov has passed.

Roughshod. Clay Phillips (Robert Sterling) and Mary Wells (Gloria) take a walk to sort out their feelings for each other in one of Gloria's few westerns.

Each time he fails her, she vows to run wild in Sonora, yet she never stops believing that Clay could be the man for her, if he would only accept her for who she is. For his part, he does have a lot on his mind, and once Lednov is dead he attends to Mary, admitting that he was planning to visit her the next day and declare his feelings for her before she left for good.

The other women find varying degrees of comfort away from Aspen. Marcia is rescued from a life of dance halls by Jim Clayton, who loves her and wants to marry her. He is the man that Clay would be if Clay weren't so busy herding his horses back home, looking after his younger brother and evading a vicious killer bent on revenge. Elaine finds sanctuary at home, although it is fear of facing her parents after her disgrace that nearly drives her mad. Yet it is an uneasy sanctuary, as Elaine will never reveal some of her experiences with her parents and is frightened that Mary or Helen will. The fate of Helen is more troublesome. Caught with the miner Fowler by Lednov and his men, she sees the outlaw kill the man she has just met and joined. Lednov knocks her to the ground and then turns to her as the shot dissolves, thus intimating that she is about to experience the Fate Worse Than Death — and probably death as well. Leaving this to the audience's imagination is very smart filmmaking — and rather nasty to think about.

Most Westerns would focus on the trouble between Clay and Lednov as their main area of conflict. Yet by minimizing this conflict and subordinating it to the fate of the women, the film sneakily sharpens this menace. Steve actually talks more about Lednov than does Clay, and the women who should probably be terrified that their guide is being hunted by a psychopathic killer hardly mention it at all. On the other hand, Lednov's ruthlessness is portrayed in scenes involving the killings of the three men at the campfire, the bullying of the Wyatts and the killing of Fowler. The audience is left to wonder how Clay, who has barely raised a hand against anyone during the film, can face the deadly Lednov and his cohorts, especially alone. The dramatic imbalance is highly effective in highlighting Clay as an underdog and providing suspense at the rather routine climax.

Eventually *Roughshod* returns to familiar formula: The hero gets the girl, the villain gets his comeuppance, the wounded boy recovers. Yet for most of its succinct running time, director Mark Robson's film avoids following the familiar formulas. It has *noirish* elements that work well in its western setting. Joseph Biroc's cinematography is superb, capturing the beauty of the California highlands between Yosemite National Park and Reno, Nevada, and framing the interplay between characters quite meaningfully. The film seems fresh and absorbing due to its well-developed characters, authentic situations and genuine emotions. It was designed as a B-western but approaches the A level in terms of its script, direction, production values and at least some of its casting.

While Robert Sterling is earnest but a bit bland in the lead, Gloria, Claude Jarman Jr. and John Ireland are particularly diverting in their roles. Jarman is terrific as Steve, whose young age provides an enlightening perspective regarding the relationship between Clay and Mary. It is Steve's loss of innocence during this trail drive that resonates more than any other theme. Ireland is wonderfully menacing as Lednov, dressed in a dark shirt and unshaven, bullying the Wyatts, yet cowardly when it comes to facing Clay at the final showdown. The three other women don't have nearly as much to do as Gloria, but Myrna Dell makes a strong impression. Martha Hyer has an excuse for her abbreviated role as Marcia: she suffered an attack of appendicitis while on location and underwent emergency surgery in a small mountain hospital. As for Gloria, she enjoyed the location work and developed a close relationship with Jeff Donnell, who plays Elaine. It was one of the few strong female friendships that Gloria would cultivate; she simply preferred to be with men most of the time.

The role of Mary Wells provided Gloria with her third trampish part, though it isn't nearly as dark as that of Ginny Tremaine in *Crossfire*. Ginny was still trapped as a "hostess," while Mary is, at the moment, not practicing the part. Between saloons, she is free to be herself, although she certainly uses her feminine wiles to try to persuade Clay to transport her and her friends to Sonora. Mary also encourages Clay to kiss her, but not because she wants anything from him but the companionship to which she is accustomed. She's quite independent in her thinking and she isn't afraid to speak her mind. When Helen decides to stay with Fowler, Mary tells Fowler, "It's nice to meet a man who doesn't want to own a girl from the day she was born. I never had the luck. The only kind I ever meet are tramps and dirty-minded hypocrites." Clay doesn't respond to the jibe (which is aimed at him) and Mary is again left alone with herself, knowing that she could love a man like Clay if he could just love her in return.

With her golden hair and gorgeous face, Gloria positively glows at times in the outdoor sunshine. She looks fine all dolled up but even better when she's wearing a flannel shirt, jeans and a rope belt. Gloria exudes energy and vitality, making her an easy focal point for the movie's advertising, which is dominated by her large portrait and the tagline, "Dare you say I'm not good enough to marry?" Some actresses would have complained about the lack of niceties on the location shoot, but Gloria took it all in stride. Once director Robson succeeded in persuading Gloria's mother to go home, Stanley Clements was able to join her (they were still married when this was filmed). The result was that Gloria had a blast. She was able to enjoy Stanley's company when he was around, and she was often the center of attention when he wasn't. She also liked the experience of shooting predominantly outside, which was new to her. All in all, it was a terrific adventure.

It also helped that the film was pretty good. Its weaknesses are few. It seems odd that Clay doesn't know that the Wyatts have a grown daughter, considering that he knows them personally; logic dictates that he should have been aware of who she was and how she ran away from home. The character of Elaine is very melodramatic, perhaps too much so. Supporting characters such as Jed Graham and Jim Clayton move in and out of the plot with alacrity. And the conclusion feels somewhat rushed, particularly involving Lednov's death. Yet these are minor quibbles; *Roughshod* is a solid, modestly produced western adventure that offers something a bit out of the ordinary for the genre, in addition to casting women such as Gloria and Martha Hyer in parts unusual for them.

Critics were generally upbeat. Bosley Crowther of the *New York Times* wrote, "It rep-resents an effort to get a wee bit away from the usual literal formula of the low-budget Western film," but ultimately termed its direction "muddled," and Gloria "rather silly" in her role. *Time*'s critic called it "a modest little film which offers several minor but pleasant surprises," and touted Mark Robson as "one of the most sought after young directors in the business." The British Film Institute's *Monthly Film Bulletin* was perhaps more observant, referring to *Roughshod* as a "quite unambitious but very beguiling Western" and noting, "Robson's intelligent direction of his players is matched by an admirable visual control; the film is smartly edited and well photographed; almost all the time it is a joy to watch."

Roughshod was Gloria's first Western and could easily have led to further roles in the genre. She seems well cast as an Eastern girl looking for adventure and fortune in the West, dressed in frilly frocks and dolled up to attract as many men as possible — although at just 24 she seems awfully young to be running a gambling house-dance hall-saloon. Gloria seems equally at home later as she gets comfortable in flannel and jeans, destined to live and work in the great outdoors. Yet Gloria made few westerns as her career progressed, and the later ones she did make were not top-flight productions, and made after her career was past its prime. Producers didn't see her as the out-doorsy type; her come-hither looks and slinky sexuality were deemed more urban in nature and best presented after dark. *Roughshod* offers a different view of Gloria, in a role that expands upon her developing "bad girl" persona but also encourages her best instincts. It is a shame that Gloria rarely had the opportunity to make other outdoor adventures. As evidenced here, she was capable of a great deal more than the studio executives for whom she worked could surmise.

In a Lonely Place (1950)

CREDITS Santana Productions. *Distributed by* Columbia Pictures. *Directed by* Nicholas Ray. *Produced by* Robert Lord. *Associate Producer*: Henry S. Kesler. *Screenplay by* Andrew Solt. *Adaptation by* Edmund H. North. *Story by* Dorothy B. Hughes. *Director of Photography*: Burnett Guffey. *Film Editor*: Viola

Lawrence. *Art Director*: Robert Peterson. *Set Decorator*: William Kiernan. *Assistant Director*: Earl Bellamy. *Gowns by* Jean Louis. *Makeup by* Clay Campbell. *Hair Styles by* Helen Hunt. *Sound Engineer*: Howard Fogetti. *Technical Adviser*: Rod Amateau. *Musical Score by* George Antheil. *Musical Director*: Morris Stoloff. *Orchestrator*: Ernest Gold. *Script Supervisor*: Charlsie Bryant. *Camera Operator*: Gert Andersen. *Gaffer*: William Johnson. *Grip*: Walter Meins. *Stunt Double*: Rod Amateau. *Still Photographer*: Irving Lippman. Black and White. Flat (1.37:1). Monaural Sound. 94 minutes. Released on May 17, 1950. Currently available on DVD. Previously available on VHS.

CAST *Dixon Steele*, Humphrey Bogart; *Laurel Gray*, Gloria Grahame; *Detective Sergeant Brub Nicolai*, Frank Lovejoy; *Captain Lochner*, Carl Benton Reid; *Mel Lippman*, Art Smith; *Sylvia Nicolai*, Jeff Donnell; *Mildred Atkinson*, Martha Stewart; *Charlie Waterman*, Robert Warwick; *Lloyd Barnes*, Morris Ankrum; *Ted Barton*, William Ching; *Paul*, Steven Geray; *Singer*, Hadda Brooks; *Frances Randolph*, Alix Talton; *Henry Kesler*, Jack Reynolds; *Effie*, Ruth Warren; *Martha*, Ruth Gillette; *Swan*, Guy Beach; *Junior*, Louis Howard; *Joe*, Arno Frey; *Second Hatcheck Girl*, Pat Barton; *Bartender*, Cosmo Sardo; *John Mason*, Don Hanin; *Waiter*, George Davis; *Young Boy*, Billy Gray; *Tough Girl*, Melinda Erickson; *Officer*, Jack Jahries; *Dr. Richards*, David Bond; *Post Office Clerk*, Myron Healey; *Airline Clerk*, Robert Lowell; *Himself*, Mike Romanoff; *Lady Wanting Matches*, Laura K. Brooks; *Angry Husband in Convertible*, Charles Cane; *Actress in Convertible*, June Vincent; *Bartender*, Jack Chefe; *Dave (Parking Attendant)*, Frank Marlowe; *Flower Shop Employee*, Davis Roberts; with Hazel Boyne, Oliver Cross, Joy Hallward, Mike Lally, Tony Layng, Harold Miller, John Mitchum, Allen Pinson, Jack Santoro, Evelyn Underwood.

Gloria was induced to make a second movie for her husband, director Nicholas Ray, which, because of the casting of Humphrey Bogart in the lead, promised to be a major motion picture, Gloria's first since *It's a Wonderful Life*. It was an easy role for Gloria to play: an aspiring actress who tends to fall for older men who are no good for her. Although the story is based on fiction — a popular novel by Dorothy B. Hughes — Ray altered it to suit his own perspective, shaping Bogart's role to mirror his own struggles with relationships, drink and temperament. Even as his marriage to Gloria began to unravel, Ray continued to inject elements of their life together into the story, resulting in a record of a failed romantic relationship that was decidedly close to home. This reflection of their reality, sharpened and tinted by Ray's personal knowledge of their most intimate secrets, provides *In a Lonely Place* with a verisimilitude that surprised and even shocked audiences at the time, and it remains both convincing and troubling yet today. It remains one of the most fascinating movies in which Gloria Grahame ever appeared.

In a Lonely Place begins with the threat of violence, as a woman in a car stopped at a traffic light talks to Dixon Steele (Humphrey Bogart), who is driving another car. This makes her husband jealous. Dix offers to fight but the other man drives away.

Dix stops at a bar and is joined by film industry cronies. His agent, Mel Lippman (Art Smith), wants Dix to read a particular book and adapt it into a screenplay. Dix is dubious, so when the hat check girl, Mildred Atkinson (Martha Stewart), gushes over it, Dix persuades her to tell him the story so he won't have to read it himself. Dix gets into a brief fight before he leaves the bar, and Mildred accompanies him home. There, she describes the book's story to him, even acting out some of the parts, before he sends her home with some cab money and some extra cash for her time.

Detective Brub Nicolai (Frank Lovejoy), an old friend of Dix's, awakens Dix at 5:00 A.M. and takes him in for questioning. Captain Lochner (Carl Benton Reid) reveals that Mildred Atkinson has been killed, and Dix is the last person known to have seen her alive. Dix recalls that a woman in his apartment building saw them together, very much alive. Laurel Gray (Gloria Grahame) is brought in for questioning and states that she saw Mildred leave. Dix is intrigued by Laurel. He is freed and walks home, pausing to buy some flowers for Mildred Atkinson. News of Dix's questioning spreads and Mel Lippman arrives in a panic. Dix pretends to be guilty just to revel in his agent's anxiety, then asks him about Laurel, an aspiring actress. Laurel meets them in the courtyard and introduces herself; Dix presses her for romance rather quickly, but she doesn't want to be rushed. Meanwhile, Captain Lochner reads extensive notes on Dix's volatile temper and violent past, and tells Brub to keep his eye on Dix. Lochner is not at all convinced of Dix's innocence.

At dinner with Brub and his wife Sylvia (Jeff Donnell), Dix talks about the crime and

In a Lonely Place. Something about Dix Steele (Humphrey Bogart) catches the eye of Laurel Gray (Gloria Grahame) when they first meet in this Columbia drama. The woman between them is Mildred Atkinson (Martha Stewart), soon to be murdered.

even restages it. Sylvia poses as Mildred and is unnerved by Dix's intensity. "He's a sick man, Brub," she tells her husband later. "There's something wrong with him." Dix sees Laurel, who has decided to be with him exclusively. They kiss and fall in love.

Mel Lippman visits and is astonished to see Dix sober and writing, with Laurel acting as his secretary and inspiration. They are as happy as can be. Captain Lochner interviews Laurel again, telling her he still suspects Dix. The cops also interview Henry Kesler (Jack Reynolds), Mildred's boyfriend. Dix and Laurel go to a nightclub but Dix is bothered by the presence of a cop and his wife, and they leave. The next day Laurel gets a massage from masseuse Martha (Ruth Gillette), who tells her how Dix once broke a woman's nose. Laurel doesn't want to hear it and orders Martha away. Dix and Laurel join Brub and Sylvia for a beach party, which ends abruptly when Sylvia indi-

cates that Dix is still under suspicion. Dix drives home angrily and almost hits another car. Laurel is frightened when Dix and the other driver get into a fight. Dix knocks out the younger man and nearly crushes his skull with a rock. Later, after he calms down, he discusses a line from his screenplay with Laurel: "I was born when she kissed me; I died when she left me; I lived a few weeks while she loved me."

Dix feels guilty about beating up the other driver and sends him $300. He sees Brub at the police station and meets Kesler; Dix tells Brub that Kesler would be the prime suspect in fiction. Laurel sees Sylvia and confesses that Dix's temper is frightening her. Dix is very attentive to Laurel, so much so that she is becoming anxious. Laurel also confesses her fears to Mel, who stands up for his client: "You knew he was dynamite. He has to explode sometimes." Unconvinced, Laurel calls Martha and makes arrangements to get away. Dix has finished the script and Mel takes it to a producer. At the bar, friends stop by and one mentions how good the script is, which so angers Dix that he slaps Mel for showing it around without his permission. After Laurel leaves in disgust, Dix apologizes to Mel, after a fashion. Meanwhile, Captain Lochner discovers that Kesler was the murderer; Kesler has just tried, unsuccessfully, to kill himself.

Returning home, Dix pressures Laurel to go away with him, eventually forcing his way into her bedroom when she demurs. He apologizes to her but is still upset. Laurel is so anxious that she is shaking, and that sets off Dix again. He begins choking her with passion, declaring, "I'll never let you go!" He stops, realizing what he has become. The phone rings; it's Brub, with the news that Kesler confessed to killing Mildred Atkinson. Laurel tells him that yesterday the news would have meant so much, but today it doesn't matter at all. She hangs up and turns toward Dix, who is already walking out of her life forever. "I lived a few weeks while you loved me," she whispers. "Goodbye, Dix."

In a Lonely Place deviates from the Hughes novel in a couple of important ways. First, Hughes' story is written exclusively from the perspective of Dix, firmly bonding the character to the reader, and vice versa. Nothing in the book happens about which Dix isn't aware or involved. The film takes an omniscient approach, adding scenes involving other characters and aspects which Dix could not possibly witness. The effect is to provide viewers with a larger frame of reference and significantly deeper understanding. Thus, Laurel is a much more important character in the film, and is so because director Ray wished to make Laurel an equal partner in his view of the formation and subsequent disintegration of a relationship. Ray's primary goal with this project is to analyze how a romantic relationship deteriorates, even though the film's ostensible purpose is to function as a mystery-thriller. Second, in the story, Dix Steele *is* the murderer. And a rapist. The novel's power derives from the continuous conflict surrounding Dix; readers are faced with the probability that Dix is guilty (he doesn't confess until the end) and yet because everything is seen and felt as it pertains to Dix, readers cannot help but feel for the guy. The

film, on the other hand, places Dix under suspicion without ever truly convincing viewers that Dix might have killed Mildred. This, despite the fact that Andrew Solt's original screenplay actually shows Dix strangle Laurel, with Brub arriving too late to stop him (reportedly the scene was filmed). Instead, having changed his mind regarding the nihilism of the ending (of both novel and screenplay), Ray opted for ambiguity, gradually building the case that Dix is capable of such a murder; it seems just a matter of time before he "explodes" so violently that someone else is permanently destroyed, and that prospect is what ultimately frightens Laurel away.

Although the film is structured as a mystery, the murder of Mildred is largely irrelevant, especially to Dix. Other men in his situation, having sent her away into the night only to be murdered, might be racked with guilt. But not Dix. His sorrow extends to privately buying flowers for her funeral, but his seeming lack of remorse is a major reason why Captain Lochner continues to suspect his involvement in her death. Dix doesn't visibly grieve for Mildred because he considers her just another victim of Hollywood's relentless appetite for human souls. Having been partially devoured himself — essentially blacklisted within the industry for his argumentative nature, despite what seems to be enormous talent — Dix simply cannot feel much empathy for a girl who, with questionable taste in books and a tendency for histrionics, is unable to defend herself properly. Dix's remarks throughout the movie indicate that he cares for very few people outside of himself. And of course as a man who often bullies women, Dix is unable to feel much sympathy for any female victim.

What the film really wants to convey is that all men as a group, and Dix Steele specifically, are capable of murder, particularly within the parameters of a romantic relationship. Ray provides clues as triggers for such behavior, and rather slyly suggests that such behavior is not abnormal at all, but is to be expected from the aggressive male species, especially in the then-current postwar environment. In Hughes' original story, Dix is a veteran who began killing in England during World War II and is unable to stop. In the film, Dix is a screenwriter with a long history of bad behavior that may

In a Lonely Place. Laurel Gray (Gloria) is happy to have had a positive, calming effect on the volatile personality of Dix Steele (Humphrey Bogart); he is absolutely crazy about her. Unfortunately, it will not end well.

be, and possibly must be, compounded by the realities, longings and frustrations of life in the goldfish bowl of Hollywood. This unflattering view of Tinseltown is definitely indicative of Ray's own feelings toward the film industry and its jaded commerciality, particularly in regard to its treatment of gifted people such as himself.

It is no accident that the film turns Dix into a screenwriter, a man with skills in a town where talented people are coaxed by the promise of big money and a comfortable lifestyle to devote their talent to making mostly empty movies. This environment, from Ray's perspective, creates hostility that can upset just about any relationship, as demonstrated by Dix's relations with almost everyone. Some of Dix's anger can be attributed to external, typical Hollywood pressure: Dix is urged to write a script from a book in which he has no interest; despite an alibi, the police still consider him, as a

minor celebrity with a colorful past, a prime suspect; after finishing the script, Dix's agent shows it around without Dix's permission. Each of these situations causes Dix grief; he feels so betrayed by the last that he slaps his agent in anger, later mumbling what for him is an apology. But none of these incidents would, in and of themselves, lead Dixon Steele to murder.

The "lonely place" of the title might refer to Dix's position in Hollywood. He is described as a good writer who seems to be wasting his talent writing scripts based on bad books. That puts him, as an artist, in an uncomfortable position. Should one accept Danny Peary's premise in his review of the film in *Cult Movies 3*, the paranoia Dix feels extends from the House Un-American Activities Committee–instigated witch hunt of the Hollywood Ten, eight of which were screenwriters. Peary is convinced that Ray was framing Dix's troubles as a response to the political climate of the time, depicting the psychological effects of a crushing, relentless persecution upon one man. Dix is pushed into violence by the paranoia caused by constant surveillance, questioning and gossip about his life, and he reacts as would a hunted animal under those conditions.

More convincing is Peter Biskind's argument in *Seeing Is Believing: How Hollywood Taught Us to Stop Worrying and Love the Fifties* that Dix is persecuted because he is "superior." Dix sees, feels and writes about things that others cannot because his talent makes him "superior." And that superiority sets him apart, even from his friends (Sylvia calls her husband Brub "attractive and average" in comparison with Dix); it makes him a target. Mildred describes her boyfriend Kesler (her actual murderer) thusly: "He's nice and substantial, the easygoing type. He lives with his folks and has a good job." But because Kesler is so average, he is not "a person of interest." Due to Dix's temperamental nature, incident-filled past and apparent lack of remorse (most likely due to his wartime experiences), however, Dix remains the police's prime suspect. To be "superior" in the 1950s, argues Biskind, was to invite suspicion and unwanted attention, and Dix Steele certainly fits that profile.

On a personal level, Ray explores that "lonely place" where Dix resides to show how a man, respectable and well respected in his field, could push himself so close to murder. Ray's direction makes it pretty clear from the start that Dix did not kill Mildred, but by the end of the story the audience feels that Dix could have done it, had she irritated him sufficiently. This is shown by the contempt Dix shows the young driver whom he sideswipes and confronts, nearly killing him with a rock for calling Dix a, "blind, knuckleheaded squirrel," and by the fear of betrayal he shows when Laurel finally confesses that she is leaving him, nearly strangling her — in the same manner of Mildred's death. The key to the drama is that Dix doesn't transform into a psychopath; all the elements are there, and it is just a matter of time before they coalesce into a rage that Dix cannot control.

Brub tells his wife Sylvia that Dix has been "that way" since the war, but that he was a good officer and his men liked him. Mel tells Laurel,

"You knew he was dynamite. He has to explode sometimes." Dix's former girlfriend Frances Randolph (Alix Talton) asks him, "Do you look down on all women, or just the ones you know?" After Dix and Brub re-enact the murder of Mildred, Sylvia notes, "He's a sick man, Brub. There's something wrong with him." It takes Laurel a long time to recognize Dix's basic instability and it greatly disturbs her once she realizes its implications as they pertain to her and her future with him.

Those implications are at the heart of the film. Mildred's murder is the story's McGuffin. What Ray is really after is to convey the feeling to the audience that Dix *could have* killed her, just as he might eventually have killed Laurel if they had stayed together. A relatively normal guy, Dix is so volatile, especially around women for whom he has feelings, that he might not be able to control his rage. As Laurel shows fear, Dix becomes increasingly agitated, tightening his tenuous hold on her affections. When she finally admits that she's leaving, he cries, "I'll never let you go!" and almost refuses to, before rationality reappears. The implication is that Dix is so lonely and desperate that he will almost certainly destroy any chance for happiness he ever finds again, and that Laurel is lucky to escape alive.

Ray purposely leaves the ending ambiguous. Instead of Solt's original ending where Dix strangles Laurel before finishing his script, Ray opted to let Laurel live. In the 1975 documentary *I'm a Stranger Here Myself*, Ray explains:

> I just couldn't believe the ending that Bundy [Solt] had written. I shot it because it was my obligation to do it. Then I kicked everybody off stage except Bogart, Art Smith and Gloria. And we improvised the ending as it is now. In the original ending, we had ribbons so it was all tied up into a very neat package ... and I thought, "Shit! I can't do it, I just can't do it." Romances don't have to end that way. Marriages don't have to end that way, they don't have to end in violence for Christ's sake, you know. And let the audience find out and make up its own mind about what's going to happen to Bogie when he goes outside of the apartment area.

For all of Dix's predilection toward violence, he's not a bad guy. Even the people that he has harmed in the past — Fran and Mel — remain friendly and stand by him. Dix shows great regard for a Shakespearean actor, Charlie

Waterman (Robert Warwick), a drunk whom nobody else in town wants around. But Dix always has a kind word for him and some ready cash. Perhaps Charlie reminds Dix of his possible future condition. Several reports state that Warwick was hired because he had befriended Bogart back in 1922 when they appeared together in a play, and Bogart was still looking out for his old friend. It is also likely that Ray fashioned the character and his treatment at the hands of Dix as a reminder that Hollywood, just like anywhere else, has its own history, and that such history should be respected. Charlie Waterman's inclusion also imparts an important air of decency around Dix, indicating that he has redeeming qualities and, regardless of his questionable disdain for women, demonstrates loyalty and compassion. Of course, this differentiates the cinematic Dix from the killer in Hughes' story, but that is to be expected in any filmic adaptation. And it also follows that

Ray needed Dix to display empathy, as Dix was representing the director himself.

If one accepts that Ray interjected many of his personal thoughts, feelings and history into this material, then it cannot be denied that Ray is himself represented by Dix Steele, and that the potential for violence shown by Dix also must also apply to Ray himself. It is certainly true that the marriage between Ray and Gloria was tempestuous; when they eventually divorced in 1952, Gloria testified that he had hit her on two occasions. Gossip columns told of screaming matches and all-too-public displays of temper on both sides. So when Ray crafted the part of Dixon Steele, tailoring it to fit Bogart (the decision to make Dix a screenwriter had been made before Solt was hired to write the script), it can be presumed that Ray was openly scrutinizing his own attraction to Gloria's "type" and even predicting how their relationship would turn, given time and his own tendency toward jealousy and paranoia.

Not everyone accepts this premise, including Ray himself. In his biography of Gloria, author Vincent Curcio states that Ray himself described the film "not as objective events in his marriage but ... his perspective on those events." Ray claimed that he wasn't Dix Steele, but that "the emotional temperature was his." This seems like a case of semantics, considering that, like Dix, and Bogart as well, Ray was undeniably ambivalent toward women, had a history of fighting and violence, and was appreciably older than his leading lady (Ray was twelve years older than Gloria). Perhaps Ray was simply too close to the situation. He could recreate various elements of his troubles with Gloria on the screen in the guise of fiction, yet he could not bring himself to publicly accept his movie efforts as

In a Lonely Place. **In this publicity shot, Dix Steele (Humphrey Bogart) demonstrates the type of physical control he wants over Laurel Gray (Gloria), and she is none too keen about the idea.**

anything but the artistic exploration of character. Even the setting of the apartments where Dix and Laurel live extends from Ray's experience: That complex is a replica of where Ray lived when he first moved to Hollywood.

Never before and never since had Gloria's life been so solidly attached to and reflected in a film role. Ray and Gloria had been married for little more than a year when they began *In a Lonely Place*, but they separated soon after filming began. Their problem was that they couldn't tell the producers—including Bogart, whose company, Santana Productions, was backing the project—because both were afraid that the production would be shut down if they did, or that one of them would be fired. So they pretended that everything between them was fine and they behaved professionally. Ray had an area of the set made into an apartment of sorts where he could stay overnight, claiming that there was so much work to do that he didn't want to spend the time commuting home. Gloria listened to her husband's direction and did everything required of her with no objections; indeed, she had been pressured before filming commenced to sign an agreement for the studio in which she agreed to obey Ray in all matters while on the set, six days a week, a document which was prepared because the producers feared what a breakup between their director and leading lady would do to their production.

Ultimately, public and critical fascination with the gossipy behind-the-scenes aspects of the film have little to do with its actual quality. And despite all the problems that he was enduring at the time, Ray fashioned *In a Lonely Place* into a remarkable movie, and guided Gloria to one of her finest performances while doing so. Perhaps the greatest irony for Gloria was that while her private life was in utter turmoil, the person with whom she could no longer cohabitate offscreen was guiding her onscreen with tremendous skill, patience and understanding. Ray believed in the film, and he believed in Gloria. He had pushed for her in the part, lobbying for Columbia to hire her instead of Ginger Rogers, the studio's first choice to play Laurel Gray, and over Bogart's preference for his own wife, Lauren Bacall. Ray honestly felt that Gloria was right for the part, and once he got her there, he worked with her ex-

tensively to coax the best performance possible from her.

It is Gloria's first major co-starring role and she is terrific. Unlike the shadier parts for which she would gain greater fame (and which would typecast her to a large degree), Laurel Gray is a classy, intelligent, sophisticated woman. Laurel meets Dix, decides that she likes his face, and within a day arranges her life so that she can get to know him better. As she discovers that she loves Dix, Laurel devotes herself to him, basking in his adulation and putting her struggling career aside to care for him. Gloria plays this very straightforwardly, with as much realism as she can muster. It was Ray's intention to make Laurel uncomplicated, driven by the clear agenda to find in Dix a love that has so far eluded her in Hollywood, and Gloria never loses sight of that goal. She is completely believable, especially as the relationship begins to sour, when Laurel is faced once again with the prospect of personal unhappiness—or possibly worse.

Gloria's early scenes with Bogart are full of the tantalizing quality that would make her so memorable in *film noir* projects over the next five years. Laurel first meets Dix formally at the police station, where he is being questioned regarding Mildred's murder. Laurel is shocked that Mildred is dead, but after carefully looking at Dix she concludes that he had nothing to do with it. She gives Dix a solid alibi and Captain Lochner asks her why she had noticed him the previous evening. "I noticed him because he looked interesting. I like his face." This admission, of course, thrills Dix, who offers to take her home. Laurel refuses. "I always go home with the man who brought me," she says, referring to the cop who is waiting for her. Later, Dix talks to Laurel and tries to make quick inroads to her affection. They're talking about his face and Lauren compliments it again. Dix says, "You're out of your mind! Look at it," as he closes in for a kiss. "I said I liked it," states Laurel calmly. "I didn't say I wanted to kiss it." She turns away with a smile.

Right after that, it is Dix who articulates Laurel's appeal: "You know, when you first walked into the police station I said to myself, 'There she is. The one that's different. She's not coy, or cute, or corny. She's a good guy and I'm glad she's on my side. She speaks her mind and

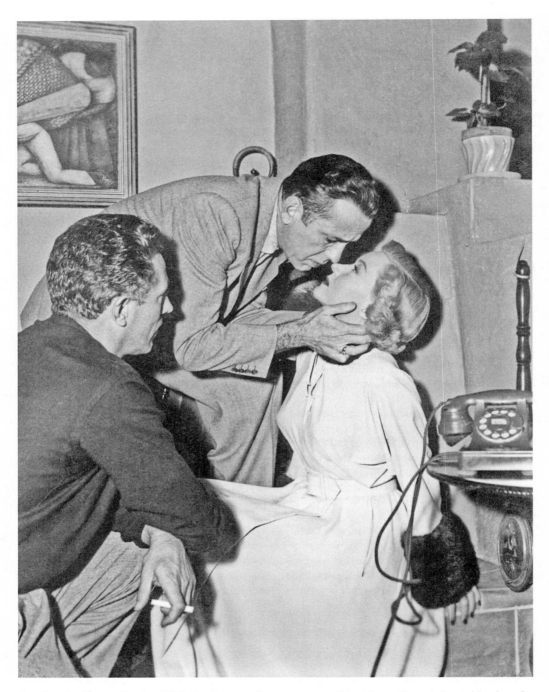

In a Lonely Place. Director Nicholas Ray watches intently as Humphrey Bogart shows him how he intends to kiss, or strangle, Gloria. Ray altered the film's final scene because he did not want Bogart's character to kill Grahame's.

she knows what she wants.'" Indeed, Gloria portrays Laurel in just this manner. She looks Bogart, and all of the other actors, in the eyes during her scenes, directly and without pretense. She thinks about the dialogue rather than simply reciting it, and that thought conveys the intelligence of the character. A *Screen Album* reviewer detailed her approach and was right on the beam. "When she looked, she really looked, and when she listened, she really listened, and her appearance in a scene guaranteed that scene a certain mood, value and vitality. As an actress, she's well trained; as a woman, she has an original quality which sets her apart from a good many of the young blonde starlets that infest Hollywood. In a melodramatic situation she quite admirably refuses to be melodramatic, and when she's in love, you trust her, and when she's in trouble, you're worried."

In the scenes where Dix returns to writing, Laurel is the very picture of chic 1950s domesticity, bringing him coffee and tidying the apartment in a high-collared dress. She makes the bed and hides the telephone so he won't be disturbed. Mel (Art Smith) appears and tells Laurel that if Dix had met her ten years earlier, Mel wouldn't have ulcers now. Gloria is at her best here, relaxed and luxuriating in the easy humor of the script. Her light touch is just right for this sequence, especially as Laurel teases Dix about winning the Mr. America contest. It is clear that they are exactly right for each other, and director Ray refuses to poison this moment in any way. Perhaps this is the way he always imagined life with Gloria, with her gentle devotion and subservience to him no matter the situation. Life, of course, turned out much differently.

The spectacle of a happy relationship does not last long, for Ray merely needed to establish the potential for happiness before he began to depict how forces both interior and exterior could erode that happiness despite his lead characters' best intentions and genuine love for each other. *In a Lonely Place* is an unusual film in this way: While most Hollywood movies (especially comedies) remained true to the formula that love would indeed conquer all and that marriage was as permanent as death, Ray's film — perhaps reflecting his own world view — recognizes the imperfect nature of human relationships and insists that people are sometimes *dangerous* to each other as they become intimate. One can only speculate as to whether Ray felt that he and Gloria would become dangerous to each other if they remained together, but it is undeniable that he turned that premise into a classic film.

In many ways *In a Lonely Place* defies description. It is often classified as a *film noir* and certainly has elements of that genre, but it doesn't fit comfortably into any description of that genre. It isn't much of a mystery, as there is little doubt that Dix is innocent of the murder of which he is accused. In fact, Dix offhandedly identifies the murderer (named, as an in-joke, for the movie's associate producer) in a scene about halfway through the film. In his treatise on the film for the British Film Institute's Classics series, author Dana Polan likens the film's structure and dialogue to that of the screwball comedies of the 1930s and '40s. Certainly much of the romantic dialogue fits that description, though the tone is decidedly different. Although set in Tinseltown, it doesn't really function as a Hollywood exposé; it's too generic and vague in terms of its film industry references to fully succeed as anything more than a general indictment of Hollywood's unique callousness. The term that probably best describes the film is "psychological study," for its dissection of the Dix-Laurel relationship is striking and exceptionally penetrating.

Columbia didn't know how to describe or promote the film, as evidenced by its ill-defined and often contradictory declarations of its contents. Despite mostly strong reviews, the film did poorly, although it would have fared better had its advertising campaign been solidly structured. Seen as an "actor's picture," it was fairly well regarded at the time, and its reputation has only grown over the years since. Today it is considered a top psychological drama with Bogart delivering one of his sharpest, most incisive performances and Gloria clearly on her way to stardom. Ray's reputation as an *auteur* has soared, with *In a Lonely Place, Johnny Guitar* and *Rebel Without a Cause* noted as films which define the 1950s and his personal style of filmmaking. *In a Lonely Place* was added to the National Film Registry in 2007.

At the time of its release, however, critics were somewhat divided. Thomas M. Pryor of the *New York Times* loved it, calling it "a dandy film" and praising everyone involved. Philip T. Hartung of *Commonweal* was impressed, too: "The climax is terrific; and the ending, the only one that would make any sense, comes as a complete surprise." *Variety* predicted it would be "a boxoffice winner." But *Time* judged that it "seems to take forever getting to the point and just about as long driving it home" and simplistically derided the story as an "over-familiar love story of a hero-heel (Bogart) and a good-bad girl (Grahame)." John McCarten of *The New Yorker* opined, "As a murder mystery the piece suffers from being a trifle incredible, but Mr. Bogart is first-rate, and so is Gloria Grahame...." *Film Daily* also appreciated Gloria's efforts: "It is another commendable example of an unusual story pattern ably delineated. Both Bogart and Gloria Grahame deliver top caliber performances. Miss Grahame, it must be added, is a most capable actress. She takes full charge of her characterization, makes it register and attracts considerable attention." John Springer concurred in his book *Forgotten Films to Remember*, calling Gloria "a revelation in her first chance to play something other than the good hearted slut."

Gloria had her husband to thank for the part, and for working diligently with her to perfect her performance. It was an odd situation, for they needed to be, and were, thoroughly professional on the set even as they cohabited separately after hours. Ray knew how much was riding on the film and he wasn't about to let his tumultuous personal life blow it. Gloria realized that co-starring in a Humphrey Bogart picture was the big time, and that it represented her second big chance. So they worked hard, singly and together, to make the film as well as it could be made. It was also a comeback for Bogart, whose last few films had been disappointments. Bogart's risk was even greater, for it was his company that produced *In a Lonely Place*.

Both stars received excellent notices, even if their film confounded the critics who were accustomed to pictures they could easily compartmentalize. And both moved on to immediate success, with Bogart winning an Academy Award the following year for *The African Queen* and Gloria working non-stop on no less than four films that would be released in 1952, one of which would win her an Academy Award of her own.

The Greatest Show on Earth
(1952)

CREDITS Paramount. *Produced and Directed by* Cecil B. DeMille. *Associate Producer*: Henry Wil-

coxon. *Screenplay by* Fredric M. Frank, Barré Lyndon and Theodore St. John. *Story by* Fredric M. Frank, Theodore St. John and Frank Cavett. *Director of Photography*: George Barnes. *Edited by* Anne Bauchens. *Additional Photography*: J. Peverell Marley and Wallace Kelley. *Technicolor Color Consultant*: Robert Brower. *Special Photographic Effects*: Gordon Jennings, Paul Lerpae and Devereux Jennings. *Costumes*: Edith Head and Dorothy Jeakins. *Circus Costumes*: Miles White. *Circus Costumes Executed by* Brooks Costume Co., New York. *Art Direction*: Hal Pereira and Walter Tyler. *Set Decoration*: Sam Comer and Ray Moyer. *Technical Advisor*: John Ringling North. *Circus Musical and Dance Numbers Staged by* John Murray Anderson. *Choreography*: Richard Barstow. *Dialogue Supervisor*: James Vincent. *Makeup Supervision*: Wally Westmore. *Sound Recording by* Harry Lindgren and John Cope. *Assistant Director*: Edward Salven. *Unit Director*: Arthur Rosson. *Music Score by* Victor Young. *Songs* "The Greatest Show on Earth" and "Be a Jumping-Jack" by Victor Young and Ned Washington. *Song* "Lovely Luawana Lady" by John Ringling North and E. Ray Goetz. *Songs* "Popcorn and Lemonade," "A Picnic in the Park" and "Sing a Happy Song" by Henry Sullivan and John Murray Anderson. *Orchestrators*: Sidney Cutner, George Parrish and Leo Shuken. *Produced with the Cooperation of the* Ringling Bros.–Barnum and Bailey Circus. *Officers of the* Ringling Bros.–Barnum and Bailey Circus: John Ringling North, *President*; Henry Ringling North, *Vice-President*; Arthur M. Concello, *General Manager*; Pat Valdo, *General Director of Performance*. *Unit Managers*: Roy Burns, C. Kenneth Deland and Andrew J. Durkus. *Assistant Directors*: Daniel McCauley and Walter Tyler. *Second Assistant Director*: Frank Baur. *Construction Coordinator*: Gene Lauritzen. *Assistant Art Director*: Jack Senter. *Designer of the Big Top*: Norman Bel Geddes. *Special Effects by* Barney Wolff. *Stunts by* Polly Burson, Chuck Hamilton, Russell Saunders and Dale Van Sickel. *Cornel Wilde's Aerialist Coach*: Lynn Couch. *Elephant Handler*: Barlow Simpson. Technicolor. Flat (1.37:1). Monaural Sound. 152 minutes. Released on January 10, 1952. Currently available on DVD. Previously available on VHS and laserdisc.

CAST *Holly*, Betty Hutton; *The Great Sebastian*, Cornel Wilde; *Brad Braden*, Charlton Heston; *Buttons*, James Stewart; *Phyllis*, Dorothy Lamour; *Angel*, Gloria Grahame; *FBI Agent Gregory*, Henry Wilcoxon; *Klaus*, Lyle Bettger; *Mr. Henderson*, Lawrence Tierney; *Harry*, John Kellogg; *Assistant Manager*, John Ridgely; *Circus Doctor*, Frank Wilcox; *Ringmaster*, Bob Carson; *Buttons' Mother*, Lillian Albertson; *Birdie*, Julia Faye; *Buttons*, James Stewart; *Themselves*, Emmett Kelly, Cucciola, Antoinette Concello, John Ringling North, Tuffy Genders. *Narrated by* Cecil B. DeMille; *Sam's Wife*, Dorothy Adams; *Vicki*, Vicki Bakken; *Bruce*, Bruce Cameron; *Dave*, Lane Chandler; *Farmer Sam*, Davison Clark; *Rus*, Rus

Conklin; *Jack*, John Crawford; *Dorothy*, Dorothy Crider; *Ann*, Gloria Drew; *Claude*, Claude Dunkin; *Rosemary*, Rosemary Dvorak; *Truesdale*, Norman Field; *Bill*, William Hall; *Charmienne*, Charmienne Harker; *Osborne*, Bradford Hatton; *Mable*, Adele Cook Johnson; *Lorna*, Lorna Jordon; *Mona*, Mona Knox; *Hank*, Ethan Laidlaw; *Tony*, Anthony Marsh; *Carson*, Sydney Mason; *Gay*, Gay McEldowney; *Chuck*, John Merton; *Gertrude*, Gertrude Messinger; *Patricia*, Patricia Michon; *Noel*, Noel Neill; *Jack Lawson*, John Parrish; *Hugh*, Hugh Prosser; *Keith*, Keith Richards; *Herself*, Iphigenie Castiglioni; *Board Member*, Everett Glass; *Ambulance Driver*, Chuck Hamilton; *Reporter*, Brad Johnson; *Pickpocket Victim*, Milton Kibbee; *Train Fireman*, Fred Kohler, Jr.; *Foreman*, Herbert Lytton; *Train Engineer*, Frank Meredith; *Truck Boss*, Howard Negley; *Man in Train Wreck*, Dale Van Sickel; *Policemen*, William J. Riley and Robert W. Rushing; *Midway Barkers*, Lester Dorr, William Ruhl, Syd Saylor and Edmond O'Brien; *Circus Midgets*, Daisy Earles, Luce Potter and Angelo Rossitto; *Circus Workers*, Eric Alden, Lydia Clarke, Jimmie Dundee, Slim Gaut, Dolores Hall, George Magrill, Harry Raven and Russell Saunders; *Little Boy Spectators*, Lee Aaker, Lonnie Burr, Malcolm Cassell, Gerald Courtemarche, Bobby Diamond, John Hamer, Joe Harper, Jimmy Hawkins, Bill Henry, Rudy Lee, Joel Nestler, Eric Nielsen, Sammy Ogg, Peter Roman, Tony Taylor, Stuart Torres and Robin Winans; *Little Girl Spectators*, Bonnie Kay Eddy, Linda Green, Kathleen Hartnagel, Frances Karath, Peggy McKim, Royce Milne, Beverly Mook, Noralee Norman, Judy Nugent, Susan Odin, Judith Ann Vroom and Beverly Washburn; *Adult Spectators*, Erville Alderson, Stanley Andrews, Ross Bagdasarian, Gladys Blake, Oliver Blake, Arthur Q. Bryan, Bobb Burns, Paul E. Burns, Charles D. Campbell, Ken Christy, Bing Crosby, Bob Crosby, Don Dunning, Art Dupuis, Franklyn Farnum, Mary Field, Bess Flowers, Kathleen Freeman, Mona Freeman, Gerry Ganzer, Nancy Gates, Joseph Granby, Greta Granstedt, Scott H. Hall, Peter Hansen, Helene Hatch, Paula Hill, Fay Holderness, Bob Hope, Jerry James, James McNally, Bill Meader, Ralph Montgomery, Lyle Moraine, Clarence Nash, Ottola Nesmith, David Newell, Ruth Packard, Queenie Smith, Robert St. Angelo, Robert R. Stephenson, Dorothy Vernon, Wally Walker, Josephine Whittell and Kay Wiley; *Bit Part*, Mary Bezemes. *Circus Personnel Photographed Under the Big Top*: Lou Jacobs, The Alzanas, Trisco, The Flying Artonys, Lilo Juston, The Chaludis, The Idnavis, The Realles, The Fredonias, Luciana and Friedel, Buzzy Potts, Ernie Burch, Felix Adler, Paul Jerome, Miss Patricia, Eddie Kohl, Tiebor's Sea Lions, Mroczkowski's Liberty Horses, The Zoppes, Bones Brown, Fay Alexander, The Flying Concellos, Lola Dobritch, The Hemadas, Christy and Gorilla, Tonito, The Bokaras, Prince Paul, Jimmy Armstrong, Paul Horompo, Paul Jung,

Charley Bell, Gilbert Reichert, C. H. Lindsey, Peterson's Dogs, Rix's Bears, Arthur Burson, La Norma, Jeanne Sleeter, Bill Snyder, The Flying Comets, Veronica Martell, Miss Loni, The Romigs, Rusty Parent, The Maxellas, Martha Hunter, Truzzi, Eugene Scott, James Barnes, Merle Evans, Frank McClosky, Mike Petrillo, Peter Grace, Bob Reynolds, George Werner. *Circus Guest Star*: Hopalong Cassidy (William Boyd).

Although *Macao* was the first of Gloria's four 1952 releases to be filmed, the first to reach theaters was Cecil B. DeMille's mammoth circus picture, *The Greatest Show on Earth*. DeMille filmed his two-and-a-half hour all-star spectacular and had it in theaters before the troubled RKO production *Macao* was fully edited and finished. Thus, a full eighteen months after Gloria's terrific job in the Humphrey Bogart drama *In a Lonely Place*, audiences were treated not to her secondary, subservient role in *Macao*, but a full-fledged co-starring role in what promised to be 1952's first really big film. The timing couldn't have been better for Gloria, who, with this movie, started the biggest year of her film career with a bang.

The Greatest Show on Earth begins with DeMille's voice narrating the scene at the Ringling Bros.–Barnum and Bailey Circus winter headquarters in Sarasota, Florida, a few days before their national tour is to begin. Circus manager Brad Braden (Charlton Heston) meets with the circus brass and insists on playing a full eight-month season, despite calls to play only big cities on a ten-week tour. The matter is deadlocked until Brad reveals that he has signed trapeze artist The Great Sebastian — a deal dependent upon playing the full season. Brad is told that the circus can tour as long as it is making money. Brad finds that a more difficult negotiation is moving resident trapeze artist Holly (Betty Hutton) out of the middle ring, which he previously promised her she could have. Sebastian (Cornel Wilde) arrives with fanfare just before the train departs, charms all the women in sight and inadvertently instigates a rivalry that will take place high above the ground during the tour.

The first time that they appear together as trapeze artists, Holly insists on doing everything Sebastian does, more spectacularly if possible. Sebastian enjoys the rivalry and soon has Holly swooning for him. Holly is warned about

The Greatest Show on Earth. Elephant trainer Klaus (Lyle Bettger) and his assistant Angel (Gloria Grahame) are stars of the Ringling Brothers and Barnum and Bailey Circus in Cecil B. DeMille's mammoth circus production.

Sebastian by Angel (Gloria Grahame), an assistant elephant trainer who had been with him in Paris. Angel also insists that Brad (whom Holly has always loved) deserves better. Angel has her own pursuer, the elephant trainer Klaus (Lyle Bettger), who declares his feelings for her at every opportunity. The circus performers stage a parade under the big top with different themes. Buttons the clown (James Stewart) sneaks away to see a woman in the audience; it is his mother, who warns him that police are still looking for him. After the show, the circus closes down and moves to the next town. DeMille intones, "The performance ends but the drama never stops," as he narrates the incredible work necessary to pack and stow the equipment and animals, move them to the next town via railroad, then put it all up again within a matter of hours.

Up in the air in another town, Holly is swinging by a rope, flipping herself up and down as the crowd counts the number of repetitions. Brad is notified of her impetuous act and he unceremoniously has her lowered to the ground, moving the crowd to laughter. Holly, furious, is comforted by Sebastian. She nearly falls prey to Sebastian's romantic moves, only to be rescued by Angel and an elephant. Brad shows Holly the rope that was coming undone as she flipped through the air, and Holly realizes that Brad probably saved her life. He loves her; she tries to make him admit it, but he won't comply. Klaus continues his pursuit of Angel, but she rejects him yet again. Meanwhile, a crooked midway barker, Harry (John Kellogg), fleeces a man of his wallet. Brad is called to the midway, sees Harry in action and physically throws him off of the grounds. Later, shady businessman Henderson (Lawrence Tierney), the man operating the crooked midway barkers, tries to convince Brad to reinstate Harry. Brad will have none of it.

At another performance, Sebastian announces he will do an especially dangerous trapeze move and, at Holly's teasing, cuts down his safety net. He attempts the trick and crashes to the ground. Sebastian is carried away and only kept alive by Buttons' quick medical response. The show goes on, with Holly moving into center ring. Lots of circus acts are seen: tightrope walkers, jugglers, acrobats, clowns, animal acts. Practicing on the trampoline between shows, Holly and Buttons sing "Be a Jumping-Jack" while the other performers watch and laugh. Sebastian returns, but declares that he is leaving the circus for another. Brad guesses the truth and forces him to reveal the full extent of his injury: a dead arm with a claw hand. Sebastian is too proud to stay, but Holly declares her love for him and finally persuades him that she is serious. During another performance parade, Angel criticizes Holly for abandoning Brad for Sebastian, and declares that she will go after Brad herself.

Angel visits Brad in his trailer and cleans up around him while he's on the phone. She makes coffee for him and persuades him that having a girl around is not necessarily a bad thing. "Women are poison," Brad states. "It's a wonderful death," Angel replies. While Angel cheerfully seduces Brad, Klaus steams. Harry sneaks back onto the grounds and goads Klaus into helping him with a scheme to get even. At the next performance Brad is warned to watch Angel, who may be in danger. Klaus poises an elephant's foot above Angel's face as she reclines on the ground. He taunts her with threats, all the while making the elephant hold its foot in the air. Brad intervenes, pulls Angel away and fires Klaus on the spot. Angel finishes the act, riding at the head of a parade of pachyderms, and even being carried in one's mouth, smiling all the while.

As the circus ends one evening, Harry is nearby running a crap game. Klaus arrives and agrees to Harry's plan; they drive away to put it into action. An FBI agent named Gregory (Henry Wilcoxon) arrives and talks to Brad, looking for a fugitive. The agent will be fingerprinting some circus people and traveling with them to their next destination on the train. Realizing that Buttons is the wanted man, Brad warns him about the agent. Buttons tells Brad that Sebastian's injury may not be permanent and suggests a way for Brad to demonstrate it. Brad makes Sebastian so angry he clenches his injured hand, proving to him that there is hope for the future. Up the tracks, Harry and Klaus set their trap, putting a flare in the middle of the tracks. The train slows and stops, giving the two men the opportunity to rob it of the night's receipts.

But the circus train travels in two sections, and as the second section comes barreling down the tracks oblivious to the situation ahead of it, Klaus realizes that Angel is in mortal danger. Ignoring Harry, he tries to warn the second train section, driving toward it on the tracks and screaming for it to stop. The locomotive smashes into Harry's car, flipping it end over end, and then smashes into the first train, sending train cars rolling and spinning. People are tossed, crushed and killed; animals crawl away from their broken enclosures and begin to prowl around the scene of chaos. Holly and Sebastian rescue Angel and help people out of their upturned car. Brad issues his orders as always, but he is trapped beneath some wreckage, and bleeding. Animals are rounded up. Seeing that Brad is trapped, Angel retrieves an elephant, which lifts the wreckage off of Brad. He is bleeding badly, and only a doctor with surgical skill will be able to help. Holly finds Buttons, who is trying to sneak away amidst the clamor, and begs him to help Brad.

Buttons returns and begins to operate on Brad, aided by the FBI agent Gregory. Brad needs a blood transfusion and the only person with matching blood is Sebastian. Although Brad protests vociferously, Sebastian cheerfully volunteers to keep Brad alive, reminding Brad that every time he sees his (future) children, he will recall that they are part Sebastian. Meanwhile, Holly takes over in Brad's stead, ordering that the circus be established in a nearby field for a performance the next day; the show must go on. The next morning Brad is approached by Henderson, who insists that the circus is finished. They are interrupted by a parade of the circus performers, led by Holly, which has returned from the nearby town and is being followed by hundreds of the town's residents. Buttons is led away in handcuffs by FBI agent Gregory after finally admitting that he is the doctor who killed his terminally sick wife years before. Brad tries to tell Holly he loves her, but (just like he did earlier in the story) she refuses to stand still long enough to listen to him. Angel sees that she has lost Brad to Holly and says so to Sebastian, who, surprisingly, offers to marry Angel. They tacitly agree as Holly sings "The Greatest Show on Earth" and the circus presents another performance.

Big, bold, brash and loud, *The Greatest Show on Earth* immediately became the classic circus picture. When Cecil B. DeMille decided that he wanted to direct it, he determined to make it first-rate all the way. He didn't dicker with a small or even mid-level circus; he approached the industry leader and offered to showcase that circus and its performers in his big-budget extravaganza. He sought use of the circus' world-famous slogan for his title, unrestricted access to all aspects of the traveling circus, a period of acclimation for himself (DeMille toured with the circus during the summer of 1949) and personalized training for key cast members doing specialized acts. In return, the Ringling Bros.–Barnum and Bailey Circus was paid a $250,000 consulting fee and even received profit participation once the film made back its costs. All in all it was a match that virtually guaranteed motion picture success.

DeMille recognized that the circus was as important a character as any of the actors and was determined that it be represented as such, and not remain merely colorful background. "It is an army. It is a family. It is a city, always on the move. It is an agile giant. It is sweat and fatigue and danger endured to send a rippling wave of thrills and laughter across a continent." His narration emphasizes the hard work and dedication necessary to reassemble the "city always on the move" in each new town, noting that some fourteen hundred people participate in the process. DeMille took great care to include quite a few behind-the-scenes shots of the circus roustabouts at work, and to populate his dramatic scenes with people in the background attending to the myriad of details requisite for keeping the show on track, and safe for the performers. He was resolved to make his picture truly authentic, even to the point of having his famous movie stars do their own acts.

According to press reports of the time, DeMille was deluged with requests by stars to appear in his picture. Not so well reported is that many aspirants changed their minds when they discovered that they would actually have to do their own acts. It really is Betty Hutton and Cornel Wilde swinging through the air on their trapeze bars. It really is Dorothy Lamour spinning in mid-air, hanging only by a leather jaw-strap. And it really is Gloria Grahame lying on the ground with a real elephant's foot poised an inch above her beautiful face. These stars and others studied with the circus pros, practiced until they were comfortable in their roles and then performed the stunts with the circus before audiences in Sarasota, Philadelphia and Washington, D.C., while DeMille filmed the proceedings as unobtrusively as possible. It was all in keeping with the director's fervor to present the circus milieu as truthfully as possible, and to provide genuine thrills to the audience. Nowadays insurance restrictions and the cost of liability insurance would probably prevent such a movie from being made in such a fashion. But DeMille had spent time with the circus, knew exactly what he wanted to do, and did it.

When touring with the circus in 1949, De-

The Greatest Show on Earth. Surrounded by the other trainers, assistants and elephants, Angel (Gloria) stands proudly atop Minyak during a center ring performance. Gloria and Minyak did not care for each other, but that did not prevent either of them from remaining thoroughly professional before the cameras.

Mille realized that filming under the big top would be difficult. Lighting was a definite problem, especially when it came to the aerial trapeze acts. By the time filming began in 1951 he had devised a system of lights on poles that could be maneuvered vertically to provide the light necessary and yet be out of the camera's line of sight. This new scheme for lighting in close quarters was quickly adopted by other filmmakers. Another challenge arose when it came time to film the performers in front of audiences. Camera and lighting equipment was kept out of sight as much as possible during the performances, so as not to distract the audience from the spectacle of the acts, and the thrill of watching real movie stars risk their lives.

Not just counting on his stars to sell the movie, DeMille included more than sixty circus acts into the film as well. Some are seen just briefly while others such as Emmett Kelly, Lou Jacobs, Tiebor's Sea Lions and Peterson's Dogs are spotlighted with their own sequences. All are credited before the film, which also notes the circus' full cooperation with the film. De-Mille had designed the film not as a drama with a circus background but a fully fleshed circus picture, a worthy substitute for a real-life visit to the circus—and then crowned it with the most spectacular train wreck ever put on film. At least one family went to the movie instead of visiting a circus in 1952. It was Steven Spielberg's family; he was just five years old and seeing *The Greatest Show on Earth* is his earliest childhood memory. The train wreck sequence later inspired him to replicate it with a model train set at home, lens it on 8mm film and begin his career as a filmmaker.

The film itself is as vivid as DeMille's imagination. It contains multiple story threads, interwoven throughout the big top canvas. Circus manager Brad Braden (Charlton Heston, in his first major success) regards romance as an unnecessary and often counterproductive distraction, yet that just makes him irresistible to both Holly (Betty Hutton) and Angel (Gloria Grahame). The arrival of Sebastian (Cornel Wilde) turns that romantic triangle into an awkward square, as Sebastian has already been with Angel and now has his sights set on Holly. Holly can't make up her mind who she loves, and Angel wants Brad. Complicating matters are Klaus' (Lyle Bettger) dogged pursuit of Angel, the element of crooked barkers on the midway, and Buttons' (James Stewart) reason for never taking off his clown makeup. Throw in the climactic robbery and train wreck and all the ingredients are present for a blockbuster.

DeMille's quest for authenticity led him to stage as much of the personal drama under the big top, during the actual performances. Thus, the rivalry for center ring between Holly and Sebastian is intensified due to their one-upping each other while swinging forty feet above the ground. When Klaus finally loses his temper with Angel, it is when he is positioning an elephant's foot above her head, with an audience watching. Buttons makes surreptitious contact with his mother while he is clowning around in the audience. Sebastian surprises Holly in mid-air by taking her catcher's place; when she objects to his kiss, he drops her into the safety net. Holly and Angel have a testy discussion about Brad while touring around the big top during one of the parades. Staging the personal drama this way enlivens the circus acts dramatically and prevents the movie from turning into a dull recording of circus performances.

Not that the film doesn't have its dull spots. Including more than sixty separate carnival acts (and spotlighting a handful of them) pushes what could have been a two-hour drama past the two-and-a-half hour mark. Most tedious are two parades, where the performers and other people don extravagant themed costumes and walk or ride around the big top as music plays and the ringmaster announces the theme. The first parade, a "Circus Serenade," offers Walt Disney characters, plus characters of seasons, representations of the Gay '90s, nursery rhyme characters, a Stephen Foster album, a South American album, a Christmas album and a "Bouquet of American Beauty." The second parade is a "Picnic in the Park," dramatizing Marie Antoinette attending the Royal Horse Show. It is during this sequence that Holly and Angel, dressed as bewigged French women, have their emotional discussion about Brad. These sequences slow down the movie, while adding very little. The "Circus Serenade" sequence in particular is interminable and deadly dull.

Another staple of the format that doesn't contribute very much is the audience reaction shot. There are dozens of shots of specific audience members enjoying the show, or being upset by the suspense of the dangerous acts taking place in front of them. DeMille uses two tricks to alleviate the tedium of such reaction shots. The first is to repeat shots of certain people, allowing them to evolve in their reactions. Thus, an adult male gradually becomes more childlike as he watches the show, while a young boy becomes so rapt that he forgets to eat his cotton candy. The second trick is somewhat distracting, and that is to place famous people in the audience. Thus, viewers are surprised to find Bob Hope and Bing Crosby watching appreciatively as Phyllis (Dorothy Lamour) does her "Lovely Luawana Lady" song. And in the final shot, it is Edmond O'Brien, dressed as a midway barker, who exhorts the audience to visit the circus when it comes to town.

Although circuses are famed for their animal acts, DeMille minimizes their screen time and impact in *The Greatest Show on Earth*. Certain acts are spotlighted, like Tiebor's Sea Lions and Peterson's Dogs, but little attention is paid to the lions, tigers and bears usually associated with circuses. They are seen being transported in their large cages, but only briefly do they score any screen time under the big top. A few escape during the train wreck but they are quickly brought under control before they can make matters worse for the injured circus personnel. Horses and monkeys receive greater attention than do the big cats or bears. DeMille reserved most of his focus for one other animal: the elephant.

Klaus' elephants are the animal kings of the circus domain. They star in the parades and they have their own specialized act with Angel. When Brad is pinned underneath the train wreckage, it is an elephant, led by Angel, who lifts it off of him. And when the circus re-forms for its performance after the train wreck, the parade from town is led by Angel and Sebastian astride an elephant. DeMille used pachyderms because they were easier to incorporate into the story, posed less risk to the actors, were easier to work with than the big cats, and were physically impressive, towering over their human co-stars.

Two elephants, Ruth and Minyak, appear with Klaus and Angel. Angel rides Ruth most of the time because Ruth was more sedate and amenable to taking orders from the actors pretending to be her regular handlers. Gloria rides Ruth in several scenes and appears quite comfortable with handling the prized pachyderm, as Angel would be under the circumstances. It is Ruth that Angel uses to grab Holly and carry her away from the romantic clutches of Sebastian. Ruth, who was one of two Ringling Bros. elephants with that name at the time, got along well with Gloria, and vice versa. Minyak was another matter. Although described to Gloria as "the soft-hearted old lady of the Ringling elephants," Minyak was somewhat aggressive, or perhaps just faster in her actions than Gloria expected.

From the moment they met, Gloria and Minyak were uncomfortable with each other. Minyak was practicing with a Ringling Bros. elephant girl, and when Gloria approached, the elephant dropped the girl. Seeing Minyak drop the girl made Gloria distrust her from the beginning, and the precise timing necessary between elephant and handler just never developed with Gloria. In the suspenseful scene where Klaus threatens to have an elephant step down on Angel's face, it is Minyak who dangles her foot a few inches above Gloria's beautiful kisser. Gloria was praying that Minyak wouldn't end the scene too quickly, and she didn't. It has been reported, and is probably true, that the close-up of Gloria's face underneath the elephant's foot was made with a convincing mock-up. This would make sense, given the time necessary for lighting, focus and other lensing issues. Even so, it is quite convincing on film. But Gloria was not quite out of harm's way with Minyak.

In a long shot where Gloria squirms out from under Minyak, the elephant lowered her foot more quickly than anticipated and bruised Gloria's leg. The scene ends as Gloria stands in front of the elephant's raised feet, and when Minyak lowers them before Gloria is ready, she is bumped forward a little bit, smiling awkwardly. Even though this take reveals that handler and animal were not in perfect synchronization, it was still used in the final film.

Minyak also appears in the train wreck segment. During the first take, when the elephant was to lift the wreckage off of Brad, Minyak accidentally stepped on a railroad spike, trumpeted loudly in agony and stamped around the set. Charlton Heston, playing Brad, pinned beneath the wreckage, was terrified. But Minyak was treated for the wound and calmed down. In another take, Minyak grasped the wreckage more quickly than planned, before Gloria could pull her hand out of the way. As the elephant lifted the wreckage, Gloria suffered a painful scratch. Once she was treated, the take was repeated, and this time worked just as DeMille had planned.

New York Times columnist Thomas M. Pryor attended a Philadelphia staging of the

The Greatest Show on Earth. The danger facing any elephant girl is evident as Minyak holds his huge foot just inches above the beautiful face of Angel (Gloria). Gloria later said this moment was the only time she had ever been genuinely frightened while making a movie.

circus while the movie was being filmed and reported upon Gloria's close call:

> Monday night was an unhappy night for Miss Grahame. She almost was hit by the elephant's foot while rolling into the clear and upon remounting just barely grasped the trapping as the elephant did a hind stand. The actress' husband, director Nicholas Ray, was watching the act for the first time. When it was over he was speechless, mopping his drenched brow with shaking hands. Miss Grahame, regarded as a fast-rising star, took the whole business with amazing calm the two nights running.

Gloria was thrilled to be requested by De-Mille. She then learned that she was a replacement for Lucille Ball, who was unable to do the picture because she had become pregnant. Paulette Goddard had also desperately wanted the part and tried to finagle her way into it, but after working with Goddard in *Unconquered*, DeMille wanted nothing more to do with her and threw her telegraphed request for the part into a wastebasket. Nonetheless, Gloria was hypnotized by DeMille's proposal. "He explained the whole thing to me thoroughly, dramatically and clearly. When he was finished I was almost ready to chuck Paramount and join the circus." That sentiment was nearly reversed when she saw Minyak drop the real elephant girl, but ever the trouper, Gloria rose to the challenge. It was difficult not to do so, when surrounded by stars bigger than herself, all being paid the same $50,000 salary and risking their lives for one of the founders of modern cinema. DeMille appreciated bravery for the sake of art, and he loved what Gloria brought to the film. Following principal photography, he presented her with one of the cut crystal balls he often gave performers who displayed courage and professionalism on his sets. When asked to describe Gloria, DeMille said, "She has the manner of a schoolgirl and the eyes of a sorceress."

DeMille provided Gloria with perhaps her most colorful role. Her beauty and "been around the block" persona fit into the circus background perfectly. Unlike star Betty Hutton, whose most important scenes take place in the air, Gloria grounds the drama with convincing realism. Her somewhat jaded but wistfully romantic character nicely counterpoints the grating perkiness of Hutton's and the lustful naiveté of Dorothy Lamour's. Gloria is vividly alive in the movie, moving amongst the circus trappings as if she belongs there, always ready with a quip or a caustic comment. She is perpetually in motion, whether riding on the back of Ruth the elephant, hurriedly dressing for one of the parades or helping rescue Brad after the train crash. Best of all, in a movie full of high-flying escapism, she is pragmatic and sensible, helping to keep the film from careening out of control.

Angel is intended to serve as a romantic red herring in the film. Holly interrupts her pursuit of Brad to focus on Sebastian, even sincerely offering to stay with him forever after his injury. But Holly is always meant for Brad, a fact that becomes clear during the train wreck sequence. That leaves Sebastian free to go after Angel, again, at the end of the story. But this time, when he offers marriage, Angel tacitly agrees! This turn of events is startling, considering the disdain that she shows for Sebastian throughout the film. It is obviously included to give Angel and Sebastian a "happy ending" but it is an ill-considered move, too abrupt and quite unbelievable.

This should be evident from Angel's attempts to steer Holly back to Brad, and from Angel's declaration that she is going after Brad herself. In the parade scene when Holly and Angel are dressed as French ladies, Gloria delivers her finest soliloquy: "Maybe I have been over the course a few too many times. But I've got a heart under this costume with room in it for one guy. You busted him apart and I'm gonna pick up the pieces. He'll never miss you, Sugar. And I'm gonna give him more than you ever could." A little bit later, Angel visits Brad in his trailer and straightens up the place while he's on the telephone. He eventually realizes what she is doing and tries to shoo her away. "You want to bite somebody?" Angel asks casually, leaning away from him seductively. "Pick your spot." That gets his attention. What really changes his mind is that Angel can pack his pipe, a trick she learned from her father. They seem right together, which makes Angel's switch at the ending seem cheap and unworthy.

But Gloria was becoming accustomed, at least in the movies, to not getting her man. She wasn't the clean-cut, All-American type of girl that moviemakers so often deigned would find everlasting happiness before the final fadeout. Gloria Grahame, the girl "with the eyes of a sorceress," was cinematically destined to find unhappiness, betrayal and tragedy with most of the men she would romance. Not all of the time, perhaps, but certainly most of the time. In this case, Gloria was fifth-billed, behind two other women, so it was natural (at least in box office terms) that they have first dibs on the leading men. So it is actually rather odd that it is fourth-billed Dorothy Lamour who is left out in the cold, romance-wise.

Lamour has the most thankless of the major roles. Her circus act is to hang by a leather jaw-strap and spin, which is certainly difficult but perhaps not spectacular to most audiences. Dramatically she always seems out of place, a major personality with very minor things to do. Cornel Wilde boasts energy, theatricality and a Maurice Chevalier–like accent that is difficult to take seriously much of the time, particularly when he is wooing the women. During filming, Wilde also discovered that he was really afraid of heights, which put him in DeMille's doghouse, as it had Paulette Goddard during the filming of *Unconquered*. Wilde completed his aerial stunts but was acutely nervous while doing so. Charlton Heston, in his fourth film, found himself boosted into stardom as the circus manager. Many critics found his playing wooden, although he is quite animated at times. He loved the moment after the premiere when DeMille showed him a fan letter that described how good the actors were, and how the real circus manager (Heston) blended into the Hollywood atmosphere so well.

Betty Hutton dominates the movie. Her aerial stuntwork is outstanding; she practiced for months, lost weight for the part, and was described as fearless. Yet her brash personality is sometimes tough to take, and it is Hutton who, for better or worse, typifies the circus performer, and this particular circus movie. Perhaps the most unfortunate aspect of her character is that it is so humorless. Because Holly is totally egotistical and spectacularly serious all the time, it is difficult to empathize with her, especially in her romantic difficulties. In the years since its release, reaction to the film has increasingly been dependent upon one's reaction to Betty Hutton.

The movie's other controversy is its use of James Stewart as Buttons. The book *Bad Movies We Love* judges the film as "the all-time weirdest, screwiest, funniest Best Picture Oscar-winner," and lampoons Stewart's role as "a clown who harbors a Terrible Secret." Buttons never removes his makeup, and his dilemma is hinted a couple of times during the drama. "Clowns only love once," he tells Holly. One of the elephants finds a newspaper on the ground with a feature story about a doctor who killed his terminally ill wife; Buttons sees it and crumples it before anyone else can read it. He keeps Sebastian alive after the trapeze artist falls to the ground, and he finally reveals his Terrible Secret after the train wreck, when he must keep Brad alive and administer a blood transfusion — aided by the FBI agent (Henry Wilcoxon) who has been searching for him. Buttons is, of course, the doctor who killed his wife. Afterwards, Buttons is led away in handcuffs, a common criminal. Would he receive the same treatment today?

The controversy lies not so much with the morality regarding mercy killing, which is ignored by the film, but rather with the hackneyed approach to the character of Buttons and his Terrible Secret. It is clear right away that Buttons is in hiding, and once he helps Sebastian and sees the newspaper it is pretty clear why. Many critics feel that Buttons is an extraneous character, despite DeMille's insistence otherwise, and that Buttons' subplot is a big flaw in the film. Stewart enjoyed the anonymity of the part. He studied clowning with the Ringling Bros.' world-famous clown Emmett Kelly, and they appear together in several scenes. It was certainly important to have a clown be a central part of the story, but DeMille might have erred by insisting on creating such a nutty background story for Buttons. It adds suspense but subtracts believability.

Despite its slow spots, DeMille's bombastic narration, trite love stories and occasional melodrama, *The Greatest Show on Earth* enthralled audiences and made a mint. Released in early January 1952, the film earned $12 million, becoming the highest-grossing film of the year. It was so popular and well received that it nabbed five Academy Award nominations, including Best Picture and Director. When it won the Best Picture Oscar, it became one of the few January releases to be so feted a full year later. It also won for Original Story, though it lost in the Director, Film Editing and Color Costume Design categories. While DeMille did not win the Best Director Oscar (the only time he was so nominated), he was given the Irving Thalberg Memorial Award for producing excellence, an honor that he felt was even sweeter.

For a Best Picture Oscar-winner, the film's reviews were pretty mild, yet if ever there was a critic-proof film, this was probably it. Bosley Crowther of the *New York Times* gushed, "Everything in this lusty triumph of circus showmanship and movie skill betokens the way with the spectacular of the veteran Mr. DeMille.... [It's] a piece of entertainment that will delight movie audiences for years." Arthur Knight in the *Saturday Review* praised the film and wrote about the director: "Here it's right for DeMille to be vulgar, obvious, gaudy. For what else is a circus? ... It's hokum, sure — but it's hokum from the hands of a master." *Variety* crowed, "This is the circus with more entertainment, more thrills, more spangles and as much Big Top atmosphere as Ringling Bros.–Barnum and Bailey itself can offer. It's a smash certainty for high-wire grosses."

On the other side of the scale was *Films in Review*, which wrote, "Mr. DeMille is so accomplished a showman that one is astonished he did not just photograph a circus performance without the synthetic story he injected here.... But he had to add love interest — and schmaltz it all up." John McCarten of *The New Yorker* declared, "As long as Mr. DeMille isn't bothering about the story, he makes an engrossing business out of the circus, but he's interrupted so often by the foolish mewlings of the various lovers that all the wonders of the Ringling Brothers and Barnum and Bailey can't save the picture from becoming rather boring."

The British Film Institute's *Monthly Film Bulletin* was positively vitriolic: "What surprises one about this long extravagant film is not the boredom of the personal stories—conceived in flat tabloid terms, with dialogue to match, the fantastic marrying-off of Angel and Sebastian, who have hardly exchanged a word throughout the picture, the endless references to Brad — the dogged manager who puts the circus above his private life — as having 'sawdust in his veins'; one expects the characterisation and dialogue to be childish in a DeMille film."

The critic for *Time* put the film in proper perspective: "If art were merely a matter of fitting form to content, the movie would be a masterpiece, for DeMille and the circus are fated for each other. By sprinkling his footage with shots of circus audiences munching all the tidbits of the refreshment stand, DeMille tightens his claim to another distinction: *Greatest Show* is likely to sell more popcorn than any movie ever made."

History has not been especially kind to the film's reputation. It is now widely considered to be the worst Best Picture choice in Oscar history, seeing as it was chosen over *High Noon*, *Moulin Rouge* and *The Quiet Man*, all classics which were nominated, as well as *Singin' in the Rain, Viva Zapata!, The Bad and the Beautiful, The Lavender Hill Mob* and *The Man in the White Suit*, all classics which were not nominated that year. (*Ivanhoe* was the fifth Best Picture nominee for 1952.) *High Noon* probably should have won, but its writer, Carl Foreman, had very publicly been hauled in front of the House Un-American Activities Committee, helping to jump-start the Communist witch hunt and blacklisting of outspoken movie industry liberals. Hollywood's reaction was to swing to the conservative side of the political fence, and no one was more politically conservative than Cecil B. DeMille. The director had also been instrumental in founding Hollywood as a film community and guiding it through its growing pains. He was a legend and the 1952 Oscars allowed the film community to honor him and his most popular film to date.

DeMille was a master showman whose films are often criticized for their excesses and for rewriting history with melodramatic flair, but audiences flocked to see them. At his best he was a hugely imaginative and creative artist, one who worked tirelessly to bring his visions to spectacular cinematic life. *The Greatest Show on Earth* is a bold, brash, sometimes silly movie that nonetheless recreates circus life better than any other film ever has, before or since. It wasn't the best film of 1952 but it was the most popular, and there were sound reasons for its becoming so. Some critics argue that the Academy Award standards were lowered when it won, but the opposite is really true. Expectations for *The Greatest Show on Earth* are inexorably heightened for modern audiences because of its win. Really, it was intended, as *Time* duly noted, to be the ultimate popcorn movie. That's the way it should be remembered, and enjoyed.

Gloria was still married to Nicholas Ray during this production, although they remained separated. He was busy directing for RKO, or being consulted on how to fix some of the studio's other films, and she was freelancing. Following *Macao*, Gloria had been able to sever her contract with RKO, with DeMille's circus film being the first subsequent project she was offered. She and Ray were largely living separate lives, although they maintained the fiction of a happy marriage for the sake of their young son Timothy and because neither wanted hostile publicity. They were really no longer on speaking terms because of an incident that occurred during the post-production of *Macao*, the effects of which would haunt both of them for the rest of their lives. But neither the public nor the film industry at large was aware of these issues; Nick was becoming a director of some note and Gloria was one of Hollywood's rising stars.

As for the film, despite her close calls with Minyak the elephant, Gloria had survived and even thrived under DeMille's direction. She had proven herself game and delivered a solid, colorful performance that had enhanced the motion picture. It was a big stepping stone for her to be associated with such a popular success, and to have risked her pretty face so dramatically in the process. Professionally, 1952 would be the finest year of Gloria's career, and it began spectacularly with the release of this movie. Gloria's next release would be a step backward, partly due to the size and scope of the role and partly because Howard Hughes took so long to get *Macao* out of the editing room and into theaters.

Macao (1952)

CREDITS RKO Radio Pictures. *Directed by* Josef von Sternberg. *Uncredited Directors*: Nicholas Ray, Mel Ferrer and Robert Stevenson. *Produced by* Alex Gottlieb. *Executive Producers*: Samuel Bischoff and Howard Hughes. *Screenplay by* Bernard C. Schoenfeld and Stanley Rubin. *Story by* Robert Creighton "Bob" Williams. *Uncredited Writers*: George Bricker, Edward Chodorov, Norman Katkov, Frank L. Moss, Walter Newman and Robert Mitchum. *Director of Photography*: Harry J. Wild. *Film Editors*: Samuel E. Beetley and Robert Golden. *Songs* "Ocean Breeze," and "You Kill Me" by Jule Styne and Leo Robin. *Song*: "One for My Baby," *lyrics by* Johnny Mercer, *music by* Harold Arlen. *Music by* Anthony Collins. *Musical Director*: C. Bakaleinikoff. *Vocal Arrangements*: Hugh Martin. *Art Directors*: Albert S. D'Agostino and Ralph Berger. *Set Decorations*: Darrell Silvera and Harley Miller. *Sound by* Earl Wolcott and Clem Portman. *Gowns by* Michael Woulfe. *Makeup Artist*: Mel Berns. *Hair Stylist*: Larry Germain. *Production Supervisor*: Jerry Wald. *Assistant Directors*: James E. Casey, William Dorfman and Lowell J. Farrell. *Second Unit Director*: Richard Davol. *Mural Painter*: Keye Luke. *Sketch Artist*: Edward Vorkapich. *Still Photographer*: Ernest Bachrach. Black and White. Flat (1.37:1). Monaural Sound. 81 minutes. Released on April 30, 1952. Currently available on DVD. Previously available on VHS.

CAST *Nick Cochran*, Robert Mitchum; *Julie Benton*, Jane Russell; *Lawrence C. Trumble*, William Bendix; *Lieutenant Felizardo José Espirito Sebastien*, Thomas Gomez; *Margie*, Gloria Grahame; *Vincent Halloran*, Brad Dexter; *Martin Stewart*, Edward Ashley; *Itzumi*, Philip Ahn; *Kwan Sum Tang*, Vladimir Sokoloff; *Narrator*, Truman Bradley; *Garcia*, Everett Glass; *Alvaris*, Trevor Bardette; *Detective Lieutenant Daniel Lombardy*, John Daheim; *Chang*, Weaver Levy; *Gimpy*, Don Zelaya; *Arabian*, Abdullah Abbas; *Bus Drivers*, Rico Alaniz and Nacho Galindo; *Woman Passenger*, Genevieve Bell; *Chinese Photographer*, George Chan; *Old Fisherman*, W. T. Chang; *Hoods*, Spencer Chan, James B. Leong and Alfredo Santos; *Portuguese Pilot*, Art Dupuis; *Merchant*, Lee Tung Foo; *Sampan Pilot*, H. W. Gim; *Sikh*, Phil Harron; *Dutch Tourist*, Sheldon Jett; *Drunken Lecherous Salesman*, Harold J. Kennedy; *Desk Clerk*, Marc Krah; *Chinese Victim*, Tommy H. Lee; *Bartenders*, Alex Montoya and Manuel Paris; *Fisherman*, Walter Ng; *Ship's Captain*, Emory Parnell; *Woman Barber*, May Takasugi; *Customs Official*, Philip Van Zandt; *Russian Doorman*, Michael Visaroff; *Croupiers*, Iris Wong and Maria Sen Young; *Rickshaw Driver*, William Yip.

It was probably *Macao* that altered Gloria's career more than any other during the early 1950s, when she had the potential to be-come one of the top actresses of the decade. *Macao* is an international mystery-thriller in the mold of *Algiers*, *Casablanca*, *Singapore*, *Saigon* and *Hong Kong* and, to its credit, it was partly filmed on location. The production was supervised by Howard Hughes, then owner of RKO Radio Pictures; it was Hughes who refused to loan Gloria to Paramount when George Stevens requested her for *A Place in the Sun* (1951). Gloria would have played the character essayed by Shelley Winters, and it might well have changed the direction of her career if she had, elevating her into even more prestigious productions. But Hughes was adamant that *Macao* was just as important a film as *A Place in the Sun* and he refused to listen to her entreaties. Ultimately *Macao* would prove to be a very troubled production and Gloria's defiant attitude toward Hughes and the film's first director, the tyrannical Josef von Sternberg, would spark the first industry gossip that she was "difficult." This, although Gloria was certainly not the only cast member to defy von Sternberg's orders. The on-set atmosphere became chillier when Nicholas Ray, still married to Gloria at the time but living apart from her, was recruited to replace von Sternberg as director for reshoots! Actually, however, Gloria's extra filming duties were handled by Mel Ferrer, the brother of Jose Ferrer, and a well-respected actor and director in his own right. Ferrer and Ray were not the only directors coaxed by Hughes into trying to better the picture; Robert Stevenson had a hand in it as well.

Macao begins with narration describing the city's dark underside which most tourists never see. A man is chased to an enclosed wharf area, running for his life from two Chinese men and a Caucasian, and is killed with a thrown knife to the back. News travels to the International Criminal Police Commission that the dead man was a New York City detective. Soon afterward, a ferry enters Macao's port on a typical, steaming hot day. In a cabin, a salesman dances to music and tries to entice Julie Benton (Jane Russell) to accompany him, without success. He tries to force his affections upon her and is interrupted by Nick Cochran (Robert Mitchum), who promptly knocks the salesman out cold. Nick then makes a pass at Julie, which she also rejects. It is only later that he realizes that while he was kissing her, she was lifting his wallet. Julie is also propositioned by a salesman, Lawrence C. Trumble (William Bendix), who provides her with a new pair of stockings, which she immediately dons on the ship's deck.

The local police chief, Lt. Sebastian (Thomas Gomez), questions Nick at length because he has no identification. Lt. Sebastian then goes directly to a local gambling hall, the Quick Reward, to tell its owner, Vincent Halloran (Brad Dexter), that he believes Nick is a detective sent to arrest Halloran for the death of the New York City detective. (Halloran was the Caucasian who helped chase and kill the detective.) Halloran directs the police chief to get rid of the American. Seeing that Nick needs it, Julie returns his money. Lt. Sebastian refers her to the Quick Reward for a singing job; she is hired at $100 a week and instructed to find some new clothes. Nick also asks for a job but is refused. Halloran tells him he thinks Nick is a cop and that Nick won't be able to get work anywhere in Macao.

Julie makes her debut in a strapless white dress, crooning "You Kill Me" to a crowd that would rather gamble than listen. Halloran teases Nick with loaded dice, tossed by Halloran's girl Margie (Gloria Grahame), and advises him to go to Hong Kong while he still can. Both men have taken a liking to Julie, but it is Nick with whom she leaves the Quick Reward that night. They ride around the harbor in a sampan swapping personal histories and Nick asks her to leave Macao with him. When he admits that he needs time to set everything in place, she refuses. The following day Trumble asks Nick to act as middleman selling a diamond necklace to Halloran, and Nick agrees. He flirts a little with Margie and shows her a diamond from the necklace, which she recognizes. Halloran agrees to buy it and to travel to Hong Kong to get the rest of the necklace to which it belonged. Meanwhile, Trumble meets with the International Police (he is the cop sent to nab Halloran).

Nick arrives at the appointed time to meet Halloran at the same wharf where the New York City detective was killed, and is sapped from behind. He awakens in Margie's house with Margie bringing him breakfast, but she answers no questions. Julie is led to him by a blind man (Vladimir Sokoloff); she finds Nick with Margie, and leaves jealous and angry. She never sees Halloran's hoods with guns pointing at Nick, forcing him to give her the wrong impression. Back at the Quick Reward, Julie sings "One for My Baby" in a gold lamé dress. Halloran argues with Lt. Sebastian about what to do with Nick, still a captive at Margie's house. With Nick under control, Halloran decides to go to Hong Kong to retrieve the necklace. But Margie helps Nick escape, asking him to take Julie out of town so that she can once again have Halloran all to herself.

Halloran's two hoods are soon on Nick's trail, following him to the wharf. Trumble is also there, and he follows the action, unseen. The chase goes to the water as Nick jumps from slippery piers to swaying sampans, through hanging nets and over many obstacles. The hoods continually close in. Trumble makes contact with Nick and gives him a gun just before he, like the New York City detective, receives a knife in the back. Before he dies, Trumble whispers an apology to Nick for involving him. Nick returns to the hotel to see Julie, who attacks him with anything she can throw and then comes after him with an electric fan! Nick wrestles it away and calms her down, explaining that he had to act as if he was with Margie or he would have been killed. She tells Nick that Halloran is going to Hong Kong; Nick asks her to help him. She agrees.

At the wharf, Margie distracts one of the hoods long enough so that Nick can kill him. He then takes the man's place at the wheel of Halloran's boat and drives it past the three-mile international limit where Halloran can be legally arrested. Halloran realizes that something is amiss and attacks Nick on the top deck. The men have a terrific fight that ends when Nick knocks Halloran overboard. Nick dives in to make sure Halloran doesn't drown. A police cruiser arrives and Nick tows Halloran over to it, leaving him in the hands of the international police. Nick then swims back to the boat and Julie Benton. They kiss as the screen fades to black.

Macao is, like the aforementioned internationally themed dramas, heavy on plot, romance and intrigue, often at the expense of character development and common sense. It is in every sense a minor film, certainly not the prestigious project that Howard Hughes considered it to be, yet it is also not without merit.

Its dialogue is sly and sassy, especially when delivered by Jane Russell, who has rarely been as alluring. The story moves along rapidly and purposefully, perhaps because it is gossamer thin. Although its sets are strictly soundstages, enough of Richard Davol's picturesque second-unit work is sprinkled throughout to provide the film with flourishes of style and an intriguing sense of the place. Despite the presence of a few handguns, the violence that does occur involves fisticuffs, thrown knives and the electric fan wielded by Russell, all of which are very menacing cinematically.

The film's greatest asset is its cinematography and visual style. Director Josef von Sternberg, though unhappy with the assignment, took care to make his visual presentation of Macao as atmospheric as possible, particularly when it came to the climactic chase through the city's dark and eerie wharf area. That chase, an almost silent, increasingly desperate run for his life by Nick from the two Chinese henchmen, remains the film's most memorable sequence. It is genuinely sinister, smartly executed and as patently evocative as von Sternberg could make it.

Von Sternberg's visual motif for the story is a sort of vertical segmentation; there are prominent door and window slats in almost every scene except for those on the ferry boat (where a steel stairway is used for visual access in the same way), while hanging fishing nets and netting, gauzy drapery and even a beaded doorway visually separate characters from each other and from action to be performed — yet they do not prevent interaction of any sort. Characters constantly see and hear each other through doors, nets, doorways and windows, and they frequently enter rooms or other private areas without knocking or waiting for an answer. The wooden slats and netting are the thinnest possible barriers between characters

Macao. Big shot businessman Vincent Halloran (Brad Dexter) prevents Nick Cochran (Robert Mitchum, center) from claiming his roulette winnings. Watching the drama unfold are Margie (Gloria) and Lawrence Trumble (William Bendix, standing at right), who has a few secrets of his own.

and also represent the insubstantial, fragile structure of Vincent Halloran's power and status in Macao. Everything seems transient here; everything except for the quiet, long-suffering people who form only a distant background to this melodramatic story.

The vertical segmentation is also present in other ways. Halloran's office in the Quick Reward is on the second floor, and it is here that the wealthiest bettors sit, high above the gambling tables, employing cages lowered to and raised from the tables to make their bets and collect any winnings. Except for Julie's crooning, almost nothing important dramatically occurs on the ground floor of the Quick Reward; all the intrigue is upstairs. The ferryboat stairway serves to separate Julie from Nick, with Nick below looking up appreciatively at Julie's newly stockinged legs, clearly an erotic emblem for von Sternberg. In the later scene at Margie's house, it is Julie looking up a stairway at disheveled Nick, whom she thinks is cavorting with Margie; now Nick is an emblem of sexuality, on an even par with Julie, as they have switched positions. Finally, on Halloran's boat at the climax of the story, Halloran and Julie are sitting cozily in the cabin while up above, it is Nick steering them toward a rendezvous with the International Police. Because of the reshoots done without his participation, von Sternberg essentially disowned *Macao* in the years afterward, but it is clear that, especially in the visual sense, he put a lot of effort into the project.

Some, and perhaps many, of von Sternberg's flourishes were excised as the film underwent its evolution. RKO executives, working under Hughes' supervision, tinkered with it for months following von Sternberg's initial version, shortening it substantially to eliminate what they considered "dead spots" of local atmosphere. Three separate directors were brought in for reshoots: Robert Stevenson reshot some scenes with Mitchum, Russell and Philip Ahn; Mel Ferrer reshot scenes with Mitchum and Gloria; Nicholas Ray shot or reshot several scenes, attempting to match von Sternberg's visual style. The opening sequence, where Halloran and his hoods kill the New York City detective, was Ray's, as was the climactic fistfight between Halloran and Nick on Halloran's boat. None of the three men were credited

for their efforts, although Ray's participation was well known at the time and, as his reputation has grown over the years, has perhaps been over-credited for this title. Best estimates are that Ray is responsible for about one-third of the finished product, including pick-up shots made necessary by editing von Sternberg's long takes into shorter takes with more frequent reaction shots.

Hughes was famous for tampering with his movies, delaying them for years while he fine-tuned and re-shot elements of the story that didn't work for him, or were already out of date. *The Outlaw* (Jane Russell's debut film) began filming in 1940, was delayed three years before its premiere, and another three after that for a wider release. In fact, many moviegoers saw Russell in *Young Widow* (1946) before they saw her in *The Outlaw*. *Jet Pilot* was filmed in 1950 (by von Sternberg) but not released until 1957. By contrast, *Macao* seemed, by Hughes' standards, almost rushed into theaters a mere eighteen months after filming had begun. Shooting commenced in September 1950, shortly after *In a Lonely Place* had been released, and the film didn't make it to theaters until after *A Place in the Sun* (the movie that Gloria had been prevented from making) had already competed for the 1951 Academy Awards.

Although Jane Greer and Joyce Mackenzie were considered for Margie, Hughes wanted Gloria. But being forced to make *Macao* simply because she was under contract to RKO at the time, and being subjected to von Sternberg's infamous Teutonic temperament, did not suit Gloria at all. She (and her mother, who was still guiding her career) realized quite clearly that *A Place in the Sun* was the far greater opportunity, and Gloria argued to no avail that she deserved that opportunity. Further aggravating her was the fact that Hughes steadfastly refused to screen *In a Lonely Place* to see that Gloria was, indeed, worthy of the prestigious projects for which she was arguing. She actually sent a telegram to Hughes as shooting was about to commence:

Dear Mr. Hughes, I have a thing to tell you. You were misinformed that I liked a part designated for me in a picture called *Macao*. At this writing there is no part in this picture for me. Also as described by one of your representatives the part itself varied in interpretation from Eurasian to

White Russian to "Marge" in a mere fifteen minutes of laborious discussion. In the meantime all I asked for was a release or a good part. No executive in your studio has admitted seeing my performance opposite Bogart, a loanout which you so kindly sanctioned. Now, according to a Mr. Bischoff, the part I am requested to play in *Macao* has not been written — this is true — his statement that I am happy with this unwritten part is misrepresentation.

Misrepresentation or not, Gloria was forced into making *Macao*. According to both Jane Russell and Robert Mitchum, they were as well. RKO had done surprisingly well with their earlier teaming, *His Kind of Woman* (1951), and the studio was eager to capitalize upon that modest hit. That seems understandable by studio standards, yet why Gloria was also forced to participate remains somewhat mysterious. Hughes always liked Gloria, and he may have had plans of becoming romantically involved with his blonde star. If so he was disappointed, because Gloria (and her mother) had, like everyone else in Hollywood, heard the rumors about his penchant for last-minute notices and midnight rendezvous. Gloria, who could flirt as well as any starlet in town, ensured that she kept her relationship with Hughes purely platonic and professional.

Gloria was right about the part. It is vague and sadly underwritten. In fact, the character is addressed as Margie just once during the film; otherwise she would simply be known as "Halloran's girl" or "the blonde." Gloria admitted in a 1978 interview that she was so vexed by having to play the part that she purposely played Margie as "a little wide-eyed innocent country girl." That may have been Gloria's memory almost thirty years later, but it isn't what she projects onscreen. Gloria's Margie is clearly a gold-digger with Vincent Halloran as her prey. When Nick arrives, she is briefly intrigued but would rather that Nick leave town and take Julie with her, especially when Halloran begins to make eyes at Julie. Margie definitely sees Julie as a threat, and enjoys the spectacle that Julie makes when she finds that Nick has spent the night at Margie's. Yet despite Margie's desire for Halloran, she unaccountably helps Nick eliminate Halloran's main henchman and deliver Halloran to the International Police! No wonder she didn't care for the part.

She also probably felt it difficult to compete, in terms of fashion and glamour, with Jane Russell, who was given lavish attention in those areas for this film.

Yet Gloria is fine as the secondary femme. While dressed demurely when compared to Russell, she is still gorgeous. Gloria slinks around the perimeter of the Quick Reward, seemingly always on the prowl for easy money and the fringe benefits that being Halloran's girl can provide. It is a quiet performance consisting of knowing glances, a raised eyebrow here and there and the self-confidence to know that, no matter how weak the script, she has the correct look of the character down pat. Shaking the large dice cup as croupier is as physical as the role ever becomes, and Gloria does that quite alluringly. Margie is a nothing role, but Gloria makes it better than it appears on the page. Preview audiences agreed, stating that they wished her role were stronger and fatter.

Aside from the size and impact of her role, Gloria also did not care for her treatment at the hands of Josef von Sternberg. An autocrat who always felt the need to belittle the cast and crews who worked for him, he reigned like a dictator. His overbearing personality alienated everyone on the set, leading to persistent grousing and complaining. Few people stood up to the director's authoritarianism; only Mitchum was openly hostile to the director's caustic comments. Gloria, who rarely if ever said anything bad about anyone else, fumed whenever von Sternberg rebuked a crew member or patronized, Russell, whom he felt had no talent. But she never confronted von Sternberg; she did what she always did when she disagreed with a director. She listened politely, nodding in agreement, then did a scene her way, over and over, each time a little differently to keep things fresh. It drove him crazy, just as it would other directors who wanted to control her expressions and reactions, and who would find it impossible to do so. Much of Gloria's reputation as a troublemaker in later years would be founded in her seeming inability to repeat each and every acting step with precision, as desired by her directors. Having been educated in the theater, Gloria found the precision of film acting rather dull. The directors who could work with whatever she gave them thrived on her spontaneity, while the others, like von Sternberg, suffered through their projects and then griped about her afterwards.

It wasn't only Gloria, however, who detested the director and his despotic personality. A short, stocky man, von Sternberg often stood upon a box while directing. He had done so years before and was accustomed to total command of a film set. But during one of his *Macao* tirades the director of photography, Harry Wild, lost his temper and kicked the box, knocking the director to the floor. Mitchum later remarked, "I think Joe [von Sternberg] sort of lost heart at that point."

After viewing von Sternberg's finished product, RKO executives decided that re-shoots were in order. Von Sternberg refused so the other directors were shuttled in to tighten the story and beef up the action. Gloria was scheduled for her retakes on July 18, 1951, but because she separated again from Nicholas Ray just before then, it was Mel Ferrer who directed them. Ray was designated as the unofficial supervisor of the re-shoots, and reportedly Gloria told him, "If you cut me out of the picture entirely, you won't have to pay me alimony." He might have been tempted, but Hughes would never have allowed it.

Ironically, after all the trouble Gloria underwent to get out of the picture, she was finally released from her RKO contract on October 3, 1950, almost immediately after principal filming was completed. If the release had occurred six or even three months earlier, Gloria could have made *A Place in the Sun* (provided, of course, that she had not scheduled anything else). Gloria was determined, like so many other stars following the example of James Stewart and others, to work independently as often as possible. She would make a couple of multiple-picture deals at other studios, but never again would Gloria sign a long-term contract. She had had enough of misguided assignments, endless waiting between them, ridiculous publicity exercises and the lack of personalized career guidance at MGM and RKO. She thought she could do better for herself, by herself, and she was thrilled to be free of the chains that tied her to one studio at a time.

Gloria was as surprised as anybody when *Macao* was finally released to poor reviews yet still did solid business. She had hated being pressured into it and had hated making it, yet people seemed to enjoy it. *Time* called the film "an amalgam of corn and cleavage ... handsomely directed by Josef von Sternberg, as if it matters." The British Film Institute's *Monthly Film Bulletin* remarked, "Macao itself is evoked mainly by stock exterior shots; the film has a rather hypnotically slow, actionless tempo more characteristic of Sternberg than other directors of Russell-Mitchum vehicles; but the whole rigmarole is made without conviction or even genuine extravagance." *Variety* termed it "a routine formula pic," but predicted strong sales because of the stars. It also noted, "Miss Grahame, who scored in *The Greatest Show on Earth*, is not shown to advantage. She's a much prettier gal than presented in the film." Other reactions to Gloria's performance were mixed. In his book *The Films of Josef von Sternberg*, Andrew Sarris states that Gloria is "unsympathetic in a part that drifts into pointlessness." In his book *Film Noir: A Comprehensive Illustrated Reference to Movies, Terms and Persons*, Michael L. Stephens argues, "Gloria Grahame almost steals the film with her subversively sexual performance as Halloran's jealous girlfriend."

Von Sternberg himself disowned the finished product. In his autobiography *Fun in a Chinese Laundry* he devotes just one short paragraph to it. "After *Jet Pilot* I made one more film in accordance with the contract I had foolishly accepted. This was made under the supervision of six different men in charge. It was called *Macao*, and instead of fingers in that pie, half a dozen clowns immersed various parts of their anatomy in it. Their names do not appear in the list of credits."

Perhaps surprisingly, the reputation of the film has grown considerably since 1952. This is probably due to a re-evaluation of the spectacular visual acumen of von Sternberg, and the rise to *auteur* status of Nicholas Ray, who supervised the retakes and who is generally credited with "tightening" the film. This, despite the fact that neither director enjoyed making the movie or felt it was very good after the fact. Bruce Eder of the Internet's All Movie Guide believes that *Macao* is "an extraordinary film for its time and its personnel" and also terms it "an underrated *noir* classic." Dennis Schwartz of the Internet's Ozus' World Movie Reviews calls it "a wonderfully tongue-in-cheek scripted

Macao. Margie (Gloria) and Julie Benton (Jane Russell) share some thoughts about the man who intrigues them, Nick Cochran (Robert Mitchum, not pictured). This time it was not Gloria who dominated the movie's ads, but Jane Russell.

RKO adventure story" and gushes, "If you are looking for an underrated film *noir* gem — that somehow got swept under the rug — this is it!" The film even rates a mention in *The Entertainment Weekly Guide to the Greatest Movies Ever Made*, summarized by the comment, "This was as hot and suggestive as it got in the '50s."

Hot and suggestive it is, benefitting from Stanley Rubin's sassy dialogue and bantering byplay of best pals Robert Mitchum and Jane Russell. One snatch of dialogue is particularly memorable, when Julie catches Nick admiring her figure and remarks, "Enjoying the view?" Nick pauses a beat, then says, "Well, it ain't the Taj Mahal or the Hanging Gardens of Babylon, but it'll do." Russell and Mitchum share the film's visual and erotic focus, with Russell in particular remarkably glamourous. Her dresses, especially in her singing scenes, are quite incredible. Viewing her in the gold lamé dress while crooning "One for My Baby" is reason enough to see the movie. The dress was made of tiny metal pieces and weighed twenty-six

pounds; adjustments were made to it with pliers! Russell perfectly embodies the character of a wandering, lonely torch singer searching for someone to help her make a real life for herself. Mitchum is his usual sleepy-eyed self, rousing only to kiss Russell at various times, run for his life during the chase sequence and vigorously clobber Halloran in the final reel. William Bendix is pleasantly subversive as the sneaky salesman with a hidden agenda; he provides the film's most consistent energy.

Stanley Rubin was also supposed to produce *Macao*, but when the studio's biggest stars Mitchum and Russell became involved, it was handed to others with the promise that Rubin would get another chance to produce (he did; the excellent *noir* classic *The Narrow Margin* [1952] was his next project as writer-producer). Rubin was not pleased about being passed by on *Macao*, but received a bonus of a sort when he began to date Gloria during the course of filming. It was rumored at the time that her involvement with Rubin was the reason that her separation from Ray became permanent, but Gloria had already moved away from the temperamental director. While her relationship with Rubin never became very serious, she stayed in contact with him for years afterward, and a few of her television appearances during the 1960s were on shows that he produced.

During the long period that *Macao* was in post-production, Gloria's marriage to Ray finally sputtered and died. The last straw for Ray came on the summer afternoon in 1951 when he found Gloria in bed with his thirteen-year-old son Tony. The boy had returned from military school unexpectedly, met Gloria at the door of the Rays' Malibu house, and had fallen spellbound at what he later termed his "lifelong image of love." Their afternoon delight ended abruptly when Ray came home, found the two in bed and nearly lost his mind. He certainly lost his temper, smashing a great deal of the house and its contents and physically ejecting his son. It is a wonder that Gloria wasn't seriously hurt or even killed in the heat of Ray's fury. While Gloria escaped physical injury that afternoon, the psychological ramifications of her tryst with Tony would reverberate for years to come. Ray was never the same; his relationship with his son was always strained because they never reconciled from the fact that Tony had slept with his stepmother. Ray never trusted Gloria again in any important way, although to his everlasting credit he never discussed the tryst publicly. Tony returned to military school and also kept his mouth shut about what had happened. He knew what they had done was inappropriate, but he never considered it to be *wrong*. The images and memories of making love with Gloria sustained him through a difficult adolescence, and when he reached adulthood, he came back and gently reached out to her, attempting to discern if the feelings he still carried for Gloria were reciprocated by her. Gradually, following the dissolution of Gloria's third marriage, Tony reconnected with Gloria and they eventually married.

Gloria certainly regretted the incident, but that was more from a professional standpoint than a personal stance. She was deathly afraid that accounts of what happened would circulate through Hollywood and shatter her reputation and career. Indeed, if the news that Gloria had

slept with her thirteen-year-old stepson were ever to have been made public, Gloria's career would have been finished. Her impetuous act, whether it was selfish sexual self-gratification or an intended act of kindness to a boy just entering the realm of adulthood, was incredibly foolish, not to mention criminal. That she got away with it was solely due to the fact that Ray did not want a public scandal. He certainly would have suffered as well had the news been made public, so Nick's solution was simply to pretend it never happened, and get Gloria out of his life.

Through it all, Gloria attempted to sustain a positive façade. Ray left, moving to the famous apartment complex called the Garden of Allah. The divorce moved forward and Gloria began to spend time with Stanley Rubin. The *Macao* reshoots were completed without incident and she buried herself in work. Although there was always time for romance, Gloria devoted herself to her career again, making an average of three movies a year for the next four years. The fears she had of public disclosure failed to materialize so Gloria rededicated herself to becoming the formidable actress that people kept telling her she could become.

Macao was a low point for Gloria at the time, not so much for the finished product, but because making it prevented her from doing work she desired to do, and because of the personal turmoil she endured during its eighteen-month gestation. *Macao* was the least of her four 1952 releases, but it did showcase her beauty and smoldering sexuality. Her part was certainly a letdown after her showy role in *The Greatest Show on Earth* a few months before, but she would rebound nicely in her next film, a dark little thriller that teamed her with an up-and-coming actor named Jack Palance and against the most celebrated — and feared — film actress of her time, Joan Crawford.

Sudden Fear (1952)

CREDITS Joseph Kaufman Productions. *Distributed by* RKO Radio Pictures. *Directed by* David Miller. *Produced by* Joseph Kaufman. *Executive Producer*: Joan Crawford. *Screenplay by* Lenore Coffee and Robert Smith. *Based on the story* "Sudden Fear" by Edna Sherry. *Director of Photography*: Charles P.

Lang, Jr. *Film Editor*: Leon Barsha. *Music Composed and Directed by* Elmer Bernstein. *Song* "Afraid" by Elmer Bernstein and Jack Brooks. *Song* "Sudden Fear" by Irving Taylor and Arthur Altman. *Art Director*: Boris Leven. *Director of Second Unit*: Ralph Hoge. *Set Decorations*: Edward G. Boyle. *Production Supervisor*: Henry Spitz. *Production Assistant*: B.C. Wylie. *Makeup for Miss Crawford*: Edwin Allen. *Makeup for Mr. Palance*: Josef Norin. *Hair Stylist*: Jane Gorton. *Sound*: T.A. Carman and Howard Wilson. *Optical Effects*: Consolidated Film Industries. *Miss Crawford's Gowns Designed by* Sheila O'Brien. *Furs Designed by* Al Teitelbaum. *Lingerie and Hostess Gowns by* Tula. *Hats by* Rex, Inc. *Jewels by* Ruser. *Assistant Director*: Ivan Volkman. *Second Unit Camera Operator*: Loyal Griggs. Black and White. Flat (1.37:1). Monaural Sound. 110 minutes. Released on August 6, 1952. Currently available on DVD. Previously available on VHS and laserdisc.

CAST *Myra Hudson*, Joan Crawford; *Lester Blaine*, Jack Palance; *Irene Neves*, Gloria Grahame; *Steve Kearney*, Bruce Bennett; *Ann Taylor*, Virginia Huston; *Junior Kearney*, Mike "Touch" Connors; *Scott Martindale*, Taylor Holmes; *Dr. Van Roan*, Selmer Jackson; *Bill — Play Director*, Lewis Martin; *Party Guest*, Estelle Etterre; *Reception Guests*, Bess Flowers and Howard Miller; with Arthur Space.

Sudden Fear, Gloria's third movie released in 1952, was a popular hit. This movie, more than any previous film Gloria had made, established her *noirish* "scheming tramp" persona that she would resurrect often in the years to come. It was the type of role to which Gloria was particularly suited, mixing brains and sensuality, cunning, lust and greed, all directed at the unsuspecting back of Joan Crawford's naïve character. Adding to the intrigue on the set was Crawford's intense dislike of Gloria; Gloria was eventually barred from the set of any scenes other than her own. As Gloria was to discover, this movie was all about Crawford, and Gloria would have to settle for whatever good moments—and costumes—happened to be left over for her.

In a New York City theater, the new play by heiress-playwright Myra Hudson (Joan Crawford) is being staged. Myra watches intently as the lead actor, Lester Blaine (Jack Palance), runs through a scene. Afterward, she confers with the producer and director, telling them that Blaine is simply not romantic enough to carry the role. He is dismissed, and told that Myra was unsatisfied with him. The role is recast and the play becomes a major hit.

Myra takes a train back to her home, San Francisco. On the train, she meets Lester and tries to explain why she let him go. He refuses to discuss the matter, yet is charming enough to pique her interest. They spend the entire train trip together and by San Francisco are infatuated. Dinner, dancing and staying up all night together only increases the attraction, and soon they are romantically involved. Myra throws a party for Lester but he doesn't appear; she is so upset that she goes looking for him, finding him as he is preparing to leave town. He tells her, "I don't belong to your world. You have so much; I have nothing." She understands.

They marry, spending their honeymoon at a California beach house with steep steps running down toward the sea. Lester remarks upon its inherent danger. Back in San Francisco they attend a party and meet Irene Neves (Gloria Grahame). Lester seems to know Irene but claims otherwise. Irene pays no attention to Lester, preferring to cuddle with Junior Kearney (Mike "Touch" Connors), the brother of Myra's lawyer. Later, Lester locates Irene — his former girlfriend in New York — and demands to know why she is there. She read about his marriage in the papers and wants in on the action. Lester warns her not to interfere. "If you ever do, you're gonna need a new face," he snarls, roughly pushing her onto a chaise lounge. "Thanks," she replies. "Thanks for still loving me." About to leave, Lester closes the door and returns to Irene.

Lester meets with Steve Kearney (Bruce Bennett), Myra's lawyer, and insists on working; he claims not to want to live on his wife's money. Lester asks for advice on looking for an appropriate job. Later, Lester meets Irene on the sly to begin planning how to spend some of Myra's wealth. Irene informs Lester that Myra is planning to give away all of her father's fortune to her charitable foundation on heart disease and live only on the money she makes by writing. This does not make Lester or Irene very happy.

Steve prepares a new will for Myra, designating that Lester receive $10,000 a year upon her death until he remarries. Myra is aghast at that suggestion, and uses her fancy dictation machine to dictate a new will leaving everything to Lester. The new will would be prepared over the coming weekend and signed on the following Monday. The next morning, Myra finds that she forgot to turn off the dictation machine. Myra listens to her own recitation of the will and is pleased with it. Then she hears Lester and Irene, who had snuck away from a party for a quick conference; Lester says he never loved Myra. Also on the recording, Lester finds Steve's proposed will and is disgusted that Myra would leave him so little, and only until he remarries. Irene coyly suggests that because the will is to be signed on Monday, perhaps something should happen to Myra over the weekend. Myra is suddenly terrified as the recording ends with Irene's voice repeating, "I know a way" over and over and over.

Myra removes the recording disc from the machine for evidence but drops and breaks it. She then retreats to bed, unable to face the situation, and

Sudden Fear. The touch of Lester Blaine (Jack Palance) is filled with affection — and menace — for his partner in crime, Irene Neves (Gloria).

imagines the ways in which Lester will kill her. The nightmare ends with her screams, bringing Lester, who considerately puts her back to bed and gives her some sleeping pills. Myra remains awake all night, waiting for Lester to make his move. He does not. On Saturday morning Myra apologizes for her behavior and suggests they go back to the summer (honeymoon) house for the weekend. Lester goes ahead by himself to prepare it for their arrival, lighting a fire in the fireplace and romancing Irene in front of it. Irene wonders if Myra suspects anything and suggests covering their tracks by ordering theater tickets for later in the week.

Myra sneaks into Irene's apartment and finds Irene's gun and blank note paper. At home, Myra writes a note to Irene (from Lester) and a note to Lester (from Irene) establish-

ing a rendezvous at Irene's apartment shortly after midnight the following night. Saturday night passes uneventfully and in the morning Myra tells Lester that they cannot go to the summer house; their friends are coming over for dinner and bridge. Lester is angry but cannot change her mind. He meets with Irene, who has retrieved a bottle of poison, and they determine to act that night, no matter what.

Before the dinner, Myra falls down a staircase, pretending to injure her ankle. She begs off dinner, as does Lester, who reads to her until she falls asleep. After he leaves to meet Irene for the rendezvous, Myra rises and puts her plan in motion. Myra hurries to Irene's apartment first and waits for Lester. But before he gets there, Myra has an attack of conscience, realizing that she cannot kill him, and drops the gun on the floor. Lester arrives, waits for Irene, and eventually finds the gun as well as a handkerchief proving that Myra knows about their plan. What he does not know is that Myra is hiding in the closet. Lester panics, running outside, yelling for Irene. Myra leaves, too, but is seen by Lester, who, in his car, chases Myra down San Francisco's dark, rainy streets. Myra ducks into an alleyway, forcing Lester to leave his car. She hides and he returns to his car. He drives some more and sees Myra walking down a steep sidewalk. Only it isn't Myra, it's Irene, returning from the rendezvous that Myra arranged to keep her out of the way. Lester aims his car recklessly, driving past a cowering Myra, whose cry of warning is too late, and runs over Irene. The car overturns, killing Lester as well. Myra trudges up the hill, heartbroken, but smiling because she's alive.

Sudden Fear is a tidy, nicely acted little thriller that in its second half ventures into complete implausibility, yet still manages to thrill and entertain. Based on Edna Sherry's novel of the same name, it churns a lot of drama out of its mix of brilliant but naïve heroine, duplicitous characters, patently obvious parameters, odd accoutrements (a music box, a wind-up dog) and unbelievable coincidence. As contrived as this story surely is, it is remarkable that it is so effective. This success — and the film is considered to be very successful both commercially and artistically — is due to its director, David Miller. He coaxes excellent performances from his leads; both Joan Crawford and Jack Palance received Oscar nominations for their work. Miller and cinematographer Charles Lang Jr. (also Oscar-nominated) work hard, especially in the film's second half, to permeate the atmosphere with danger and doom.

Miller was thrilled to be able to cast Crawford as Myra, but her casting led to certain challenges and compromises that might have been avoided by having someone else in the lead. As unofficial executive producer, Crawford wielded enormous power; before he agreed to direct, Miller made sure she understood that any on-set issues would have to be settled by the director, not the star. She agreed. She battled with Miller about casting Jack Palance, whom she felt was too ugly to play her leading man. But Miller had seen Palance in *Panic in the Streets*—which he showed to Crawford

more than once — and knew that only a forceful, rugged actor like Palance could effectively menace Crawford on screen. She reluctantly agreed to this, too, and both later received critical kudos. As filming progressed, Crawford grew to like Palance a great deal and wanted to become intimate with him; that is, until she discovered that Palance and Gloria Grahame were already enjoying a fling. Gloria had been separated from Nicholas Ray for more than a year but still had not yet divorced him, and she would soon be dating Cy Howard, the man who would become her third husband. But in between, she was enjoying herself with writer Stanley Rubin and, off the set of *Sudden Fear*, Palance.

Evidently that was the final straw for Crawford, who had a history of shunning, even bullying young actresses on her pictures. Crawford told David Miller that she didn't want to see Gloria on the set unless Gloria was in the scene. Miller, who had won all of what he considered to be the important battles, acquiesced. Gloria took the ban in stride, sneaking around to watch as filming progressed, rather hoping that Crawford would catch her peeping from behind a curtain. Crawford, always the clothes horse, also reportedly decreed to costumer Sheila O'Brien (who received the film's fourth and final Oscar nomination) that Gloria's costumes be "off the rack," so that Gloria's appearance would not compete with her own. This did not sit well with Gloria, nor her mother who, as usual, was nearby as Gloria's personal acting coach, but they capitulated. After all, Joan Crawford was essentially running the show.

Crawford insisted that the film's ending be considerably altered from Edna Sherry's original story. The film follows the story closely, having Myra discover Lester's treachery through her dictating machine and then, fearing the public shame and barrage of publicity that would accompany divorce proceedings, choose to tackle the deadly situation herself rather than more sensibly contacting the authorities. Yet in the novel Myra doesn't hesitate to kill her wayward, money-chasing husband. She calmly shoots him through the heart and barely gives it another thought. Her efforts to frame Irene Neves (Irma in the book) for the murder also work precisely. Myra's mistake comes when she purposely smashes her ankle in a window frame to give herself the perfect alibi. She smashes it too well, refuses to have it treated, and within a few days perishes of erysipelas and blood poisoning! Under no account would Crawford allow her character to die from such stupid, self-inflicted action, no matter how cleverly intentioned. And if Myra wasn't going to die for her sins, then she couldn't very well kill Lester, since the Production Code demanded that murderers inevitably pay for their crimes in some manner. So the entire last act was altered to spotlight Myra's sudden but not wholly unexpected crisis of conscience, followed by a spooky chase as the husband Myra could not bring herself to kill inexorably pursues her through the rain-soaked streets of San Francisco in the middle of the night.

Another interesting change takes place in the opening scene where Myra watches Lester rehearse her play. She wants a "romantic leading man" and concludes that although Lester is an able actor, he is not quite attractive enough for the role. In the book, the opposite is true; Lester's beauty "overpowers" the other actors, which is why Myra has him fired. But her professional analysis of his appearance's effect on stage does not prevent Myra from falling for Lester off stage, and his beauty fuels her continuing affection for him. But Lester is a far better actor than Myra recognizes until it is almost too late. Changing Lester's appearance, and Myra's reaction to it, was necessitated once Palance was considered for the role. Director Miller believed that Crawford would overwhelm any overtly handsome actor they might hire as Lester and dilute the sinister aspects of the drama that he wished to emphasize. By altering the equation involving Lester's appearance, the director was able, eventually, to persuade Crawford to accept the rugged Palance as someone who could convincingly menace her.

The film's first half, detailing the whirlwind courtship of Myra and Lester, is excellent, culminating brilliantly in the scene where Myra discovers the plot against her. This scene is a tour de force for Crawford, recalling her days in silent films, reacting simply and forcefully to the trusted voices of her husband and friend matter-of-factly discussing the need to dispatch her within the next few days in order to receive

her estate. Miller heightens the suspense by gradually tightening the focus onto Crawford's anxious face as she listens, and by cannily repeating Irene's foreboding words as the recording cylinder finishes. It's a terrific scene that some critics feel plows without pause right into melodrama. In their book *Bad Movies We Love*, Edward Marguiles and Stephen Rebello describe the action thusly: "The record starts skipping, so Grahame's voice repeats, 'I know a way,' over and over, thirty-two times while Crawford acts and acts and acts." While Crawford's detractors sneer at her histrionics, this is one instance where her character's emotional crisis needs to be powerfully depicted.

Where *Sudden Fear* really falls off the tracks is when Myra refuses to go to the authorities, or at least confer with her own trusted lawyer, regarding the things she hears. In the film, Myra is so emotionally shattered by the recording that she hurriedly attempts to hide it and drops it, breaking the only evidence of the plot against her. Then, she's so upset that ... she lies down and imagines the ways in which Lester and Irene will kill her! Myra's refusal to tell anyone else is ridiculous. In the book, author Edna Sherry describes the absolute horror that the wealthy Myra has of public humiliation, even to the extent of telling her close friends and exposing her weakness to them. Sherry makes the case that allowing others to ridicule Myra's poor judgment and marital misfortune would be worse to Myra than her own death. The movie fails to explain this so thoroughly; it just seems that Myra is haughtily stubborn and is willing to gamble her own life in the effort to turn the tables on her predators. Sherry's literary conceit works very well; Myra's playwriting expertise allows her to manipulate others to amazing effect. While the film follows the same formula, Myra's machinations seem unwise at best, and foolhardy, dangerous and unbelievable at worst. Yet that, of course, is part of the fun that *Sudden Fear* offered to enthusiastic audiences.

Thanks to Miller's expertise, the film overcomes its major weaknesses. His technique of having Myra imagine the sequence of events leading to Lester's death and Irene's punishment for it, superimposed by a clock that moves the action inexorably forward, is superb. The scenes where Myra hides in Irene's closet and secretly watches Lester while he waits for Irene are extraordinarily suspenseful, particularly when Lester, just killing time, winds up a toy dog that then marches across the floor straight toward Myra's sanctuary. Though the film is not traditional *film noir* in many respects, Miller treats it as such during the final act, using shadow and light as skillfully as any other *noir* director of the era.

Even the final chase through the slick streets of San Francisco is suspenseful — although its conclusion unfortunately relies on the coincidence that Myra and Irene both happen to be wearing coats and scarves that look almost identical. The Production Code's insistence upon evil being punished is responsible for having Lester not only run over Irene but also turn over his car and die while doing so. It is thus a weak finale that punishes the evildoers and allows Myra to escape and move on with her life, cleansed of all guilt. The final shot shows Myra walking uphill away from the crash, removing her scarf — the symbol of her active participation in the death of her betraying husband — and dropping it into the gutter, where the rainwater washes it away.

Despite these melodramatic moments, inconsistency of logic and over-reliance on tiny little details that could easily be overlooked or misconstrued, *Sudden Fear* is an exciting motion picture. It is extremely well acted by everyone involved and as a result was appreciated both by critics and large audiences. Crawford had been offered a base salary of $200,000 or a healthy percentage of the profits; she famously took the latter and made quite a bit more money than that on the deal.

A.H. Weiler of the *New York Times* enjoyed the film, labeling it a "cleverly turned melodrama, but one that is hardly spine-chilling." He also singled out Gloria, stating that she "adds an excellent portrayal as the hard, brash and sexy blonde who goads our villain to desperate deeds." *Boxoffice* decreed, "Joan Crawford sinks her teeth into a meaty and suspenseful morsel of dramatic fare which the average run of patrons — especially the femmes — probably will regard as one of her strongest vehicles in years." Even critics who found fault still seemed to want to recommend it, such as the British Film Institute's *Monthly Film Bulletin*: "This new Crawford vehicle, for-saking the rags-to-riches formula, is elaborately absurd, though it contains some masochistic suspense sequences put across with punch."

Gloria really began her roll of hard-bitten *femmes fatale* with Irene Neves. It's a startlingly masochistic role, beginning with her first private encounter with Lester. He threatens to disfigure Irene if she betrays him to Myra and she doesn't even bat an eyelid. In fact, she lustily demands that he "crush" her with his kiss, and she ensures that she's getting as much of his carnal attention as Myra. When Myra accidentally discovers the plot to kill her, it is revealed that Lester is not the active instigator — Irene assumes that role. Irene lures, cajoles and pushes Lester into vengeful rage against Myra, and it is she who imagines how to do it properly. "I know a way," the recording cylinder repeats, again and again. In the book, Irma (Irene) is even more fearsome; she essentially admits killing her drunkard father and is clearly psychopathic.

Gloria is excellent in the film. If she had not been Oscar-nominated for *The Bad and the Beautiful* this same year, she almost certainly would have been nominated for *Sudden Fear*. She is just right playing a woman glamourous and generous on the outside but petty and vindictive inside. Her sensuality makes Irene a formidable challenge to Myra in terms of keeping Lester's attention, and the manner in which she so thinly disguises Irene's baser instincts thrusts the plot forward forcefully. In a magazine feature titled "The Role I Liked Best..." Gloria indicated that Irene was her favorite part. "As Irene Neves, a sort of junior-size Lady Macbeth, I was a changeable as March weather and often twice as nasty." Gloria had always wanted to play Lady Macbeth (and finally did, onstage, in 1979), and used Shakespeare's character as her main motivation:

> This made the role both explosive, and, to me, instructive. I learned a lot by playing Irene, and while learning it I worked harder than I ever had before. I read and reread *Macbeth* in order to try to understand Irene's basic motivation, which I felt was similar to Lady Macbeth's. I even reread *Othello*, because I felt that Iago schemed to accomplish his purpose much as Irene did. Thus, by mixing Shakespeare with personal effort, and seasoning the whole with a great deal of helpful coaching from director Miller, I tried to make Irene real. I hope I was successful.

Sudden Fear. Irene Neves (Gloria) seduces lawyer Junior Kearney (Mike Connors) as part of her sinister plan.

Gloria's magazine account omits the troublesome aspects of the production, but that was her way. Gloria rarely told the press (or anyone else) anything disrespectful about the people with whom she worked. When a columnist asked her about working with Crawford, Gloria, having been shunned and banned from the set by the star, could have caused some real fireworks. Instead she said that Joan was marvelous to work with and was a true professional. Publicists could count on Gloria to keep studio secrets safe. In later interviews, Gloria would be intentionally vague on many matters involving her career, insisting that she knew the particulars of what had happened to her and around her, but that those things were not as important as the movies, television shows and plays which resulted from the creative process.

Sudden Fear was a popular hit that made Joan Crawford bankable again (and put a lot of money back into her bank account), helped promote Jack Palance to leading man status, introduced Mike Connors to cinema audiences

and forever cemented Gloria Grahame's film persona. She would not play another femme fatale role for a year, but portraying Irene Neves — and studying *Macbeth* and *Othello* for motivation — laid the foundation for Gloria to excel in those parts when she accepted them. Most of Gloria's serious films that followed *Sudden Fear* were not nearly as successful as this potboiler, meaning that audiences had the strong and lasting impression of Gloria as a scheming harlot rather than as a serious character actress. This became a factor that would also help determine the path of her career. Gloria's fling with Jack Palance remained just that, partly because he was intimidated by her and partly because she was determined to keep her energies focused on her career. But late in 1952, Gloria's career was still rising, and with a propulsive speed that would make her agent's head spin. Best of all, the industry's biggest prize would come her way for her very next picture.

The Bad and the Beautiful
(1952)

CREDITS MGM. *Directed by* Vincente Minnelli. *Produced by* John Houseman. *Screenplay by* Charles Schnee. *Story by* George Bradshaw. *Director of Photography*: Robert Surtees. *Film Editor*: Conrad A. Nervig. *Music Composed and Conducted by* David Raksin. *Art Directors*: Cedric Gibbons and Edward Carfagno. *Assistant Director*: Jerry Thorpe. *Recording Supervisor*: Douglas Shearer. *Set Decorations*: Edwin B. Willis and Keogh Gleason. *Special Effects*: A. Arnold Gillespie and Warren Newcombe. *Women's Costumes Designed by* Helen Rose. *Hair Styles by* Sydney Guilaroff. *Makeup by* William Tuttle. *Orchestrators*: David Raksin, Ruby Raksin and Lawrence Morton. *Choreographer*: Alex Romero. *Stunts*: Eric Alden. Black and White. Flat (1.37:1). Monaural Sound. 118 minutes. Released on December 25, 1952. Currently available on DVD. Previously available on laserdisc and VHS.

CAST *Georgia Lorrison*, Lana Turner; *Jonathan Shields*, Kirk Douglas; *Harry Pebbel*, Walter Pidgeon; *James Lee Bartlow*, Dick Powell; *Fred Amiel*, Barry Sullivan; *Rosemary Bartlow*, Gloria Grahame; *Victor "Gaucho" Ribera*, Gilbert Roland; *Henry Whitfield*, Leo G. Carroll; *Kay*, Vanessa Brown; *Syd Murphy*, Paul Stewart; *Gus*, Sammy White; *Lila*, Elaine Stewart; *Von Ellstein*, Ivan Triesault; *Sheriff*, Stanley Andrews; *Evelyn Lucien*, Barbara Billingsley; *Ferraday*, John Bishop; *Mrs. Rosser*, Madge Blake; *McDill*, Robert Burton; *Ida*, Marietta Canty; *Miss March*, Kathleen Freeman; *Timmy — Assistant Director*, A. Cameron Grant; *Arlene*, Dorothy Patrick; *Linda Ronley*, Dee Turnell; *Rosa*, Kaaren Verne; *Eulogist*, Francis X. Bushman; *Casting Director*, Robert Carson; *Assistant Directors*, Jonathan Cott, Ted Jordan, Joseph Keane and William "Bill" Phillips; *Real Estate Woman*, Lillian Culver; *Priest*, Alexis Davidoff; *Screaming Little Girl*, Sandy Descher; *Pawnbroker*, Phil Dunham; *Cameramen*, Steve Dunhill, George Sherwood and Ray Walker; *Publicity Man*, James Farrar; *Screen Test Actors*, Steve Forrest, George J. Lewis and Paul Marion; *Wardrobe Man*, Ned Glass; *Lighting Technician*, Dabbs Greer; *Singer*, Peggy King; *Blonde Dancing with Gaucho*, Lucy Knoch; *Preview Ticket Taker*, Mike Lally; *Pebbel's Secretaries*, May McAvoy and Perry Sheehan; *Electrician*, Patrick J. Molyneaux; *Cigar Clerk*, Roger Moore; *Amiel's Boy*, Christopher Olsen; *Theater Manager*, Paul Power; *Piano Player*, Hadda Brooks; *Heavy Woman*, Mabel Smaney; *Actor in Catman Suit*, Arthur Tovey; *Judge*, Harte Wayne; *Butler*, Eric Wilton; *Set Assistants*, Bob Davis and Franklyn Farnum; *Leading Lady*, Phyllis Graffeo; *Leading Men*, Richard Norris and Douglas Yorke; *Waiter*, William H. O'Brien; *Reporters*, Ellanora Needles, Frank J. Scannell and William Tannen; *Bobby-Soxers*, Janet Comerford and Kathy Qualen; *Poker Players*, Stuart Holmes, Reginald Simpson and Larry Williams; *Party Guests*, Jay Adler, Ben Astar, James Conaty, Bess Flowers, Frank Gerstle, Sam Harris, Kurt Kasznar and Paul Maxey; *Mourners*, Kenner G. Kemp and Harold Miller; *Men Outside Club*, Marshall Bradford and Pat O'Malley; *Hugh Shields in Portrait*, William E. Greene; *Voice of Georgia Lorrison's Father*, Louis Calhern.

Gloria's fourth and final film of 1952 was a star-studded impugnation — and vivid celebration — of the business of moviemaking, titled *The Bad and the Beautiful*. Originally called *Tribute to a Bad Man*, the title was changed when glamourous Lana Turner was signed for the lead, spurring MGM to market the film to the distaff audience. It is a serious, entertaining glimpse into the business that creates silver screen excitement, exposing the pettiness, manipulation and ego-destroying elements of the motion picture industry. Yet beyond the betrayals, power plays and penny-pinching decisions that shape what the public is shown, there is also a deep respect and appreciation for the artistry of film entertainment, which prevents the pessimism of the piece from overwhelming its subject, and its audience. The film was a big hit for MGM both artistically and commercially, ultimately collecting five Academy Awards, including one in the Best Supporting Actress race. The winner was Gloria Grahame.

The Bad and the Beautiful begins with a series of telephone calls from a producer to people with whom he formerly associated. Two refuse the calls. One man picks up the telephone, says "Drop dead," and hangs up. Later, the three phone call recipients meet after hours at the Shields Pictures Inc. studio to greet producer Harry Pebbel (Walter Pidgeon). Pebbel informs them that producer Jonathan Shields is ready to make a comeback and produce another picture, and he desires their participation. Each person immediately says no, but they reluctantly agree to wait while a transatlantic call is put through to Shields in Europe so he can hear their refusals for himself. While they are waiting, Pebbel recounts how each person met, associated with and then was betrayed by Shields. Each story is told in extensive flashback fashion.

The first subject is director Fred Amiel (Barry Sullivan). At the funeral for Hugo Shields, Amiel insults the deceased, not knowing that the man standing next to him is Jonathan Shields (Kirk Douglas), Hugo's son. Shields pays each of the mourners $11 for their attendance, but refuses to pay Amiel, who didn't properly play his part of a mourning friend. Fred Amiel seems to be the only mourner to not be attending at Jonathan's monetary coaxing. He later finds Shields to apologize and they bond. Soon they are working together, Amiel directing and Shields producing Poverty Row westerns on cheap indoor sets. They spend their evenings crashing Hollywood parties trying to network, and eating the free food. Shields worms his way into a poker game against producer Pebbel, managing to lose $6351 in one sitting. It seems like a disaster, but Shields offers to work off his debt at Pebbel's studio, with Amiel as his assistant.

Over the next few years Shields produces eleven pictures for Pebbel, and Amiel directs eight of them. They work well as a team. When they are assigned to make the horror opus *The Doom of the Cat Men*, both men are aghast, and rendered speechless when they see the cat costumes. They agree to make the movie as creepy as possible by avoiding views of the ridiculous Cat Men costumes, and their efforts lead to the best notices of their careers. Pebbel is ecstatic and immediately assigns them another film: *The Son of the Cat Men*. Amiel has had enough. He shows Shields the book *The Faraway Mountain*, considered unfilmable by Hollywood, and reveals that he has written a long outline to turn it into a major movie. They take the idea to Pebbel, who disapproves, yet contradictorily demands that they make *The Faraway Mountain* to prove once and for all that their talents are better spent making Cat Men movies.

The movie progresses and they pursue a Latin actor, Victor Ribera (Gilbert Roland), better known as Gaucho, for the lead. He is recruited, and suddenly the project becomes a "major motion picture" with a million dollar budget. Shields reconsiders his position and offers the directing post to the autocratic director Von Ellstein (Ivan Triesault). Amiel is stunned; it was his idea and his script. Suddenly he's out in the cold, betrayed by his partner and best friend. The movie, of course, is a hit and Shields' career is made. Back in the present, Pebbel tells him, "Look what he did to you, Fred. He brushed you off his coattails so you

had to stand on your own two feet. And all you've got in the world is one wife, six kids, two Academy Awards and every studio in town after you. Why, Jonathan ruined you."

Next up is actress Georgia Lorrison (Lana Turner). She had met Shields and Amiel five years earlier without ever showing her face when they visited her father's decaying mansion in the middle of the night, and Shields remembered her. Presently she plays bit parts at various studios for booze money and sleeps around. Shields recognizes her and chooses her for a screen test with Gaucho. Although the studio consensus is that Georgia lacks her famous father's acting talent, Shields hires her anyway as the lead in a costume picture. Six weeks of preparation is spent fine-tuning her but the night before shooting starts, Georgia goes on a bender. Shields finds her, sobers her up and, having calculated the odds very carefully, becomes her lover. With his constant devotion and tenderness, Georgia gains confidence and matures into a strong actress. Shooting on the picture finishes and Georgia wants to celebrate, but Shields is absent. Georgia finds him at home romantically involved with a bit player, Lila (Elaine Stewart). Georgia leaves in hysteria and nearly kills herself driving away, crying and screaming. Eventually she overcomes his betrayal and makes a career for herself. Back in the present, Pebbel says, "Jonathan certainly ruined you. You were a drunk and a tramp, playing bit parts around town, and he made a star out of you."

The third party is writer James Lee Bartlow (Dick Powell). He is a professor in a small Southern town and *The Proud Land* is his first book to be published. He is married to Rosemary (Gloria Grahame), a soft Southern belle who now luxuriates in her husband's modest fame. Shields calls Bartlow to coax him to Hollywood for two weeks, hoping to talk him into writing a screenplay based on his book. Bartlow refuses but Rosemary seems to want to go, so he changes his mind. After two weeks in Tinseltown, Bartlow agrees to stay, mainly because Rosemary is entranced with the lifestyle and benefits of fame. He tells Shields, "I'm flattered you want me and bitter you got me." Bartlow works on his screenplay but is constantly interrupted by Rosemary. She meets Gaucho at a party and is swept off her feet. Bartlow is

The Bad and the Beautiful. Mrs. Rosser (Madge Blake, center) finds a hot spot in writer James Lee Bartlow's first novel. Watching her reactions are Bartlow (Dick Powell) and his wife Rosemary (Gloria).

troubled by his wife's behavior and she agrees that she has changed since arriving in Hollywood. She is still devoted to him, however. Wanting to get Bartlow back on the beam, Shields takes him to a remote fishing cabin where they can work in peace. Shields also innocently asks Gaucho to squire Rosemary around town while they are gone. Bartlow finishes the script, but returning home he discovers that Rosemary and Gaucho have died together in a plane crash on their way to a Mexican resort.

Shields pushes Bartlow deeper into work so that grief will not overwhelm him. Shooting begins on *The Proud Land* with Von Ellstein directing, but Shields is unhappy. He finally takes over the direction himself, putting every ounce of energy he has into its creation. Seeing the finished product, Shields has to admit that the film is no good. He wants to shelve it indefinitely. Bartlow is pragmatic about the film

and agrees to go off with Shields again to finish his next book. But Shields accidentally reveals that he had prodded Gaucho to romance Rosemary, and then he infuriates the writer by telling him that Rosemary was no good for him. Bartlow punches Shields in the face and walks out. Back in the present, Pebbel holds Bartlow's new book in his hands: *A Woman of Taste*, which seems to be his tribute to Rosemary. "Yes, Jim," Pebbel sermonizes. "Jonathan destroyed you. You came out of it with nothing, nothing but a Pulitzer Prize novel and the highest salary of any writer in Hollywood."

Pebbel reminds the trio that they all owe Jonathan Shields more than they will ever admit. The call comes through from Europe, and Pebbel asks them one last time if they will agree to work with Shields again. All answer no, and they walk out of the office as a group. Still on the telephone, Shields insists on telling Pebbel his story idea then and there, so Pebbel listens. Reluctantly curious despite herself, Georgia picks up an outer office phone and eavesdrops. Amiel slowly slides over and Georgia shares the phone. And, finally, Bartlow joins them. Against their instincts, they reluctantly listen and none says a word, engrossed as Shields makes his sales pitch...

The Bad and the Beautiful is among Hollywood's finest examples of self-evaluation because it is knowingly intimate, capturing various methods of illusion at will and reveling in their dynamic power. It skewers the high-profile participants of the film industry at many moments and for many reasons, yet it also glories in their triumphs of art and commerce. The film firmly presents moviemaking as a business in which pretensions of art are certainly secondary and often accidental, and the people who make those movies to be almost solely concerned with getting ahead of the other guy and making money. The industry itself is viewed as a rather tawdry enterprise intended to find or create power to be wielded over others with less influence — and it makes no apologies for that cynical approach. MGM's glossy drama could have been fashioned with a "soap opera" approach to its characters' tumultuous personal lives—which it does, indeed, resemble during the Georgia Lorrison segment. But director Vincente Minnelli was intent upon providing an authentic glimpse of how movies are made and he concentrates upon the primary story structure with considerable success.

The movie is so true to the time and the current film industry fashion because it is so squarely rooted within it. Charles Schnee's screenplay takes great care to include as many familiar trappings as possible while avoiding the tendency to turn them into clichés. Thus, settings such as sound stages, dressing rooms, executive offices, cottages and the requisite Beverly Hills mansions (both opulent and ruined) are incorporated into the action, which in itself takes place on the studio lots during the day and at splashy parties and swanky premieres at night. Audiences are immersed in the experience of the film industry, from the "discovery" of Georgia Lorrison by Shields, through her build-up by the studio marketers, to the triumphant premiere of her movie with Shields—and her subsequent romantic betrayal. Screen tests, backstage bickering, dailies, late-night producers' meetings, costume fittings, quick set-ups and boredom between shots while lighting is re-keyed are all part of the landscape that Minnelli uses as backdrop to his story. The drama is effective because it seems authentic.

Adding to the authenticity are the thinly veiled references to industry figures represented by key roles. Jonathan Shields is clearly inspired by David O. Selznick (and David Merrick, and Val Lewton, too), while Georgia Lorrison is reminiscent of actress Diana Barrymore. Fred Amiel's early career is modeled after that of Val Lewton. Such references are necessarily vague and fuzzy, as no one at MGM wanted to be sued for unauthorized depiction — or defamation of character. But the similarities to real life do not end there. Production chief Harry Pebbel has the same penny-pinching characteristics as MGM's production chief Harry Rapf, director Von Ellstein resembles both Erich von Stroheim and Josef von Sternberg in countenance and name, while writer James Lee Bartlow bears a foggier kinship to F. Scott Fitzgerald and William Faulkner. The smaller roles of actor Gaucho, agent Gus, starlet Lila and others have their own counterpoints in real life, too numerous and familiar to identify. While it isn't necessary or even desirable to match fictional characters to their real-life models to enjoy the movie (it can be a rather distracting exercise), it was great sport at the time to do so, and various reporters and columnists such as Louella Parsons openly speculated about who was supposed to be who. For rabid movie fans, this added yet another dimension to its appeal.

Not everyone was thrilled with the idea of making a movie that skewered the industry, including former MGM head Louis B. Mayer. Mayer had hated Paramount's *Sunset Blvd.*, a 1950 movie that had excoriated aspects of the film industry, and he had told Billy Wilder after the premiere that Wilder was "biting the hand that feeds him." *The Bad and the Beautiful* would never have been made under Mayer's watch, but Mayer, one of the founders of the MGM studio, had finally resigned in May of 1951, essentially having been forced out of his own studio. New head of production Dore Schary brought in producer John Houseman, and it was Houseman who unearthed the project then known as *Tribute to a Bad Man*. Schary gave the project the green light that Mayer never would have provided and the MGM gloss was applied to cure its vitriol into the more palatable essence of self-conscious dissection. It was a bold move, just as *Sunset Blvd.* had been, for any studio, but especially for MGM. Under Mayer's reign, MGM made "beautiful stories with beautiful people." That phrase certainly didn't apply to any of *The Bad and the Beautiful*'s characters, who, conforming to the new style then sweeping through Hollywood, were increasingly tragic, psychologically complex and morally ambivalent. In contrast to Mayer, Schary desired to make gritty, important stories about realistically flawed people, just as he had while producing *Crossfire* for RKO five years earlier. He embraced Houseman's project because it spectacularly deglamorized Hollywood while cleverly humanizing the people who create the illusions and have to live and work on the thin footing between fantasy and reality in sunny Southern California.

The film stops short of claiming that the industry causes people to blackmail, betray and belittle their fellow filmmakers, though that is occasionally insinuated by the behavior of some of the characters. Rather, the story chronicles how a natural heel like Jonathan Shields takes advantage of the opportunities he is given to climb around and over others also trying to ascend the Hollywood ladder of success and makes the argument that he is morally right to do so. This story actually undermines this cynicism by stating that Shields not only betrayed Amiel, Bartlow and Georgia Lorrison, but also helped their careers by doing so (a notion central to the source material). Within the confines of Schnee's script, that seeming contradiction is true — as each has gone on to greater glory since separating from Shields' influence, and have done so with the confidence that surviving Shields' betrayal has provided the strength and fortitude to survive and prosper in the future. Yet that contradiction doesn't ring true so often in real life. The film does not offer the seamier aspects of such blatant betrayals: promising careers cut short or altered irrevocably, with the victims experiencing deep depression and even contemplating or attempting suicide. In this regard, the film is remarkably upbeat. It is, of course, a movie, one that presents its protagonists as perhaps being rather *too* resilient and capable.

The genesis for *The Bad and the Beautiful*— and its message regarding the positive aspects of betrayal —consists of two short stories written by George Bradshaw. The first to be published was "Of Good and Evil" in the February 1948 issue of *Cosmopolitan*. The second was "Memorial to a Bad Man" in the February 1951 *Ladies Home Journal*. The second story came to the attention of producer Houseman first. He immediately recognized that it had cinematic applications, although he decided to change the setting from the Broadway theatrical world (which he felt had been extensively covered in *All About Eve*) to the mercurial byways of Hollywood. "Memorial to a Bad Man" concerns the death of a megalomaniac theatrical director, whose will defends his actions to a trio of former collaborators still bitter about their experiences with him. Also in the will is a request that they work together on one final play that he has arranged for them. Reluctantly they agree, and the story ends with the trio expressing ironic laughter at the hated director's method of bringing them together again. "Of Good and Evil" chronicles the efforts of a remorseful rich heel to make amends for his past, only to find that his "victims" want no apologies or reparation from him; each person is doing well on his or her own after bouncing back from the setbacks he caused. The moral of both stories is that people are exceptionally resilient, able in time to turn personal or professional adversities into areas of growth and prosperity. It is this optimism that so attracted Houseman to the properties and that infuses the film with charm in place of bitterness.

The Bad and the Beautiful celebrates the process of moviemaking almost as much as it pillories the manner in which the cutthroat "business" of Hollywood so often degrades its own populace. From the earliest bottom-of-the-barrel efforts made by Shields and Amiel to Shields' overly opulent production of *The Proud Land*, it is obvious that these people love the industry they are in, despite its crazy economies and excesses. Nowhere is this more apparent than in the sequence dealing with *The Doom of the Cat Men*. Still operating with tiny

The Bad and the Beautiful. Writer James Lee Bartlow (Dick Powell), still sitting in his favorite chair, thinks his wife Rosemary (Gloria) is just the cutest woman in the world. "You have a dirty mind, James Lee, I'm happy to say."

budgets, producer Shields and director Amiel are assigned to make a silly horror movie about cat-suited men terrifying the world. Attending a costume conference, they sit blank faced as the wardrobe man (Ned Glass) shows them the threadbare costumes with which they'll have to work.

Glass is great: cigarette glued to his lower lip, squinting so as to not look at his wares too closely, blithely presenting the ridiculous costumes in a serious, professional manner. "This the sort of thing you had in mind?" he asks as he zips an actor into a tattered black velvet Cat Man suit and places a shabby Cat Man mask upon the man's head. "Of course they need some freshening up, they've been hanging for quite a while." Another actor is too big for his suit and the back is left open. "If they don't turn around too much, a little muslin here will cover it up fine." Yet another actor's belly prevents his suit from zipping shut. "This, this could be a problem, unless you get a thinner man," the

wardrobe man says. But one actor is in the full costume and Glass presents him with pride. "Here, a perfect fit. This will give you the full effect. See, lots of character in the tail, plenty of fright, you need a little puffing up but it will be all right. Of course, you gotta visualize it in the lights, you gotta use your imagination." He moves to another man zipped into his costume, but without the mask, and raises the loose costume above the man's shoulders. "Shoulder pads. Straighten it right out. This will give you the effect. It'll be good!" Meanwhile, Shields and Amiel just stare at the sight before them, and the looks on their faces are priceless. It's a perfect little scene that has undoubtedly been played at movie studios innumerable times.

What to do? Conferring in a screening room later, Shields and Amiel know full well that audiences will howl at the ridiculous costumes, so they must do something to save the picture. Shields asks, "What scares the human race more than any other single thing?" and he shuts off the room's overhead lights. "The dark!" answers Amiel. There and then they decide not to show the Cat Men. Instead, they will show "two eyes, shining in the dark!" "A dog, frightened, growling, showing its fangs!" "A bird, its neck broken, feathers torn from its throat!" "A little girl, screaming! Claw marks down her cheeks!" This scene illustrates the basic essence of great filmmaking, the creative use of imagination — and it smartly echoes the movie's moral point about making the most of an unfortunate situation to create something memorable and exciting. The notion of concealing the origin of a film's terror was certainly not original to this story, but it is expressed here with supreme clarity and effect. (The same principle was forced upon Steven Spielberg when his mechanical shark continually malfunctioned during the making of *Jaws* more than two decades later, proving its viability — and profitability). Shields and Amiel forge their reputations with the success of *The Doom of the Cat Men*, thanks to their creativity under pressure and a positive audience response. But what is their reward? Depicting the authentic Tinseltown reaction, production chief Pebbel assigns them to make *The Son of the Cat Men*.

Another facet of the process is explored when Shields takes over the direction of *The Proud Land* from Von Ellstein. Artistry and movie magic are the subjects of this sequence, which the film presents as difficult to quantify and harder to capture than moonbeams. Normally a harsh taskmaster as producer, Shields completely alters his persona when directing. He is patient, understanding and intuitive as a director, a completely different man. Von Ellstein had told him that a director needs humility and Shields had listened. *The Proud Land* is made with delicacy and care. Nevertheless, it fails. After a studio screening, Shields praises the individual departments for their work and then castigates his own direction. "I butchered it!" he exclaims. "I have no tension, no timing, no pace, nothing! I took a beautiful, sensitive story and turned it into a turgid, boring movie." Shields shelves the movie, essentially shuttering the studio and ending his career in Hollywood, at least for a time.

Before he is fired from the picture, Von Ellstein handles a large dinner scene with a restraint that irks Shields, who argues that "there are values and dimensions in that scene you haven't even begun to hit." Von Ellstein retorts, "Perhaps they are not the values and dimensions I *wish* to hit. I could make this scene a climax. I could make *every* scene in this picture a climax. If I did, I would be a bad director. And I like to think of myself as one of the best. A picture all climaxes is like a necklace without a string, it falls apart. You must build to a big moment. And sometimes, you must build slowly." Shields rejects that philosophy and discovers too late that Von Ellstein knows what he is talking about. Von Ellstein's approach, measured and reserved, does not seem "complete" enough to satisfy Shields, yet the man's reputation for directing good movies should have conquered Shields' worries. Instead, Shields' own meticulousness subsequently overwhelms the story he is filming, resulting in a movie without rhythm and the breath of life. Even on his best behavior and with the best intentions in the world, Shields is unable to produce the masterpiece he craves.

Movie magic is difficult to manufacture. Against all odds, Shields and Amiel find it in the dark with *The Doom of the Cat Men*. With everything in his favor, Shields is unable to produce it with *The Proud Land*. The important thing, the overriding concern of *The Bad and the Beautiful* is that Shields keeps trying to find, produce, or create some sort of movie magic. One way or another. With every project. Even if that means using a director other than his best friend (and who brought the project to his attention), or coaxing a performance out of an alcoholic actress with little experience, or doing whatever it takes to keep a writer focused on the project at hand. Anything is allowed, in Shields' eyes, as long as it's for the good of the picture. Sure, he's a heel. But he often produces great movies. Before he finally makes his telephone call from Paris, Harry Pebbel reminds the director, the star and the writer that they all owe Shields their careers. Even Pebbel himself, who admits he would probably still be making Cat Men movies if not for Shields. "You know, when they list the ten best movies ever made, there are always two or three of his on the list. And I was with him when he made them." The pride in Pebbel's voice is unmistakable. He alone admits that the quality of Shields' work is ultimately more important than the vicissitudes of Shields' friendship and trust. Those two sentences justify everything that Shields has done and everything he will do in the arena of filmmaking. One may not agree with this decree, but the film is adamant in its conviction that Jonathan Shields is an important figure because of the quality of his work and that he deserves the chance to try again.

In the film's final shot, Georgia Lorrison lifts an extension phone receiver to listen to Shields' sales pitch to Pebbel. As she does so, she moves into a light from overhead, leaving her two comrades in darkness. One by one, they also move into the light to listen to Shields describe the story he wants to film. The film ends on that optimistic note, with David Raksin's lush score rising to a crescendo, indicating that perhaps, despite their bruised egos, the director, the actress and the writer may yet agree to join with Jonathan Shields to make some more movie magic. One can only hope that it will be so.

The Bad and the Beautiful was a big hit for MGM, earning $2,367,000 in its domestic run, with another million dollars of ticket sales outside of America. The reviews were quite mixed. The British Film Institute's *Monthly Film Bulletin* appreciated Minnelli's direction, which it termed "brilliantly assured, clever and ingenious," yet finally decided, "For all the cleverness of the apparatus, it lacks a central point of focus." John McCarten of *The New Yorker* felt that the film "doesn't lack for action, but I doubt if all the scurrying about really adds up to much." He liked some of the performances, especially Gloria, "who is first-rate as Mr. Powell's spouse from the magnolia belt," but also wrote that Dick Powell "plays the part [of author Bartlow] as if he were posing for a shirt advertisement."

Time seconded that opinion: "Dick Powell bases his characterization on tweedy suits and a pipe," and praised Gloria's "fluttery Southern belle, smartly played." Bosley Crowther of the *New York Times* was not convinced of the film's clarity: "It is a crowded and colorful picture, but it is choppy, episodic and vague." Even Hollis Alpert of *The Saturday Review*, who absolutely loved the performances, still had qualms regarding the story. "The ring of it all is faintly phony and faintly hollow, and I still felt what was shown to be closer to the Hollywood of the fan magazines rather than the Hollywood of reality."

At least Alpert understood and addressed the film's moral center, rather than simply dismissing it as so many other critics did. "Are the ends worth the means of Jonathan's behavior? the picture seems to ask. The value of the particular ends might be just a little questionable, however, and maybe a better question would have been: are any ends worth the betrayal of all human feeling? Perhaps the picture never intended to get that serious. If so, then the fact that it leads to speculation is all to the good." The question of whether Shields' betrayals are justified must be at the center of any discussion involving this movie, and it is evident that one's personal reaction to his actions often dictates how one feels about *The Bad and the Beautiful* in general. The film itself, of course, intimates that the overall greatness of Shields' work overrides any other concern, and that his betrayals directly lead to career breakthroughs by his "victims." This is all based squarely upon George Bradshaw's source stories. Bradshaw makes convincing arguments for his stance, and these are repeated in the film. Viewer opinions differ based on their own worldview and personal experience; people who have been so betrayed are less likely to take an objective view, or, unlike Bradshaw's characters, are less liable to be so forgiving about it.

One area that most critics could agree was that the performances were above average. Kirk Douglas was feted in the majority of reviews for bringing his special energy and intensity to a role especially suited to him. *Newsweek* stated, "Kirk Douglas is close to perfection," while Tony Thomas in his book *The Films of Kirk Douglas* termed the performance "a tour-de-force. The role of Jonathan Shields is one of the meatiest ever handed a Hollywood actor — not only as a subtle, dramatic vehicle but as an opportunity to reveal the character of the film kind of film producer actors know but do not love." Douglas was prodded by director Minnelli to turn on his charm, for Minnelli believed that Shields had to be charming enough to cajole and persuade all these people to trust him. In a letter to Minnelli, Douglas wrote, "I was very pleased with what I did, because you got out of me a much more quiet quality than I have ever been able to get in any picture." For his efforts, Douglas snagged his second Academy Award nomination as Best Actor, ultimately losing the award to Gary Cooper in *High Noon*.

Lana Turner's turn wowed many pundits who had rarely considered her more than a voluptuous sex symbol. *Boxoffice* judged both Turner's and Douglas' performances as "definitely of Oscar-nominating caliber." Hollis Alpert wrote, "Most astonishing of all is Lana Turner, who seems to have been surprised into giving the performance of her life." The Turner scene that everybody remembers is Georgia Lorrison's frantic drive away from Jonathan after she has discovered him with another woman. It was shot eleven weeks after the rest of the film was finished, with Lana placed into the chassis of a car mounted on springs and

planks on a soundstage. While the camera circled the car and men made the contraption bounce and pitch and blew water onto it to simulate a violent rainstorm, Lana dug into her own painful past to resurrect the emotions commensurate to Georgia's despair. Lana spent an entire day in the car contraption while Minnelli and his crew filmed her panicking, crying and screaming. The result was a scene that is among the most memorable of the 1950s, and one that forever proved that she was an actress of formidable power when given the chance to truly emote.

The rest of the cast is impeccable. Walter Pidgeon, Barry Sullivan, Dick Powell, Leo G. Carroll, Sammy White, Ned Glass and Ivan Triesault are all superb in supporting roles. At the time Powell, as noted, received a fair amount of criticism for his acting choices, but those critics failed to see his artistic underplaying of the part. Powell had been offered the Fred Amiel director role but was more intrigued by the part of the snobbish intellectual writer. Once he donned the tweed jacket and pipe, Powell became the gentrified Southern writer in both appearance and temperament. Pidgeon removed his trademark tuxedo, opted for a crewcut and leaped into the role of producer Harry Pebbel with relish. Barry Sullivan, originally cast as the writer, studied the methods of low-budget directors to enhance his understanding of the Fred Amiel role. And director Minnelli took his time with everybody, from Lana Turner to singer Peggy King (she sings "Don't Blame Me" in a party sequence) to establish a convincing atmosphere in every scene.

The Bad and the Beautiful. James Lee Bartlow (Dick Powell) begins to wonder if their stay in Hollywood is changing his starstruck wife Rosemary (Gloria) for the worse. He will soon find out.

Perhaps the film was too authentic for the industry to fully appreciate it.

With its heel of a hero, downbeat tone and penchant for shattering illusions, it may have made film people uncomfortable. This is reflected in the fact that, despite its overall classiness and a December release date, Minnelli's drama was not heavily feted at awards time. The film was nominated for a number of awards by groups such as the Golden Globes, the Directors Guild of America, the Writers Guild of America and BAFTA (the British Academy of Film and Television Awards), but it failed to win any. In most cases the film garnered just one nomination per group, sometimes two. It scored best at the Academy Awards, where it was nominated for six Oscars and came away with five. In fact, *The Bad and the Beautiful* still holds the record for the most Oscars won by a film that was not nominated for Best Picture. Only Kirk Douglas lost (to Gary Cooper in *High Noon*) in his category. The film won for Best Art Direction–Set Decoration, Black and White; Cinematography, Black and White; Costume Design, Black and White; Best Writing, Screenplay, for Charles Schnee's flawless script; and Best Actress in a Supporting Role, for Gloria Grahame.

This was Gloria's second Oscar nomination, following her nod for *Crossfire* five years earlier, and her first win. She was a favorite for the award, having accrued major parts in four popular films in 1952. Cases were made for nominating Gloria for *The Greatest Show on Earth* or *Sudden Fear*, but it was the December drama for which Gloria was honored by the Academy. She received some of the best notices of her career, with some industry pundits even suggesting that Lana Turner had been passed over for an Oscar nomination because Gloria's charming appearance had undermined it. It is a fact that Gloria and Lana had no scenes together, and Gloria is said to have curiously peeked around studio sets in order to get a glimpse of the movie's star, as she had done so with Joan Crawford earlier in the year.

Gloria is superb in what is really quite a small role, one that doesn't appear until late in the story. Assuming a Virginian accent that she acquired by studying with Los Angeles disc jockey Joe Adams, she is all chiffon and cotton candy on screen. Her sweet-smiled charm enhances her character's sensuous approach to life; Rosemary's signature saying seems to be

"James Lee, you have a dirty mind, I'm happy to say." It is because of Rosemary's eagerness that her husband, leery of the trap that he senses in Hollywood, agrees to go. Once there, he has a difficult time controlling her, for Rosemary is quickly and powerfully entranced by the glamourous Hollywood lifestyle. Parties, music and dancing sweep the Southern belle off her feet and threaten to overwhelm their marriage. James Lee Bartlow becomes so distracted that he cannot write, and Rosemary is oblivious of the effect she is having on him. That's when Shields casually asks Gaucho to squire her around town while Bartlow goes off to write.

In the original story, the writer's wife is seduced by the producer (the Shields character) in New York while the writer is off finishing a script. She leaves the writer, divorces him, and spends "a month or two" with the producer before he kicks her out. Meanwhile the writer goes to France and writes two new plays, proving that without distraction, his true artistry can emerge. The film softens the blow to the writer (and the audience) by having Shields' request be largely innocent; it is Gaucho, ever the romantic leading man, who acts on his own, taking Rosemary to Mexico. Her death frees Bartlow to become the writer Shields suspects he can be. When Bartlow discovers Shields' part in the tragedy, he rewards his producer with a punch to the jaw. Later, Bartlow writes a memoir in his late wife's honor, and wins the Pulitzer Prize for it.

Gloria thoroughly enjoyed making *The Bad and the Beautiful*. She was chosen for the role by studio head Dore Schary, who felt she was perfect for the part. Schary saw himself in the part of the writer and believed that Gloria was the actress in Hollywood most like his wife Miriam. Gloria loved being flirtatious and sweet, for the films she had previously made rarely offered her the opportunity to show those sides of her personality. She worked on her timing to deliver her comic lines with just the right finesse. Having grown up in Hollywood, the spectacle of premieres and parties was not new to her, yet Gloria made the sensation seem fresh and special to Rosemary. This is also the most "girlish" portrayal of Gloria's gallery of characterizations; she softened her look, her speech and her manner. She required little direction from Minnelli, who in any case was devoting a lot of time and attention to Lana Turner. Shooting was a nice, rewarding experience for Gloria.

It became more rewarding when the announcements were made for the 1952 Academy Award ceremony. As fate would have it, this was the first Oscar ceremony to be televised, ensuring that millions of people would witness it as it happened. Gloria was nominated in the Supporting Actress category, along with Jean Hagen for *Singin' in the Rain*, Colette Marchand for *Moulin Rouge*, Terry Moore for *Come Back, Little Sheba* and Thelma Ritter for *With a Song in My Heart*. Gloria was the early favorite, thanks in part to the versatility she had displayed in three other 1952 movies. Nevertheless, when Edmund Gwenn announced, "Gloria Grahame in *The Bad and the Beautiful* ... she's the beautiful," Gloria was stunned. "I didn't think I was going to get it. I thought Thelma Ritter would be the winner," she said later. Striding uncertainly to the stage to receive her prize, Gloria tripped on the stairs because she couldn't see them — the lights for the telecast were blinding her. She murmured, "Oh, shit," then straightened and walked to the podium. Gwenn whispered, "Smile, you're on television," and Gloria responded with an awkward smile. She said, "Thank you," and walked backstage to thunderous applause.

Rumors began that night and circulated around Hollywood for weeks that Gloria was drunk when she accepted the Oscar, but that was untrue. She was among the first winners to have to climb the stage from the audience and she had no idea how blinding the lights would be. She was also nearsighted, which compounded the problem. Furthermore, she had been a nervous wreck for weeks, trying on four different dresses and arguing with new boyfriend Cy Howard about how much makeup she should wear. Gloria had finally divorced Nicholas Ray on August 14, 1952, but had started dating comedy writer Howard in April. Finally, she hadn't really believed that she would win the award. The result of all of this was that she looked confused and disoriented when she won. Her behavior afterward didn't win her any defenders, either. She refused to give interviews because she was busy filming *The Big Heat*. The day after the ceremony she took her Oscar to the set and left it alone. Later she couldn't find it; it had been mistaken for a prop and locked in a prop cabinet. Word also spread that she was treating her Oscar poorly, giving it to her son as a toy. That is partly true; young Timmy commandeered it, calling it "his doll" and sleeping with it. Gloria told an interviewer, "As for what I think of my cherished Oscar, no fond mother takes away her child's favorite plaything."

Gloria spent the next few months defending herself in sporadic interviews, arguing that she didn't have "Oscar-itis," the affliction that makes movie stars pompous and arrogant when their heads swell from so much adulation. Since mid–1951 Gloria had worked almost constantly, making six movies with almost no breaks in between. That's how she was able to appear in four films in 1952 and four more in 1953. She would stay busy with three more in 1954 and three more in 1955 before finally taking time off in 1956 to raise her new daughter, Marianna (Paulette). It was Gloria's greatest period of production, but by the end of it she was exhausted and had pretty well ruined her reputation in Hollywood. Part of that damage was caused on Oscar night and by the perception that Gloria had become completely self-centered. Gloria would, unfortunately, exacerbate those perceptions with her behavior and demands on certain productions over the next few years.

Yet there was a sweet irony for Gloria when she won the Oscar, for she had done so in a movie from MGM, the studio where she had started. They had given up on her, selling her contract to RKO in 1947, yet five years later she had returned when the new management (ironically, former RKO head Dore Schary) had found the right role for her. It would be another three years before she would again return to the studio, to work for the same director, on another project with a great deal of potential. In the meantime, the majority of her work would take place at Columbia.

The authors of *Hollywood on Hollywood* noted in 1978: "Interestingly, as the years have gone by, the movie has grown in stature, becoming a minor classic that seems destined to rise even higher in estimation in future generations. After all, considering some of the amateurish trash distributed today, the facileness of *The Bad and the Beautiful* looks very good indeed." The *Motion Picture Guide* bestowed it with a rare five star review and called it "The quintessential movie on the movies ... graced with performances that approach and/or capture perfection from all the leads." In 2002 it was chosen for inclusion on the National Film Registry. Today in discussions regarding movies about moviemaking — and there have been many such movies over the last fifty years to add to the discussion — few of them offer the impact or cachet of *The Bad and the Beautiful*. Thanks to its discerning script, sterling performances and unflinching contemplation of the film industry, it is that rare example of a movie about moviemaking that actually has a great deal to say regarding the process, in terms both professional and personal. It is among the greatest of Hollywood's self-examinations, and it is certainly among the five best films that Gloria Grahame ever made. Her contribution to its brilliance is somewhat minor, all things considered, yet she undeniably enhances it and adds to its effectiveness. It is the kind of project she should have done more often.

The Glass Wall (1953)

CREDITS Columbia Pictures. *Directed by* Maxwell Shane. *Produced by* Ivan Tors. *Associate Producer*: Ben Colman. *Screenplay by* Ivan Tors and Maxwell Shane. *Director of Photography*: Joseph F. Biroc. *Supervising Film Editor*: Stanley Frazen. *Film Editor*: Herbert L. Strock. *Production Design*: George Van Marter. *Music by* Leith Stevens. *Production Manager*: C. M. Florance. *Assistant Director*: Richard Dixon. *Assistant Director — New York Unit*: Ben Berk. *Art Director*: Serge Krizman. *Lighting Effects*: Robert Jones. *Sound*: William H. Wilmarth. *Special Effects*: Jack Rubin and David Commons. *Orchestrator*: Gus Levene. Black and White. Flat (1.37:1). Monaural Sound. 78 minutes. Released on March 20, 1953. Currently available on DVD. Previously unavailable on commercial home video.

CAST *Peter Kuban*, Vittorio Gassman; *Maggie Summers*, Gloria Grahame; *Nancy*, Ann Robinson; *Inspector Bailey*, Douglas Spencer; *Tanya Zakolya*, Robin Raymond; *Tom*, Jerry Paris; *Mrs. Hinckley*, Elizabeth Slifer; *Eddie*, Richard Reeves; *Freddie Zakolya*, Joseph Turkel; *Mrs. Zakolya*, Else Neft; *Toomey*, Michael Fox; *Monroe*, Ned (Nesdon) Booth; *Zelda*, Kathleen Freeman; *Girl Friend*, Juney Ellis; *Lieutenant Reeves*, Barney Phillips; *Police News* *Broadcaster*, Roy Engel; *Dock Inspector*, Kenner G. Kemp; *Club Manager*, Lou Krugman; *Louie*, Dick Monda; *Sammy*, Alvin Freeman; *Zelda's Friend*, Dorothy Neumann; *Giggling Man in Arcade*, Richard Collier; *Restaurant Patron*, Sammy Finn; *Musician in Men's Room*, Joseph Mell; *Taxi Driver's Pal*, Frank Mills; *Man in Alley*, Snub Pollard; *Themselves*, Jack Teagarden, and Shorty Rogers and His Band; with Sayre Dearing and Valerie Vernon.

For many years the rarest and most difficult of all early Gloria Grahame films to locate was this independently made post–World War II immigration drama distributed by Columbia. Filmed largely on location in New York City by producer Ivan Tors and director Maxwell Shane, the film presents timely social commentary within the context of a ten-hour manhunt for a "displaced person" who is attempting to find a friend who can substantiate his claim for asylum in America. It is a message movie about the need for public and personal consciousness regarding the plight of less fortunate people, a reminder that compassion is the finest human quality. It offers the opportunity to view Gloria Grahame in a rare deglamorized role, in the type of movie that was increasingly popular in Europe.

An ocean liner steams into New York harbor carrying 1,322 displaced persons ... and one stowaway. Peter Kuban (Vittorio Gassman) was born in Hungary and had escaped from German captivity after years of imprisonment during World War II. He has stowed away on the transport ship to find a new life in America, and freely declared himself once the ship docked. But Inspector Bailey (Douglas Spencer) of the Immigration Service needs proof of Kuban's tale before he can allow him to enter the country. Kuban is missing three fingernails on one hand "because they [the Nazis] thought I knew something," but that disfigurement is not conclusive evidence. Kuban relates how he saved an American soldier named Tom during the war, but since he does not know Tom's surname, nor Tom's address, the inspector does not believe him. Kuban is termed "Excluded," and confined to the ship, which is due to sail back to Europe the following morning.

Desperate, Kuban escapes, leaping from the ship to the dock and injuring his ribs in the process. Policemen chase and shoot at him, but Kuban jumps onto a passing truck and avoids capture. The truck carries Kuban to Times Square where he begins to search for Tom, the American soldier he had saved, and who he knows to be a clarinet player in the city. When he stops for rest and a quick meal in a coffee shop, he sees a young woman (Gloria Grahame) eat the remainder of a donut left behind by somebody and then attempt to steal a coat. The coat's owner protests and the young woman flees. Kuban follows, hides with her in a park and leads her safely away from the vigilant police. The young woman is Maggie Summers, and Kuban pressures her to take him home with her, intimating that he will turn her in if she does not comply.

At Maggie's apartment, the landlady Mrs. Hinckley (Elisabeth Slifer) demands a rent payment, so Kuban gives up his last seven dollars to delay Maggie's eviction. Seeing that she is worse off than he, Kuban tries to leave, but collapses. With her help, Kuban lies down to rest, revealing his injured ribs. She sees Kuban's picture on the front page of the newspaper on top of the headline "EXCLUDED!" and begins to understand his predicament.

In another part of the city, Tom (Jerry Paris) finally lands an audition with Jack Teagarden's band. Tom is thrilled with the opportunity, but he is troubled when he, too, sees Kuban's photo in the newspaper. Tom wants to find Kuban but his fiancée Nancy (Ann Robinson) insists that he audition instead. Thinking of his own future, Tom relents.

Back at Maggie's apartment, the landlady's truck-driving son Eddie (Richard Reeves) makes a move on Maggie, provoking Kuban to defend her. Eddie beats the tar out of Kuban before Maggie smashes a chair over Eddie's head. Maggie and Kuban escape while the landlady calls the police. Nearby, Tom plays several songs with Jack Teagarden's band, causing the famous trombonist to exclaim, "He's really got it!" Finally, however, Tom cannot wait to help his friend any longer. He packs his clarinet away and leaves for the nearest police station to help find the man who once saved his life.

Kuban and Maggie walk the streets for a while before Maggie gathers enough change — by bullying some kids, a tactic of which Kuban disapproves—for them to ride the subway. There, they can rest and avoid their pursuers. Before they can board the train, however, police arrive and grab Maggie. Kuban leaps past an approaching subway train and escapes. At a police station, a chastened Inspector Bailey explains to Tom (who has arrived to help find Kuban) and Maggie (captured by the police but turned over to the inspector) that Kuban must be located before the ship sails at 7:00 A.M., or he will be considered a fugitive and never granted entry into the United States. Bailey divides Manhattan into four quadrants and directs police officers and his own men to search for him.

Kuban wanders the streets alone. He rests in an arcade but awakens to find people harassing him and runs. He finds a quiet spot in the back seat of an empty taxi cab and falls asleep immediately. A burlesque stripper named Tanya (Robin Raymond) finds him in the cab that has been waiting for her, recognizes him from the newspaper and takes him home, after checking why he is wanted by the police. Tanya is, like Peter Kuban, also Hungarian, so she decides to help him. Kuban rests while Tanya and her elderly mother (Else Neft) prepare a meal for him. Tanya's brother Freddie (Joseph Turkel) arrives, discovers the visitor and demands that he be thrown out immediately. The family argues heatedly, waking Kuban, who leaves quietly while they quarrel about his presence.

At dawn, Kuban has given up searching for Tom. He asks a newspaper vendor about the United Nations. "It's a big tall building with a glass wall," replies the man, pointing in its direction. As Kuban nears the U.N. building he is spotted by Tom, Maggie and Inspector Bailey, who have spent the night in a squad car searching for him. Fearful of capture by the police, Kuban enters the U.N. building. In the empty "Commission on Human Rights" meeting room, Kuban screams for someone, anyone, to listen. He begs for mercy, reminding the empty chairs that "to each man, *he* is the world!" With pursuers close behind, Kuban sprints painfully to the roof. He is on a ledge, contemplating the long fall, when Tom calls out to him. Kuban turns and, seeing his friend, collapses onto the roof. Tom assures him that he will be free and Inspector Bailey nods his assent. Supported by Tom and Maggie, Kuban rises and for the first time faces a future filled with promise.

The Glass Wall is a movie that preaches tolerance, understanding and compassion yet does so in a suspenseful, entertaining format. The movie's publicity downplayed any social commentary, emphasizing instead the more exciting aspects of the story. ("It's a 10-hour manhunt through the jazz-joints and sin-spots of New York!" boasts the poster.) Only at the climax, when Kuban begs an empty U.N. chamber to listen to him, does the film enter the realm of social propaganda. Yet even that sequence carries some emotional impact simply because Kuban has been through so much and cannot seem to catch a break.

The film falls short of stating that the "system" has let Kuban down although viewers may jump to that conclusion themselves. Even though it is the Immigration Service which refuses Kuban entrance into America (on valid grounds, it should be noted), and the police do shoot at him when he first jumps ship, it is also that same Immigration Service and police force that search all night to find him and save him from fugitive status—and permanent banishment from America. It is important thematically that Inspector Bailey locates Kuban—but it is just as important that the Hungarian refugee probably would have jumped to his death if Maggie and Tom hadn't been with the inspector. The movie's point is that political and social positions taken by governmental officials need to be tempered with human understanding and compassion for people affected by such positions. Peter Kuban is such a person and he is saved not by American justice, but by the efforts of people who barely know him, yet believe in him nonetheless.

The film implies that a tacit obligation to help people in need exists, yet also acknowledges difficulties in doing so. The best example is Tanya (Robin Raymond), a rather mature burlesque dancer ("She's Atomic!" exclaims her billboard) who welcomes Kuban into her home and lets him rest with her sleeping children simply because she and he share a Hungarian heritage, which convinces her that he is not dangerous. Tanya's mother agrees and prepares a meal for him. But Tanya's brother Freddie has been Americanized to the point of despising his own parents' background. Freddie, whose own business dealings do not appear to be legitimate, immediately balks at having Kuban in the house and demands his ejection. Freddie calls Kuban a "lousy foreigner," causing his

mother to slap him sharply. "Don't forget, your dead father was a lousy foreigner!" she reminds him. Kuban awakens, hears Freddie's protests and quietly leaves, not wishing to cause anyone any problems. Tanya is saddened and she too, slaps her brother for causing Kuban to leave. But at least she tried to help a man in need.

Another person who aids Kuban is the woman whom he aids first. Maggie Summers (Gloria Grahame) is penniless and hungry when Kuban first sees her. She tries to steal a coat just to keep warm and would probably have been captured and incarcerated if not for Kuban's help. Finding Maggie even more poverty-stricken than himself, Kuban gives her his last seven dollars to appease her impatient landlady.

Maggie doesn't know what to think about Kuban. He pressures her into taking him home with her and she assumes it is for companionship. "You got me buffaloed," she frets, realizing that he could turn her in for grabbing the coat. But in her apartment he doesn't make a pass at her. After he gives her the money, apologizes and leaves, she realizes she may have misjudged him. Hearing him collapse on the staircase, she rushes to his side and helps him back inside her apartment, thus risking the further wrath of her nosy landlady.

It is Maggie who cements audience empathy for Kuban. Inspector Bailey doesn't believe Kuban's story of strife and there is no reason—other than Vittorio Gassman's obvious sincerity in the role—that viewers should either. As the inspector remarks, people will say anything to get into America. But any doubt about Kuban's character is erased when he reaches out to help Maggie, a person in circumstances nearly as dire as his own. Once Maggie realizes that he needs her help, she responds in kind. They connect, which is precisely the film's goal. Although Maggie has only known Kuban for a few hours, when questioned about him by the police she states unequivocally, "He's the first guy I met in my life who treated me decent," and begs the police to let him alone.

Movie romances are often sugar-coated fantasies, meetings of predetermined destiny or witty, verbal bantering between people leading to inevitable happy endings. The relationship between Kuban and Maggie does not follow any of those patterns. Theirs is a rela-

The Glass Wall. Maggie Summers (Gloria) and Peter Kuban (Vittorio Gassman) hide in a park from the New York City police. She has just tried to steal a coat and he is a fugitive newly arrived in America without the proper papers.

tionship based on mutual need, and the recognition that they cannot help but assist and support each other through a troubled time. At no time do they flirt or act suggestively toward each other, nor do they (as so many modern movie couples do) find time for a quickie in the middle of their dangerous and exhausting adventures. This is a realistic and compelling relationship: two people who meet by chance and connect strongly enough to affect the rest of their lives. Maggie — and Tom the clarinetist as well — are ultimately willing to spend the night hunting for a man they barely know merely because he assisted each of them when they needed it. The bond they feel for Kuban isn't obligation, it's human affinity.

The only sequence that goes over the top is the final one at the United Nations building. It is Tanya's brother Freddie who puts the idea of going to the U.N. in Kuban's head, so in lieu of finding Tom he staggers toward his last hope

for remaining free. The U.N. building is the "glass wall" of the title, which is also symbolic of Kuban's plight. Introduced as a towering and inspiring symbol of power and destiny (especially when seen by Kuban with the Empire State Building in view behind him and music swelling in the background), the U.N. building is also revealed to be an empty shell when it is without people to make and execute fateful decisions.

Pursued, Kuban dashes into a side entrance of the building, then into a chamber marked "Commission on Human Rights." It is empty, being just after 6 A.M. Kuban finally unburdens himself in the chamber, begging for justice. "Somebody, somebody listen! You, you come here to bring peace to the world, but what is the world? As long as there is one man who can't walk free where he wants, as long as there is one displaced person without home, there won't be peace. Because to each man, *he is the*

The Glass Wall. Maggie Summers (Gloria) tells Lieutenant Reeves (Barney Phillips, right) about fugitive Peter Kuban (Vittorio Gassman, not pictured). Listening to her story are Kuban's friend Tom (Jerry Paris) and Inspector Bailey (Douglas Spencer) of the Immigration Service.

world!" Kuban ends his outburst helplessly, muttering, "Nobody listens."

While this scene and the threatened suicidal leap from the roof that follow are certainly heartfelt, these events do not quite fit the film's previous path. This is a case where thematic material overwhelms the carefully constructed realism of the story, weakening its effectiveness. There are several points during the final chase where Kuban might have been stopped simply by Tom or Maggie calling out to him. And yet, these dramatic oversights still reinforce the main theme that Kuban cannot survive on his own; he needs the support of other people to stay alive and to find meaning in his life.

One other oddity involves the newspaper account of Kuban's plight. A large photo of the stowaway graces the front page of the *New York Daily News* along with the large-type headline "EXCLUDED!" and a brief caption. Tom and Maggie are each informed about Kuban's situ-ation by reading the paper, thus avoiding any long-winded expository sequences. Yet Kuban seems unaware of his fleeting fame. At no time during the film is there an explanation of how Kuban's situation has been related to the newspaper, nor is a reporter part of the plot. This seems quite strange, since the newspaper story and photo are so crucial to the action. The film's brief running time (78 minutes) hints that perhaps more of this angle was to be involved, but dropped, for any number of reasons.

Much of the film was lensed on the streets of New York City (although a few rear projection shots are apparent) and the gritty, semidocumentary style employed by director Maxwell Shane suits the material to a tee. *The Glass Wall* generally follows the tenets of Italian neorealism for most of its duration, focusing on the small yet significant details of modern city life and emphasizing its difficulties, although the melodrama and heightened reality of the final sequence strays from the concept of depicting life as it truly is rather than as it should be. By the time of the film's production, the neo-realist movement was in decline, as audiences demanded escapist entertainment and producers attempted to provide it. Thus, the film may have been a bit too bleak for the public taste, despite its handsome, exotic leading man and beautiful leading lady.

The Glass Wall was the first American film for Italian star Vittorio Gassman (billed in publicity material as a "Latin Lover"), who had recently wed Shelley Winters. Gassman (sometimes spelled with two n's, which was the family name spelling) is excellent and totally convincing as the troubled Hungarian, making an auspicious American debut. Gassman made several undistinguished Hollywood films before returning to Italy, but did periodically come back to America for assorted films much later in his life. The actor (and former Olympic basketball player) did his own stunts in *The Glass Wall* and reportedly copied Hungarian producer Ivan Tors' accent for the part. Later he became a writer and director as well.

Gloria Grahame co-stars as Maggie Summers, a different kind of woman-in-trouble role for the actress. This is one of the rare 1950s roles in which Grahame is not called upon to unleash her considerable sex appeal or suffer the fates of cinematic bad girls. "Down on her luck" best describes Maggie, and Gloria portrays the character with a shell-shocked vulnerability. Maggie is still feisty at times, yet most of her hope is gone until Kuban demonstrates how to crawl one's way out of trouble. Gloria is just right in the role, especially in the middle scenes as she explains her unfortunate circumstances and begins to display feelings for the man she is helping.

Her best scene occurs when Maggie describes how she fell into poverty. "Did you ever put tips on shoelaces?" she asks Kuban. "That's what I did for two years." She enacts the process of cutting shoelaces from a spool and having a machine stamp the plastic tips on them. "There's a big steel machine here, see, and over here a giant spool of shoelace. You pull it out like this [*gesturing*] twenty-seven inches at a time, all day. You stamp a pedal and a ton of steel bangs down, cuts the lace and rolls the tip

on — bang! — like that, and again — bang! — all day. You're scared you'll smash your finger. At the same time you gotta keep your eye on the assistant foreman 'cause every time he comes by he pinches you. You do this 'til your brain goes numb, and you get thirty-five bucks a week. And then all of a sudden you have an appendix attack, an operation. You're out, flat on your back, and you just can't get back on your feet. You get fed up. And you want to strike back at somebody, *anybody*! And so you steal a coat."

It's a great monologue, and Grahame delivers it with smoldering anger. Vincent Curcio critiques it this way: "[Gloria] is too hard-boiled for pathos in this scene and yet too believable not to achieve our sympathy." It's the type of scene that Gloria loved to perform and sought in the scripts she read, realizing that often just one scene can define and cement a character in the public eye. Maggie is also a non-glamourous role, which was another switch for the actress. Although her wardrobe is limited to just one very plain sweater and skirt combination, the film's publicity calls Gloria "Tawny and Terrific!," and emphasizes the growing attachment between Kuban and Maggie.

Shelley Winters had desired the part of Maggie, mostly to be able to work with her new husband on his first American film, but Universal wouldn't release her for the role. Gloria enjoyed the change of pace that the role provided, but attempted to steer it her own way a few times. This so infuriated director Maxwell Shane that he vowed to have her brought up on charges before the Screen Actors Guild (Gloria had threatened to walk off the set if changes to her character were not made to her liking). This incident made it into the Hollywood trade papers. Although Shane later termed it "a little disagreement over the story," it helped turn Gloria's working reputation somewhat sour. Despite this incident, she fulfilled her obligation and delivered an excellent performance.

One of the factors behind this incident, possibly the main reason, was Gloria's dedication to her new beau, Cy Howard. When Gloria romanced a man, he became the primary focus of her life. Friends at the time recall Gloria dropping everything, cutting dinners short, cancelling other engagements, just to be with

Cy as she got to know him. Gloria was to marry Cy, but that wouldn't occur until 1954. Cy was in show business, primarily known as a comedy writer, but unlike Gloria's first two husbands, he wasn't part of the film community. When Stanley Clements or Nicholas Ray gave her advice, she knew that it had the weight of experience. Cy also liked to give Gloria advice on her career, but it was from a different perspective, a selfish perspective. Cy's advice wasn't designed to improve her film as a whole, but rather to enlarge and expand Gloria's role, sometimes to the detriment of other performers. Cy warned Gloria to watch her back and get what she could out of every role, to always try to improve her position in Hollywood, and he did not understand or seem to care that the best way to do so was simply to produce good collaborative work.

As Cy's influence took hold, Gloria became more demanding on movie sets, because Cy had told her to be assertive. Directors and producers would try to limit Cy's input on Gloria's roles, and her mother Jean was still around to ensure that her daughter gave quality performances, but it was sometimes difficult to prevent Gloria from calling Cy, even in between individual takes. *The Glass Wall* is the first film to feel the effects of Cy's input, which would reach its zenith on the *Oklahoma!* set.

The Glass Wall also "introduces" Jerry Paris, the likable actor best known for portraying Dick Van Dyke's affable neighbor on TV's *The Dick Van Dyke Show*. In fact, Paris had previously appeared in seventeen films before *The Glass Wall*, but this film did provide him with his biggest part to date. Douglas Spencer, perhaps best known as the reporter in *The Thing from Another World* (1951), also has a nice supporting role as Inspector Bailey. Ann Robinson is wasted in a shrill and unsympathetic role as Tom's fiancée.

A jazzy score is provided by Leith Stevens, one of the better but least known film composers of the era. Musical performances by the bands of trombonist Jack Teagarden and Shorty Rogers lend the film extra atmosphere, provide an authentic jazz background to the dramatics and give Peter Kuban a reason to wander around the city until dawn. Director Shane made only two more feature films but later found success as the producer of television's *M*

Squad and *Thriller* series. Producer Ivan Tors later took to the water for such TV projects as *Sea Hunt, The Aquanauts* and *Flipper*.

The Glass Wall was not very successful commercially, and critics generally felt that the film lacked luster. According to *Newsweek*, "The film's hints at historical significance never amount to a great deal; its stature remains that of a Grade B escape story." Similarly, *Time* termed it "a standard chase yarn whose only novel ingredient is a United Nations backdrop." The British Film Institute's *Monthly Film Bulletin* noted, "This is another of the Individual-versus-The State films. When it sticks to the chase it succeeds, but when it becomes propagandist it merely embarrasses. Vittorio Gassman is bewildered and sympathetic as Peter and Gloria Grahame gives a very good performance in a trite part." *Variety* decided that "it lives up to its entertainment intentions sufficiently to rate as regulation heavy-drama screen fare," and also praised Gloria.

The film is virtually unknown today, being almost impossible to find for many years. It was recently broadcast on the Starz Mystery Channel and Turner Classic Movies and has just recently made it to DVD. *The Glass Wall* is unusual in Gloria's career in that her character is neither hedonistic, homicidal nor hellraising. Maggie is an unlucky woman whose luck begins to change when she helps a man in need. It is one of her most satisfying, human roles, although it is not particularly deep. The part marked Grahame's effort to vary her film appearances and perhaps to strive for an acting credibility above and beyond the Hollywood blockbusters in which she had recently been appearing. *The Glass Wall* provided her with cinematic integrity and proved conclusively that she was capable of far more than most Hollywood producers were willing to offer her, and that she was willing to battle to improve roles in which she believed, even if some of her battles were ill-chosen.

Man on a Tightrope (1953)

CREDITS 20th Century–Fox. *Directed by* Elia Kazan. *Produced by* Robert L. Jacks. *Associate Producer*: Gerd Oswald. *Screenplay by* Robert E. Sherwood. *Story by* Neil Paterson. *Director of Photography*: Georg

Krause. *Film Editor*: Dorothy Spencer. *Musical Direction*: Franz Waxman. *Art Direction*: Hans H. Kuhnert and Theo Zwirsky. *Wardrobe Direction*: Charles LeMaire. *Costumes Designed by* Ursula Maes. *Orchestration*: Earle Hagen. *Makeup Artists*: Arthur Schramm and Fritz Seyfried. *Sound*: Martin Mueller and Roger Heman. *Assistant Director*: Hans Tost. *Property Master*: Don B. Greenwood. Black and White. Flat (1.37:1). Monaural Sound. 105 minutes. Released on April 1, 1953. Not currently available on commercial home video.

CAST *Karol Cernik*, Fredric March; *Tereza Cernik*, Terry Moore; *Zama Cernik*, Gloria Grahame; *Joe Vosdek*, Cameron Mitchell; *Fesker*, Adolphe Menjou; *Barovic*, Robert Beatty; *Rudolph*, Alex D'Arcy; *Krofta*, Richard Boone; *Konradin*, Pat Henning; *Jaromir*, Paul Hartman; *The Chief*, John Dehner; *Secret Police Captain*, Peter Beauvais; *Madame Cernik*, Madame Brumbach; *Captain*, Willy Castello; *Police Agent*, Gert Fröbe; *Kalka*, Hansi; *The Sergeant*, Philip Kenneally; *Konradine*, Edelweib Malchin; *Mrs. Jaromir*, Margarete Slezak; *Police Agent*, Rolf van Nauckhoff; *Duchess*, Dorothea Wieck; with The Brumbach Circus.

For her second circus movie in two years, Gloria Grahame joined director Elia Kazan and a notable cast on a trek to Germany to re-enact the escape of the Brumbach Circus from behind the Iron Curtain, as had been reported in *Life* magazine and elsewhere. This time Gloria would not be in the ring with petulant pachyderms, but the shoot was grueling nonetheless. Filming in Germany was a dreary affair, as the weather alternated between rain, fog and sunshine dulled by the heavy, moist air. Most of Gloria's time was spent in a small trailer. For the sake of art, the real names and locations of this true story were changed, but the story's basis in fact provides it a *gravitas* that few other circus movies ever attain. Of course, that didn't stop 20th Century–Fox's publicists from promoting the film with screaming taglines such as "Peril in Pink Tights!," "Love Behind a Curtain!," "Death in the Driver's Seat!" and "The Most Dangerous Thing a Man and Woman Ever Did Together!" With dramatic exclamations like these, it is no wonder that this low-key drama failed to meet many audience expectations. In fact, it is among the lowest-grossing movies ever released by 20th Century–Fox.

Man on a Tightrope begins in 1952 Czechoslovakia. A convoy of trucks comprising the Cirkus Cernik is forced off a dirt road by a military procession of trucks carrying political prisoners. The circus owner, Karol Cernik (Fredric March), takes stock of items damaged, including rotting rope. "Everything's rotten," he mutters. Cernik sees his daughter Tereza (Terry Moore) fraternizing with tent man Joe Vosdek (Cameron Mitchell) and warns her to stay away from him. The circus moves on and establishes camp down the road. A performance showcases clowns; Cernik is the lead clown, frolicking with the dwarf Kalka (Hansi) and balancing on a tightrope (thus, the title) to the delight of the crowd. Following his performance, Cernik returns to his trailer where his second wife Zama (Gloria Grahame) idly listens to music while trying to write using just her toes, hoping to create a role for herself in her husband's circus.

Cernik is taken from the circus to Pilsen by police agents and questioned about his political beliefs by the Chief (John Dehner). He is reminded that the State now owns the circus, and he is merely its manager. Cernik is ordered to pay a fine, follow specific orders regarding the content of the performances, and fire one of his performers, a Frenchwoman. He agrees. While Cernik is being questioned, bored Zama makes a play for Rudolph the lion tamer (Alex D'Arcy). Joe and Tereza spend the time horseback riding, then swimming in a nearby river, kissing passionately. After Cernik leaves Pilsen, police agent Fesker (Adolphe Menjou) expresses interest in placing Cernik under surveillance; Fesker believes Cernik is up to something.

Cernik returns to the circus and dismisses the Frenchwoman, then changes his mind. In the ring he performs a dance with a mannequin, then after the performance sees his daughter throw herself at Joe. The dwarf Kalka steals a crucifix and is ordered away from the circus, despite protests from Zama. Six of the top circus men meet secretly in a trailer and Cernik announces that someone has been spying on them. He feels that things are closing in around them. The following day Tereza demands that Joe take her away from the circus. Joe confesses that he is a deserter from the American army, a Czech citizen who has been trying to find his father, and who has only recently found proof of his father's death. Cernik sees them together and again tries to make

Tereza leave Joe alone. "I'm a woman and I'm going to act like one," Tereza states, adding that Cernik should be paying more attention to Zama.

A rival circus owner, Barovic (Robert Beatty), arrives to have a conference with Cernik. Barovic knows all the details concerning Cernik's secret plan to take the circus across the border into American-occupied Bavaria. Barovic confesses that Kalka hid under the trailer and heard everything, then sold the information to him instead of the police. Cernik admits to the plan and furthermore announces that the escape will have to be moved up — to this very day. Barovic asks for some of the equipment that will be left behind and, in his own way, agrees to help. Cernik cannot understand Barovic's attitude but his rival supplies the answer: "We hate the government." They stage a mock fight to convince everyone (then, and later) that Barovic is not helping Cernik and that the two men still despise each other. Barovic loses the fight and leaves in disgrace while Cernik cleans up in his trailer. Zama derides him, telling him that he's not a man any more. He slaps her, hard. Zama is stunned, but happily so. "You should have done it a long time ago," she purrs.

The circus makes preparations to move, and to stage a small performance along the border for the troops stationed there. Cernik and his top two men, Konradin (Pat Henning) and Jaromir (Paul Hartman), reconnoiter and return. The head foreman, Krofta (Richard Boone), objects to the sudden change in plan and demands that they adhere to the original schedule. Cernik clobbers Krofta with a mallet and binds him, stuffing the spy into an equipment box. Fesker realizes what Cernik is planning and goes after him. After Fesker leaves, the other police agents call Prague for further instructions regarding Fesker, who is disobeying orders by issuing a pass to the circus on his own authority (he hopes to trap Cernik as the circus prepares to cross the border).

Zama is finally told of the plan, which she heartily approves. But Tereza is gone. She left with Joe in an equipment truck — one which Cernik planned to leave behind, as he has always suspected Joe of being the spy. He goes after Tereza and brings both her and Joe back to the circus, which is ready to depart. He also agrees to take Kalka with them, despite the dwarf's bad behavior. Fesker is intercepted by fellow police agents who accuse him of treason for illegally issuing the circus pass. Fesker begs his colleagues to stop the circus, telling them that Cernik is trying to escape, but his pleas are ignored. Back with the circus, Krofta gets loose and grabs a gun. He demands that Cernik surrender, realizing that they plan to escape the country. Kalka intercedes and he and Zama force Krofta outside. Cernik is shot during the scuffle that follows. Kalka shoots Krofta to death.

With Cernik bleeding in his trailer, the circus moves toward the border, slowly, marching and parading, as Communist guards watch from their towers. The American guards across the border crossing can see them approach. The band plays, the clowns clown, the animals parade. The guards begin to relax and enjoy the show. Suddenly, Joe yells the signal and throws a bomb that destroys one of the guardhouses. A truck with a reinforced front frame rams the border gate, creating an opening toward the bridge separating Czechoslovakia from Austria. Metal grates are quickly laid over the fence wreckage and the circus performers and animals stream over it toward freedom. Joe holds off the guards with a revolver. On the bridge that separates the two countries, Cernik's trailer is dislodged. Rudolph the lion tamer tries to help but is killed. Konradin moves an elephant to push it the rest of the way, but he is too shot. Cernik's trailer, still pushed by the elephant, is the last one to reach freedom in Bavaria, where Cernik dies, a fulfilled man. The circus promises to continue, now led by Zama and Tereza.

Man on a Tightrope is less a circus movie than a politically driven escape drama. This is true even considering the participation of the Brumbach Circus, the actual troupe upon which this fact-based story is based. Director Elia Kazan refused to make the film until he had met the people who had inspired the story. He was impressed by their resilience and worked as many of them into the movie as he could. Most are in the background as circus performers, but two — Hansi, who plays Kalka, and Madame Brumbach, who plays the mostly silent, regal Madame Cernik — are quite important to the story.

Man on a Tightrope. Even in the midst of her husband's circus, Zama Cernik (Gloria) feels isolated and alone, for she has never been fully accepted as part of the circus family.

And it is a story. This is a fictionalized version, complete with fictional characters and a melodramatic storyline, of a real-life event. Writer Neil Paterson had fictionalized the event for a magazine article titled "International Incident," later expanding the tale into his short novel *Man on the Tightrope*. It is this book that forms the basis of the movie. Screenwriter Robert E. Sherwood's script follows the book faithfully, yet is disappointingly routine and rather shallow in terms of human drama. Kazan recognized this, yet was intrigued by the dramatic possibilities the story offered. Initially hesitant to make the movie, Kazan changed his mind after meeting the circus people and concluding that he "was dealing with an event in history," as he notes in his autobiography, *A Life*. Even with a script he considered inferior, he felt he could imbue the action sequences with enough energy and vitality to overcome that weakness.

An even bigger factor in Kazan's decision to make the film was the reaction to his recent (1952) testimony before the House Un-American Activities Committee. An admitted Communist, Kazan had named names when called upon to do so and his reputation had suffered greatly because of it. Darryl F. Zanuck, president of 20th Century–Fox, pressured Kazan to make this movie because of its anti–Communist stance. For his part, Kazan was nervous about making an anti–Communist diatribe in response to his own troubles, but he could not deny the essential truth of what had happened to Europe in recent years. In his autobiography, Kazan claims, "I had to make this film to convince myself — not others — that I was not afraid to say true things about the Communists or anyone else, that I was still capable of free inquiry, that I was no longer a Party member in my head." Therefore, soon after Kazan's controversial testimony, the director found himself in Europe making a movie damning the constrictions of a political philosophy he had previously supported.

Filming far away from the testimony controversy allowed Kazan to immerse himself in the work and rededicate his life. He found the circus people remarkable in their stolid constancy despite the hardships in their lives, and resolved that he would face his own difficulties in the same way. To the benefit of the film, much of Kazan's admiration for the circus folk is conveyed, whether directly or indirectly. Everybody in the circus takes their duties seriously, practices often and with diligence, and tries to contribute to the circus's welfare. They are professionals. Even Zama, Cernik's second wife and an outsider to the circus world, feels the desire to become part of the troupe.

Yet the film doesn't sentimentalize their dilemma. Kazan's naturalistic style is well suited to portraying this particular time and setting. He doesn't sermonize about how the circus people are being oppressed; he demonstrates it through their treatment by the military men and police agents. And the director symbolizes their desire for freedom in a simple example that Cernik relates to the Chief. When asked why one of the routines which Cernik had been ordered to change has not been altered, Cernik explains that it was no longer funny after the alteration. Removing the subtleties from the comedy routine robs it of its humor, just as forbidding individuality and diversity robs life of its variety. But of course the Chief doesn't care. He demands adherence to political guidelines above all else. Cernik publicly agrees, though it is evident that privately he despairs.

Even Fesker, the individualistic police agent, suffers the consequences of thinking outside Party lines. His fellow police agents distrust him and his habit of following hunches instead of following standard procedure. They are only comfortable in their closeted offices, receiving and relaying orders, whereas Fesker thinks on his feet and gathers impressions out in the field. When Fesker is taken into custody, he has already deduced that Cernik is planning to escape, but his colleagues find the need to eliminate his individuality more imperative than persecuting a run-down circus. Arrogance is also a factor, as Fesker's superior states he will deal with the circus "in due time," despite Fesker's pleas to arrest Cernik at once. But the most telling remark occurs as Fesker glances up at the monolithic police headquarters where interrogations are conducted, and where he is due to spend much of his future. "Sooner or later," he tells his arresting officer, "it happens to all of us."

Man on a Tightrope is certainly anti–Communist propaganda, yet it is more than that. Even working with this rather routine screenplay, Kazan manages to delve past its political ramifications to depict the human struggle beneath. Not everything works; the relationship between Cernik and Zama is awkward at best, and the turmoil surrounding Tereza's blooming sexuality is overwrought. Still, the film succeeds in portraying a group of people grinding out entertainment for others despite their own personal desperation. And it also works as an escape drama; after all, Cernik doesn't even reveal his intention to evade the Communist regime till past the story's halfway mark. Even with poor staging of the climactic escape, the film is exciting and suspenseful.

One area that should have been improved concerns the circus performances. They are desultory at best, which may be unavoidable given the run-down condition of the circus. Kazan may have staged these scenes so raggedly to emphasize the extent to which the Communists have impoverished the circus, but they are singularly unimpressive and unfulfilling (especially when compared to those of *The Greatest Show on Earth*). Even with the participation of the Brumbach Circus, the scenes are disappointing. The animal acts are similarly depressed. Late in the story, Cernik makes reference to "releasing the wolves" during the escape attempt, yet the animals released are very clearly dogs, not wolves. In any case, very few of the actual circus acts are seen, as opposed to Cecil B. DeMille's opus, where the circus acts were heavily featured. It is partly due to this, as well as the basic story, that *Man on a Tightrope* is not considered a top circus film.

Of course that wasn't Kazan's goal. What he was trying to do—and largely succeeded in doing—was to frame a historical event in terms of its participants. How the men and women involved in the risky escape attempt act and react is the crux of the story. The big picture is that the circus escapes from behind the Iron Curtain. Smaller vignettes illustrate how Cernik leads people to freedom; how his wife Zama rediscovers her passion for him; how

Man on a Tightrope. **Zama Cernik (Gloria) and her husband Karel (Fredric March) have a heart-to-heart discussion regarding the future of the Circus Cernik.**

Tereza's newfound maturity reflects that of her father in ways she does not understand; how people band together for a cause in which they believe; how Krofta's political beliefs eventually supersede his loyalty to Cernik; how Rudolph's cowardice is overcome by guilt; how Communism rots people from the inside out; how a shared cause can overshelm rivalry; how one cannot escape one's own beliefs; and how freedom is worth any price. All those smaller pictures are the human elements of the larger drama, and they make that drama interesting.

To lead his fictional circus, Kazan chose Fredric March, whom he had directed in the play *The Skin of Our Teeth.* The actor was having difficulty finding work because of an industry blacklist, but Kazan fought for his participation and prevailed. March studied the Brumbach Circus clowns and did most of his own tricks, dances and stunts, including the scene where Cernik and Barovic (Robert Beatty) beat each other bloody in Cernik's trailer. It was a physically demanding role for

March, who is onscreen the majority of the time, but he carries the film with great dignity. Another dignified presence was Adolphe Menjou, an actor whose conservative political views directly clashed with the liberal Kazan's. However, the director hired Menjou for his performance and was quite happy with it, and with Menjou's professional behavior on the set.

Young Terry Moore was cast as Tereza. Her dramatic highlight is swimming in a cold river with curly-haired Cameron Mitchell and convincing the audience that it isn't freezing her solid. There isn't much to her role, although she sports some of the same characteristics as her fictional father. In smaller roles, Richard Boone, Alex D'Arcy, Robert Beatty, Pat Henning and Paul Hartman lend authenticity to the drama.

Gloria Grahame is Zama, a role first offered to Marlene Dietrich. Zama is Karol Cernik's second wife; no background is presented regarding her past. She is an outsider when it comes to the circus, though she half-heartedly pretends to be working up an act of her own. She still loves Cernik but no longer respects him since the Communists have taken over. Bored out of her mind, she makes a play for lion tamer Rudolph. Her catharsis is harsh: when she verbally emasculates Cernik, he slaps her. That slap is a revelation to her. Suddenly subservient and startlingly aroused, she murmurs, "You should have done it a long time ago."

That one scene pretty much summarizes Gloria's persona at the time. Kittenish and unabashed about following her sexual instincts into trouble, Zama is concurrently shrewish and docile, selfish and generous, angry and expectant. She's tough on men, but once Cernik resumes control, her passion runs rampant. She needs a firm hand to keep her in line, but she's worth it. Nowadays the notion of a woman needing — or wanting — to be so manhandled is far out of fashion, but in the classic era of movies a woman who could take a little punishment (and sometimes even desire it) represented a tough, gritty femininity that men found enticing and even admirable. And if there is anyone who could maintain the thin line between victim and instigator, whether she was performing for the camera or arguing about what to have for dinner, it was Gloria Grahame.

Gloria has a few nice scenes. The first is when we meet Zama, lying on her back in bed with her long bare legs up in the air. She is trying to write or draw with a piece of chalk between her toes. She looks great and has an insolent attitude that speaks volumes about Zama's wandering state of mind. The next morning Zama encourages Cernik to fight back against the State police or else she may leave. After Cernik is taken away, Zama puts on lipstick and visits Rudolph. It's evident that she is much more dangerous to him than any of the lions. Later, she defends Kalka the dwarf against her husband's wishes.

Her best scene is the dramatic confrontation where Cernik slaps Zama. The gauzy close-up of her sensuous face after the slap conveys not only her newfound respect for Cernik but a desire that may never fade away again. Her next scene finds her supple and pliant for her husband, getting him coffee and bread, ecstatic with the exciting news of the imminent escape plan. Then she realizes that Tereza is already

gone and she covers her face in distress before telling him. Later, she waits patiently with the others for his return with Tereza. And when Krofta threatens Cernik, it is she and Kalka who push Krofta out of the trailer. She comforts her dying husband and expresses much grief when he passes away. Zama tells the company that Cernik is dead, and it is she who angrily prods the circus people — now her people — to get moving.

Gloria is good in the part, but she is undeniably miscast. Even without much makeup, she is too glamourous for the role, which itself is rather stunted. Only at the confrontation and the climax is she given anything of substance to do. She never seems convincing as an outsider to the group, as Gloria was social enough to blend in virtually anywhere, especially in a culture dominated by men. In hindsight, it is extremely easy to envision Marlene Dietrich in the role.

Kazan recalled, "Gloria Grahame ... was a slightly over-the-hill siren, intent on reinforcing her career." He recounts in his autobiography the story of how Gloria brought a set of heavy barbells in her luggage to Germany, meaning to exercise and increase her bustline, which she felt was too small. Evidently curious about the Communists across the border, Gloria reportedly snuck into East Germany in order to see them firsthand and found them quite large and imposing. Gloria was on her own in Europe, which proved to be a welcome break from all the romantic anxiety she had been experiencing in Los Angeles. While stationed in Europe making this movie, Gloria also submitted to more dental surgery. She had long been insecure about her face and between movies often sought surgeons who would be willing to help her "improve" her appearance. This time, however, something went wrong and a nerve to her upper lip was severed. She returned to America with a literal stiff upper lip and underwent more reconstructive surgery to fix the problem, which, unfortunately, never quite entirely repaired the problem. This became the origin of a nickname that would plague her throughout the rest of the decade: the Girl With the Novocaine Lip.

Kazan found the experience of making this movie rejuvenating. However, neither he nor Fox president Zanuck were completely happy with the finished product. Kazan found it too syrupy; Zanuck found it too lumpy. Without Kazan's participation or consent, Zanuck edited the film, reshaping it into a "conventional action melodrama" (Kazan's words), with the hope of "saving it in the editing room," as the saying goes. Kazan muttered his contempt and walked away from the experience determined not to let it occur again. The final film as it exists is Darryl Zanuck's cut.

Despite all the issues during and after production, *Man on a Tightrope* found favor with many critics. A.H. Weiler of the *New York Times* termed it "not only an arresting melodrama but a vivid commentary on a restricted way of life in our parlous times," praising the filmmakers' "artistic acumen to concentrate more on movement and characterization than on politics." Weiler also wrote, "Gloria Grahame is excellent as his erring wife, who draws courage and admiration from her husband's heroic deed." *Newsweek*'s critic called it "a highly atmospheric and timely melodrama, jammed with talent...." According to *Saturday Review*'s critic, "the whole adds up to an unusually absorbing picture given added stature by its implications in our world today."

Regardless of all the talent and effort that went into making the movie, it bombed. Audiences simply weren't interested in the travails of this tiny little circus, nor in the timely anti–Communist message. It has remained a minor title ever since, noteworthy mainly for its role in rejuvenating director Kazan (his next movie was the classic *On the Waterfront*). *Man on a Tightrope* is a good little movie that, like many others over the years, had enormous potential but did not completely fulfill its promise. For Gloria it was the second commercial failure in a row.

The Big Heat (1953)

CREDITS Columbia Pictures. *Directed by* Fritz Lang. *Produced by* Robert Arthur. *Screenplay by* Sidney Boehm. *Based upon the Saturday Evening Post serial by* William P. McGivern. *Director of Photography*: Charles Lang. *Film Editor*: Charles Nelson. *Gowns by* Jean Louis. *Art Director*: Robert Peterson. *Set Decorator*: William Kiernan. *Makeup by* Clay Campbell. *Hair Styles by* Helen Hunt. *Sound Engineer*: George

Cooper. *Assistant Director*: Milton Feldman. *Musical Director*: Mischa Bakaleinikoff. *Original Music by* Henry Vars. *Additional Music by* George Duning, Fred Karger, Hans J. Salter, Daniele Amfitheatrof, Arthur Morton and Ernst Toch. Black and White. Flat (1.37:1). 89 minutes. Released on October 14, 1953. Currently available on DVD. Previously available on VHS and laserdisc.

CAST *Dave Bannion*, Glenn Ford; *Debby Marsh*, Gloria Grahame; *Katie Bannion*, Jocelyn Brando; *Mike Lagana*, Alexander Scourby; *Vince Stone*, Lee Marvin; *Bertha Duncan*, Jeanette Nolan; *Tierney*, Peter Whitney; *Lieutenant Wilks*, Willis Bouchey; *Gus Burke*, Robert Burton; *Larry Gordon*, Adam Williams; *Commissioner Higgins*, Howard Wendell; *George Rose*, Chris Alcaide; *Hugo*, Michael Granger; *Lucy Chapman*, Dorothy Green; *Doris*, Carolyn Jones; *Baldy*, Ric Roman; *Atkins*, Dan Seymour; *Selma Parker*, Edith Evanson; *Dr. Kane*, Joe Mell; *Bartender*, Sid Clute; *Jill*, Norma Randall; *Joyce Bannion*, Linda Bennett; *Martin*, Herbert Lytton; *Mrs. Tucker*, Ezelle Poule; *Dr. Jones*, Byron Kane; *Butler*, Ted Stanhope; *Segal*, Mike Ross; *Reds*, Bill Murphy; *Mike*, Phil Arnold; *Dixon*, Mike Mahoney; *Intern*, Pat Miller; *Fuller*, Paul Maxey; *Hopkins*, Charles Cane; *Marge*, Kathryn Eames; *Harry Shoenstein*, Al Eben; *Hank O'Connell*, Harry Lauter; *Hettrick*, Phil Chambers; *Bill Rutherford*, Robert Forrest [Robert Stevenson]; *Al*, John Crawford; *Mark Reiner*, John Doucette; *Policeman*, John Close; *Councilman Gillen*, Douglas Evans; *Cabby*, Donald Kerr; *Moving Man*, Lyle Latell; *B-Girl*, Laura Mason; *Janitor*, William Vedder; *Men*, Jimmy Gray, John Merton and Nico Lek; *Lagana's Mother in Portrait*, Celia Lovsky.

Although *Man on a Tightrope* and *The Glass Wall* are quality products, neither film provided Gloria with the first-rate role one might expect of a recent Academy Award winner. That role arrived when she signed to play Debby Marsh in *The Big Heat*, a mere two weeks before production began. The part of a perky, fun-loving gangster's moll who learns the hard way that crime doesn't pay is perfect for Gloria, who has never been sexier, nor acted with more skill. What's more, the film itself is one of the best crime dramas of the decade, one which remains surprisingly potent, shocking and meaningful even today.

Less than ten seconds into *The Big Heat*, Tom Duncan shoots himself at a desk. His wife Bertha (Jeanette Nolan) finds the body and a suicide note addressed to the city's District Attorney ... and makes a telephone call. The coverup begins. Detective David Bannion (Glenn Ford) believes the widow Duncan's story until it is refuted by a hostess at the Retreat bar, Lucy Chapman (Dorothy Green), who had been seeing Duncan for over a year and who provides evidence that Duncan had been on the take. Mrs. Duncan admits the affair, but insists that her husband was an honest cop and that his suicide was due to worries over poor health. Bannion begins to wonder about the real cause of Duncan's suicide.

Word arrives that Lucy has disappeared, and Bannion finds her — in the morgue. He learns that Lucy had been tortured before being murdered (she is covered with cigarette burns) and he again questions Mrs. Duncan. His boss, Lieutenant Wilks (Willis Bouchey), cites pressure from "upstairs" and urges Bannion to lay off of this developing case. Undeterred, Bannion visits crime boss Mike Lagana (Alexander Scourby) at his home, essentially notifying him that he is on the case to stay. He roughs up one of Lagana's men and vows to get to the bottom of the Duncan-Chapman mystery. Lt. Wilks reprimands him again, but Bannion's cheery wife Katie (Jocelyn Brando) tells her husband not to compromise. Shortly thereafter, Katie is killed by a car bomb meant for Bannion.

Assured by corrupt Police Commissioner Higgins (Howard Wendell) that his wife's killers will eventually be brought to justice, Bannion disgustedly resigns from the police force and warns Lt. Wilks and his former partner Gus Burke (Robert Burton) to stay out of his way while he tracks down the killers himself. To protect his young daughter, Bannion moves into a hotel. Meanwhile, Lagana's right-hand man, Vince Stone (Lee Marvin), has his hands full with sarcastic girlfriend Debby Marsh (Gloria Grahame), who constantly teases him about jumping through Lagana's hoops like a trained animal, and about the bungling ways of Larry Gordon (Adam Williams), whom Vince had trusted to dispose of Lucy Chapman and, later, Bannion.

While tracing Larry, Bannion runs into Vince and Debby at a bar, where he sees Vince burn a woman's (Carolyn Jones) hand with a cigarette. Bannion steps in and forces Vince to leave, then refuses Debby's offer of a drink. Debby follows Bannion outside and persuades him to take her to the hotel where he is staying. He pumps her for information about Larry but gets nowhere and sends her back to her cronies.

When Vince catches Debby lying about where she has been, he angrily twists her arm behind her back, then throws a pot of scalding coffee into her face (offscreen). Still angry, Vince forces poker buddy Police Commissioner Higgins to take Debby to a doctor, then calls Lagana to arrange for Debby's permanent disposal.

After seeing the doctor, Debby slips away from Higgins and returns to Bannion, begging him to help her and making sure he understands that her face was scalded because she was seen with him. She tells him about Larry, whom Bannion tracks down and beats for information. Larry blames the murders on Vince. Bannion almost strangles him but then leaves him alive to run, knowing that he won't get very far. Larry is killed (offscreen) by Vince, who tells Mike Lagana straight out that he refuses to be the fall guy if Bannion exposes them. They agree to put pressure on Bannion's most vulnerable point — his young daughter.

Bannion visits Mrs. Duncan again and almost strangles her, but the police, notified by Lagana, arrive before he can summon the rage to do it. Back at his hotel, Bannion tells Debby that Larry confirmed that Mrs. Duncan has her husband's records on Lagana, and that they would be brought to the public's attention if anything were to happen to her. That is why Lagana wants Mrs. Duncan kept alive and is having her protected by the police. Bannion learns that the police protection of his daughter has been retracted through Lagana's influence, so he rushes to her side, only to find that she is well protected by his brother-in-law and his old Army buddies. Even Lt. Wilks and Burke arrive to help. Meanwhile, Debby takes matters into her own hands, visiting and killing Mrs. Duncan.

Bannion goes to Vince's apartment, but Debby has beaten him there. She surprises Vince by throwing a pot of scalding coffee in *his* face and tells him that she has killed Mrs. Duncan. He shoots her, then shoots at Bannion as he arrives. They have a brief gunfight, which ends as Vince runs out of bullets and tries to escape. Bannion beats him up but can't bring himself to kill him. Lt. Wilks and Burke arrive and take Vince into custody as Debby dies on the floor, tenderly asking Bannion to tell her about his deceased wife. In the last scene,

The Big Heat. Mob moll Debby Marsh (Gloria) turns her charm on Lt. Dave Bannion (Glenn Ford) in response to his questions about her boyfriend Vince Stone (Lee Marvin, not pictured).

Detective Bannion again sits at his desk in the police station, gets a call and joins Burke to investigate another crime.

The Big Heat follows the path of many classic crime films, exploring the morally gray area between the law-abiding citizenry and the greedy gangsters who prey upon them. The focal point of the movie, as well as William McGivern's source novel, is the exceedingly thin line that separates the cops from the robbers, and how each group finds benefit from moving toward or emulating the other. Lagana, once a petty thug, has risen to a place of prominence in Kenport, a typical American city. He even receives 24-hour police protection at the taxpayers' expense. But no matter how "legitimate" Lagana becomes, he continues his criminal activities, thinking nothing of eliminating people who won't cooperate or look the other way.

Bannion's investigation of Lagana moves slowly until Bannion begins to use threats and force to gain information. After his wife's death, he becomes more and more like the people he is hunting. Bannion almost resorts to murder himself but cannot bring himself to do so; his inability to cross that moral line is the thematic essence of the film. He hardens himself to become like the criminals but eventually reclaims his humanity by telling dying Debby about Katie and what she meant to him.

But it's more ambiguous than that. While Lagana is morally lost (despite his love and respect for his deceased mother and seemingly genuine feelings for his family) and Bannion remains redeemable, Debby Marsh is the swing character. She is introduced as the traditional gangster's moll, a decorative trophy sent out of the room while the bad boys talk. Debby certainly realizes what Vince and his henchmen are and what they do to people, but she enjoys her materialistic lifestyle enough to blind her-

The Big Heat. Mob enforcer Vince Stone (Lee Marvin) interrupts his poker game with Larry Gordon (Adam Williams, left), Commissioner Higgins (Howard Wendell, right) and George Fuller (Paul Maxey, far right) to talk to his girl, Debby Marsh (Gloria). He has learned that Debby was questioned by the police, and he wants to hear what she has to say about it. His manhandling of her is about to become extreme, in one of the most shocking scenes in 1950s American cinema.

self to her own complicity. This changes when she meets Bannion and is attracted to him; she's looking for something better and perhaps more exciting, and she recognizes it in the tough detective. He rejects her on moral grounds, genuinely hurting her feelings. Vince senses her change of allegiance and punishes her with a face full of scalding coffee.

Realizing that Vince or Lagana will kill her now that she poses a danger to them, Debby turns to Bannion. Although the death of Katie has removed most of his empathy, Bannion is still able to take pity on Debby and agrees to protect her. She helps him with his investigation, though most of her help is an effort to convince him to like her. When she sees that Bannion cannot kill Bertha Duncan to force the public release of her husband's hidden records, she handles it herself. Debby's cold-blooded

killing of Mrs. Duncan is morally repulsive, yet it is fully understandable. Since all of the violence and killing that have taken place have sprung from Mrs. Duncan's telephone call following the suicide of her husband, it is dramatically fitting that she should become a victim of her own actions as well. By killing her, Debby consigns herself to the criminal side of the law even though she continues to help Bannion smash and expose Lagana's empire. The final vision of her, dying on the floor with Bannion holding her hands, asking him to tell her about Katie, suggests that Debby is certainly worthy of one's empathy.

Another figure is ambiguous as well. Lieutenant Wilks (Willis Bouchey) is totally corrupt in the novel. In the film, he bows to unseen pressure from "upstairs" and castigates Bannion for "bothering" Mrs. Duncan. He doesn't protest his best detective's resignation and seemingly ignores the situation that leads Bannion to resign. However, he keeps tabs on Bannion, and even personally offers to help when his superiors remove the police protection surrounding Bannion's daughter. He arrives in time to arrest Vince and prevent Bannion from killing him. He may not be an exemplary cop, but he at least fulfills some of his duties. In contrast to Wilks, Bannion seems like a knight in shining armor, even while using excessive force to clean up the crime-ridden town.

Bannion has the same capacity for violence as Vince, but, unlike the psychopathic killer, he doesn't *like* it. Vince thinks nothing of extinguishing a cigarette on the back of a pretty girl's hand or getting his way by literally twisting an arm or two, particularly those of women. And that's when he's not angry. The really frightening thing about Vince is his temper; when he loses it, he grabs the nearest weapon and attacks without thinking. It is this brutality, this out-of-control ferocity, which makes such an impact on audiences because it strikes suddenly and violently. No matter how angry or vengeful Bannion becomes, he somehow retains control of his temper, and that's a big difference between the two men.

There is more of a difference in McGivern's original novel. Vince Stone is Max Stone in the book, and he's not quite as loutish as Lee Marvin portrays him in the film. Dave Bannion, however, is much more of a thinker in the book, in which he habitually reads "the gentle philosophers, the ones who thought it was natural for man to be good, and that evil was the aberrant course, abnormal, accidental, out of line with man's true needs and nature." That is, until Katie dies, at which point Bannion feels that they have nothing important left to say. It isn't until after Debby's death (self-inflicted in the book after shooting the Mrs. Duncan character) that Bannion is able to even recall any of the philosophy by which he once lived his life.

McGivern's book is adapted fairly faithfully, although many of the names have been altered or changed entirely. Debby Marsh is Debby Ward, Mrs. Duncan is Mrs. Deery, Lucy Chapman is Lucy Carroway, Larry Gordon is Larry Smith, etc. The book also offers a professional county detective, an inquisitive re-porter and a grateful young black man, all of whom help Bannion make inroads into his investigation. Plus, there's a killer named Biggie Burrows, credited with much of the action the film leaves to Vince and Larry. Although the film boasts fewer important characters, it does add Selma Parker (Edith Evanson), a secretary at an auto graveyard who tips Bannion to Larry's involvement and who positively identifies him. In fact, it is the women in the movie — Lucy Chapman, Selma Parker and Debby Marsh — who supply Bannion with his best leads, despite the danger they place themselves in by doing so.

Director Fritz Lang's film was considered to be quite violent for its time, especially towards women, which actually led a sizable number of reviewers to criticize it on those grounds. The scene most often noted is the coffee-throwing scene, which is still shocking today because it happens so quickly, and because coffee is so rarely used as a weapon. (It should be noted that the actual scalding occurs offscreen.) Lang's film also seems more violent than it really is because the violence is *personal*. Lots of crime films depict innocent bystanders or anonymous gang members brought down by gunfire during robberies and escapes, when bloodletting seems expected. Here, the violence is one on one, and it escalates. Tom Duncan shoots himself. Bannion socks one of Lagana's henchmen at Lagana's house. Vince burns a woman's hand with a cigarette. Kate is killed by a car bomb. Bannion pushes another henchman down at the Retreat and threatens Vince. Vince scalds Debby. Bannion chokes Larry Gordon, then releases him. Bannion chokes Bertha Duncan, and is forced to release her. Debby shoots Bertha Duncan. Debby scalds Vince, who then shoots her. Bannion beats Vince into submission. By the time the movie ends, it feels as if a lot of people have died.

By today's standards, the violence in *The Big Heat* is minimal, yet it still packs a wallop. Much of this is due to the depictions of the *consequences* of the violence. Katie's death shatters Bannion's happy home; his daughter is sent to live with relatives while he roots out those responsible. The last time the Bannion home is seen, it is cold and barren, as he closes it while he moves to a hotel. As critic Colin McArthur in the British Film Institute's volume on the movie remarks, this is the moment when Bannion "is propelled into the twilight world of the mob, virtually indistinguishable in his actions from those he hunts."

After Vince tosses coffee into Debby's face, her whole life changes. Debby has prided herself on her appearance — note how many times she looks into a mirror — and now she's disfigured. Half of her face covered in bandages; she cannot even walk the streets without being stared at or ridiculed. That one act moves her from casual indifference of her gangland pals to avenging angel. The moment when Debby rips off the bandages to show Vince her disfigured face is one of the most ghastly moments in cinema history, especially as she has just scalded *his* face and is showing him what he can expect. (Hot coffee would never leave such hideous scarring, but Lang simply used dramatic license, to very powerful effect.)

Debby visits Bertha Duncan at her home and they are both wearing mink coats. Before Debby shoots Mrs. Duncan, they share a brief dialogue in which Debby famously says, "We should use first names, Bertha. We're sisters under the mink." Debby then shoots her without any remorse. Debby's dialogue not only notes her parallel with Mrs. Duncan in terms of materially benefitting from their criminal lifestyles, but solidly links them in terms of destiny. As Mrs. Duncan is about to be shot for her actions, so will Debby. Such are the consequences of violence.

Ultimately, justice is served in *The Big Heat*. At the end of the film, Bannion is back where he belongs, Mike Lagana and Police Commissioner Higgins are indicted, Vince Stone is in jail and the secret which killed Tom Duncan is out in the open. The price for the urban clean-up is high — especially for Dave

The Big Heat. Vince Stone (Lee Marvin, second from left) has just hurled scalding coffee (the pot is still in his hands) onto the face of Debby Marsh (Gloria), which is already beginning to scar. This vicious act changes the destinies of everyone in the room. From left to right: Larry Gordon (Adam Williams), Police Commissioner Higgins (Howard Wendell), George Fuller (Paul Maxey), and Councilman Gillen (Douglas Evans).

Bannion — but necessary. Justice has also arrived over time for this unheralded gem, as *The Big Heat* has slowly been recognized as a classic of the cynical, hard-boiled school of mystery-thrillers, a worthy successor to John Huston's *The Maltese Falcon* and Howard Hawks' *The Big Sleep*.

Most of the credit for upgrading a familiar one-man cop crusade into a genuine work of art must be given to director Lang. Austrian by birth and trained in Germany during the silent film era, he learned how to tell stories visually. *The Big Heat* is a most welcome return to the smart and exciting top form of Lang, who had previously helmed such classics as *Metropolis*, *M*, *Fury* and *The Woman in the Window*, among many other gems. His style visually separates honest detective Bannion from the illegally wealthy hoodlums, contrasting the luxurious, seemingly ceilingless Lagana house with the brightly lit, tiny but happy Bannion home; comparing Vince Stone's huge apartment to the messy, cramped police station where Bannion works and the plain hotel room where he later stays; dressing the criminals and their molls much more glamourously than the working-class cops and their wives. The effect is obvious, but it works: The criminals make and have money and its benefits, but the working-class detective is the one who has the inner satisfaction and, ultimately, the happy home.

Bannion's home life is explored in some detail so that when it is ripped apart by the sudden, unexpected murder of his wife, his grief greatly moves the audience. While Lang's version of Bannion's domestic bliss seems dated now, it provides a clear contrast to the dark streets which, as a detective, he regularly prowls. The lighting is much brighter and the dialogue is lighter, filled with playful banter. It is a happy home. It isn't a coincidence that before the car bombing, Bannion tries to help his daughter build a castle out of blocks but clumsily knocks it down, just as he is about to destroy his own family due to his investigation. Realizing that the odds are stacked against him bringing Lagana to justice at the office, Bannion offers to just let events play out, but Katie (Jocelyn Brando) refuses to let him. She tells him not to compromise, and her words force him forward after her death.

As critic Danny Peary notes in *Cult Movies*

2, "Lang's films are about the territorial imperative, about how inhabitants of an environment react to trespassers." This is certainly true in *The Big Heat*, where violence occurs not in public places, rainy streets or shadowy wharfs, but in the main characters' homes and apartments, again and again. When Bannion's home is invaded by a threatening phone caller, then the car bomb, he closes it up, creates a refuge in a hotel room and takes the battle to Bertha Duncan's home and Vince Stone's apartment, with a side trip to defend his brother-in-law's apartment when his daughter is endangered. This just serves to continue to make the film's violence more personal and upsetting.

Even the very first shot of the film is startling. The camera is in the position of someone sitting on the desk, on top of which lies a revolver. A hand — ostensibly that of the audience, since the camera is placed behind the desk — reaches in, lifts the gun out of frame and shoots. The camera pulls back revealing a man — Tom Duncan — slumping over the desk, dead, in place of the audience, which is shocked by becoming directly involved in the sudden, unexpected violent beginning of this tale. Lang actually wanted to show Duncan pulling the trigger on himself but standards of the time wouldn't allow it, so he turned inventive and pulled the audience into the action immediately.

Besides Lang's impeccable direction, which conveys much of the film's meaning without expository dialogue, critics and audiences responded to the movie's great performances. Glenn Ford is excellent as Dave Bannion, convincingly conveying the detective's unshakable sense of right and wrong. It is certainly among Ford's finest performances, as much for the restraint he shows as for his intensity. The role of a one-man wrecking crew might have become cartoonish with a more heroic, imposing actor, so the prosaic persona generated by Ford is far more dramatically appropriate. Just as good is Lee Marvin in his first truly malevolent performance. Marvin shines after Vince Stone's angry rampages subside and he struggles to control himself. He is masterfully in control of the tone and inflection of his voice and body language.

As good as Ford and Marvin are — as well as performers in smaller parts such as Alexan-

The Big Heat. Before any of the trouble begins, mob moll Debby Marsh (Gloria) thoroughly enjoys her life of leisure. This is a quintessential Gloria pose, artfully relaxed and effortlessly alluring.

der Scourby, Willis Bouchey, Jeanette Nolan and Dorothy Green — it is Gloria Grahame who delivers the knock-out performance. As Debby, the bubbly B-girl who endures Vince's occasional tantrums for the sake of her preferred lifestyle, Gloria perfectly embodies the traditional gangster's moll. Whether languorously lying on the sofa or being totally absorbed in applying lipstick, Gloria is utterly convincing as the blissfully disregarding doll whose only concern is that Vince is beginning to bore her. Debby is clearly more than Vince can handle; Lagana and his henchmen all note it and tease Vince about it, which just gives him more reason to hurt her. Gloria is perky, smart and sassy as Debby, until the moment when her life changes unalterably. From then on, she is at first weak and pitiable, then vengeful, quietly determined and finally tender. It's a remarkable performance that hits a great many dramatic notes.

Gloria had won an Oscar the previous year for her work on *The Bad and the Beautiful*, been nominated six years before for *Crossfire*, and she had also been excellent in *The Greatest Show on Earth*, *Sudden Fear*, *In a Lonely Place* and others, but she topped them all in *The Big Heat*. That she wasn't even nominated for this role is a sad oversight by Academy voters, especially in the lightweight competition (in Oscar standards) of 1953. In his book *Alternate Oscars*, Danny Peary lauds Gloria as the best choice for Best Actress that year, noting, "Grahame makes sure Debby emerges as someone we can truly admire," praising her skill in capturing Debby's hidden self-esteem. Oversight of her great work was probably due to the middling reaction the film received and the beginning of Hollywood rumors about her on-set behavior becoming "difficult," but there is no question that some of Gloria's finest film work is captured for eternity in *The Big Heat*.

Gloria was worried that she didn't have enough strong dialogue to recite, and turned to Cy Howard for help. Known for his quips, he contributed two to the script: "We're sisters under the mink" and Debby's reaction when she first walks into Bannion's hotel room: "I like it — early nothing." This was one instance of Cy being more helpful than obtrusive. His humor helped leaven the dry script.

Although Gloria stated that she wanted to work with directors who kept a tight rein, she had difficulties with Lang. First of all, she had a great deal of trouble repeating specific actions, moves and expressions. A creature of the moment, Gloria liked to remain "fresh," which resulted in doing things a little differently from take to take, which drove perfectionist director Lang crazy. Although Lang hounded everybody on the set, he zeroed in on Gloria, who, by most accounts, took his curt and sometimes angry direction good-humoredly. The result, whether reached amicably or not, is a performance of great depth and force. The experience did not prevent them from working again within a year in *Human Desire*.

Why was this film, now considered to be a classic by so many critics and historians, then ignored? First was its perceived level of violence, which disgusted as many viewers and critics as it excited. The film did not receive as wide a release as it otherwise might have because of that perceived level of violence. Second, perhaps the public was tiring of movies about organized crime. Following Senator Estes Kefauver's televised hearings on organized crime in 1951, motion pictures were rushed into production which tackled the subject, such as *Hoodlum Empire*, *Kansas City Confidential* and *The Captive City* (all 1952), the latter a Robert Wise film followed by an epilogue featuring Kefauver himself. Two years after the hearings, perhaps organized crime stories were considered old news, though movies revolving around them would continue for another decade. Third, *The Big Heat* was a modest production for Columbia; the studio did not saturate the market with advertising or publicity. When it was released, a surprising number of magazines did not even bother to review it.

The reviews it did receive were all over the map. *Boxoffice*'s critic opined, "It's an oft-told story ... but this time around the yarn is sparked by exceptionally persuasive performances and an aura of hard-hitting realism." Bosley Crow-

ther of the *New York Times* wrote, "Mr. Lang can direct a film. He has put his mind to it, in this instance, and he has brought forth a hot one with a sting." Manny Farber of *The Nation* called it "a compelling crime show," while *Newsweek*'s critic termed it "a tough, smoothly written cops-and-robbers melodrama directed by Fritz Lang with something of the flair for suspense and violent action that he exhibited in a half dozen other films, including *M*, *Fury* and *Man Hunt*."

On the other hand, the critic for *Time* judged that it "gets off to a fast start and then slows to a walk." The British Film Institute's *Monthly Film Bulletin* called it "a tough and brutal thriller," but then remarked that "the main impression left by the film is of violence employed arbitrarily, mechanically and in the long run pointlessly." Moira Walsh of *America* was more condemning: "This aggregation of horrors succeeds in being so repellent, and also so unreal and ultimately ludicrous, that I would have not mentioned the picture except that, strange to say, it has been given quite favorable mention in other quarters." Robert Kass in *Catholic World* tallied the body count in the first paragraph of his brief review, then wrote, "There is, of course, no excuse at all for a film like *The Big Heat* but, in case you care, it is extremely well-performed by Glenn Ford, Gloria Grahame, Lee Marvin and Alexander Scourby."

As should be evident, it was the perceived violence factor with which many critics found fault, even though many of the movie's deaths occur offscreen. Actually, only three characters die onscreen: Tom Duncan, Bertha Duncan and Debby Marsh. Over the years since its original release, *The Big Heat*, much like other now-lauded classics such as *It's a Wonderful Life*, *High Noon*, *Touch of Evil* and *The Man Who Shot Liberty Valance*, has steadily grown in reputation. Perhaps it was ahead of its time.

Aside from its level of violence, which was noted in almost every review, the other constant is the universal praise for Gloria's performance. Though she made just a handful of *film noirs*, her portrayal of Debby Marsh is one of the most indelible portraits of the genre, both before and after the coffee scalding. Hers is a thoroughly charming and shattering performance, remarkably sensuous and deft, which instantly grants class to the gangsters with whom she spends time before revealing them to be thoughtless, despicable men unworthy of her loyalty. Gloria doesn't just act in *The Big Heat*; she fully inhabits her character with an intensity that is remarkable. From her sarcastic asides to her steady gaze as she mercilessly guns down Bertha Duncan, Gloria is *all there*. Debby is the story's true heroine; it is she who pulls Vince Stone and his lit cigarette off of the girl's hand at the Retreat bar, it is her horrible disfigurement which constantly reminds everyone (and the audience) of the utter vileness of Vince and his associates, it is her understandable (if still immoral) dispatching of Bertha Duncan which blows open the case, and it is her tender emotion for Bannion and his dead wife even as she lies dying on the floor which provide the story with its most powerful sentiments. Credit Gloria for maximizing the potential of this role and creating an enduring, unforgettable cinematic portrait. It is, arguably, her finest hour as a film actress, and her acting excellence is a key reason why *The Big Heat* is now widely considered to be at least a minor masterpiece.

Prisoners of the Casbah (1953)

CREDITS The Katzman Corporation. *Distributed by* Columbia Pictures. *Directed by* Richard Bare. *Produced by* Sam Katzman. *Screenplay by* DeVallon Scott. *Story by* William Raynor. *Director of Photography*: Henry Freulich. *Film Editor*: Charles Nelson. *Technicolor Color Consultant*: Francis Cugat. *Art Director*: Paul Palmentola. *Set Decorator*: Sidney Clifford. *Assistant Director*: Charles S. Gould. *Special Effects*: Jack Erickson. *Sound Engineer*: Josh Westmoreland. *Musical Director*: Mischa Bakaleinikoff. *Unit Manager*: Herbert Leonard. *Additional Music by* George Antheil, David Buttolph, Arthur Morton, Ben Oakland, Heinz Roemheld, Paul Sawtell, Marlin Skiles and Gregory Stone. *Stunts*: Bob Herron. Technicolor. Flat (1.37:1). Monaural Sound. 78 minutes. Released on November 3, 1953. Not currently available on commercial home video.

CAST *Princess Nadja*, Gloria Grahame; *Firouz*, Cesar Romero; *Ahmed*, Turhan Bey; *Marouf*, Nestor Paiva; *First Thief*, Paul Newlan; *Soura*, Lucille Barkley; *Selim*, Philip Van Zandt; *Second Thief*, Frank Richards; *Third Thief*, John Parrish; *Yagoub*, Wade Crosby; *Zeida*, Gloria Saunders; *Abdullah*, Eddy (Eddie) Fields; *Snake Charmer*, William Fawcett; *Emir*, Nelson Leigh; *Yussem*, Ray Singer; *Ayub*, John Marshall; *Mokar*, John Mansfield; *Rashid*, Eddie Fos-

ter; *Arab Dog*, Paul Marion; *Soldier*, Frank Ellis; *Slave Girls*, Mimi Borrel and Willetta Smith; *Guards*, Baynes Barron and John Crawford; *Thief*, Leonard P. Geer.

Surely the silliest of Gloria Grahame's motion pictures must be this sword-and-sandal programmer courtesy of producer Sam Katzman, which casts Gloria as a princess of 18th century Algiers. An incredibly prolific producer, Katzman specialized in making B-grade westerns, East Side Kids comedies, the Jungle Jim series and fantasy-adventures with historical settings such as *Serpent of the Nile*, *Siren of Bagdad*, *Prisoners of the Casbah* and *Slaves of Babylon*, all four of which were released in 1953. Many of Katzman's adventures were set in far-off lands and shot in color; however, they were filmed on flimsy, unconvincing soundstages and backlots as quickly as possible, employing the bare minimum of performers to tell their complicated and often ridiculous stories.

Prisoners of the Casbah begins as any good exploitation feature should, with the lovely princess Nadja (Gloria Grahame) taking a cleansing dip in an oasis pool. She is returning to Algiers with her father, the emir (Nelson Leigh), and a contingent of guards, harem girls, etc. While the guards amuse themselves wrestling, one of them dares to spy on the princess but is caught when he falls from his perch in a tree. Nadja demands that his eyes be put out but the captain of the guards, Ahmed (Turhan Bey), persuades her that a good beating will suffice. The grand vizier, Firouz (Cesar Romero), asks the emir if he may marry Nadja and is refused yet again. Firouz leaves camp to arrange the emir's welcome in Algiers. The emir decides that Nadja should marry, and offers her to Ahmed. The captain of the guards is flabbergasted, because he considers the princess a spoiled brat. He tells her so when she insults him, and she orders him dragged into the desert behind a horse. She changes her mind, rides after the horse and rescues Ahmed, only to threaten to have him boiled in oil.

Instead of riding into Algiers, Firouz stops at the camp of his own guard unit. They are to disguise themselves as Bedouins, attack the emir's camp, kidnap the princess and hold her until Firouz can pretend to rescue her, thus earning the emir's approval to wed the princess. After giving his final instructions, Firouz continues to Algiers. His troops don scarves to hide their faces and ride toward the oasis. The phony Bedouins attack suddenly, killing and wounding many of the emir's guards. The emir is shot and mortally wounded. One of the harem girls is also killed, and the princess quickly switches clothing with her. When the phony Bedouins enter the emir's tent, they are fooled into believing that the princess is dead. Ahmed is captured, but he recognizes the Bedouins as Firouz's men. Nadja remains unaware that Firouz is responsible for the death of her father.

Tied to stakes buried in the sand, Ahmed awaits certain death, but he cunningly escapes and takes Nadja with him toward Algiers. Knowing that Firouz will have him arrested and boiled in oil, Ahmed rides directly into the Casbah, the section of the city completely controlled by criminals. Firouz's men try to follow but are turned back by the Casbah's guards. Ahmed and Nadja are taken into custody by the criminals and given a hearing. Ahmed admits to the mob that he was a guard but now wants to be a thief; he offers Nadja the harem girl as proof of his thievery. The criminals, led by the so-called King of Thieves, Marouf (Nestor Paiva), are not convinced, but when Ahmed offers to bring them the gold of the palace treasury they decide to let the newcomers stay. Watching how Marouf leers at Nadja, however, Marouf's woman Soura (Lucille Barkley) insists that Ahmed and Nadja be married. They are, and the party lasts long into the night. Ahmed considers pressing his new wife for pleasure on the wedding night, but changes his mind when he sees her new companion, Allipasha, a large (but, unknown to him, toothless) cobra.

Marouf sets the Casbah's criminals to digging a tunnel to the palace, but the effort takes days. Ahmed enjoys his newfound leisure and begins to change his mind about Nadja. In the meantime, Firouz mourns the death of Nadja and her father; he had wanted to take control of the country legally. Now Firouz is forced by circumstance to assume control amidst the unrest of the populace.

When the tunnel is completed, Ahmed leads six criminals into the palace coffers. While they are looting the treasury, Ahmed finds Firouz and attempts to kill him, but the

Prisoners of the Casbah. A publicity portrait of Princess Nadja (Gloria) in seductive glory reveals a change in persona. Gloria wore a brown wig for the part and felt the dark look made her seem more serious, so she kept her hair that color for years afterward.

palace guards chase him back into the Casbah. Ahmed and the six criminals return with bags of gold and jewels, causing the people of the Casbah to proclaim him King of Thieves. Marouf, jealous of Ahmed and desirous of Nadja, visits Firouz and arranges for an ambush of Ahmed, in exchange for power at the palace. Firouz is astonished that Nadja is still alive and agrees; marrying the princess will end the country's unrest and ensure his future as its ruler. The ambush takes place; Ahmed kills his assassins but is wounded. Soura nurses him back to health. Ahmed is stunned to find that Nadja has been returned to the palace by Marouf.

As Ahmed and Nadja are already married, Firouz is furious. A go-between, the merchant Selim (Philip Van Zandt), arranges for Ahmed to divorce the princess in exchange for 200,000 dinars. Firouz, Marouf and Nadja enter the Casbah with a large contingent of guards and Ahmed keeps his word. He divorces Nadja, watches as Marouf is killed by a knife thrown by one of his own men, and attacks Firouz as the criminals jump and overwhelm the palace guards. Ahmed kills Firouz in a fight and then remarries Nadja while the criminals celebrate.

As should be evident from the synopsis, *Prisoners of the Casbah* is so full of nonsense that it is impossible to take seriously on any level. It is intended to be a witty, action-packed escape into the exotic 18th century milieu of Algiers, but Richard Bare's adventure is sadly lacking in wit, action or intelligence. Although it is lensed in pretty Technicolor hues, the script and direction are devoid of any meaningful color. The stars—particularly Gloria, who is wildly miscast—are unable to prevent the sheer silliness of the project from undermining their acting and dialogue, no matter how hard they try. The result is a fatuous, self-conscious exercise in escapism that barely qualifies as motion picture entertainment.

The problems begin early. In the oasis pool, Princess Nadja is supposedly nude. Yet director Bare allows her to be seen emerging from the water in a very visible flesh-colored tunic before her female attendants swathe her in towels. It's also evident that the oasis water is not blue. According to the movie's pressbook, it was discovered that Algerian princesses of the era often bathed in perfume. Hence, the water is dyed bluish-green to simulate a perfume bath. This fact is, of course, never mentioned in the film, with the result that the water simply looks dirty.

Firouz utilizes his own guard unit to attack the emir's encampment—and only wearing scarves to hide their faces—yet no one except Ahmed recognizes them. It also seems odd that Firouz's men have no compunction about slaughtering their ruler's guards. Surely they would be loyal first to the emir, then to Firouz. When Nadja switches clothing with her dead attendant, none of Firouz's men recognize either woman. Wouldn't they know what their princess looked like? The emir's blunt refusal to allow Firouz to marry his daughter is puzzling as well. As the grand vizier, Firouz would be an important and trusted personage. Nadja indicates that she likes Firouz, so the emir's refusal to allow her to wed Firouz—as well as his ignorance of Ahmed's true feelings regarding his daughter—seem utterly artificial.

Even more ridiculous is Ahmed's turn from stalwart captain of the guards to brazen raider of the palace treasury. It makes sense that Ahmed would promise riches to the Casbah criminals to ensure his survival; it makes no sense that he would actually allow the criminals to carry off the booty. Even with Firouz in charge, Ahmed's honor would lie with the country to which he pledged allegiance, not the Casbah criminals. Furthermore, when Ahmed kills Firouz—in one of the poorest sword battles ever put on film—he celebrates with the conquering criminals, who themselves have just slaughtered the palace guards. Are they now to rule Algiers?

The only noteworthy element is the color photography. The sets, both indoor and outdoor, are all too obviously studio-based. The action sequences are brief and shoddily directed, culminating in the aforementioned pathetic duel between Ahmed and Firouz. Gloria was 30 when the movie was released, Turhan Bey was 33, but Cesar Romero was 46; perhaps that is why the emir didn't want Firouz to marry Nadja. Nelson Leigh, who plays the emir, was only 48. This was also Bey's final film.

To its credit, the movie does have a sense of humor. Bey in particular delivers his lines with tongue firmly planted in cheek, and Gloria manages a few laughs here and there. The funniest thing in the movie is Allipasha, the toothless cobra, but it only makes three appearances. Writer DeVallon Scott intended charm to infuse the banter between Ahmed and Nadja, whose dislike for each other gradually grows into respect and, finally, love, but their repartee is usually more painful to hear than charming.

Some of the film's atrociousness can be laid at Gloria's feet. Turhan Bey was comfortable with this kind of movie and even Cesar Romero doesn't seem out of place. Gloria, however, is completely miscast. In a brown wig and exotic costumes, she looks fine, but her personality simply isn't suited for the part. In an interview with *Silver Screen*, she said, "A while back, I read in a column where Columbia Pictures wanted a glamourous, sexy princess for *Prisoners of the Casbah*, and I turned the page because I figured a role such as that didn't fit me. Then my telephone rang, and my agent informed me that I was being seriously considered for the role. 'Me—an Eastern princess—never!' I said, and yet a few days later I was signed for it, my first costume picture." Gloria should have trusted her first instinct.

Prisoners of the Casbah. **Princess Nadja (Gloria) meets Allipasha, the toothless cobra, for the first time and it is love at first sight. Gloria was spectacularly ill-suited for this ridiculous costume comedy-drama.**

Gloria was quoted later as saying she took the role as a "change of pace" from the *film noir* projects she was usually handed, and she also said she did it for her son Timmy, who wished to see his mommy in an adventure story. Closer to the truth is the notion that Gloria was pushed into it by Cy Howard because it represented the first film for which she would be the primary star. No Humphrey Bogart, no Glenn Ford, no Joan Crawford in front of her. Gloria would be top-billed, which to Cy meant that she was finally at the top. This was, in fact, to be Gloria's only top billing in the movies she made in her prime. She would not again receive top billing until *Blood and Lace* in 1971 and *Mama's Dirty Girls* in 1974. It should be noted that the below-average quality of these three particular movies, the only ones for which Gloria received top billing, is not coincidental. That is not to say that Gloria could not headline a premier project; the fact is, however, that she never did.

Gloria properly portrays Nadja as a spoiled brat, yet she is never convincing in her exotic costumes. Gloria's contemporary sensibility and streetwise experience simply do not match the princess's sheltered upbringing. There are moments when Gloria tries to convey her trademark sensuality in scenes with Bey, but director Bare evidently found the original takes too hot and excised them. In a *Motion Picture* profile, two instances are noted when Bare "had to restrain the natural Grahame tendency to light up the sound stages with high potency womanhood." Indeed, while the film's advertising spotlights "The Lady with the Golden Earrings ... whose tantalizing kisses inspired the crime that made the Casbah gasp!" and "Searing Sensations in color by Technicolor," the film itself is quite restrained in terms of prurience.

The advertising must have worked, as *Prisoners of the Casbah* made a great deal of money for Columbia. Gloria's name, plus the promise of her in revealing costumes, brought plenty of people into theaters. The critical response, however, was not kind, nor should it have been. *Variety* judged, "This trite costumer in Technicolor is strictly a filler booking offering a minimum of entertainment, even for the least discriminating filmgoer." The *Variety* reviewer called Gloria's acting "wooden," and other critics agreed. The most astute judgment came from the British Film Institute's *Monthly Film Bulletin*. The final line of its review stated, "Gloria Grahame deserves something better than this."

Gloria received better parts over the next few years, until she more or less voluntarily retired from the screen in the late 1950s. *Prisoners of the Casbah* was Gloria's only "costume" picture, and it was the first film in which she donned dark brown hair (in this case, a wig). Nevertheless, either she liked the brunette look or Cy insisted that she change her hair permanently to appear more serious, because she would not make another movie as a blonde for many years. While some of her later films were certainly popular, Gloria's personal popularity as a brunette was never as high as when she was young and blonde.

Prisoners of the Casbah also unfortunately proved that an important key to Gloria's successful screen persona was for her to remain modern and contemporary. Learning her lesson, Gloria returned to the modern era with a bang in her next three films, all of which promoted her sex siren image as spiritedly as possible.

The Good Die Young (1954)

CREDITS Remus and Romulus Films. *Distributed by* Independent Film Distributors, Ltd., and United Artists. *Directed by* Lewis Gilbert. *Produced by* John Woolf. *Associate Producer*: Jack Clayton. *Screenplay by* Vernon Harris and Lewis Gilbert. *From the novel The Good Die Young* by Richard Macaulay. *Director of Photography*: Jack Asher. *Film Editor*: Ralph Klempen. *Art Director*: Bernard Robinson. *Music by* Georges Auric. *Musical Director*: Lambert Williamson. *Production Manager*: Bill Kirby. *Camera Operator*: Harry Gillam. *Assistant Director*: Denis Johnson. *Continuity*: Angela Allen. *Sound Recording*: Bert Ross and Red Law. *Makeup*: David Aylott. *Hairdressing*: Joan Carpenter. *Chief Production Electrician*:

Louis H. Lavelly. *Dubbing Editor*: Stanley Hawkes. *Dresses Designed by* Rahvis. *Second Assistant Directors*: Robert Sterne and Ted Sturgis. *Draughtsmen*: David Butcher and Thomas Goswell. *Boom Operator*: Peter Dukelow. *Dubbing Crew*: Norman Daines and Bob Jones. *Special Effects by* Reg Johnson and Bryan Langley. *Stunts*: Robert Porter. *Clapper Loaders*: Alan Hall and Dennis C. Lewiston. *Focus Puller*: Ronnie Maasz. *Assistant Editors*: Stanley Hawkes and Roy Hyde. *Filmed at* Shepperton Studios. *Sound by* Western Electric Recording. Black and White. Flat (1.37:1). Monaural Sound. 98 minutes. Released on March 2, 1954, in London; November 29, 1955, in America. Not currently available on DVD. Previously available on VHS.

CAST *Miles "Rave" Ravenscourt*, Laurence Harvey; *Denise Blaine*, Gloria Grahame; *Joe Halsey*, Richard Basehart; *Mary Halsey*, Joan Collins; *Eddie Blaine*, John Ireland; *Angela Morgan*, Rene Ray; *Mike Morgan*, Stanley Baker; *Eve Ravenscourt*, Margaret Leighton; *Sir Francis Ravenscourt*, Robert Morley; *Mrs. Freeman*, Freda Jackson; *David*, James Kenney; *Doris*, Susan Shaw; *Tod Maslin*, Lee Patterson; *Girl*, Sandra Dorne; *Stookey*, Leslie Dwyer; *Carole*, Patricia McCarron; *Bunny*, George Rose; *Woman*, Joan Heal; *Dr. Reed*, Walter Hudd; *Burns*, Thomas Gallagher; *Milton*, Alf Hinds; *Simpson*, Edward Judd; *Winnie*, Patricia Owens; *Carruthers*, MacDonald Parke; *Hospital Doctor*, Harold Siddons; *Molly the Barmaid*, Marianne Stone; *Referee*, Joe Bloom; *Boxing Master of Ceremonies*, Patsy Hagate; *Policeman*, John McRae; *Doctor at Baths*, Hugh Moxey; *Promoter*, Philip Ray; *Air Hostesses*, Zena Barry and Sheila McCormack; *Young Man*, Alexander Davion; *Young Woman*, Stella Hamilton.

At the height of her career popularity, Gloria Grahame was struggling through personal problems. Divorced from director Nicholas Ray, she was living a paradox. She was never more in demand as an actress, but she was also unsure of her talent, apprehensive about her looks (resulting in unnecessary and damaging surgery on her mouth and lips) and uncomfortable being alone. She decided to travel to England for a month to film a British heist melodrama, and so sailed across the Atlantic on the *Ile de France* (the ocean liner later deliberately and memorably scuttled during the filming of *The Last Voyage*) with the man she was currently seeing, future third husband Cy Howard. It was a tumultuous month, as Gloria and Cy battled most of the time; when they weren't arguing, they were making up or doing the town. Cy was advising Gloria in every aspect of her career, and sometimes Gloria re-

HARVEY · GRAHAME · BASEHART · COLLINS   THE GOOD DIE YOUNG   JACKSON
IRELAND · RAY · BAKER · LEIGHTON · MORLEY

The Good Die Young. A U.S. serviceman stationed in Britain, Eddie Blaine (John Ireland), wants to keep his marriage to Denise (Gloria) alive, despite her repeated infidelities.

belled against his control, resulting in very public spats. As for the film, Gloria was paid $25,000 for three weeks work. Although she is second-billed, her role in the proceedings is disappointingly small, consisting of just three brief sequences with her friend John Ireland, who had menaced her in *Roughshod*.

The Good Die Young begins at night, with four men in a car parked near a post office. One of them distributes guns to the others and narrated flashbacks then relate how each of the men found themselves in the car this particular night...

Joe Halsey (Richard Basehart) is a Korean War veteran who asks for a week away from his job to which he has only recently returned, to travel to England and bring back his wife. His request is refused but he goes anyway. In England, Joe meets wife Mary (Joan Collins) at the airport; she tells him that she is pregnant. He's ecstatic, but he cannot convince her to leave her needy, hypochondriac mother Mrs.

Freeman (Freda Jackson). Boxer Mike Morgan (Stanley Baker) needs one more payday to reach his goal of having saved enough money to quit for good. His wife Angela (Rene Ray) is sick of the fight game and begs him to give it up. Mike fights one last time, with a broken hand, but wins the match. In the crowd, watching intently, is Miles "Rave" Ravenscourt (Laurence Harvey). After the bout, Mike and Angela are met by Angela's brother Dave (James Kenney), who needs money to pay off a gambling debt. The Morgans refuse to help Dave, even though he threatens to turn to crime to get the cash he needs. Mike gives his winnings to Angela.

Eddie Blaine (John Ireland) is an Air Force sergeant whose film actress wife Denise (Gloria Grahame) is clearly stepping out on him, ostensibly to further her career. She brings co-star Tod Maslin (Lee Patterson) home to her apartment and is surprised to find Eddie there. They argue and Eddie leaves angrily.

Rave asks his wife Eve (Margaret Leighton) for some money to pay off a gambling debt. She refuses, announcing that they will soon be traveling to Kenya. Rave ignores this and romances her, returning sporadically to the subject of the money he needs. Eve continues to stall.

The stories then begin to intertwine. Mike begins looking for a job, then accidentally crushes his broken hand, leading to its amputation. Eve writes a check to pay Rave's gambling debt, but destroys it when she receives proof of his infidelities, for which he apologizes. Joe and Mary Halsey are ready to leave England when news reaches Mary that her mother has attempted suicide. Mary refuses to leave her mother. Joe gets confirmation from a doctor that Mary's mother's suicide attempt was a ploy; Joe castigates Mary's mother, but Mary persuades him to stay in England a while longer. Joe goes to a tavern to cool off and meets Mike, who has been unable to land a job.

Rave visits his father (Robert Morley), who refuses to allow him access to his inheritance, questions his military valor (Rave had been decorated for bravery in World War II) and gives him this advice: "You could better employ your talents planning to rob a bank. You'd have more chance of success." At the tavern, Joe and Mike are joined by Eddie, who is acquainted with Joe through the armed services. Rave observes the men together and begins to hatch a plan. Eddie goes home and waits for Denise. She arrives with Tod Maslin again and Eddie loses his temper. Due to travel to Germany for the Air Force for a month, Eddie cannot contemplate life without Denise and remains in London. Denise goes on holiday with Tod for five days. At the tavern, Rave makes his move, befriending the three men, buying them drinks. They agree to meet on a regular basis.

Things get worse for all of them. Mike discovers that Angela has used his savings to bail out her brother, who quickly left the country, leaving them penniless. Joe and Mary fight bitterly about her mother's unnatural dependence on her. Denise returns from holiday still in Tod's arms; Eddie throws him out of the apartment and dumps her screaming into a bathtub full of water. Rave returns home to find his gambling debt paid and Eve expecting him to

accompany her to Kenya. He is ambivalent, close to activating his alternative plan. Knowing that his compatriots are as desperate for cash as he is, he unveils to them a plan to rob a post office of bank money passing through late at night. When the plan is presented to him, Joe refuses, but he doesn't leave. The four men reluctantly agree to think about it.

Back to the present. The men in the car await the cash delivery to the post office. When it arrives, a local constable sees their car and becomes suspicious. He approaches it and Rave shoots him. Constables close in as the men quickly grab the money sacks. Rave shoots at a female bystander and trades shots with approaching policemen. Eddie and Joe run with the money into a churchyard. Mike decides to give up and walks toward the police, unarmed. Rave shoots him in the back, then follows the other men into the churchyard as Mike dies in the street. They quickly hide the money sacks in a mausoleum, hoping to return for it later. They run to a rail yard and cross the tracks in between passing trains. Rave pushes Eddie onto a live rail, electrocuting him. He then follows Joe into a train tunnel, escaping the police, and they board a train. Joe accuses Rave of enjoying the act of killing and forcefully tells him that he won't be killed like the others.

They leave the train but Joe hops back on as it moves away, leaving Rave behind. At Mary's mother's place, Joe demands that Mary make a choice, and she decides to leave with him; they head to the airport with resolve. Eve waits for Rave at the airport, hoping that he'll accompany her to Kenya, but she doesn't see him. Arriving at the airport, Joe telephones the police to confess—but he is stopped by Rave. Joe shoots Rave, but before dying, Rave also shoots Joe. Rave dies on the floor, alone. Eve, giving up on her husband accompanying her, boards the plane to Kenya. Joe joins Mary but cannot make it to the plane. He drops dead on the tarmac, proving that for these men, crime certainly did not pay.

The Good Die Young is a gritty, *noirish* tale of how desperation can drive even the most honorable of men to acts as self-destructive as they are foolish. It presents the reluctant robbers as driven to crime by circumstance, and by society's neglect of them. All but Rave are honorable: Joe is a war veteran trying to pry his wife away from her mother's selfish clutches; Eddie is an Army sergeant trying to keep the wife he loves from other men's arms; Mike, also a veteran, is a boxer whose final injury eventually costs him his hand, and who is cheated out of his winnings by his wife's brother. These three men, and the women they love, are in trouble. Two of them are penniless, and the third needs to make money to end his wife's philandering. These men are the "Good" of the title, for their financial travails are commonplace and their destinies are foretold.

Then there's "Rave" Ravenscourt. Compared to the other men, Rave has led a life of luxury. He's had every advantage, including a wife who rescues him when need be. Yet Rave is morally bankrupt. He piles up debt but refuses to work it off. He shamelessly asks his wife for money using the promise of romance and sex as blatantly as any prostitute. When she delays helping him, he deserts her in favor of a greedy, dangerous enterprise that appeals to his increasing discontent and his penchant for killing. He persuades his new acquaintances to help him execute the robbery by plying them with drink and exploiting their anxieties. He constructs the robbery plan so that when (not if) violence occurs, everyone will be involved. And once the killing starts, Rave remembers that he likes the power that the gun gives him. He has no compunction about shooting at innocent bystanders or policemen, plugging Mike in the back and pushing Eddie onto a live electrical rail. The only thing that matters to Rave is his own self-interest.

The film, based on Richard Macaulay's novel, presents a compelling portrait of how such honorable men can be led astray by a charming devil and the alluring promise of easy money. It is grim and uncompromising in its portrait of how human pressures brought to bear against other people — especially by and toward one's own loved ones—can lead to unhappiness, despair and ruin. It is layered in irony, from the spectacle of boxer Mike Morgan losing his hand while trying to secure estimable employment, to the final resting place of the cash taken in the robbery. It purports that escape is an illusion, that debt must always be paid one way or another, that one's class is no guarantee of one's character and, finally, that the best of intentions sometimes cannot pre-

vent the good from turning bad and dying young.

The Good Die Young is a robbery film where the robbery is secondary, not to elaborate preparations, as in caper movies, but to the motivation and development of its participants. It's really a character piece about four couples, each in a different stage of marital evolution. All of them are unhappy, at least partially due to money worries. The majority of them are repairable, if attention and commitment were to be applied. The movie's point, stated succinctly by the closing narration, is that the money would not have helped the men, despite their faith that money could restore happiness. In the end, the quest for cash leads, quite literally, to dead ends.

Part of the blame for the men's troubles, the movie argues, falls on society as a whole. Rave is quite persuasive when he puts it this way: "You're all three good boys. There's no room in the world for good boys, don't you know that? All the good boys got themselves killed in the war, or should have done. The good die young. That's what we were meant to do. You ask the ones who stayed at home. But we didn't die. Oh, no. We fooled 'em. We stayed alive. And worse than that, we came back. So now we're in the way. We're redundant. We're not wanted." This argument, though it contains germs of truth, is certainly not powerful enough to coax men into crime. But these men are in deep trouble and are anxiously looking for the easiest way out of it. Rave is able to turn his new friends' bitterness in his favor. He also times events so that there is little opportunity to think things over. A master manipulator, Rave is able to control everything, except the men's basic integrity.

Lewis Gilbert directs *The Good Die Young* with immediacy and vitality. Filming mostly at night or indoors, Gilbert creates a *noirish* atmosphere more familiar to Los Angeles than London. He utilizes quite a few point-of-view shots, especially during the boxing sequence, which is filled with close-ups of Mike and his opponent punching right into the camera. When Mike discovers his savings are gone, the camera tilts for effect, throwing him — and the audience — off balance. When Rave delivers his "good die young" soliloquy, the camera zooms in on him for emphasis, then backs away as he

The Good Die Young. A romantic tryst between actress Denise Blaine (Gloria) and her new co-star Tod Maslin (Lee Patterson) is interrupted by the arrival of her husband Eddie (John Ireland, not pictured) in this British crime drama.

finishes. When Mary is forced to make her final choice, the camera is behind her, showing her between husband Joe on the left and her mother on the right. As Rave dies on the airport floor, the camera pulls back to reveal a sign reading "This Way Out." This was Gilbert's tenth feature film as a director and it shows much of the promise he would bring to later projects such as *Sink the Bismarck!* (1960), *Alfie* (1966), his James Bond films and *Educating Rita* (1983), among others.

Gilbert cast his film with stars both established and upcoming. The international cast blends Brits Joan Collins, Margaret Leighton, René Ray and Robert Morley with American actors Gloria Grahame and Richard Basehart, Canadian-born John Ireland, Welshman Stanley Baker and, finally, Laurence Harvey, a British subject who was actually Lithuanian by birth. Harvey, incidentally, married co-star

Margaret Leighton three years after making this movie, in which they play an unhappily married couple. Their real four-year marriage would end in divorce in 1961. Several of the players including Harvey, Collins and some lower-billed cast members had worked with Gilbert in his first half-dozen movies.

It was Gilbert's notion to adapt Macaulay's American bank robbery novel to the milieu of working-class London, and he co-wrote the script with longtime collaborator Vernon Harris. Because British banks refused to fund a movie in which a bank was robbed, Gilbert and Harris were forced to alter the locale of the robbery to a post office. There was also some fuss made about the climactic shoot-out, as British constables are not armed. This was addressed by having the unarmed police quickly call for back-up by a special unit of armed policemen. In any case, it was essential to show Rave shooting at everything in sight to depict his desperation and lust for violence and retribution.

According to *Suicide Blonde*, Gilbert considered Gloria "quite a character." Only three years older than she, Gilbert was surprised to find that Gloria was quite nervous about the film and her performance in it. He boosted her confidence by constantly complimenting her and by conferring with her romantic interest, Cy Howard, on how best to keep her in good spirits. Still insecure about her appearance, Gloria had dental work performed and surprised the production company by submitting the bills to them. She was also quite picky about her wardrobe, not wanting to wear certain items in the film, yet desiring to take others home with her once filming was completed.

Gloria was certainly the most famous star in the cast at that time, yet her part is subservient not only to all four leading male roles but most of the female roles as well. Of the four wives, her story is the least important — and the least interesting. She plays the part of a philandering actress well enough; indeed, it probably should have been second nature by that time. And the scene in which she is dumped into the bathtub and then dunked repeatedly is a highlight. But dramatically, one wonders just what drew Gloria to this project. Her role is the most glamourous of the wives, but that's the nicest thing one can say about it. Any viewers — then or now — hoping for a great Grahame performance are bound to be disappointed.

The rest of the movie, however, is solid, if somewhat predictable. After all, the title preordains what will happen. Some critics took aim at Harvey's callow character and praised Baker's work more than the others. Of the ladies, little-known Rene Ray delivers the best performance as the world-weary wife of Stanley Baker's boxer.

Boxoffice loved the film. "A taut, tingling and suspenseful crime melodrama, studded with fine performances by a strong cast, this is one of the best British-made pictures to reach these shores in recent months." *The Motion Picture Guide* termed it "a gripping crime tale" and "an atmospheric thriller." But the British Film Institute's *Monthly Film Bulletin* called it a "synthetic and pretentious melodrama ... increasingly implausible as it progresses." No

major American magazines and few newspapers reviewed it, indicating that despite Gloria's formidable star power, not to mention that of the rest of the cast, the film was barely released in America. In fact, though it was released in March of 1954 in England, it was not seen in the United States for another year and a half, and then only on a very limited basis. Thus, of Gloria's output at the height of her career, it is this film (and the obscure drama *The Glass Wall*) that remain the least seen by her fans.

Soon after *The Good Die Young* was completed, Gloria and Cy returned to the States where she immediately began filming *Naked Alibi*, the *Big Heat* clone set south of the border, which, along with Gloria's next four films, was released well before this film in America. Yet despite Gloria's nervousness about the film, her looks and her performance, England made a strong impression on her. She returned briefly in late 1955 to film *The Man Who Never Was*, and made many more trips to Britain over the years. In fact, after her film career wound down, Gloria spent quite a bit of time on theater stages in London and rural England. Gloria had good reason to appreciate the United Kingdom; on her father's side, she was distantly related to King Edward III, and on her mother's side, to the Scottish kings of the Hebrides.

Human Desire (1954)

CREDITS Columbia Pictures. *Directed by* Fritz Lang. *Produced by* Lewis J. Rachmil. *Screenplay by* Alfred Hayes. *Based on the novel La Bete Humaine by* Emile Zola. *Director of Photography*: Burnett Guffey. *Film Editor*: Aaron Stell. *Gowns by* Jean Louis. *Art Director*: Robert Peterson. *Set Decorator*: William Kiernan. *Assistant Director*: Milton Feldman. *Makeup by* Clay Campbell. *Hair Styles by* Helen Hunt. *Recording Supervisor*: John Livadary. *Musical Score by* Daniele Amfitheatrof. *Music Conducted by* Morris Stoloff. Black and White. Matted Widescreen (1.85:1). Monaural Sound. 91 minutes. Released on August 5, 1954. Currently available on DVD. Previously available on VHS.

CAST *Jeff Warren*, Glenn Ford; *Vicki Buckley*, Gloria Grahame; *Carl Buckley*, Broderick Crawford; *Alec Simmons*, Edgar Buchanan; *Ellen Simmons*, Kathleen Case; *Jean*, Peggy Maley; *Vera Simmons*, Diane DeLaire; *John Owens*, Grandon Rhodes; *Brakeman*, Paul Brinegar; *Davidson*, Victor Hugo Greene; *Yard*

Dispatcher, Don C. Harvey; *John Thurston*, Carl Lee; *Chief of Police*, John Maxwell; *Matt Henley*, John Pickard; *Prosecutor Gruber*, Dan Riss; *Duggan the Bartender*, Dan Seymour; *Lewis*, Olan Soule; *Gruber's Assistant at Inquest*, Hal Taggart; *Russ Russell*, John Zaremba.

Gloria Grahame returned to melodrama for Columbia Pictures, reteaming with co-star Glenn Ford and director Fritz Lang on what the studio considered a follow-up to *The Big Heat*. The temperamental German director had wanted Peter Lorre and Rita Hayworth for the leads of his filmization of Emile Zola's novel *La Bête Humaine*, but Lorre refused to work again with the director who had mercilessly bullied him during the filming of *M* almost a quarter century before, and Hayworth was prohibited from leaving the United States during a testy divorce. So when Lang chose to make the movie in Canada — due partly to criticism that too much of *The Big Heat* took place indoors— Hayworth was out, and the studio pushed for a re-teaming of Ford and Gloria. It is in this movie that Gloria's screen persona began to solidify once and for all. After *Sudden Fear*, for instance, Gloria had still been able to vary her subsequent performances; in fact, the range she showed in four 1952 releases undoubtedly led to her winning the Best Supporting Actress Academy Award. But once she was cast as a vixen with infidelity, criminal gain or murder on her mind in *The Good Die Young, Human Desire* and *Naked Alibi*— all of which were released consecutively within sixteen months— Gloria was unable to break away from the stereotype of a despicable dame; her persona was no longer very sympathetic.

Human Desire begins on a train. It is the Central National #153, and Jeff Warren (Glenn Ford) is working as an engineer, heading home after three years and forty-three days in the Army, serving in Korea. He is welcomed back by Carl Buckley (Broderick Crawford), an old buddy who works as a supervisor at the train yard and has recently married. Jeff bunks in the home of another engineer, Alec Simmons (Edgar Buchanan), his wife Vera (Diane De-Laire) and their grown daughter Ellen (Peggy Maley). Jeff likes Ellen; he gives her a kimono that he bought for her in Tokyo. It is obvious that Ellen likes him, too.

Carl loves his new wife Vicki (Gloria Gra-

hame) and while she seems bored, she also loves him. But one day he loses his temper at the rail yard and is fired. Vicki offers to get a job but Carl pressures her into asking a wealthy shipping magnate, John Owens (Grandon Rhodes), to give Carl his job back (she is acquainted with Owens, who does a great deal of business with the railroad). Vicki refuses but Carl insists. She makes the call. Vicki's visit with Owens lasts five hours, and the first thing she does upon returning is shower, which sends Carl into a rage. She taunts him and he slaps her around. Carl forces Vicki to write a letter to Owens, arranging another rendezvous, this time on the train to Chicago that evening.

Carl and Vicki board the train; Jeff is also on board, having filled in for another engineer and needing a ride back. Carl forces Vicki into Owens' compartment and knifes him in front of her. He also grabs Vicki's letter. Carl cannot leave without being seen by Jeff, so he sends Vicki to distract him. Intrigued by Vicki, Jeff has a drink with her and then makes a pass, which is rebuffed. He becomes suspicious when he sees Vicki with Carl at the station. Jeff hears about the murder from Alec the next day, and attends the medical inquest into Owens' death. Jeff has the opportunity to identify Vicki as being present on the train, but he doesn't. He realizes she is involved somehow and determines to find out what really occurred.

In a neighborhood bar, Jeff joins Carl and Vicki for drinks. A man asks Vicki to dance and Carl starts a fight with him. Carl is drunk, so Jeff and Vicki walk him home and put him to bed. Jeff asks Vicki for an explanation and she lies to him, implicating Carl as insanely jealous. Jeff considers her situation but remains aloof. Later, Vicki complains to Carl that she can't live with him any more but he refuses to let her go, or to give her the incriminating letter. "It's the end of everything," she cries. "This letter is going to keep us together," he replies. Vicki finds Carl's stash of cash and a pocket watch but not the letter. Desperate, she calls Jeff, telling him that Carl beats her and that she doesn't feel like a woman or a wife. Then she asks him how hard it is to kill someone. "It isn't difficult, Vicki," Jeff says. "It's the easiest thing in the world." Aroused by their baser instincts, they kiss passionately.

Ellen discovers that Jeff and Vicki are

Human Desire. Crafty Vicki Buckley (Gloria) uses the old "I've got something in my eye" ploy to get close to railroad engineer Jeff Warren (Glenn Ford) in Fritz Lang's adaptation of Emile Zola's novel *La Bête Humaine.*

having an affair; it disheartens her. Alec tries to warn Jeff about Vicki but he doesn't listen. Jeff asks Vicki to leave Carl but she cannot. She tells him that Carl killed Owens and about the letter. Jeff agrees to do whatever he can. Meanwhile, Carl is a broken man, trapped in a mess of his own creation. He gets fired again from the rail yard and decides to move away with Vicki. Unwilling to accompany him, Vicki prods Jeff to kill him, and Jeff is amenable to the idea. In the rail yard at night, Carl is drunk and Jeff has a wrench; still, he cannot bring himself to do it. Jeff and Vicki argue about killing Carl, so she tells him that Owens raped her when she was 16. Nonplussed, he finally realizes that she is manipulating him. He gives her up, but before he leaves he gives her the letter, which he had secretly taken from Carl.

The next day Jeff is running the train and Vicki gets on, alone. Jeff is thinking about Ellen, whom he is going to ask to a dance. Vicki is startled when Carl enters her compartment and begs her forgiveness. She spurns and ridicules him. Carl's jealousy grows when he thinks about her and Jeff, and she confesses that she wanted him dead, but that Jeff wouldn't do it. Then she confesses that she willingly seduced Owens when she was 16, wanting the wealth that he had. They fight. In a rage, Carl strangles Vicki to death. He sits dazedly, confused and without hope or reason, as the train rolls on.

Human Desire Americanizes the original Emile Zola novel, reducing Zola's complex vagaries of life, love, jealousy and murder to an allegory of deceptively simple people driven by their base instincts, and emphasizing the setting of the train. In this allegory, the train represents the pace of life: rolling forever forward, forcing everyone to keep to its schedule, bringing new people into the picture and taking others away, providing comfort and refuge for passenger and killer alike. Everything important in the story happens either on the train, in the train yard or close to the train yard.

The further the characters get from the train yard, the less important the individual details of their lives become. The film begins and ends from the perspective of the train zooming powerfully through the modern, curiously barren landscape of America (though parts of it were filmed in Canada).

Because this is more allegory than actual story, the characters rarely rise above the level of ciphers or symbols. Jeff is a war veteran who yearns for a simple, uncomplicated life of relative ease and comfort. He tells his aspirations to Ellen and she is amenable to the same dream; their budding romance is interrupted by his encounter with Vicki. Jeff wants to do the honorable thing by marrying Vicki, but she has other plans. Jeff is surprisingly sympathetic to the idea of killing Carl, and that is key, for the movie's moral point is that "human desire" can persuade anybody to do almost anything. No one is immune, no one is so honorable that they cannot be corrupted. Ultimately, of course, Jeff comes to his senses, leaves Vicki and makes plans to court Ellen. He fulfills his sense of obligation to Vicki by returning to her the letter that implicates her; after that, she's on her own.

Carl is the pitiable victim in all of this melodrama. He has a good job and one that he does well, although his boss rides him too hard when things go wrong. He loves Vicki and likes to provide for her; he refuses to let her work when he loses his job. But his intense jealousy — well founded, it turns out — leads him to ruin both of their lives. Carl's inability to control his temper is his downfall. He beats Vicki, prompting her to consider getting rid of him, and he kills Owens with full premeditation. Eventually, he kills Vicki with his bare hands. And yet, though he murders two people, it is Carl who suffers the most in this drama, for he must live with the guilt, as well as the anger that boils from being wronged in the first place.

Vicki is the catalyst. Having learned at an early age that wealth is not easy to attain no matter what the method, she gets a simple job at the railroad newsstand and then accepts Carl as her husband. "He looked big, solid, decent," she tells Jeff about Carl. "That's what I wanted most, I guess. Somebody decent." But Carl is anything but decent when he gets mad. Forced to distract Jeff on the train, Vicki sees an opportunity, for she witnessed the full extent of Carl's jealousy when Carl killed Owens. She cultivates Jeff as an ally, then as a lover. Jeff is decent; he wants to marry her. Vicki recognizes that she may never find a better man. But when she cannot pry the letter away from Carl — the letter that symbolically represents letting her go — she determines that he must die, and she tries to persuade Jeff to do it without actually asking him directly to do so.

Like the men, Vicki succumbs to her base instincts, which warn her to survive at any cost. But where Jeff only succumbs for a time to his lust for her and Carl simply cannot control his violent impulses, Vicki actually *descends* into depravity from a relatively high moral position. She tries to be a faithful, helpful wife, and only becomes unfaithful to regain Carl's job for him. Carl takes it the wrong way — even though he deliberately pushed her into the situation — and beats her savagely, then kills Owens out of spite. As their marriage hardens into a sterile prison, Vicki turns to sex with Jeff to free her from its futility, and, she hopes, from Carl. Even at this point, Vicki is still sympathetic. But she continues to descend. She lies to Jeff, attempting to lure him into murder. She pushes Carl away even as he begs for forgiveness. Finally, after Jeff gives her the letter but leaves her anyway, she strikes out on her own. Even here, Vicki is still somewhat sympathetic. She accepts what has happened and is doing the only thing she can to save herself. But then Carl enters and the bare-boned truth is finally told, in one of Gloria's wonderful monologues:

> See if you can understand this. I'm in love with Jeff and he walked out on me. Do you know why? Because I wanted him to kill you and he couldn't. You never knew me. You never bothered to figure me out. Well, I'm gonna tell you something. Owens did have something to do with me. But it was because I wanted him to. I wanted that big house he lived in. I wanted him to get rid of that wife of his. But he wasn't quite the fool that you are. He knew what I was after. And you know what? I admired him for it. If I'd have been a man, I'd have behaved exactly as he had. Now get out of here and let me unpack!

Naturally, Carl strangles her. At the bitter end, Vicki is just as depraved, if not more so, than the men who love her and who at least consider resorting to murder to keeping her for

Human Desire. Vicki Buckley (Gloria) displays marks of the manhandling she has received at the hands of her husband Carl (Broderick Crawford, not pictured) to Jeff Warren (Glenn Ford), in the hopes that Warren will murder the beast.

themselves. She's just as vicious and selfish as everyone else in the world.

Director Fritz Lang had intended *The Human Beast* (the film's working title) to signify the tragedy of doomed men caught up in the inexorable ebb and flow of life. The casting worked against him; Peter Lorre's innate desperation would, Lang felt, have proven very effective as Jeff became enmeshed in Vicki's machinations. Instead, Lorre was replaced by Glenn Ford, a solid but sometimes bland actor who would not allow his screen image to be sullied. Questioned, perhaps, but not sullied. Broderick Crawford, an Academy Award–winning actor, seemed perfect for Carl, but he was drinking heavily, was surly on the set and, unfortunately, contributes the least amount of acting prowess of the leads, disappearing almost entirely in the second half of the story.

The film's production had bigger problems than the casting. Producer Jerry Wald was insistent that the tone be lightened. "Everybody is bad in your picture," he told the director and writer Alfred Hayes. "Naturally, because Zola wanted to show that in every human being is a beast," Lang replied. Wald snorted, "You both don't understand it. The *woman* is the human beast." The producer would not budge, and so the film became more a triangle tragedy than the universal indictment of human emotionalism that writer and director envisioned. Lang was further enraged when the title was changed from *The Human Beast* to *Human Desire.* "Have you ever seen any other kind of desire?" he asked critic Peter Bogdanovich.

Nothing was more important to the film than its trains, yet no American railroad company would cooperate with the studio, as the script indicated that a mad sex maniac was killing people in sleeping compartments. Columbia finally found a Canadian railroad that agreed to let the studio film its tracks, yard and equipment, but at the last minute even that agreement almost collapsed. Director of photography Burnett Guffey did yeoman work collecting interesting railroad shots of Canada in the weeks leading up to Christmas in between bouts of bad weather. Then exterior shots were lensed in the town of El Reno, Oklahoma, for two weeks with the cast. The interior train shots were shot on studio mock-ups in Hollywood — evidenced by the width of the train's rooms and hallways, not to mention how wide and quiet the area is between the cars where Jeff and Vicki first meet.

Perhaps because of the physical difficulties, perhaps because of the philosophical differences he was having with the Columbia brass, Lang was not happy. Never known as a warm and caring man, he was tyrannical on the *Human Desire* set, especially toward Gloria. At one point Crawford had heard enough of Lang's bullying of Gloria, stepped in and lifted the director off his feet, threatening to show him some genuine method acting. Afterward, Lang was said to be aloof and indifferent on the set, just trying to bring the film in on time and under budget.

That he did, but the result was disappointing to both studio executives and the audiences who viewed it. Except in France, where it was embraced. In *Arts*, young critic François Truffaut wrote, "It is a solid and strong film, a beautiful block whose sharp edges follow the classical rules of cutting; the images are frank, brutal, each of them has its own beauty...." Even Truffaut, however, admitted that *Human Desire* was inferior to the Jean Renoir adaptation that predated it. *La Bête Humaine* (1938) had starred Jean Gabin, Simone Simon and Fernand Ledoux in a naturalistic and far more downbeat version of the Zola novel. Truffaut recognized that Lang approached the material from an utterly different perspective. Andrew Sarris in the *Village Voice* best clarified that, writing, "Whereas Renoir's *The Human Beast* is the tragedy of a doomed man caught up in the flow of life, Lang's remake *Human Desire* is the nightmare of an innocent man enmeshed in the tangled strands of fate. What we remember in Renoir are the faces of Gabin, Simon and Ledoux. What we remember in Lang are the geometrical patterns of trains, tracks and fateful camera angles. As Renoir is humanism, Lang is determinism. As Renoir is concerned

with the plight of his characters, Lang is obsessed with the structure of the trap."

Most critics felt that Lang had missed the mark. Bosley Crowther of the *New York Times* wrote, "Mr. Ford seems no closer to madness when he finds himself lusting for Miss Grahame than he might be if he were yearning for a chocolate malted milk," and found the proceedings quite dull. *Variety*'s critic concluded that "the development is contrived and the characters shallow." The British Film Institute's *Monthly Film Bulletin* concurred: "Such of the story as remains is reduced to a rather violent and depressing blood-and-thunder level by the near-sadistic manner in which the incidents are, whenever possible, handled. Apart from this, the film lacks any sort of style or atmosphere such as his distinguished even some of the weakest of Lang's recent work."

Apart from Guffey's cinematography, there is one other good reason to watch the film — Gloria Grahame. It can be convincingly argued that her male co-stars were miscast. But not Gloria. In his comparison of the Zola filmizations, Truffaut wrote that directors Renoir and Lang "also have in common a predilection for catlike actresses, feline heroines. Gloria Grahame is the perfect American replica of Simone Simon...." And in his book *Film Noir: A Comprehensive Illustrated Reference to Movies, Terms and Persons*, Michael Stephens opines, "Gloria Grahame's performance as Vicki Buckley is masterful, the film's saving grace. Vicki is the archetypal femme fatale, sadistic and masochistic at once. Grahame spends much of the film lounging around in lingerie, and Lang's camera seems to linger on her like an irresistible erotic angel of death. It is Gloria Grahame's finest performance."

Although the film degenerates into melodrama pretty quickly, Gloria prevents it from submerging into turgidity. Her Vicki is smart, adroit and *likable* all the way to the climax, when the real Vicki is finally revealed. Vicki tells just enough of the truth in every scene to justify her emotions and actions; her reactions to being beaten by Crawford are pitch-perfect and the terror on her face is utterly convincing. In fact, Vicki is so believable as a victim and persuasive as a reluctant would-be murderess that when she ultimately tells her husband what she really thinks of him, it is a genuine shock.

That climactic scene embodies Zola's theme ("in every human being is a beast") to perfection, while at the same time fulfilling producer Jerry Wald's position that "the *woman* is the human beast." She is superb.

Gloria did not enjoy making the film, as it was a very physical shoot for her and Lang was less than friendly. The scene in which Crawford slaps her around required twenty-six takes. At one point, Vicki shows Jeff the bruises on her shoulder where Carl had manhandled her. The fingerprints are Lang's, painted in by the director (a shot of Lang's hand, handprint or fingerprints appears in just about all of the director's films). Gloria was not the first choice for Vicki; Barbara Stanwyck, Olivia de Havilland and Rita Hayworth had each been asked before Gloria. But Gloria never minded about being second (or third, or fourth) choice. She often called herself "the replacement" due to the number of parts she took after other actresses had bowed out. Gloria accepted parts that interested her and always found ways to make them her own. In *Human Desire* her triumph is that final scene where she really lets loose, convincing everyone that Vicki truly is "a human beast," just as Zola proffered some sixty years previously. Gloria had once again fulfilled her role in somebody's artistic vision.

Just ten days after *Human Desire* premiered, Gloria married Cy Howard. For all their constant bantering and bickering, some of which evolved into real battling, they were inseparable. They had been together for more than two years, and finally agreed that it was time. Cy was now steadily writing gags for the biggest comedians in Hollywood, Dean Martin and Jerry Lewis (both attended the wedding), and Gloria was busy making an average of three movies a year. She increasingly relied on his advice on what parts to accept and how to play them. It was a happy time for Gloria, especially once she finished shooting *Human Desire*. Twenty-six takes of a slapping scene had been, in her opinion, somewhat more than necessary.

Naked Alibi (1954)

CREDITS Universal Pictures. *Directed by* Jerry Hopper. *Produced by* Ross Hunter. *Screenplay by* Lawrence Roman. *From the original story Cry Copper by* J. Robert Bren and Gladys Atwater. *Director of Photography*: Russell Metty. *Film Editor*: Al Clark. *Art Direction*: Alexander Golitzen and Emrich Nicholson. *Set Decorations*: Russell A. Gausman and Ray Jeffers. *Sound*: Leslie I. Carey and Robert Pritchard. *Dance Numbers Staged by* Kenny Williams. *Gowns by* Rosemary Odell. *Hair Stylist*: Joan St. Oegger. *Makeup*: Bud Westmore. *Assistant Director*: Tom Shaw. *Musical Supervision by* Joseph Gershenson. *Original Music by* Hans J. Salter and Frank Skinner. *Additional Music by* Herman Stein. *Stunts by* John Daheim, Sol Gorss and Eddie Parker. Black and White. Matted Widescreen (1.85:1). Monaural Sound. 86 minutes. Released on October 1, 1954. Not currently available on DVD. Previously available on VHS.

CAST *Chief Detective Joseph E. Conroy*, Sterling Hayden; *Marianna*, Gloria Grahame; *Al Willis*, Gene Barry; *Helen Willis*, Marcia Henderson; *Detective Lieutenant Parks*, Casey Adams [Max Showalter]; *Petey*, Billy Chapin; *Captain Owen Kincaide*, Chuck Connors; *Matt Matthews*, Don Haggerty; *Chief A.S. Babcock*, Stuart Randall; *Tony*, Don Garrett; *Felix*, Richard Beach; *Irish (Bartender)*, Tol Avery; *Gerald Frazier*, Paul Leavitt; *Commissioner F.J. O'Day*, Fay Roope; *Otto Stoltz*, Joseph Mell; *Detective Sergeant Jenkins*, John Daheim; *Jean Jenkins*, Kathleen O'Malley; *Stu*, John Alvin; *Lois*, Dee Carroll; *Councilman Edgar Goodwin*, Frank Wilcox; *Lieutenant Fitzpatrick*, Bud Wolfe; *Charlie*, Paul Newlan; *Henchman*, Eddie Parker; *Waiter*, Dick Crockett; *Guard*, Dean Cromer; *Motel Proprietor*, Alan DeWitt; *Communications Officer*, Herbert Ellis; *Round Man*, Michael Fox; *Counterman*, Phil Garris; *Man in Bar who Starts Fight*, Sol Gorss; *Employee*, Brett Halsey; *Bride*, Beverly Ruth Jordan; *Man in Mexican Bar*, Kenner G. Kemp; *Drunk*, Frank Marlowe; *Bartender*, William H. O'Brien; *Guard # 2*, Carlos Rivero; *Highway Patrol Officer*, Robert Stevenson; *Hood*, Jack Stoney; *Border Patrol Officer*, Lewis Wilson; *Detectives*, Byron Keith and Mike Mahoney; *Bit Parts*, Cheryll Clarke, Barbara Marshall, Alan Paige, Byron Poindexter, Ray Quinn and Max Trumpower; *Gloria Grahame's Singing Voice Dubbed by* Jo Ann Greer.

Fully enmeshed within her *film noir* persona by this time, Gloria moved from the cold steel railroad yards of the poorly titled *Human Desire* to a smoldering little California town on the Mexican border in the luridly titled *Naked Alibi*. Gloria, once again playing a small-time songstress, is at least provided with some sexy dresses to wear, but her part is ill-conceived and somewhat cumbersome. *Naked Alibi* bears some resemblance to *The Big Heat*, but retains little of that film's stark glory. Yet strangely enough, though *The Big Heat* is a far superior film, Gloria enjoyed making *Naked Alibi* more than any other motion picture during the most successful phase of her career.

In a police station in a town near Los Angeles, three detectives question a man in regard to some local jewel robberies. The man is Al Willis (Gene Barry) and he is obviously intoxicated. He refuses to answer their questions and socks Lieutenant Parks (Casey Adams) with an ashtray before the detectives subdue him. Willis swears vengeance on Parks ("I'll get even! I always do!") even though it was Willis himself who started the fracas. Witnessing Willis' outburst is Chief of Detectives Joe Conroy (Sterling Hayden). But Willis' record is clean and he is freed. Willis is shown to have a wife (Marcia Henderson) and young daughter, and he owns a bakery. He seems to be an honest, ordinary citizen, evidently just having a bad night.

Lieutenant Parks is gunned down on a city street. Willis is questioned intently but never cracks, and Conroy is forced to let him go because there is no proof. The two other detectives who questioned Willis are killed when their squad car explodes (in a scene very similar to one in *The Big Heat*). Conroy is convinced that Willis is behind the murder spree, and puts

Naked Alibi. Publicity shot of Marianna (Gloria). It may be the sexiest pose of Gloria's career.

continuous pressure on him, finally leading to a public confrontation that results in Conroy's firing. Conroy doesn't give up, however; he teams with private detective Matt Matthews (Don Haggerty) to follow Willis around the clock. Paranoid from the surveillance, Willis convinces his wife that he needs to get away. He flees to Border City, a town just north of the U.S.-Mexico line. At the El Perico Cantina, Willis watches a saloon singer shimmy her way through the song "Ace in the Hole." The singer is Marianna (Gloria Grahame) and she is romantically involved with Willis—and unaware that he is married.

Conroy follows and soon falls prey to three men who rob him and beat him senseless. A young shoeshine boy named Petey (Billy Chapin) finds Conroy in an alley and persuades his uncle Charlie (Paul Newlan) to offer Conroy shelter so he can heal. Purely by coincidence, Marianna is also there, and she finds a newspaper clipping with Willis' picture, which she keeps for herself. Conroy rests for a couple of days before resuming his search for Willis. He sees Willis with Marianna, and guesses that she is ignorant of Willis' other life. Marianna and Conroy each try to subtly make the other talk about Willis, but without success. Marianna presses Willis to marry her, but to no avail. They have an argument and she accuses him of being married. Willis beats her up, then apologizes and tells her he means to get a divorce so he can marry her. Marianna no longer believes him, and she tells Conroy that Willis is nearby, and that he knows Conroy is in town looking for him. Conroy sees the bruises caused by Willis and realizes that she is in danger. He tells her about the murders and shows her a telegram from Nashville, where Willis is suspected to be the leader of a hijacking ring.

Conroy is caught by Willis and two of his henchmen and taken to the El Perico. Willis is ebullient, gallantly forgiving Conroy for persecuting him, and insists on buying him dinner. At the El Perico, Marianna is forced to join them; seeing them together, Willis becomes insanely jealous. Willis stages a bar fight and arranges for the lights to go out, during which time his two dinner guests will be knifed to death. But Conroy is ready and he and Marianna escape through the darkness. Willis follows, armed with a gun, and he and Conroy have a terrific fight. After Conroy knocks Willis unconscious, the two men and Marianna head for Conroy's home town, where he plans to force Willis to surrender the weapon that killed Lieutenant Parks. Willis' henchmen report his disappearance to the police and a manhunt begins for Conroy, who is suspected of kidnapping the ostensibly innocent Willis. Conroy eludes the police by ditching the car and hiding Willis and Marianna in the back of a semi-trailer headed north.

Back in town, Willis frees himself, jumps Conroy and gets away, but Conroy guesses where he is headed. Cops nab Conroy so Marianna follows Willis to the Church on the Square, where Willis hid the murder weapon. Desperate, Willis forces Marianna to accompany him up to the roof when the cops arrive. They are led by Conroy, now back in the good graces of the police force. Marianna tries to escape and Willis shoots her in the back. Willis tries to make a rooftop getaway but is shot by a police officer, falling from the roof. Conroy finds Marianna, who dies in his arms after wishing that they had met sooner. Alone again, Conroy slowly walks away, leaving the crime scene and the recent, violent past behind him.

Naked Alibi, though based on an original story called *Cry Copper* by J. Robert Bren and Gladys Atwater, seems to owe a lot to *The Big Heat*. Once again a detective hot on the trail of crime is thrown off the force, only to continue the investigation on his own. In both movies people are killed when cars explode. Once again a Gloria Grahame character is caught between the criminal she's seeing and the sensitive cop who represents salvation. In both movies she is killed by the wicked man and dies in the arms of the honest cop who tries but cannot save her. And once again the disgraced cop returns to the fold, the only place he will ever feel safe and secure. There are certainly differences but *Naked Alibi* unmistakably has a similar structure. *The Big Heat* had not been a big hit but it was recognized throughout the industry to represent a substantial and potent formula, one which established certain parameters that promised solid commercial results if followed. Those parameters included casting a hard-boiled lead actor and teaming him with a hard-boiled dame — someone like Gloria, if not Gloria herself. Those parameters also called for a

high degree of luridness, and here *Naked Alibi* outshines its predecessor.

A great deal of nastiness pervades *Naked Alibi*, most of it surrounding Al Willis. At first the film gives Willis the benefit of the doubt, presenting him as an ordinary, honest working man with a wife and child. But once he reaches Border City he is unveiled as the sadistic bully he really is. He slaps around Marianna on-screen twice, once severely, and is constantly seen to be hitting people, knocking them over for fun, or shooting at them. He bullies Marianna psychologically as well, once he has perceived that she has feelings for Conroy. The scene where he buys Conroy dinner and then spends most of the meal trying to make Marianna admit that she has switched allegiances is all about humiliating her. Finally, when Marianna tries to escape him on the roof, Willis savagely shoots her in the back. Even in his final moments he's yelling and firing at the cops with all the venom that remains in him.

The film deserves some credit for presenting one situation and then reversing it, thus flipping audience expectations. At the beginning, when Willis is being questioned, sympathy is generated for Willis and against the cops. Conroy believes that Willis is guilty but he has no evidence, just a hunch. And when he begins to follow Willis all over town, it seems that Conroy is the crazy man who should be stopped. But in Border City, when Conroy is robbed and beaten, he becomes the empathic hero and the real story structure is set in motion. From that point onward, viewers realize that Conroy was right all along and that Al Willis is a deviant sociopath.

Willis' character is the film's greatest flaw, because there is such an unexplained, unbelievable discrepancy between the kind, loving husband and father seen early in the film and the rabid, cop-hating madman viewed later. It's one thing for a character to be duplicitous, to lead a secret life; however, there is absolutely no connection between the two disparate personalities of Al Willis. His wife seems to love him and the people who work for him at the bakery appear to get along fine with him. He even seems conscientious about his work. Yet when he goes to Border City he carries himself like a hardened criminal — with henchmen, yet! — accustomed to being able to act any way

Naked Alibi. Marianna (Gloria) cozies up with Joe Conroy (Sterling Hayden), unaware that he is a detective looking for her current boyfriend, Al Willis (Gene Barry, not pictured).

he likes. This evil side is reinforced by the telegram Conroy receives that identifies Willis as the suspected leader of a hijacking ring in Nashville. Hijacking? What has that got to do with anything else in the movie? Willis was brought in for questioning at the start of the story in regard to jewel store robberies. And he is evidently innocent of that, since the subject is never mentioned again and stolen jewels are never seen or discussed! The only criminal talent Willis displays is attacking the police officers who wish to question him, and shooting at the ones who chase him in Border City. It is inferred that he goes to Border City on occasional "business trips," but how could someone who only gets into town once in a great while have such criminal power or henchmen? Willis' background, like much of the film, doesn't stand up to close scrutiny.

The most interesting aspect of Willis is that he is portrayed by Gene Barry, a suave, dapper, almost genteel actor cast here firmly against type. Best known at the time for playing scientists in *The Atomic City* (1952) and *The*

War of the Worlds (1953), Barry reveled in the opportunity to change his cinematic image. He is most effective early in the story, when Willis' innocence is still a possibility. Once in Border City, Barry tends to ham it up, using broader strokes to paint his picture, and the effect is diffusion.

Better suited to his role is Sterling Hayden. Tall and ruggedly handsome, Hayden could play either side of the law effectively. He's solid as a rock as Conroy and his doggedness is completely believable. Hayden was born for this kind of film, although he was usually better than the material, which is certainly true here. However, one aspect of his performance which fails to impress is the growing emotional attachment that Conroy is supposed to have for Marianna. There just isn't much chemistry at all between Hayden and Gloria, despite Gloria's attraction to him. In *Suicide Blonde* Vincent Curcio states that Hayden was scared silly by Gloria's advances, and it's apparent in the film that she makes him nervous. That is a shame because their personas are so well suited to each other. It is entirely possible that Gloria's attention to Hayden was meant to bolster his performance, or perhaps even to make husband Cy Howard jealous (Gloria was known to do that once in a while).

Gloria dazzles the eyes in *Naked Alibi*. She is introduced almost 30 minutes into the story wearing a sexy black satin gown with spaghetti straps keeping it legal, singing "Ace in the Hole" to a very quiet crowd in the El Perico Cantina. She looks great in the dress and shimmies a bit during the song, but it isn't Gloria's voice. It is Jo Ann Greer's voice, and it unfortunately is quite obvious that Gloria is dubbed. Greer's voice gives the song some pop, while Gloria's physical performance of the song is rather subdued. Of Gloria's four performances as a singer, this is the least impressive. But with her brown hair cut short and curled around her face, wearing a pair of long earrings and boasting bountiful red lips, Gloria is at her sexiest. Curcio, in fact, chose a *Naked Alibi* pose for the cover of his biography of Gloria, and with good reason. Rarely has Gloria looked more sensuous in a movie than she does in *Naked Alibi*.

Like Hayden, Gloria was born for this type of movie, and also like him, she was often better than the material. *Naked Alibi* is a classic case of the performers having to do what they can to make a mundane movie palatable. Gloria tries, but she doesn't seem to find a handle for her character. According to the backstory Marianna provides Conroy, she was with Willis in Nashville, so it can be presumed she knew about his nefarious past. That would make her at least an accomplice to his crimes. But Marianna never acts like she knows anything about Willis' misdeeds. She keeps expecting him to marry her! And when she discovers that he is already married, it still doesn't clue her into the fact that he is a cop-killing criminal. Gloria simply acts like she loves Willis because the script has told her to; there is no deeper underlying understanding of Marianna's motives because they would not make sense when held up to examination. Marianna is alleged to have singing talent, so why is she wasting her time at the El Perico, a dump of a place? She's a smart girl, so why can't she see that Willis is no good for her? Nothing concerning Marianna's circumstances is either convincing or engrossing.

Despite the poor script and the flightiness of her character, Gloria truly enjoyed making *Naked Alibi*, much of which was filmed in Tijuana, Mexico. It was a male-oriented movie and Gloria loved being surrounded by men, especially virile guys like Hayden and Barry. She and Barry became fast friends; Gloria later appeared with him in two *Burke's Law* episodes and one *Name of the Game* episode after her film career faded. The crew loved Gloria for her sense of humor and straight-talking personality. After filming was finished, she sent a note to producer Ross Hunter saying that she had never felt more appreciated on a movie set. By contrast, it was a year later that Gloria had so much trouble on the *Oklahoma!* set, and effectively got herself blackballed.

Ross Hunter was so impressed with Gloria that if he had been in a position to sign her to a studio contract, he stated that he would have. He felt she had the makings of a major star, given the right material. *Naked Alibi* was not the right material, but it was popular anyway and received mixed notices from critics. The British Film Institute's *Monthly Film Bulletin* termed it a "slightly above-average crime story" and praised the photography. Its critic also added, "The heroine's one absurdly casual song-and-dance number alone makes the film worth seeing." *Boxoffice* praised the film as "a taut and spine-tingling crime melodrama ... [Gloria Grahame] once again excels as a sultry honky-tonk singer." *Variety*'s critic wrote, "Miss Grahame makes as much as possible of the blatant sex so obviously spotted in her character," but judged the final product to be "highly improbable." Bosley Crowther of the *New York Times* complained about the violence quotient, terming *Naked Alibi* "a very sluggish and slug-nutty film."

Nevertheless, it made money. Its advertising focused on Gloria in the black satin dress and hinted that she was the subject of the title, which she was not. But combine Gloria Grahame with "*Naked*" anything and prurient interest is stirred. The film was successful but has gradually faded into relative obscurity. It has yet to be released on DVD and received only a token release on VHS many years ago. The vast majority of Gloria's films are available today but this is one that is not. Quite a few of Sterling Hayden's films are also missing today, so perhaps its absence is more indicative of his box office standing.

Except for specific elements such as its cinematography and lighting, *Naked Alibi* is not particularly artistic. Yet it does feature Gloria at her most voluptuous and she has moments that reveal that her talent was more than skin deep. Gloria loved making the film; for her it was a blast. It would prove to be her next to last foray into *film noir*, with her final effort still five years away. Gloria was aware that the industry was changing. Fewer movies were being made and many of those were being shot in color or the new widescreen processes. *Film noir* was disappearing quickly, and Gloria was determined to adapt. Her next projects would be bigger and brighter productions, advancing with the trends of the times.

The Cobweb (1955)

CREDITS MGM. *Directed by* Vincente Minnelli. *Produced by* John Houseman. *Associate Producer:* Jud Kinberg. *Screenplay by* John Paxton. *Additional Dialogue by* William Gibson. *From the novel by* William Gibson. *Director of Photography:* George Folsey. *Film Editor:* Harold F. Kress. *Assistant Film Editor:* Conrad A. Nervig. *Art Directors:* Cedric Gibbons and Preston Ames. *Set Decorations:* Edwin B. Willis and Keogh Gleason. *Color Consultant:* Alvord Eiseman. *Assistant Director:* William Shanks. *Graphic Designs Executed by* David Stone Martin. *Music by* Leonard Rosenman. *Recording Supervisor:* Wesley C. Miller. *Hair Styles by* Sydney Guilaroff. *Makeup Created by* William Tuttle. *Costumes Designed by* Helen Rose. *Unit Manager:* William Kaplan. *Sound Editors:* Kurt Hernfeld and Van Allen James. *Sound:* Charles Wallace. Eastman Color. CinemaScope (2.55:1). Monaural Sound. 124 minutes. Released on June 7, 1955. Currently available on DVD. Previously available on laserdisc.

CAST *Dr. Stewart "Mac" McIver*, Richard Widmark; *Meg Faversen Rinehart*, Lauren Bacall; *Dr. Douglas H. Devanal*, Charles Boyer; *Karen McIver*, Gloria Grahame; *Victoria "Vicky" Inch*, Lillian Gish; *Steven "Stevie" W. Holte*, John Kerr; *Sue Brett*, Susan Strasberg; *Mr. Capp*, Oscar Levant; *Mark McIver*, Tommy Rettig; *Dr. Otto Wolff*, Paul Stewart; *Lois V. Demuth*, Jarma Lewis; *Miss Cobb*, Adele Jergens; *Mr. Holcomb*, Edgar Stehli; *Rosemary "Rosie" McIver*, Sandra Descher; *Abe Irwin*, Bert Freed; *Regina Mitchell-Smythe*, Mabel Albertson; *Edna Devanal*, Fay Wray; *Curley*, Oliver Blake; *Mrs. O'Brien*, Olive Carey; *Shirley Irwin*, Eve McVeagh; *Sally*, Virginia Christine; *Mr. Appleton*, Jan Arvan; *Mrs. Jenkins*, Ruth Clifford; *Miss Gavney*, Myra Marsh; *James Petlee*, James Westerfield; *Sadie*, Marjorie Bennett; *Mr. Wictz*, Stuart Holmes; *Lieutenant Ferguson*, Roy Barcroft; *Dr. Tim Carmody*, Dayton Lummis; *Albert*, John Bennes; *Barber*, Ed Agresti; *Messenger*, Harry Harvey, Jr.; *Switchboard Operator*, Lenore Kingston; *Intern*, Harry Landers; *Deputy Sheriff*, John McKee; *Telephone Operator*, Patricia Miller; *Usher*, Norman Ollestad; *Waiter*, Lomax Study; *Recital Attendee*, James Conaty; *Patients*, Alvin Greenman, Kay E. Kuter, Henry Sylvester and Moria Turner.

In June of 1955, Gloria Grahame appeared in two highly anticipated medical-themed melodramas, both featuring all-star casts and excellent production values, and based on popular books. The first of these is *The Cobweb*, which takes place in and around a mental health clinic in a town somewhere in the American Midwest (in William Gibson's novel, it is in Nebraska). Although billed fourth, Gloria has the second most important role; indeed, her presence utterly dominates the movie's first half. Familiar with her talent from directing her to an Oscar in *The Bad and the Beautiful*, Vincente Minnelli allows Gloria full rein in *The Cobweb* to invest herself into the character of the neglected wife of a progressive psychoanalyst (Richard Widmark). Although not a part of the clinic itself, Gloria's character interacts with several of its staff members and patients, and instigates "the trouble" that propels the plot. Alluring, vulnerable, bitchy and selfish, Gloria finds just the right tones to play; the result is her finest work since *The Big Heat*. The movie itself provokes a huge range of reaction, from strong appreciation to wild derision, but few people deny that Gloria is very good in it. It was to be her last major film for MGM, the studio that gave her a start a decade earlier.

"The trouble began..." in *The Cobweb* with an innocent remark by young Stevie Holte (John Kerr). Walking along the road, Stevie is given a ride by Karen McIver (Gloria Grahame), and he happens to tell her that the clinic where he is staying, the Castle House Clinic for Nervous Disorders, needs new drapes for its library. Karen takes it upon herself to measure the room and call the chairman of the board of the clinic, Regina Mitchell-Smythe (Mabel Albertson), to discuss purchasing drapery material. Meanwhile, the clinic's accountant, Vicky Inch (Lillian Gish), plans to order cheap muslin

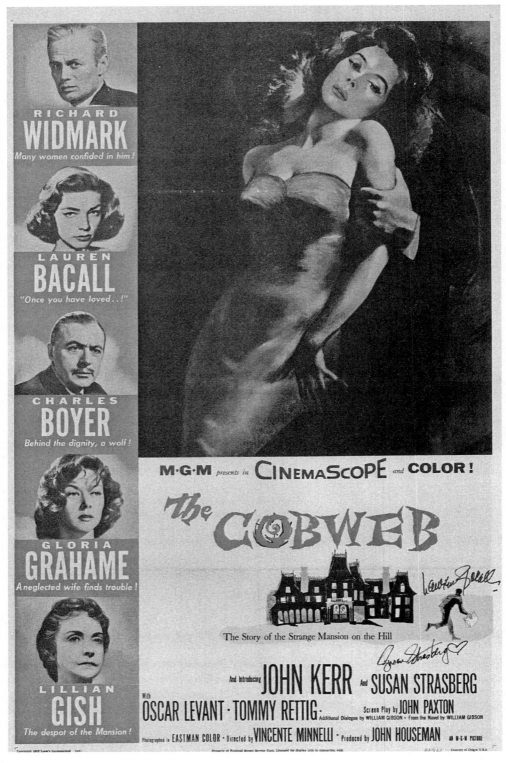

The Cobweb. MGM was not sure how to market this psychological drama so the studio resorted to artwork depicting Gloria as a sex siren and, just for added punch, tagged her character thusly: "A neglected wife finds trouble!" This particular poster is signed by Lauren Bacall and Susan Strasberg.

material for the same purpose. At almost the same time, a patient group led by new employee Meg Rinehart (Lauren Bacall) suggests allowing artist Stevie to design illustrations depicting life at the clinic and to transfer those illustrations onto drapery material for the library. This plan delights Dr. Stewart McIver (Richard Widmark), who views it as therapeutic for the patients, as well as a step forward in his progressive plan to allow the patients to self-govern their day-to-day activities at the clinic. McIver believes that only by assuming responsibility for their lives can the patients achieve stronger mental health and, ultimately, self-sufficiency.

Karen attempts to tell her husband about her plans, but her timing is poor and he rebuffs her, only increasing the distance that already exists between them. In session, Stevie tells McIver about meeting his wife. McIver tells the young man it is perfectly natural to be attracted to such a beautiful woman, and that he is not angry or offended about it. At home, McIver and Karen argue about Stevie's attraction to her, and the fact that McIver spends all his time at the clinic instead of with his family. Karen calls Vicky Inch about the drapes, which insults Vicky because she considers redecorating the library to be under her purview. Thoroughly offended that Karen is meddling, Vicky goes ahead with the muslin order. Karen goes around Vicky by approaching the clinic's director, Dr. Devanal (Charles Boyer), and asking him to intercede on behalf of herself and the chairman of the board, who, she assures him, is already ordering the new drapes.

Stevie creates several designs that meet with enthusiasm and McIver affirms the idea of the patients making their own draperies. Meg Rinehart learns that Vicky has purchased muslin for the drapes and approaches her about the possibility of saving the clinic money by allowing the patients to make the drapes themselves. Vicky is dubious and calls Meg "a cat's paw" in a plot to allow Karen McIver to do what she wants. Meg reports this to McIver, who is unaware of his wife's involvement. McIver appreciates Meg's direct honesty and is increasingly drawn to her. McIver visits Vicky at home, bullies her into obeying him, and makes peace with her. He goes home to confront Karen and learns that she has visited Dr.

Devanal, which angers him. They fight about the clinic but the subject turns quickly to their own problems, and she accuses him of neglecting her. "I'd be home more, Karen, if there were more to come home to," he quietly replies.

The next day Vicky taunts Dr. Devanal at work, learning that he no longer has the power to fire her — authority that he abdicated upon Dr. McIver's arrival. Vicky humiliates him; he responds by drinking heavily, going to the McIver home and making a pass at Karen. When she rebuffs him, Devanal decides to take action to save his position, and issues a memo that the new library drapes will not be provided by the patients. This angers Stevie, whose rampage is cut short by McIver. The analyst is able to calm Stevie and reassure him that Devanal's memo is a mistake. Devanal asks Vicky to prepare a report showing the turmoil at the clinic since McIver assumed control, and enlists Regina to look into the matter personally. The patients hold another meeting and ask for consistency in their treatment; McIver promises that he will take care of the staff issues that are causing disruptions. He spends an evening with Meg, leading to a romantic kiss and possibly more. Karen discovers that her husband is with Meg and loses her temper. She takes her new drapes to the clinic and hangs them in the library while everyone else is preoccupied.

The next morning, Stevie sees the new drapes and loses his temper, injuring the clinic's gardener. Stevie destroys the designs and runs away toward the nearby river. McIver spends all day looking for Stevie but to no avail. The police are contacted and, finding a shoe, begin the task of dragging the river for Stevie's body. McIver returns to the clinic, sees the new drapes and rips them down himself just as Dr. Devanal and Regina arrive to find the place in chaos. McIver threatens Devanal but walks away before he completely loses his temper. Devanal's wife Edna (Fay Wray) shows McIver a report that proves Devanal was having affairs and wasting the clinic's resources; the report is from Vicky Inch in response to Devanal's request to dig up dirt on McIver. McIver finds Vicky, rips up Edna's copy of the report, and requests that Vicky not present it at the upcoming board meeting. Back at the river, waiting for the police to find Stevie's body, McIver complains to Meg that he isn't sure of anything any more and asks her what he should do. "Who do you think I am?" she cries. Their romantic tryst is over.

The clinic's board of directors meet in the library, where no draperies hang on the windows. Vicky shelves her damning report on Devanal. McIver states that despite Stevie's apparent suicide, the clinic was moving in the right direction, and that if he remains its leader, he will continue to work toward the goals he has enumerated. He departs, leaving the decision in the hands of the board members. Dr. Devanal silently hands his resignation to Regina, who reads it aloud. Later, McIver and Karen are talking together in a quiet wooded area. "What do we do now?" she asks. "Try to help each other as much as we can," he replies, willing to work to save his marriage and family. They drive home, only to find a ragged Stevie waiting in the garage, barely able to stand. They help him into their home, where he collapses upon the sofa. Karen wraps him to keep him warm, using the new drapery material that McIver had removed from the clinic library. Stevie, barely conscious, notices it and mumbles, "Seem to keep running into these things" before he falls asleep. "The trouble was over..." appears on the screen and the picture fades to black.

The Cobweb is an intricate dramatic web spun around the seemingly mundane idea of new draperies being ordered at a mental clinic. William Gibson's novel is based on the concept that such a relatively insignificant task can and often does, because of human interaction and interference, create a multitude of human reverberations. These reflections and repercussions echo off of each other and the people who create them, causing anxiety, confrontation, conflict and even destruction — all emanating from a very simple act. The ordering of new draperies is the act. It rightfully ought to belong to the accountant, Vicky Inch, who ordered the last pair some forty years earlier, because Vicky is the person who traditionally handles such mundane matters, leaving the medical staff time to work their magic. Meg Rinehart has the idea to use the opportunity to create new drapes from scratch as a therapeutic tool, and Dr. McIver heartily agrees. In his mind, and because he is the clinic's highest authority, McIver automatically puts the treatment of the patients ahead of the economic considerations of installing cheap draperies. This merely confirms McIver's progressive outlook, which tends to rankle some of the clinic's older employees; they were accustomed to doing things more traditionally under Dr. Devanal's administration.

This simple conflict is exacerbated when Karen McIver, on her own, decides to update the library's old-fashioned muslin with elegant draperies chosen with the help of Regina Mitchell-Smythe. Karen's intentions are honorable: She wishes to beautify the clinic, to become more involved in her husband's career, to strengthen the McIver ties to the clinic's chairman of the board, and to exercise her own artistic expression. Karen even tries to tell her husband about her inspiration twice and is rebuffed both times. Had she been able to talk to him about it, it is probable that the whole situation could have been effectively handled with little fuss. But this lack of communication — in a medical clinic driven by the concept of people communicating with each other — is the key as to why this simple conflict spirals out of control. After Karen is rebuffed and insulted by Vicky Inch, she determines to continue the project with or without her husband's help, eventually leading to Stevie's near-suicidal rampage. Karen's refusal to withdraw is also incredibly personal for her. The draperies themselves are not the real issue, but they seem to her to be the only thing able to catch her husband's interest.

It is clear that Karen is sexually neglected by her husband. In their home, though they share a bedroom, Stewart McIver is shown sleeping by himself in another room most of the time. The first night, after Karen goes to the concert by herself, she lies awake in bed waiting for McIver to return. When he does, he peeks into the bedroom, stares at Karen (who pretends to be asleep), thinks about joining her, and then quietly closes the door, leaving her alone. It is that moment that signifies the damage to their marriage. Karen's insistence on staying involved with the drapes is a direct plea to remain involved in her husband's life. At home she is almost completely cut off from McIver, and this is a way to remain close to him at work, to prove that she is worthy of his attention. She still wants him and

The Cobweb. Stevie Holte (John Kerr) is a patient at the Castle House Clinic for Nervous Disorders, while Karen McIver (Gloria) is the wife of his primary care psychiatrist, Dr. Stewart McIver (Richard Widmark, not pictured).

him only; she refuses Dr. Devanal's pass even after subtly encouraging his desire for her, and she doesn't want Stevie's attention either. Karen's life revolves completely around her husband and children, and she feels her familiar levels of love and comfort slipping away.

McIver's inability to fulfill his wife's desire is the key to his character, and to their relationship. As much as he loves her, he feels more responsibility for the patients under his charge at the clinic than he does for his family. The irony is that everyone else thinks McIver has it made, living with the most beautiful woman in town, but both he and his wife are desperately hungry for love. McIver gradually falls for Meg Rinehart (and in the book eventually leaves Karen for her), but their relationship stalls when, at the river, McIver feels unable to control his life, or those of his patients, any longer. He asks Meg what he should do, and his impotence overwhelms her. "Who do you think I

am?" she cries, and turns away from him for good. It is his work, in the pitiable form of Stevie, which ultimately reunites McIver with Karen. When Stevie is found in McIver's garage, the psychoanalyst regains his emotional and professional footing. Karen helps care for the young man, even wrapping him in the new drapes she had taken so much trouble to install (and which her husband had forcibly removed from the clinic after assuming that Stevie was dead). Once Stevie is safe, McIver's impotence is symbolically cured. He and Karen have a long conversation and vow to make the effort to repair the damage that they have done to their marriage and to each other. It isn't a simplistic happy ending, but in keeping with the themes of the movie it is progress, and that is what drives Dr. Stewart McIver: strong, steady progress for the people under his care.

Gibson's book does not settle even for this generally happy ending: Although Stevie survives, McIver cannot return home to his empty life with Karen, instead turning to a new life with Meg Rinehart. Meg is more prominent in the book than in the film. Having lost her husband and son a few years earlier, she is waiting for life to once again involve her; this finally occurs when she bonds romantically with McIver and maternally with Stevie Holte. Her presence allows McIver to escape from his loveless marriage and start afresh. This is posited in the movie as well, but with the moral guidelines that filmmakers were forced to follow at the time, McIver leaving his family was not a realistic option.

Establishing this multi-dimensional conflict on a foundation of the simple act of replacing drapes is a brilliant literary conceit that Gibson handles very well in his novel, but which is not quite as effective when translated to film. What seems reasoned and intelligent on the page can seem silly and trite on the big screen. Fans of the film enjoy the complexities and ramifications of the story, as well as the solid acting of its stars, but others dismiss the film as much ado about nothing. Even at the time of its release there was a great divide regarding the film's core idea, and that has only widened over time. Unfortunately, as snide sarcasm has gradually overtaken real film criticism (especially on the Internet), *The Cobweb*'s reputation has plummeted. In 1955, Philip T. Hartung of *Commonweal* gave the film a strong review, but also famously, hilariously, subtitled his piece "Drapes of Wrath." It was a funny jibe that didn't interfere with his intelligent review. Now, most references to the film — which has only recently been released on DVD are full of scorn for its central conceit.

Upon first glance, the notion of choosing a set of drapes can seem like a weak foundation for a sophisticated movie, but that simply proves that first glances rarely reveal the inherent depth of any motion picture story. The drapes function as the plot device that sets the characters in motion, working with, around and against one another. The story's primary concerns are communication and pride.

The clinic depends on open communication, particularly between doctor and patient, but also between doctor and staff. It is the communication at the upper levels of the clinic that is so problematic. Relieved of his authority when McIver was hired, Dr. Devanal has never told anyone, particularly Vicky Inch, that he is no longer the clinic's actual director. Devanal's pride won't allow him to tell anyone, and McIver plays along with the charade. McIver has trouble getting his progressive messages about the patients across to the staff, particularly nurse O'Brien, partly because he has avoided taking full charge of the clinic. Staff accustomed to doing things the old ways under Dr. Devanal still resist McIver's new methods. Gradually this will change, as personified by new hire Meg Rinehart, whose views parallel those of McIver; but without full disclosure of his authority, McIver is making the job much harder on himself. McIver has stopped trying to communicate with Karen, which not only places his own marriage in jeopardy but also throws the clinic into tumult when Karen attempts to take matters into her own hands. Karen's pride smashes directly into that of Vicky Inch, and their clash over the drapes turns into a battle royal. Devanal's pride leads him to a rash attempt at a last stand to control the clinic, but it is too late to recover what he has lost.

About the only person with whom McIver actually communicates well is Stevie Holte, and it has taken months of therapy to get Stevie to the point where he begins to take some responsibility for his own life. Although several patients are depicted in some detail, Stevie is the key; his designs for the drapes symbolize therapy for all, and if they are not allowed to hang, McIver's therapeutic method grinds to a standstill. Stevie reluctantly assumes the role of group leader as the story unfolds, and it is his friendship with shy Sue Brett (Susan Strasberg) that promises to overcome her fears about people and ultimately bring them both into adulthood. Stevie comes to represent Meg Rinehart's lost son and threatens to displace Karen in McIver's own heart. He and the drapes are inextricably tangled up together throughout the story, so it is deliciously ironic that Karen literally wraps him in them at film's end.

Symbolically Stevie also represents artistic freedom of expression, which was dormant under Dr. Devanal's old-fashioned reign (illustrated by Vicky Inch's cheap, ugly original set of library drapes) and augurs to blossom under Dr. McIver's progressive management. Stevie talks of painters to McIver and Karen, as well as Meg Rinehart, and they are all able to discuss those painters and their styles with familiarity. It is also not coincidental that the McIvers' first fight presages a community music concert, which Karen attends on her own. Clearly, even this small Midwestern town has its share of Culture, and maintaining that Culture is important to the filmmakers. In the film's progressive vision, Art is the key to unlocking Stevie's self-destructive nature, to opening lines of communication amongst everyone and to entertaining the clinic's well-educated staff and community. Yet Art should also be functional: Stevie's designs are to be used to make new library drapes, and when Meg Rinehart is shown painting, she is painting her apartment.

The décor of the film was important to director Vincente Minnelli, an aesthete who had begun his film career as a set and costume designer. Because of his background, Minnelli is rare among directors, a true stylist whose films accurately reflect his personal vision of how they should appear. And because he understood elements of design so clearly, he was able to treat the dramatic dilemma about the drapes with respect, whereas another director might well have been unable to avoid the impulse to emphasize the seeming triviality of the situation, thus undermining the entire plot. Minnelli took the drapes seriously; the battle over them was merely representative of the conflicts they inspired in the characters. "Woven throughout were separate stories of members of the staff and patients. It was so rich in possibilities that I volunteered to direct," he wrote in his autobiography, *I Remember It Well.* Evidence of the director's passion for visual clarity is everywhere, from the chic magazine-spread look of the McIver home to the opening conversation between Stevie Holte and Karen McIver, who discuss painter Les Fauves and his use of "color and form."

Lauren Bacall recalled Minnelli's obsession about the picture's look in an interview with Mark Griffin. "On *The Cobweb*, I'd arrive on the set and there he'd be up on the boom, zooming up to the drapes, and I thought to myself, 'He's really in heaven now.' The bloody drapes. It was all about the goddamned drapes in *The Cobweb*. I loved Vincente and we were friends, but I used to joke with Oscar Levant about Vincente's direction because he was so totally involved with what everything looked like...." That approach may have baffled or irritated the performers, but it was imperative to Minnelli that the décor visually reflect the dramatic situations of each scene and the dilemmas present within each major character.

Minnelli and producer John Houseman hired screenwriter John Paxton to adapt Gibson's novel, but both were disappointed with Paxton's end product. When Gibson showed interest in rewriting it, the creative team jumped at the chance to bring in the original author to instill some of the drama that had faded away in Paxton's script. Gibson felt Paxton's script was "miserable," and worked every day for three weeks before shooting began to improve upon it. After viewing the edited end product, Gibson decreed, "I found it totally boring."

One of the compromises that producer and director were forced to make involves the ultimate solution to the film's primary romantic triangle. In his autobiography, Minnelli discussed why the book's original ending was changed: "The film veered from the book in one very important regard. After stacking the deck against the Gloria Grahame character, at the end of the picture Richard Widmark returns to her instead of leaving her for Lauren Bacall. It seemed dishonest, since we'd established extraordinary bonds between the doctor and the staff member, but the conclusion was very much within the existing movie code."

The biggest battle the director faced occurred at the end of production. Minnelli also confessed that his rough cut was some two and a half hours long. Producer Houseman insisted that it be cut to nearly two hours, and that is what eventually happened; Houseman supervised the cutting himself. Houseman wrote in one of his autobiographies, *Front and Center*, "When I ran it for him after hacking close to half an hour out of the film, including entire scenes he had shot with loving care, he made a violent, lachrymose scene in the projection room, accusing me of insensitivity and treachery. I offered to let him recut the film, but he refused." Both men were pleasantly surprised when, even after the drastic revisions, the film still won praise in audience previews, and the animosity between them lessened considerably as the film went into release to generally favorable response.

The Cobweb. Dr. Stewart McIver (Richard Widmark) tries to repair the fractured relationship with his wife Karen (Gloria) after neglecting or ignoring her for the majority of the movie.

Minnelli had one other compelling reason for making *The Cobweb*. Due to the instabilities of his wife Judy Garland, he had become quite familiar with the inner workings of mental clinics and institutions. He deeply understood the need that people had for places like the Menninger Clinic, where Garland had been committed for a time, and was determined to present such a place in a balanced light. Despite the clamor about the drapes, Dr. McIver and the staff do make positive strides to help the patients under their care. His progressive theories and attempts to allow the patients to self-govern themselves are, in Minnelli's eyes, absolutely essential steps in the treatment of people with neuroses. One can make the case that the Castle House Clinic for Nervous Disorders is Minnelli's wishful vision of a place that he could have taken his troubled wife for treatment.

Yet he takes care to follow Gibson's lead, refusing to worship the place and canonize the staff. Gibson's novel presents the clinic staff as troubled people themselves, just as human as their patients. Minnelli's film reasserts that point again and again. Stevie tells Karen McIver, "You can't tell the patients from the doctors." Karen replies, "Oh, but I can." "How?" "The patients get better," Karen replies. The doctors and staff bickering over the drapes is shown to actually interfere with the patients' well-being and treatment. When this is brought to McIver's attention, he assures the patients that the staff will address their problems and then turn their full attention back to the patients. Indeed, in the book *Celluloid Couches, Cinematic Clients,* Jerrold R. Brandell praises the film for its flawed clinic staff:

> *The Cobweb* is a remarkable film, but not because it represents psychiatrists as the "secular saints" of what has been called the Golden Age of movie psychiatry. Rather, the film rises in my estimation — and I would deem it more progressive than *The Snake Pit* — because its psychiatrist characters are fallible and they, and psychiatric authority itself, are subject to what I consider to be a very

appropriate critique, given the power and history of these elements.

The Cobweb was conceived with one main cast yet began production with another. Originally, Robert Taylor and Lana Turner were cast as the McIvers, with Grace Kelly touted as Meg Rinehart and James Dean as Stevie Holte. But production delays, mainly due to Minnelli's insistence upon a stronger script, led to Taylor and Turner looking for work elsewhere. Kelly, claiming exhaustion, took a break from films for a few months, costing her the Meg Rinehart role. Warner Bros. wanted too much money to loan out young James Dean, whom they were grooming for stardom.

So instead, *The Cobweb* boasts a sterling cast of other stars, five of whom were or would become Academy Award nominees. Interestingly, of those five, only Gloria Grahame ever won one. Richard Widmark took a break from all the tough guy villains and antiheroes he was playing throughout the '50s to essay the intellectual role of the liberal-minded psychoanalyst McIver. Being one of the smartest actors in Hollywood, Widmark responded to the challenge superbly. He balances the cockiness inherent in the character with a vulnerability that overwhelms McIver as everything in his life falls apart when Stevie disappears. Sensitive and smart, yet inattentive enough to allow events to spiral out of control, Widmark is dynamic as the flawed hero. Widmark's expertise is matched by that of Gloria Grahame; this is one of Gloria's more colorful and sharply defined roles. She particularly dominates the first half. It is interesting that Gloria, so often accustomed to playing the "other woman," is here portraying a woman desperately trying to hold onto her man. Gloria also looks fabulous, so much so that the advertising poster's primary image is a voluptuous pose of her inciting the lust of a figure standing behind her.

Second-billed Lauren Bacall is effective in a smaller role. Bacall creates a very likable, sympathetic Meg Rinehart, at least until she is melodramatically overwhelmed by McIver's loss of confidence in himself. Had the film followed the path of the book, Meg would have assumed greater importance, but the film standards of the era prevented MGM from allowing McIver to leave Karen for Meg. As Dr. Devanal, Charles Boyer is rather pompous and silly. It's more the part than the actor but Devanal is only once a convincing character, and that is when he gazes nostalgically at the book he had written some two decades earlier and wonders what happened to the man who wrote it. The strongest performance is delivered by Lillian Gish as the clinic's business manager, Vicky Inch. Prickly to the point of rudeness, Vicky is a powerhouse of bundled nerves and imagined slights. It is very much a *tour de force* by Gish, who steals the spotlight from everyone else in her scenes.

Two young performers, John Kerr (as Stevie Holt) and Susan Strasberg (as Sue Brett), made their film debuts in *The Cobweb*. Kerr made a big splash as a troubled youth in this, quickly followed by *Gaby* and *Tea and Sympathy*, both 1956 releases. Following *South Pacific* (1958), Kerr spent the remainder of his career mostly as a television guest star. He is forceful and articulate as Stevie, usually able to keep the melodramatic aspects of his role under control. Strasberg has quite a bit less to do but is convincing, especially in her sensitive scenes with Kerr. Following *Picnic* (also 1955), Strasberg also spent the majority of her career on television. Of the other performers to portray patients, the most noteworthy is Oscar Levant (Mr. Capp), whose performance was probably enhanced by the fact that he had spent time in several mental institutions over the years. His acid-tongued character was very much a reflection of his own personality: blunt to the point of rudeness but vulnerable beneath the grumpy veneer. *The Cobweb* was to be the last of his thirteen movie appearances.

Critics seemed to appreciate the cast's efforts more than the movie itself. According to *Newsweek*, "All this sounds a little like either farce or snake-pit horror, but the material is handled with such respect that it emerges as adult drama. One might challenge the likelihood of certain circumstances in this movie, were it not for the persuasive acting." Moira Walsh of *America* decreed, "Much of the movie is unusually intelligent and absorbing, and the cast ... is first rate." According to *Variety*, "The quality of the performances ... is, as expected, very good as developed under the sensitive, but not too probing, direction by Vincente Minnelli." The *Variety* critic was also impressed by the production values, but nevertheless complained that the film "fails to impress as screen entertainment of wide popular appeal."

The British Film Institute's *Monthly Film Bulletin* described *The Cobweb* as "markedly inferior" to *The Bad and the Beautiful*: "The characters—staff and patients—seem to come straight from an elementary textbook in psychiatry, and the point at issue, the complex affair of the drapes, appears altogether too slight a foundation for the weight it has to bear." *The Motion Picture Guide* described the film thusly: "An all-star cast, a brilliant director, an eminent producer, and a script from a fascinating book all contribute to making this a very dull movie."

Lee Rogow of the *Saturday Review* confessed, "There are several things about *The Cobweb* which make me feel it is one of the most rewarding films I have recently seen come out of Hollywood. It appears to me to be a completely new story, which is headline material in itself. More, it's a mature story of the most exciting kind, in which the interior dramas of the individuals are brought together in outward dramatic events which have revelation and consequence." *Commonweal*'s Philip T. Hartung thoroughly enjoyed the film's fine performances and expanding complexities. In the *New York Times*, Howard H. Thompson wrote, "Yes, what a cast! But what an institution! And jumping Jehosaphat, what a picture!"

The Cobweb was a major film of 1955 but it was also a boxoffice disappointment. It made $1.5 million, which was a respectable figure at the time, but that failed to cover the costs of its production. Despite its prominent cast and profile it has only recently been released on DVD; only a widescreen laserdisc release in the 1990s and occasional television broadcasts have kept it alive in the public eye. It is a better film than its reputation would suggest, offering an insightful, engrossing glimpse of men and women working to help heal the minds of others, yet often failing to use their knowledge and access to treatment to help themselves. It is a dated film, to be sure, but was rather progressive for its time. It is low-key rather than sensational, tempered rather than sharp, and amusing rather than grotesque, all characteristics that reflect the good taste and judgment of its producer and director. Despite the protestations of those who mock its central conceit and find it all a big, bloated fuss about nothing, *The Cobweb* is a very worthwhile motion picture.

Gloria Grahame is terrific in one of her most colorful roles. She was paid $75,000 for seven weeks of work. She, like the movie itself, received wildly differing reviews, but she enjoyed the experience, especially the aspect of not being "the other woman" again.

Not as a Stranger (1955)

CREDITS Stanley Kramer Pictures Corporation. *Distributed by* United Artists. *Produced and Directed by* Stanley Kramer. *Written for the Screen by* Edna and Edward Anhalt. *Based on the novel by* Morton Thompson. *Director of Photography*: Franz Planer. *Film Editor*: Fred Knudtson. *Production Design by* Rudolph Sternad. *Music by* George Antheil. *Song* "Not as a Stranger" by James Van Heusen and Buddy Kaye. *Art Director*: Howard Richmond. *Set Decorator*: Victor Gangelin. *Costume Supervision*: Joe King. *Makeup*: Bill Wood. *Hair Styles*: Esperanza Corona. *Sound Engineer*: Earl Snyder. *Camera Operator*: Bud Mautino. *Dialogue Director*: Anne Kramer. *Script Supervisor*: John Franco. *Production Assistant*: Sally Hamilton. *Company Grip*: Morris Rosen. *Production Manager*: John E. Burch. *Assistant Director*: Carter DeHaven, Jr. *Gowns*: Don Loper. *Music Conductor*: Paul Sawtell. *Technical Advisor*: Morton Maxwell, M.D. *Assistant Technical Advisors*: Josh Fields, M.D., and Marjorie Lefevre, R.N. *Orchestrator*: Ernest Gold. *Sound Recordist*: Watson Jones. Black and White. Matted Widescreen (1.85:1). Monaural Sound. 135 minutes. Released on June 28, 1955. Currently available on DVD. Previously available on VHS.

CAST *Kristina Hedvigson*, Olivia de Havilland; *Lucas Marsh*, Robert Mitchum; *Alfred Boone*, Frank Sinatra; *Harriet Lang*, Gloria Grahame; *Dr. Aarons*, Broderick Crawford; *Dr. Dave Runkleman*, Charles Bickford; *Dr. Clem Snider*, Myron McCormick; *Job Marsh*, Lon Chaney, Jr.; *Ben Cosgrove*, Jesse White; *Oley*, Henry (Harry) Morgan; *Brundage*, Lee Marvin; *Bruni*, Virginia Christine; *Dr. Dietrich*, Whit Bissell; *Dr. Lettering*, Jack Raine; *Miss O'Dell*, Mae Clarke; *Carlisle Emmons*, William Vedder; *Mr. Revere*, John Dierkes; *Intern*, David Alpert; *Patient*, Robert Bailey; *Mrs. Fields*, Gail Bonney; *Men in Nightclub*, Ralph Brooks, James Conaty and Franklyn Farnum; *Mr. Clyde*, Jack Daly; *Mr. Slocum*, King Donovan; *Patient*, Marlo Dwyer; *Morgan*, John Goddard; *Mr. Burt*, Paul Guilfoyle; *Policeman*, Don C. Harvey; *Boy*, Jimmy Hawkins; *Sam*, Earle Hodgins; *Mrs. Payton*, Gertrude Hoffman; *Patients*, Stuart

Holmes, Donald Kerr, Frank Mills, Al Murphy, Dorothy Neumann and Frank Orth; *Mr. Parrish*, Frank Jenks; *Gertrude*, Nancy Kulp; *Harry*, Harry Lauter; *Mrs. Ferris*, Eve McVeagh; *Mrs. Clara Bassett*, Juanita Moore; *Mrs. Fields' Son*, Scotty Morrow; *Thompson*, Jerry Paris; *Man in Immunization Line*, Bob Perry; *Orientation Doctor*, Stafford Repp; *Ed*, Harry Shannon; *Unexpected Father*, Carl "Alfalfa" Switzer; *Nurse Snowl*, Irene Tedrow; *Kristina's Father (in Photo)*, Arthur Tovey; *Lou, Pharmaceutical Salesman*, Herb Vigran; *Man with Cast*, Mack Williams; *Mr. Roberts*, Will Wright; *Bit Part*, Suzanne Ridgeway; *Patient Being Restrained*, Al Murphy (scenes deleted).

Gloria's second all-star project of 1955 was Stanley Kramer's version of Morton Thompson's best-selling medical novel *Not as a Stranger*. Though billed fourth, Gloria has a small role compared to the others; it is, however, a memorable one. Once again she is called upon to play the incendiary love interest, so she seduces star Robert Mitchum in a scene staged so melodramatically that modern audiences hoot with derision — but it startled its original audience with its sexual candor. The rest of the film is an earnest soap opera about a young doctor who succeeds despite a lack of empathy, and the love of the compassionate nurse whom he marries for her money.

Lucas Marsh (Robert Mitchum) is a medical intern intent on becoming a great doctor. Though morally supported by fellow internists Al Boone (Frank Sinatra) and Brundage (Lee Marvin), he is in trouble financially. His poor fiscal condition leads him to court nurse Kristina (Olivia de Havilland), the rather plain "Swedish Nightingale" of the hospital who puts half of her paycheck into savings each week. Marsh convinces Kristina that he loves her and they marry, to the chagrin of Al, who knows his true motive. Throughout their internship, Marsh and Al maintain their friendship despite Al's misgivings about the marriage and Marsh's ever-increasing arrogance. At one point Marsh is threatened with expulsion for arguing with a surgeon regarding a procedure. Marsh eventually backs down, even though he was correct, and transfers his frustration to Kristina.

Once he graduates from medical school, Dr. Marsh establishes a practice in a small town called Greenville with aged Dr. Runkleman (Charles Bickford) while Kristina settles into housework. Runkleman introduces Marsh to many patients and their ailments, including Harriet Lang (Gloria Grahame), a lonely, bored widow who operates a horse-breeding farm and likes the new doctor's looks. Over time Marsh finds himself drawn to Harriet and begins seeing her, even as Kristina becomes pregnant. Kristina believes that Marsh doesn't want the baby, so she doesn't tell him about it. The culmination of Marsh's affair with Harriet takes place at night, during a storm, as their passion explodes just like that of her stallion and mare. Marsh does not return home that night or the following morning.

Marsh discovers a patient at the hospital with typhoid fever, isolates him and calls in Kristina as a nurse; together, working all night, they save the man. Not knowing about the baby, Marsh asks Kristina to return to nursing, thus confirming her belief that he does not want to begin a family. Marsh feels guilty about the affair with Harriet and ends it just before Al tells him that Kristina is pregnant. It doesn't matter; Kristina learns of the affair and throws her husband out of the house anyway.

Marsh tries to find solace in work, but that backfires when Dr. Runkleman has a heart attack and dies on the operating table as Marsh tries to save him. As Marsh leaves the operating room in a daze, another doctor watches and says, "God help him; he made a mistake." Marsh wanders around town, finally finding himself at home. Kristina opens the door to see her husband in tears. "Help me, Kris, for God's sake, help me," he begs. She holds him silently, forgiving him and accepting him because he finally needs *her*.

Not as a Stranger is top-grade soap opera, given plenty of dramatic weight by its extraordinary cast, which includes no less than five past or future Academy Award winners, plus two other nominees. It is based on a remarkable best-selling novel by Morton Thompson (who died just two weeks after completing it) and boasts a cogent screenplay by respected scribes Edna and Edward Anhalt. It was extremely popular at the box office, ranking as the fifth highest-grossing film of 1955. And yet, it is a solid film but never extraordinary. This is probably due to the direction of Stanley Kramer. He was an outstanding producer, and this was his first film as a director.

His film truncates the book's story of

Lucas Marsh, a man seemingly born to become a physician. The script eliminates virtually all of Marsh's life prior to entering medical school, material which filled the first hundred pages of Thompson's novel and inexorably formed Marsh's character. It updates the story from the 1920s to the 1950s. It shrinks Marsh's stormy relationship with his father down to two scenes (in one of them, Marsh is unexpectedly confronted with his father's corpse). It expands the melodramatic aspects of Marsh's situation while restricting his exploits with patients to a scant few and a couple of montages. Perhaps most importantly it alters the conclusion of the story, thrusting upon Marsh a necessary humility he only achieves in the novel by becoming hopelessly lost in the woods(!), for the sake of redeeming the arrogant doctor and reuniting him with his faithful wife Kristina. Ultimately, author Thompson could not allow his creation Marsh to fail at his shrine of medicine; director Kramer felt it was essential to humble the person, to detail his imperfect humanity, by showing that he could fail even at the most sacred thing in his life.

Not as a Stranger. **This publicity shot of Harriet Lang (Gloria) emphasizes her sophistication and sensuality. Gloria's face is still gorgeous, though the area around her upper lip is a bit puffy, a result of several facial surgeries.**

Lucas Marsh's obsession with practicing medicine is the crux of the story, and the film honors that. Yet the film is less interested in Marsh's personal fixation than on the means he uses to attain his goal. The central question is not whether Marsh will succeed as a doctor; that is a given. It is whether he will ultimately and fully accept Kristina as his wife and life partner, having married her only so that she could finance his way through medical school. That is why the climax forces Marsh to finally face his own limitations; until the moment that Dr. Runkleman dies on *his* operating table, Marsh does not need anybody else. When he cannot save his beloved friend and mentor, he conclusively realizes that medicine will not fulfill him on a human level. For that he needs Kristina, and it is to her, finally, that he returns.

The novel is awash in medicine; Marsh's obsession with it permeates every page. The film establishes his interest, then turns to how Marsh's obsession affects him and those with whom he comes in contact. Few other doctors are as thorough or relentless in their need to grasp the intricacies of the human body. Only Dr. Aarons and Dr. Runkleman command Marsh's firm respect in that regard. Indeed, the other medical students are more interested in establishing practices and making money. Such talk alienates Marsh; it is the human, outside-of-the-body practice of medicine that he has difficulty understanding. Marsh thinks of "Medicine" as pure science: the healing of illness, the repair of injury and the postponement of death; science which can only be soiled by its intersections with human imperfection and weakness. The film captures some of this feeling yet cannot convey it with the power that Thompson does in the novel. Yet, the film's medical scenes are compelling and realistic. Indeed, its two medical montages are among the most interesting, truthful and amusing sequences in the entire film.

Its human stories are not as well executed. Marsh's relationship with Kristina forms the crux of the drama and it is perfectly clear why Marsh pursues her. Just what Kristina sees in Marsh is less clear. Kristina is painted as a plain, serious fuddy-duddy from Sweden with few friends and no prospects for romance, making her an easy target for Marsh's romantic interest. Yet she is a smart, perceptive woman, wonderfully able in the operating room, who ought to be aware of his ploy. Perhaps she doesn't care that she's being used, but that is difficult to accept. One cannot help but think that Kristina certainly deserves better.

A larger problem involves the romance between Marsh and Harriet Lang. Their eventual entanglement is easy to predict, partly due to the construction of the script and partly due to Gloria Grahame's predatory persona. There is simply no question that Harriet likes what she sees and she wants Marsh for herself. As single-minded (and even puritanical) as Marsh seems to be, his interest in an affair is somewhat surprising, yet he is easily swayed by Harriet's beauty, sophistication and hints of carnal delight. Even with dark brown hair, Gloria is the perfect choice for this type of part, effortlessly conveying sophistication, sexual heat and easy access. The dark hair was the idea of Gloria's husband Cy Howard, who advised her to vary her appearance so that audiences would think of her as a versatile actress rather than as a blonde movie star. This was Gloria's seventh consecutive picture with dark hair, and yet some reviewers still mentioned their dislike for Gloria's appearance.

The real problem with the Harriet Lang–Lucas Marsh affair is the obvious symbolism with which Kramer stages its consummation. Marsh arrives at Harriet's horse-breeding farm at night, with a storm a-brewin', foreshadowing the passion yet to come. As the wind whistles through the trees, a stallion is heard whinnying in the barn, hungrily awaiting his rendezvous with a nervous mare, trotting around the corral. Marsh opens the barn door for the stallion, then approaches Harriet just as the stallion corners the mare. Harriet moves into the camera and her lips blur just as the stallion meets the mare and the symbolic union is complete. At the time, the scene's sexual candor made audiences gasp, yet its overt carnal symbolism was roughly derided by both audiences and critics. Today, viewers howl with laughter at the melodramatic scene. Even director Kramer wishes he would have staged it differently, as he confesses in his autobiography *A Mad, Mad, Mad, Mad World*:

> Gloria also paid a price for something that was my fault, not hers. During her last love scene with Mitchum before Marsh returns to his wife, I chose

a barnyard setting in which a stallion gets loose to cavort with a mare as a symbol of what the two humans are doing off camera. I would never do that again. The audiences and some of the critics found it a silly device, and they were probably right.

It was during this film that the rumors swirling around Gloria's penchant for padding her upper lip finally went public. For the past two or three years, Gloria had attempted to change her appearance by discreetly placing a wad of tissue paper, or sometimes cotton, between her upper teeth and lip. She believed that a puffier upper lip was somehow sexier (she never liked the ridges in her lip, which she felt were too deep) and used this trick to achieve the desired effect. Various costars had discovered it upon kissing her in their scenes and discovering, to their surprise, the tissue or cotton in their own mouths when the kiss was finished. This ploy had remained a trade secret until *Not as a Stranger*. Kramer explains:

> As "the other woman" in Mitchum's marriage, Gloria apparently decided to make herself look sexier by slipping tissue paper or some kind of paper under her upper lip, which was needless since Gloria needed no enhancements to make her sexy enough for any man. Whatever she did, the trick was so insignificant I didn't even notice it, but somebody on the set did and soon the word was spread so far that even the critics heard about it. The result was that some of them made fun of her performance, which I thought was unfair because Gloria, while not an intellectual by any means, was a fine, instinctive actress, as her Academy Award for her role in *The Bad and the Beautiful* attested.

Whether it was the rumors about tissue paper, the dark brown hair, the lurid symbolism of lovemaking or a genuinely poor performance, Gloria received the worst notices of her career for the part. *Boxoffice* praised virtually everyone, but wrote, "Disappointing is the part of Gloria Grahame as Harriet Lang, largely because the character is so materially altered." The British Film Institute's *Monthly Film Bulletin* commented, "Gloria Grahame appears annoyingly affected as the socialite...." *Time* declared, "Mitchum meets and at first nobly resists the town siren, played by Gloria Grahame in a manner suggesting that someone has paralyzed her upper lip with Novocain." *The Hollywood Reporter* chastised, "She was so wonderful in *The Bad and the Beautiful*, but she seems to have gone into her blue period of acting. She seems bent on playing every scene without moving her upper lip, as though she were a British colonel stoutly holding Fort Chutney during the Indian Mutiny."

Gloria was stung by the criticism, especially as she had asked Kramer to help her delineate the role. "It's in the script. Don't ask me," he replied. But Gloria was not the only performer whose efforts were criticized. Olivia de Havilland, portraying the blonde, Swedish nurse Kristina, was noted for her vague accent and uncertain character motivation. Criticism fell most heavily, however, on the broad shoulders of Robert Mitchum, whom the majority of critics felt was either miscast, overwhelmed by or just not up to the demands of the role. Mitchum's sleepy-eyed demeanor and lack of emotion became magnets for claims that he didn't know how to act in general or had no clue as to what to do with this role in particular. What reviewers somehow failed to comprehend was that making Marsh an unemotional, self-contained, ascetic individual was exactly what Kramer was trying to do.

Mitchum is, in fact, very good in a role that demands that he repress his feelings until the climactic catharsis. He studied and practiced the medical procedures for realism and delivers a reserved but tenacious portrait of a man subduing his emotions for the sake of his very honorable, altruistic ambition. There's even some humor in his portrayal, which most critics either slept through or ignored. Mitchum's understated style is exactly what prompted Kramer to choose him for the role. Thematically, Marsh refrains from emotional displays; he considers such outbursts unnecessary weakness, detracting from the serious business of medicine. Mitchum plays this perfectly, allowing his livelier co-stars, particularly Frank Sinatra, to deliver the histrionics.

Sinatra is the surprise of the film, creating a memorably warm portrait of Al Boone, Marsh's best friend. Al is the one human connection that Marsh maintains, someone who constantly reminds Marsh what real life is all about. He warns Marsh away from Kristina, yet gradually realizes that she is the only person who can possibly humanize his friend. Al tells Marsh that Kristina is pregnant, because he understands that Marsh needs to know, regardless of Kristina's apprehension. Al Boone is not the doctor that Marsh is, but he understands people in ways that Marsh never will. Sinatra plays him with a cordial, unassuming manner that makes him more memorable than the star; it is Al Boone whom more people would choose to be their personal physician rather than Lucas Marsh, simply due to their personalities.

Kramer's film was controversial at the time because it reflected negatively upon the medical profession, a trade that aggressively defended itself against any and all criticism. Story elements emphasize Marsh's disgust with doctors who fail to learn all they can in medical school; who neglect to remain appraised of recent advancements; who discriminate against expert instructors due to ethnic prejudice; who seek practices with wealthy patients in favor of more needy, but poorer patients; who continue to work long after their professional value has vanished; and who fail to take medicine seriously. Marsh's idealism, however, is established not as the standard to which every doctor should be held, but as the standard to which every doctor should aspire. Kramer's film understands that only a select few ever come to medicine with Marsh's discipline and talent; it is those few who must inspire others and impart as much wisdom and knowledge as can be taught. Even with this deliberate approach, Kramer himself felt he did an injustice to the profession:

> For my part, I think I could have been a little more deft and serious about the profession. I should have given more attention to the Broderick Crawford character's lecture about the ideal nature of proper medical practice. I didn't prove, in the story, what the Crawford character said on-screen. That still bothers me about *Not as a Stranger*. I didn't get into the picture a sense of my own convictions about the nobility that the profession can and usually does represent. I didn't do as much justice to the virtues of the profession as I did to its vices. That will always bother me.

Despite Kramer's later misgivings, he injects a great deal of positive feeling about medicine into the film. The clinical scenes in medical school are as accurate as he could make them, aided immeasurably by technical advisors Dr. Morton Maxwell, Dr. Josh Fields and nurse Marjorie Lefevre. Many of the principal actors

Not as a Stranger. The new doctor in town, Lucas Marsh (Robert Mitchum), meets some of Greenville's prominent citizens (and drinkers): Ben Cosgrove (Jesse White) and Harriet Lang (Gloria Grahame), with whom Marsh will embark on a passionate affair. The film marked producer Stanley Kramer's debut as a director.

attended a few medical procedures to prepare, and most of them reacted with fainting or sickness when they witnessed real operations or autopsies. During the climactic operation on Dr. Runkleman, a heart can actually be seen beating inside an opened chest; this was one of the first times a movie had ever shown such a sight. (This scene was snipped in Great Britain.) And for all of Marsh's railing against the evils of the profession, there is no doubt whatsoever that he will rise to become a great doctor, and that there must be others like him who value idealism and professionalism over the financial rewards that becoming a doctor brings.

The film is pretty cleanly divided into two halves. The first half consists of the medical school scenes; the second takes Marsh and Kristina to Greenville, and private practice. The medical school scenes are clinical and efficient. They contain both drama and humor, establish the characters and explore medicine in impres-

sive detail. The first half is without doubt the better portion of the film.

The second half expands the Marsh-Kristina relationship, introduces the wedging elements of private practice (no longer do Marsh and Kristina share a profession, at least not until he brings her in to help cure the typhoid patient), Harriet Lang, and boredom. Marsh's affair with Harriet turns the drama into soap opera, with its blatant symbolism undermining the subtlety of what has gone before. Marsh's problems in Greenville seem to stem from boredom. No longer frazzled in medical school, he has the time to contemplate dissatisfaction with Kristina, carnal thoughts about Harriet and the future of a physician with his talents languishing in a small city. Acting on those thoughts is what gets him into trouble. Finally, the catharsis involving the death of Dr. Runkleman shocks Marsh into understanding what people, including his own father, have been telling him all along, "You have to have a heart."

This, ultimately, is the message that Kramer delivers. Only after he confronts his own fallibility does Marsh become fully human, capable of empathizing with his patients, wife and friends. It is this, finally, that will complete his evolution into a valuable doctor.

Reviews for the film were all over the place. *Time* liked it, but with reservations. "It is a better than adequate film, but that stud horse should have been kept quiet in its stall." Arthur Knight of *Saturday Review* concluded, "The result ... is a kind of super-suds— the very finest consistency, but still soap." On the other hand, Robert Hatch of *The Nation* decided, "All the high-grade acting and expensive surgical equipment is wasted on a journey to nowhere." *Variety* called it "strong screen diversion." Moira Walsh of *America* declared, "The film's clinical aspects have a vitality that covers a multitude of script deficiencies." According to *Commonweal*, "The picture is as clinically cold as some of the operating scenes with which Kramer has decorated the plot so generously, but it doesn't use its scalpels to show us what its people are really like." The British Film Institute's *Monthly Film Bulletin* termed it "a conventionally glossy and long-winded affair." *Boxoffice* declared, "There can be no doubt that it will be one of the most widely discussed motion pictures of the decade," and praised "the magnificence of Kramer's accomplishment as both producer and director."

Despite mixed critical response, the public flocked to *Not as a Stranger*. Its all-star cast helped, of course, but at the time the American public was heavily interested in medical dramas, especially on television. This version of Thompson's best-seller was the premier blockbuster on the subject and its elements of medical drama, romantic intrigue and sexual candor made it a must-see. It was nominated for one Academy Award (Best Sound Recording). The National Board of Review selected Charles Bickford (Dr. Runkleman) as Best Supporting Actor, and the British Film Institute nominated Frank Sinatra as Best Foreign Actor. Sinatra lost to Ernest Borgnine in *Marty*.

Today the film is hardly remembered. It has only recently been released on DVD, perhaps because it seems so dated next to the innumerable medical dramas in both cinema and television that have followed it. It looks downright quaint next to *Grey's Anatomy* or *ER*. That is a shame, for it is a good, solid, meaningful exploration of the medical profession.

For the first time, audiences rebelled against Gloria's performance (and appearance). She had played the trampy woman next door once too often, betrayed by a director who wouldn't help her focus the character and finally-out-in-the-open rumors about the silly tissue paper stunt. Her performance really isn't bad, blurry though it may be. She fits the role to a tee. But it is a thankless role, not written with the clarity and precision to which she was accustomed. Other elements in the film overwhelm her, as they should, and the one big scene she has with Mitchum out in the windy corral is laughable. What was a prestige project turned, in her case, into an embarrassment. Despite the film's popularity, as well as a $50,000 paycheck for making it, Gloria felt *Not as a Stranger* was a personal failure.

Oklahoma! (1955)

CREDITS Magna Productions and Rodgers and Hammerstein Productions. *Distributed by* Magna Productions (Todd-AO version), 20th Century–Fox (CinemaScope version) and RKO Radio Pictures (CinemaScope version). *Directed by* Fred Zinnemann. *Produced by* Arthur Hornblow, Jr. *Executive Producers*: Richard Rodgers and Oscar Hammerstein II. *Screenplay by* Sonya Levien and William Ludwig. *Adapted from* Rodgers and Hammerstein's Musical Play. *Based upon a dramatic play* (*Green Grow the Lilacs*) by Lynn Riggs. *Play Originally Produced on the Stage by* The Theatre Guild. *Music by* Richard Rodgers. *Book and Lyrics by* Oscar Hammerstein II. *Director of Photography*: Robert Surtees. *Film Editor*: George Boemler. *Dances Staged by* Agnes de Mille. *Production Designed by* Oliver Smith. *Art Direction by* Joseph Wright. *Music Conducted and Supervised by* Jay Blackton. *Musical Arrangements by* Robert Russell Bennett. *Background Music Adapted and Conducted by* Adolph Deutsch. *Costumes by* Orry-Kelly and Motley (Sophie Devine). *Set Decoration*: Keogh Gleason. *Color Consultant*: Alvord Eiseman. *Production Aide*: John Fearnley. *Assistant Director*: Arthur Black, Jr. *Music Coordinator*: Robert Helfer. *Sound Supervisor*: Fred Hynes. *Makeup*: Ben Lane. *Hair Stylist*: Annabell. *Wardrobe*: Frank Beetson and Ann Peck. *Additional Cinematography by* Floyd Crosby. *Additional Film Editing by* Gene Ruggiero.

Additional Costuming by Charles Arrico. *Makeup Artist*: Ben Nye. *Unit Manager*: Samuel Lambert. *Assistant Director*: Jack Voglin. *Second Assistant Director*: Robert E. Relyea. *Sound Recordist*: C. J. "Mickey" Emerson. *Dubbing*: Joseph I. Kane. *Sound Editor*: Milo B. Lory. *Camera Operator*: Bobby Moreno. *Still Photographer*: Schuyler Crail. *Helicopter Pilot*: Bob Gilbreath. *Orchestrators*: Alexander Courage and Albert Sendrey. *Music Editor*: Ralph Ives. *Production Executive*: Barney Briskin. *Todd-AO Technician*: Schuyler A. Sanford. *Dialogue Coach*: Jus Addiss. *Production Assistant*: John Emerson. *Unit Publicist*: H. Thomas Wood. *Stunt Double*: Ben Johnson. Eastman Color. Todd-AO (2.20:1) and CinemaScope (2.55:1). Orthosonic Stereo Sound. 145 minutes (CinemaScope version). 147 minutes (Todd-AO version). Released on October 11, 1955 (Todd-AO version). Released in late 1956 (CinemaScope version). Currently available on DVD. Previously available on VHS and laserdisc.

CAST *Curly McClain*, Gordon MacRae; *Ado Annie Carnes*, Gloria Grahame; *Will Parker*, Gene Nelson; *Aunt Eller Murphy*, Charlotte Greenwood; *Ali Hakim*, Eddie Albert; *Andrew (Pa) Carnes*, James Whitmore; *Laurey Williams*, Shirley Jones; *Jud Fry*, Rod Steiger; *Gertie Cummings*, Barbara Lawrence; *Ike Skidmore*, Jay C. Flippen; *Marshal Cord Elam*, Roy Barcroft; *Dream Curly*, James Mitchell; *Dream Laurey*, Bambi Linn; *Principal Dancers*: Jennie Workman, Virginia Bosler, Kelix Brown, Evelyn Taylor, Lizanne Truex, Jane Fischer and Marc Platt; *Minister*, Russell Simpson; *Farmer at Dance*: Donald Kerr; *Cowboys at Auction*: Al Ferguson, Rory Mallinson and Buddy Roosevelt; *Wrangler*: Ben Johnson; *Dancers*, Charlene Baker, Joanne Genthon, Sheila Hackett, Nancy Kilgas, Alicia Krug, Raimonda Orselli, Gloria Patrice, Christy Peterson, Donna Pouget, Celia Rogers, Salli Sorvo, Dolores Starr, Sally Whelan, Robert Cole, Fred Hansen, Hugh Allen, Chad Block, Bob Colder, Bill Chatham, Bob Hanlin, Loren Hightower, Carey Leverette, Paul Olson, Bob Petrovich, Felix Smith, Jack Tygett, Eddie Weston and Jerry Dealey.

Although Gloria Grahame had appeared as singers in *Song of the Thin Man, A Woman's Secret* and *Naked Alibi*, it had not been Gloria actually singing in any of those movies. In fact, she was largely tone-deaf. She had a pleasant singing voice, but was unable to stay on pitch very long. So in those movies Gloria's warbling was actually dubbed by professional singers. This practice was common in Hollywood and remains so today. But such is the strange, twisted landscape of Hollywood that, while it was widely known that she could not sing, Gloria found herself under serious consideration

for a key role in the filming of Broadway's most revered musical, *Oklahoma!* And in one of the greatest ironies in show business history, it is indeed tone-deaf Gloria singing — with her songs pieced together phrase by phrase, sometimes note by note, in the recording studio — on what would quickly become the top-selling soundtrack in movie history.

The experience of filming *Oklahoma!* (on location in Arizona and on MGM's soundstages in Hollywood) also changed Gloria's career in other ways, mostly negative. Due to a variety of factors, she was not comfortable in the part and by many accounts she behaved very unprofessionally on the set. There had been whispers or rumors before that Gloria was becoming "difficult," and on location for *Oklahoma!* those rumors turned into cold, hard fact. She finished the film and her performance was widely lauded, but the word had spread throughout the filming that she was no longer reliable. The result is that this long-awaited musical was her last major American film for four years, and essentially ended her Hollywood stardom.

Oklahoma! begins with cowboy Curly McClain (Gordon MacRae) riding his horse Blue across the Oklahoma prairie singing "Oh, What a Beautiful Mornin'." He visits with Aunt Eller Murphy (Charlotte Greenwood) and her niece Laurey Williams (Shirley Jones), with an eye toward asking Laurey to accompany him to the box social dance that evening. They banter playfully and Curly turns on the charm, singing "Surrey with the Fringe on Top" to persuade her. It almost works, but Laurey stubbornly refuses to admit that she really likes Curly. Instead, she accepts an invitation to the dance from Jud Fry (Rod Steiger), Aunt Eller's burly farm hand. Curly resignedly asks Aunt Eller to accompany him to the dance, and she agrees at once.

Aunt Eller takes a carriage to the Claremore train station to meet Will Parker (Gene Nelson), arriving from Kansas City with something for Aunt Eller to wear at the dance. Will is delighted to announce that he won a rodeo event worth fifty dollars, just the amount needed to claim the hand of his beloved Ado Annie. He shows the cowboys hanging around the station a gadget he purchased called a "Little Wonder," essentially a kaleidoscope tube with naughty pictures inside — as well as a spring-

Oklahoma! Ado Annie Carnes (Gloria) sits all prim and proper with Persian peddler Ali Hakim (Eddie Albert), but he has some rather fresh ideas of his own. Those ideas will cost him dearly before the final fade-out.

loaded knife blade. Aunt Eller sees the pictures and teases Will, who launches into the song and dance "Kansas City." Meanwhile, Laurey takes a swim close to home and is met by the Persian peddler Ali Hakim (Eddie Albert) and Ado Annie Carnes (Gloria Grahame). Ali Hakim suggests a swim for all three the Persian way — with no bathing suits — but he is not taken seriously. Laurey asks Ado Annie why she is with the peddler when Will Parker is coming back to town that very day. Ado Annie describes her feelings about men in the song "I Cain't Say No."

Ali Hakim sells Laurey some Egyptian smelling salts and then meets Will Parker, who arrives with Aunt Eller. Will announces his attention to marry Ado Annie, which is just fine with the peddler. But Ado Annie is not so sure, as the fifty dollars necessary to make her father happy has all been spent on gifts for her. A crowd of people arrives at Aunt Eller's, stopping there on the way to Ike Skidmore's, where the dance is to take place. The women go into the house to freshen themselves, and there Lau-

rey sings "Many a New Day" when it becomes clear that another girl, Gertie Cummings (Barbara Lawrence), has her eye set on Curly. Ado Annie tells Ali Hakim that she has to marry Will, but her father Andrew Carnes (James Whitmore) arrives and sees an opportunity to marry off his daughter to the peddler. Andrew's shotgun pointed at Ali Hakim helps the peddler make up his mind about Ado Annie, although he would rather not be so committed.

Laurey joins Curly in Aunt Eller's peach orchard and they sing "People Will Say We're in Love," but Laurey is still promised to Jud for the dance. Vexed, Curly visits Jud Fry in the smokehouse where he lives and they sing "Pore Jud Is Daid." Curly and Jud develop into rivals for Laurey's affections, and Jud warns Curly to stay out of his way. Laurey hears Jud warning Curly and is troubled. She takes a nap before leaving for the dance, using the Egyptian smelling salts to "make up my mind for me." Laurey's dream, begun by the song "Out of My Dreams," turns into an impressionistic ballet sequence in which Curly and Jud fight over her, and Jud wins! She awakens as Jud is carrying her away, only to find the burly farm hand in his best clothes, reminding her that it's time to leave for the dance. The Todd-AO version of the film has an intermission at this point (the CinemaScope version has no intermission).

Riding to the dance, Jud slows his carriage well behind the others and declares his feelings for Laurey. She reacts violently, causing the horses to run wild. The carriage flight is finally interrupted by a train, which frightens the horses into stopping. Jud calms the horses but before he can climb back into the rig, Laurey pushes him away and drives off alone. The box social is underway at the Skidmore property, part of which has been donated to build a schoolhouse. It is at this partially completed structure that the dance is to occur. Ike Skidmore (Jay C. Flippen) hosts the event, singing "The Farmer and the Cowman" as everyone hoots, hollers, briefly fights, and dances. Skidmore now ushers the crowd toward his porch, where an auction will take place of ladies' food baskets, and the company of those ladies for the duration of the meal.

Laurey arrives alone, donates her basket, and is chagrined to see Curly. Ali Hakim arrives and is hassled by Will Parker, who doesn't like the peddler moving in on his girl. Ali has the smart idea to buy Will's gifts for Ado Annie, thereby giving him the cash that Annie's father demands. He is negotiating when Jud sees Will's "Little Wonder" and buys it. Ali purchases the rest of Will's gifts. The last two hampers of food are Annie's and Laurey's. Annie's fetches bids from Ali, who is pressured to bid by Andrew Carnes, until Will bids fifty dollars for it. Will's bold declaration of love for Annie is rejected by Andrew, because Will is then broke again, so Ali bids fifty-one dollars and wins the hamper, leaving Will with enough money to marry Ado Annie according to her father's promise. Laurey's hamper also sees multiple bids, but Jud tops every one of them. Curly steps up and sells his saddle, his horse, and finally his gun to win the auction — and win Laurey's affections by doing so. After the auction, Jud shows Curly the "Little Wonder," but Ali Hakim warns Aunt Eller in time to keep Jud from using its hidden knife blade against Curly.

The dance continues, but Will pulls Ado Annie aside and demands her fidelity in the song "All 'er Nothin'." The song ends with their tacit agreement to remain true to one another. Meanwhile, Jud privately threatens Laurey and she fires him on the spot. Laurey tells Curly about it, and they kiss for the first time. Their song "Let People Say We're in Love," an altered reprise of "People Will Say We're in Love," seals their intentions, and Curly agrees to marry her. Meanwhile, Ali Hakim leaves, but not before giving Annie a passionate "Persian good-bye." Will sends him on his way and gives Annie an even more passionate "Oklahoma hello." The dance has run its course.

A short time later another gathering is held, this time at Aunt Eller's place, for the occasion of a marriage at sunset. Curly marries Laurey inside while Jud skulks around outside. After the ceremony, Curly leads everyone outside where he and the company sing "Oklahoma!" Then the men and women separate, for Andrew Carnes is arranging a "shivoree" for the couple. Curly and Laurey are led outside and placed on top of a large haystack where the surrounding crowd taunts and teases them. Curly sees a burning haystack and the crowd hurries to put out the fire. Jud appears with a torch and sets the haystack with the newlyweds afire. Curly pushes Laurey off in one direction and then jumps toward Jud, who has pulled a knife and is yelling for Curly to come and get it. The men collide and Jud falls on his knife. Jud is carried to a doctor's while Curly is restrained by the crowd. At Aunt Eller's, word arrives that Jud has died. The federal marshal (Roy Barcroft) wants Curly to turn himself in, but Aunt Eller won't hear of it. She pressures the local judge, Andrew Carnes, to hold an impromptu court in her crowded kitchen. Curly is found "not guilty" by reason of self-defense, and the newlyweds are sent off toward an awaiting train and their honeymoon. The departing crowd sings a reprise of "Oh, What a Beautiful Mornin'" and the movie ends.

Oklahoma! was the highly anticipated film version of the Broadway musical that forever changed the direction of American musical theater. Historians claim that *Oklahoma!* (originally titled *Away We Go!*) was the first fully integrated musical; that every one of its songs was character-driven, sung from one or more characters to or for the other characters on stage (instead of primarily to the audience) and designed to move the story forward. Previous musical plays featured specialty acts or specialty numbers, musical interludes included for their entertainment value rather than any intrinsic story value. A good example is Lynn Riggs' play *Green Grow the Lilacs*, from which *Oklahoma!* is adapted. Several folk songs and traditional Western tunes populate *Green Grow the Lilacs*, but they are sung as performance pieces, because that was the practice in 1900, when the play was set. The songs essentially serve the same purpose as those written by Rodgers and Hammerstein for *Oklahoma!*; that is, to convey the emotions and feelings of the characters singing them, yet the effect is not the same because they are staged as someone (usually Curly) publicly singing a song that suits his temperament at the moment, while others listen and enjoy the serenade. Furthermore, previous plays often featured performers such as Ethel Merman who, even when singing a character-driven song, would step out of character, move to the front of the stage and bellow her show-stopping number directly to the audience. *Oklahoma!* changed all that, and the public responded. The first musical partnership of composer Richard Rodgers and lyricist Oscar Hammerstein II debuted on March 31, 1943, was an immediate success and eventually played for 2,212 performances. It won Rodgers and Hammerstein a special Pulitzer Prize and made them rich.

Was *Oklahoma!* the first fully integrated musical play? Perhaps not; Jerome Kern and Hammerstein had already developed *Show Boat*, another classic show with similar aims. *Oklahoma!* took the concept of seamlessly blending story and song to its logical extreme, however, and it was the first tremendously successful play to do so. It set the pattern for all of subsequent Rodgers and Hammerstein projects, allowing them the financial independence to develop their works in any manner they chose. More than any other factor, this led to the film version of their first hit being made in the unusual fashion that it was.

With the success of the play, its creators were besieged by Hollywood offers to bring it to the big screen. Virtually every studio tried to wrangle the rights to what was fast becoming Broadway's greatest success story. But Rodgers and Hammerstein were unwilling to let anybody make an *Oklahoma!* movie but themselves. Rodgers, in particular, was not enamored of the way the studios changed aspects, themes, characters and even the music of various projects without any regard for the originals. He had seen those tendencies up close during his earlier partnership with Lorenz Hart, when several Rodgers and

Oklahoma! This publicity shot of Ado Annie Carnes (Gloria) and Will Parker (Gene Nelson) is flattering to both performers, yet absolutely no chemistry is evident between them. Gloria alienated everyone on the production with her behavior; it was her last major Hollywood role.

Hart properties had been made, in his opinion, to disappointing standards. Rodgers and Hammerstein were convinced that *Oklahoma!* was special, and they were determined to control every aspect of its evolution. They eventually formed a company, funded by investors independent of the Hollywood studios, to make their movie when they were ready, and they utilized Michael Todd's distributing company, Magna Corporation, to distribute it. But it was a long time before they were ready.

The Broadway show played for five years, and the road companies that took it all over America (and eventually to Europe as well) played for ten. Rodgers and Hammerstein realized that as long as the stage version was running strong, any movie version could wait. And so they waited. Once the road companies began to close down in the early 1950s, finally there was serious consideration of a movie. Because of Rodgers' distrust of the studio system, they decided to produce the movie themselves. In fact, *Oklahoma!* would become the only major motion picture musical not produced by a Hollywood studio. Because they were inexperienced in moviemaking they hired Arthur Hornblow, Jr., to produce their film, and because they were determined to protect the story, they eventually hired Fred Zinnemann to direct. Zinnemann had never made a musical before, and never would again. At the time it was a controversial choice. But Zinnemann was a humanistic director, known for keeping his stories focused on character, and had made such classics as *The Search*, *The Men*, *High Noon* and *From Here to Eternity*. The latter film had won Academy Awards for Best Picture and Director (and six others), making Zinnemann the hottest director in town. So he got the nod.

The biggest hurdle to overcome was where to shoot the project. The first choice was the state of Oklahoma. It was found, however, that in the ensuing years much of the Sooner State had evolved from rural, pastoral land to modern, managed property. Gone were the vast plains and prairie. Roads, telephone lines and especially oil wells stretched on every horizon, and the filmmakers could not settle upon an Oklahoma location that actually evoked the Oklahoma of the past. They settled on a locale outside Nogales, Arizona, where it was felt that the landscape and skyline best represented the

visual motif that they wanted. Even this solution had its anachronisms and difficulties, however. Oklahoma is rather notoriously flat, yet there are mountains in most of the movie's backgrounds. A large thematic conflict is between "the farmer" and "the cowman," yet in the background of the shots of Aunt Eller's place is an oil well, and oil is never discussed. Nowadays such an anachronism would be digitally removed. The difficulties of the location derived from rain. The Nogales area was chosen in part because of the beautiful cloudscapes that were so visually appealing. But those are rain clouds, and it rained nearly every day on the set, which delayed or postponed much of the filming. The rain was so heavy in certain arroyos that several cars driving to and from the set, including some carrying a day's worth of processed film stock, were lost in flash floods. One area was so notorious it was nicknamed "Cadillac Gulch" for an incident when a Cadillac was swept several hundred feet by the roaring water.

The picturesque location also caused some political contentiousness. Because the milestone play was so revered in its home state, the decision to film elsewhere was highly unpopular to Oklahoma's citizenry. Oklahoma's governor famously decreed that the Nogales, Arizona, filming location was, at least temporarily, part of Oklahoma territory, and he made a similar declaration when the movie premiered in New York City. The play was so beloved in the Sooner State that its rousing title song was adopted as the state's official song in 1953.

Rodgers had partnered with Lorenz Hart for many years and successful shows, but the partnership had ended in 1942. Rodgers and Hart had been approached by the Theatre Guild to provide music and lyrics for Lynn Riggs' play *Green Grow the Lilacs*, but Hart was uninterested and the partnership dissolved. Meanwhile, Jerome Kern and Oscar Hammerstein II had also been approached, but Kern was likewise uninterested. But Rodgers and Hammerstein, who had known each other for years and had composed together for a Columbia University varsity show in 1920, decided to try their luck as new partners. They worked extremely well together from the start. Although the play proved to be full of challenges, when it opened on March 31, 1943, as *Oklahoma!*, theater history was altered forever and the two men found themselves the toast of Broadway.

Rodgers was a master of melody, as evidenced by the wonderful songs he composed over his long career, and he was at the top of his form when he wrote the score for *Oklahoma!* Hammerstein's lyrics perfectly complement, and sometimes even improve upon, Rodgers' music, ably and memorably evoking not only the emotions of the characters but the spirit of the time and place as well. Rodgers' music runs the range from supremely lyrical to rousingly boisterous, with unforgettable melodies and beautiful orchestrations that made the *Oklahoma!* soundtrack the bestselling movie soundtrack album of its time. Hammerstein's lyrics capture every nuance of character and truly thrust the narrative forward. They are full of colloquial charm, description and humor that contribute layers of meaning and enjoyment to Rodgers' eminently hummable tunes. Together, Rodgers and Hammerstein created music for the ages in plays and movies like *Carousel, The King and I, South Pacific* and *The Sound of Music*, yet, in purely musical terms *Oklahoma!* ranks among the best work they ever produced. Their theatrical legacy was assured with this, just their first work together, but *Oklahoma!* was followed by some of the greatest musicals in Broadway history.

It is somewhat odd to note, then, that those milestone musical plays did not always translate into classic movies. Some did: *The King and I* is a delightful movie, probably the best screen translation of a Rodgers and Hammerstein play; and of course *The Sound of Music* became, for a long time, the most popular musical movie ever made. But *Carousel, South Pacific, Flower Drum Song* and *State Fair* are simply not the runaway classics, nor the box office powerhouses, that their respective studios expected when those expensive projects were bankrolled. Nor is *Oklahoma!*

The film itself is, despite its nearly two-and-a-half hour running time, notably slight. In essence it is, after all, the simple question of who will accompany who to a dance. That humble structure, however, is complicated by various aspects that fuel it with drama: the rivalry between two men for both Laurey and Ado Annie; the sexual coming of age of those women in markedly different ways; the land-based thematic conflict between "the farmer" and "the cowman," or in other words, tradition versus progress; the prospect of statehood for the Oklahoma territory; the specter of violence that Jud Fry represents; the quaint customs of the citizenry in regard to love, sex and marriage; and, of course, the beautiful music of Rodgers and Hammerstein which sets all of these elements into musical perspective.

The two romantic triangles establish every important conflict, and the manner in which they play against each other provides humor, clarity and perspective. The primary triangle finds Curly and Jud vying for Laurey, and the various actions and ramifications of this relationship are quite serious. The secondary triangle, Will Parker and Ali Hakim wooing Ado Annie, is largely played for comic effect, but also serves to parallel the primary triangle. Whenever Laurey's predicament becomes melodramatic, Ado Annie steps in for some laughs, reminding everyone that courtship can be silly, too. Laurey and Annie are similar, in that they are attractive young women just learning how to deal with men, yet they represent opposite positions. Laurey is as chaste as can be; she has no real notion of what effect she has on men, or any sense of physical love. With her golden hair, pure voice and white dresses, Laurey is the absolute picture of virgin beauty; it is no wonder that Curly and Jud are after her. Her notions of love are firmly idealized, as evidenced in the songs "The Surrey with the Fringe on Top" and "People Will Say We're in Love," which present romanticized versions of how she and Curly will appear to all who see them together.

Annie, on the other hand, has sampled physical affection, and finds that she likes it more than just about anything else. Roughly the same age as Laurey, Ado Annie is by comparison a nymphomaniac. Of course, her experience is limited to kissing, as this is a family show, yet Annie is undeniably aware of her effect on men, and she enjoys all the attention she is causing and receiving. Her outlook on romance is not idealized at all; she enjoys the physical aspects that she has experienced. Her song "I Cain't Say No" says everything about her character. Of her two suitors, Will has honorable intentions for her, although he is quite aware of her amorous proclivities. Ali Hakim has no such honor — he just wants to have sex with her. Thus, Will is Curly's parallel, while Ali Hakim is the comic equivalent (if that is possible) to Jud Fry. In both triangles, the girl is almost lost to the lecherous man, but the honorable man eventually wins her hand. In Laurey's case, Jud is eventually killed with his own knife and Curly is exonerated of manslaughter. In Annie's case, Ali Hakim actually buys his way out of matrimony by allowing Will to keep his fifty dollar betrothal payment. It is interesting to note that although Ali Hakim eludes Ado Annie's marriage-minded clutches, he is later caught by the cackling Gertie Cummings (Barbara Lawrence), in circumstances very similar to those which had threatened his cherished freedom when he was dallying with Annie.

A hallmark — and apparent self-contradiction — of the Rodgers and Hammerstein oeuvre is that many of their stories have as a foundation a need or desire for sex or sexual fulfillment. This may not seem so if one considers their plays to be family entertainments — which they undoubtedly are — but nevertheless it is true, especially in the case of *Oklahoma!* Curly wants to be with Laurey; Jud desperately wants to be with Laurey; Will wants to be with Ado Annie; Ali Hakim wants to take advantage of Ado Annie; Laurey is just blossoming into womanhood and is unsure what she wants; Ado Annie wants to be with both Will and Ali Hakim. Their sexual preferences and desires form the drama which propels the story's narrative, even if they are couched in quaint terms, customs, song lyrics and witticisms. The material is handled quite delicately, of course, yet it is undeniable that Ado Annie is (or could become) a nymphomaniac, and that Jud is (or could become) a rapist.

Being a mainstream entertainment in the era in which it was written, of course, those terms and what they really implied couldn't be proffered. The promise of sex was conveyed by the act of kissing and wanting to kiss, and all the discussion about marriage was really shorthand for forming permanent relationships. The central sexual tension, of course, is between Curly and Laurey, and their relationship consists of familiar banter and teasing, followed by beautiful intimate moments of kinship, followed by Laurey's inability to reconcile her feelings. That lasts until she finally kisses Curly, and then backs away in stunned surprise. Laurey, finally understanding what Ado Annie kept singing about, then throws herself into Curly's arms wholeheartedly and her inhibitions vanish. Naturally, the next words out of her mouth are about marriage.

Further conflict is established between the farmers and the ranchers, most visibly during the song "The Farmer and the Cowman." In fact, it is really only there that the adversarial relationship is addressed, and even then, only briefly. The box social dance is interrupted by a quick fight between those two groups, but Aunt Eller puts a stop to the roughhousing at once and forces everyone to keep dancing — at gunpoint! Nevertheless, the inclusion of this conflict at all, as well as two transitory discussions regarding the aspects of Oklahoma becoming a state, provide a wider historical context with which to anchor the film's story and give it a broader perspective. The statehood issue is established to indicate the need for change and progress, on both social and personal levels. Curly, in fact, prods himself into marrying Laurey and becoming a farmer partly because of the impending statehood, which he views as attaining maturity on both levels.

It is said that any story involving conflict is only as good as its villain, and the villain of *Oklahoma!* is Jud Fry. Director Zinnemann was determined to humanize the character, not wanting a standard, stock villain to rival Curly for Laurey's affections. With the removal of Jud's signature song "Lonely Room" from the movie, Zinnemann had yet another reason to boost the part. And because Jud represents the only darkness in the entire venture, the director felt that the role had to be forcefully portrayed. He got his wish, as Rod Steiger — in both the narrative and the ballet sequence — solidly upstages the rest of the cast with apparent ease. Yet it is this relentlessly realistic and downbeat portrait of a social outsider, shunned by everyone in the Oklahoma community, that throws the musical off its balance, stylistically and thematically.

Thematically Jud seems necessary to try to counterbalance the play's innate sunniness. Everything is light and airy, charming and homespun, lyrical and playful — except for Jud Fry. From the moment he walks onto the

Oklahoma! Aunt Eller Murphy (Charlotte Greenwood) gives Ado Annie Carnes (Gloria) a friendly pat on the rump during the song "The Farmer and the Cowman," to the delight of the neighbor folk.

screen, dark and powerful, beefy and unsmiling, he is instantly recognizable as a threat to the flaxen-haired Laurey. But the movie overemphasizes Jud. It portrays him as the serpent in this Garden of Eden, hiding in his dark, underground smokehouse, a place where only evil can flourish. He even has pictures of naked women on his dirty smokehouse walls! Although Jud's attraction to Laurey is perfectly understandable and probably inevitable for anyone in his position, the movie (and the play, too) turns Jud's feelings into a twisted, sordid obsession that eventually leads him to try to destroy her for rejecting him. Sure, some counterpoint to the rampant sunshine of this narrative is desirable, but Jud is an anachronistic character (that's why everybody shuns him), and one who detracts from the film's effectiveness.

Stylistically Jud's presence disrupts the gentle harmony that the film's other relationships and subplots balance rather nicely. Jud and his dark dominion are given so much intensity that they overwhelm everything else.

What is known about Curly, other than he is a happy-go-lucky cowboy who takes a shine to Laurey? Compare that with the backstory provided for Jud, an itinerant farm hand, whose interior life is shown quite intimately (although with no song of his own). Furthermore, Jud's actions— spying on Laurey, trying to force himself upon her, threatening her after the dance, skulking around after he's been fired, eventually trying to kill her and Curly with fire — seem better suited to a serial killer movie than a pastoral musical. *Oklahoma!*'s façade is the essence of Americana, but it's heart is Jud's festering rage. Zinnemann later sensed that he had unbalanced the play's drama, writing, "Rod Steiger's performance as Jud is excellent, but I gave it too much weight. I ought to have spotted this break in style during the film, but I didn't."

It is somewhat strange that Jud's presence so forcefully disrupts the proceedings, because he is of even greater significance in the original play. He is named Jeeter Fry in *Green Grow the Lilacs*, and much of the play revolves around

Jeeter's and Curly's rivalry for Laurey. This is, in fact, the only romantic triangle in the play, and it is very clearly staged as a battle of good and evil for Laurey's affections. No auction occurs in which Jeeter is ostracized by the community; his place in the story is clearly defined as Curly's rival for Laurey. The story unfolds straightforwardly as Jeeter tries to pressure Laurey into liking him, she rejects and fires him (privately) at a dance, and then he tries to kill Laurey and Curly on their wedding night in the same manner as occurs in the later film. None of this seems unbalanced in the original play because it is the primary focus. But *Oklahoma!*, while keeping the basic story of the play and much of the dialogue as well, shifts the focus away from the dangerous romantic triangle to a greater sense of the pastoral open West, soon to be fenced in the name of statehood, and the resilient practicality and common sense of its population, most notably in the character of Aunt Eller. In this bountiful, agreeable, sun-blessed environment, it is inevitable that a maleficent, black-hearted character such as Jud would seem unnatural. Perhaps Rodgers and Hammerstein were too successful in their effort to fashion *Oklahoma!* as a Utopian paradise.

Jud also figures prominently into the other element that unsettles the movie: the dream ballet sequence. The scene is worth discussion because it is now so polarizing. At the time the film was made, Rodgers and Hammerstein debated whether to keep it intact. Laurey's dream ballet was an integral part of the stage show, and the central idea behind the film was to bring to the screen the elements of the theatrical show that had been so memorable and successful. Gene Kelly and Fred Astaire were successfully putting ballet sequences in their movies, so the decision was made to keep it. Laurey's dream ballet is fifteen minutes long in the CinemaScope version, fourteen in the Todd-AO version. Its artistic pretention directly upstages the smooth, lyrical feel of the narrative and stops it dead in its tracks. The ballet sequence is a microcosm of the movie's narrative, albeit with a twist: At its conclusion, it is not Jud, not Curly, who carries Laurey away.

Supporters of the dream ballet point to the larger issue of dance within the film's context, noting that this musical is flush with Agnes de Mille's exuberant choreography and that removing any of it, particularly the dream ballet, would damage the artistic integrity of the whole. It is beautifully danced by James Mitchell (as Curly) and Bambi Linn (as Laurey), and creditably performed by Rod Steiger, who remains as Jud because no one else of his physicality could be found to replace him. It hints at Jud's mental state more expressively than does the narrative, especially considering that Jud's song "Lonely Room" was not transferred to the movie. Because it is a dream sequence, it is the one occasion that imagination is allowed to float free, leading to elements like the staircase that goes nowhere and the painted tornado and wind effects that express Laurey's fears. And like dreams are wont to do from time to time, it ends badly for the dreamer, transmogrifying into a sexually charged nightmare.

Critics of the dream ballet argue that it brings the narrative to an abrupt standstill; that it doesn't further the story at all, but instead simply recounts what is already clear and apparent; that the appearance of a different Curly and Laurey (despite an interesting changeover method) is jarring. Why couldn't the real (so to speak) Curly and Laurey have done their own dancing? Jud did! Shirley Jones, for one, is glad that she didn't have to try. She explains on a DVD audio commentary that she was not then and has never become a dancer, and that it would have been much too hard for her to handle, especially in her first feature film. Jones gives great credit to Rod Steiger for accepting the challenge and for strengthening his character by doing so.

Nevertheless, the dream ballet is a pivotal sequence, and it divides the audience into those who are enthralled by the wordless musical spectacle and those who take the opportunity for a bathroom break. It is the apotheosis of de Mille's remarkable choreography, which blends the flavors of Aaron Copland and rural Americana with a distinctly feminine edge, hinting at volatile sexuality beneath a cornpone façade. The de Mille choreography is powerfully spotlighted in the numbers "Kansas City," "Many a New Day," "The Farmer and the Cowman" and the dream ballet, and, to a lesser degree, in "All 'er Nothin'" and the title song. De Mille's choreographic contributions are integral to the musical concept embraced by Rodgers and Hammerstein, that of having the story propelled forward by the music. The large film frame actually provides her with more space with which to work than she had on the New York stage, and she takes full advantage of it. She reworked her original dances and tweaked them here and there for the film. One of her more intriguing contributions involves two young dancers, Lizanne Truex and Jane Fischer, known colloquially on the set as the "Goon Girls," though they are not identified as such in the film. The two, a bowl-haired blonde tomboy (Truex) and a brunette beauty (Fischer), appear in every one of the dances, almost always together, usually doing their own thing apart from everyone else. The Goon Girls (named that way for their "gooning," or goofing, around) are the Rosencrantz and Guildenstern of the piece, delightfully popping in and out all the time, including the ballet sequence. On repeat viewings, they tend to upstage the dancers in the center of the frame as they cavort in the background, yet they are absolutely adorable.

Director Zinnemann emphasized the music, of course, and allowed de Mille to fill the Todd-AO and CinemaScope frames with her athletic, energetic dances, but he handled the rest of the story with a realism that occasionally undermines the act of creating what is in essence a fantasy musical. Musicals by nature are colorful, escapist entertainment, often blissfully unattached to the realities of life. Zinnemann largely eschewed the fantasy approach, even in the musical numbers, electing to bring as much authenticity and verisimilitude to the story, just as he had in his earlier dramatic triumphs. One of his many touches is to occasionally film characters with their backs to the camera, even while they are speaking, which is a technique eschewed by most directors. The result is dramatically solid, yet the very credibility of Jud's obsessive anger, or Laurey's spite at Curly's casual arrogance, or Annie's romantic confusion about sex, or the community's refusal to accept Jud as one of their own, prevents this famous musical from taking flight in the way that *Singin' in the Rain* or *Seven Brides for Seven Brothers* is able to do. Neil Sinyard, in his analysis of Zinnemann's work *Fred Zinnemann: Films of Character and Conscience*,

judges his movies in this way: "*High Noon* has been described as a Western for people who do not like Westerns. To some extent, *Oklahoma!* is a musical for people who do not like musicals. It does not have the genre's requisite bounce and joy, but it does have its moments of drama."

The failure of *Oklahoma!* to be ranked with the greatest musicals of its era, much less of all time, is due to several factors. Zinnemann's realistic approach to the material actually dampens this musical's zest and buoyancy. The dramatic weight given to Jud Fry unbalances an already slight storyline. The ballet sequence is exceedingly long, jarring in its interruption of the narrative, and dramatically unnecessary. Three of the secondary performers — Rod Steiger, Gloria Grahame, Eddie Albert — are noticeably miscast, although they deliver strong, provocative performances. The twelve-year delay between the theater and movie versions, as well as the immense popularity of the play, eliminated any mystery about a movie version; most people in 1955 were well aware of the play and its music. The film's billing was misleading, listing non-lead Gloria Grahame right next to Gordon MacRae, probably confusing the public as to who she played; and movie fans had no idea who Shirley Jones was yet. Finally, a dozen years after the play had taken Broadway by storm — and with the similarly folksy *State Fair* in the meantime — the setting, colloquialisms and simple charm that *Oklahoma!* offered were perceived as being quaint and old-fashioned. By 1955, the play was dated; the pastoral Utopia simply did not exist any more, if indeed it ever had.

But that perception did not prevent Rodgers and Hammerstein from working very hard to bring their first collaborative vision to the screen. Musicals were still big business in 1955, as evidenced by the productions of *Young at Heart, Daddy Long Legs, Guys and Dolls, Three for the Show, Jupiter's Darling, Love Me or Leave Me* and *It's Always Fair Weather*. Other than *State Fair*, which was written directly for the screen after the success of *Oklahoma!* in 1945, no other Rodgers and Hammerstein project had yet been transferred to film, and the two impresarios were determined to bring each and every one of their blockbuster musicals to cinematic fruition. Their baby, *Oklahoma!* was to be the first. Aside from hiring the best director and department heads they could, they considered the next most important factor to be inspired casting. And while Zinnemann and producer Hornblow certainly had crucial input, the final casting decisions were made, for better or worse, by Richard Rodgers and Oscar Hammerstein II.

Casting Curly was indicative of the issues the production faced. Zinnemann wanted a real actor in the part; Paul Newman and James Dean (both pre-stardom) were auditioned and strongly considered but neither one could sing well enough to suit the executive producers. It is fascinating to imagine *Oklahoma!* as Zinnemann did in preproduction, with Newman, Dean or even Montgomery Clift as Curly and Joanne Woodward as Laurey, not to mention Marlon Brando or Eli Wallach also vying to play Jud Fry. Now that is a cast for people who don't like musicals! But Rodgers, in particular, had definite casting ideas and he wanted someone with a powerful singing voice to play Curly. So Gordon MacRae, a "light" actor with a gorgeous voice, got the call and set the tone for the film. MacRae was not an actor on par with Newman, Dean or Clift, but he is ideally suited to portray a relaxed, lovestruck cowboy. Hearing him softly croon the final stanza to "The Surrey with the Fringe on Top" with Shirley Jones' Laurey leaning on his shoulder, it is evident to all that the right choice was made.

Jones had also been chosen by the duo, well before the movie went into production. On a chance audition on her way to college to study veterinary medicine, Jones had been summoned before first Hammerstein and finally Rodgers in turn, asked to sing songs from the play, and then offered a personal contract. College was abandoned, and Jones was placed in the chorus of *South Pacific* on Broadway, and then transferred to a featured role in *Me and Juliet* to provide her with experience and prepare her for the role they really wanted her to play: Laurey Williams. *Oklahoma!* was Jones' film debut, although she had appeared briefly in three television episodes a few years earlier. Jones was nervous about her big break, but she was kept so busy that she didn't really have time to think about the circumstances, and she had great faith in the judgment of the producers, who were certain that she was right for the part.

Again, judging the final result, Rodgers and Hammerstein knew exactly what they were doing. Jones is as fresh as a spring blossom, invigorating the story with her flaxen-haired beauty and lilting voice. Her acting is occasionally unpolished, yet her vitality and enthusiasm is undeniable, resulting in a very memorable, positive film debut.

It has been reported occasionally that Rodgers plucked Jones out of one of the *Oklahoma!* touring company choruses to portray Laurey on screen. This is not true; Jones eventually did play in a stage version of the play, but it was *after* the film, when a European tour of the play was mounted, and Jones played Laurey again. Jones continued her association with Rodgers and Hammerstein through their next film project, *Carousel*, before breaking out on her own professionally.

Gene Nelson was another Rodgers and Hammerstein choice, with strong backing from Agnes de Mille, because unlike the leads, Nelson could dance and loved doing so. His easygoing charm nicely parallels that of MacRae, and his comic timing is essential in keeping the tone of his scenes light and enjoyable. The presence of Nelson allowed de Mille to make "Kansas City" the film's first big dance number; it is the fourth song to be performed, so unlike the play, the dancing doesn't really start until the film is well underway. Nelson did not utilize a stunt double for any scene, not even when the train begins to pull away with him on it, and he has to transfer to his horse while the train is moving. This is done in a long shot, so it's difficult to tell that it's really Nelson, but it is.

Rod Steiger was Zinnemann's selection, and as he could sing well enough, no objection was raised to it. Later, when the European play version was put together, Rodgers unceremoniously fired Steiger, calling his labored performance "a cancer" on the production, an insult that the actor never forgave. Steiger is excellent as Jud Fry, delivering perhaps the finest performance in the film (rivaling that of Charlotte Greenwood as Aunt Eller), but it is precisely Steiger's intense, raw acting that takes attention away from the leads and leaves a bad taste in viewers when Jud's intentions are so publicly foiled at auction and he then dies without much comment in the final reel. The song "Pore Jud Is Daid" is sung mainly by MacRae,

Oklahoma! A four-page German film program treats Gloria Grahame and Gene Nelson as the real stars, not only on the pictured cover, but throughout its pages.

but Steiger nicely holds his own in his few verses. And, of course, he is the only one of the principal cast to perform in the dream ballet, and does a creditable job, even lifting dream Laurey (Bambi Linn) over his head and carrying her away as the dream ends.

Charlotte Greenwood was a natural choice for Aunt Eller; she was the first choice for the original play, but had been unable to accept it due to a prior commitment. In the movie she is the voice of reason and a remarkably enthusiastic participant in several of the musical numbers. It is a wonder that she did not receive an Academy Award nomination for her work, which is truly outstanding.

Two other stars were cast against type, and rather controversially. Eddie Albert appears as Ali Hakim, the Persian peddler who dallies with Ado Annie. With a phony accent and all–American looks, Albert looks and sounds nothing like a Persian. His is the most comic role, deflecting Annie's thoughts of marriage while avoiding Will Parker's enmity and trying to sell his junk to the community. (In the play but not the movie, Ali Hakim has a song, "It's a Scandal! It's an Outrage!," regarding the habit of fathers of pretty girls to have shotguns at their quick disposal whenever he is around.) Albert plays the role broadly, emphasizing Ali Hakim's licentiousness and ribald charm, highlighting his tendency to get into situations with women that are bound to lead to trouble and personal danger. But Albert's considerable talent is never enough to make one forget that he is abominably miscast.

There is an opposite view, however, based on the notion that the film's situations would not play the same should Ali Hakim be played by a genuine Middle Eastern actor. Ali Hakim (pronounced Alley Hackem by the community) is accepted, if not exactly trusted, by the Oklahomans. As personified by all–American Albert, he is one of them, even if he sounds different. What would the community's reaction be to the character if he were played by a dark-skinned foreigner, as the part ostensibly demands? Remember, this is a character who habitually romances the pretty daughters of the farmers and ranchers he meets, with the idea of bedding them without wedding them. Moreover, what would be the reaction of the audience? Would thoughts of racism, even if never

introduced by the script, enter their minds? Perhaps Rodgers and Hammerstein foresaw such a predicament and simply decided to avoid any hint of racial conflict by casting the part with a white actor, preferably one with comic talent and a somewhat overbearing temperament, hoping to outweigh the character's written attributes with entertaining perks of personality. The result is that Albert was hired for the thankless role, and he does his best to make Ali Hakim palatable.

And then there is Gloria Grahame as Ado Annie Carnes. Rewarded with second billing for her clearly secondary part, Gloria was personally selected to play the girl "who cain't say no" by Richard Rodgers. Shirley Jones has confirmed that Rodgers wanted no one other than Gloria, always insisting that she was the right woman for the role in his film despite her lack of musical talent. Gloria felt that Celeste Holm, who had established the role on the stage, was great and should have been hired, but when husband Cy Howard insisted that Gloria accept the part and the $100,000 being offered for it, Gloria reluctantly consented. Hollywood insiders, viewing Gloria as the premier *femme fatale* in town, were surprised by the offer, and everyone who knew that Gloria could not sing was dumbfounded. Others were startled because they had never seen Gloria play flat-out comedy, something she had not done on film since 1947. Yet the casting makes some sense, judging solely by the character.

In the original play *Green Grow the Lilacs*, Ado Annie is described as "an unattractive, stupid-looking farm girl" by Lynn Riggs' stage directions, and her function in the story is to tag along with Laurey when Jeeter takes her to the dance. But Rodgers and Hammerstein saw potential in the part and boosted it. In *Oklahoma!* Ado Annie is the community's bad girl. That persona fits Gloria to a tee. The difference is that Annie's romantic wildness is mild when compared to that of Gloria's earlier characters. Gloria recognized this, however, and delightfully restrained her performance, leaving intact her ability to convey sexual desire through the way she looked at the men and, most notably, when she sang Annie's signature song "I Cain't Say No." It is this song, combined with Gloria's well-known propensity to burn through the men in all her movies, which makes her an almost perfect fit for the part, and Rodgers recognized this. He downplayed the issues of perceived miscasting, knowing that Gloria would essentially be portraying yet another sexually unfulfilled but somewhat predatory woman, this time with a comic bent. He believed she could do it, and he continually told her so.

Gloria's offbeat, delightful performance offers still more proof that Rodgers was a skilled judge of talent. Gloria's Annie is a bundle of repressed nerves and hormones just waiting to blast into ecstasy. Her primary need is affection, and she's happy to accept it from whoever she's with — provided, of course, that marriage is the ultimate target. Gloria restrains herself physically, particularly during her songs, acting mostly with her torso and arms. She bounces and rocks lightly from foot to foot during parts of "I Cain't Say No," as if wanting to jump with orgasmic joy, but then slows and stops, as if realizing that she cannot just explode with rapture; it just wouldn't be proper. Her Ado Annie is stiff with propriety most of the time, especially around Ali Hakim. There are only a few moments where she lets herself visibly relax; one is at the box social, when she participates in the number "The Farmer and the Cowman," another is during "All 'er Nothin'," when she recognizes that she and Will Parker are right for each other, and a third is just before the conclusion, when she and Will emerge out of the cornfield, having finally sampled bliss for the first time. That moment is vintage Gloria Grahame.

The most interesting aspect of Gloria's performance is that even when she is in Annie's stiff, repressed mode, she is completely convincing. She plays Annie almost as a kewpie doll come to life, comically unaware of how things, especially involving men, are supposed to work. Yet she knows intuitively how to get what she wants. Gloria's southwestern accent is flawless and the idioms that she spouts are often hilarious. As in the original play, when Annie is frustrated by something her response is to say, in a startled manner, "Foot!" Gloria positively glows with lines like, "I like it so much when a feller talks purty to me I get all shaky from horn to hoof!" And of the two formats, Gloria is better in the Todd-AO version; she's just peppier and funnier. Gloria's greatest moments are revealed when a sly, secret smile

reveals just what Annie is thinking, even as her dialogue states something else entirely. The strangest aspect of her performance occurs during the songs "The Farmer and the Cowman" and "Oklahoma!," when Ado Annie is visible at times, and then disappears entirely, only to pop back on screen at key moments and again when the songs end. In "Oklahoma!," for instance, Will and Annie are on the porch when the song begins, and once the dancing starts, they disappear, replaced on the porch by older folks. The song ends, and they're back in place.

Because of Rodgers' insistence on casting Gloria, several actresses were disappointed, among them Celeste Holm, Debbie Reynolds, Betty Hutton and Mamie Van Doren, each of whom wanted the role for themselves. Gloria accepted because of the paycheck and Cy Howard's insistence. However, she was nervous and even hostile throughout the shoot, insecure because of the musical demands to be placed on her. The songs were pre-recorded prior to location filming, and then the singers simply synchronized their voices to the songs already recorded. This was absolute horror to Gloria, partly because she took so long to record her tracks, phrase by phrase and often note by note, and partly because she could not summon the professionalism necessary to repeat her takes the same way. Gloria had always liked to give slightly different interpretations during takes, but on the *Oklahoma!* shoot, such behavior was harshly frowned upon, especially as most takes had to be shot twice to utilize the two different formats, and the results were supposed to be essentially the same. Gloria spoiled take after take because she could not or would not repeat the same movements, inflections and actions in consecutive takes. Shirley Jones remembers that Gloria was quite nervous about the part, and feels that Gloria regretted accepting it because it required so much musical ability — ability that Gloria just didn't have.

Moreover, her co-stars grew to complain that Gloria would go out of her way to upstage them. Gene Nelson stated later, "She did terrible things — she would step on my feet or on Ali Hakim's lines, and would do all sorts of physically gimmicky things, like playing with her gloves, to draw attention away from him." Most of the trouble seemed to emanate from Cy Howard, with whom she spoke by telephone at every available moment. Howard continually reminded Gloria that *she* was the movie's biggest star and urged her to assert herself on the set. And because Gloria was so insecure, she constantly asked his advice, describing the scene she was currently in, and Howard would suggest something to improve it. The result was that Gloria was constantly in a state of flux regarding her performance, while everyone else was seeking stability, repetition and constancy.

It was this behavior that, more than any other factor, led to the rather speedy descent of Gloria's career. By the time the *Oklahoma!* shoot was complete, the word had spread that working with Gloria was a nightmare. At the wrap party Gloria finally relaxed and became her humble, gracious self, but it was too late, and she was shunned by the entire cast and crew. Nelson said, "After that, she was blackballed all over town and didn't do any more pictures, except with people who didn't know how bad things had been. It haunted her until the day she died." Indeed, after *Oklahoma!* Gloria traveled to England to make *The Man Who Never Was*, far away from the glaring, public spotlight of Hollywood.

Gloria's poor behavior on the set was one of *Oklahoma!*'s real problems, but there were others, too. Agnes de Mille threw a fair number of temper tantrums, at one point locking both Rodgers and Hammerstein off the set until she was satisfied with the choreography she was to show them. They didn't hire her back for their next production, *Carousel*. The Arizona weather was always a factor, with daily rainstorms in particular causing problems in front of and behind the cameras. Corn had to planted a full year in advance by the agricultural department of the University of Arizona, and then it actually grew higher than needed ("as high as an elephant's eye"). And then there were the two rival photographic formats, Todd-AO and CinemaScope, both of which were utilized on this important film project.

Although the timing was finally right to make the film after the touring shows finally wound down, the other factor that persuaded Rodgers and Hammerstein to press ahead was the development of the Todd-AO camera. Impresario Michael Todd had helped develop Cinerama, but was positive that the widescreen image could be captured by one camera, instead of Cinerama's three, and sold his interest in the Cinerama process. When he learned that a 65mm, 30 fps, single-camera widescreen process was developed by the American Optical Company in Buffalo, New York, Todd quickly purchased the rights to promote it. The 128-degree image was designed to be projected onto a curved screen, with a resultant clarity and depth of field never before attained through a single camera lens. The 65mm format also had the capability to hold a six-track stereophonic soundtrack, which greatly appealed to moviemakers. Todd called the process Todd-AO (for American Optical) and presented screen tests to Rodgers and Hammerstein, who were delighted with the result and realized that the process alone was a publicity treasure trove. They made the decision to photograph their first film in this format, no matter what the difficulties; but they really had no idea of the issues involved. The main difficulties were that there was only one Todd-AO lens in existence, and that the 65mm dailies had to be shipped from the Nogales, Arizona, location to Buffalo to be processed, and then back to Hollywood for review. It was an expensive, time-consuming process, but everyone was thrilled with the visual results.

Having to photograph everything twice proved to be quite costly, especially involving the travel for all the Todd-AO material. Thus, the budget escalated past the $5 million mark, finally settling at $6.8 million, making it the most expensive musical film ever made at that time. Having to use two separate camera formats was also time-consuming, with at least two acceptable takes necessary for every shot. This was necessary because of the different film speeds for each format, the standard 24 fps CinemaScope process and the 30 fps speed of the Todd-AO process which led to greater depth of field and clarity. On their next picture, *Carousel*, Rodgers and Hammerstein used the same technique, but they famously did not bother to tell Frank Sinatra, hired to play Billy Bigelow. Sinatra discovered that he was supposed to film everything twice and immediately quit, telling them that they weren't paying him to make two movies! On that film, Gordon MacRae stepped in to fill Sinatra's vacant shoes, with results that many viewers felt were disappointing.

Oklahoma! Ado Annie (Gloria) and Ali Hakim (Eddie Albert) watch Will Parker (Gene Nelson) smooch Ali's bride Gertie Cummings (Barbara Lawrence).

Zinnemann discovered that the cast was a bit stiffer for the new Todd-AO camera and relaxed for the more familiar CinemaScope camera, so at length he decided to switch them around without the cast's knowledge. The pace and tempo of the Todd-AO version is a bit quicker than the CinemaScope version, which comes across as the one made with retakes. The Todd-AO version is two minutes longer, because of the overture, exit music and intermission music that is included. However, it also includes extra action, particularly in shots involving Jud and Laurey's runaway carriage, an increased quantity of cattle shots before the wedding sequence, and quite a few extra snippets of dialogue. This extra dialogue, though seemingly quite minor, is helpful in revealing tone and meaning in the individual scenes in which it appears. It is also evident that certain musical numbers, such as those featuring Gloria in action, have greater energy, vitality and movement than the CinemaScope takes. Thus, the Todd-AO version is definitely, noticeably superior.

An irony is that the CinemaScope version is the one seen by most people. The Todd-AO version was released on March 31, 1955, and it played around the country for most of a year before the CinemaScope version was ever released. But there were only a few theaters that could properly show the Todd-AO version, and as a roadshow attraction it was more expensive than other movies, so even though it made strong profits it was not seen by a truly large audience during its first year of release. The subsequent CinemaScope version, released in late 1956, reached a much wider audience during its run, and it is this version that was rereleased over the years (mainly because most theaters could play it, and did not have the equipment to exhibit the faster Todd-AO prints), as well as exhibited on television. It is only recently that the Todd-AO version has been restored and made available to audiences. 20th Century–Fox and the Rodgers and Hammerstein company recently released a DVD two-disc set that offers both versions, as well as audio commentaries for both versions.

Critical reaction to the roadshow premiere in 1955 was generally favorable. Bosley Crowther of the *New York Times* loved it, calling *Oklahoma!* "a production that magnifies and strengthens all the charm that [the play] had on the stage." *Variety* judged, "All things weighed in the scale, *Oklahoma!* rates with the industry's best," and praised everyone in the cast. *Time* called the picture "a handsome piece of entertainment," despite carping about the project's cost and occasional technical issues of the presentation. *Newsweek* summarized it thusly: "Bigger than ever, and just as good." The *Motion Picture Daily* stated, "The show comes through fresh as today's rain, and it would seem the *Oklahoma!* screen sun will be shining for many a year."

On the other hand, John McCarten of *The New Yorker* wrote, "In its picture form, it has an air of magniloquence hardly suited to the simple rusticity of its theme.... Rod Steiger is a very menacing customer — maybe just a bit *too* menacing, since occasionally the character he depicts seems to be a type better adapted to a psychiatric clinic than to musical comedy." Robert Kass of *Catholic World* complained, "*Oklahoma!* on screen is not quite so fresh and crisp as we remember it thirteen years ago," and faulted the direction as "too heavy-handed for what should have been a brisk, smooth-as-starch musical comedy." Robert Hatch of *The Nation* felt the film was overproduced: "But the screen is not the stage and two hours and twenty minutes of edible Technicolor is too much. I was upset to discover that long stretches of *Oklahoma!* are insipid, that a number of the 'great moments' felt forced."

Even those critics who found fault with the dramatics, however, agreed that the music was top-notch and well presented. It is the wonderful music, of course, that evokes audience emotion, and that music is timeless, whether it is Gordon MacRae's lyrical opening on horseback, "Oh, What a Beautiful Mornin'," or Shirley Jones' lilting hymn of female freedom, "Many a New Day," or Gloria Grahame's deadpan ode to romantic fun, "I Cain't Say No," or the rousing renditions of "The Farmer and the Cowman" or "Oklahoma!" It is the music that viewers remember, and the way it was delivered by a wonderful cast. If the drama is a bit heavy at times, or some scenes prolonged beyond necessity, it's only a matter of time before another beautiful song comes

along. Audiences responded to the movie despite its problems, and despite its roadshow pricing. It made upwards of $7 million, showing a small profit, and in occasional re-releases made even more money. In 2007 it was named to the National Film Registry.

Oklahoma! is a movie with individual parts — performances, scenes and specific songs and dances — greater than the whole. Certain moments remain rooted in memory more so than a grand impression of the entirety. And most of those moments revolve around its music. For better or worse, *Oklahoma!* is a better soundtrack than it is a film. It's a good film; it's a great soundtrack. For her part on the soundtrack, Gloria was offered either $10,000 cash or a two percent royalty. Gloria chose the royalty, and was still collecting payments when she died. The *Oklahoma!* soundtrack was immediately and eternally popular, outselling the original Broadway cast album and redefining the way in which movie soundtracks were perceived by the public. It still sells well today, and is the single source that allows listeners to hear Gloria actually sing. No, her singing is not continuous, but it is her voice and it is delightful to hear, even if it is pieced together little by little. Gloria suffered a great deal of anxiety making *Oklahoma!* and her colleagues suffered a great deal from her. Yet while she is admittedly miscast (because she is not a singer), she brings a mannered goofiness to Ado Annie that is very endearing, as well as a couple of terrific songs that prove the old adage that, indeed, "anyone can sing." For better and for worse, Gloria had risen to the challenge. Her movie career would never be the same again.

The Man Who Never Was (1956)

CREDITS Sumar Productions. *Distributed by* 20th Century–Fox. *Directed by* Ronald Neame. *Produced by* André Hakim. *Associate Producer*: Bob Mc-Naught. *Screenplay by* Nigel Balchin. *From the book by* Ewen Montagu. *Director of Photography*: Oswald Morris. *Editor*: Peter Taylor. *Music Composed by* Alan Rawsthorne. *Conducted by* Muir Mathieson. *Played by* Sinfonia of London. *Art Director*: John Hawkesworth. *Camera Operator*: Arthur Ibbetson. *Dubbing Editor*: Winston Ryder. *Sound Mixers*: Basil Fenton-Smith and J. B. Smith. *Assistant Directors*: Gerry O'Hara and Erica Masters. *Makeup*: Harold

Fletcher. *Photographic Effects*: Tom Howard. *Clapper Loader*: Derek V. Browne. *Wardrobe Supervisor*: Sam Benson. DeLuxe Color. CinemaScope (2.55:1). Monaural Sound. 103 minutes. Released on April 3, 1956. Currently available on DVD. Previously available on VHS.

CAST *Lieutenant Commander Ewen Montagu*, Clifton Webb; *Lucy Sherwood*, Gloria Grahame; *Lieutenant George Acres*, Robert Flemyng; *Pam*, Josephine Griffin; *Patrick O'Reilly/Phillips*, Stephen Boyd; *Admiral Cross*, Laurence Naismith; *General Nye*, Geoffrey Keen; *The Father*, Moultrie Kelsall; *Taxi Driver*, Cyril Cusack; *Sir Bernard Spilsbury*, André Morell; *General Coburn*, Michael Hordern; *Vice-Admiral*, Alan Cuthbertson; *Landlady*, Joan Hickson; *Larry*, Terence Longden [Longdon]; *Club Porter*, Gibb McLaughlin; *Scientist*, Miles Malleson; *Joe*, William Russell; *Lieutenant Jewell*, William Squire; *Shop Assistant*, Richard Wattis; *Adams*, Ronald Adam; *Consul Laurence*, D.A. Clarke-Smith; *Admiral Canaris*, Wolf Frees; *Bank Manager*, John Welsh; *Admiral Mountbatten*, Peter Williams; *Customs Officer*, Gordon Bell; *Doctor*, Michael Brill; *French*, Robert Brown; *Club Matron*, Everley Gregg; *Passport Officer*, Lloyd Lamble; *Wills Officer*, Brian Oulton; *Secretary*, Cicely Paget-Bowman; *German Colonel*, Gerhard Puritz; *Air Marshal*, Ewen Montagu; *Sailor on Submarine*, Michael Peake; *Clerk of British Embassy*, Francois Périer; *Voice of Winston Churchill*, Peter Sellers.

Based on a true episode in World War II, *The Man Who Never Was* is typically British in tone: understated, even-handed and gallant. It is a story of espionage and deception; there is no battlefield action. However, the episode had a profound effect on the Allied invasion of Sicily in 1943 and its skillful execution undoubtedly saved many hundreds, if not thousands, of lives. Some of the movie characters were based on real people while others were fictional, developed for dramatic purposes. The central character is Lieutenant Commander Ewen Montagu, a British naval intelligence officer who not only conceived and managed the original plan, but later wrote a book about the experience and even makes a cameo appearance in the film as an air marshal.

In the spring of 1943, General Montgomery reports that the African campaign has been successfully concluded. Prime Minister Winston Churchill (voiced by Peter Sellers) decides that Sicily should be the next area of operation and instructs his staff to devise a diversion of some sort so that the German defenses on the island will be considerably lessened. Lieutenant

Commander Ewen Montagu (Clifton Webb) and his assistant, Lieutenant George Acres (Robert Flemyng), imagine that the body of a courier transporting secret papers, indicating that Greece is the target, would suffice. They develop a plan whereby a body, disguised as a Royal Marine major and carrying top secret personal papers, would be found in Spain after presumably having drowned in an aircraft crash.

Montagu and Acres construct a personal background for the imaginary officer, whom they name Major William Martin, collecting ticket stubs, receipts and other items to personalize him. Their assistant, Pam (Josephine Griffin), is enlisted to write a love letter, ostensibly from Martin's fiancée. She has trouble with the task, but is aided by her roommate, Lucy Sherwood (Gloria Grahame), who is just beginning a serious relationship with Royal Air Force pilot Joe (William Russell). Lucy's letter is so convincing that it is included with Martin's other effects, along with a photo of Lucy, since she wrote the letter. General Nye (Geoffrey Keen) and Admiral Mountbatten (Peter Williams) contribute personal letters containing key (falsified) military information, which the courier (Martin) is to deliver to General Eisenhower and others.

In order to fool the Germans, the body needs to have drowned, or to appear that it has. Pam locates a recently deceased man who has perished from pneumonia, a condition that would be masked by submersion in ocean water if the body were to be closely examined. Montagu meets with the man's father (Moultrie Kelsall) and persuades him to allow them to use his son's body, without revealing its ultimate purpose. The body is, in a detailed and reverent scene, dressed by Montagu, Acres and pathologist Adams (Ronald Adam). Now identified as Major Martin, it is put into a steel container with dry ice, driven to the shore and ferried out to a waiting submarine. The submarine arrives off the Spanish coast and unloads the body, which drifts toward the distant shoreline.

Major Martin is found on the beach and Spanish authorities investigate his appearance, eventually sending his effects back to Britain. Montagu wonders if his intricate plans have been for nothing until it is confirmed that the

The Man Who Never Was. Lucy Sherwood (Gloria) is reluctant to let go of Joe (William Russell), who will soon be leaving her to go to war. Joe's fate will directly affect a top secret World War II military operation.

letters accompanying the body have been opened, copied and resealed, presumably by German agents. In Germany, despite Hitler's belief that the letters are genuine, orders are issued to have Major Martin's background authenticated. An agent with an Irish identity, Patrick O'Reilly (Stephen Boyd), is sent to London.

O'Reilly has copies of the receipts in Martin's possession, and thoroughly investigates each of them. The results of his search are inconclusive, so he turns to the letter from Lucy Sherwood, which has her actual address. He waits at her apartment and watches Pam arrive home. Pam is surprised when he walks into her apartment and is startled to hear that he claims to be a friend of William Martin, whom she knows to be a figment of her boss' imagination. Her attempt to deflect his questions is interrupted by Lucy's arrival. Lucy convinces O'Reilly that Martin was real and that her grief over his death is real — but she is actually grieving for her fiancée Joe, who had been reported as killed earlier in the day.

O'Reilly gives his address to Pam with the expectation that if Martin is not real, he will soon be arrested. Indeed, Pam reports O'Reilly to the authorities, who speed to apprehend the enemy agent. Montagu divines O'Reilly's intent and convinces General Coburn (Michael Hordern) that the agent must be left alone. Finding no interference, O'Reilly contacts Germany confirming that Martin was genuine.

The result of the operation is that, based on O'Reilly's confirmation, German forces are diverted from Sicily. Three batteries of soldiers, one panzer division and six flotillas of ships are moved from Sicily to Greece, thus softening the defense of the island for the Allied assault. Montagu is decorated with the Order of the British Empire for his efforts. After the war, Montagu visits the grave in Huelva, Spain, where the body identified as William Martin is buried. He places his medal upon the gravestone and walks away, alone in his knowledge of the man's true identity.

The Man Who Never Was is based upon

Ewen Montagu's same-titled account of the story. The film is very faithful to the spirit of Montagu's 1953 book, although some alterations have been made, two of which are quite important. First, the character of Lucy Sherwood (Gloria Grahame) is entirely fictional. In real life, Pam was assigned to write a personal letter to Major Martin, and while she enlisted the help of a friend, she never identified her helper. Screenwriter Nigel Balchin simply added Lucy as a plot point, the lynchpin to persuading the enemy agent (Stephen Boyd) that Martin's identity was genuine. Although some critics would argue the point, it makes sense to include the character, because involving Pam directly in the matter would have led any investigator directly to Naval Intelligence. If it was determined that Pam worked there, the deception would not have worked. An intermediary character was necessary, though it can be persuasively argued that it should have been someone with no direct connection to Pam — such as her roommate — because of the risk of detection.

Second, there is no evidence that the Germans ever sent an agent to authenticate Martin's identity. Montagu's book includes the German response to the attempted ruse, based on files and letters found during and after the war. The Germans were indeed fooled by Martin's papers — Hitler himself decreed them "absolutely genuine" — but the matter of an enemy investigator is entirely a dramatic one, created by scriptwriter Balchin. Again, this is a decision that makes sense. The film is barely an hour old when Major Martin is found on a Spanish shore, and the story would have been wrapped up in ten minutes after that, if no investigation were launched. Moreover, such an ending would have been anticlimactic. In real life, the British had no substantive proof that the Germans had fallen for the deception until Sicily was invaded and it was found that much of the island's defenses had been shifted away. A movie, however, needs a strong conclusion, so Balchin created agent Patrick O'Reilly and sent him to London.

The film is effective because of its basis in fact, and the semi-documentary style with which director Ronald Neame chronicles the development of deception. War movies often indulge in bloody battles, clichéd microcosms of men and grand statements regarding the waste of life entailed by combat. *The Man Who Never Was* features none of these elements. Indeed, there is but one onscreen fatality — the poor lad who died of pneumonia and was selected to be Major Martin — and not a single shot is fired during the film. Events do occur outside, but most of this war story takes place indoors and at night, inside cramped offices, small, dark flats, a submarine and a morgue. It chronicles the private, secret war behind the war. Its most public moment is the discovery of Major Martin's body on a beach in Spain; otherwise, affairs are conducted and strategy is planned behind closed doors.

The use of intelligence, in both of its definitions (personal and military), is the key to its approach. Montagu and Acres create a scheme with a good chance of fooling the Germans. British military intelligence puts the plan into place and runs the operation. German commanders fall for the ruse, though not before testing its authenticity. The enemy agent uses his brains to investigate the matter, and Montagu smartly divines the agent's intent and prevents British military police from apprehending him, thus confirming the deception's false genuineness to the Germans. It is intelligence rather than might which wins this battle, with the spoils of war received by the audience.

Proper casting was necessary to reinforce the intelligence of the characters, and Clifton Webb became Lieutenant Commander Ewen Montagu. The Indiana-born actor was not British, but certainly seems so, with the proper carriage and posture befitting a military man in the service of the queen. Webb restrains most, but not all, of the sarcastic mannerisms he displayed so vividly in *Laura* and the three *Mr. Belvedere* films, preferring to play the role relatively straight. He is thoroughly appropriate and quite effective, anchoring the film with dramatic weight and purpose. Robert Flemyng is fun as Lieutenant George Acres, allowing a boyish persona to show through his naval stripes. And Stephen Boyd is terrific as the Irish agent for Germany, Patrick O'Reilly. In just his third film, Boyd commands the screen as the secretive yet rather bold provocateur.

Josephine Griffin is sterling as Pam, the always reliable assistant. It's not a flamboyant role, and Griffin plays it just right. More troublesome is Gloria as Lucy Sherwood. The role of Lucy is never as fully developed as it should have been, particularly as Gloria is afforded co-star status with Webb. It is definitely a secondary role, consisting of two major scenes and four smaller ones. Her "big" scenes are the ones which people remember, since they convey a civilian's perspective on war with a passion not found in other sequences.

When Pam has trouble writing a letter to Major Martin, she asks Lucy for help. Lucy has just committed herself to a flyer named Joe, and dictates her own feelings for the letter:

Darling, when you went away tonight, something went with you. It must have been my heart, 'cause now I'm cold and empty. It's always bad when you go away but it was worse tonight, because the day was so good. You shouldn't have bought the ring, and I know you shouldn't, and you did because you love me. And I let you because I love you. There isn't much more than that to be had from any day. I won't wear it, darling, I told you I wouldn't, 'cause if I did that would mean you were real, that you belonged to me and that they couldn't take you away from me. Whereas now they can send you away, and lead me to wonder if I'll ever see you again. Whether I may wake up and find I've dreamed you. Maybe there'll be a time when it's all over and you're still there, and real, and love me. And then I'll put your ring on and wear it — and wear it until I die! Oh God, darling, take care of yourself, as if you ever could or would. I suppose I mean, Oh God, take care of you. I love you! I love you!

The passionate nature of Lucy's dictation (and the music which accompanies it) is almost out of place in this quiet drama, yet it is precisely this passion that personalizes the letter and provides its persuasiveness. For those are Lucy's feelings, and they are quite sincere, even if they are not directed toward William Martin. There is a similar scene at the climax, where Lucy persuades O'Reilly that her true love has died, even though she is actually grieving the death of Joe, the flyer to whom she had pledged her love, and who had been reported as killed just minutes before. It is the coincidence of these scenes, the timing by which Lucy is able to write such an impassioned letter just as it is needed and then mislead O'Reilly with her grief surrounding the death of Joe, which critics disliked and noted, as well as Gloria's awkward appearance in them.

At the height of her fame, Gloria was still suffering from the aftereffects of surgery on her upper lip. The botched operation in Europe three years earlier had made her face rather immobile, and that, combined with a strange and curious sheen of her makeup, makes Gloria look, sound and act differently than anybody else in the picture. Although the condition had been present for three years, it is never more apparent than in this movie, perhaps because of her many close-ups. Additionally, Gloria's makeup is so oily that one of her shorter scenes ends with her in the bathroom applying makeup to her face, as if to somehow help explain the extreme look. Critics took notice of Gloria's appearance and wondered why such a beautiful woman would resort to such measures. Many argued that her looks and facial immobility led to a poor performance.

Variety complained, "Gloria Grahame, assigned (without her knowledge) to be the girlfriend of 'Major Martin,' seems an unhappy choice for the part, and she overplays it badly. Also, there is something very much amiss with her makeup in this picture." The British Film Institute's *Monthly Film Bulletin* commented, "Gloria Grahame, left to convey the atmosphere of a wartime romance in a couple of contrived emotional scenes, makes an unconvincing job of it." Moira Walsh of *America* termed Gloria's part as "ill-defined and unappetizing," while John McCarten of *The New Yorker* noted, "She emotes all over the place ... but I'm afraid that she offers nothing very engrossing in the way of dramatic art except an ability to talk without moving her upper lip." The critic for *Time* observed, "Its chief flaw is some romantic embroidery concerning Gloria Grahame, who is done a bad turn both by the scriptwriter and the makeup man (she often looks as if she had been doused in oil for a Channel swim)." And Hollis Alpert of *Saturday Review* stated unequivocally, "The worst moments occur when Gloria Grahame is called upon to convince the spy that the corpse is not a counterfeit, and I suspect she stands a chance of being nominated the worst actress of the year by the *Harvard Lampoon*." (She was not.)

While Gloria's appearance in the film is startling, and rather sad considering her great beauty, there are those who feel her reading of Lucy Sherwood's emotional lines is quite powerful. Gloria liked to pick scripts that offered meaty dialogue, so Lucy's dictation of the letter and emotional outpouring of grief regarding the fate of "Dearest Willie" in front of O'Reilly appealed to her. Despite the excessive makeup and unfortunate stiff upper lip, Gloria supplies the requisite emotion without histrionics. Critics hated her in this movie but it seems likely that many were reacting to the clumsiness of the part and her odd appearance. In terms of acting, this movie may not be Gloria's high point but it certainly isn't her lowest, either.

Critics were divided upon the ultimate rewards of the film. Some found it intriguing but not thrilling. *Time*'s critic wrote, "So long as the film remains a documentary, its detail is fascinating," but then bemoaned the fictitious second half. Bosley Crowther of the *New York Times* enjoyed it until the final coincidence, then wanted it to end, quickly. More positive are reviews in *Variety*, which termed it "well-made and unusual entertainment"; *Boxoffice*, which called it "a fascinating insight into the complexities of espionage and counter-espionage during World War II"; *Newsweek*, which judged it "a genuine thriller"; *America*, in which Moira Walsh labeled the film "deftly reconstructed, stranger-than-fiction fact"; and *Commonweal*, in which Philip T. Hartung decreed the film "the best cloak-and-dagger film since *Five Fingers*."

The Man Who Never Was is a fascinating glimpse into the world of subterfuge and deception. Thoroughly British, it is understated and thoughtful rather than histrionic and tumultuous. It tells its story with pacing that suits its subject, showcasing the tiny but important details which are so important in cases of large-scale deception. It is handsomely produced in CinemaScope and with a marvelous cast, down to the voice of Peter Sellers as Prime Minister Winston Churchill. Most of all, it is intelligent drama which ably reflects the tenor of intelligence-gathering and usage during wartime conditions. It is a smart movie about a smart subject, which is quite unusual. It is one of the better espionage movies ever made, one which, like its spies, does not call undue attention to itself. And while this is one of Gloria Grahame's least appreciated roles, it remains one of the better films in which she appeared.

One final question remained following the film's release. Who really was "the man who never was"? For more than fifty years, nobody knew. When Ewen Montagu wrote his book, he pledged to keep the true identity of William Martin secret, as he had promised the man's father. The movie follows the same path, stating in its prologue, "Military security and respect for a solemn promise have made it necessary to disguise the identity of some of the characters in this film...." Then, in 1996, a theory was put forward that one Glyndwr Michael, a homeless alcoholic who had allegedly committed suicide by ingesting rat poison, was the man, and that no familial permis-

***The Man Who Never Was*.** Gloria and Clifton Webb pose for a portrait shot on the set of their World War II true-life adventure. The actual identity of the sailor used in the secret British operation remained secret for half a century.

sion to use the body had been received or even requested. The discovery was reported worldwide and widely accepted, despite the very basic problem that a man dissipated by disease and containing at least traces of rat poison in his system would hardly be suitable to pose as a ranking officer of the Royal Marines. Even an autopsy in Spain would probably have found the poison, rendering the deception futile.

In 2002, television documentary makers argued that one Tom Martin, a sailor who had died in the explosion and sinking of the HMS *Dasher* in 1943, was the man. Clues in Montagu's writing pointed to the "Martin" surname being more than just coincidence, although other evidence seemed circumstantial. Then, in June 2002, a new book, *The Secrets of HMS Dasher* by John and Noreen Steele, posited that one John Melville, also of the *Dasher*, was the man, and this fact was ultimately verified by the Royal Navy late in 2004. A memorial service for Melville was conducted on the current HMS *Dasher*, a patrol boat operating around Cyprus, in October of 2004, with Lieutenant Commander Mark Hill stating, "In his incarnation as Major Martin, John Melville's memory lives on in the film *The Man Who Never Was*. But we are gathered here today to remember John Melville as a man who most certainly was."

It is Melville's actual grave in Spain that appears at the end of *The Man Who Never Was* (as that of Major William Martin), and it is he who, some sixty years after the fact, has finally been recognized as an important, if unwitting, figure in British history.

Ride Out for Revenge (1957)

CREDITS Bryna Productions. *Distributed by* United Artists. *Directed by* Bernard Girard. *Produced and Written by* Norman Retchin. *Associate Producer*: Victor Orsatti. *Based on a novel by* Burt Arthur. *Director of Photography*: Floyd Crosby. *Film Editor*: Leon Barsha. *Music Composed and Conducted by* Leith Stevens. *Art Director*: McClure Capps. *Production Manager*: Barney Briskin. *Assistant Director*: Ralph Black. *Set Decorations*: Rudy Butler. *Sound*: Jack Goodrich. *Makeup*: Lee Greenway. *Wardrobe Supervisor*: Elmer Ellsworth. *Stunts*: Regis Parton and Calvin Spencer. Black and White. Flat (1.37:1). Monaural Sound. 78 minutes. Released on November 1,

1957. Not currently available on commercial home video.

CAST *Marshal Russ Tate*, Rory Calhoun; *Amy Porter*, Gloria Grahame; *Captain Albert George*, Lloyd Bridges; *Pretty Willow*, Joanne Gilbert; *Little Wolf*, Vince Edwards; *Garvin*, Richard Shannon; *Chief Yellow Wolf*, Frank de Kova; *Billy Horton*, Michael Winkelman; *Preacher*, Cyril Delevanti; *Lieutenant*, John Merrick [John Frederick]; *Cheyenne Indian*, Iron Eyes Cody; *Sergeant*, John Mitchum; *Townsman*, Jeffrey Sayre.

Gloria's second of three westerns is a grim parable regarding the pointlessness of hate. It is definitely a second-tier western in terms of its budget, production values, writing and casting, yet its ambitions are higher than might be expected. Based on a novel by the prolific Burt Arthur (who is not listed in the credits), *Ride Out for Revenge* is a cynical and foreboding treatise on race relations (whites vs. Indians) which begins and ends with the Cheyenne losing their culture and heritage.

Ride Out for Revenge takes place around a windy, dusty little town called Sand Creek in the Dakotas region in the autumn of 1868. Two Cheyenne Indians, Little Wolf (Vince Edwards) and his father, Chief Yellow Wolf (Frank de Kova), walk miles from the tribe's camp toward town to plead for food and clothing to protect the tribe during the upcoming winter; they are met with hostility. Marshal Tate (Rory Calhoun) escorts them to meet with Captain George (Lloyd Bridges), who runs the Army post and oversees Indian affairs. George scorns their pleas, reminding them that they are to relocate to a reservation in Oklahoma, as the U.S. government has ordered. Yellow Wolf has one final counteroffer: He produces gold nuggets and asks to trade them (and more gold) for permission for his people to stay on their ancestral lands. George offers to think about it, and accepts the gold. On their way out of town, Yellow Wolf is shot and killed by an unseen assailant. Little Wolf jumps on a nearby horse and rides out of town.

Tate is disgusted that Yellow Wolf has been killed; not a single witness will attest to what happened. In his office, George meets with Garvin (Richard Shannon), the murderer of Yellow Wolf. It had been George's intention to scare the chief, but Garvin took matters into his own hands. Tate arrives, warning George that Little Wolf will go to war with the town, but George argues that the Indians are weaponless and dispirited. Tate tells the Army captain that he knows George is too scared to start a fight with the Cheyenne, and leaves. On the way to his boarding house, Tate is joined by Billy Horton (Michael Winkelman), his late sister's child, an adolescent for whom Tate is responsible. Tate tells him to prepare to pack and move; he doesn't want Billy around when the Indians attack. Billy objects, refusing to leave a life he loves.

The boarding house is run by Amy Porter (Gloria Grahame), an attractive widow who doesn't want either Billy *or* Tate to leave town. She tries to talk to Tate, but he leaves hurriedly. Garvin and a handful of men meet Tate in the street and tell him his marshalling days are over. Tate allows Garvin to remove his star, and goes on his way. At the river, Tate greets Pretty Willow (Joanne Gilbert), Yellow Wolf's beautiful and proud daughter. They kiss and discuss leaving the area, but when Tate tells her of her father's death, she turns cold. She agrees with Tate that Little Wolf will fight, and returns to the Indian village, for her place is with her people. Tate returns to town and tries to warn George that a raid is imminent, but the Army captain is carousing in the saloon and refuses to listen. Back at the boarding house, Amy talks to Tate, asking why he feels he must leave. "I don't think we have the right to pass our hate onto kids like Billy," he replies. She suggests that Billy needs a real family, and that Tate marry her. "I'm so lonesome, and I love you. I love you, Tate," she pleads. When he rejects her, she castigates the Indians who she feels are causing the problem. "It's the Indians' home, too," he reminds her. Amy's prejudice against the Indians who killed her husband and Tate's sister (Billy's mother) turns Tate against her. He tells her that he and Billy will be moving out the following day.

That night, Billy sneaks out of bed, determined to run away rather than leave town with Tate. When he reaches the corral where his pony is kept, Billy witnesses the beginning of the Indian raid. He tries to escape on his pony, but an Indian brave, not knowing that he's just a child, shoots him. The Indians ride through town yelling and shooting, having looted the Army's supply of weapons and horses. Tate ar-

rives in the street to find Billy dead, surrounded by angry townspeople. At the funeral the following day, the town's preacher (Cyril Delevanti) rails against the Indians, and against George, who was supposed to run them off months earlier. When he hopes that the Indians will all soon be killed, he reflects the mood of the town. Tate is repulsed at the town's attitude. George asks Tate for help, realizing that Little Wolf will attack again, now armed with the Army's rifles. George suggests that Tate use his influence with Pretty Willow to make peace, and Tate socks him in the jaw.

At the boarding house, Tate and Amy argue about the Cheyenne. Tate arms himself and sets off after Little Wolf, believing that if he kills the new leader of the tribe, he can prevent the massacre of the town. Tate follows Little Wolf to an area with a lot of boulders and aims carefully, but he cannot pull the trigger. He cannot kill his enemy in cold blood. After Little Wolf leaves, Tate examines a boulder and finds that it contains gold. He takes a chunk back to the boarding house, where Amy finds it and secretly shows it to George. The captain concludes that Tate has made a deal with the Cheyenne, and determines to trap Tate and Little Wolf. He sends Garvin to the Indian camp with the message that Tate is trying to kill Little Wolf. The Cheyenne do not believe him and hold Garvin until Pretty Willow can verify his claims. She meets with Tate, who acknowledges that he went after her brother, and she tries to kill him with a knife. Tate wrestles it away, telling her that he couldn't kill Little Wolf, and they embrace. She realizes that events are now beyond their control.

Garvin is freed when Pretty Willow returns and corroborates his story. Little Wolf plans to meet Tate at the river and kill him, which Garvin overhears. Garvin, George and about a dozen cavalry troops surround the river meeting place and open fire after Tate and Little Wolf fight for a while. Tate is shot and disappears beneath the water; Little Wolf runs toward the cavalry troops and stabs Garvin to death before he is killed by George. The Army captain takes Pretty Willow into town and asks Amy to take care of her until the Cheyenne are herded out of town by the Army reinforcements that are arriving. Amy and Pretty Willow discover that they have much in common;

Amy is no longer jealous of Pretty Willow, and she is more accepting of Indian culture. She chastises George for causing so much trouble.

George returns Pretty Willow to the Indian village, but demands she take him to the gold deposit. When they reach it, Tate interrupts and tells her to hide. George tries to bargain with Tate, but then pulls his gun — too late. He is killed by Tate. Later Tate and Pretty Willow are together, watching the Cheyenne begin the long trek to Oklahoma. "Things change," remarks Tate. "You either fight it, or learn to live with it." Pretty Willow asks Tate what will happen when someday the whites will have to fight for their homes just as the Cheyenne did. Tate agrees that such a scenario could happen some day. But for the moment, they are together at last, ready to begin a life together far away from Sand Creek.

Ride Out for Revenge is representative of the "new breed" of westerns that appeared in the 1950s. Traditional westerns were long on action but short on story, but during the post–World War II era, that began to change. As movie characters became more psychologically complex in mainstream movies, that effect bled into westerns as well. And no longer would most westerns consist of good cowboys vs. bad Indians. Fifties films such as *Broken Arrow*, *Devil's Doorway*, *The Savage*, *Apache* and *Run of the Arrow* began to treat Indian characters and culture with a respect not seen since the silent days of cinema. It became valid to depict and explore the negative effects of destroying Indian culture and sending red people to reservations in movies, and this in turn created dramatic opportunities that led to further and often better movies.

The crux of *Ride Out for Revenge* is the Cheyenne's desire to remain on their ancestral lands in the Black Hills region of what is now South Dakota. The movie (and the book upon which it is based) do not faithfully follow history, but the use of Sand Creek as the center of the action is no coincidence. Many Cheyenne women and children were butchered at Sand Creek, Colorado, in 1864, in a cavalry raid that was so horrific that it bound several tribes together in active revolt against the U.S. government for years afterward. The violent western *Soldier Blue* (1970) is based upon that incident. Further, the Black Hills gold rush of 1874 displaced the Cheyenne and Sioux quite rapidly, as wishful prospectors and miners ignored treaty boundaries and rushed into the protected area to find their fortunes. These events are not explicitly alluded to in the film, but they certainly frame the onscreen action.

The Sand Creek townspeople feel entitled to their land and dislike the "dirty" Indians who reside nearby. As Amy Porter remarks, there isn't a person in town who hasn't lost a relative or friend in skirmishes with the Indians. Almost everyone would prefer Captain George to complete his assignment and force the Cheyenne south toward Oklahoma, where they have been ordered to go by the government. The only person in town with any feeling for the Indians is Marshal Tate. It is never explained why Tate is so forgiving while everyone else is so condemning, other than his good nature and the fact that he's in love with the chief's daughter, Pretty Willow. This relationship makes Tate an object of scorn in the community, but it's a guarded jealousy, as she is more beautiful than any other girl in town.

The fact that everyone, including young Billy, wants to be rid of the Indians once and for all makes this movie more heavy-handed than it ought to be. Tate is alone in his respect for the Cheyenne and therefore seems both too good to be true and too foolish to still be alive. One wonders how Tate has been able to remain town marshal when everyone disapproves of the Indians that he alone is protecting. When the Indian chief and his son ask George for help to meet the coming winter, George replies by asking, "Who cares what your people need? It's what my people need that counts. And we need food and clothing, too." The night before he dies, Billy wishes all the Indians were dead. After the killing of Billy, the preacher calls for action against the Indians, even if the civilians have to take care of it themselves. Nobody wants them around, except for Tate, and it can be persuasively argued that he has a special reason to care about them (Pretty Willow). A more balanced script would have positions both for and against the Indians presented by various townspeople. Yet, for the era in which this was made, this low-budget movie represented thematic progress. At least the film demonstrates that the Cheyenne have as much innate dignity, or more, than the whites who

Ride Out for Revenge. Widow Amy Porter (Gloria) tries to interest Marshal Russ Tate (Rory Calhoun) in staying with her permanently, but he has stronger feelings for a Cheyenne girl named Pretty Willow (Joanne Gilbert, not pictured).

persecute them. And the conclusion, when Pretty Willow asks Tate how whites would react in the same situation, poses a darn good question, quite profound for the era.

The star of the film, Rory Calhoun, contributed this perspective to the movie's publicity: "What [the movie] has to say is merely that progress is inevitable, but people are neither all black nor all white in their motivation. It presents a fresh and valid look at the Indian's view of the white man's 'progress' and, in a final ironic twist, it makes the hero see things from the redskin's point of view and thus come to the realization that he would have reacted the same way had he been in their position. And I feel it is this quality which will keep the good western in favor for many years to come, no matter how many mediocre ones may glut the market."

Calhoun is stalwart and active in the lead role, but Tate is not a particularly deep character, which is probably why Bryna Produc-

tions boss Kirk Douglas failed to take the role for himself when his company produced this project. Douglas might have done more with it, but the result would probably still have been quite similar. More effective is Lloyd Bridges as cowardly Captain George. Bridges sinks his teeth into the role, particularly in the scenes of carousing and drinking, to convey his character's selfish nature. Joanne Gilbert is quite fetching as the Indian "princess" Pretty Willow, and her dramatic scenes are convincing. Frank de Kova and Vince Edwards are likewise strong and commanding in their Cheyenne roles.

Gloria is identified as "the town-woman" in the ads. Two taglines appear with her picture: "She'd do anything to get her man ... even start a massacre!" and "What has that Cheyenne got that I can't give you!" Both, of course, exploit Gloria's persona of sensuality, although these tend to emphasize her desperation rather than her ability to manipulate men. Gloria is seen in an attractive pageboy haircut and a welcome minimum of makeup in the film; her appearance is quite natural and refreshing when compared to her previous job, *The Man Who Never Was.*

As good as she looks, though, Gloria's acting at first seems not quite up to her usual standard. Her initial scenes with Rory Calhoun are somewhat uncomfortable, although this may be explained because Amy is aware that Tate is seeing the Indian girl, and is hurt and offended by that relationship. When Amy declares her love for Tate, Gloria is better, but then they argue and she turns cold. Gloria's best acting comes near the end of the picture, when Amy spends time with Pretty Willow and discovers that her prejudice is rather ill-advised, and when she relates her feelings regarding what has occurred to Captain George. Amy's brief exchange with George is nicely understated, encapsulating the movie's message:

AMY: We beat them, didn't we?
GEORGE: Yeah, we sure did. They're nothing but the losers now.
AMY: Are they? I wonder. Tate lost his life, I lost two people I loved and you, you don't even know it, but you lost more than any of us.
GEORGE: No, Mrs. Porter, not me.
AMY: Oh, yes you have, captain. You're in real trouble now. With them gone, there's no one left here to hate, but yourself.

While the dialogue is admittedly awkward, its message is clear and truthful: Hate and prejudice harm not only the victims but their perpetrators as well. This message, and Gloria's skillful conveyance of it, provides this western with a moral punch that other routine westerns lack. Tate consistently stands by the Cheyenne, while the townspeople consistently dislike the Indians. Amy is the only white character to make the switch from prejudice to acceptance, and Gloria's job is to bring the audience along with her. The resignation in her voice during the dialogue with George is just right, leaving no doubt as to the devastating impact of losing the men in her life, yet imparting her newly gained insight into George's soul candidly and without rancor. Other actresses might have played this scene with great emotion, but Gloria realized that at this point, Amy is empty. She has nothing left, and grief will come later.

In Burt Arthur's original novel, Amy is even more important to the story; she has a

brief affair with Tate, is quite hysterical when Billy is killed, befriends Pretty Willow more earnestly and actually sets out to kill Captain George when she is convinced that he is going to rape the Indian maiden. Her transition from Indian-hater to sympathetic defender of Pretty Willow is again the plot's moral compass, steering the audience from a traditional perspective of anticipating the massacre of the red men to thoughtful consideration of their place in the world.

Gloria had another reason to seem dispirited, because her volatile marriage to Cy Howard was finally ending. This, after Gloria became pregnant in 1956 and bore Cy a daughter, Marianna, on October 1. The baby, known as Paulette (her middle name) for the rest of her life, did not bring Gloria and Cy closer for very long. The couple had been separating and reconciling in cycles over the previous two or three years. Their antipathy for each other eventually overwhelmed their love, causing Gloria to file for divorce in May of 1957. The divorce was finalized on Halloween, October 31, 1957, the day before *Ride Out for Revenge* opened in theaters across the country.

Despite Gloria's second-billed presence, *Ride Out for Revenge* was not well received, and it was barely released in many areas as the bottom half of double features. *Boxoffice* called it "a routine western, which is short on action and long on tolerance toward the Indians.... Miss Grahame's sophisticated appearance and purring delivery of lines seem out of the place in the Old West of 1868." *Variety* labeled it a "haphazard and heavyhanded western, employing all the 'new' clichés." In his book *Western Films*, Brian Garfield concluded: "Brisk brief oater has all the standard clichés but it's reasonably diverting." *The Motion Picture Guide* opined, "This is a film full of good intentions, almost an apology for the countless number of films where the Indians were sadistic and mindless. However, the action here is too melodramatic and overwrought with the new clichés. Direction is never sure of which way to go, resulting in a film of mixed quality. Still, it is an honest effort at changing some past Hollywood (as well as historical) misdeeds and worth a look."

Gloria worked for one week on the picture and was paid $10,000. Considering that just a couple of years earlier she was earning $100,000 a picture, this was certainly a step down. But it was work, and it was a pretty good role, even if the project wasn't very prestigious. As her marriage to Cy Howard finally ended, new mother Gloria determined to spend more time with her baby (as she had with Timmy back in 1949), putting her career on the back burner. She would make just one more movie two years later, going into semi-retirement, at least where motion pictures were concerned. The golden era of Gloria Grahame performances was coming to a close.

Odds Against Tomorrow (1959)

CREDITS HarBel Productions. *Distributed by* United Artists. *Produced and Directed by* Robert Wise. *Co-Producer*: Harry Belafonte. *Associate Producer*: Phil Stein. *Screenplay by* John O. Killens and Nelson Gidding (and, uncredited, Abraham Polonsky). *From a book by* William P. McGivern. *Photographed by* Joseph Brun. *Film Editor*: Dede Allen. *Music Composed and Conducted by* John Lewis. *Production Manager*: Forrest E. Johnston. *Settings by* Leo Kerz. *Assistant Director*: Charles Maguire. *Sound*: Edward Johnstone and Richard Voriseck. *Costumes*: Anna Hill Johnstone. *Set Decorator*: Fred Ballmeyer. *Makeup*: Richard Jiras. *Script Supervisor*: Marguerite James. *Camera Operator*: Saul Midwall. *Gaffer*: Howard Fortune. *Grip*: Edward Knott. *Sound Editor*: Kenn Collins. *Title by* Storyboard. Monaural Sound. Black and White. Flat (1.37:1). 96 minutes. Released on October 15, 1959. Currently available on DVD. Previously available on VHS and laserdisc.

CAST *Johnny Ingram*, Harry Belafonte; *Earl Slater*, Robert Ryan; *Lorry*, Shelley Winters; *Dave Burke*, Ed Begley; *Helen*, Gloria Grahame; *Bacco*, Will Kuluva; *Ruth Ingram*, Kim Hamilton; *Annie*, Mae Barnes; *Coco*, Richard Bright; *Kittie*, Carmen De Lavallade; *Moriarty*, Lew Gallo; *Edie Ingram*, Lois Thorne; *Soldier in Bar*, Wayne Rogers; *Girl in Bar*, Zohra Lampert; *Police Chief*, Alan Nourse; *Bank Guard*, William Adams; *Gas Station Attendant*, Chris Barbery; *Carousel Boy*, Ron Becks; *Bank Secretary*, Mary Boylan; *Solly*, Floyd Ennis; *Bus Station Announcer*, John Garden; *PTA Member*, Stanley Greene; *Jonesy*, Burtt Harris; *Bank Manager*, Fred Herrick; *Garry*, Paul Hoffman; *Club Employee*, Robert Earl Jones; *Guard*, Robert Jones; *Captain of Waiters*, Lou Martini; *Ambulance Attendant*, Maro May; *Hotel Juno Clerk*, Ed Preble; *Club Hostess*, Diana Sands; *Cannoy*, Fred J. Scollay; *Hotel Juno Elevator Operator*, Mel Stewart; *Man with Dog*, Ronnie Stewart; *Jazz Club Bartender*, Cicely Tyson; *Policeman*, Clint Young; *Bartender*, Bill Zuckert; *Bit Parts*, Eric Burroughs and David Clarke.

Occasionally cited as the last genuine example of American *film noir*, Robert Wise's gritty *Odds Against Tomorrow* seems like a throwback to the 1940s, with an underlying social message that suddenly overwhelms its taut narrative at the climax. Utilizing only the first half of William P. McGivern's source novel, Wise's film explores how and why racial discrimination is a social cancer, disrupting and eventually ravaging everything it touches—from ordinary, normal human relationships to a perfectly planned bank robbery. The message underscores the action from the moment the two protagonists meet, promising a violent, disturbing confrontation that finally occurs at the film's explosive conclusion.

At New York City's Hotel Juno, former cop Dave Burke (Ed Begley) is interviewing candidates to help him rob a bank of $200,000. The first man to visit Burke is Earl Slater (Robert Ryan), a middle-aged Southerner who doesn't seem to care for black people. Slater leaves to consider the offer and Johnny Ingram (Harry Belafonte) arrives. He's a slick-looking black man whom Burke knows is deep in debt to a local bookie. Ingram, too, is reluctant to get involved, but he is desperate for cash. After he leaves, Burke visits the bookie Bacco (Will Kuluva) to ensure that pressure remains on Ingram to pay up, and soon.

Slater returns to an apartment he shares with Lorry (Shelley Winters), who knows all about Slater's criminal past and wants him to stay honest. When he needs cash, she gives him some. But Slater wants to retain his independence. "They're not gonna junk me like an old car," he says. Slater agrees to go over the plan with Burke, who wants to know more about it. They drive to Melton, about one hundred miles north of New York City along the Hudson River (the film was actually lensed in Hudson, New York). Slater sees that Burke's plan is thoughtfully conceived — but he is aghast at the idea that the third man needed to pull off the robbery is black. He backs out of the deal.

Ingram plays xylophone in a nightclub, singing "When That Cold, Cold Sun Goes Down," when Bacco arrives. The club manager, sensing trouble, gives Ingram a small gun with which to protect himself. When Bacco demands payment and threatens Ingram's family, Ingram draws the gun but is overcome and beaten by Bacco's henchmen. He is given one more day to find the $6,000 he owes Bacco, or else. Ingram goes back on stage and takes over the song "All Men Are Evil" from the singer Annie (Mae Barnes), using the forum to express his indignation at the world. The following day Ingram takes his daughter to a fair where he notices Bacco's henchmen watching him. He uses the presence of local cops to make them back off. After leaving his daughter with his ex-wife Ruth (Kim Hamilton), Ingram agrees to help Burke rob the bank, and Burke pays his $6000 debt to Bacco.

Slater is bored sitting at home while Lorry works. He is bothered when their neighbor Helen (Gloria Grahame) asks him to babysit her young child, and goes instead to a local bar. There, he sees a soldier (Wayne Rogers) demonstrate a judo move on a friend. Trying to impress upon the soldier that more than a knowledge of judo is necessary to defend oneself, Slater brings the soldier to his knees with a quick punch to the solar plexus. For his trouble, he is evicted from the bar. Angry that another thing in his life has backfired, Slater returns home. Lorry nags at him to stay straight, which just angers him. Slater contacts Burke and confirms that he wants back in. When Helen comes back to visit Lorry, who isn't home, Slater invites her in for a drink. He apologizes to her, and she asks him how it felt to kill people in the war. Realizing her intent, he tells her how intimate killing can be: "He dared me, just like you are now." Slater unties Helen's nightgown, revealing her slim upper body, clad in just a bra. He pulls her to him and closes the door; she does not object.

Slater meets Burke and Ingram for the final stages of planning. Slater insults Ingram but Burke intercedes and stops the taunting

Odds Against Tomorrow. Lonely Helen (Gloria) lives in the same apartment building as Earl Slater (Robert Ryan). She finds him most charming and virile, especially when he tells her about his violent past.

immediately. He sets down rules and the two men agree to them. Ingram is to pose as a delivery man, bringing coffee and sandwiches to the bank after hours. After the planning session, Slater returns to Lorry. She apologizes for getting mad, but he takes the blame: "I spoil everything. I can't help it, I just spoil everything." She begs him not to leave and he agrees, although he is determined to complete this one final job, for which he will receive $50,000 if all goes well.

Slater drives a souped-up station wagon to Melton, picking up Burke along the way. Ingram takes the bus into town, and is stopped by the sheriff after witnessing a traffic accident. Slater is suspicious, seeing Ingram talk to the sheriff, and tries to pick a fight with the black man. Burke separates them and demands that they behave. The three men separate for the day, waiting for darkness to fall. At the appointed time, Slater picks up Ingram, who changes into the delivery man's uniform. Ingram wants the keys to the station wagon, but Slater refuses to give them to him, instead handing them to Burke. When the real delivery man leaves the local diner, Burke jostles him, causing the box of coffee and sandwiches to spill all over the sidewalk. This is Ingram's cue; he approaches the bank with a box, and his face hidden. When the guard opens the door, Ingram and Slater push through. Slater and Burke gather the money while Ingram stands guard. They fill a large satchel with cash and exit the bank, but the sheriff just happens to be walking past. The sheriff yells and Slater shoots. The sheriff fires back, hitting Burke, who has both the cash and the keys to the getaway car. Burke is shot two more times as Slater and Ingram escape down the block. Burke has a gun but, being a former cop, refuses to fire at the sheriff; instead, he shoots himself.

Realizing the robbery has failed, Slater takes a shot at Ingram and runs for his life. Ingram grabs Burke's gun and follows. The police are forgotten as the two men run through Melton's industrial yards, shooting at each other in raw hatred. Finally, Slater climbs a ladder onto a high cylindrical structure and Ingram follows. The police remain at a distance, as they are afraid of what may happen in the oil refinery. Ingram corners Slater and they fire at each other, turning the refinery into a flaming inferno. Later, a coroner tells the sheriff that he cannot identify either man — their bodies are burned beyond recognition, charring their skins colorless.

Odds Against Tomorrow is tough and gritty, uncompromising in its depiction of unlucky men hoping for one big score, and, for the era, uncommonly raw in its display of sexuality. Source novelist William McGivern was no stranger to the world of urban crime; films had already been made of his earlier novels *The Big Heat* (1953, with Glenn Ford and Gloria), *Shield for Murder* (1954, starring and directed by Edmond O'Brien), *Rogue Cop* (1954, starring Robert Taylor and Janet Leigh) and others. All of these McGivern novels depict the criminal temptations facing cops and detectives and chronicle the trouble that follows whenever a good cop goes bad. Dave Burke is not the central character in *Odds Against Tomorrow*, but he is the catalyst, turning to crime after being sent to jail for a year for contempt of court. Having seen criminals fail over and over again, Burke devises a simple but brilliant plan to steal $200,000, which he believes he is owed because he was an honest cop sent to jail for refusing to cooperate with a crime commission. Burke recruits the right men for the job, but finds that Slater's inherent racism must be carefully controlled or chaos will result.

In McGivern's original book, Burke is not the mastermind behind the caper, but rather another henchman. Frank Novak is the book's ringleader, but Novak was deemed to be superfluous by the screenwriters and dumped. The bank robbery marks the halfway point of the book; McGivern's story sees Burke killed by the sheriff while Ingram helps an injured Slater get away. The two men hide at a nearby home; Ingram goes for help and brings back Lorry and, later, a doctor to tend to Slater's gunshot wound. Gradually a respect builds between the racist and the black man, but Slater nevertheless meets a violent end, due in part to Lorry's cynical selfishness. McGivern's account is hopeful, conveying the idea that racism can be overcome, or at least abated, by mutual respect.

Director Robert Wise's film takes the opposite approach. It remains faithful to McGivern's novel until the robbery is foiled; at that point, Wise hammers home the idea that Slater's innate racism and Ingram's intolerance of Slater are responsible for its failure, and that racism will always lead to disaster. Wise was not interested in making another hopeful social statement, such as Stanley Kramer's *The Defiant Ones*, which had been a big hit the previous year. Wise wanted to show that hate destroys everything it touches. Thus, he abandoned McGivern's hideout story and brought his two protagonists into direct conflict. Once the bank robbery is foiled, Slater and Ingram are left with nothing but hatred for each other, and Wise allows them to abandon everything else — including common sense — in their narrow-minded fury. They chase and shoot at each other, oblivious to the police officers who are following and slowly closing the net surrounding them. In a truly explosive finale reminiscent of *White Heat*, Wise's film ends in irony, as the two men destroy themselves in hate, wherein they finally become equal. Their bodies are so disfigured by the heat of the blast that they are unrecognizable. Which one is which? It doesn't matter.

Until the bank robbery goes awry, *Odds Against Tomorrow* is a taut, grim, sharply acted tale of societal cast-offs trying to regain some of their former glory through one last, desperate gamble. The situation is crisply presented, the characters are beautifully rendered and their desperation is palpable. The ominous undercurrent of hatred running below the drama promises a powerful confrontation, while John Lewis' memorable jazz score encapsulates the human turmoil. But then Burke dies, still holding the car keys. As they cannot escape, Slater and Ingram instinctively turn on each other. The final phase of the picture is certainly dramatic, but for many viewers it crosses the line from suspense into strained allegory, all for the sake of irony. It's a weak ending to a terrific film.

Until that ending, Wise utilizes a semi-documentary style to chronicle the hard lives of his world-weary protagonists. Nothing comes easy for these people, from Ingram's visits with his young daughter to Slater's encounter with a soldier in a bar. Burke lives in a run-down hotel room with only a German shepherd for company. Slater is reduced to baby-sitting once in a while to keep peace with his woman. The odds seem stacked against them ever finding real happiness or significance in their lives—which is, of course, the point of the title. The point of the movie, and the book upon which it is based, is that the odds are worse for those who cannot overcome their intolerance. Ingram's life is hell due to gambling and a combative disposition; Burke's reputation is shattered because he wouldn't cooperate with the crime commission. But Slater, despite a relatively cozy existence, is truly the man without a future because his hatred will allow him no future satisfaction. Everything is tainted to him, and will remain so. He is doomed to a violent, virulent death because of the poison within his soul.

Because the subject matter lent itself to an air of intense conflict, Wise utilized infra-red shots in the beginning sequence and in the quiet pause before the bank robbery. He felt the infra-red shots altered and intensified the moods he wanted to convey. *Odds Against Tomorrow* is one of the last true *film noir* products; the advent of color and widescreen processes hastened its demise, but so had the tastes of audiences. Viewers wanted something, it was believed, that television couldn't offer, and television was clogged with westerns and crime dramas (as well as medical dramas and family comedies).

And while the film may not precisely be the punctuational period of the *film noir* genre, it can certainly be viewed as its exclamation point. Slater, Ingram and Burke are as hard-boiled, yet well-defined, as any other characters in the oeuvre. Lorry and Helen are also archetypal, and a bit more dimensional than usual. Lensed with a great deal of contrast by Joseph Brun, the film offers images of stark squalor and desperation. Night scenes are particularly effective, and the city of Melton (actually Hudson, New York) is viewed as just as hostile to these unlucky men as New York City itself. Furthermore, the explosive climax—as overblown as it is—recalls that of *White Heat*, and its spectacular nihilism. Wise's message that hate destroys also recalls one of the highpoints of the genre, *Crossfire*, which also starred Robert Ryan as a bigot and Gloria Grahame as a woman of ill repute. *Odds Against Tomorrow* is a good companion piece to *Crossfire*, due to both films' casting, and their uncompromising looks at how racism leads to big trouble for those whose intolerance overrules common courtesy. One could make the argument that in *Odds Against Tomorrow*, Gloria's Helen could be the older and no wiser version of *Crossfire*'s Ginny Tremaine.

For Gloria, the movie was both a blessing and a step down. It was her first film in two years, and a major one at that, but hers was a supporting role consisting of two scenes. She filmed those scenes in a week and was paid just $5,000 for her work—yet she is as memorable as ever. At first perky to the point of irritation, Helen (known as Margie McMillin in the novel) intrudes into Slater's apartment to persuade him to babysit her child. When he refuses in a huff, she is offended, but just slightly, as if she expects the slight. Later, she returns, and Slater is much more amenable. Helen likes the danger that Slater represents, and when he

Odds Against Tomorrow. Gloria pals around with Robert Ryan and Shelley Winters on the set. Gloria and Shelley were good friends despite vying against each other for numerous roles throughout the 1950s.

brazenly opens her dressing gown she doesn't stop him.

Gloria's role in that second scene is reminiscent of her seductresses of the past, and seeing her in a black lace brassiere is an unexpected surprise. This time, however, she doesn't have to work to seduce the man in question; as he is obviously already in the mood, it's really up to her whether the tryst goes forward or not. Gloria's Helen is more languid than her earlier vamps, but the look in her eyes conveys the same sexual heat. Slater is going to have his hands full. The movie's advertising exploits Grahame and her persona's naughty past; one ad describes Helen as "the next-door neighbor who dropped in to borrow another woman's man!" while another describes Helen thusly: "Even if you washed her face and dressed her up ... she'd still be a tramp!" At this stage of her career, Gloria was not pleased about being the picture's sexy focal

point, and actually threatened to sue the filmmakers if photographs showing her with her dressing gown open were utilized to promote the film. She understood that the movie's sexual candor was pushing boundaries, but she felt that it would be demeaning to be thrust in front of the public wearing nothing but a bra beneath her dressing gown in those photographs. Today such a situation would not raise an eyebrow, but back in 1959 it was a big deal to Gloria.

But Slater's women are forgotten as the robbery takes center stage. In the book, Lorry returns to Slater and even attempts to persuade him to abandon Ingram to the police. In the movie, no mention of Lorry or Helen is ever made once the robbery begins. At that point, they become superfluous.

Slater is yet another bigoted role for Robert Ryan, who was so memorable as the murderer Montgomery in *Crossfire*. Slater, like Montgomery, is an ex-military man with too much time on his hands and too much antagonism running through his brain. Ryan provides Slater with the necessary bitterness, but he also infuses the character with hopefulness. Slater tries to do the right thing several times but is always rebuffed in one manner or another. Ryan's portrayal provides Slater with enough empathy to keep the audience involved in his fate. Ryan played just a few prejudiced villains throughout his long career —*Crossfire, Bad Day at Black Rock* (1955), *Odds Against Tomorrow*— but they were so convincing that they dominated his screen persona. Yet he was known in Hollywood circles as a caring man and dedicated civil rights activist. Ryan was once quoted as saying, "I have been in films pretty well everything I am dedicated to fighting against." That is certainly true with this performance.

The star of the picture is Harry Belafonte, who also produced it through his own film company, HarBel Productions (a contraction of *Har*ry and *Bel*afonte). The singer-actor brought the project to Wise's attention and hired the director to bring it to the screen. Belafonte was looking for film projects that would reflect the black experience in America without traditional stereotyping, and without excessive sanctity. His goal was to produce films that showed blacks living life just like anyone else. In McGivern's book, Ingram is inured to slights from whites; he doesn't seem to mind much when Slater repeatedly calls him "Sambo." That did not sit well with Belafonte, an articulate and outspoken crusader for black equality. Belafonte's Ingram reacts to insults and innuendoes; he doesn't allow snide remarks to pass by unnoticed. When Slater gives him trouble, he gives it right back. As a performer, Belafonte uses his forceful personality to ensure that Ingram has a backbone, and as a producer, he also guarantees that Ingram has the same universal type of problems as everybody else.

In the book, Ingram is a loner. In the movie, he is trying to maintain a good relationship with his ex-wife Ruth (Kim Hamilton) and his young daughter Eadie (Lois Thorne), a task made much more difficult because of his gambling habit. He chastises Ruth when he discovers a PTA meeting being held in her apartment; he doesn't want his daughter exposed to the hypocritical race relations he believes are

being represented by the mostly white middle-class committee. He loves Eadie and wants to protect her, yet he also wants her to grow up proudly black instead of agreeably black. Ingram is unhappy with his role as the stereotypical "delivery boy," yet he acknowledges the sense of the plan and even suggests an improvement to Burke's robbery scheme.

Furthermore, Belafonte provides Ingram with a style that is absent from the book, both as star and producer. Ingram drives up to the Hotel Juno in a fancy sports car, and his inimitable clothing style is pure Belafonte: turtleneck, slacks, sports jacket. Ingram sings in a nightclub, allowing Belafonte to please fans of his music, and his wails to "All Men Are Evil" reflect Ingram's feelings about his current predicament, supporting the storyline in dramatic fashion. Ever tuned in to current trends, Belafonte the producer hired John Lewis to provide a jazzy music score for the film. Lewis co-founded the Modern Jazz Quartet, the group which provides the rhythmic, dynamic music that accompanies this dark adventure.

Robert Wise always professed to care more about story than message, yet *Odds Against Tomorrow* uses an allegorical climax to push his message regarding the evils of intolerance past the film's logical conclusion. Wise's ending has nothing to do with McGivern's original concept, nor with the screenplay by Abraham Polonsky. The movie credits novelist John O. Killens and Nelson Gidding with the script, but the majority was penned by the blacklisted Polonsky. Killens, at Belafonte's urging, served as Polonsky's "front," but he actually did not write any of the script (even though he accepted the credit because he wanted to break into the screenwriting field). Gidding revised and polished Polonsky's script after Polonsky became busy with other projects. The Writers Guild officially awarded screenplay credit to Polonsky in 1997. It is no accident that Burke's motivation for the heist is for spending a year in jail for contempt of court charge; having felt the long-lasting effects of the Hollywood blacklist, Polonsky certainly emphasized the bitterness that Burke felt at being so unfairly maligned.

The script's tautness and effectiveness is due to Polonsky, who envisioned a "simple death" for these petty criminals. But he was overruled by Wise, who wished the climax to demonstrate the insignificance of racial designation. In death, the two men become equal, especially as they can no longer be differentiated from one another. In this case Wise is just as obvious as Stanley Kramer, whose well-intentioned but often sermonizing films were often castigated by critics. Yet Kramer's films almost always met with commercial success, while *Odds Against Tomorrow* did not, despite its high-powered cast and director. It failed to recoup its costs and collected very mixed reviews.

Boxoffice predicted it would be "a box-office winner," and lauded its star: "Harry Belafonte achieves new stature as a dramatic actor in this exciting suspenseful picture...." Moira Walsh of *America* found the film to be "continuously absorbing.... It has human dimension and moral perspective, which are values not usually present in crime melodramas." *Time* called it "a peculiar plea for racial integration in the underworld." Hollis Alpert of *The Saturday Review* wrote, "Crime and prejudice not only don't pay in this story; the seem, on the whole, rather boring." Perhaps the British Film Institute's *Monthly Film Bulletin* had the sharpest perspective when its critic wrote that the film "is strongly reminiscent of the sort of socially significant melodramas that Hollywood was making ten years ago.... Ten years ago, in fact, the film would probably have seemed a good deal more striking than it does now."

Odds Against Tomorrow holds up pretty well. It's taut and suspenseful, with sharply defined characters and a dark, ominous edge that never fades away. The ending is a bit much, but there are plenty of rewards to compensate for its excess. It boasts excellent acting, top-notch cinematography, a jazzy score and an exciting story. The movie deserves greater recognition than it has received.

It was the last major motion picture featuring Gloria Grahame for two decades. Gloria would spend time with her children, nurturing her young daughter Paulette and ensuring that Timmy, eleven years old in 1959, matured into a fine, strong, healthy teenager. To keep her hand in show business, Gloria began to appear regularly on stage and she turned up on television now and again. The 1950s had been a wild rollercoaster ride for Gloria, and at least she was able to end the decade with an impor-

tant film. The 1960s would challenge her in mostly negative ways she could not yet imagine. Gloria's most difficult period would ensue with the return of a person from her past — Tony Ray — who intended only the best for Gloria, and with whom Gloria would bear and raise two more children over the next six years.

Ride Beyond Vengeance (1966)
(aka *Night of the Tiger*)

CREDITS Mark Goodson–Bill Todman Productions; Sentinel Productions; Fenady Associates; The Tiger Company. *Distributed by* Columbia Pictures. *Directed by* Bernard McEveety. *Produced and Screenplay by* Andrew J. Fenady. *From the novel The Night of the Tiger by* Al Dewlen. *Director of Photography*: Lester Shorr. *Film Editor*: Otho Lovering. *Art Direction*: Stan Jolley. *Set Decoration*: William Calvert. *Production Manager*: Harry F. Hogan. *Assistant Director*: Lee H. Katzin. *Script Supervisor*: George A. Rutter. *Music Editor*: John Caper, Jr. *Orchestration*: Willard Jones. *Casting Consultant*: Marvin Paige. *Properties*: Richard M. Rubin. *Makeup Artist*: Fred B. Phillips. *Hair Stylist*: Virginia Darcy. *Men's Costumer*: Gordon T. Dawson. *Women's Costumer*: Frances Hamilton. *Special Effects*: Lee Vasque. *Sound Recording*: Terry Kellum and Joel Moss. *Music by* Richard Markowitz. *Song* "You Can't Go Home Again" *by* Richard Markowitz (music) and Andrew J. Fenady (lyric), *sung by* Glenn Yarbrough. *Executive Associate for Sentinel Productions*: Ann St. Lawrence. *Stunt Coordinator*: Bill Catching. *Stunts*: Fred Carson and Luke Saucier. Pathé Color. Matted Widescreen (1.85:1). Monaural Sound. 101 minutes. Released in April, 1966. Currently available on DVD. Previously available on VHS.

CAST *Jonas Trapp*, Chuck Connors; *Mrs. Lavender*, Joan Blondell; *Bonnie Shelley*, Gloria Grahame; *Dub Stokes*, Gary Merrill; *Johnsy Boy Hood*, Bill Bixby; *Elwood Coates*, Claude Akins; *Lee Hanley*, Paul Fix; *Brooks Durham*, Michael Rennie; *Census Taker*, James MacArthur; *Bartender/Narrator*, Arthur O'Connell; *Aunt Gussie*, Ruth Warrick; *Mr. Kratz*, Buddy Baer; *Tod Wisdom*, Frank Gorshin; *Hotel Clerk*, Robert Q. Lewis; *Jessie Larkin Trapp*, Kathryn Hays; *Maria*, Marissa Mathes; *Vogan*, Harry Harvey, Sr.; *Bartender*, William Bryant; *Pete the Blacksmith*, Jamie Farr; *Mexican Boy*, Larry Domasin; *Drunk*, Bill Catching; *Storekeeper*, Chuck Hamilton; *Barfly*, Bill Coontz.

This was Gloria's third and final appearance in a theatrically released western; she would return to the west one final time in the TV-movie *Black Noon* for the same producer five years later. Once again she has little to do and is almost superfluous to the story. That has less to do with Gloria's ability than the violent, male-dominated script. Gloria had been away from the big screen for seven years, and her third-billing in the advertising is surprising evidence of her remaining star power. Other than the violence quotient, which is high (especially for 1966), this could pass for a made-for-television movie, peppered as it is with familiar faces and directed by Walt Disney veteran helmer Bernard McEveety. Yet, like most of the other westerns of 1966, it passed through theaters without attracting much notice.

Ride Beyond Vengeance begins in the present day with a census taker (James MacArthur) tallying names in Coldiron, Texas, where many of the citizens are rather inexplicably named "Reprisal." Finished with his assignment, the census taker stops at the local bar and grill and asks the bartender (Arthur O'Connell) about the name. The bartender tells him that August 16, 1884, was "the night of the reprisals," and then goes on to narrate the story of Jonas Trapp, shown in flashback.

Jonas (Chuck Connors) is heading home to Coldiron after having spent the past eleven years collecting buffalo skins worth $17,000. He spies a campfire on the trail and rides up after dark. The place is deserted but then three men emerge from the shadows with guns drawn. They accuse Jonas of cow thievery, finding a tied calf nearby in the brush. Jonas protests and two of the trio beat him mercilessly. One man prevents the others from hanging Jonas on the spot, but the other two take a poker from the campfire and brand a large T (for "thief") onto Jonas' chest and leave him to die from the effects of the branding. Jonas then dreams of his life: of swimming with Jessie (Kathryn Hays), of marrying her despite the opposition of her Aunt Gussie (Ruth Warrick), of the shame of not being able to provide for Jessie (who is relatively rich), of planning to take her with him to Kansas and hunt buffalo, of her refusal to go, of his fateful decision to leave eleven years ago and strike out on his own, planning all the time to return with the means to provide for her.

Jonas awakens to find an old man named Lee Hanley (Paul Fix) caring for him and his money stolen. With his chest searing from pain, Jonas determines to retrieve what is his, no matter what the cost. He returns to Coldiron after dark, still dirty, smelly and bedraggled. He sees Jessie leave her store, a woman's emporium, and approaches her, but she doesn't recognize him in his battered condition and hits him, thinking he is just another drunk. Jonas wanders into a saloon and orders a bottle of whiskey. He can't pay the $2 but frightens the bouncer Mr. Kratz (Buddy Baer) enough to let him alone. In the hotel, Johnsy Boy Hood (Bill Bixby) impatiently taunts his Mexican girlfriend Maria (Marissa Mathes) and her cat. She wants a ring from him to display to her mother, proving that she is still respectable, but he doesn't care. They argue and he pushes her around some before he leaves. Jonas is outside, drinking under a staircase, when he sees one of his assailants ride past. It is Johnsy Boy Hood.

At a nearby ranch, Bonnie Shelley (Gloria Grahame) is waiting for someone, so she spurns the advances of her ranch hand Tod Wisdom (Frank Gorshin). She goes for a walk and meets Johnsy Boy out in the woods. He implores her to remove her savings from the bank before her husband returns (in three weeks) so they can run away together to St. Louis. Bonnie reluctantly agrees, stating that she loves Johnsy Boy; he reassures her that everything will be wonderful in the big city. Returning from his rendezvous, Johnsy Boy is stopped by Jonas in the road. Johnsy Boy tries to escape, repeatedly whipping Jonas, but Jonas eventually gets the upper hand. Johnsy Boy begs for his life and implicates the two men that were with him. Jonas threatens to brand him in the same manner and is astonished when Johnsy Boy suddenly grabs the branding iron, pulls it into his own gut and runs away with it, screaming in pain ... and in sado-masochistic ecstasy. In town, Tod Wisdom staggers into the saloon and tells the cowboy crowd how Johnsy Boy returned to Bonnie's house with burned hands and belly, then shot himself in front of her mirror. Among the men paying rapt attention are Jonas' two other assailants.

One of them, Elwood Coates (Claude Akins), is fascinated by Tod's repeated mentions of $17,000 in cash. Despite drinking heavily, he finds Hanley the next day, questions him about the stranger and demands his share of the stranger's cash. Hanley denies having any cash and so Coates knocks him senseless, ties him to a horse and sends the horse away, dragging Hanley behind it. Then Coates goes to meet Jonas' other assailant, Brooks Durham. In town, a cleaned-up Jonas finally meets Jessie, who hits him again and snarls, "Why did you come back?" They talk in her shop and he discovers that she, believing Jonas to be dead, is to marry banker Brooks Durham (Michael Rennie). As he leaves, stunned, he is accosted by Mr. Kratz, still looking for the $2 to settle Jonas' bar bill. A fight ensues and Jonas tosses Kratz through a store window. Jonas is prevented from killing him by Dub Stokes (Gary Merrill), Jonas estranged foster father.

Coates visits Durham at the bank and demands his share of the money that he believes Durham stole from Jonas. Durham refuses. Coates withdraws but tells Durham that Jonas is Jessie's husband, knowing that Jessie is planning to marry Durham. This sets Durham to thinking, as it was Durham who prevented Coates and Johnsy Boy from killing Jonas in the first place. Jonas moves into the hotel, in Johnsy Boy's old room. Maria offers herself to him, but Jonas isn't interested. He pets her cat, the one that Johnsy Boy didn't like. Maria gets food for him and offers herself again. This time Jonas accepts. Meanwhile, Bonnie waits for the stagecoach out of town, alone. Durham visits Jessie, tells her everything and says that he'll return the money to Jonas. He still wants her, though, and he will not run from Jonas. The inevitable showdown between Brooks and Jonas is interrupted by Coates, who tries to trample Durham and Jonas in the street. Neither is hurt, and Durham confesses the whole story to the townspeople gathered around. He apologizes to Jonas, who knocks him down disdainfully.

Jonas goes after Coates, who ambushes him from a rooftop. Their subsequent fight moves from the street into the saloon and is a real humdinger. It finally ends with Jonas winning, but the beaten Coates then pulls a gun. Maria distracts Coates so that Jonas can fill him full of lead. Jonas gives Maria his gun so she can swap it for a ring. The following day, the whole town is out to see what Jonas will do

Ride Beyond Vengeance. **This costume test shot was used before the film's release to announce the fact that Gloria was making her first movie since 1959.**

next. He brings out the cat and lets it run free. He says goodbye to Jessie, telling her he'll go south to hunt the last few remaining buffalo. She implores him to stay, even as Durham hovers in the background, but he refuses. He tells her to keep the money and rides out of town. Dub coaxes Jessie to ride after him but she cannot, convinced that Jonas no longer wants her.

Back in present day, the census taker asks the bartender what happened after that. "Nobody knows," the bartender replies. Jessie never married Durham but left a few weeks later and was never heard from again. The census taker does not believe Jessie ever found Jonas, or stayed with him if she did. As he leaves Coldiron, he reflects on the single most important event in the town's history, the night of the reprisals, and he begins to understand the significance of the name.

Ride Beyond Vengeance is a very faithful rendering of Al Dewlen's novel *The Night of the*

Tiger, which also serves as an alternate title for this film. Very few elements have been changed, although Jonas Trapp was Julius Rupp in the book. The biggest change involves the character of Maria, Johnsy Boy's Mexican girlfriend. In the movie, Maria is left behind when Johnsy Boy kills himself, so Jonas pays her hotel bill for a week, befriends her and eventually leaves her his gun so that she can pawn it for the ring she so strongly desires (and which Johnsy Boy promised her). Jonas never tells Maria that it was because of him that her boyfriend died. In the book, Maria discovers Julius' part in Johnsy Boy's death and angrily exhorts Coates to kill him. Yet as Julius is about to leave, Maria returns his gun to him and decides to ride away with him — and with the cat. The cat also appears in the film but neither it, nor Maria, accompany Jonas out of town. In terms of the overall structure, however, these are exceedingly minor alterations, and this is almost unheard of in adaptations from page to screen. Even the prologue with the census taker is included!

One scene from the book, however, is missing from the movie and it involves Bonnie Shelley, Gloria's character. In the movie, Bonnie is seen waiting in the hotel lobby for the stagecoach out of town following the death of her lover Johnsy Boy, and that is the last time she is seen. Bonnie is obviously agitated, crying softly, anxious to get out of town and away from the gossip that is certain to swirl around her affairs for months to come. It is inferred that she leaves town in total shame on the departing stagecoach, but the money she removed from her (and her husband's) bank account is never addressed. In the novel, before Bonnie leaves town she meets with Brooks Durham, returns most of the money to her husband's account that Johnsy Boy had illicitly persuaded her to remove — all except for $200, which she figures is a fair wage for fifteen years of marital servitude. Bonnie leaves Coldiron without a husband or a lover, but with at least a trace of her dignity intact.

If such a scene was included in the script, it was not included in the final film, probably for reasons of time. That ultimately missing scene could have explained why Gloria accepted the part, since it is a rather weak role in every other respect. Gloria always liked parts with intricately written character flourishes, and the novel's scene between Bonnie and Durham has incisive, thoughtful dialogue and underlying layers of meaning that would have greatly appealed to Gloria's acting instincts.

Gloria is fine in the role of the lonely farm wife, lonely enough to fall prey to the silky attentiveness of narcissistic Johnsy Boy Hood. The romantic scene between Gloria and Bill Bixby is vacuous, due entirely to Johnsy Boy's moral transparency more than the acting chops of its participants. It doesn't help that in the previous scene Johnsy Boy's nefarious intentions are revealed to his girlfriend Maria — as is his predilection toward sado-masochism. (In the book this is revealed immediately after his rendezvous with Bonnie, which is considerably more effective.) Thus, when Johnsy Boy meets Bonnie, there is no doubt at all that he is after her money and will discard her with distaste once he has it. Bonnie, of course, is unaware of this, and Gloria imbues her with an anxious hopefulness that is entirely appropriate. Gloria's finest scene, actually, is her brief but sorrowful vigil for the stagecoach in the hotel lobby. With her head downcast, mumbled responses to the hotel clerk's polite comments and a single tear drifting down her cheek, Gloria is absolutely convincing as a woman trying not to surrender to her emotions as she releases one life and prepares to chart another, utterly alone.

But Gloria was no longer alone. Before she started filming *Odds Against Tomorrow* she began seeing Tony Ray, who was her stepson while she was married to Nicholas Ray. Their relationship gradually developed from reluctant friends to intimate lovers and they married on May 13, 1960, in Mexico. Knowing that news of their nuptials would cause an uproar, they managed to keep it quiet for nearly two years. Eventually people found out and Gloria's name was trashed in the tabloid press. Nicholas Ray was stunned and furious. But Tony loved Gloria and she loved him. They had two children, Anthony Jr. on April 30, 1963, and James on September 21, 1965. Tony and Gloria remained married until May 4, 1974 — almost fourteen years, about four times longer than Gloria's marriage to Nicholas Ray.

Tony Ray suffered from some of the same issues his father did, but not to the same extent.

He never fell out of love with Gloria as his father had. But their union followed the same pattern that all of Gloria's previous marriages had: cycles of separation and reunion. Some of their troubles were caused by the public reaction to their marriage; some of them were monetary; some were caused by Cy Howard, who didn't want his daughter Paulette in a household he considered to be unstable. Gloria suffered so much from Cy that in 1964 she endured shock treatments to try to free her mind of some of the guilt he pushed upon her. Because of the money issues, since Tony was not working steadily (he did not seem to have the talent that his father displayed behind the camera), Gloria accepted television jobs when they were offered to her by friends like Stanley Rubin. She also found jobs on the stage, and discovered that they were far more rewarding artistically than doing films. Movies just weren't offered to her because of her bad publicity. It wasn't until 1966 that she landed the role in *Ride Beyond Vengeance*. She did not land another movie role for five more years.

And the rest of the time she raised her family. Now with four kids, Gloria devoted herself to motherhood and housework, a lifestyle she had trouble sustaining when she was hot in Hollywood. She fought continually to protect her three boys and one girl from the prying eyes of the press and to maintain a normal, healthy environment for them. It wasn't always easy, given her celebrity and the frequent legal rumblings from her former husbands, but she tried. She spent as much time with them as she could, playing with them in the backyard, throwing neighborhood parties for them and attending as many school activities as was possible. During the 1960s, Gloria's life was radically different from what it had been before, but she assured anyone who asked that raising the family was far more rewarding.

Filmed in the hiatus between seasons of the television series *Branded*, *Ride Beyond Vengeance* shared not only its star (Chuck Connors) with that series, but many of its crew members and more than a few of its supporting cast and guest stars as well. It is often considered sensible — and relatively inexpensive — for the cast and crew of a series to film a movie while not shooting their series, when the right project can be found and agreed upon. Being familiar with each other, and filming a story that shared the same time period as their series, the *Branded* crew felt perfectly at home making this movie.

Perhaps the predominant variation from television involves the savagery of the script. Unremittingly bleak and nihilistic, the physical and emotional torture of Jonas Trapp was notoriously rough for its era, at least on American shores. Critics have since declared that the savage tone of the film came in direct response to the first wave of "spaghetti westerns" made in Europe. Those films, most famously starring Clint Eastwood and Charles Bronson, combined sturdy tales of the old west with a new, grimy aesthetic, startling stylistic flourishes and an abundance of colorful death and destruction. *Ride Beyond Vengeance* has been termed an artistic, and American, response to the emergence of those films — and a blatant attempt to cash in upon the barbarous trend. It is impossible to refute such claims after witnessing Jonas viciously branded, Johnsy Boy throw a cat, Johnsy Boy mercilessly whip Jonas, Johnsy Boy astonishingly brand *himself*, Coates slug Hanley with the butt of his gun before tying him to a horse to be dragged to death, and Jonas beat Mr. Kratz to a pulp. Jessie seems to slap Jonas every time she meets him! Then, the film's action highlight is the four-minute fight scene between Jonas and Coates, a sequence that essentially destroys a barroom. Legendary director William Wyler called it "one of the greatest fight scenes I've ever seen on the screen."

It isn't just the physical action that is punishing. The tone of the film is harsh and nasty. Even Johnsy Boy's suicide, an offscreen event, is related by Tod Wisdom with such fervor (as it is in the novel) that it is remarkably grisly. No relationship can be described as normal or healthy, from Jonas' anger with his foster father Dub Stokes to Jessie's lies to her Aunt Gussie in order to marry Jonas. Brooks Durham wants no part of hanging unproved cow thief Jonas, but he deftly steals the man's life savings with little compunction. Coates is so eager to get the money that he kills his own rustling partner, Hanley, and then goes after Durham without pause. Yet these selfish characters and their actions all pale in comparison with Johnsy Boy Hood.

From the crazy moniker (pronounced Jonesy Boy) to his spectacular narcissism, Johnsy Boy is one of a kind. His defining characteristic is his streak of sadism. He hurts everyone he touches, even the cat, and he cannot seem to stop himself. In one brief scene with Maria, he is both sweet and sadistic. Then, when Jonas threatens him with the same treatment that Johnsy Boy and Coates had so gleefully applied to Jonas, he literally takes matters into his own hands and maims himself with a branding iron. Such masochism was, at the very least, unexpected; most critics found it downright ugly. It is due to Johnsy Boy, and to a lesser degree Coates, that the film owes its memorably repulsive reputation.

That reputation belies its intriguing story, designed to make larger than life the legend of "El Tigre," Jonas Trapp. Jonas is a flawed character, having pridefully left his wife for eleven years just to prove himself capable of providing for her. But once he is branded, he becomes a sympathetic figure in every respect. It is notable that, for all the film's violence, the only killing attributable to Jonas is that of Coates, who draws his gun as Jonas is walking away from him. And, of course, the film's point is that Jonas is, finally, able to "ride beyond vengeance." Although the title hints at the opposite, at being destroyed by vengeance, it actually means mentally moving past vengeance in order to survive and function as a human being. Jonas does not forgive his assailants; when Durham apologizes Jonas tells him to go to hell and slugs him for good measure. But he does not kill them in cold blood either. Withstanding the physical agony and betrayal surrounding his return home to Coldiron, Jonas survives to begin his life anew. In the movie, when he leaves he's alone, with the possibility that Jessie will, in time, follow; in the book, Julius is accompanied by Maria and the cat.

The conceit of the story is that Jonas' reprisals have passed into local legend that, even eighty years after the fact, still grips the town, causing the town's inhabitants to name their newborns Jonas, Jessie, and, yes, Reprisal. In the book, the census taker cannot resist including Jonas, Jessie and the other principals as alive and well in Coldiron, though they are long dead, such is their impact upon him.

It is this conceit that ought to provide the story its lasting impact, yet because Jonas fails to wreak the vengeance that is so luridly advertised, this claim seems invalid. Had Jonas wiped out half the town, as the movie's advertising suggests, then perhaps an ascendancy to legend would be understandable. But only Johnsy Boy, Coates and Hanley die, and Jonas' ultimate act of vengeance is to turn his back on his hometown and ride away. Proclaiming such events to be legendary, even to a small town such as Coldiron, seems a bit of a stretch, if not positively preposterous.

The movie, however, is well crafted and entertaining. Chuck Connors is commanding and intense as Jonas, and physically perfect for the part. It was his favorite movie role, one he relished because of its complexities and physicality. He performed many of his own stunts, too. He is billed in the advertising as "the New Giant of Western Adventure." Columbia was obviously hoping that this movie would do for Connors what *A Fistful of Dollars* (1964) had done for Eastwood. That didn't happen; Connors followed *Ride Beyond Vengeance* with the second season of *Branded* and then one season of *Cowboy in Africa*. His next film was, indeed, a "spaghetti western" made in Italy in 1968 but not released in America until 1970, variously titled *Go Kill Everybody and Come Back Alone* or *Kill Them All and Come Back Alone*.

The supporting cast offers excellence: Claude Akins as the drunken cow rustler Coates, forever mumbling to his invisible friend and alter ego, the Whiskey Man; Gary Merrill as Jonas' foster father Dub Stokes, trying unsuccessfully to rekindle a friendship lost long ago; Michael Rennie as the complicated banker Brooks Durham; Gloria as the lonely farm wife; and Kathryn Hays in her movie debut as Jessie. Hays ages gracefully from sweet but selfish western maiden to bitter, forlorn, deserted wife, hoping to salvage some sort of a normal life by marrying Durham. Hays' performance is probably the best of the bunch; had the movie been made a dozen years earlier, hers is the type of role that Gloria could have essayed with aplomb. Also notable are Paul Fix and Frank Gorshin in atypical roles. Whether Bill Bixby is effective as the neurotic Johnsy Boy is heavily dependent upon one's reaction to the character. It is certainly Bixby's most outlandish cinematic character.

Because the film so strongly resembles a western television show, it is often critically disparaged, which does not give it due credit. Bernard McEveety's film is robust, hard-edged, stylistic, smart, dramatic and unsentimental. It has flaws, of course, and is sometimes over the top and tough to take. Yet it is among the better westerns of 1966 and contains a most memorable barroom brawl, among several other fine sequences and the performances already mentioned.

Western writer Brian Garfield, in his book *Western Films*, wrote, "It's a relentless one-note movie, wretchedly overacted, and it includes some of the most ludicrously savage brutality this side of the nauseating *Forty Guns*. Filled with sado-masochism and leering sexual innuendo, it nevertheless manages somehow to be utterly boring."

On the plus side, Kevin Thomas of the *Los Angeles Times* loved it: "*Ride Beyond Vengeance* really isn't a western in the usual sense of the word. Yet, if considered as one, it is a classic. Few films of any genre crowd so many flesh-and-blood characters on the screen. Few westerns, with their traditional black-and-white morality, have people of so many shades of grey." W. Ward Marsh of the *Cleveland Plain Dealer* judged it "a first-rate western in the manner and mood of the high-class oater which placed William S. Hart, Tom Mix, Art Acord, Ken Maynard and a few others in the celluloid halls of sagebrush fame." When asked about the film years later, producer Andrew J. Fenady stated, "As time goes by it will gain stature as a classic, much as the John Wayne film *Chisum* is gaining stature as the years go by. *Ride Beyond Vengeance* is more cerebral than the spaghetti westerns, but it probably falls into that category as a cult classic."

But the fact is that the film was not even reviewed in the major magazines of the era and is barely remembered now. Connors is recognized for starring on TV's *The Rifleman* and little else, while the movie is just a footnote on the résumés of its participants. For Gloria it represented a missed opportunity in terms of creating a memorable character, as well as re-staking a claim to box office stardom. It would be another five years before she landed another feature film role, and her career would thereafter consist of large parts in small, mostly inferior, films, and small parts in more prestigious projects.

Blood and Lace (1971)

CREDITS Contemporary Filmakers and The Carlin Company. *Distributed by* American International Pictures. *Directed by* Philip Gilbert. *Produced by* Ed Carlin and Gil Lasky. *Associate Producer*: Chase Mishkin. *Written by* Gil Lasky. *Director of Photography*: Paul Hipp. *Film and Sound Editing*: Dennis Film Services. *Art Director*: Lee Fischer. *Camera Assistant*: Ric Eisman. *Key Grip*: Bob McVay. *Electrician*: Jim Feazell. *Continuity*: Carol Littleton. *Sound Recordist*: Douglas Kennedy. *Sound Assistant*: James Maura. *Editorial Assistant*: Marcus Tobias. *Creative Makeup*: Dennis Marsh. *Production Stills*: Jean Pagliuso. *Title Lettering by* Lettergraphics. *Music Editing*: John Rens. *Titles and Opticals by* Cinefx. Rated PG (originally rated GP). Movielab Color. Flat (1.37:1). Monaural Sound. 87 minutes. Released on March 17, 1971. Not currently unavailable on DVD. Previously available on VHS.

CAST *Mrs. Dorothy Deere*, Gloria Grahame; *Harold Mullins*, Milton Selzer; *Tom Kredge*, Len Lesser; *Calvin Carruthers*, Vic Tayback; *Ellie Masters*, Melody Patterson; *Bunch*, Terri Messina; *Walter Barnes*, Ronald Taft; *Pete*, Dennis Christopher; *Ernest*, Peter Armstrong; *Jennifer*, Maggie Corey; *Nurse*, Mary Strawberry; *Edna Masters*, Louise Sherill; *Unidentified Man*, Joe Durkin.

After a five-year hiatus from the screen, Gloria Grahame came back very visibly with the top-billed role in the gruesome, twisted horror film *Blood and Lace*. Because it is rated PG, there isn't a lot of blood (nor is there much lace), so the title is more suggestive than descriptive. However, the story and its tone are gruesome and perverse enough to have merited a harsher rating, and it would probably have been more frightening and effective had the filmmakers not held back on its violence and sexuality. It is an odd movie, to say the least, but it put Gloria back into the public eye, albeit in front of an audience that she had not had before.

Blood and Lace begins with the point-of-view perspective of someone creeping around a house in the dead of night. The person sneaks into the house and picks up a hammer in the kitchen. The camera follows the hammer as the person enters a bedroom where a couple is sleeping and then slaughters them with it. The

Blood and Lace. **Young Ellie Masters (Melody Patterson, left) is unhappy being sent to a county youth home run by Mrs. Deere (Gloria).**

killer is never seen; the woman's skull is crushed and the man is terribly injured as the house begins to burn and the killer exits.

Pretty Ellie Masters (Melody Patterson) awakens screaming in a hospital; it is only a short time after her sluttish mother was killed — hammered to death while sleeping with her latest lover. Because Ellie is still a minor, social worker Mr. Mullins (Milton Selzer) makes arrangements to send her to the county's youth home. Ellie sneaks away from the hospital at night but is followed and caught by Calvin Carruthers (Vic Tayback), now a detective working on her mother's murder case. Carruthers takes Ellie back to the hospital and warns her to be careful; he believes that the killer saw her in the house and may wish to eliminate the only possible witness. Meanwhile, Carruthers meets with Mullins to discuss Ellie; both men seem to have a personal interest in the nubile young woman.

At the Deere Youth Home, teenager Ernest

(Peter Armstrong) runs away, chased by the home's handyman, Tom Kredge (Len Lesser). Kredge teases the boy by throwing a meat cleaver which chops off Ernest's right hand. Ernest runs and hides in thick underbrush; Kredge cannot find him and returns to the home with the boy's suitcase and hand. The proprietress, Dorothy Deere (Gloria Grahame), is quite angry with Kredge, because the boy represented $150 a month in county payments to her. Knowing that the social worker Mullins will be bringing Ellie the next morning, and that he will be expecting to make a head count of the kids during his inspection, Mrs. Deere has Kredge bring three frozen bodies from the meat locker in the basement to the infirmary. Ellie sees them, but thinks they are sleeping. The Deere Youth Home is home to about a dozen teenagers who no longer have families. As the teens do chores outside (as demanded by Mrs. Deere for their keep), Mullins and Mrs. Deere find some afternoon delight in her room.

Dinner is awkward, as Mrs. Deere demands silence. After dinner, Ellie finds a girl chained in the attic as punishment for trying to run away. Kredge prevents Ellie from helping the handcuffed girl.

Calvin Carruthers arrives to check on Ellie. She tells him that kids have run away, but he doesn't believe her because there are no records to prove it. Meanwhile, a bald figure with a burned face (presumably either the original killer, or the man who survived, out for revenge) begins to prowl the grounds. Kredge knows that Ellie wants to run away and lures her into the cellar, where he tries to rape her, only to be interrupted by Mrs. Deere. After Ellie is sent to her room, Kredge demands to be made a partner; he knows enough to cause real trouble, so Mrs. Deere reluctantly agrees. The next day Ellie is sent to clean a shed, but not before Mrs. Deere slaps her around and tells her that dead people will someday be restored to life. Later, alone, Mrs. Deere talks to her dead husband, who is frozen in the meat locker.

Mrs. Deere realizes that Ellie knows too much about her evil ways, and decides to let Kredge eliminate her. In the attic, Ellie sees the burned man with the handcuffed girl and runs away screaming. Kredge catches Ellie and locks her in the meat locker where she is to freeze to death; there, Ellie finds the corpses of missing kids and Mr. Deere. Mullins arrives, angrily demanding to make a head count because he's been informed that kids have gone missing. As Mullins waits to inspect the freezer, Kredge thrusts a meat cleaver into his back. Mullins is being put into the meat locker when the burned man interferes, allowing Ellie to escape. Kredge and the burned man fight. Ellie tries to get the other kids to run for their lives, but they won't listen. The burned man knocks Kredge unconscious and chases Ellie. Mrs. Deere drags Kredge into the meat locker, but is locked inside with him by the girl from the attic, who has been freed. The burned man chases Ellie through the woods, where she gives herself away by screaming when she stumbles across the dead, decomposing body of Ernest. The burned man removes his mask, revealing himself to be Calvin Carruthers. The lovesick detective confronts Ellie, telling her that he surmised that she killed her mother and her

mother's lover with a hammer, but that he won't turn her in if she will marry him. Posing as the surviving man (who actually died in the fire), Carruthers used Ellie as bait because he knew something was wrong at the youth home, and now he has rescued her (and the other kids) from it. Ellie is disgusted with Carruthers' proposition but, facing a certain prison sentence, she agrees to marry him. Then he tells her that he was the first man who ever made love to her mother. Ellie's mother had always said that the first man to make love to her was Ellie's father; Ellie begins laughing hysterically, and the movie ends.

Between a girl who murders her own mother (and her mother's lover) with a hammer, a handyman who enjoys assaulting people with a meat cleaver, a detective who pretends to be a deformed killer, a proprietress who has conversations with her dead husband in a meat locker and teenagers who would rather remain at a youth home where they are underfed and overworked — and with a killer on the loose — than run away and embrace the freedom that awaits them, this is one seriously twisted movie. It begins with a gruesome (though not particularly realistic) hammer murder and ends with the specter of incest, and it's all rated PG. A decade before Michael Myers, Jason Voorhees and Freddy Krueger stalked and slaughtered movie teens by the busload, such teenagers had to fend for themselves against less supernatural, but no less freakish, predators such as Mrs. Deere and Tom Kredge in drive-in fare such as *Blood and Lace*.

While the violence quotient is relatively low, the film does not skimp on luridness or salaciousness. Its heroine is pretty Ellie Masters, not yet 21 and thus still considered a minor. Her mother Edna (Louise Sherill) is the town slut (described as a prostitute in the film's pressbook), of whom Ellie is suitably ashamed. Edna seems to have known every man in town, including Harold Mullins and Calvin Carruthers. Nobody seems very disturbed about Edna's murder, but Mullins and Carruthers are both highly interested in the fate of young Ellie. Mullins openly lusts for the girl, and Carruthers tells him that Ellie would be "good breeding stock." At the youth home, Kredge tries to rape Ellie, although he doesn't seem to notice any of the other young nubile girls. And at the conclusion, Carruthers is disguised as the burned killer and chases Ellie through the woods with a hammer before finally revealing himself. His proposition will keep Ellie out of jail, or prevent her from being hung for the murder of her mother, but marrying the older man is obviously distasteful for Ellie — especially when she realizes that Carruthers is her long-lost father!

There isn't much mystery to the story either. Viewers see the initial murders committed with a hammer, and then the house burns down. Ellie tells detective Carruthers that she was in the house and saw a man leave, but she doesn't remember a hammer. Later, examining the wreckage of the house, Carruthers finds the burned claw of the murder weapon. Since Ellie told him (without provocation) that she didn't see a hammer, and yet a hammer was the murder weapon that the detective finds in the ashes, it is obvious to Carruthers that Ellie is her mother's killer. As soon as Carruthers is seen finding the hammer claw, it should be obvious that Ellie is guilty of matricide. The story then switches to Ellie's peril at the Deere Youth Home. There, she is menaced by Mrs. Deere, Kredge, the burned man and even her jealous roommate, Bunch (Terri Messina). It is clear right away that Mrs. Deere and Kredge are taking as much advantage of their teenage charges as possible, and killing them when they attempt to run away. That just leaves the identity of the burned man, which provides the only suspense generated by the story.

The youth home scenes are pretty silly, especially when contrasted with the behavior of similarly aged teenagers today. The *Blood and Lace* kids accept without protest the meager rations doled out by Mrs. Deere, although Pete (Dennis Christopher in his film debut) tries to sneak an extra bread roll at dinner — and is promptly caught by Mrs. Deere. They wander around the grounds raking leaves, planting flowers, cleaning, scrubbing and polishing whatever they are told with nary an argument. When Ellie escapes from the meat locker, she warns the kids to run because there's a killer in the basement — but they simply stand around. Pete, who knows that something is wrong, wants to follow Ellie, but Walter (Ronald Taft) stops him. "Go where, Pete?" he asks. *People are being killed in the basement*, but the kids

cannot work up enough gumption to save themselves!

The saving grace of this pernicious motion picture is that it doesn't take itself very seriously. It is intended to be scary and creepy and uncomfortable to watch, but it also exhibits a streak of welcome wit at odd moments. When Mullins peeks into the infirmary to see the three sick kids, he hopes they will recover quickly. "Just a little cold," says Kredge, who only recently carried them up from the meat locker. Later, when Mullins wants to conduct a full inspection, Kredge breaks the news to Mrs. Deere. "He wants in the freezer," Kredge says. "Then that's where we'll put him," she replies. The moment that reveals Mrs. Deere as seriously crazy comes after she slaps Ellie and tells her that dead people will, someday, be restored to life. "Death may be only the temporary absence of life," she declares. Right then, Ellie knows that she has to get out of that house if she is to remain alive.

Because this is drive-in fodder with little pretense at realistic moviemaking, its surreal moments should not be unexpected. Yet every once in a while, it surprises with a moment of convincing normalcy. One night Ellie has a nightmare about the burned man with the hammer (it really isn't a nightmare, but she doesn't realize that). Ellie screams, waking the other kids, and Mrs. Deere comes to see what the trouble is. Surprisingly, Mrs. Deere actually acts like a real house mother, and consoles the young woman. No tantrums about waking her, no warnings not to do it again, just honest caring. Likewise, when Tom is trying to rape Ellie, Mrs. Deere interrupts with genuine concern. But such moments are few and far between.

It is no coincidence that those moments are Gloria's. Although she had not appeared in a feature film in five years, or co-starred in one for fifteen years, Gloria had not lost the talent that she had painstakingly developed. Gloria portrays Dorothy Deere as a no-nonsense woman trying to take every advantage of a lousy situation. She plays the part with little makeup and tousled hair, befitting a woman who has no time for niceties. Mrs. Deere is convincingly stern to keep the teenagers in line, showing only a glimpse or two of compassion when caught off-guard, and Gloria knows exactly how to play such a hardened soul. She is particularly strong in a scene where she finally brings the handcuffed girl in the attic, Jennifer (Maggie Corey), a glass of water, then sadistically drinks the water herself. Gloria portrays the widow Deere as a lonely woman determined to get whatever benefit she can out of the rest of her ignoble life, even if that requires the deaths of some kids that no one cares about. And, of course, Mrs. Deere's conversations with the late Mr. Deere, frozen in the meat locker, only confirm that her sanity is slipping away.

One wonders why Gloria would return to the screen in such a project. She was not a horror fan, and this was a role that was bound to shock, and probably disappoint, many of her fans. Well, Gloria wasn't sure that she still had any fans. It had been a long time since she had been in a meaningful picture, and the handful of television parts she had played had not kept her in the front of casting agents' thoughts. Her youngest son, James, had been born in 1965, so

all of her kids were, as of early 1971, between five and twenty-two years old. Gloria had spent most of the last decade as a housewife and mother, subordinating the urge to act to the necessity of caring for her children. As the seventies dawned, Gloria realized that maintaining a career was still important and, she hoped, still viable. She couldn't just jump back into leading parts; she was nearing fifty years of age and had long been virtually invisible in the industry. So she and her agent looked at what was making money, and the answer was horror flicks and youth pictures. Logically, then, Gloria determined to prove herself in those areas.

Gloria is the best thing about *Blood and Lace*. Although she receives star billing, hers is not the central role. That is Ellie Masters, as essayed by the girl from *F Troop*, Melody Patterson. This movie did nothing for Patterson career-wise, and she only made a couple of other appearances before disappearing from the industry. Patterson is weak in the central role,

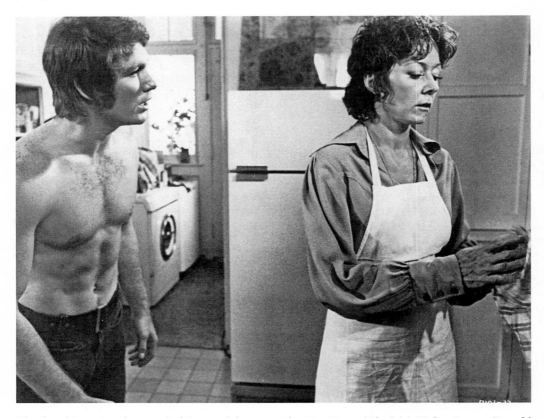

Blood and Lace. Another ward of the youth home run by Mrs. Deere (Gloria) is Walter Barnes (Ronald Taft), who is concerned that Ellie Masters (Melody Patterson, not pictured) is about to run away.

mainly because she is not convincing as a woman so schizophrenic that she would kill her mother. She and Vic Tayback, who later gained fame playing diner owner Mel Sharples on *Alice*, share the same peculiar propensity, particularly in the final scene, of pausing midway through each of their sentences. Tayback is rather sleazy as detective Calvin Carruthers, but at least he gets to have fun dressed in a plastic burn mask and chasing Patterson around the woods with a hammer. Len Lesser is solidly disreputable as Tom Kredge, and he has the funniest lines in the film to boot.

Blood and Lace was shot on a tiny budget at an empty Hollywood mansion, and promoted with a grisly marketing campaign emphasizing a bloody hammer. It became one of those movies that continually found playdates in drive-ins and on ultra-shock double features around the country throughout the 1970s, and then played endlessly on early cable systems during the 1980s. It has yet to receive a DVD release, but that is only a matter of time. The film was ignored by most critics and reviled by those who did bother to watch it, but that didn't keep people from seeing it. *The Motion Picture Guide* begrudgingly admitted that it "manages to keep some tension despite murky photography and muddy sound." On a technical level, that about summarizes its effectiveness. *Variety* judged, "Pic should suffice for chill bills." Ann Guarino of the *New York Daily News* wrote, "The cast tries to bring believability to the plot, but the audience couldn't help laughing in the wrong places. Terri Messina manages to stand out as a teen-aged sexpot." And the *New York Post* decreed, "The story manages to keep you guessing all the way to its macabre end, if you can stand it that long."

For 1970s horror fans, *Blood and Lace* remains a vivid memory. Other than its gory first murder there is hardly anything spectacular about it, yet its nasty tone and twist ending (Ellie realizes that her father has just proposed to her) are unforgettable. Gloria had returned to the movies in a very unconventional way, in a film that her fans would probably never see, yet it fulfilled the purpose of putting her back in front of the public eye — a new public with decidedly different tastes. *Blood and Lace* jump-started the second phase of Gloria Grahame's film career and initiated her into the realm of horror queens, although she would never embrace the genre, and her subsequent projects would never quite attain the same impact as this film. It was a radically different Hollywood that Gloria was trying to rejoin, and she never felt fully comfortable in her later efforts, mostly because Hollywood still didn't know what to do with her.

The Todd Killings (1971)

(aka *A Dangerous Friend*; *Skipper*)

CREDITS National General Pictures. *Directed and Produced by* Barry Shear. *Executive Producer*: Walter Wood. *Associate Producer*: Robert Levy. *Screenplay by* Dennis Murphy and Joel Oliansky. *Story by* Mann Rubin. *Director of Photography*: Harold E. Stine. *Film Editor*: Walter Thompson. *Art Director*: Arthur Lonergan. *Set Decorator*: James Payne. *Makeup Supervision*: Jack P. Wilson. *Hair Stylist*: Annabell Levy. *Titles by* Pacific Title. *Unit Production Manager*: Jerome M. Siegel. *Assistant Director*: John H. Roe. *Sound*: John Kean. *Music Editor*: John Mick. *Post-Production Supervisor*: Gary Gerlich. *Music*: Leonard Rosenman. Rated R. Technicolor. Panavision (2.35:1). Monaural Sound. 93 minutes. Released on October 20, 1971. Currently available on DVD. Previously available on VHS.

CAST *Skipper Todd*, Robert F. Lyons; *Billy Roy*, Richard Thomas; *Roberta (Robbie)*, Belinda J. Montgomery; *Amata*, Sherry Miles; *Haddie*, Joyce Ames; *Norma*, Holly Near; *Sam Goodman*, James Broderick; *Mrs. Roy*, Gloria Grahame; *Mrs. Mack*, Fay Spain; *Fred Reardon*, Edward [Ed] Asner; *Detective Shaw*, Michael Conrad; *Mrs. Todd*, Barbara Bel Geddes; *Jackie*, Tanis Montgomery; *Police Officer*, Sugar Ray Robinson; *Reporter*, Clete Roberts; *Policeman*, Jason Wingreen; *Man Who Offers Skipper a Recording Contract*, Jack Riley; *Mr. Carpenter*, Guy Wilkerson; *Mr. Carpenter's Son*, Geoffrey Lewis; with Frank Webb, William Lucking, Sandy Brown Wyeth, Sherry Lynn Diamant, Georgene Barnes, Robert Williamson, Billy Bowles, Mike Rupert, Meg Foster, Ronwen Proust, George Murdock, Harry Lauter, Eddie Firestone, Eve Brent, Morgan Sterne, Forrest Lewis, Barbara O'Mallory, and Michelle Art.

For her return to the movie scene, Gloria Grahame concentrated on what was then popular: horror movies and disaffected youth films. *Blood and Lace* had been surprisingly profitable; she had higher hopes for *The Todd Killings*, even though she was just one of several familiar veteran actors appearing in it. The unbridled, astonishing success of *Easy Rider* had convinced studios that the youth market was burgeoning, but few filmmakers were able to capitalize upon it. Nevertheless, studios invested a great deal of time, effort and money to make movies about and for Young America. Some were comedies; others were dramas; a few were musicals. *The Todd Killings* (which was re-released under the titles *A Dangerous Friend* and *Skipper*) is a drama based upon a true-to-life 1965 murder spree that shocked an Arizona community. This fictional film depicts the atmosphere and factors that surrounded the thrill killings and attempts to place the killer's actions in the context of the society of the time. As opposed to those youth films that celebrate and even demand anarchy in the streets, *The Todd Killings* is a cautionary tale warning parents that their kids may be up to no good.

In the aftermath of a girl's killing by Skipper Todd (Robert F. Lyons), Skipper, Andy and Norma (Holly Near) are hurriedly burying a teenage girl's body in a dry California riverbed. When they are finished, Skipper refuses to dwell on the matter, taking the younger teens to a party in his dune buggy. On the way, they stop to pick up a hitchhiker, Billy Roy (Richard Thomas). Billy has just left reform school and is still ashamed of his crew cut. Skipper takes a shine to him — so much so that Skipper informs Billy that he has actually killed somebody that very day, and he blithely composes a song about the experience.

Skipper Todd is 23. He harangues his mother (Barbara Bel Geddes) for money but refuses to work with her in the small nursing home that she runs. He hates the place and what it represents; he is determined to live life to the fullest. Skipper expresses his philosophy to Billy after meeting Billy's mother (Gloria Grahame): "This rat bucket is sinkin' and everybody knows it. So groove!" Skipper likes to hang around with the local teenagers, supply them with dope and drink, have sex with the pretty young girls and act on whatever fantasies spring into his mind. Billy becomes beholden to him when Skipper pressures a blonde girl named Amata (Sherry Miles) to pay attention to Billy, despite her obvious attraction to the more mature Skipper.

A brunette named Robbie (Belinda J. Montgomery) catches Skipper's eye, even though (or perhaps because) she is only 16. She rebuffs him several times but finds herself drawn to him anyway. He finally attacks her in her bedroom one night, and despite the violence of his approach, she whispers "I love you" to him as he takes her. They become a couple. Meanwhile, the police investigate the disappearance of Sue Ellen Mack, and there are several juxtaposition cuts of Skipper being questioned throughout the narrative, either by the police or by military officers (Skipper is being considered for military duty, and brags about beating it to his friends). Mrs. Mack (Fay Spain) publicly accuses Skipper of being involved in her daughter's disappearance, and Skipper's mother forcefully defends her son. A local teacher, Sam Goodman (James Broderick), also begins to question Skipper about his life, and informs him, "You are the epitome of everything you hate."

Skipper and Robbie break up for a little while, then Skipper arranges for Robbie to be brought to him by one of the local kids. They fight, but Skipper admits that he has feelings for Robbie. At one of his parties, someone mistakenly begins to play a tape of Skipper's song about killing Sue Ellen, and he flies into a rage and stops it. Norma sees him kissing Robbie and becomes so jealous that she blurts out something about burying the girl; frightened, Robbie runs away. A few nights later, Robbie visits Skipper while her sister Jackie (Tanis Montgomery) is seeing a movie in town. Robbie demands the truth and Skipper tells her that he killed Sue Ellen to find out what it would be like. Robbie is horrified when he tells her it could have been anyone; Sue Ellen was the fourth girl he had called that fateful day. Robbie tearfully asks Skipper if he is going to kill her too; given a chance to think about it, that is exactly what Skipper does. As Robbie drops to the floor, strangled, Jackie arrives looking for Robbie. She is also killed.

The next day Skipper enlists Billy's help but the two boys are questioned by the police and a man named Fred Reardon (Ed Asner) before Billy learns why Skipper needs him. Skipper does his innocent act and the young men are released. Skipper and Billy drive the dune buggy to the river bed and bury the two girls, who were in the back seat of the buggy, covered, the whole morning. Billy demands to know if

Skipper is going to kill him, too, so Skipper leaves him there. Billy walks back to town and takes a position patrolling the street in front of Amata's home with a large dog at his side. Amata's parents demand to know why Billy is behaving so strangely and he finally tells them about Skipper's acts. After his confession, Billy runs to Skipper and tells him what he's done. Skipper can't believe it: "You killed me, man!" He sends Billy away, cut to the soul by Billy's betrayal but unwilling to kill him for it.

The police and many other people dig at the river bed looking for the bodies. None are found. Finally, Billy realizes that Skipper has moved them. Skipper is in jail, reading about himself in the newspaper. He is visited by a lawyer who advises him to blame his actions on the drugs he had taken. ("You'll emerge out of it a national hero. Best actor I've ever seen.") Skipper finally confesses to the police that he killed Robbie because "I didn't want her to control my life." He leads the cops to the bodies, buried at another spot along the river. Several of the teenagers follow Skipper and the cops, and yell at Billy, calling him a "fink." Robbie's body is recovered; she no longer has a face. A few of the kids are sickened by the sight, but others ask, "What are we gonna do without Skipper?" One by one the teenagers turn and shuffle away.

The Todd Killings is a film that, despite its dated jargon and fashions (and dune buggy) was years ahead of its time in terms of probing the cultural malaise gripping young people and the cult of celebrity that murderers could (and would) attain. It is a precursor to the "teens who experiment with murder" subgenre that has flourished since the 1980s and boasts many of the same themes and attitudes as such films as *River's Edge*, *Bully* and *Mean Creek*. It captures the ennui of a bored generation without sensationalism or sentimentalism. Its psychology is dead on target regarding not only its central psychopath but also the reactions of the youth for whom he provides excitement and leadership. And perhaps scariest of all, *The Todd Killings* is a fact-based film that depicts a trio of actual killings in mid–1960s Tucson, Arizona. While the dates and locale of the events have been changed and the story fictionalized, the movie is quite faithful to the murderous exploits of Charles Schmid.

The Todd Killings. Mrs. Roy (Gloria) begins to wonder about her son's new friend Skipper Todd. The movie is a slightly fictionalized version of serial killer Charles Schmid's exploits in the early 1960s.

Schmid was not quite 22 when he decided to kill a local girl, Alleen Rowe, because he wanted to experience what it would be like to murder someone. He and two friends, John Saunders and Mary French, were involved in killing the girl and burying her in the Arizona desert on May 31, 1964. On August 16, 1965, Schmid killed a former girlfriend, Gretchen Fritz, when she threatened to reveal his involvement in the Rowe murder. He strangled her and her sister Wendy, who had accompanied her sister to see him after watching an Elvis Presley movie in town. The disappearance of the Fritz girls caused a commotion in the Tucson area but the police, as they had in the Alleen Rowe case, felt that the girls were runaways.

Schmid told another friend, Richard Bruns, about the murders, and they were reportedly visited by mob figures also looking into the disappearances. Again, Schmid proclaimed his innocence, and Bruns held his tongue. But after a time Bruns began to believe that Schmid was planning to kill his girlfriend, too, since she had dated Schmid before Bruns.

Bruns was eventually sent to Ohio to live with his grandparents because of his increasingly erratic behavior (he was "protecting" his girlfriend day and night), and it was there that he finally revealed what he knew about Schmid and the murders. Following a notorious trial, Schmid was sentenced to death, which was eventually reduced to fifty years in prison when California abolished its death penalty. On March 10, 1975, Schmid was stabbed forty-seven times by two fellow prisoners and took almost three weeks to die.

The Schmid trial was sensationalized by the press. Both *Playboy* and *Life* magazines assigned correspondents to cover it, and Don Moser's March 4, 1966, *Life* story, titled "The Pied Piper of Tucson," was extremely well-received. John Gilmore followed up with a book, *The Tucson Murders*. Schmid was presented as a somewhat improbable but charismatic, gregarious ladies' man with a strong affinity for being the center of attention of Tucson's younger crowd. In 1966, Joyce Carol Oates based her short story "Where Are You Going, Where Have You Been?" on the Schmid case. Oates' story, in turn, was developed into the 1985 film *Smooth Talk* with Laura Dern and Treat Williams. And in 1994, Schmid's story was the focus of a film titled *Dead Beat*, with Bruce Ramsay in the killer role and Balthazar Getty as his friend who eventually turns him in, with Natasha Gregson-Wagner and Sara Gilbert as the female leads.

But long before *Dead Beat*, which has yet to be released on DVD, and *Smooth Talk* — which has little in common with the Schmid case other than the predatory character of the story's antagonist, named Arnold Friend — Schmid's story was fictionalized and planned for motion picture treatment as early as 1967. It underwent several title changes and several people were attached to write, direct or produce it, including acclaimed screenwriter Abby Mann. Eventually the directing job fell to veteran Barry Shear, a highly professional television director who in 1968 had found solid success directing *Wild in the Streets*. This youth parable about teenagers coming to power in America once the voting age is lowered to 14 was a sleeper hit that proved Shear had a strong connection to the youth movement — even as his movie questioned its methods and ultimate

aims. Looking for other feature film projects, Shear saw in *The Todd Killings* some of the same themes, as well as a similar opportunity to throw into question some of the darker, seamier aspects of youth run amok. When Abby Mann bowed out of the production due to "a dispute," Shear assumed producing chores as well as the directorial reins. Ultimately, it is Shear's movie.

With this picture, Shear intended to capture discontent and alienation on two fronts: an intimate, personal level felt by individual characters as they fail to connect with their parents (or children), or each other; and a larger, generalized one that applies to American culture at the time. It is palpable malaise that prevents solid interaction between the parents who are letting their kids run wild and the kids who cannot seem to find worthwhile ways to spend their free time. The police don't take Mrs. Mack's claims about Skipper's involvement with her daughter's disappearance seriously; to them, he's just another lazy hippie kid. Teacher Sam Goodman has trouble communicating with the teens, including Skipper, and his efforts to reach the suburban housewives by talking to them about *Moby-Dick* seem fruitless as well. None of the kids who suspect Skipper's guilt bothers to tell an adult, much less betray his trust. Robbie doesn't want to believe that Skipper killed Sue Ellen but finally asks him if it is true ... which leads to her own death, as well as that of her sister.

It is really the issue of the kids' silence that forms the crux of Shear's film. Sure, Skipper Todd killed Sue Ellen Mack, and later killed Robbie and Jackie. But two other kids, Andy and Norma, witnessed Sue Ellen's death and helped Skipper bury the body. Later, everybody at a party hears Skipper's song about killing the girl. And when Robbie and Jackie disappear, nothing happens to Skipper until Billy Roy confesses to Amata's parents. Billy betrays Skipper because he is afraid that Skipper will murder Amata, just like the others. The silence of the teenagers makes them complicit with Skipper's crimes, yet not one of them shows any remorse about the deaths of their friends. Their adulation of Skipper continues even after he leads them to the bodies. Billy is called a "fink" and shunned. Even when the kids see Robbie's faceless body up close, they don't turn on the man who killed her. "What are we gonna do without Skipper?" one asks, and they slowly turn away, ending the film. That line of dialogue was, at one time, considered for the film's title, and it deftly puts everything in perspective.

To Shear, the kids' behavior is the most shocking element of the whole story. Why did they idolize this older guy and let him get away with killing three of their own? What was it about Skipper that convinced them to remain quiet? Or was there some larger issue at work that prevented them from doing the right thing? Shear lays much of the blame upon that malaise he so skillfully depicts. When Robbie asks Skipper why he killed Sue Ellen, Skipper replies, "Boring evening. We just didn't have anything else to do." It is exactly that attitude, that "looking for kicks" thrill-seeking, that Shear pinpoints as the primary factor in Sue Ellen's death. Skipper's nihilistic attitude is the core of the problem, but everyone of his generation seems to share it. Nothing is enough any more. Shortly after Sue Ellen's death, Andy is looking for something to do. Skipper suggests having sex with Fay, the group's easy girl. "What, again?" replies Andy. Later, Skipper tells Robbie, "You know, fornication isn't much, but it's about all Darlington has to offer." After hearing Skipper's song about killing the girl, Robbie is bothered that Skipper places a low value on people. "There's living the way *you* want to live," he assures her.

However, it isn't just the kids' behavior that is reprehensible. The final act of the film takes place at the river bed, where most of the town is looking for the buried girls. Though some are honestly searching for them, many others are merely gawking, hoping to see something gruesome. Amidst the chaos are popcorn, ice cream and drink vendors, calmly hawking their wares in the afternoon heat. This scene is sharply satiric, yet painfully realistic at the same time. Then, in jail, a lawyer advises Skipper how to talk his way to freedom and even evinces admiration for the boy's acting skills. The message is that everyone is guilty of creating and sustaining an atmosphere of casual antipathy, and that such an atmosphere fosters acts like Skipper's curious murder spree.

The movie's script bases all of this, of course, on Charles Schmid's acts of just a few years earlier. Schmid callously killed Alleen

Rowe just to see what it would be like, and was so sure that none of the kids he knew well would squeal that he showed several of them the girl's body. It was more than a year later when, faced with an ex-girlfriend threatening to go to the authorities, he killed the ex-girlfriend and her sister. Only after the trial, where he pled guilty to second-degree murder yet continued to maintain his innocence, did he lead police to Rowe's remains. *The Todd Killings* changes a few of the details and doesn't go into courtroom trial scenes at all, but it faithfully follows the path that Schmid took through Tucson. When the film was announced, Tucson leaders protested, fearing that further publicity about their notorious killer would harm business and the town's reputation. This caused some delay in filming, and led to its being set in California rather than Arizona.

Shear could have been more faithful to Schmid's appearance; Schmid was a rather short man who wore makeup, stuffed rags and flattened tin cans in his cowboy boots to increase his height and even attached an artificial mole to his cheek as a beauty mark. He was also known for singing Elvis Presley songs. Instead, Shear decided on a more conventional approach and hired charismatic Robert F. Lyons to portray Skipper Todd. Skipper is, like Schmid, a would-be musician, but little is seen to make anyone believe that he has any real talent. Lyons' Skipper is a handsome guy who likes girls and hates just about everything about modern culture. And his skill as an actor is to present Skipper as someone perhaps worth knowing, even as he happens to kill three local girls, one of whom he actually loves. Lyons' magnetic performance anchors the movie, actually providing credence to its closing question, "What are we gonna do without Skipper?"

Richard Thomas contributes a high-pitched, nervous, almost brittle performance as Billy Roy, the crew-cut kid befriended by Skipper who ultimately renounces Skipper to ensure the safety of Amata, the girl he loves. His actions are convincing, although it is not clear exactly what Skipper sees in Billy to confide in him so completely. As Roberta (Robbie), Belinda J. Montgomery is excellent, delivering a performance that makes the character seem years older and wiser than Skipper. And that's Belinda's sister Tanis as Robbie's sister Jackie. Unfortunately, many of the other actors are not properly identified with their characters, including the young man who plays Andy, a fairly major role in the production.

The adult actors in *The Todd Killing* are not particularly noteworthy, because this movie is all about the kids. James Broderick, as teacher Sam Goodman, puts Skipper in his place a couple of times, but his scenes seem almost intrusive into the narrative. Ed Asner has one solid scene as a local bigwig unmoved by Skipper's innocent act. Asner's role is inspired by the shadowy mob figures who reportedly interviewed Schmid and Bruns about the disappearance of the Fritz girls. Barbara Bel Geddes has the movie's most thankless role, that of Skipper's put-upon mother. Mrs. Todd operates a nursing home and has tried to get Skipper to live a life of consequence, but she, too, gives up too easily on directing her charming son. Bel Geddes has a terrific scene when Mrs. Mack stops by to blame him for her daughter's disappearance; Mrs. Todd defends her son like a momma bear defending her cubs. Yet even Bel Geddes' commendable contributions are slight in the film's focus, as her character is not seen or heard once Skipper's guilt is assured. In real life, as has happened all too often, Schmid's mother was left bankrupt and broken-hearted by the actions of her adopted son. The film might have had greater impact had it presented Mrs. Todd's grief, but Shear kept the focus on the kids and their ambivalent feelings about their idol's actions.

Gloria has a tiny role as Billy Roy's mother, and is in just two scenes. Mr. and Mrs. Roy welcome their son home with open arms in the first, after his "dropping out for a while" and going to reform school. She comments on Billy's weight loss and bears witness to a tension between Billy and her husband, although that tension is never openly addressed. In the second scene, Mrs. Roy is among the Darlington housewives attending the extension course offered by Sam Goodman as he lectures about *Moby-Dick*. Mrs. Roy sees Skipper arrive and offers to find Billy for him. He politely refuses, and shocks her by loudly asking Sam Goodman, "Wasn't Herman Melville a fag?" A few moments later, she turns away from him, finally beginning to see through his lies when he says something polite but smarmy while asking her to find Billy for him. In that one simple backward glance over her shoulder, Gloria conveys a shrewdness and complexity that the rest of the movie's adults completely lack.

Gloria was thrilled that Shear thought of her and hired her for the small role, which was actually filmed before *Blood and Lace*. It had been five years since Gloria had been in front of a movie camera, and she was happy to be directed by a man who had been working steadily in television and film since 1950. "It isn't that you forget your craft — it's just that so many things today seem different," she told her friend Larry Kleno. For her return to films, Gloria was also happy to have a secondary role, to be part of an ensemble cast. And she appreciated that her name added prestige to the project. Moreover, *The Todd Killings* was a noteworthy project with a hot-button subject that she hoped would be popular as well as controversial.

As fate would have it, the film was neither. Despite its strong cast and excellent quality, it was a big commercial disappointment. Part of this was due to the rapidly changing culture involving serial killers. In the half-decade since Schmid's final killings and trial, other murderers took his place in the public eye — particularly Richard Speck, who in July 1966 brutally stabbed eight nurses to death; Charles Whitman, who only a month later shot and killed fourteen people from his perch atop the University of Texas Tower after slaying his wife and mother at home; Robert Benjamin Smith, who walked into a beauty parlor in November 1966 and shot four women and a child because he wanted to become famous; and Charles Manson, who in August 1969 directed his "family" to murder a number of people, including pregnant actress Sharon Tate. Thus, the murderous exploits of Charles Schmid, as horrific and sensational as they were, soon paled in comparison to those of Speck, Whitman, Smith and Manson, and "The Pied Piper of Tucson" faded into obscurity.

Part of the film's failure was due to National General's handling of it. The studio took four full years to bring its fictionalized version of Schmid's killings to the screen, and the film underwent quite a bit of turmoil before Shear finally finished it. It was the final production of National General Pictures, which had positioned itself to be a major Hollywood player over a number of years, but which ultimately lost the financial backing to continue. National General continued to distribute films for two more years before shutting down entirely. The studio's marketing campaign was less than ideal: The poster shows Skipper dragging a girl into the desert with the tagline "SKIPPER TODD DIGS GIRLS. It's his idea of killing time...."

Incidentally, this tagline forms the basis of a song by the punk rock group The Angry Samoans. Their song, "The Todd Killings," recites the name of the movie and that tagline combined with a few other lyrics and is part of their regular set. That song was later covered by the band The Briefs on their album "Joy of Killing." The songs can be sampled on YouTube clips on the Internet.

Perhaps the biggest factor in the film's failure to attract audiences was Shear's subversive tone. The studio, not unexpectedly, positioned *The Todd Killings* as a youth film. However, the film doesn't play that way at all. While many examples of the youth films of the time celebrated freedom and advocated at least a certain amount of social anarchy, *The Todd Killings* is an exploration of how such freedom and anarchy result in murder and heartbreak. Sure, the film shows teenagers having good times with sex and drugs and (very little) rock 'n' roll. But it also shows how they are rather easily manipulated by sex and drugs into the control of a psychopath, and that even after being shown the consequences of trusting such an individual, they seem incapable of regret or remorse. At the end of the film, Skipper's friends are not grieving for the dead Robbie; she has become a faceless curiosity to them. What they regret is that they will no longer share Skipper's companionship. This self-absorption is what the film is indicting, the idea that contemporary teenagers put their own selfish interests so far above everyone else's, especially society as a whole. This message improves the film's effectiveness, but it also marked it as a bummer for the youth of 1971 who might have wanted to see it.

The Todd Killings opened in New York in October 1971, quickly fading out of sight. It was re-released seven years later as *A Dangerous Friend* and did even less business; by then

Schmid had been dead for three years. The ignominious fate of National General Pictures sealed the film's rapid descent into obscurity. Nevertheless, *The Todd Killings* remains one of the finer films of the early 1970s, with a reputation that steadily grows.

It received mixed reviews at the time, ranging from Ann Guarino's take in the *New York Daily News*: "Another tiresome contemporary drama about the youth scene" to Judith Crist's belief in *New York* that "this tight little melodrama reaches beyond its central concern with a young psychopath to the surrounding emptiness of his society." Some critics damned it mercilessly: Newton North of the *New York Daily Mirror* opened his review, "Now littering up the screens..." and termed the film, "pure schlock." *The Motion Picture Guide* decried, "This film which attempts to delve into the psychology of youth, but winds up as a long list of clichés."

Others, however, appreciated Shear's artistry. Howard H. Thompson of the *New York Times* wrote, "The sure brilliance of producer Barry Shear's direction and Harold E. Stine's photography, and the subtle meshing of the incidents make for an engrossing, often gripping eyeful." The most astute review came from William Paul of *The Village Voice*: "*The Todd Killings* is a genuine sleeper, the kind of film that is overlooked by audiences and critics alike in the great flood of new releases, a good movie against all expectations, a surprise success in a setting of minimal artistic pretension." Paul also appreciated seeing Gloria Grahame again. "And nothing could have made me miss finding out whatever happened to Gloria Grahame, favorite bad girl of my childhood, here playing the bit part of a middle-aged housewife, a role in which she seems properly uncomfortable."

It is curious that no critic mentioned the real-life source of the film's plotting; in fact, a few critics commented that the story was "illogical" (*Variety*) or "absurd" (*New York Times*). This fact illustrates the notion that despite the film's opening declaration ("The story you are about to see is a fictionalized dramatization of actual case histories"), few if any critics connected it to Schmid's murders of just a few years previously. In hindsight it might have benefitted the marketing department to simply declare, "Based on a True Story," and to discuss, or at least mention, the actual Schmid case in its press material. Yet there are more than sufficient parallels between the film and its true-life inspiration for critics to have made the connection themselves.

Though the film failed commercially, it reminded people within the industry that Gloria Grahame was not only still around but available for work. It must be admitted that Gloria's contribution to its quality is slight, due solely to the size of her part. Gloria fully embraced her small part of the whole with enthusiasm, hoping only to help improve it and gain some recognition from being associated with it. Unfortunately, feature film parts for the now forty-seven-year-old actress were shrinking rather than growing.

Chandler (1971)

CREDITS MGM. *Directed by* Paul Magwood. *Produced by* Michael S. Laughlin. *Associate Producer*: Gary Kurtz. *Screenplay by* John Sacret Young. *Story by* Paul Magwood. *Director of Photography*: Alan Stensvold. *Photographic Advisor*: Louis Horvath. *Film Editors*: Richard A. Harris and William B. Gulick. *Art Director*: Lawrence G. Paull. *Unit Production Manager*: John Wilson. *Assistant Director*: Robert Dijoux. *Sound*: Les Frescholtz and Hal Watkins. *Action Scenes Coordinated by* Eric Cord. *Casting*: Lee Wenner. *Assistant to the Producer*: Dorothy Alsup. *Music by* George Romanis. *Stunts*: Jesse Wayne. Rated GP. Metrocolor. Panavision (2.35:1). Monaural Sound. 85 minutes. Released on December 1, 1971. Currently available on DVD. Previously unavailable on commercial home video.

CAST *Chandler*, Warren Oates; *Katherine Creighton*, Leslie Caron; *Ross J. Carmady*, Alex Dreier; *Charles Kincaid*, Mitchell Ryan; *John Melchior*, Gordon Pinsent; *Bernie Oakman*, Charles McGraw; *Leo*, Richard Loo; *Zeno*, Walter Burke; *Selma*, Gloria Grahame; *Sal Sachese*, Royal Dano (scenes deleted); *Smoke*, Scatman Crothers; *Angel Carter*, Marianne McAndrew; *Waxwell*, Lal Baum; *Binder Ransin*, Charles Shull; *Rudy the Bartender*, John Mitchum; *Salesgirl*, Vickery Turner; *Captain of the Security Guard*, Ray Kellogg; *Assistant Station Master*, Ernest Lawrence; *Shoe Shine Boy*, Eugene Jackson; *Taxi Driver #1*, Eddie Marks; *Taxi Driver #2*, Frederick Stanley II; *Bogardy*, James B. Sikking (scenes deleted).

Gloria Grahame completed her busy 1971 with one scene in *Chandler*, a misbegotten private investigator flick that squanders the talents of everyone involved in its production. For one day of work she was paid $500; her screen time is one minute and ten seconds. In an era that witnessed a renaissance of cop films and crime dramas, *Chandler* is near the bottom of the proverbial barrel. Aside from its intriguing casting, a jazzy George Romanis score and some beautiful California coast scenery, it has almost nothing to recommend it. Indeed, the behind-the-scenes wrangling that took place when MGM studio chief James Aubrey recut the film without consulting the writer or the producers is far more interesting than the movie itself.

For Chandler (Warren Oates), a low-heeled California gumshoe with no discernable first name, his latest case is more than he can handle. He tries to work as a security guard but he just can't stand the boredom and walks out in the middle of his shift without a word. Back home, he is given an assignment by his friend Bernie Oakman (Charles McGraw) to meet a Frenchwoman at a train the following morning. She is a material witness who needs protection. Chandler refuses, but Oakman gives him the details anyway, hoping he'll take the job. What Chandler does not know is that Oakman has chosen him to be a patsy for Ross J. Carmady (Alex Dreier) in order to lure the Frenchwoman's lover from the East Coast.

Chandler has second thoughts, collects money from those who owe it to him, retrieves his gun from a pawn shop, gets some clothes from his friend Selma (Gloria Grahame) and sobers up for the job. He meets the train and trails Katherine Creighton (Leslie Caron) to a funeral home. She picks up a phony I.D. from the funeral director, Zeno (Walter Burke). Chandler knows Zeno and learns where Katherine is going. He boards the same train to Monterey and introduces himself as "a rent-a-cop." She brushes him off but he keeps tabs on her. At Monterey, Katherine is grabbed by two men and stuffed into a cab. Chandler follows in another cab along with Angel Carter (Marianne McAndrew), his contact at the train station. The car chase along the California coast ends in sand when Katherine leaps from her cab. She calmly gets into the empty second cab and leaves everyone else behind wondering what is going on.

The persistent P.I. finds Katherine further

up the coast, sketching. She thinks he has been sent to kill her but his amused expression convinces her otherwise. Katherine explains that she loved a man back East but left him, and that the two men were hired to bring her back to him. In a restaurant they are joined by Carmady, who fawns over Katherine, irritating her immensely. Katherine leaves with Charles Kincaid (Mitchell Ryan), evidently under duress. Chandler identifies Carmady as a government agent and is taken to Kincaid's estate along with the girl.

Kincaid phones John Melchior (Gordon Pinsent), the man from the East Coast, and tells him that Katherine is safe. Melchior will be coming west to claim her. Carmady plays golf with Kincaid and explains that when Melchior, a powerful organized crime figure, is eliminated, government agent Kincaid will take his place. Katherine is the bait to lure him out into the open. Katherine asks Chandler for help; she claims to have found a dead man. He checks, finds no body, but evidence of a killing. She confides her past to him; he responds by kissing her. They escape from Kincaid's estate in an old truck that runs out of gas on the road to Carmel. They walk and talk, cementing their relationship. The bad guys arrive and take Katherine back after beating Chandler and leaving him lying in the mud. After recovering, Chandler locates Oakman and learns the truth. He locates Angel Carter and learns from her that the government has been planning to infiltrate the East Coast criminal organization for years; this is their chance. She tells him where Katherine is.

Melchior arrives at a hotel and meets Kincaid, whom he doesn't suspect, but whose story doesn't ring true, either. Melchior leaves to find Katherine. Chandler beats up Kincaid and tries to warn Melchior but is interrupted. Melchior finds Katherine but she refuses to stay with him. She goes into a bathroom, followed by Chandler. They kiss, just as Melchior enters and sees them. Melchior still wants Katherine and warns that he'll come after them if they run. "Come," dares Chandler. He and Katherine leave while Melchior puts his people into action to stop them. They drive into the night but eventually become stuck driving along the foggy coast and find themselves on a beach.

The next morning Chandler and the girl

are located by Melchior. But Melchior has been unobtrusively followed by Kincaid and Carmady, who murder him and then come after the couple. Chandler is shot in the arm and drops to the sand. The two men come down from the surrounding hills to finish the job. Once they confirm that Melchior is dead, they turn away, leaving Chandler alone. Katherine lifts Chandler's gun and kills Kincaid. She doesn't have any bullets left for Carmady, who shrugs and slowly walks away. Lying on his back, Chandler looks at the woman kneeling above him. "You'll do," he says, smiling.

Chandler is, in all respects, a mess. It's intended to be an homage to old-style private-eye movies; at one point Chandler says of himself, "That's Chandler, as in Raymond"—but old-style private-eye movies contain interesting storylines, characters thicker than cardboard and an abundance of mood, all of which are absent here. Nothing is convincing, from the callous government agents who do not act or look anything like government agents, to the rain that suddenly begins falling during Chandler and Katherine's walk toward Carmel. Nothing is sensible, from the puzzling plot point of hiring Chandler in the first place (why is he needed at all?) to the villains' generous decision to leave Chandler and Katherine alive after killing Melchior (they are witnesses!). Nothing is smart about this movie.

The story is confusing and muddled, paralleling ruthless governmental agents with the mob organization they wish to infiltrate. Ultimately, their plan makes no sense and offers them little opportunity to control events, especially once Chandler becomes involved. The film wants to construct and sustain an aura that nobody can be trusted, but apart from Chandler, its basic structure and characters are so uninteresting that it does not matter. This is connect-the-dots filmmaking with no shading, nuance or color.

It's not just the plotting which is substandard. There is little action in the picture, and what there is of it is poorly handled. The taxi cab chase is blasé and ends abruptly in the sand when Katherine leaps out. There should be a good fight, but Chandler merely pulls one guy out of the taxi and then just lays him down on the sand. Later, what could have been a big escape chase is cut short when Chandler's old

Chandler. Private eye Chandler (Warren Oates) asks his friend Selma (Gloria) for a hot shower and clean clothes before he embarks on an involved case. The movie's press material indicates that Selma is a former hooker, but that is not at all clear in the film.

truck runs out of gas! Finally, what could have been a spectacular chase at the climax as Chandler and Katherine run from Melchior loses its steam in the California fog. This film does not deliver even routine thrills; any episode of *Starsky and Hutch* or *The Streets of San Francisco* boasts more action and intrigue.

Rickety, cryptic dialogue does not help matters. Much of Chandler's dialogue consists of monosyllabic responses like, "So what?" The crux of the scene in which Chandler finally connects emotionally with Katherine is delivered with these words: "Why me?" "Why not?" "Thanks." Katherine's dialogue is abruptly succinct, which is often followed by her walking away from someone. At least a dozen times during this movie she simply moves away from the person to which she was talking (usually Chandler). It seems to be a visual metaphor for her running away from her past, but it's rude and annoying taken to such an extreme.

Casting is the one area where director Paul Magwood was sensible. Warren Oates was an inspired choice for the role of the bedraggled detective. *Chandler* was his first solo starring role and Oates fits the part perfectly. He is not called on to do very much and his character is rudely referred to as "Monkey Face" at one point, but Oates is fine. Leslie Caron is indeed French, as the part demands, but she was hired because she was married to the producer, Michael Laughlin. And some time after she divorced Laughlin in 1980, she married Paul Magwood! Caron is appropriately enigmatic as the woman who drifts from one lover to another; it is probable that she had no conception of what she was supposed to be doing because the script was so poorly developed.

Scatman Crothers has two brief scenes as a piano player Chandler knows who is being pressured by Carmady's thugs. Robert Mitchum's brother John Mitchum has one scene as Rudy the bartender. Royal Dano and James B. Sikking were cast but their scenes were deleted before the movie was released. Charles McGraw is afforded co-starring status, but his contribution consists of three scenes.

And then there's Gloria Grahame. Gloria is cast as Selma, the wife of a friend of Chandler. He sees her to get some proper clothes for his assignment. Selma lets him have some of her husband Vince's clothes as he is in jail for another "four years, two months and eight days." Selma lectures Chandler about working and advises him, "Change your line. Adopt." He kisses her sweetly and goes on his way. It's a tiny part and Gloria does not impress in it. She's a bit shrill and rather unconvincing, although the kiss is a nice moment. Her part lasts just seventy seconds. For Gloria, this kind of filmmaking was a hollow echo of what she had experienced in the past. "I don't know how I feel about it," she said when asked about her comeback. "It's hard to get a good script. Maybe I should just keep doing housework and not try to come back at all, you know what I mean?"

MGM was not pleased with the final product and barely released it to theaters at the end of 1971. Producer Laughlin later reportedly claimed that the studio butchered the movie, but, to be frank, there isn't much here to spoil. Laughlin and Magwood rather infamously purchased an ad in the *Hollywood Reporter* around the time of *Chandler*'s release that read, "Regarding what was our film *Chandler*, let's give credit where credit is due. We sadly acknowledge that all editing, post-production as well as additional scenes were executed by James T. Aubrey, Jr. We are sorry." Laughlin and Magwood claimed that MGM studio chief Aubrey locked them out of the editing room, restored scenes that had been previously cut from the picture and changed the music score without consulting them. Legal action was forthcoming, but the case was dropped before it ever went to court.

The men behind *Chandler* were not the only filmmakers at the studio who were suffering at the hands of the studio chief. Producer Bruce Geller had his name removed from his first film, *Corky*, because of Aubrey's unwelcome editing. Herbert B. Leonard claimed that the studio chief "unilaterally and arbitrarily raped" his picture, *Going Home*, by removing more than twenty minutes of footage. Blake Edwards stopped production on his film *A Case of Need* (later retitled *The Carey Treatment*) because of Aubrey's changes to the production schedule. MGM was in deep financial trouble in the early 1970s, and Aubrey's financial wisdom led the way back to profitability. However, the writers and producers on the lot at the time viewed him mainly with disdain.

Aubrey felt that he was improving *Chandler* when he made his editing room changes, but the result is astonishingly bad for a major studio release. History shows that his changes were unsuccessful at best. Few people remember *Corky*, a stock car racing movie with Robert Blake. *Going Home* featured Robert Mitchum and Jan-Michael Vincent in a potent drama, but it was barely seen. *The Carey Treatment* was more successful, because Blake Edwards refused to give up on his medical thriller and its star, James Coburn, was a hot commodity at the time. And *Chandler* was a disaster.

Variety was generous when its critic called *Chandler* a "mediocre crime film." *The Motion Picture Guide* is closer, terming the feature a "disappointing crime story.... scripting and direction are less than inspired in this mediocre debut by Magwood." *The Great Detective Pictures* offers this appraisal: "Warren Oates here essays the title role of the snooper, but to little avail, as he and the rest of the uncomfortable cast are swept away by a foggy script." Donald J. Mayerson of *Cue* wrote, "Since neither the plot nor the characters are worth any investment of time or energy, one searches for facets of occupy one's interest," and found a few. "A mauve wall in a private club caught my eye, as did some attractive wallpaper in a ladies' room where the mistress, her erstwhile boyfriend, and her new one, the dull detective, have an encounter. But these hardly justify seeing the film."

The listless and pointless *Chandler* isn't as lurid as Gloria's previous *Blood and Lace* or her still-to-come *Mama's Dirty Girls* or *Mansion of the Doomed*, but in terms of entertainment quality, it is among the worst films in which Gloria was ever to appear.

The Loners (1972)

(aka *Julio and Stein*; *The Deathly Riders*; *Police Trap*)

CREDITS Four-Leaf Productions. A Fanfare Films Release. *Directed by* Sutton Roley. *Produced by* Jerry Katzman. *Executive Producer*: Sam Katzman. *Screenplay by* John Lawrence and Barry Sandler. *Story by* John Lawrence. *Director of Photography*: Irving Lippman. *Film Editor*: John Woelz. *Music Scored and Conducted by* Fred Karger. *Assistant Director*: Gary Grillo. *Script Supervisor*: Ray Quiroz. *Makeup*: Douglas Kelly. *Sound Effects*: Marvin Kerner. *Production Manager*: Robert Stone. *Titles*: Pacific Title. *Post-Production Supervision*: William Martin. *Prints by* Movielab. Rated R. Metrocolor. Flat (1.37:1). Monaural Sound. 79 minutes. Released in April, 1972. Currently unavailable on DVD. Previously available on VHS.

CAST *Stein*, Dean Stockwell; *Annabelle Carter, Jr. (Julio)*, Pat Stich; *Allan*, Todd Susman; *Sergeant Joe Hearn*, Scott Brady; *Annabelle Carter*, Gloria Grahame; *Police Chief Perkins*, Alex Dreier; *Howie Rudd*, Tim Rooney; *Sheriff*, Ward Wood; *Mrs. Anderson*, Hortense Petra; *Driver (Mr. Taylor)*, Richard O'Brien; *Stein's Father*, Hal John Norman; *Man in Diner*, Duane Grey; *Woman in Diner*, Jean Dorl; *Bridegroom*, Stuart Nisbet; *Officer Kelly*, Larry O'Leno; *Waitress in Diner*, Wilma Black.

Gloria's only feature film of 1972 is an interesting, if oddly edited, counter-culture melodrama that ultimately pits a large Southwest police force against a polite motorcyclist, his simple friend, and the rebellious local girl he encounters. Advertised as being in the vein of *Bonnie and Clyde* and *Easy Rider*, this is instead a rather tame tale of misunderstood youth that fails to echo either of the two cultural touchstones that it emulates. Gloria provides a jolt of energy as the girl's shrewish, harried mother and easily outclasses the rest of the cast, particularly in an impressive one-take scene that lasts nearly three minutes. Gloria is so impressive that it almost seems as if she is in another, better movie.

In a Southwestern desert, a pair of policemen stop to aid a motorist whose car has been driven off the road, its windshield shattered. The man claims a motorcyclist tried to kill him. A quick flashback reveals otherwise, as the driver speeds up behind the motorcyclist, laughing with glee while he bumps the rider while traveling down the highway at 80 MPH. In retaliation the motorcyclist throws some-

thing backwards which shatters the driver's windshield and causes him to crash. Back in the present, the policemen leave the man behind and pursue the cyclist, cursing the hippies ruining the country as they close the distance between them. When the cops catch up to the cyclist he leads them off-road, creating massive dust clouds as they race around an abandoned mining operation. The squad car drives through the dust and off a steep cliff, crashing below and killing the driver. When the motorcyclist, Stein (Dean Stockwell), climbs down to see if he can help, the other cop, Sgt. Joe Hearn (Scott Brady), battered and bloody, shoots at him.

Stein gets away and joins his friend and mechanic Allan (Todd Susman) in a nearby town. Stein explains that he cannot stay and tries to make Allan go his own way. Allan (who is described in the press material as mentally handicapped) refuses to listen and leads Stein out of town before the cops arrive in pursuit.

In another town, a young woman named Annabelle Carter Jr. (Pat Stich) is fooling around with a friend, Howie Rudd (Tim Rooney), when her mother comes home. Howie sneaks out through the window and Annabelle Jr. pretends to have been sleeping. Her mother Annabelle Carter (Gloria Grahame) berates her for wasting time and insists that she get a job. They argue until Annabelle Jr. can no longer stand it, leaving the house in a huff.

Annabelle Jr. is hanging out at a drive-in with loud music when Stein and Allan arrive. Stein immediately takes a shine to her and within a few minutes they are making out in the men's room. Howie Rudd and his friends take offense to Stein's hippie-like appearance and start trouble. Allan scares two away by swinging a chain at them while Stein dumps Howie into a garbage can as onlookers cheer. Stein and Allan hop on their bikes for a quick exit and Annabelle Jr., whom Stein has decided to call Julio, joins them. (From now on she will be known as Julio, pronounced "Julie-O"). They drive to a park with a pond. Julio strips and jumps into the water, enticing Stein to join her. After making love they lie in the grass and talk. He wants to be the fastest motocross racer; she has little ambition other than wanting some excitement in her life. He reveals that he is half–Navajo and half–Scotch-Irish: "I never scalp on Saint Patrick's Day." He tells her that the cops are after them and that excites her. She persuades him to let her come along and help them steal whatever they need to survive and escape. Allan is upset by her intrusion but he is devoted to Stein and accepts what he cannot change.

The trio breaks into a store at night. The proprietor hears them and starts shooting at Stein and Allan without warning. Julio comes to the rescue, clobbering the man with a shovel. Realizing that she has killed him, Julio cries and screams in horror. Later, the trio finds a honeymooning couple canoodling in the grass by a river. They tease them with guns, stealing the man's wallet and tuxedo and the woman's wedding dress. They check into a motel's wedding suite, where Stein and Julio take to the connubial bed. When Allan tries to join them, Stein chases him away. The next morning, when cops arrive, Stein and Julio blast through the motel window on his motorcycle and Allan sneaks away on his. The cops fire and miss, and a chase is averted because of a resulting traffic tie-up.

Police Chief Perkins (Alex Dreier), who espouses tough crime control and never removes his sunglasses, runs the town. A political rally supporting Perkins takes place at night and Stein and Julio, still fancily dressed, sneak inside. After the police chief leaves, Stein robs the place at gunpoint. They hide in a junkyard, as their cycles need repair. They decide to head to the Navajo reservation where they can appeal to Stein's father for help. While Stein goes to check for roadblocks, Allan goes to a diner and orders lots of food, but he is distracted by a woman who flirts with him. The woman argues loudly with her husband, and the husband then attacks Allan, beating him up. Finally unleashing his temper, Allan shoots the man, the woman and four other people, killing them all. He returns to the junkyard covered in blood. Julio comforts him, reminding him that "we're all the same," and that the three of them have to rely upon one another to survive.

Stein returns and the trio retire to a nearby church for sanctuary. Stein asks Allan to marry Julio and himself, but the ceremony is interrupted when a woman and her daughter enter the church. Meanwhile, Annabelle Carter begs Chief Perkins to spare her daughter, exclaiming that Annabelle Jr. (Julio) is a good girl, kidnapped by hooligans and forced to have sex

with them. As she leaves, Chief Perkins remarks, "She's crazy!" Back at the church, the trio leaves their excess food for the woman and her daughter. Stein sneaks up to a nearby roadblock and throws a Molotov cocktail into a squad car, causing it to explode. The trio rides past the fiery wreckage. They arrive at the Navajo reservation and Stein acts penitently with his father (Hal Jon Norman), from whom he has been estranged for years. Julio begs the man for help but before anything can be done, the police arrive, startling Allan. He runs toward the house and is shot down in a hail of bullets. Stein and Julio run outside, with Stein shooting at the cops, and they, too, are shot. Stein's father watches sadly from the window. Stein dies yelling, "You made me do it! You made me do it!," a sentiment that is echoed as the closing credits roll.

The Loners is a standard rebellious youth versus militant establishment drama, inspired by the social temperament of the previous decade and fueled by the notion that films were still needed to depict the struggle of the young against "the establishment." This notion is refuted by the fact that the vast majority of the biker films and the anti-establishment movies that *The Loners* emulates had already had their vogue. By 1972, few moviegoers were still interested in the conflict that had defined the mid- to late 1960s. Hollywood's cinematic revolution had already occurred, led by films like *The Graduate, Bonnie and Clyde* and *Easy Rider,* with dozens of others branching off on their own unique tangents. The rating system instituted in 1968 regulated a freedom of expression that filmmakers had never before experienced. *Easy Rider* (1969) essentially capped the '60s with its slick portrayal of cultural malaise and nonconformity, laced with casual sex, drugtaking and cathartic violence that was no longer viewed as merely hippie culture, but as representative of mainstream America. *The Loners* followed three years later, and three years is an eternity in terms of cinematic cycles. Hippierelated stories were passé; Hollywood had already turned to black-themed dramas and action movies, while all-star disaster films were just starting to hit their stride.

Had *The Loners* appeared five years earlier, it might have found an audience, for its message of intolerance against the young would have reverberated with some force. The story of one man being hounded by ordinary citizenry as well as a militant police force evinces dramatic power, particularly because the young man is never allowed a chance to explain or defend himself. Stein is immediately thought to be guilty by everyone in authority, despite the fact that he is the most mild-mannered of men. To be honest, Stein's gentleness and passivity might have doomed the film even had it been made and released earlier, for his characteristics are not those that audiences would have been ready to accept. Biker films were popular in the late '60s, with such actors as Peter Fonda, Dennis Hopper, Tom Laughlin, Bruce Dern and Jack Nicholson riding their hogs to stardom. They portrayed tough but intelligent guys able to take care of themselves and their biker chicks, at least until the establishment unleashed superior firepower. Stein, in contrast, doesn't have a gun when the story starts and when he gets one doesn't fire it at anybody until the final minute of the movie, after Allan is killed. Stein is hardly the type of character to head a typical biker movie.

That is because *The Loners* does not aspire to be a typical biker movie. To its credit, it has higher aspirations. It is intended as a symbolic representation of an entire generation of young adults misunderstood and mistrusted by those generations that have come before it. If not for his long hair and predilection for riding fast motorcycles, Stein would be perfectly acceptable to the older crowd. He's not a typical cinematic biker thug in any sense; his biggest thrill is to ride in motocross races. He is not criminally inclined; he is led into stealing by Julio and circumstance, and to violence only when necessary to gain his freedom. Allan is similar in that he is polite and avoids trouble when he can. He isn't afraid to defend himself and he won't hurt anyone unless attacked. Of course, when he *is* attacked, Allan reacts with more force than necessary, killing not only his attacker in the diner but five other people as well. It is never explained in the film but it is obvious that Allan has some intellectually limiting condition, and that his friend Stein has taken the responsibility of looking after him. They are innocents who are persecuted and ultimately killed for the crime of being "different" in a world that does not tolerate any such differences.

Julio is a separate case. Born as Annabelle Jr. and hating the name, she allows Stein to casually rename her, even though he confesses that Julio is the name of a girl he used to know (this is not something most girls would care to be told). Julio craves any kind of excitement in her life, obviously rejecting her mother's practical understanding of how the world works ("Get out of bed! Get a job!"). In some ways she represents what is considered the worst traits of the young: She's lazy, spiteful to her mother, enjoys casual drug use and exhibits no ambition whatsoever. But in other ways she is quite specifically herself. Her need for excitement leads her from embarrassing Howie Rudd by leaving with Stein to stealing and, in short order, inadvertently killing. Her mother thinks she has been kidnapped, but the police know better. Julio's taste for danger and excitement, as much or more than any other factor, is the primary spur for her own inexorable demise.

It is natural that Julio be attracted to Stein, a handsome guy who carries himself confidently and only reluctantly confesses that he is in trouble. His trouble is what seals the deal, as she desires to leave the drudgery of her ordinary life behind and experience the thrills promised by the law's pursuit of Stein. Stein's attraction to Julio is less binding. Apart from the lure of sex and companionship that she willingly offers, there doesn't seem to be anything special enough about her to keep him interested. Perhaps he looks upon her as he does Allan: that Julio is someone for him to watch over and protect; his personal responsibility. Stein's offer to marry Julio is surprisingly old-fashioned under the circumstances, even if the wedding (conducted by Allan) would not be legal. It is yet another aspect of the film that is not in tune with its intended audience.

An aspect that is very much in tune with its intended audience is the inexorable combative and reactionary nature of most of the film's authority figures. The policemen simply accept that Stein is guilty of trying to kill the driver at the beginning of the story. When Stein climbs down the cliff to help the stricken policemen, Sgt. Hearn assumes he is there to finish the job of killing them and shoots at Stein without warning. Julio's mother continually berates her, essentially driving her out of the house. The store owner shoots at the intruders in his store, causing Julio to clobber him with a shovel. Police Chief Perkins tells anyone who will listen that a closed fist is the only thing that will keep the young people in line. The couple in the diner behaves atrociously, with the wife first winking at Allan and then yells at her husband that Allan is more of a man than he is. The husband cannot abide his wife's flirtatiousness with other men, screams at her to act decently and then turns on Allan, beating him almost senseless. It's no wonder that the young people rebel against these bigots, harpies and hypocrites. The film captures quite sharply the generation gap when the young people encounter these adults.

Like *Bonnie and Clyde*, the film understands that turning to crime carries a certain allure for its protagonists. This is seen when they rob and tease the honeymooners lying naked by a lake. Stein and Allan point their newfound guns (collected at the general store they robbed) at the pair and hector the couple, amusing themselves by taunting them about the money being stolen from them. The way they elude the cops at the motel, when Stein and Julio crash through a wall, and again at the bridge when Stein destroys the squad cars, is lighthearted. The film's treatment of their crimes turns dark just twice. The first time is when Julio kills the shop owner; she cries and screams unremittingly. The second time is the massacre at the end of the movie.

The film's most serious scene involves Gloria Grahame. As widow Annabelle Carter, she wears a straight dark-blonde wig and eschews glamourous makeup. Upon entering the house and finding her daughter still in bed, Annabelle castigates her for staying out all night and refusing to get a job, and threatens to throw her out when she turns twenty-one, all while collecting and washing the laundry and drinking beer. It is a stark, belligerent scene that compactly explains why Julia wants to get away and expertly establishes the generation gap that exists between a harried working woman and her spoiled, spiteful daughter. Its tone and technique are so far removed from that of the rest of the story that it seems lifted from another film altogether. The first part of that scene is a 2:40 single take that follows Gloria around the house. Director Sutton Roley described it this way:

The whole crew applauded her when she did [it all] in one take. In this scene she had to find her daughter in bed, start screaming at her, pop open a beer and drink it, walk down the hall to the laundry, load her wash into the machine, walk back down the hallway and pop open and drink another beer, all without ceasing to yell at the top of her lungs. There aren't a half-dozen actresses in Hollywood who could do that in a single take, but Gloria took it all in stride.

Gloria is superb in the vignette, attending to the physical demands of the scene—continuous movement, picking up clothing strewn around Julio's bedroom, stuffing it into the washing machine, opening and drinking cans of beer—all the while chastising her lazy daughter. "You've got a serious physical handicap," she yells at Julio from the laundry room. "You can't move your ass!" There is no trace of self-consciousness or satire in Gloria's tone; her Annabelle is all business. The scene ends somewhat ironically, when Annabelle finds cannabis next to Julio's bed; after harshly scolding Julio for smoking pot in her home, Annabelle lights it up herself to enjoy the puff or two that is left. The insinuation here is that Annabelle, alone of the story's authoritative adults, still recalls what it was like to be young, carefree and rebellious.

Oddly, Gloria's second scene ends quite differently. Annabelle is walking along with Police Chief Perkins, begging him to spare her daughter when the youths are caught. "She's a good girl," declares Annabelle. Gone is her anger at her recalcitrant daughter; she just wants the only person in the world that she cares about to return safely to her. And then comes a bizarre moment, when she says she has to get to work at the Green Onion and one of the lawmen asks if she is a waitress. "A waitress!" she scoffs. "I am a dancer!" With that, Gloria turns and struts away. "She's crazy!" remarks Perkins. Like mother, like daughter, he is probably reasoning. Unlike Gloria's sincere first scene, the way this second scene ends smacks of parody. Perhaps it was felt necessary to ridicule this adult, as most of the other adults are also ridiculed. Nevertheless, that moment feels wrong.

It is in this fashion that *The Loners* undermines its own intentions and ultimately fails to provoke its intended response. Filmed on a twenty-four-day schedule around the Albuquerque, New Mexico, area, the film boasts evocative cinematography, including some fine vantage point perspectives to tell its story. Its editing, however, is clumsy. There are moments when the dialogue heard is obviously not what is being said by the characters, and in the final shooting spree while Stein is shot to death, Julio's fate is never shown, only inferred by the number of bullets shot by the cops. Likewise, when Allan goes on his rampage in the diner, it is impossible to tell precisely what is happening or how many people are being killed. The film doesn't hesitate to show Julio topless in several scenes, but it refrains from depicting the graphic violence that its characters cause or endure. This is yet one more reason why it failed to catch on with its intended audience.

Changed from its original title of *Julio and Stein*, *The Loners* was released regionally to theaters beginning in April 1972, rather than nationally. Thus, it rarely received any traditional reviews, as it suddenly popped into an area, played for a week or two and then quickly disappeared. *Variety* called it a "fast-paced [melodrama]," adding, "*The Loners* is packed with action and enough interest to rate good reception in situations where this kind of attraction pays off."

Writer Barry Sandler was hired to rewrite John Lawrence's original script and recalls working with Gloria, whom he described as "so nice, so friendly, and a total pro" on and off the Albuquerque set. He was a young, aspiring screenwriter at the time, and was very taken with Gloria. They hung around together on the set, talking about movies and Hollywood, and she asked him to escort her to a party held by Bette Davis, who was in Albuquerque filming *Bunny O'Hare* at the time. Sandler recalls specifically writing the line "You can't move your ass!" for Gloria, as they worked together to make Annabelle "sassy, tough-talking and sarcastic." He explains that the line "I am a dancer!" was designed to show that Annabelle knew that she was aging but was "still clinging to some form of desirability." And he also stated that filming took place in either 1969 or 1970, indicating that the film was on the shelf for some time before its release. The 1970 date seems more likely, and indicates that it may have Gloria's first feature film after a long ab-sence, perhaps even predating *The Todd Killings, Chandler* and *Blood and Lace*.

Gloria had been recruited by executive producer Sam Katzman, whose son Jerry produced the film. Sam Katzman had hired Gloria back in 1953 for the colorful costume picture *Prisoners of the Casbah* and when he discovered that she was available for *The Loners* he didn't hesitate to make an offer, knowing that her name would add an air of prestige to the picture. Having already recruited two-time Cannes Film Festival Best Actor winner Dean Stockwell for the lead, the elder Katzman was hoping that the addition of Oscar winner Grahame would really boost the profile of his son's project. Ultimately, it didn't seem to make any difference, either critically or commercially.

Despite Gloria's excellence, particularly in her first scene, the film did nothing for her career. It was barely seen and few people in the industry were ever aware of it. *The Loners* was briefly released on VHS in America, and also in Australia (as *Deathly Riders*) and in Britain (as *Police Trap*). Even so, it remains one of Gloria's most obscure titles. That's a shame, because it contains some of her finest acting of the '70s. Otherwise, it's an uneven melodrama that isn't raucous enough to satisfy biker film fans and was made too late to capitalize on its commentary about the generation gap. For Gloria it was a demanding test of her acting skills, and an enjoyable on-location experience with a young cast and crew.

Tarot (1973)

(aka *Tarots*; *Angella*; *Autopsy*; *Game of Murder*)

CREDITS Orfeo Film Productions/Comptoir Française du Films Productions. *Distributed by* Eric Biedermann and Vagar Films. *Produced and Directed by* José María Forqué. *Story and Screenplay by* Rafael Azcona and José María Forqué. *Cinematography by* Alejandro Ulloa. *Film Editor*: Mercedes Alonso. *Music by* Michel Colombier. *Sound Editor*: Antonio Alonso. *Art Director*: Luis Vazquez. *Assistant Production Supervisor*: Ricardo Bonilla. *Still Photography*: José Salvador. *Sound Recordist*: Eduardo Fernandez. *Assistant Cameraman*: Ricardo Poblete. *Sculptor*: Francisco Baron. *Art Director*: Juan Antonio Arevalo. *Script Supervisors*: Olga Muller and Nicolle

Guetard. *Dialogue Coach*: James M. Fox. *Production Assistants*: Mario Morales and Juan De La Flor. *Camera Assistants*: Guillermo Peña and Andres Torres. *Makeup*: Manuel Martin. *Makeup Assistant*: Antonio Gentil. *Hairdresser*: Carmen Alberdi. *Boom Operator*: Manuel Ferreiro. *Wardrobe Mistress*: Teresa Iglesias. *Assistant Film Editors*: Dolores Laguna and Luisa Hernandez. *Props*: Vazquez Hermanos. *Special Effects*: Antonio Molina. *Electrician*: C. Dendra. *Interiors*: Estudios Cinematographicos, Roma, S.A. *Lighting*: S.A.D.I.L.G.A. *Set Construction*: Decoraciones Generales, S.I. *Film Processing*: Madrid Films, S.A. *Sound*: Estudios EXA. *Titles and Opticals*: Cinefectos. A Spanish-French Co-production. Eastmancolor. Panavision (2.35:1). Monaural Sound. 91 minutes. Released in 1973. Currently available on DVD in a full-screen version as *Autopsy*. Previously unavailable on commercial home video.

CAST *Angela*, Sue Lyon; *Arthur*, Fernando Rey; *Natalie*, Gloria Grahame; *Marc*, Christian Hay; *Maurice*, Julian Ugarte; *Rosa*, Mara Goyanes; *Inspector 1*, Jorge Rigaud; *Coco*, Anne Libert; *Official*, Barta Barri; *Connie*, Marisol Delgado; *Inspector 2*, Frank Clement; *Doctor*, Adriano Dominguez.

Unfulfilled by her return to feature films in America, Gloria traveled overseas to Spain to accept a co-starring role in a suspense film to be titled *Game of Murder*. The project eventually underwent a myriad of title changes, most of which made little sense. It finally arrived in America to play exclusively in the San Francisco area on a very limited run as *Angella*, but seems best known as *Tarot*, signified by the deck of tarot cards so highly prized by Sue Lyon's character. It is also known as *Tarots* (the Spanish spelling) and *Autopsy*, the title under which it has been released on DVD. To further complicate matters, there are two European movies also titled *Autopsy* (1973 and 1975) with which *Tarot* is sometimes confused (and one of them also stars Fernando Rey!). *Tarot* is barely known in America because it never received a proper release, yet the film proved to be fairly popular in Spain and around Europe at the time. It remains Gloria's least-seen feature film, which is somewhat peculiar because it was made so late in her career.

A beautiful young American girl, Angela (Sue Lyon), is almost penniless in Spain except for the clothes on her back and the motorcycle she rides. At a bar she is contacted by Marc (Christian Hay), a man to whom she is obviously attracted, and whom she follows to a swank Spanish villa. It is there that he informs her, "Coco didn't tell you? That I'm not the one who pays." The one who pays is Arthur (Fernando Rey), a blind man of wealth who wants to get to know Angela much better. She refuses and rides away, also refusing the money. Marc finds her a few days later posing for his sculptor friend Maurice (Julian Ugarte). Marc punches Maurice for taking advantage of Angela and gives her Maurice's money. It is not long before Angela finds herself in Marc's bed.

Arthur wants Angela for himself, and gradually entices her to visit him. Arthur remains unaware that his valet, Marc, is sleeping with Angela, and neither of them wants him to know. Arthur's housekeeper Natalie (Gloria Grahame) can see what's going on, but she also keeps her mouth shut. Arthur uses Angela's prized tarot cards to show her he wishes to marry her. Angela wants to leave, but Marc openly admits that he cannot provide for her — but Arthur can. If she marries Arthur, they can be together. Angela is unhappy with the situation but she is learning to enjoy wealth, so she stays. In a small ceremony, Arthur and Angela are married. On her wedding night, Angela panics and tries to leave, but is prevented by Marc, who assures her she is doing the right thing. "You're married to me, not to him," Marc whispers. Angela begins her double life.

Maurice the sculptor delivers a wedding present, a decorated life mask of Angela, accompanied by a smarmy note to her. Natalie tells Arthur about the mask, then "accidentally" breaks it. Arthur orders six more such life masks. When Maurice personally delivers them, Arthur forces him to eat the insulting note. Marc and Angela continue their affair; Natalie watches, keeping track of their activities. Arthur, too, is getting suspicious, and one day he leaves with Natalie toward town but walks back alone from the road to the villa just to be sure of what his young wife is doing. He finds her in a bathtub chatting with Marc, planning their next rendezvous. Arthur enters, startling both young people, and threatens to drown Angela for her transgressions. When Marc moves to defend her, Arthur draws a gun from his pocket. Marc and Arthur wrestle while Angela wails in the bathtub. Marc gains the upper hand and drowns Arthur in the tub as Angela continues to scream.

Marc and Angela clean the bathroom as

Natalie returns from her trip to town. Marc orders Angela to distract Rosa the cook (Mara Goyanes) and Natalie as he drags Arthur's body outside to the swimming pool. Later, Rosa screams as she discovers Arthur's body in the pool. Police question everyone except Angela, who is so distraught she needs sedatives. But it is Natalie who does the detective work, finding the master bathroom wet, physical evidence of Arthur's presence in the bathtub and wet clothes in a closet. At dinner, she presents Marc and Angela with her findings and demands half of the inheritance she would have received had Arthur not married Angela. They agree, although Marc later infers to Angela that they will have to kill Natalie. "Is there any other way?" she asks, already knowing the answer.

A large new palm tree is being installed on the property, and Marc leaves the hole for it open so that Natalie's body can be planted underneath. He lures Natalie to Maurice's studio, then calmly teases her before he begins to strangle her. Natalie, however, has a gun in her purse and she fires it three times. Natalie drives Marc's body back to the villa and dumps him in the hole where the palm is to be planted.

Angela comes back after spending the night with Maurice (her alibi for Natalie's murder). Natalie tells her that Marc is dead, when suddenly the police arrive. They arrest Angela and Natalie for Arthur's murder, as he had bathwater in his lungs. Angela does not resist; she is crying, "I killed him!" repeatedly, even though she means Marc, for she foresaw his death in her tarot cards. Natalie wants to blame Marc, the real culprit, but she has already killed and buried him. Realizing that her smartest move is to remain silent, she calmly accepts her fate. Both women are led away and Rosa the cook is left with the care of the villa (and, it seems likely, the remainder of Arthur's estate).

Tarot is a Spanish-French co-production, yet in tone it is an Italian *giallo*, telling a dark crime story with enigmatic characters, a bright color scheme, sharp visual accents, light eroticism and contemporary music. *Tarot* is less formalized than traditionally recognized *giallos*; it is rather mild for a psychological thriller, not particularly gruesome, hardly suspenseful at all, only lightly stylized and not especially erotic. For these reasons, the film is not well known outside of horror circles; and because it does not compare well to the films of Mario Bava, Dario Argento, Lucio Fulci or Sergio Martino, it is not a favorite of *giallo* fans either.

Giallo is an Italian term meaning "yellow," which was first applied to a series of mysteries titled *Il Giallo Mondadori* by the Mondadori publishing house in the 1930s. These mysteries, many of which were translations of Agatha Christie, Raymond Chandler and other American and British authors, were dressed in distinctive yellow covers, and became quite popular. Other publishers followed suit, keeping the yellow covers, and *giallo* entered Italian parlance as crime story literature. *Giallo* films followed in the 1960s, turning away from established literature and increasingly encompassing horror elements and stylized violence. By the 1970s *giallo* films were explicitly violent and quite erotic as well, often combining sex and death in almost ritualistic fashion. As mainstream cinema gradually embraced those elements, the popularity of the *gialli* has faded, although new examples arrive from time to time.

Compared to popular *giallo* films, *Tarot* is viewed as a disappointment. While it has an offbeat feel, it is never as weird or intense as its progenitors. There are just two killings and neither is particularly bloody. Its eroticism consists of a nude shot of star Sue Lyon waiting to take a bath, and then having Lyon in a sheer top that becomes quickly transparent while she's taking that bath. The combination of sex and death is accomplished by staging Arthur's fight with Marc in the bathroom as Angela is bathing; the men struggle as Angela screams, with Marc eventually drowning Arthur almost right on top of Angela, who is, of course, still wearing her transparent top. Yet this is about as stylish and intense as *Tarot* ever becomes. The other death scene is Marc's. He is killed with a gun, when Natalie defends herself. This scene is staged well at its beginning, as Marc teases Natalie before attacking her, until she unexpectedly shoots him through her purse. But then, like some ridiculous unkillable horror creature, Marc rises, lifts a large concrete or plaster block over his head and advances toward Natalie. She shoots him again, twice, and he dies bleeding all over the tree sculpture that Maurice has made featuring Angela's life masks.

Tarot. This Spanish poster emphasizes the beauty and sexuality of Sue Lyon, and paints Gloria as the silently suffering caretaker of blind Fernando Rey — all of which is surprisingly accurate for a movie poster.

Spanish writer-director José-María Forqué intends for irony to permeate his film from beginning to end. It is ironic for Angela the penniless beauty to meet wealthy Arthur and marry him; for the blind Arthur to have more foresight than anyone else; for Natalie's machinations involving getting rid of Marc's body to backfire against her complete innocence in Arthur's death. However this irony is more intended than realized. *Tarot* is never as clever as it wishes to be; it telegraphs all of its plot developments in advance of their actual arrivals, and its limited stylization fails to divert attention from its rather static drama. For every interesting visual touch there is a corresponding dullness of dialogue or tired movement toward murder.

Two elements stand out. One is the villa itself, which is quite beautiful. Its elegance often seems quite lost on the characters who live there, but this is probably intentional by Forqué, to convey yet more irony. The other element is the color scheme of the characters' costumes. Angela, the innocent one, is almost always dressed in shades of white. Natalie is blue, purple or mauve, while Arthur is always in beige or brown. Marc is often shirtless, thus emphasizing that beautiful tanned skin is the embodiment of greed and evil. While the costuming and production design are excellent, the script simply fails to use them to any intriguing advantage.

In what is essentially a four-character play, the acting is decent but not outstanding because everyone, at one time or another, is presented as enigmatic and unfathomable. Sue Lyon is gorgeous as Angela and shows more skin than in any other film she ever made. She is not always convincing but she is quite good in Arthur's murder scene, crying and screaming and thrashing about in the tub very realistically. Fernando Rey is solid as the rich blind man Arthur, even with distracting dark glasses. It is odd that twice Angela removes Arthur's glasses and both times he reacts as if he is being blinded by light, and yet he is described as completely blind. Rey portrays Arthur with a quiet dignity perfectly appropriate for the role. Best of all is Christian Hay, the amoral Marc, who beds Angela whenever he can (he had been sleeping with Natalie before Angela's arrival) and enjoys each and every perk of serving a wealthy man. Marc is the piece's instigator, and Hay provides the character with energy, wit, a hint of danger and sensuous physicality.

Gloria Grahame is good in Natalie's early scenes, remaining largely silent and servile in the background. At first impression, Natalie might be Arthur's mistress, and this is neither confirmed nor denied. As the housekeeper, Natalie runs the villa for Arthur and ensures that he is surrounded by luxury. He confides in her and trusts her; she has been at the villa for twelve years. As Angela moves in and takes over, Natalie begins to burn inside, and Gloria illustrates this well by sharp glances and an icy tone in her voice. It is that voice, however, that betrays her after Arthur's death. Once Natalie realizes what has occurred, she informs Marc and Angela of her knowledge and demands half of Arthur's inheritance. It is here that Gloria puts on her "patrician" voice, which, unfortunately, sounds phony and artificial in these surroundings. Gloria is always at her best when acting naturally; in many of *Tarot*'s scenes she is not allowing herself to do so.

Gloria loved the opportunity to travel overseas and essay a leading role in a film that promised to at least *look* really good. Filming commenced in Marbella and Madrid, and Gloria was startled by the media attention her arrival in Spain caused. During lulls in the filming she and her mother (who was still accompanying Gloria on most of her movie shoots) toured the Spanish countryside and really enjoyed the scenery. Gloria befriended Sue Lyon, who stayed in Spain another few months and made a second film, *Clockwork Terror*, which is even less well known than *Tarot*.

Although the making of the film was newsworthy in Spain, partly because of its casting and partly due to the strong reputation of director Forqué, *Tarot* never received a proper American release. According to Vincent Curcio's biography of Gloria, the film did play in San Francisco for a short while under the title of *Angella* (why two "l"s?; this is never explained). No reviews for the film under any title. That is yet another reason why *Tarot* is almost unknown to most film fans. It was released on DVD as *Autopsy* (another of its many aliases) in 2007 by a company called Substance, although not in its proper widescreen format. But it remains more of a curiosity than anything else in Gloria's career, the primary focus of a nice trip to Spain.

Mama's Dirty Girls (1974)

CREDITS The Carlin Company. *Distributed by* Premiere Releasing Organization. *Directed by* John Hayes. *Produced by* Ed Carlin and Gil Lasky. *Written by* Gil Lasky. *Director of Photography*: Henning Schellerup. *Film Editor*: Luke Porand. *Production Manager*: Peter Cornberg. *Assistant Film Editor*: Milt Citron. *Sound Recordist*: Tony Vorno. *Sound Assistant*: Dan Ansley. *Script Supervisor*: John Dorr. *Assistant Cameraman*: Ray Isley (Icely). *Costumes*: Jodie Tillen. *Art Director*: Jim Newport. *Makeup*: Jan Hines. *Re-Recording*: Glen Glenn Sound. *Negative Cutter*: Clay Marsh. *Key Grip*: Robert Decker. *Grip*: Paul Dillingham. *Gaffer*: John King. *Still Photography*: Peter Cornberg. *Titles, Opticals and Processing*: Consolidated Film Industries. *Music by* Don Bagley and Steve Michaels. Rated R. CFI Color. Matted Widescreen (1.85:1). Monaural Sound. 82 minutes. Released in August, 1974. Not currently available on DVD. Previously available on VHS.

CAST *Mama Love*, Gloria Grahame; *Harold Stritch*, Paul Lambert; *Addie Love*, Sondra Currie; *Becky Love*, Candice Rialson; *Sheriff Roy Collins*, Christopher Wines [Lofton]; *Paul Carruthers*, Dennis Smith; *Cindy Love*, Mary Stoddard; *Willie*, Joseph Anthony; *George*, John Dennis; *Charity Collins*, Anneka de (di) Lorenzo; *Rummy*, Tony Vorno.

Certainly the sleaziest of Gloria Grahame's films is *Mama's Dirty Girls*, a violent melodrama in the *Bloody Mama–Big Bad Mama–Crazy Mama* mold. All of them headline well-known actresses (Gloria, Shelley Winters, Angie Dickinson, Cloris Leachman, respectively) as rebellious women with strong criminal tendencies that they pass along to their teenage and adult offspring. Usually the mothers are forced by circumstance into crime, but they take to it with little hesitation, trying to collect some cash to provide security for their families. All of these exploitative "Mama movies" are sexually charged and some boast abundant nudity and sex scenes, usually involving the beautiful daughters (although Angie Dickinson famously strips and gets hot and heavy with William Shatner in *Big Bad Mama*). They are also rather violent, particularly against the men who have wronged the mamas, for they are first and forever exploitation flicks.

Mama's Dirty Girls begins with one of the girls, Becky Love (Candice Rialson), naked in the bathroom, combing her hair. She puts on a bikini and goes out to the pool, where she notices her stepfather George (John Dennis) ogling her. Becky joins him in the house and teases him until he attempts to rape her. They are interrupted by Mama Love (Gloria Grahame), who threatens to call the cops on George. Mama dictates a "confession" which George reluctantly writes and signs, promising to behave himself around her daughters. Later that night, after the youngest daughter has been sent to a movie, Becky lures George into the bathroom by stripping. "No, Becky, no," says George, draping a towel around her shoulders. Suddenly Mama and older daughter Addie (Sondra Currie) push George into the tub and slash him to death with a straight razor. The youngest girl, Cindy (Mary Stoddard), finds the body in the tub when she arrives home.

After the funeral, Mama informs her girls that there is no property; George did not own the house. She reasserts her philosophy: "A man can go just about as easy as he can come, unless he owns property. Property is security." They begin to drive north, looking for a new future. In the town of Willard, Mama is pulled over by Sheriff Roy Collins (Christopher Wines), who recommends that they stay at a local health resort. The resort is run by Harold Stritch (Paul Lambert), who recently lost his wife Jenny in a boating accident. When Harold talks about the spa property, he gets Mama's attention, and the Love family decides to stay for awhile. Sheriff Roy warns Harold that he will be watching him, because he isn't convinced that Jenny's death was an accident.

Each of the women soon has a man: Mama makes out with Harold, but deflects his carnal intentions until marriage is discussed; Becky teases Willie (Joseph Anthony), the simple-minded handyman; Cindy finds romance with deliveryman Paul Carruthers (Dennis Smith); Addie starts an affair with Sheriff Collins. The sheriff doesn't love his young wife Charity (Anneka di Lorenzo) any more, but he cannot persuade Charity to divorce him. Harold has a scare when a hobo informs him that he saw Harold drown his wife in the lake, but Harold takes care of the hobo

Mama's Dirty Girls. A rare happy moment occurs when Mama Love (Gloria) marries Harold Stritch (Paul Lambert) following a whirlwind courtship.

with an axe. The sheriff tells Addie that he cannot marry her, so Addie visits Charity, demands a divorce and stabs Charity to death using Paul's switchblade when she refuses.

Mama and Harold get married, and Mama makes an honest effort to be domestic. Once they make each other their death beneficiaries, however, accidents begin to occur. Mama is almost crushed by a falling water barrel, pushed over by Harold. Harold is almost run over when Mama drives backwards suddenly; Harold, doing electrical work, is nearly electrocuted when Mama unexpectedly turns on the power. When Cindy finds a stash of jewelry, proving that Harold had murdered his wife Jenny and kept it after reporting it was stolen, Mama decides to end things once and for all. The women devise a deadly plan. Meanwhile, Becky teases Willie with the promise of sex, and Willie accidentally kills her when she refuses and makes fun of him. Mama has Cindy confront Harold with the jewelry, threatening to go to the police. When Harold tries to stop Cindy from calling the police, Mama bursts into the room and shoots at him, but she misses. Harold takes Cindy hostage, holding

her at knifepoint. Paul tries to stop Harold but fails, and Harold drives away into the hills with Cindy.

Completely distraught (for she loves her daughters very much), Mama follows Harold, still carrying the gun. Paul calls Sheriff Collins and tells him he is going into the hills after Harold, Cindy and her crazy mother. The sheriff catches up to Paul and threatens to kill him; Addie has convinced him to shoot Paul, since Paul's knife was the weapon that killed the sheriff's wife. In the end, however, Collins cannot shoot Paul. They join forces and drive into the hills in pursuit. Harold gets the car stuck in a ditch and Cindy escapes. He finds a board and frees the car, attempting to flee when Mama arrives. She shoots into the car as he runs her down. The car crashes and burns. Collins and Paul arrive to find Mama and Harold dead, and Cindy alive. The sheriff arrests Addie for the murder of his wife, Charity. Cindy and Paul drive away, hopefully to a happier future.

Mama's Dirty Girls probably marks the nadir of Gloria's feature film career, in as much as she headlines the cast list and willingly participates as an actress in the gruesome killings of her character's two husbands. Moreover, Mama forces her youngest daughter, Cindy, to confront Harold about his former wife's jewelry, hoping to lure him into attacking her — an attack which she plans to stop with a revolver. This, after leaving the body of her previous husband, George, for Cindy to find in the bathtub, stabbed and mutilated. The older girls, Becky and Addie, are sluts. Becky isn't happy unless she is teasing someone with provocative sexuality, while Addie proves repeatedly that she will kill to get the man she wants, and she doesn't hesitate to frame an innocent man for the murder. Mama sets quite an example for this brood of beautiful crazies; it's a wonder that Cindy is even close to normal, considering the lack of morality to which she has been exposed.

Throughout the film, it is Cindy who represents the only innocence and hope for redemption. Cindy is not involved in George's murder; she is sent to the movies and told not to come home until midnight (though it seems a cruel trick that Cindy is then forced to find George's bloody body). Cindy's relationship with deliveryman Paul is the only male-female relationship shown to be based on love. Mama hates George, eventually killing him, and her marriage to Harold is based on greedy deceit. Addie desires Sheriff Roy, who is married, and kills his wife in order to free him for herself. Becky flirts with every man she meets but isn't satisfied with any of them. However, Cindy and Paul fall in love; their sex scene, in contrast with those of her sisters, is loving and tender. Paul and Cindy survive the climactic showdown and end the distasteful proceedings by starting a new life together, no longer tethered to the deadly salaciousness of her sluttish sisters and avaricious mother.

The ladies are generally viewed as scheming, conniving, sex-starved liars, and the men are not treated much better. George is a pig who cannot help but lust after his luscious stepdaughter. At least he tries to resist her seductive advances; his last words are "No, Becky, no." Alas, his conscience arises too late. Harold is a

Mama's Dirty Girls. They didn't get that way on their own. Mama Love (Gloria) decides that yet another of her marriages must end, and end quickly.

little better; at least he has no designs on the young girls. But he's already offed one wife and seems quite willing to do it again, all for money. Willie the handyman is mentally handicapped, much like the character Lennie in John Steinbeck's *Of Mice and Men*. Sheriff Roy Collins readily cheats on his wife with Addie and looks the other way when Addie kills her; for a time he even accepts the idea of killing Paul so that Charity's death can be blamed on Paul. Eventually his conscience overwhelms his lust, but it's tough going for a while. Only Paul Carruthers seems like a decent guy, and he is rewarded by becoming Addie's scapegoat for murder.

This cinematic mishmash of lust and murder might have generated some trashy exuberance, but it is poorly written by co-producer Gil Lasky and ineptly filmed by director John Hayes. It attempts to revel in self-conscious satire, which mostly falls flat. Instead of creating a sense of outrageousness covered with a satiric sheen — as the other "Mama movies" at least attempt to produce — *Mama's Dirty Girls* is an exercise in moral turpitude. It is exploitation at its lowest level: scenes of sexuality, greed and violence without any artistic merit. The film was made by the Carlin Company, run by the folks who brought *Blood and Lace* to the screen three years earlier. Producer Ed Carlin mined the same exploitative vein with other titles such as *The Manhandlers*, *The Swinging Barmaids* and *The Student Body*. None of them had the impact of his two films with Gloria Grahame — probably because they didn't feature a star with Gloria's status. Just how Carlin and Lasky, who wrote both features and partnered with Carlin to produce them, were able to persuade Gloria to participate remains a mystery. Hopefully she earned a hefty paycheck — because unlike her cinematic daughters, she refused to appear naked.

It must be admitted that the ladies do look great. Candice Rialson, Sondra Currie and Anneka di Lorenzo were in the midst of appearing in such exploitation fodder as *Candy Stripe Nurses* (1974, Rialson), *Chatterbox* (1977, Rialson), *Teenage Seductress* (1971, Currie), *Jessi's Girls* (1975, Currie), *The Centerfold Girls* (1974, di Lorenzo) and *Rape Squad* (1974, di Lorenzo) so the various strippings, slashings and stabbings in this film were no great challenge for

them. Di Lorenzo followed this movie with a stint as *Penthouse* magazine's Pet of the Year in 1975–76. Gorgeous blonde Rialson makes the strongest impression of the three, though her fate is the silliest. This was Mary Stoddard's only film role (as Cindy, the youngest daughter).

As Mama Love, Gloria looks superb for her fifty-one years of age. She is seen to her advantage in short dresses, open-necked blouses and tight slacks. While her acceptance of this project is certainly questionable, there is no doubt what the producers saw in Gloria. She's tough, sexy and energetic, easily capturing the inherent sordidness of her character. With her long, wavy hair luxuriantly wrapped around her attractive but curiously austere face, Gloria retains the retreating indications of beauty that daughters Rialson, Currie and Stoddard so strongly manifest. Had her role (and the movie) been more fully developed, Gloria might have tapped into some of her earlier, sluttish, downtrodden roles to really deliver a powerhouse performance; perhaps that possibility occurred to her when agreeing to this project. Mama Love could have been the middle-aged version of some of Gloria's previous, troubled characters, one who never quite managed to adapt to society's standards. But such depth is not to be found in this movie.

Unfortunately the level of Gloria's acting does not match that of her appearance. She tends to take the material too seriously. Her dialogue about finding a man with property is delivered with a gravity which overwhelms the speech's flimsy artifice. When planning Harold's demise, Mama and her oldest daughters cackle with glee in a scene so phony it's painful to watch. Gloria is overly theatrical in the scenes where Harold and Mama narrowly miss killing each other, and it is unbelievable that Mama remains blind to his deadly intentions (and vice versa). Although she is the nominal star of the film and has quite a bit to do, Gloria does not showcase her talents well in this particular forum.

No newspaper or magazine reviews could be found for this movie. *Mama's Dirty Girls* absolutely made money, as that type of movie so often does, yet they do so without ever seeming to attract mainstream attention or play in theaters like other, better movies. There is certainly a market for this type of film, evidenced by the fact that so many of them have been produced, yet few of them ever attain the notoriety that *Mama's Dirty Girls* did. And part of its status, its allure, is that it is led by an Academy Award–winning actress. Gloria's participation ensured that it would receive attention; its other characteristics kept it in circulation at drive-ins and on cable television for years.

In addition to the ignominy of starring in *Mama's Dirty Girls*, Gloria was to have a really rotten 1974. She and Tony Ray filed for divorce and spent weeks in court battling over money and custody issues; their relationship deteriorated while the divorce proceedings would drag on for two years. Gloria also discovered, in March, that she had breast cancer. On the advice of her physicians she stopped smoking, drastically reduced her alcohol intake, and turned to a mostly vegetarian diet. With radiation treatments and a new regimen for healthy eating, the cancerous tumor shrank within three months and could not be found in six. With a huge sigh of relief, Gloria resumed her career while remaining on the health regimen that had helped her keep her life. Because of the cancer, and more especially her ongoing disputes with Tony, Gloria curtailed her work commitments, especially in feature films. She was not happy with what she was being offered anyway, so she concentrated on family issues, remaining healthy, and convenient stage and television work as it came along. Anything but another movie like *Mama's Dirty Girls*. Yet, just two years later, Gloria was to land in another gruesome horror spectacle; she needed the work.

Mansion of the Doomed (1976)

(aka *Eyes*; *Eyes of Dr. Chaney*; *House of Blood*; *The Terror of Dr. Chaney*; *Massacre Mansion*; *Eyes of the Living Dead*)

CREDITS Charles Band Productions/Group 1 International Distribution Organization, Ltd. *Directed by* Michael Pataki. *Produced by* Charles Band. *Executive Supervision by* Albert Band. *Written by* Frank Fay Perilli. *Cinematography by* Andrew Davis. *Edited by* Harry Keramidas. *Makeup Designed by* Stanley [Stan] Winston. *Music by* Robert O. Ragland. *Production Manager*: Richard Shore. *Assistant Director*: Richard Band. *Production Assistant*: Bobby Herbeck. *Second Assistant*: Lynn Hayes. *Art Director*: Roger Pancake. *Set Decorator*: Patrick McFadden. *Script Supervisor*: Monica Dunlop. *Production Secretary*: Kathryn Cunha. *Assistant Cameraman*: Jim Dennett. *Second Assistant*: Robert Hale. *Gaffer*: Moishe [Moshe] Yakobovesky. *Grip*: Schmulik Firstenberj [Sam Firstenberg]. *Sound*: John Hayes. *Boom Operator*: Tony Vorno. *Wardrobe*: Tommy Hasson. *Still Photographer*: Steve Vaughn. *Makeup Artists*: Mike Bacarella and Tom Hoeber. *Food Supervisor*: Linda Turley. *Medical Consultant*: Nunzio Nerbo. *Assistant Editor*: Sandra Estrin. *Sound Editor*: Mary McGlone. *Music Editor*: Lee Osborne. *Re-recording*: Glen Glenn Sound. *Titles by* Cinefx. Rated R. DeLuxe Color. Matted Widescreen (1.85:1). Monaural Sound. 89 minutes. Released in October, 1976. Currently available on DVD. Previously available on VHS.

CAST *Dr. Leonard Chaney*, Richard Basehart; *Katherine*, Gloria Grahame; *Nancy Chaney*, Trish Stewart; *Dr. Dan Bryan*, Lance Henriksen; *Al*, Al Ferrara; *Georgio*, Jo Jo D'Amore; *Sylvia Porter*, Donna Andresen; *Miss Mathews*, Marilyn Joi; *Elevator Girl*, Katherine Fitzpatrick; *Hitchhiker*, Katherine Stewart; *Detective Simon*, Vic Tayback; *Ambulance Doctor*, Simmy Bow; *Wino*, Arthur Space; *Libby*, Libby Chase; *Landlady*, Sally Marr; *Miss Dunn*, Patsy Sublime; *Dr. Del*, Del Negro; *Delivery Boy*, Barry Chase; *Young Doctor*, Sandy Champion; *Girl on Street*, Barbara Sloane.

Gloria's next project isn't much better than *Mama's Dirty Girls*. It isn't quite as sleazy, focusing its energies on medical mayhem conducted by a rogue surgeon, and its quotient of violence and gore is lower. However, its central plot device — eyeball transplants!— is enough to make anyone squeamish, which is why it has a solid reputation among horror aficionados. Adding to its reputation is the involvement of cinematographer Andrew Davis, who would later direct such hits as *Code of Silence*, *The Fugitive* and *Under Siege*, and makeup man Stan Winston, who became one of the makeup and special effects wizards of 1970s and '80s Hollywood. The film also benefits from the participation of acting greats Richard Basehart in the lead, and Gloria as his faithful assistant — although Gloria is, rather criminally, given almost nothing of value to do. Gloria looks fantastic, but even her looks cannot make this movie palatable to viewers offended by scenes of eyeballs being removed from people's faces without their permission.

Dr. Leonard Chaney (Richard Basehart), a brilliant, renowned eye surgeon, is rather conservative in his approach to surgery — until his lovely daughter Nancy (Trish Stewart) is blinded in an auto accident. Chaney realizes that current treatments will never restore her sight, so he decides to take matters, literally, into his own hands. His assistant Katherine (Gloria Grahame) raises objections to his idea of transplanting entire eyeballs, but she is overruled. Nancy is devastated by her injury, spending her time sitting in her dark bedroom crying. Chaney invites a young colleague, Dr. Dan Bryan (Lance Henriksen), to visit. Dan hopes to cheer Nancy, his fiancée, but Chaney has other plans. Dan is drugged, dragged into the basement and told that he will be sacrificing his own sight. In just under twenty minutes, Chaney transplants Dan's eyes into Nancy, with Katherine assisting.

The operation is successful; when Nancy removes the bandages she can see! Light scarring around the eyes is evident but Chaney assures her that it will fade. Within days Nancy is back to normal, lounging by the swimming pool. One day she drives over to Dan's place but (obviously) he hasn't been around lately. She goes swimming, and her eyes develop a deep infection which re-blinds her. Chaney is crushed; he had not foreseen the risk and had not limited her activity. Since he has proof that the procedure works, he decides that he will just have to do it again. As he walks the Los Angeles city streets looking for a suitable donor, Katherine takes a plate of food down to Chaney's basement laboratory, giving it to Dan, who is still alive, locked in an electrified jail cell-like cage, raging about his newly blinded state. Chaney sees a pretty hitchhiker (Katherine Stewart) about Nancy's age and moves quickly to give her a lift. When she awakens in the cage next to Dan, she is blind as well. But Nancy remains sightless; an "inner wall" has developed that somehow prevents the operation from succeeding. Chaney goes looking for another subject.

This time Chaney actually interviews women, ostensibly looking for a nurse for Nancy. He chooses Miss Mathews (Marilyn Joi), a beautiful black woman with no family in the area, and soon she has unwittingly donated her sight. Nancy, however, still cannot

see, and the scarring around her eyes is readily apparent. Sick from the surgeries, Nancy murmurs, "I don't care any more," but her father refuses to listen. Katherine begs him to stop, too. "Get rid of those people, Len," she urges. "Kill them." Chaney is horrified; he plans to restore their sight, too, in the same fashion once he has perfected the technique and Nancy has regained her sight. A realtor named Sylvia Porter (Donna Andresen) is next, and then she joins the growing coterie in the basement cell. Dan tries to control the group and influence the women but no one listens. Chaney tries again, this time with a woman (Katherine Fitzpatrick) he meets on an elevator. Again, it doesn't work.

Fixated on the idea that the eyes are being rejected because they are not young and fresh enough, Chaney goes to a park and charms a little girl named Libby (Libby Chase), but she escapes after causing his car to crash into another. The two men in the other car, Al (Al Ferrara) and Georgio (Jo Jo D'Amore), follow him home. Chaney calmly writes them a check for the damages, then invites them for a friendly drink. Both men awaken in the basement, also blind. Neither set of eyes work for Nancy, who is now bedridden in agony. Almost insane at losing his sight, Al attacks Georgio and has to be restrained by Dan and the others. Gradually he calms down and agrees to help Dan with his escape plan, which involves digging through the concrete wall with a piece of wire. Meanwhile, Chaney stalks the city streets looking for another "donor" and is mugged by a wino (Arthur Space) he is trying to lead back to his home.

After one of the women dies in the cell, Katherine once again begs Chaney to put the others out of their misery. He refuses. The cellmates succeed in digging a hole large enough for the smaller women to escape through. Miss Mathews makes it outside but is caught by Chaney, who leads her back inside before she can raise an alarm. Sylvia also escapes and makes it to a busy roadway, where she is run down as Chaney watches, sickened by the image of a life lost for nothing. Detective Simon (Vic Tayback) investigates and is puzzled by the victim having being blinded *before* she was accidentally run over on the highway. Simon consults with the local eye expert, Chaney, and enlists his help in studying the body for an explanation.

Katherine brings food to the cage and is grabbed from behind by Al. Chaney turns on the electricity to make him let her go, which works, but it electrocutes Katherine in the process. Chaney takes her eyes and transplants them into Nancy, who now has terrible facial scars from so many operations. Nancy awakens with limited vision and stumbles to the basement while Chaney is digging Katherine's grave out in the yard. Nancy hears voices and finds the blind people, including her fiancé Dan. She unlocks the cell just as Chaney approaches, desperate to stop her. Chaney is pushed inside with Al, who begins to strangle him and then switches tactics, ripping Chaney's own eyeballs out with his bare hands. The end credits roll as the blind people stagger outside, free at last.

Mansion of the Doomed is obviously inspired by Georges Franju's famous 1960 French film *Eyes Without a Face*, in which a surgeon tries to replace his daughter's entire face, which was disfigured in an automobile accident. The films are remarkably similar in plot detail, although the tones are very different. *Eyes Without a Face* (which, like *Mansion of the Doomed*, is also known by another lurid name, *The Horror Chamber of Dr. Faustus*) is a moody, almost poetic film that spends much time with its faceless victim Christiane (Edith Scob), conveying her ambivalence about the efforts of her father to restore her to beauty, and the cost of those efforts in human life. *Eyes Without a Face* is more disturbing psychologically than visually (except for the first transplant scene, in which a woman's face is removed in startlingly vivid detail). Christiane's tight-fitting face mask is remarkably beautiful, allowing her eyes to give her blank, rigid, white face gentle expression. There is no such beauty or poeticism in *Mansion of the Doomed*.

Instead of full-face transplants, Dr. Chaney needs to transfer entire eyes. This, of course, is considerably more difficult in terms than the facial grafts needed in *Eyes Without a Face*. In fact, Chaney's methods are impossible, particularly considering the speed at which he operates and the primitive conditions in his basement operating room. His assistant Katherine even asks about the optic nerve when he first announces his new methodology, but his double talk sidesteps the issue. Director Michael Pataki attempts to infuse a sense of nasty reality into the proceedings by using actual medical footage of eyes being operated upon (seen on camera monitors), but this footage doesn't match anything in his movie and appears distinctly out of place. It was a good idea to utilize medical footage in place of scenes that obviously could not be shot of characters losing their eyes, but the footage that was chosen does little to strengthen the film or horrify viewers.

Indeed, the most horrifying aspect of *Mansion of the Doomed* is that Dr. Chaney keeps his blinded victims alive and caged in his basement. *Eyes Without a Face* dispensed with such melodrama; its victims, dead, were dumped in the local river. The result is a leaner narrative that focuses full attention on the actions and consequences of Dr. Génessier's (Pierre Brasseur) toil to provide his daughter Christiane with a new face, and her responses to his misguided efforts. *Mansion of the Doomed*, on the other hand, isn't satisfied with just documenting Dr. Chaney's well-intentioned but gruesome scheme to restore his daughter's sight; it replaces death with human suffering and the need for revenge upon the good doctor. Gradually this part of the story overwhelms the other part, as the number of Chaney's victims increases to a small gang and retribution becomes inevitable.

This dramatic difference between the two otherwise very similar films demonstrates a fundamental divergence between European horror and American horror, at least in the latter quarter of the twentieth century and beyond. The European film, while visually horrifying in its way, has a larger scope and purpose structured to explore the human psyche, realizing that the inner thoughts, jealousies and emotions that govern the actions of its characters form the foundation of the essence of horror. The American film follows the dictums that horror must be *seen* in all its graphic glory to be effective, and that outward human suffering, suffering which must be witnessed to be believed, is the most terrible thing of all. Dr. Chaney's eyeball-popping operations are not considered gruesome enough, so his victims are kept barely alive, denied even the most basic comfort and care, until they can finally rise up as one against their tormentor. This key differ-

Mansion of the Doomed. This is a Spanish lobby card with wild artwork that barely reflects what the movie actually depicts. Note that Trish Stewart's name is misspelled, while the other stars' monikers survive intact.

ence demonstrates why American horror films are often so distasteful to view while European horror films usually compel and fascinate.

Thus, *Mansion of the Doomed* has little of the skill, subtlety or poeticism of the film it is so clearly based upon. The one scene in the movie that generates genuine discomfort and suspense occurs when Chaney reasons that his daughter needs eyes that are young and fresh, so he travels to a local park and invites a young child named Libby to go with him to Disneyland. The effectiveness of this creepy scene has been heightened over the years as American society has become aware of the pedophile; the scene is stronger because of our preconditioned reaction to pedophilia, even though this character has nothing sexual in mind for the child. It is also notable that this scene results in nothing more dramatic than a minor traffic accident, yet because of the imminent peril of the child, it is easily the most effective sequence in the movie.

Much of the movie's intended terror depends on one's squeamishness and discomfort at the thought of losing one's sight. Director Pataki tries to heighten this natural discomfort by including the shots of medical eye operations, and with Stan Winston's makeup effects of Dan, Miss Matthews, Sylvia and the others with vacant sockets where their eyes should be. The makeup is minimally effective because it is obvious that actors are simply playing their parts with their real eyes covered. The film might have benefitted by having real blind people with removable glass eyes in small victim roles (such as the hitchhiker, whose face is not clearly seen before she is blinded) and then filming their faces, close-up without their eyes in place, in the basement cage. Obviously this was not done, and the film suffers from unconvincing makeup effects.

The film is not helped by Richard Basehart's lethargic portrayal of Dr. Chaney. Basehart certainly has the intelligence to convey Chaney's brilliance, but his countenance is far too low-key and sedentary to demonstrate Chaney's fiery descent into madness. It may be that Basehart figured Chaney never actually did go mad, but anyone who would disfigure and blind other people in an effort to restore sight to a loved one has definitely lost at least some of their reason. Basehart never loses his cool, even in his running narration of how things are going. It is a one-note performance, and it is the wrong note.

Gloria is little better as Katherine, but that is due almost entirely to the emptiness of the role. At first glance it would seem that Katherine is married to Chaney but that is not the case; he comments that Nancy is not her daughter and that he appreciates Katherine's attentiveness to Nancy over the years. There seems to be a deeper relationship between the two characters, but it is never fully fleshed out. Katherine raises realistic objections to Chaney's methods, and yet always aids him in his operations. It is also up to Katherine to feed and take care of the ever-increasing crowd in the basement cell and it is this duty that spooks her. "Get rid of those people, Len. Kill them!" she says. Is this demand made out of fear, or pity? Because Katherine's character is paper thin, it is difficult to say. Probably both.

Gloria had no love for the project, but it was work, and she was determined to do it well. She worked with Basehart on the medical scenes, learning to assist him the way a nurse would assist a real doctor, and studied eye structure so her dialogue wouldn't sound forced or phony. Even so, there is no sparkle or conviction in her scenes. She may have been reflecting Basehart's cool performance, but Gloria is simply uninteresting in this movie. The only asset she brings is her appearance. Gloria is gorgeous at various moments during the picture, slim and trim, and with beautiful flowing hair. It is a shame that she is so rarely the focus of the frame, for she was in full flower. Director Pataki remarks in Vincent Curcio's biography of Gloria that her beauty proved to be a problem in the scene after Katherine is killed and Chaney is about to remove her eyes. Gloria was in full makeup and refused to remove it even though she knew she was playing a corpse. Pataki had to resort to smearing her makeup all over her face and threatening to film her like that before she acceded to his wishes.

Following this project, Gloria was not seen in another feature film for three years. Strong roles were simply not being offered to Gloria, so she turned increasingly to television and sought to rebuild her personal life. Having burned through four husbands in thirty years, she was not anxious to marry again. Nevertheless, Gloria embarked on another romance or two after she left Tony Ray behind her for good. Just as or more important to Gloria was her return to the stage. Between 1976 and 1982 Gloria starred or co-starred in a dozen theatrical productions, averaging two per year, staged from Darien, Connecticut, to Los Angeles, California, and many places in between. She also returned to England for four different productions and was in London in late 1981 for another when her health rapidly deteriorated. But she continued to make movies, too, even if her parts were small or the type of movie, like this one, did not suit her tastes.

Mansion of the Doomed marked Lance Henriksen's sixth appearance in front of film cameras, and his career has largely continued down the horror and science-fiction path ever since. Henriksen is energetic as Dan, especially in the cage scenes where he is trying to get his blind colleagues to band together for escape. It's a thankless role that he fulfills with gusto. And that is Vic Tayback as Detective Simon, who calls upon Dr. Chaney to consult on the body of Sylvia. Tayback is purely a stock detective character here, but this is notable as his second appearance as a detective investigating Gloria's murderous exploits, following the 1971 film *Blood and Lace*.

Mansion of the Doomed was filmed over twenty-three days on the shoestring budget of $270,000, which, unfortunately, is quite evident. Despite the talents of makeup man Winston and cinematographer Davis, whose careers were just beginning, as well as director Pataki, who was better known as an actor, this horror opus just does not work very well. It has none of the magic of *Eyes Without a Face* and its additional gore adds little of value. It is poorly edited, badly lit (especially in the basement scenes), muddily recorded and glumly acted. An early horror effort by the Band brothers, who later founded Empire Pictures and Full Moon Entertainment, it is probably best described as a training ground for the filmmakers and a mistake for the cast.

It did not receive a standard release, as its multiple titles would suggest. Best known as *Mansion of the Doomed*, it was also sent to theaters as *Eyes, The Eyes of Dr. Chaney, The Terror of Dr. Chaney, House of Blood, Massacre Mansion* and *Eyes of the Living Dead*. Only *House of Blood* and *Massacre Mansion* sound effective because of their similarity to *Mansion of the Doomed*, although *Eyes* is evocative and *The Terror of Dr. Chaney* is the closest explanation of the story. Incidentally, this is the first of two Gloria Grahame films to be titled *Massacre Mansion* at one time or another. The other is the last movie she made, *The Nesting*. This film did not do well under any of its many monikers and no magazine or newspaper reviews could be located for it. *The Motion Picture Guide* gave it a zero star rating, and recommended that the audience "keep its collective eyes closed...." In Welch Everman's book *Cult Horror Films* he makes the case that films like *Mansion of the Doomed* "are one way in which we can get a bit of revenge against the medical profession," but also argues that the film "never takes advantage of the fear all sighted people have about losing their eyes. As a result, it manages to be pretty disgusting at times, but it never really manages to be frightening."

Mansion of the Doomed was notorious in its day, and because so few people have actually seen it some of its notoriety has remained intact. But Welch Everman is right; no list of memorable movies about losing one's sight include this one. *Zombie* (aka *Zombi 2*), yes! *Theater of Blood*, yes. Even *Saturn 3*, yes. But not *Mansion of the Doomed*. It is a misbegotten imitation of the lyrical *Eyes Without a Face* that wastes the talent of everyone involved. Richard Basehart and Gloria Grahame should have fired whoever persuaded them to make this dud. Fortunately, there was more work to come for each of them, including major motion pictures that would attract critical acclaim and awards attention.

A Nightingale Sang in Berkeley Square (1979)

(aka *The Biggest Bank Robbery*; *The Mayfair Bank Caper*; *The Big Scam*)

CREDITS S. Benjamin Fisz Productions. *Directed by* Ralph Thomas. *Produced by* S. Benjamin Fisz. *Associate Producer*: Joyce Herlihy. *Original Story and Screenplay by* Guy Elmes. *Director of Photography*: John Coquillon. *Editor*: Peter Boita. *Production Design*: Lionel Couch. *Assistant Director*: David Tringham. *Camera Operator*: Herbie Smith. *Casting Director*: Maude Spector. *Art Director*: Tony Curtis. *Costume Designer*: Emma Porteus. *Set Dresser*: Peter Young. *Makeup Artist*: Freddie Williamson. *Hairdresser*: Betty Glasow. *Continuity*: Ceri Evans. *Stills Photographer*: Barry Peake. *Sound Recordists*: Simon Kaye and Gerry Humphries. *Dubbing Editor*: Peter Best. *Construction Manager*: Jack Carter. *Chief Electrician*: Nobby Cross. *Executive Accountant*: Wally Eggleden. *Production Assistant*: Jennie Raglan. *Music by* Stanley Myers. *Painter*: Adrian Start. *Best Boy*: Reg Parsons. *Wardrobe Supervisor*: Daryl Bristow. *Processed by* Rank Film Laboratories. *Cameras and Lenses by* Joe Dunton Cameras. *Lighting by* Lee Electric (Lighting) Ltd. *Music Recorded at* Anvil Film and Recording Group. Color. Matted Widescreen (1.85:1). Monaural Sound. 106 minutes. Released in 1979. Currently available on DVD. Previously available on VHS under the titles *The Big Scam* and *The Mayfair Bank Caper*.

CAST *Lucius Percival "Pinky" Green*, Richard Jordan; *Fred "Foxy" Fox*, Oliver Tobias; *Ivan*, David Niven; *Miss Pelham*, Elke Sommer; *Ma*, Gloria Grahame; *Inspector Watford*, Richard Johnson; *Pealer Bell*, Michael Angelis; *Charlie the Chubb*, Dicken Ashworth; *Mavis*, Minah Bird; *Major Treadwell*, Peter Cartwright; *Gregory Peck*, Brian Croucher; *Nobby Flowers*, Derek Deadman; *Aussie*, James Galloway; *Sid Larkin*, Hugh Griffith; *Clint*, Charlie Hawkins; *Legs Eleven*, Anthony Heaton; *Sid the Yid*, Davy Kaye; *Jack Diamond*, Edward Peel; *Stan the Spinner*, Brian Protheroe; *Solicitor*, John Rhys-Davies; *Phil*, Gerard Ryder; *Blakestone*, John Washbrook; *Judge*, Robert Raglan; *Prison Officer*, Graham Padden; *Jill*, Sally Harrison; *Doris*, Yvonne Costello; *Sergeant George*, Ian Collier; *Mac*, Raymond Skipp; *Ibrahim*, Stefan Kalipha; *Fletcher*, John Pennington; *Kersey*, Rex Robinson; *Mr. Beddings*, Michael O'Hagan; *Waitress*, Carolyne Argyle; *Commander Ford*, Ewen Solon; *Dolman*, Chris Sullivan; *Sergeant Trimm*, Stacey Davies; *Sergeant Dunbar*, Mike Lewin; *Morgan Stanfield*, Bruce Boa; *Barrister*, Elizabeth Adare; *Warder*, Godfrey Jackman; *Policeman*, John McCarthy; *Police Car Driver*, Duncan Preston; *Constable*, Howard Bell; *Security Guards*, Eamonn Jones, Roy Boyd, Christopher Coll and Nicholas Donnelly; *Prison Warden*, Joss Ackland; *Policeman*, Harry Fielder; *Port Official*, Alfred Molina; *Gang Member*, Dave Cooper.

Gloria had returned to England to appear in a stage production of *Rain* at the Watford Palace Theatre in London. It was a four-week run and afterward she remained in England in the company of her new beau, Peter Turner. Gloria had not made a feature film in Great Britain since 1956, but she was happy to oblige when an opportunity to do so suddenly appeared. She was hired for a small role in a bank caper movie that underwent several title changes but is best known as *A Nightingale Sang in Berkeley Square*. The film is a fictionalized account, and subtle parody, of an actual bank robbery that occurred in the Mayfair district of London on April 24, 1975. The names and places (and, in some cases, destinies of characters) have been changed for legal reasons, yet the robbery in the film is quite faithful to that which actually emptied the vault of a Bank of America branch on that fateful day. Gloria's participation is very minor, as are the contributions of all the women in the cast; this is an instance of women's roles being almost completely subordinated to those of men. Her part in the filming required just a day or two; then it was back to the stage, preparing for a role in *A Tribute to Lili Lamont* at the New End Theatre in Hempstead.

The day that "Pinky" Green (Richard Jordan) is released from prison, he returns home to Brighton and vows to his mother (Gloria Grahame) and stepbrother Fred (Oliver Tobias) that he will pursue a career as an electrician and turn his back on crime. With a recommendation letter in hand, Pinky stays true to his word, quickly finding work at the Global Group fixing their fluorescent lights. Impressed by Pinky's electrical knowledge, charm and willingness to work late hours and weekends, he is assigned to the Atlantic and Pacific Bank. His immediate supervisor, Miss Pelham (Elke Sommer), likes Pinky enough to have him hired by the bank; soon he is working in all three of the bank's offices and local branches, even in high security areas. Pinky is so trusted that he is given permission (and keys) to come and go as he pleases. He couldn't be happier.

That is, until he is summoned to a conference with Ivan (David Niven), the local crime boss. Ivan has been informed of Pinky's newfound status with the bank and wants to use it to his own advantage. Ivan pressures Pinky to give him the combination for the vault, but that proves to be beyond Pinky's ability. Nevertheless, Ivan and his gang determine

to rob the place, and Pinky is told to work at one of the other branches the night of the robbery so that he'll have an alibi. The robbery takes place but is surprisingly unsuccessful; the robbers try to drill through the vault door and cannot due to a faulty electrical outlet that causes a power failure. Only Pinky knows that he rigged the outlet to fail, yet the bank staff recognizes Pinky as a hero and awards him a personal bank account as a reward for thwarting the robbery.

Pinky celebrates by dancing with his mother at a party and deciding to move into his own apartment. Back at work, Pinky is assigned to install a new alarm system near the vault. In doing so, he accidentally pokes a hole in the ceiling above the vault entrance and discovers that he can see the combination lock through the hole. One night he hides above the ceiling and watches the managers open the vault. Not trusting his view of the numbers, Pinky buys a telescope to double check the process. Upon hearing that Pinky has purchased a telescope, Ivan deduces the real reason and again pressures Pinky to aid with another attempt. Pinky reluctantly complies.

Pinky tells his stepbrother Fred about the upcoming robbery, arranging for Fred to accept Pinky's share of the money and hide it. Pinky arranges to be with Miss Pelham at the time of the robbery; he goes to her apartment ostensibly to fix a fan, but remains most of the night on more personal business. The robbery takes place on schedule but ends more quickly than planned when the overnight computer programmers discover the plot and are locked inside the vault by Ivan and his gang. Even so, the gang gets away cleanly. When divvying the loot, someone suggests that Pinky's share need not be as big as everyone else's, but Ivan stands up for his inside man. Pinky's share is dropped in Fred's car; Fred buries most of it according to Pinky's instructions, using a suitcase to hide the rest. The total take is £4 million in cash, plus another £8 million in gold and jewelry, making the robbery one of the largest in history.

The only hitch is that Pinky gets a parking ticket near the bank before going to visit Miss Pelham, and that ticket ultimately leads Scotland Yard and Inspector Watford (Richard Johnson) to him. Pinky denies everything, of course, but when Watford is shown the telescope and, in Pinky's jacket, a slip of paper with the combination numbers written on it, the jig is up. Eventually Pinky cuts a deal with Watford and tells his story to the incredulous police. Everyone involved is corralled.

Pinky advises Fred to move his share of the loot, but he is too late; Fred watches with dismay as Pinky is forced to lead Watford to the stash. The sound of gunshots suddenly attracts everybody's attention and Watford investigates them. Fred grabs the loot and gets away before the cops return. The robbers are sentenced to ten, fifteen or twenty years in prison. Ivan, as the mastermind, gets a twenty-five-year sentence. Pinky is sentenced to seven years; he's astonished, because his deal with Watford called for three years. After the sentencing he is allowed to use the courthouse restroom, where he grabs a judge's robe and, pretending to be a judge, walks out of the building. He runs and is met by Fred; they escape with their share of the money. The film ends with the note that only half a million pounds (of the four million taken) was ever recovered by Scotland Yard.

A Nightingale Sang in Berkeley Square is saddled with a terribly non-descriptive title (but recognizable, as it is shared with that of a popular British song; the song is heard in the movie at least twice). It's an amusing recreation and parody of one of the largest bank robberies in world history. The real heist was, somewhat mysteriously, not widely publicized in Great Britain at the time, although the trial a year later was quite well covered. And, astonishingly, the theft received almost no mention in the United States—perhaps because the target of the April 24, 1975, robbery was a London branch of the Bank of America. The only American ties to the film are star Richard Jordan, and the actress who portrays his mother, Gloria Grahame. The vast majority of the cast is British, as is the writer, Guy Elmes, and the director, Ralph Thomas. This was Thomas' final assignment behind the cameras; he is best known for helming most of the rambunctious "Doctor in the House" medical comedies in the 1950s and '60s.

Elmes and Thomas choose to treat the heist not just as a caper — encompassing all the traditional humorous and anti-establishment elements inherent in popular caper movies— but also as a comedy of circumstance. Pinky Green really wants to go straight, but time and again he's pushed back into crime. The bank is a modern facility in a busy, well-policed area that should never fall prey to such a robbery, but actually it's not just vulnerable but amazingly assailable. Pinky provides himself with an airtight alibi, but his own stupidity leads the investigation straight to him. Then, when justice is being rightfully administered to everyone involved, including Pinky, Pinky finds the only possible route of escape. This atmosphere of circumstance, or possibly divine fate, overwhelms the story's dramatic and suspenseful elements, making it more farcical than the material warrants. For everything that happens in the movie happened, in one fashion or another (more often another), to the perpetrators of the real crime.

The film portrays Pinky as a reluctant participant in the robbery; despite his best efforts to go straight, opportunity continually falls into his lap. The real inside man, Stuart Buckley, was not at all reluctant. The robbery progressed according to Buckley's well-conceived plan, just as it is staged in the movie. There was indeed an attempt of drilling the vault that failed only because of mechanical mishaps. Incredibly, the ex-convict Buckley came under no scrutiny; in fact, the bank that hired him never performed a background check and was totally unaware of his criminal past. It was Buckley who discovered the method of hiding in the ceiling and watching as the combinations were dialed on the vault door, and in court testimony, he did claim that his discovery was accidental. In the film Ivan attempts escape out of the country in disguise but fails; in real life, Frank Maple did evade prosecution for several years by fleeing to Europe. Maple fled to Morocco, was nearly extradited from Spain and ultimately was extradited from Austria following prosecution for armed robbery there. In the film, Pinky escapes custody by stealing a judge's robe. Stuart Buckley made no such escape, having quickly confessed to the robbery and implicated the other gang members. However, fellow conspirator Jimmy O'Loughlin did escape custody at the courthouse, in the same manner as Pinky does in the film. After several months on the run, O'Loughlin was recaptured just before he was, reputedly, about to turn himself in, and he, along with most of the other robbers, spent more than a decade behind bars. Buckley was, like Pinky, sentenced to seven years, although he only served about three before being released and provided with a new identity. From there, he simply vanished. Finally, just as the movie notes, most of the money has never been recovered.

With an event brimming with such inherent drama, suspense, action and irony, it is perplexing why this particular bank robbery is not better known by the public, and why it has not served as the basis for any other films. It may also seem odd that the one film that does dramatize the Mayfair bank robbery does so with tongue in cheek. The real-life robbery does not seem like a barrel of laughs. Yet as its bizarre elements were revealed in the trial that followed, screenwriter Elmes became convinced that the event had all the hallmarks of cheeky comedy. And that is exactly how Ralph Thomas directed it: with a light touch, bright and breezy, manipulating the various components and characters for maximum ironic effect. Thus, conniving Stuart Buckley becomes hapless Pinky Green, an ex-con whose determination to go straight leads him directly to the grandest criminal opportunity he could ever have imagined. Frank Maple becomes dapper Ivan, an urban crime lord who seems to own every other business in Mayfair but wants more. Jimmy O'Loughlin's daring escape becomes Pinky's, so that the movie can have a Hollywood-type hopeful ending.

The casting is unusual in some respects, yet reflected sound business sense, at least to the producer. American Richard Jordan is Pinky Green, cast presumably for the American audience. It makes no sense for Pinky to be American, nor to have British half-brother Fred (Oliver Tobias), and it makes no sense for their mother (Gloria Grahame) to also be American, but there it is. (It can also be surmised that Pinky is *not* related to Fred and his mother, but simply calls her "Ma" as the family's closest friend, but the literal dialogue seems more believable). Jordan was, at the time, an up-and-coming Hollywood actor and Gloria was still considered "a name," so they were hired to lure U.S. audiences. Another international personage is German actress Elke Sommer, cast as the

bank manager Miss Pelham, with almost as little to do as Gloria. Elke, however, was called upon to take a quick nude shower as her character waits for Pinky to arrive on the night of the robbery. The shower scene was excised in British prints, and it does seem completely gratuitous in this otherwise very innocuous movie.

The story is British through and through, and the movie would have been better served by keeping it that way, casting someone like a young Daniel Day-Lewis in the lead and eliminating Pinky's strange family triangle. However, that is not what happened. Jordan is quite jaunty and effective as Pinky, ably handling each odd new situation as it develops. His brash confidence is just what the character needs. David Niven essentially cruises through his role as Ivan, but he still delivers some verbal zingers and adds *gravitas* with his presence. Gloria does what she can with her few lines, but her part seems just as much ad-libbed on the spot as scripted beforehand. Her single characteristic of note is that "Ma" was, and evidently still is, an actress. She tells Pinky that she was recently in a film and had five lines. "I could have been a star," she tells him, "only his [Fred's] dad liked to go to bed early." Unfortunately, as with so many other caper films and tales of espionage, character development is almost always the weakest aspect.

Where the film succeeds is portraying the methodology needed to rob the bank, and having fun with the notion that it so easily falls prey to these opportunists. Caper films excel when they demonstrate a solid sense of humor about their illegal endeavors, and *A Nightingale Sang in Berkeley Square* is no exception. Not only is the ex-con Pinky assigned to work at the Atlantic and Pacific Bank without a background check, but he is assigned so much work that he is paid double time to work late to accomplish it, thus providing him with access to the entire building in the middle of the night when there is nobody around to monitor him. The first robbery is a washout and, because he rigged an electrical outlet to fail, Pinky is hailed as a hero by the bank staff—and given even more access and trust. The big break comes when Pinky drops a tool while working in the suspended ceiling near the vault, in the exact spot needed to get a clear view of the vault's combination locks. Pinky has the notion to keep his idea to himself, but the news spreads like wildfire when he overpays for a telescope and soon Ivan deduces exactly what Pinky has in mind. Fred's involvement is a huge risk on Pinky's part, yet it is because of Fred that when Pinky escapes he has most of his loot waiting for him. And, of course, the biggest bank robbery in British history is undone, at least at first, by a simple parking ticket that leads the authorities to Pinky.

Then there are the escapes—first, the attempted escape by Ivan, who puts on a silly disguise and takes a hovercraft (!) across the English Channel to supposed freedom in France; unfortunately for Ivan, Watford is there waiting for him. Outside of a James Bond adventure, it's quite unusual for a hovercraft to make an appearance in any movie. Pinky's escape is delicious in its execution. Almost sick at the seven-year sentence he receives, Pinky needs to visit the loo. Once there, he sees inspiration hanging on the wall and uses it to bluff his way out of the courthouse. Pinky's bravado once again wins the day.

These elements, most of them inspired by actual events, give the film its vibrancy and bounce. Not everything works: There is simply no reason for Pinky to still have the piece of paper with the combination numbers in his jacket. And one wishes that Miss Pelham had a larger role in the story, for she is the only female character of any interest. Another liability is the score by Stanley Myers, which consists almost entirely of bluegrass music! Myers' music generally reflects the film's jauntiness but tends to undermine every dramatic scene that it underscores. Nevertheless, the majority of this story is intriguing and entertaining, the more so for reflecting the reality behind it with humor and vitality. It's a movie that tweaks history a little bit but does so with a great deal of charm.

Despite its casting of Americans Jordan and Gloria, and despite the fact that it is based on a remarkable moment in British history, the film barely received a theatrical release anywhere. Finished in 1979, it did virtually nothing under its original title. In 1980 it re-emerged under the title *The Biggest Bank Robbery*, which is the title it was known as when it appeared on British television as early as 1981. Strangely,

even then just six years after the Mayfair robbery, it seemed to exist outside of history. Two *London Times* television listings refer to the film's implausibility, despite the fact that virtually everything that happens in it really occurred during and after the actual robbery. Two video releases eventually followed, under two more titles: *The Big Scam* and *The Mayfair Bank Robbery*. Regardless, the film still remains obscure no matter what title it uses, which explains why there are no reviews to quote.

The film, under any of its titles, is worthy of at least one viewing. For Gloria it was only a quick bit of unrehearsed, and seemingly unscripted, film work between stage jobs in England. She was just entering the last really busy part of her career on both stage and film, a period which, had she lived to pursue and enjoy it, promised to lead her into some major character roles throughout the 1980s. Any proof needed for this statement can be found in her next film, Gloria's last important role.

Chilly Scenes of Winter (1979)

(aka *Head Over Heels*)

CREDITS Triple Play Productions. *Distributed by* United Artists. *Directed by* Joan Micklin Silver. *Produced by* Mark Metcalf, Amy Robinson and Griffin Dunne. *Screenplay by* Joan Micklin Silver. *Based on the novel Chilly Scenes of Winter by* Ann Beattie. *Director of Photography*: Bobby Byrne. *Edited by* Cynthia Scheider. *Music by* Ken Lauber. *Production Designer*: Peter Jamison. *Production Manager*: Paul Helmick. *First Assistant Director*: Lorin Salob. *Second Assistant Director*: D. Scott Easton. *Script Supervisor*: Hannah Scheel. *Publicity*: Maslansky Koenigsberg, Inc. *Camera Operator*: Ray De La Motte. *First Assistant Cameraman*: Ted Sugura. *Second Assistant Cameramen*: Eric Engler and Jeffrey Gershman. *Gaffer*: James Boyle. *Best Boy*: Peter Davidian. *Electricians*: Steve Shaver and John Hawn. *Sound Mixer*: Ron Curfman. *Boom*: Richard Thornton. *Costume Design*: Rosanna Morton. *Assistant Art Director*: Robert [Bo] Welch. *Set Decorator*: Linda Spheeris. *Leadman*: William Wright. *Key Grip*: Paul Borchardt. *Best Boy Grip*: Ophelious Braxton. *Dolly Grip*: Robert Gaynor. *Grip*: Mitch Lookabaugh. *Property Master*: David Scott. *Stills*: Jack Gereghty. *Makeup*: Ben Nye II. *Hairdresser*: Lola "Skip" McNalley. *Costumers*: Agnes Lyon and Julie Dresner. *Construction Coordinator*: Joe Acord. *Transportation Captain*: Joseph Sawyers. *Assistant Editor*: Mindy Byer. *Apprentice Editor*: Deedra Bebout. *Looping Editor*: Harriet Fidlow. *Assistant to the Director*: Laura Morgan. *Production Office Coordinator*: Betty Atkinson. *Locations* (*Salt Lake City*): Hal Schlueter. *Sound Effects Editor*: Don Sable. *Assistant Effects Editor*: Lowell Mate. *Re-recording Mixer*: Jack Higgins. *Production Accountant*: Rita Damon. *Assistant Production Accountant*: Cathy Freckleton. *Production Assistants*: Charles Wessler, Neal Hoffberg and Cathy Lehne. *Music Editor*: La Da Productions, Inc. *Guitar, Harmonica and Whistle by* Jean "Toots" Thielemans. *Driver*: Jerry Sidwell. *Orchestrator*: Ken Lauber. *Songs*: "Get It While You Can," *written by* Jerry Ragovoy and Mort Schulman, *performed by* Janis Joplin, *courtesy of* CBS Records; "Skylark," *written by* Hoagy Carmichael and Johnny Mercer, *performed by* Bette Midler, *courtesy of* Atlantic Records. *Prints by* Technicolor. *Optical Effects by* Film Opticals. *Titles by* Hillsberg and Meyer. *Panaflex Cameras and Lenses by* Panavision. Rated PG. Metrocolor. Panavision (1.85:1). Magno Sound (monaural). 92 minutes (as *Chilly Scenes of Winter*). Originally 96 minutes (as *Head Over Heels*). Released on October 19, 1979 (as *Head Over Heels*). Re-released on August 13, 1982 (as *Chilly Scenes of Winter*). Currently unavailable on DVD. *Chilly Scenes of Winter* previously available on VHS.

CAST *Charles Richardson*, John Heard; *Laura Connolly*, Mary Beth Hurt; *Sam McGuire*, Peter Riegert; *Pete*, Kenneth McMillan; *Clara (Ma)*, Gloria Grahame; *Betty*, Nora Heflin; *Mr. Patterson*, Jerry Hardin; *Susan*, Tarah Nutter; *Jim Connolly (Ox)*, Mark Metcalf; *Blindman*, Allen Joseph; *Mrs. Delillo*, Frances Bay; *Doctor Mark*, Griffin Dunne; *Elise*, Alex Johnson; *Woman in Park*, Beverly Booth Rowland; *Man in Store*, Oscar Rowland; *Rebecca*, Angela Phillips; *Dancing Nurse*, Margaressa Peach Taylor; *Waitresses*, Ann Beattie and Mags Kavanaugh; *Optician*, Linda Alper; with Amy Robinson (scenes deleted).

Chilly Scenes of Winter (1976) was an acclaimed first novel by Ann Beattie that examined a romantic relationship in sometimes excruciating detail. Just three years later that story was made into a film by a group of young producers and a director who sought to make a movie about the everyday experiences of authentically real people, which was quite trendy at the time (*Kramer vs. Kramer, Ordinary People*, etc.). However, as seems to be the case with many films, the distributor was unsure how to market it. United Artists changed the title from the "cold and dreary" *Chilly Scenes of Winter* to the jocular expression *Head Over Heels*, which, while being eminently forgettable, actually summarizes the romantic state of its protagonist quite appropriately. Naturally, the movie failed to attract audiences—despite some excellent reviews—and faded from sight. Three years later, United Artists surprisingly decided to give it another chance, restored the original title and, encouraged by the director and producers to do so, agreed to drop its conventional happy ending. Therefore, the only version available to view since 1982 is *Chilly Scenes of Winter*, the version that ends with its protagonist, Charles, running in a park.

Charles Richardson (John Heard) is leaving the Salt Lake City, Utah, office building where he works, ruminating on his romantic fate. "I don't have Laura," he says to himself. Entering his frozen car, he imagines that she is there, but it's just his heartbroken imagination. At home, his friend Sam McGuire (Peter Riegert) stops over for dinner, and Charles' sister Susan (Tarah Nutter) is there with her college roommate Elise (Alex Johnson). Dinner is interrupted when Charles' mother Clara calls, saying she is going to kill herself. Charles turns to the audience (breaking the "fourth wall"; he does this periodically throughout the story) and describes how he met Laura. Flashbacks show him at work, meeting Laura (Mary Beth Hurt) and pestering her to go out with him, even though she is (unhappily) married. Their date ends in Laura's empty apartment with Laura crying about her life. Back in the present, Charles and his sister Susan drive over and fish their mother Clara (Gloria Grahame) out of the bathtub, where she is sitting, soaking in an evening dress. As they put Clara to bed, her husband Pete (Kenneth McMillan) returns home, and Pete asks them over for Sunday dinner. Returning home, Charles finds Sam and Elise having sex in his bed. He sleeps on the couch.

The narrative then bounces between the present, with Charles pining after Laura (who has returned to her husband) and Sam moving into the spare bedroom after losing his job, and flashbacks detailing the burgeoning romance between Charles and Laura. In the present, Charles and Sam visit Charles' parents on the following gloomy Sunday afternoon. Pete is, inexplicably, in Atlanta. Clara, dressed in a black evening gown and white sneakers, gives Sam a deep smooch and asks about Sam's parents, whom she knows (but claims not to know) divorced many years earlier. Sitting at the table with empty china and glasses before

Chilly Scenes of Winter. The relationship between Charles Richardson (John Heard) and his mother Clara (Gloria) is strained due to her increasingly eccentric behavior, such as halfheartedly trying to commit suicide by eating a box of laxatives.

them, Charles asks where their dinner is. Clara slyly smiles and says, "There is no dinner!" In the past, romance blooms for Charles and Laura, beginning with a chair that Charles buys for Laura and peaking when she moves in with him for two months. Gradually feelings turn sour, however, and after two months Laura finally returns to her husband. Charles copes by starting to build a model of Laura's A-frame house and watching her in her real house whenever he can.

Charles visits his mother in a psychiatric ward; she has eaten an entire box of laxatives, threatening to kill herself again. Pete is there, saying he has enrolled Clara and himself in a dancing class. He exhibits his dancing prowess by twirling by himself and then with a nurse in the hallway, impressing Charles, who is finally beginning to accept his stepfather. Still unwilling to let go of his feelings for Laura, Charles takes Sam to her husband's business to meet him. Jim Connolly (Mark Metcalf), better known as Ox, builds A-frame houses, and leads Charles and Sam to his own house nearby to

show it to them. Laura is startled by their appearance, but says nothing before Charles boldly declares his love for Laura. Ox throws out Charles and Sam.

Clara is back at home, preparing for bed wearing a silk dress, asking Charles why he can't find himself a girl. He laughs at his own misfortune. "I'm working on it," he replies. Weeks go by, and he hears nothing from Laura. He hosts dinner with an acquaintance from work, Betty (Nora Heflin), who tells him Laura has left her husband. Charles bursts with happiness, rushes her out of the house with Sam, buys some flowers and goes to Laura's new apartment to see her. They talk, then argue. Charles gives her an ultimatum; he will not wait for her any longer. She does not respond, and Charles leaves. He throws away the model A-frame he had built and tells Sam, "It's over." Charles carries on with his life. After work one day he walks to a park and then runs, flat out and as fast as he can. He pulls up and catches his breath. Life goes on. Fade out.

Chilly Scenes of Winter is a straightforward, honest attempt to capture a genuine slice of life on film. It is not quite a character study but rather a glimpse into one man's psyche as he deals with his feelings for a woman who does not love him as much as he loves her. This is the movie's strength, conveying Charles Richardson's (John Heard) very understandable emotions through sharp dialogue and intricate detail of his plain life — but it is also the movie's weakness, for Charles' largely unrequited love life is rather dull. The film's ambitions are both simple and honorable, striving to present one ordinary guy's story without fanfare or sensationalism, and the film achieves that goal quite admirably. The argument can be made, however, that the basic story undermines its own intent, since Charles does not always seem like a regular guy. This is only emphasized by the *Head Over Heels* poster's tagline "Love does strange things to people. And Charles is a little strange to start with," which appears over a stylized drawing of Charles' smiling face, with snow atop his head and windshield wipers cleaning his glasses.

Charles' life is pretty ordinary. He works as a report writer for the Department of Development for the state of Utah, writing reports on the reports he reads. He has no idea what happens to *his* reports, but he's been promoted twice and now enjoys a private office at work. But outside of work, his primary interest is pining after Laura. Nothing else interests him; most everything he thinks, says or does revolves around the fact that he loves her and wants her back. Charles' single-minded obsession is the crux of the story, which director Joan Micklin Silver exhibits with merciless precision. Silver allows her protagonist to sulk, wallow and eventually yell in self-righteous pity, knowing that everyone watching the film has experienced the same frustration regarding love, yet she keeps the story moving forward even if Charles doesn't want to himself. Everything is about Charles' reaction to feelings (his own and Laura's) over which he has no control.

If the story's presentation of Charles' unrequited love for Laura isn't obvious or poignant enough for some viewers, it reinforces those themes with the subplot involving Charles and Betty. Betty (Nora Heflin) works for Charles, typing his reports every day.

Charles has no feelings whatsoever for Betty, but talks to her because she is friendly with Laura, and he can keep tabs on Laura through Betty. When Charles suggests having a "get-together," Betty offers to coordinate the snack food, and soon develops a large notebook of ideas and suggestions for what to serve. It is obvious that Betty has some feelings for Charles but he is completely oblivious, even at the scene where Betty tells him Laura has finally left her husband. Betty is clearly unhappy being interrogated by Charles and rushes out of the house, but Charles doesn't even notice. At least Betty finds some solace with Sam, going to a movie with him after her poor treatment by Charles. This subplot solidifies the movie's overriding theme, which is that love is blind and often cruel.

There are also hints that such obsession can be dangerous. When Charles learns that Laura went to a gynecologist without telling him about it, he turns jealous, and even jokingly states that he wants to beat up the doctor and then beat *her* up. And when Laura finally leaves him, Charles' immediate response is to growl, "I'm going to rape you!" Charles will not follow through on such threats, but the script clearly indicates that the prospect of losing the woman he loves is pushing him toward violence. Eventually this leads to an awkward, rather comic confrontation with Ox, Laura's husband, and this scene, given harsher characters, could very easily have turned violent. But that is not the film's intent; this story merely illustrates the craziness to which love (either the obsessive nature of it or the pain of rejection when it is denied) drives everyone.

More than most movies, *Chilly Scenes of Winter* is a collection of moments that provide meaning for its characters and understanding for the audience ... little moments that might seem insignificant in the larger scheme of things but which Charles will always treasure, such as him buying a chair for Laura's empty apartment, bantering about whose chair it is once the gift is given, and then rushing to be the first person to sit in it. Or the scene when Charles watches Laura (Mary Beth Hurt) jump on a trampoline, clearly enjoying just watching her bounce, twist in mid-air and joyously bounce again as she must have bounced in high school. Or the scene when Charles and Pete

(Kenneth McMillan) discuss the possibility of Pete buying a new car (punctuated, importantly, by Charles asking if Pete ever danced with his mother); finding, for perhaps the first time, common ground between them. These moments authenticate the drama, give it shape and form because they are real, and telling. These moments reveal who these people are and what they want out of life. They also bind the audience to the characters because of shared experience.

Such moments are not just dramatic. They include humor, for Charles and Sam (especially sarcastic Sam) recognize how crazy life often is. For example, Charles' obsession with Laura is certainly dramatic (especially to him) but it is comic as well, particularly when he takes Sam (Peter Riegert) to visit Laura's husband Ox (Mark Metcalf). The following scene, when Ox brings the two men he thinks are home-buying prospects to his home, is bursting with coiled energy just ready to explode. And yet even here, the humor is character-driven rather than the slapstick mugging that other directors might have employed, such as Charles declaring his love for Laura, with Ox then chasing him around the house. There are few laugh-out-loud scenes, but a plethora of amusing, chuckle-inducing moments abound throughout the script, often reaction shots to something kooky that has just happened. Sam has a great reaction after Charles' mother Clara gives him a long, unexpected kiss; Sam turns away as she talks to Charles and he waves his left arm around, as if trying to regain his balance. But Clara is his friend's mother, so he doesn't say anything at all.

Charles' life is ordinary, but that isn't true for the people surrounding him. Sam is an "unemployed jacket salesman" who takes up residence with Charles and soon slows his own life to a crawl, barely rising out of bed during the day. Sam is clearly troubled by his predicament, but he cannot seem to find a solution to it — and at the end of the story, he has not yet made a change. Charles' sister Susan (Tarah Nutter) is in college; she seems happy to be away from the turmoil surrounding their mother, and eager to make a life apart from her zany family. She may be the only "normal" person in the Richardson family. Charles' mother Clara (Gloria Grahame) is the least ordinary of all; she is prone to depression and ridiculous suicide attempts that merely result in bringing her the attention she craves. Clara is the story's most troublesome character; her husband Pete doesn't know what to do with her, Charles is resigned to staying nearby for the times she needs him, and Susan wants little to do with her. Clara's antics force things to happen now and again, but with no real direction or purpose.

Gloria Grahame's best role of the 1970s should have been in this darkly comic romantic drama, for it provides her with a role, Clara, full of possibility. That role is, unfortunately, underdeveloped to the point of anemia. Clara is more caricature than character because the script (based faithfully on Ann Beattie's novel) never permits her to be as serious or authentic as her children. Clara is the story's running gag, the crazy mother always garbed in evening clothes who often takes baths in those fancy dresses. Charles (and, to a lesser degree, Susan) are accustomed to fishing her out of the tub and putting her to bed. Pete is so exhausted from the effort of keeping Clara happy that every now and then he disappears, which usually leads to another pseudo-suicidal episode. Clara demonstrates that she is completely competent while speaking, yet her actions belie her conscious sanity. A good example occurs when she hosts Charles and Sam for a Sunday dinner, yet fails to provide any food to eat. Silver's script treats Clara's inconsistencies as humorous fodder, all but ignoring the deeper issues of the character and their effect on Charles and Susan. All this follows Beattie's book, and does provide comicality, but it doesn't move Charles' story forward, it just complicates matters. Charles tries to explain Clara's behavior to Susan this way: "I think one day she just decided to go nuts because it's easier that way. That way she can lie around in the bathtub, and say whatever she wants, and hit the Scotch whenever she feels like it, and just not do anything. Sorta tempting, isn't it?"

Gloria is excellent in the few scenes she has: doting on Charles, acting perfectly sane in a psychiatric ward, crying all dressed up in a bathtub. She looks great, especially in the silver silk evening dress in which she takes a bath in one scene and lies on her stomach in bed in another. She plays Clara with her charm on full

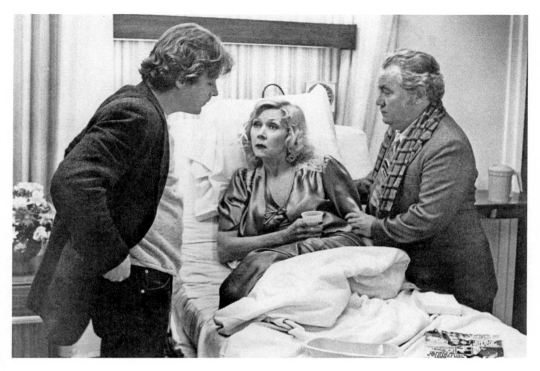

Chilly Scenes of Winter. Clara's (Gloria) wacky suicide attempts land her in a psychiatric ward, where she is visited by son Charles (John Heard) and husband Pete (Kenneth McMillan).

blast; the kiss she bestows on befuddled Sam is hilarious. Gloria also seems to have a real handle on the character, which is not so true for the audience, given its brevity. With fuller scripting and greater poignancy, the role could have been truly memorable instead of rather odd. Silver was thrilled that Gloria was available for the role; it's just a shame that she did not do more to take advantage of Gloria's talents.

The other cast members have similar issues with oddity. As Pete, Kenneth McMillan demonstrates an uncommon penchant for dancing at the hospital; as Sam, Peter Riegert spends a crucial scene tossing lit matches skyward into a hanging electrical light fixture — and then having to climb onto the dinner table and pour water on the fire he has started; as Charles' boss Mr. Patterson, Jerry Hardin asks for Charles' help dealing with his grown son's lack of social ability. The only character not specifically afflicted with oddness is Laura. Mary Beth Hurt portrays Laura as an enigma, even to herself. Laura loves her husband, but not enough to constantly remain with him. She

is disgusted by her own perfidy and the guilt she feels dooms her relationship with Charles, who genuinely loves her. Laura is not given enough screen time to steal the movie, but Mary Beth Hurt delivers an affecting performance as the woman who simply doesn't know what or who she wants strongly enough to make a choice. And while Laura is a largely unsympathetic character because she is seen as the woman driving Charles crazy with her romantic indecisiveness, Hurt's performance goes a long way to add dimension, depth and verisimilitude to their relationship.

Charles is adeptly played by John Heard, in 1979 an actor moving rapidly up the ladder toward Hollywood stardom. Heard never reached the top rungs, largely because his movies *Chilly Scenes of Winter*, *Heart Beat* (1980) and *Cutter's Way* (1981) failed to reach wide audiences, despite his excellence in them. Heard is the heart and soul of *Chilly Scenes of Winter*, perfectly embodying the stressful mix of dutiful son, lonely man, faithful friend and unrequited lover. He brings a true "everyman" quality to the role and never overplays his character. He is a sensitive actor who is just right as Charles Richardson.

The film was constructed by a team of young professionals eager to make their marks in cinema. Producers Mark Metcalf (who appears as Ox), Griffin Dunne (who appears as Doctor Mark) and Amy Robinson (whose part was eventually cut) were actors who longed to work behind the camera as well. They formed Triple Play Productions specifically to make this movie. Director Silver had made a splash helming *Hester Street* in 1975 and *Between the Lines* (which starred John Heard) in 1977. She later directed television's *Finnegan Begin Again* (1985) and the feature films *Crossing Delancey* (1988) and *Loverboy* (1989), but after the commercial failure of *Chilly Scenes of Winter* her opportunities became more infrequent and less exciting. Silver adapted Beattie's novel herself, so the strengths (and weaknesses) of the script are hers and hers alone. *Chilly Scenes of Winter* was shot on location in Salt Lake City, Utah, and at the Culver City Studios in California during a 45-day shooting schedule. The story's location was shifted to Utah because it was cheaper to film there than in the northeast, where the book is set, and that location accurately reflects the original title.

United Artists officials didn't like the title, referring to it as "cold and dreary" in discussions with Silver. So the producers began looking for one that would communicate Charles' obsession with Laura. They found "head over heels" in *Roget's Thesaurus* as an expression that reflected such obsession. The studio executives liked it, and it was adapted. But the public never warmed to the new title, probably because it is generic and meaningless. The film did poorly on its first go-round, and was shelved as a commercial failure, despite generally good notices. However, for once, that wasn't the end of the story. Three years later, the Classics division of United Artists took a second look at it and decided it deserved a second chance. With the blessing of the producers and director Silver they changed the title back to *Chilly Scenes of Winter* and constructed a new advertising campaign. One other change was made: the original ending was dropped.

Head Over Heels continued past the point where Charles goes running in the park. He returns home to find Laura ensconced in his kitchen, where she has made his favorite dessert. "She kept the keys!" he tells himself over and over again during the four-minute scene, and he is the happiest guy in the world. That happiness may or may not extend to Laura, who is ostensibly happy to be back with Charles but whose history suggests that this move might be more transient than Charles would prefer. Indeed, the prevailing feeling in Beattie's book — which also ends with a similar "happy" ending — is that the arrangement suits Laura for now, but that nothing should be considered permanent. In preparing the film for its reissue, Silver and the producers concluded that ending the film with Charles running off his frustration in the park was more realistic and effective, permitting Charles to move on with his life. United Artists officials agreed to the change and simply lopped off the final four minutes, beginning the end credits just as Charles gets his second wind.

Beattie's book was a literary success story, heralding a "new voice" in American literature, but although film companies were interested in the success it represented, no studio felt that a profitable film could evolve from it. That is how Triple Play Productions was able to grab the film rights for the relatively low sum of $30,000 ($2000 down, the rest to be paid upon completion of the picture). Scriptwriter Michael Weller was hired to write the script, but he had to back out when other projects he was completing ran beyond their deadlines. So Silver stepped in, convinced the producers that she was the right person to direct, and wrote the script herself, trying to remain faithful to the book. Silver expanded Laura's part (she doesn't appear until the final fourth of the novel), diminished the project's emphasis on personal loss, allowed Charles to "break the fourth wall" by speaking directly to the camera at times (and narrate at others), and fashioned the complex flashback structure that chronicles Charles' present and past simultaneously. For her part, Beattie wanted nothing to do with writing the screenplay, and was content to make a cameo appearance as a waitress in one scene. She was so pleased with the film that she happily participated in promoting the updated version when it was unexpectedly resuscitated in 1982. Again, the film did middling business, but it was more successful than it had been in its earlier incarnation and it had reportedly turned a profit by the time it disappeared for the second time.

Both times, critical reaction was mixed, although a few influential critics championed it. Andrew Sarris of *The Village Voice* called it "an unusually intelligent adaptation" of the novel. David Sterritt of the *Christian Science Monitor* wrote, "[It's] the most involving and intelligently filmed love story we've seen in ages...." Michael H. Seitz of *Progressive* was even more positive three years later, calling it one of the best films of the year: "The film's virtues are those often associated with the best European imports: intimacy, psychological subtlety, literate scripting. Yet in content and cultural context, this is a thoroughly American work: Its characters and idiom spring from the domestic experience of the past couple of decades." Michael Sragow of *Rolling Stone* called it one of his favorite films of 1982, "a brisk, cheerful comedy about ... depression."

Taking the other side was Rex Reed in the *New York Daily News*: "Joan Micklin Silver ... makes films that have a nice, casual feel for the way people think and move and feel, but they aren't movies. They're pages of a manuscript photographed by a camera.... The result is a nice, dull movie." Stephen Farber of *The New West* concurred: "*Head Over Heels* ... proves that little movies can be every bit as empty as colossal disaster epics." Vincent Canby of the *New York Times* opined, "*Head Over Heels* ... is a tantalizing movie, seeming to be on the verge of some revelation of profound feeling that, at long last, never comes." *Variety*'s critic decided that the film was too similar to Woody Allen's *Annie Hall* to recommend it, and other critics voiced the same complaint. Still other pundits enjoyed its individual acting accomplishments but felt that the film itself was disappointing.

Having allowed critics three years to revise their opinions, *Chilly Scenes of Winter* enjoyed nicer reviews than *Head Over Heels*. And over time, the film's reputation has grown. Danny Peary championed it in his book *Cult Movies 3*, writing, "*Chilly Scenes of Winter* is lovingly made, exceptionally written (the dialogue is terrific) and charmingly played by a talented ensemble." According to *The Entertainment Weekly Guide to the Greatest Movies Ever Made*, "This isn't so much a cerebral film

or a romantic comedy as it is a mature charmer about people using absurdity to keep loneliness from the door." Perhaps because it has never been released on DVD, the film now boasts an aura of unusual quality that it never achieved at the theaters where it played. Over the years it has gained a fervent group of followers who consider it to be among the finest romantic dramas of the 1970s, a film that, with quiet effectiveness, speaks volumes about the ways in which love generally affects everyone everywhere, but these ordinary characters in particular.

Gloria received generally positive notices, with many critics taking note of her for the first time in years. Lawrence O'Toole in *Macleans* cheered her "welcome, marvelous return to the screen," while Martin A. Jackson of the *East Side Express* remarked, "Grahame is wildly lipsticked and shockingly blonde, and she does her role with dash and excitement that is all but missing from the rest of the cast." Vincent Canby of the *New York Times* called her (and co-star Kenneth McMillan) "especially fine," and Stephen Farber of *The New West* noted, "Gloria Grahame makes a welcome comeback as Charles' flamboyantly suicidal mother, who in one choice scene invites Charles to dinner and then gleefully announces that there is nothing to eat." Had Gloria survived her second cancer ordeal, notices like these would certainly have encouraged further work and, most likely, better character parts. Gloria was pleased with the results, feeling that she fully understood the role of Clara, but was disappointed that the film was shelved so quickly. She died before it was re-released in 1982. Before she shed her mortal coil, however, Gloria was determined to stay busy and productive as an actress. And her next film garnered even better notices than this one.

Melvin and Howard (1980)

CREDITS Universal Pictures. *Directed by* Jonathan Demme. *Produced by* Art Linson and Don Phillips. *Associate Producer*: Terry Nelson. *Written by* Bo Goldman. *Director of Photography*: Tak Fujimoto. *Edited by* Craig McKay. *Casting by* Michael Chinich. *Music by* Bruce Longhorne. *Production Designer*: Toby Rafelson. *Art Director*: Richard Sawyer. *Set Decorations*: Bob Gould. *Sound*: David Ronne. *Associate*

Film Editor: Nancy Kanter. *Assistant Film Editor*: Karen Stern. *Supervising Sound Editor*: Lou Cerborino. *Sound Rerecording*: Thomas Fleischman. *Music Editor*: Rich Harrison. *Unit Production Manager*: Terry Nelson. *First Assistant Director*: Don Heitzer. *Second Assistant Directors*: Carol Jean Smetana and Wally Wallace. *Production Associate*: Sandy McLeod. *Camera Operator*: Gary Kibbe. *Assistant Cameramen*: Tony Palmieri and Eugene Earle. *Second Unit Director*: Evelyn Purcell. *Sound Editors*: Angelo Corrao, Peter C. Frank and Maurice Schell. *Makeup*: Dorothy Pearl. *Hair Stylist*: Toni [Toni-Ann] Walker. *Costume Supervisors*: Eddie Marks and Nancy McArdle. *Script Supervisor*: Paul Tinsley. *Titles and Optical Effects*: Computer Opticals, Inc. *Post Production Services by* Trans/Audio, Inc. *Transportation Captains*: Don Newton, Tom Garris and Vince Del Castillo. *Property Masters*: Doug Madison and Gary Fettis. *Key Grip*: Tom Ramsey. *Gaffer*: Mel Maxwell. *Special Effects*: Karl Miller. *Additional Casting by* Loril McKeehan. *Production Assistants*: Kay Hoff and Steve Meyers. *Assistant Sound Editors*: Bill Scharf, Cindy Kaplan, Joan Cameron and Marc S. Shaw. *Dolly Grip*: George Schrader. *Boom Operator*: John Schuyler. *Painter*: Bert Rotter. *Lead Man*: Don Krafft. *Best Boy*: Dave Morton. *Unit Publicist*: Susan Pile. *Stills*: Elliott Marks. *Second Grip*: Dwayne Redlin. *Construction Coordinator*: Walton Hatfield. *Men's Costumer*: Charles Velasco. *Grips*: Tom Lamont and Dick Sullivan. *Electricians*: Dusty Huber, Keith Pallant, Pat Thompson and Tony Grillo. *Craft Service*: Jesse Quiroz. *Location Projectionist*: Charles Howe. *Producer's Secretaries*: Dottie Morey and Patti Roberts. *Research*: Sherry Seeling. *Special Thanks to* Judge Keith Hayes, Calvin Aberle, Ron Bayless, Louis Bertini, Roger Dutson, Morgan Cavett, Jan Gregson, Charles House, Bessie Jackson, J. J. Johnson, Richard D. Keefe, Dan Keyes, Annemarie Korzeniowski and Geraldine Roberts. *Stunts*: Richard E. Butler, Jeannie Epper, Donna Garrett, Robert Herron, Alex Plasschaert, Walter Robles, Bob Terhune, Chuck Waters and Henry Wills. *Poster Artist*: John Alvin. *Additional Camera Operator*: Howard Block. *Assistant Camera*: Michael Simpson. *Drivers*: Chris Haynes and Roger Wooge.

SONGS: "Amazing Grace Used to Be Her Favorite Song," *performed by* Amazing Rhythm Aces, *courtesy of* CBS Records; "Downtown," *performed by* Crazy Horse, *courtesy of* Warner Bros. Records, Inc.; "Fortunate Son," *performed by* Creedence Clearwater Revival, *courtesy of* Fantasy Records; "Gone Dead Train," *performed by* Crazy Horse, *courtesy of* Warner Bros. Records, Inc.; "Hard Way to Go," *performed by* Daniel Dean Darst; "Hello Walls," *performed by* Faron Young, *courtesy of* Capitol Records; "It Came Upon a Midnight Clear," *performed by* Ray Conniff, *courtesy of* CBS Records; "Love Can't Hold a Ramblin' Man," *performed by* Daniel Dean Darst; "Motlow's Lament," *performed by* Elise Hudson;

"My Kingdom for a Car," *performed by* Phil Ochs, *courtesy of* A&M Records; "San Antonio Rose," *performed by* Bob Wills and His Texas Playboys, *courtesy of* MCA Records, Inc.; "Satisfaction (Can't Get No)," *performed by* the Rolling Stones, *courtesy of* ABKCO Records; "Shake the Ground," *performed by* the Bait Brothers; "She's About a Mover," *performed by* Sir Douglas Quintet, *courtesy of* Crazy Cajun Records; "Southern Belles," *performed by* Daniel Dean Darst; "Steel Guitar Rag," *performed by* Buddy Emmons, *courtesy of* Flying Fish Records; "Tennessee Stud," *performed by* Eddy Arnold, *courtesy of* RCA Records; "Windmills of Your Mind," *performed by* Henry Mancini and His Orchestra, *courtesy of* RCA Records; "Santa's Souped-Up Sleigh," *performed by* Paul Le Mat and Jason Robards; "Bye, Bye Blackbird," *performed by* Jason Robards and Paul Le Mat; "Rockwood Dairy Song," *performed by* Paul Le Mat. *Lenses and Panaflex Camera by* Panavision. Rated R. Technicolor. Matted Widescreen (1.85:1). Stereo Sound. 95 minutes. Released on September 19, 1980. Currently available on DVD. Previously available on VHS.

CAST *Melvin Dummar*, Paul Le Mat; *Howard Hughes*, Jason Robards; *Lynda Dummar*, Mary Steenburgen; *Jim Delgado*, Jack Kehoe; *Little Red*, Michael J. Pollard; *Bonnie Dummar*, Pamela Reed; *Judge Keith Hayes*, Dabney Coleman; *Attorney Freese*, John Glover; *Ventura*, Charles Napier; *Mrs. Melva Worth*, Charlene Holt; *Darcy Dummar*, Elizabeth Cheshire; *Wally "Mr. Love" Williams*, Robert Ridgely; *Chapel Owner*, Susan Peretz; *Mrs. Sisk*, Gloria Grahame; *Melvin's Lawyer*, Rick Lenz; *Clark Taylor*, Chip Taylor; *Attorney Maxwell*, Joseph Ragno; *Melvin's Cousin Fred*, Gary Goetzman; *Lucy*, Denise Galik; *Bus Depot Counterman*, Melvin E. Dummar; *First Go-Go Club Owner*, Gene Borkman; *Go-Go Dancers*, Lesley Margret Burton, Wendy Lee Couch, Marguerite Baierski, Janice King, Deborah Ann Klein and Theodora Thomas; *Joan "Rocky" Reese*, Elise Hudson; *Justice of the Peace*, Robert Wentz; *Hal*, Hal Marshall; *Woman Witness*, Naida Reynolds; *Man Witness*, Herbie Faye; *Milkman George*, Sonny Davis; *Milkman Ralph*, Brendan Kelly; *Milkman Pete*, Danny Tucker; *Patient Debbie*, Shirley Washington; *Patient Ronnie*, Cheryl Smith; *The Bait Brothers*, Jason Ball and Darrell Devlin; *Easy Street Announcer*, Danny Dark; *Easy Street Models*, Linda Cardoso, Melissa Prophet and Garrie Kelly; *Chief Thundercloud*, John Thundercloud; *Realty Agent*, Martine Beswick; *Sherry Dummar*, Melissa Williams; *Terry*, Antony Alda; *Gas Station Customer*, James Lyle Strong; *Reporters*, John M. Levin and Kathleen Sullivan; *Holdup Man*, Jack Verbois; *Lynda's Husband Bob*, Robert Reece; *Bailiff*, Charles Horden; *Third Attorney*, Joseph Walker, Jr.; *Second Go-Go Club Owner*, Joe Spinell; *Faron Dummar*, Matthew Hiers; *Bus Station Traveller*, Robert S. Holman; *Kissing Cowboy*, Tom Willett.

Gloria was involved with one final prestigious project, *Melvin and Howard*, before her career was cut short by terminal illness. The film chronicles the very important story of Melvin Dummar, who claimed that he had met and aided Howard Hughes in the Nevada desert, and then years later mysteriously received a will in which Dummar was granted one-sixteenth of the Hughes fortune. It is a lively, spirited picture which was critically acclaimed; it received three Academy Award nominations, winning two of them. Despite glowing reviews it was not a commercial hit, nor did it re-ignite a public mania regarding the notorious case, although it did accelerate Jonathan Demme's directorial career. Gloria's part in it is limited to remaining in the background of her scenes and delivering only a few words of dialogue. To be sure, her role of Mrs. Sisk, the mother of Mary Steenburgen's character, is ancillary. But Gloria seems nearly invisible in the picture, an odd fact considering her former stature in the industry.

Howard Hughes (Jason Robards) streaks across the Nevada desert on a motorcycle, jumping over a small pond, laughing with glee. He tries it again but this time hits the pond's edge and crashes to the ground. He cannot rise, and the credits roll as darkness falls. Melvin Dummar (Paul Le Mat) is driving home at night, staying awake by singing song lyrics he invented. Melvin pulls off the road to relieve himself and then hears moaning nearby. He finds Howard and assists him into his pick-up truck. Howard refuses medical attention and doesn't care for Melvin's singing. But cheerful Melvin forces Howard to learn the lyrics to a song he has written, "Santa's Souped-Up Sleigh," and then persuades him to sing a solo, "Bye, Bye Blackbird." Howard tells Melvin who he is but Melvin doesn't believe him. Melvin takes pity on the man he thinks is a bum, drives him into Las Vegas (to the Sands casino) and even gives him all the change he has. They say goodbye and Melvin drives back home to the tiny town of Gabbs, Nevada.

Melvin sneaks into bed as the morning begins and makes love to his wife Lynda (Mary Steenburgen) before going to sleep. Later, Lynda hears noises outside their tiny trailer and sees the pick-up truck and Melvin's motorcycle being repossessed. She and adolescent daughter Darcy (Elizabeth Cheshire) pack their things and leave while Melvin sleeps. Lynda and Darcy stay with a man for a few days but that doesn't work out, and Lynda is left with bruises. Darcy misses her father so Lynda tearfully sends her back to him on a bus. Melvin is thrilled to have Darcy return, and he determines to win Lynda back as well. Melvin travels to Reno where Lynda is dancing in a go-go bar. He tries to persuade her to come home but she refuses, gushing, "But I love to *dance!*" The commotion Melvin causes at the bar results in him being thrown out and Lynda losing her job. Later, at another strip club, Melvin serves Lynda with divorce papers. She throws a fit upon learning that the papers promise Darcy to Melvin, causing another commotion. Melvin is again thrown out and Lynda strips off her costume and quits.

Months later, Lynda calls Melvin from California, where she is living with her mother, Mrs. Sisk (Gloria Grahame). Lynda is pregnant with his child; Melvin still loves her and wants to remarry. In Las Vegas, accompanied by Darcy and Melvin's friend Little Red (Michael J. Pollard), Melvin and Lynda tie the knot again and stick around the wedding chapel as witnesses for other people's weddings to make some money. They honeymoon in the city, even taking time to gamble a little bit — under the watchful eye of Howard Hughes' man Ventura (Charles Napier). They move to Glendale, California, where Melvin gets a job as a milkman for the Rockwood Dairy. Still broke, Melvin has the idea to win money on the television show *Easy Street* and persuades Lynda to get on the show, where she tap dances and wins furniture, a piano and $15,007. The money serves as a down payment on a house, but Melvin cannot prevent himself from buying a Cadillac and a boat, causing Lynda, Darcy and their new baby, Faron, to leave him again, this time for good.

Melvin toils for the dairy but cannot get ahead. At the company Christmas party Melvin sings a satiric song about the company that emboldens the dairy's cashier, Bonnie (Pamela Reed), to declare her love for him. They quit immediately and take over a Salt Lake City, Utah, gas station formerly owned by her cousin. With Bonnie's two kids and a new business to run, Melvin is extremely busy, but money is still hard to find. He sees on the news

Melvin and Howard. In a scene that does not appear in the film, Mrs. Sisk (Gloria) cares for her pregnant daughter Lynda (Mary Steenburgen). Gloria hovers in the background of several scenes but has very little dialogue.

that Howard Hughes has died and reminds Bonnie that he had once met the man, although he still isn't sure it was actually him. Then one day a mysterious stranger, Ventura, drops off an envelope for Melvin at the gas station. It is Hughes' handwritten will. Melvin takes it to the Church of Jesus Christ of Latter-day Saints in Salt Lake City with the hope that it will be processed in due course. Sure enough, Bonnie receives a telephone call that Hughes has left $156 million to Melvin Dummar.

The announcement spawns a media circus and leads to a court date at the Clark County Courthouse in Las Vegas, where Hughes' "Mormon Will" case is heard by Judge Keith Hayes (Dabney Coleman). The court case is brief, dominated by the efforts of two attorneys — and the judge himself — to pressure Melvin to admit that the document is a forgery. Melvin sticks to his story about meeting Hughes and receiving the will at the gas station; he never wavers, answering every question bluntly and politely. In the courtroom he is silently sup-

ported by Bonnie, Lynda, Lynda's mother and Little Red. As the case winds down, his attorney tells Melvin that he's won, for there is no other will. Melvin knows better, saying he knows he'll never see any of the money. But he smiles and recalls Howard singing his song on the road to Las Vegas. Melvin takes Darcy and Faron for the summer and kisses Lynda one last time (Bonnie is nowhere to be seen). As he drives through the desert with his kids toward his Utah home, Melvin recalls Howard wanting to drive his beat-up pick-up truck. With reluctance, Melvin allows him to do so, then drifts off to sleep. Howard drives happily, lightly singing "Bye, Bye Blackbird" as the end credits begin to roll.

Melvin and Howard is a modern American fable based on a real story that may have actually happened. Nobody is truly sure except for the central figure involved, Melvin Dummar. Melvin has steadfastly maintained that in 1967 he found and helped a disheveled man who claimed he was Howard Hughes, and that in

1976, shortly after Hughes' death, Melvin received a will that named him a beneficiary of the vast Hughes estate. The so-called "Mormon Will" was disputed in Nevada in 1978 and found to be a forgery, despite expert witnesses who claimed it was Hughes' genuine handwriting. Of course, there were also expert witnesses who deemed it a forgery. Melvin and his second wife Bonnie have, from time to time since 1978, continued to pressure the Hughes estate to cut them in on Melvin's one-sixteenth share of the Hughes estate that the will promised him, but to no avail. This very public case for a high-stakes inheritance was big news during the late 1970s, and was thought to make great fodder for a movie.

Universal Pictures developed the project, assigning writer Bo Goldman to conduct research into the lives of the Dummars and offering the directing job to Mike Nichols. Goldman was dubious but spent three weeks with Melvin that changed his mind. Well into the process, Nichols backed out, evidently not being able to cast the film to his liking (he reportedly wanted Jack Nicholson for Melvin). Jonathan Demme was next offered the project; it immediately appealed to his instincts of what comprises Americana, and he signed on without hesitation. According to the movie's publicity packet, Demme insisted that the film did not try to convince anyone of Melvin's claim on the Hughes fortune. "It's a 'What if...?' What if Melvin was telling the truth? I believe it was true, but I'd never dream of trying to talk anyone into it." Time has not changed his opinion; on the DVD commentary, Demme remarks, "We believed in this encounter." Demme also believes the film's message shines through unabated by the legal wrangling that Melvin endures: "Life's experiences are what's important, not how much you get for them."

That refreshing sentiment is what sets *Melvin and Howard* above and beyond most contemporary movies. Other writers and directors would have focused their energies on the courtroom case, on delving into the financial motivations on both sides of the $156 million question. But that wasn't what attracted Goldman, Demme or the producers. One producer, Don Phillips, was present in Utah when Melvin had his first press conference after the Mormon Will was made public, and it was then that the idea for *Melvin and Howard* was born. Phillips relates, "What has always fascinated me about this story is the idea of one of the world's richest men and one of the poorest coming together on equal terms." This humanistic approach is why the movie works so well. Hughes is fabulously wealthy, but he's also a crazy old coot, riding recklessly around the desert without telling anybody where he has gone. Melvin can barely feed his family but he's a nice guy who gives away his last quarter to a man he thinks is worse off than himself. Hughes (according to the movie's fanciful script) keeps an eye on Melvin from afar, remembering his generosity, and upon his death, rewards him for it. Melvin certainly wants the money and dreams of buying lots of expensive toys, yet refuses to endorse a crass T-shirt design to capitalize upon his newfound fame. Even with $156 million in the balance, the story is focused on Melvin keeping the gas station open and keeping his distended family together.

Focusing the story on Melvin rather than Hughes completely alters its perspective, prompting viewers to consider Hughes differently, and no more importantly than Melvin. No details about Hughes are presented, keeping him a mysterious specter that Melvin may or may not have imagined. The film accepts Melvin's story at face value and presents it without sensationalism; indeed, their ride from the desert into Las Vegas is artfully mundane. On the other hand, nuances about Melvin's life abound, establishing his hard-working, faithful personality, yet also indicating his penchant for dreaming big and his lackadaisical management of money. It isn't Howard Hughes' story, it is Melvin Dummar's; they are two individuals with opposite lifestyles who happened to intersect one evening in the desert, sharing a little bit of themselves with the other, with the effect of eventually altering Melvin's life. The intersection itself is fascinating but the film is concerned more with the change of direction it causes in Melvin's destiny, and how Melvin confronts its challenges and heartaches, opportunities and rewards.

Despite the dramatic aspects of this story, it is almost all presented in the guise of a gentle, genial comedy. Anything that anybody does, even with the greatest sincerity, is a possibility for humor. Lynda dances at a go-go club along-side a woman wearing an absurd cast on her right arm. Melvin changes from a cowboy hat to a captain's hat when he is sitting in his boat, parked in his driveway, calling the Coast Guard for a weather report. The elderly witness at Melvin and Lynda's second wedding (Herbie Faye) nearly has a heart attack when Lynda kisses him too passionately after the service. Melvin and Darcy watch *Easy Street* on TV while wearing star-shaped sunglasses in the early morning. Reporters question anyone who ever had anything to do with Melvin after the will is announced; Melvin's former boss states that Melvin still owes the dairy $4500. Demme skillfully depicts the fact that humor can be found everywhere, in the most random acts that people perform. And it isn't the cruel, vulgar, sexual humor that is so popular today; these are laughs primed from the pump of ordinary human folly.

Melvin is an eternal optimist in a society where hope is usually squashed flat by the weight of universal greed, a general lack of compassion and special interests that do not hesitate to crush those who confront them. Melvin's simple pursuit of happiness with Lynda, and then again with Bonnie, against the backdrop of some of the United States' most iconographic centers of vulgar commercial intercourse (Reno and Las Vegas) is not only historically accurate but absolutely telling in its affectionate satire of modern America. If Frank Capra were a modern filmmaker, this story and its situations and settings would very likely appeal to his sense of what the common man must face in the modern world. Demme's vision is similar, but isn't as strident as some of Capra's films; this is not an indictment of society's neglect of the individual. It's a chiding reminder that, rich or poor, people are essentially the same, especially when they interact without society's interference, as Melvin and Howard are able to do out in the cold Nevada desert.

The script's main comedic target is Melvin's sincere but sometimes hare-brained pursuit of the American Dream. Lynda leaves Melvin the first time because, as hard as he works, he cannot prevent their car, their pick-up truck and his motorcycle from being repossessed. The fact that in their dire financial circumstances

Melvin even has a motorcycle is not discussed, only off-handedly presented. Later, Melvin delivers milk, ferociously determined to win the "Milkman of the Month" contest and a television for Lynda and the kids, even if it means allowing his boss to withdraw some of his pay for faulty equipment that Melvin did not break. Melvin's quest is the personification of the wholesome American work ethic; yet he can't get ahead because his manager is cheating him at every turn. Whatever he does simply isn't enough.

When Lynda wins the *Easy Street* prizes and for the first time begins to chart the family's path toward financial independence, Melvin nonetheless comes home with a Cadillac towing a boat! That is the last straw for Lynda, who grabs the kids and leaves him then and there. As she leaves she calls him "a loser," deeply wounding Melvin's pride, but she is really describing his predilection for buying things he cannot afford simply because he thinks he has to have them. This compromise of the American Dream is at the heart of Melvin's story, because it is now universal. Melvin finds his greatest success betting on long shots, entering Lynda on the *Easy Street* game show, and finding a will from Howard Hughes with his name on it. The final irony, of course, is that Hughes represents everything that Melvin wants — and yet Melvin is unaware that wealth and power have clearly not made Hughes a happy man. The truth is that the American Dream has always been an illusion.

Melvin and Howard was filmed on location in Nevada, California and Utah, places where the events (supposedly) occurred. One fact that had to be fudged concerned the game show. Melvin and Lynda had appeared on *Let's Make a Deal* (among other shows) and host Monty Hall had agreed to let the filmmakers use the show in the movie, but Hall changed his mind after reading the script and objecting to its adult situations. As a result, the crew had to imagine and create a set for a fictitious game show in a matter of weeks. *Easy Street* was put together as a mix of *The Gong Show* (which Demme admits "ripping off" in the DVD commentary; even the act "The Bait Brothers" first appeared there) and *The New Treasure Hunt*, both Chuck Barris productions popular in the 1970s. It was an inspired idea, for *Easy Street* and its host, Wally "Mr. Love" Williams (Robert Ridgely), perfectly embody the style of glitzy but empty and slightly tasteless shows that pass for entertainment in our modern era. Several critics also picked up this thread and complimented Demme on creating a show that sharply parodied silly shows that demonstrate how our national tastes have devolved.

Once Demme was involved with *Melvin and Howard*, he tried to persuade the studio to hire Roberts Blossom for the Hughes role, but, as Demme recounted, "they wanted an actor of recognized muscle to do it." So Jason Robards got the part, and received his third Academy Award nomination in five years for his performance. Robards had to endure more than two hours of makeup each day. The scene where Melvin initially finds Hughes was shot in one continuous take, so viewers would be convinced that nothing was omitted or edited out of the sequence that might be important later. And one directorial touch was so subtle that few people actually recognized it: The opening credits are partially written in cursive writing, and that cursive writing is modeled after samples of Hughes' handwriting.

Universal wanted Gary Busey as Melvin, but Demme hired Paul Le Mat, with whom he had worked on *Citizen's Band* (aka *Handle with Care*) three years previously. Le Mat is perfect for the part, beefy and rural, simple and sincere, conveying the essence of a man whose dreams always outstrip his ability to achieve them. On the set Le Mat was dedicated but sometimes overstepped his authority as a hired actor. Demme wanted to film the final flashback sequence twice; once in the truck, as it is shown in the movie, and again in Melvin's car with the kids, as Melvin imagines Hughes joining him in the present day. Le Mat refused to film the scene in the car, arguing that Melvin would only remember Hughes in the pick-up truck where the encounter took place. Le Mat had definite ideas of what his character would or would not do, and he would not compromise the character, even at the director's prodding. Demme was disappointed, though he acknowledged that the pick-up truck scene probably would have been the version chosen for the final film.

Mary Steenburgen reached stardom as Lynda in *Melvin and Howard*. It was just her third movie role, having co-starred in *Goin' South* (1978) and *Time After Time* (1979). She is adorable as Lynda, whether tap dancing rather awkwardly across the *Easy Street* stage or stonily informing Melvin that she has prepared bell peppers for dinner, knowing that he hates them. She is at her most appealing at odd moments, such as when Melvin storms a go-go stage to pull her off and take her home. "But I love to dance!" she insists and keeps boogying as Melvin is thrown out. Or when she agrees to let Melvin take the kids for the summer at the movie's conclusion, but asks him for a kiss before they leave. She also looks fantastic, even appearing nude in the scene where Lynda quits the second strip club. Steenburgen became a star via this picture, graduating to ever larger (if not as challenging) roles, and she has worked steadily ever since. She was nominated for a Best Supporting Actress Academy Award as Lynda Dummar and won, giving the film one of its two Oscars; the other was awarded to Bo Goldman's perceptive script. Steenburgen also won six other awards for this performance, including a National Society of Film Critics award and a Golden Globe.

Gloria Grahame essays the tiny, almost insignificant role of Mrs. Sisk, Lynda's mother. Mrs. Sisk is in the background when Lynda moves back home, fixing breakfast for her pregnant daughter. After Lynda's second wedding to Melvin, she is present when they watch *Easy Street*; in this scene, Gloria receives her one and only close-up. And Mrs. Sisk is present at the trial, the furthest of Melvin's family from the camera. According to Vincent Curcio's *Suicide Blonde*, "It was not at all an easy shoot for Gloria," but no further details are provided. Curcio claims that Gloria was to have a part in an extended courtroom scene, "but she was cut out, reportedly because of problems with Le Mat." Curcio's claims are not supported by Goldman's script, which has no such extended courtroom drama, nor by director Demme: "Ms. Grahame's part in the film was in no way truncated. Everything that appears in the script wound up in the film. It was a relatively small, but, we thought, a key and juicy role. I was overjoyed when Gloria agreed to grace the film with her presence. We had a blast working together. Ms. Grahame approached her work as she would have a leading part. Everybody concerned on both sides of the camera — most especially me — was humbled and thrilled by being on the same set as this great American actress. I treasure my memory of the experience."

Yet in an era of trendy character-driven "small" films that gained accolades and won Oscars— best represented by *Kramer vs. Kramer* and *Ordinary People*— *Melvin and Howard* had trouble finding theaters in which to play. Universal had encouraged the project and developed it, but they had no idea how to promote it and actually considered not releasing it at all. Demme showed it to friends and the good word spread; ultimately it opened the New York Film Festival in 1980, the first Universal picture to do so. The film found quick critical acclaim, if not a substantial audience.

Richard Schickel of *Time* loved it: "Anyone looking for the poetic truth about Dummar, and most especially about the sweetly dreaming life of the American underclass that produces characters like him, is advised to see this movie, which is just about as good as American films get: sly and funny and, in the end, terribly touching." Charles Michener of *Newsweek* concurred: "*Melvin and Howard* takes on the deeply satisfying glow of a classic folk tale, lovingly told." Gerald E. Forshey of *Christian Century* called the film "probably the worst-marketed good film in a decade." Michael Sragow of *Rolling Stone* opined, [Demme and Goldman] imbue it with a lyricism and humanity that overflow the big screen. And Demme and Goldman transcend blue-collar realism. They conceive Melvin's accidental meeting with Hughes as if it were a close encounter with a UFO." David Robinson of the *London Times* intimated it was his new favorite film: "It has qualities that belong to a very few works of art: a palpable, living spirit within; an unimpeachable, embracing benevolence, that leaves you afterwards happier and more hopeful." Perhaps Gene Shalit found the perfect epilogue in his *Ladies' Home Journal* review: "[Goldman and Demme] have done such an endearing job with this movie that if Howard Hughes had seen *Melvin and Howard* he might have put *them* in his will."

The film takes Melvin's account of his meeting with Hughes at face value and presents it without hyperbole. Whether it is true or not

is almost irrelevant, for the story is Melvin's, not Howard's. The Nevada court found that the will was a forgery, but never prosecuted Melvin for producing it. The presiding judge later confided to Demme that he was no longer positive that Melvin faked the will, as he felt during the trial. Evidence uncovered by former FBI agent Gary Magnesen and chronicled in his 2005 tome *The Investigation* sheds positive light on Melvin's account, though questions about the will itself still remain. The Dummars filed suit the following year against the Hughes estate, but the judge upheld the findings of the first court case and dismissed the new suit. Public opinion has always been divided; many people viewed Melvin as a greedy crackpot, while others have noted that the Hughes company, the Suma Corporation, stood to be dissolved if the will was found to be real, and therefore had every motivation to fight it, sparing no expense. The absolute truth will never be known, if, indeed, such truth even exists.

What does exist is a superb movie, one that begins with the now-mythic encounter between these two men and expands into a wonderfully crafted study of an often ignored segment of American society: regular people merely trying to live their ordinary lives. Its characters vibrate to the tensile oscillations of desires, dreams, disappointments and realities of modern life, all the while trying to sustain a pulse that keeps time with those of the people they love. This simple movie deftly illustrates how elusive the American Dream has become for everyone, from the usually broke Melvin to the insanely wealthy Hughes. Yet it also illustrates that those two men were essentially similar, and conveys a great satisfaction in that fact.

Melvin and Howard was, ultimately, a non-factor in Gloria's career. It did well but not exceedingly well, considering its acclaim, and she was essentially invisible in it. The title looked good on her résumé, but she neither received — nor deserved — any of the credit for it. Like *Chilly Scenes of Winter* it suffered distribution problems, and offered Gloria no tangible career benefit. She had great fun making it, but it did not lead her, as she had hoped, into other cutting edge film projects. So it was back to the horror genre she disliked for one final film. Although she was beginning to feel the effects of her cancer recurrence, Gloria never really considered the idea that *The Nesting* would be her final film. It was simply another job.

The Nesting (1981)

(aka *Phobia*; *Massacre Mansion*)

CREDITS The Nesting Company. *Distributed by* Feature Films and William Mishkin Pictures. *Produced and Directed by* Armand Weston. *Executive Producers*: Sam Lake and Robert Sumner. *Associate Producer-Production Manager*: Don Walters. *Screenplay by* Daria Price and Armand Weston. *Director of Photography*: J. [João] Fernandes. *Editor*: Jack Foster. *Original Music by* John Malken and George Kim Scholes. *Assistant Director*: Fred Berner. *Art Director*: John Lawless. *Scenic Designer*: Pat Mann. *Soundman*: Bill Meredith. *Special Effects*: Matt Vogel. *Costume Designer*: Alexis Blasini. *Makeup*: Lyzanne Goodson. *Special Makeup*: Richard Alonzo and Jay Pearlman. *Script Supervisor*: Clea Pricetti. *Assistant Camera*: Michael Duff. *Gaffer*: Frost Wilkinson. *Key Grip*: Doug Armstrong. *Second Electric*: Craig Nelson. *Grip*: Miles Strassner. *Loader*: David Frederick. *Best Boy*: Robert Steivers. *Stunt Coordinator*: Jery Hewitt. *Stunts*: Cliff Cudney, Jery Hewitt, Jake Plumstead and Tiffany Lynne. *Boom Operator*: Nicki Tzanis. *Assistant Art Director*: Fred Isola. *Props*: Will Scheck. *Production Secretary*: Pat Finnegan. *Second Unit Camera*: Michael Duff. *Second Assistant Director*: Philippe Rivier. *Assistant Scenic Director*: Paul Everett. *Assistant Special Effects*: Jeff Schecter and Bruce Martin. *Seamstress*: Edith Frederick. *Still Photographer*: Marco Nero. *Graphics*: Cheryl Amatuzzo. *Production Assistants*: Michelle Solatar, Gary Hill, Bob Rudis, Allison Hickey, Bruce Shell and Jill Lashley. *Bookkeeping*: Bondi Walters. *Assistant Editor*: Dave Frederick. *Location Coordinator*: Paul Giacobbe. *Publicist*: R. Allen Leider. *Legal*: Walter Gidali. *Music Mix*: Secret Sound. *Optical Effects*: Videart Opticals. *Camera Equipment*: Panavision. *Head Animal Trainer*: Brian McMillan. Rated R. Color. Matted Widescreen (1.85:1). Monaural Sound. 104 minutes. Released in May, 1981. Currently available on DVD. Previously available on VHS.

CAST *Lauren Cochran/Rose Henderson*, Robin Groves; *Mark Felton*, Christopher Loomis; *Daniel Griffith*, Michael David Lally; *Colonel LeBrun*, John Carradine; *Florinda Costello*, Gloria Grahame; *Frank Beasley*, Bill Rowley; *Abner Welles*, David Tabor; *Dr. Webb*, Patrick Farrelly; *Catherine Beasley*, Bobo Lewis; *Saphire*, June Berry; *Gwen*, Ann Varley; *Helga*, Cecile Liebman; *Leland LeBrun*, Ron Levine; *Young Abner*, Bruce Kronenberg; *Young Frank*, Jim Nixon; *Earl*, James Saxon; *Joseph the Butler*, Jeffrey McLaughlin; *G.I. # 1*, James Hayden; *G.I. # 2*, Jery Hewitt; *Sheriff*, Cliff Cudney; *Doctor*, Lee Steele.

Gloria Grahame's final feature film is an eerie ghost story regarding a young woman connected to spirits in an unusual, abandoned house. After *Mansion of the Doomed* Gloria had attempted to put horror roles behind her, but of the three feature films she made before *The Nesting*, one was barely exhibited at all and the other two, despite critical kudos, endured distribution problems and were not widely seen. Even with its Academy Award attention, *Melvin and Howard* was a box office disappointment—and it did little to further Gloria's career. Fearing that her time was limited, Gloria wanted to work constantly, so she accepted the role of a ghostly madam with a deep desire for vengeance. Since the movie was lensed on location in Irvington, New York, just north of New York City, it was a relatively easy shoot. And Gloria was assured that it would not be as trashy as either *Blood and Lace* or *Mama's Dirty Girls*. This despite a director, Armand Weston, who had directed only X-rated films before raising the money to enter the world of mainstream cinematic horror. Nonetheless, Gloria accepted the role and did the best she could.

The Nesting is not only the name of this movie, but also that of a book that appears in the opening shot. An office is surveyed, and the book is prominent on the desk. The office belongs to writer Lauren Cochran (Robin Groves), who has recently begun to fear leaving her New York City residence. Her therapist, Dr. Webb (Patrick Farrelly), diagnoses her anxiety as agoraphobia and suggests that she get away from the city. Her platonic boyfriend Mark Felton (Christopher Loomis) drives her to a small town called Dover Falls, where their car breaks down. They walk until they find a strange, octagonal Victorian-style house that seems to be abandoned. Mark is astonished that the house looks exactly like the one on the cover of her mystery novel *The Nesting*, but Lauren shrugs off the coincidence. She immediately decides to stay there to write, and does so once they locate the owners.

The house is rented to Lauren by Daniel Griffith (Michael David Lally); it belongs to his grandfather, Colonel LeBrun (John Carradine). When Daniel takes Lauren to meet the colonel, he has a paralytic stroke at the sight of her. Nevertheless, Lauren moves into the house. Handyman Frank Beasley (Bill Rowley) is a gruff alcoholic who doesn't like the new tenant but makes repairs to the place for her anyway. At night Lauren begins to have strange dreams, largely of a sexual nature. Lauren contacts Dr. Webb and persuades him to visit her at the house, which she starts to imagine is haunted. Lauren hears voices and music in the house but finds no explanation for them. The voices lead her up to the outside of the house's observatory, where she becomes so frightened she cannot move. Dr. Webb arrives and quickly climbs up to rescue her. Instead, she screams at the sight of a woman (who wasn't there moments before and quickly disappears) and Dr. Webb falls to his death.

Lauren refuses to leave the house and asks Daniel, a quantum physicist(!), to help her prove that the house is haunted. Frank makes some more repairs the following day, waking Lauren, and they have a fight. She apologizes and invites him inside to ask him about the house. Frank takes her invitation as a come-on and attacks her. Suddenly he is flung about the room by an unseen force; furniture flies at him from every direction. Frank is lifted in the air and then dropped by the force. Terrified, Frank runs out of the house. In his truck he sees a vision of dead young women, so he runs away through the trees. In a terrified state Frank wades into shallow Estes' Pond, where he gathers his breath. Suddenly, arms reach up from the dark water and pull him underneath. He is never seen again.

Having witnessed the force in action, Lauren tries to leave, but her agoraphobia recurs and she cannot. She hears more voices and music, leading her upstairs. She witnesses people fornicating, runs back to her own bed and hides. She is attacked there, seemingly by her own imagination. Meanwhile, Daniel discovers that the house was actually a notorious bordello during World War II. After the war, a nearby Army base closed and the business was abandoned. Daniel questions another local, Abner Welles (David Tobin), who reveals that Daniel's father was killed at the former bordello and insinuates that his mother was a prostitute there. Lauren gathers her courage and drives to Daniel's, but he is not at home. From there she calls Mark and asks him to come and get her; she is ready to leave. Upon learning that Daniel went to see Abner, she goes to find him. Abner

instantly dislikes Lauren and her questions. When she asks him about the house, he loses his temper and chases her away.

Lauren drives away, but Abner follows and tries ramming her car off the road with his own. He sees visions of a woman in the road which cause him to swerve into a ditch. Lauren checks on him and he attacks her again, yelling that he is going to kill her. She runs to a nearby farm and hides, but he finds her. She grabs a hand scythe and he grabs a pitchfork. As Abner is about to kill Lauren, the pitchfork is yanked out of his hands by an unseen force and flung across the barn. Lauren buries the scythe into his face and he collapses, dead. Lauren runs back to the octagonal house, crying hysterically. Lauren thinks she is becoming certifiably crazy, and the newly arrived Daniel doesn't disagree. They argue about it and he leaves.

Another erotic dream awakens Lauren, but this time Daniel is in it. When he checks on her the next day, she kisses him. Mark has not arrived, so Lauren asks Daniel to check on him. Lauren waits all day, but nothing happens. Then she finds a pile of photographs of the old bordello; the ghost of its madam, Florinda Costello (Gloria Grahame), appears and speaks to her. Florinda shows Lauren around the bordello, now clearly visible as it looked in the 1940s. Meanwhile, Colonel LeBrun also revives long enough to describe a tragic story about the bordello to Daniel. The colonel's son Leland (Ron Levine) had returned from the war and fallen for a prostitute named Rose. A baby was born. The colonel could not stand the idea of his son marrying a whore so he persuades three young local men to kidnap the baby. The men were Frank, Abner and another man. They lost their tempers and started killing everybody with rifles and shotguns. The murder rampage is shown in slow motion as Leland, other men who happened to be there for sex, and all of the girls are shot to death. Florinda tries to protect the baby and kills the third man with an axe, but the others overpower her and Abner beats her to death with a candlestick. The baby is brought to Colonel LeBrun, who gives it to a foundling home.

Upon finishing his story and admitting that he is not Daniel's real grandfather, the colonel dies. Lauren finally understands that she is Rose's baby, all grown up. Her mother Rose died on that terrible night along with everyone else. Lauren begs Florinda to reunite her with her mother, but that cannot be. The murders of Florinda and the girls have been avenged and the ghosts can now rest. Lauren refuses to leave without her mother; Florinda disappears and the house erupts in wind and flames all around Lauren. She is trapped, to be burned alive. But then Lauren conquers her fear, accepts her fate and the flames recede; they were never really there. She leaves the house calmly, ready to move on with her life.

The Nesting is a somewhat convoluted horror tale, especially concerning its complicated backstory involving the bordello and the LeBrun family ties. Like a great many supernatural mysteries, it loses punch once its mystery is explained. The film's concluding flashback sequence, narrated by Colonel LeBrun, depicts the murders in slow motion and grisly detail, but questions remain. Leland fights back and is killed, but why is it that the three men then shoot everybody else in sight? Nobody else is armed, or presents a threat to them. The story insinuates that bloodlust inflames them, resulting in the bloody massacre to follow, but that is not very believable. Surely the deaths and/or disappearances of the bordello staff, not to mention the men visiting the place, would be noticed by the neighbors. Even Colonel LeBrun should not be able to cover up such a massacre. But that is exactly what happened, according to the script. Thirty years later, the former bordello is simply part of local legend and the massacre remains unknown. This situation seems totally unbelievable, although it does provide strong motivation for the ghosts of Florinda and the girls to seek revenge through Leland's baby, who has now (unknowingly) returned to the scene of the crime.

Then there is the question of Daniel. Colonel LeBrun admits, at the film's climax, that Daniel is not his grandson, but this is obvious from the start, as Daniel has a different surname! Daniel is told that Leland's wife ran off with another man (and had Daniel) while Leland was still at war. But with the death of Leland at the bordello, the colonel evidently brought Daniel to stay with him. "You're the closest thing I had to a relative," the colonel tells Daniel. "That's why I wanted you to come home." The colonel's deathbed confession is certainly dramatic — especially when he realizes exactly who Lauren really is, and then dies in a paroxysm of fear — and it clears the way for romance between Daniel and Lauren. If Daniel were indeed the colonel's grandson, and Lauren is truly his granddaughter, then they would be brother and sister. By separating Daniel from the family somewhat, any hint of incest is averted and it also spares Daniel from the wrath of the bordello ghosts, as he is an innocent bystander.

Of course, Dr. Webb is an innocent bystander who dies as he tries to help Lauren come down from the roof. Lauren hears voices and music and climbs up to the windowed observatory at the top of the house. There, because rotten floor boards start to break beneath her, Lauren climbs *outside* onto the ledges around the observatory. Why not simply back up and run back down the stairs? Anyway, Lauren finds herself cowering on a ledge, trembling in fear, when the doctor arrives. Once he gets up to the observatory to help her, Lauren sees a "painted lady" cackling in delight (it isn't Florinda) and she starts screaming like a banshee. Why would the vision of a strange woman laughing cause Lauren fright? It is Lauren's screaming that frightens Dr. Webb so much that he falls and is impaled on a roof spike below. Daniel assures her that the doctor's death is not her fault, that it was an accident, but she and the audience know better. Apart from the frightening aspects of the doctor's death (this is a horror film, after all), the only other purpose it serves is to distract attention away from the otherwise obvious explanation of ghosts seeking revenge.

The film's most preposterous sequence involves Abner Welles. When Lauren visits Abner, it is already established that Abner is nuts, but that he knows something critical about the mystery. Her questions about the house raise Abner's suspicions so high that he actually chases Lauren out of his home, and then follows her in his station wagon, ramming her car and trying to drive it off the road. The car chase footage is poorly done, and rather unintentionally amusing when Abner runs over Florinda twice without even slowing down. After crashing, Abner pretends to be dead to lure Lauren close, bites her face (although in later scenes, no marks are visible), and then chases her on foot to a quiet nearby farm (where is everybody?); they're both yelling and screaming at the tops of their voices. A rather boring cat-and-mouse game commences before Abner finally corners Lauren with a pitchfork. As he moves in for the kill, it is yanked out of his hands (he sees a vision of Florinda, cackling with delight) and Lauren uses the diversion to bury her hand scythe in Abner's face. David Tabor's portrayal of Abner can kindly be described as florid; Abner seems certifiably insane as he's chasing Lauren and yelling that he is going to kill her. It isn't until the very end, during the flashback massacre, that his motivation in keeping Lauren permanently quiet becomes clear.

A similar situation involves Frank Beasley, the handyman who resents having to work on the house just because Lauren has moved into it. He attacks her in a sexual manner when she invites him to coffee. "Since when has your kind every wanted *my* company in for coffee?" he exclaims, grabbing her to forcibly kiss her. Then Florinda appears and Frank is thrown about the room by an unseen force as Lauren watches in horror. Frank runs away as fast as he can and finds himself, for no apparent reason, wading into Estes' Pond; the spirits of the men and women buried there drag him under the water to join them forever. It's an effective visual motif but makes little sense dramatically. Frank, like Abner, has kept his silence for thirty years, and has evidently become accustomed to working in and around the house where they massacred so many innocent people. Why haven't the ghosts been haunting him? Because the story posits that Lauren's presence is necessary (she is the baby they kidnapped) to allow the ghosts to wreak vengeance. "We've avenged our deaths through you," says Florinda to Lauren at the film's conclusion, neglecting to explain how Lauren had anything to do with Frank's death at the pond.

Other problems include minor story details. Lauren kills Abner at the farm and then runs all the way back to the octagonal house; how does she know where it is? She is supposed to be new to the area. There are shots of a typewriter that has missing keys and which leaves strange words on the page. Lauren attributes this to Frank but nothing more is ever made of it. There is not just one clichéd scene of a car

breaking down in the middle of nowhere, for no reason, but three! Apart from the story concerns that weaken the film's effectiveness, it is also somewhat amateurishly made. The car chase scene is pathetic compared to standard Hollywood chase sequences. The film is rather slow and sometimes so dark it is difficult to see what is happening. And apart from Robin Groves' portrayal of Lauren, the film's performances are less than adequate, especially from the male leads, Christopher Loomis and Michael David Lally. Even Gloria is unimpressive, but that is more a criticism of the part than her performance.

Gloria looks pretty nice as the brothel madam, Florinda Costello, in a dark, backless dress that suits her very well. She certainly does not have much to do, although she pops in from time to time to frighten Abner and Frank and guide Lauren toward an understanding of her destiny. Unfortunately the film is so dark that even when Gloria is onscreen, it is often difficult to see her clearly. Of course, that's one of the difficulties with ghosts; they are often hard to see. Gloria was very helpful to the crew, particularly in the car chase scene. She demonstrated how to stage the action backwards, standing up and walking backwards off the road as the car which has supposedly hit her backs away at a rapid pace. When projected backwards, the resulting footage looks convincingly like the car runs over poor Gloria. Fortunately Florinda's death scene is not as grisly as it could have been, for she is just offscreen as Abner beats her to death with a candlestick.

Not all of the movie is problematic. Lauren Cochran's mental state is quite effectively dramatized as she experiences the panic attacks that mark the onset of agoraphobia. Handheld point-of-view shots from her perspective in the city deftly demonstrate the anxiety she feels. A genuine spookiness pervades the early part of the story, beginning once Mark and Lauren find the house and notice that it looks exactly like the one on the cover of her book *The Nesting*. Indeed, the Victorian-style house is the film's most interesting element.

It is the Armour-Stiner Octagon House in Irvington-on-Hudson, New York, built in the 1860s on the principle that the rooms in an octagonal house had greater access to sunlight and handier accessibility than rooms in those of square design. After being in private hands for more than a century, the house, in rather poor condition, was sold to the National Trust for Historic Preservation and was named a National Historic Landmark in 1976. The house is thought to be the only remaining domed octagonal residence in the United States. It proved to be a bigger project to renovate than the Trust could handle, so in 1979 it was sold to architect Joseph Pell Lombardi, under whose ownership it remains today. Lombardi allowed the producers of *The Nesting* to film at the house in the summer of 1979, before he had made any renovations or repairs. The new owner wanted a visual record of the place in its then-current condition, warts and all, for historical purposes, and to compare many years later with the refurbished, rejuvenated house that would result from his many renovations. As soon as filming finished, Lombardi began his reconditioning process. He thinks the resulting film is "not a bad little movie," and one that definitely benefits from its unique setting.

Even in its relatively poor condition — which, of course, was exaggerated for the cameras — the house exudes a wonderful character of its own. From its initial appearance it is clear that this structure is key to the story. Its imposing height, large windows, spiky ironwork crenellations and wide, darkened porch richly convey the preternatural ambience the story demands. The producers were lucky to obtain permission to film there; it was a case of good timing that greatly enhanced their modestly budgeted fright flick.

The Nesting was the first and only mainstream motion picture written and directed by Armand Weston. He had previously made a few "revenge porn" titles such as *The Defiance of Good*, *Expose Me, Lovely* and *The Taking of Christina*. He made one more movie, a pornographic horror flick called *Blue Voodoo*, in 1984. Weston's earlier films had combined sex and violence in sensational fashion, so he thought he would try to make a mainstream movie that would be light on the sex but heavier on the violence. To his credit, *The Nesting* (which was originally titled *Phobia* until John Huston used that title for his 1980 horror film with Paul Michael Glaser) is not a gorefest, at least not until the Peckinpah-esque slow-motion massacre. Weston hired professional actors (Robin

Groves, Gloria Grahame, John Carradine) to carry the dramatic load (and to sell the picture) and genuinely tried to make the best film that he could. In the post–*Halloween* era of slasher flicks like *Friday the 13th* and *Mother's Day*, this movie is psychologically thoughtful rather than kill-crazy.

Even with the involvement of Gloria and Carradine, *The Nesting* was barely exhibited. *Variety* reviewed it in April, 1981: "[Weston demonstrates] a strong visual sense and narrative skill. Atmospheric film boasts solid special effects, but the musical score is trite library music.... Gloria Grahame unfortunately is wasted in a bit as the brothel madam and lead ghost." The film didn't play in New York for another year, where it crept into grindhouse theaters doubled with other cheaply made exploitation pictures. Bruce Williamson of *Playboy* sort of liked it, remarking that it was "Slick and grisly, carefully rigged to induce shock at regular intervals." *The Motion Picture Guide* didn't care for it: "Direction has a tendency to rely too much on standard 'gore' picture techniques. This almost destroys an interesting story which is a departure from the usual plots of horror flicks."

It was Gloria's final film. She went back to the stage and never had another opportunity to appear before a movie camera. On October 5, 1981, Gloria passed away in a New York City hospital, hours after being flown back from London where she had been rehearsing for a play. Although she was well aware during her final year that she was ill with cancer, Gloria was determined to live as fully as possible. She filled her time with movie roles, concluding with this one, while appearing in as many plays as she could. She denied being sick to prospective employers, her friends, her family, even herself. Gloria could have simply retired, disappeared from public view, rested and taken care of herself as her illness progressed. But that wasn't her way. Restless, edgy and certainly fearful, she distracted herself with work. Work that she loved. *The Nesting* represents her final film work, appearing after her death in most places where it played. Armand Weston honored Gloria in the end credits in this manner, concluding the cast list: "With the grateful participation of Gloria Grahame as Florinda Costello."

Feature-Length Made-for-Television Movies, Miniseries and Specials

Escape (1971)

CREDITS Paramount Television. *Originally telecast on* ABC-TV. *Directed by* John Llewellyn Moxey. *Produced by* Bruce Lansbury. *Associate Producer*: Robert Williams. *In Charge of Project Development*: Thomas L. Miller. *Written by* Paul Playdon. *Director of Photography*: Al Francis. *Film Editor*: John Loeffler. *Music by* Lalo Schifrin. *Music Supervisor*: Kenyon Hopkins. *Art Director*: Walter M. Jefferies. *Assistant Film Editor*: Steven C. Brown. *Supervising Music Editor*: Jack Hunsaker. *Supervising Sound Editor*: Douglas H. Grindstaff. *Post-Production Coordinator*: Carl Mahakian. *Unit Manager*: Wally Samson. *Assistant Director*: Ray DeCamp. *Set Decorators*: Richard Friedman and John Dwyer. *Men's Costumer*: Tom Costich. *Women's Costumer*: Pat Barto. *Stunt Coordinator*: Hal Needham. *Main Title Designed by* Phill Norman. *Special Photographic Effects*: Cinema Research. *Sound Mixer*: Glen Anderson. *Recorded by* Glen Glenn Sound. *Casting by* Jim Merrick. *Makeup Artist*: Lee Harman. *Hair Stylist*: Kathy Blondell. *Property Master*: Bob Anderson. *Special Effects*: Lee Vasque. *Camera Operator*: Owen Marsh. *Chevrolet Automobiles Furnished by* General Motors Corporation.

For Paramount Television: Supervising Art Director: Bill Ross. *Post-Production Supervisor*: Edward Milkis. *Casting Supervisor*: Mildred Gusse. *Executive Production Manager*: Ted Leonard. *Production Manager*: Sam Strangis. *Executive Vice-President in Charge of Production*: Douglas C. Cramer. Color. Flat (1.37:1). Monaural Sound. 73 minutes. Initially telecast on April 6, 1971. Not currently available on commercial home video.

CAST *Cameron Steele*, Christopher George; *Nicholas Slye*, Avery Schreiber; *Evelyn Harrison*, Gloria Grahame; *Susan Wilding*, Marlyn Mason; *Senator Lewis Harrison*, William Schallert; *Dr. Charles Walding*, John Vernon; *Dr. Henry Walding*, William Windom; *Gilbert*, Huntz Hall; *Dan*, Mark Tapscott; *Roger*, George Clifton; *Trudy*, Lucille Benson; *Vicki*, Lisa Moore; *Frank Carter*, Chuck Hicks; *Customer*, Ed Call; *Man on Phone*, Frank Jamus; *Designer*, Lester Fletcher; *Model*, Merriana Henriq; *Photographer*, Caroline Ross.

Gloria made just one movie during the 1960s but appeared in various television series almost a dozen times during that decade. She had learned to appreciate the opportunities that television offered, and she, like other stars in the film industry, noted with interest the sudden upswing of made-for-television movies that began in earnest in 1969. A few TV-movies were so popular and acclaimed (*My Sweet Charlie, Tribes, Duel*) that they subsequently received theatrical runs domestically and/or overseas. By the time Gloria agreed to appear in *Escape* in early 1971, such familiar motion picture heavyweights as Barbara Stanwyck, Melvyn Douglas, Stewart Granger, Edward G. Robinson, Gene Tierney, Laurence Olivier, Glenn Ford, Fred Astaire, Bing Crosby and Richard Widmark had already tested the new format. Many more would follow.

Approximately three-quarters of the TV-movies being made at the time were "stand-alone" entertainments—projects which were either specifically designed for television or were not considered strong, timely, dramatic or explicit enough to make it as feature films, and thus relegated to television broadcast. The other one-quarter were designed as pilots for prospective television series. Many of the early 1970s dramatic television series, from *San Francisco International Airport* and *Dan August* to *The Rookies* and *Charlie's Angels* were first tested in the ninety-minute or two-hour TV-movie format. Some TV-movies, like *Charlie's*

Angels, translated into standard series with little or no change. Others, like *The House on Green-apple Road*, which became *Dan August*, kept the basic premise but underwent complete cast changes before the series aired. Still others, such as *Escape*, were pilot films that never got to make the switch to serial television fare.

Escape artist Cameron Steele (Christopher George) is contacted to meet fugitive scientist Henry Walding (William Windom) at midnight at a warehouse. The scientist is a jittery man who tells Steele that he expects to be kidnapped and gives him $25,000 to find him when it happens. Sure enough, three thugs appear, kidnap the scientist and toss Steele into a nearby river, tied to a cement block. Being an escape artist, Steele escapes to live another day. This all happens before the opening credits.

Wilding is wanted for murder, having burned down a laboratory and killed his brother, Dr. Charles Walding, by doing so. Steele sends his right-hand man, investigator Nicholas Slye (Avery Schreiber), to interview Charles' widow Evelyn (Gloria Grahame), who is now married to a U.S. Senator. Evelyn is an art collector who takes offense at Slye's questions and sends him away. Steele focuses on Henry's daughter Susan (Marlyn Mason), now a fashion designer. The same thugs attempt to kidnap Susan, but Steele is able to prevent it. For Susan's safekeeping, Steele has her accompany him back to his apartment, which is located over a bar called the Crystal Ball.

Henry awakens to find himself face to face with his brother Charles (John Vernon), who is facially scarred but still very much alive. Charles has faithfully reproduced their former laboratory and now pressures Henry to provide the final step in their scientific quest to produce synthetic life. Henry refuses, reminding Charles that he destroyed the first laboratory just so Charles could not use the new synthetic life for his nefarious purposes. Charles confines his brother, certain that he can force Henry to reveal the secret. Meanwhile, Susan explains some of her father's scientific background to Steele and Slye, noting that the brothers disagreed about the progress their discovery was taking soon before the laboratory burned. Slye reveals that Evelyn's lucrative art collection is phony; that she has been privately selling the real works of art and jewelry almost as soon as she gets them from her husband, and that the husband is unaware of her activity.

While Steele tracks one of the kidnappers and Slye is called to an interview with Senator Harrison (William Schallert), Susan is tricked and kidnapped by the other thugs. Senator Harrison warns Slye to leave his wife alone. Steele is captured at Happyland, an amusement park where he had followed one of the kidnappers. Steele and Susan are reunited in a laboratory built beneath Happyland. Charles explains to them that the synthetic life that he wants to create will act like a virus when set loose, altering people's genetics and essentially allowing Charles to bend them to his will. Henry opposes Charles' plan to create a "scientific elite" to rule the world, but Charles plans to use Susan as leverage to force Henry to cooperate. Steele is strapped into a straitjacket and hung upside down in a locked cell. Susan's screams as she is mistreated persuade Henry to give his brother the secret he had once destroyed.

While Charles concludes the experiment, Steele escapes, frees Susan and Henry and laboriously leads them up to Happyland. The experiment works and Charles places the synthetic life inside a small metal canister. He and Steele confront each other before Charles and the organism escape into the amusement park. Steele follows close behind while Henry and Susan call the cops. Slye arrives with the police, and the park is evacuated while Charles is surrounded. Charles is cornered by Steele on a rollercoaster platform; Charles falls to his death. The canister falls toward the ground but Steele is able to grab it before it breaks open. Later, Slye tells Steele and Susan that Evelyn has confessed to financing Charles' laboratory by selling the artwork and jewelry. Susan provides Steele with an I.O.U. from her father for an extra $25,000 and then thanks him herself with a languorous kiss.

Escape was intended to sell the series concept of Cameron Steele utilizing his talents as an escape artist to find and release people wrongly imprisoned or held captive against their will. It is probably this limitation that doomed the concept as a continuing series, since most people never experience being illegally or criminally constrained. One can see how a number of one-hour stories could be developed from this idea, but only with a rather limited range that would become quite repetitive after a while. To combat this obvious limitation, the pilot introduces not only the political aspects that one might expect from such a story, but also a detour into science fiction.

The Walding brothers have discovered the secret to creating synthetic life. Henry foresees the moral and political dangers, which is why he burned down the original laboratory to destroy the first batch. Charles wants to use the synthetic life to control the collective will of the world and, in Henry's words, create a "scientific elite" to rule the new world. Very little scientific explanation is offered for this "synthetic life" discovery or its potential effect on the world's populace. Henry describes it as a virus that would spread like an epidemic, turning people into soulless automatons. This concept is certainly dramatic and explains why Charles works so diligently to recreate what his brother has destroyed. But with only a few lines of dialogue to establish the terrifying consequences to the outer world, the situation remains highly implausible and utterly unconvincing. This scientific mumbo-jumbo is easily the weakest aspect of the pilot and may have been the deciding factor in its rejection as a continuing series.

Another area of concern had to be the action sequences, which vary wildly in quality. For instance, the pre-credits fight between Steele and the three thugs in the warehouse is action-packed, but ridiculous because those are obviously empty cardboard boxes that they keep crashing into. What warehouse would stack rows of empty, sealed boxes? When Steele is dumped into the river a few moments later, the effect is far better. Genuine suspense mounts as Steele frees himself from the rope and cement that binds him. It is far too bright underwater at night to be realistic, but the photography is good and the scene works really well. The first big action sequence is when Steele, Henry and Susan are trapped on the rope in the elevator shaft. Just what a rope is doing hanging down into the elevator shaft is never quite explained, especially one that cannot support the weight of just three people for very long. And, of course, it breaks as Susan reaches the top of the shaft, causing Steele to

heroically rescue her. Way too much time is wasted in that elevator shaft, and that sequence is more solemn than suspenseful.

The second action sequence concludes the film, with Steele chasing Charles around the Happyland amusement park. It is silly — and perhaps intentionally ironic — to stage the chase for the deadly synthetic life canister in an amusement park, yet it is unusual and compelling, too. Here again, good photography and crisp editing make the sequence more effective than it should be. Having Steele (or his stuntman) grab onto two different rides as they speed by to help him catch up to Charles is a neat addition, one that reinforces his daredevil character and is visually exciting. Such action sequences as the series would require are often expensive, which may have been another factor in the network's decision not to pick up the show.

On the other hand the scenario is intriguing, with one brother returning from the (assumed) dead to resume his relationship and rivalry with the brother who caused his facial disfigurement and (assumed) death. The only person who can prevent Charles from forcing Henry to divulge his scientific secrets is Steele, the charming escape artist with a penchant for helping people in trouble. Toss in Henry's beautiful daughter who is unaware of the real situation, some political intrigue, an odd, potentially interesting sidekick, Nicholas Slye, and the basic structure is set. A series could have evolved from this, with Steele and Slye finding various people to help, especially if the writers developed the Steele and Slye characters and relationship as they created unusual cases for them to crack. But this was not to be.

Yet another reason why the series was not chosen may have been the availability of star Christopher George, who was an extremely busy actor at the time. In 1969 he had made the TV-movie *The Immortal*, like *Escape* a Paramount project with a science fiction slant that *had* been picked up by ABC for the 1970-71 season. *Escape* aired just three months after the fifteenth and final episode of *The Immortal* aired. In 1970, he had starred as police detective Dan August in *The House on Greenapple Road*, also for ABC-TV. The series went forward without him (with Burt Reynolds in the leading role) in 1970, as he had already committed to

The Immortal. Dan August lasted a full season of twenty-eight episodes. George continued to make TV-movies and feature films until his early death in 1983 from a heart attack.

Gloria Grahame has just one two-minute scene, which she plays with Avery Schreiber as Nicholas Slye. She portrays Evelyn Harrison, a Senator's wife seemingly consumed by her hobby of collecting artworks of all kinds from around the world. They meet in her salon, which is filled with statuary, a suit of armor, paintings and fancy, decorative *objets d'art.* Slye tries to interest her in a Rembrandt but she is aware that it burned in 1953. When he tries to ask her about Henry Walding, she chokes up about the death of her first husband and orders him to leave. Her grief seems genuine as she holds a portrait of her late husband Charles (John Vernon) and that segues right into the brief reintroduction scene between Henry and Charles, who has a disfigured face from the fire some two years earlier. That transition, linked by Charles Walding's face, before and after the fire, may be the most artistic and effective moment in the telefilm.

Until she displays her character's grief, Gloria is not very convincing in the role. She employs an affected, aristocratic manner of speech and tries to project a regal bearing in keeping with Evelyn Harrison's position as a Senator's wife. Unfortunately, her affectations are just that instead of the acting immersion she was attempting. The only time that Evelyn seems real is when she becomes upset at the mention of the man who (supposedly) killed her husband. The grief and anger that follow are much more convincing than anything that has come before. This is Gloria's only scene, although the character is important in the plot (she who finances Charles Walding's laboratory beneath Happyland). Just before Steele's final clinch with Susan, he tells her that Evelyn has confessed and that her father is now free of the murder charge that has haunted him for the past two years.

Gloria's part demanded little — although she should have put more effort into finding a realistic, convincing persona. She found that the filming moved faster than on traditional film sets, which suited her, and that the pay was decent. This motivated her to accept other TV-movie offers that came her way, regardless of the subject matter or the presumed prestige of the project. A job was a job, she reasoned.

Escape aired April 6, 1971, on ABC to respectable ratings. George was a popular draw and the guest stars, including Gloria, were designed to attract viewers. When a series failed to materialize, the telefilm quickly slipped into oblivion. It was rarely broadcast and has never been released on home video, it can be found on the private collector's market.

While Gloria fails to shine in the telefilm, *Escape* is an entertaining way to spend 90 minutes. The science is silly but that's natural for a plot that has a megalomaniac force his brother to reveal the secret to using a biological virus to conquer the world. The cast is engaging and the premise is intriguing. Just not intriguing enough, it was judged, to be developed into a regular series.

Black Noon (1971)

CREDITS Andrew J. Fenady Productions/Screen Gems Television. *Originally Telecast on* CBS Television. *Directed by* Bernard L. Kowalski. *Written and Produced by* Andrew J. Fenady. *Director of Photography:* Keith Smith. *Film Editor:* Dann Cahn. *Music by* George Duning. *Art Directors:* Ross Bellah and John Beckman. *Set Decorator:* William Stevens. *Makeup Supervision:* Ben Lane. *Special Effects:* Chuck Gaspar. *Properties:* Richard M. Rubin. *Assistant Director:* Floyd Joyer. *Casting Executive:* Renée Valente. *Music and Special Effects:* Sunset Editorial. *Opticals by* Photo Effex. *Gaffer:* Carl Boles. *Women's Costumes:* Andrea E. Weaver. Color. Flat (1.33:1). Monaural Sound. 74 minutes. Originally telecast on November 5, 1971, on CBS. Not currently available on commercial home video.

CAST *Reverend John Keyes,* Roy Thinnes; *Deliverance,* Yvette Mimieux; *Caleb Hobbs,* Ray Milland; *Bethia,* Gloria Grahame; *Lorna Keyes,* Lyn Loring; *Moon,* Henry Silva; *Joseph,* Hank Worden; *Jacob,* William Bryant; *Man in the Mirror,* Stan Barrett; *Towheads,* Joshua Bryant, Jennifer Bryan, Charles McCready and Leif Garrett; *Man,* Dan Cass; *Wife,* Suzan Sheppard; *Boy,* Bobby Eilbacher; *Ethan,* Buddy Foster.

Gloria's fourth project (and second made-for-television movie) of 1971 is an unusual project that assigns to an occult story a desolate western setting. An intriguing little horror movie, *Black Noon* builds its suspense gradually and then socks the audience with an unexpected

Black Noon. This unique publicity shot frames Gloria, Ray Milland and Yvette Mimieux amidst dozens of burning candles. It was an intriguing way to promote the telefilm's handling of devilish, bewitching themes.

twist at the end. Because it has never been re-leased commercially on home video, this TV-movie has gained a cult, almost legendary, rep-utation over the years and is highly sought by horror movie fans. And of the horror projects in which Gloria participated in the latter stages of her career, this is the classiest and most evocative — although Gloria has almost noth-ing to do in it, or with its sublime effectiveness.

A church burns to the ground as a beau-tiful woman in a long white dress (Yvette Mimieux), holding a cat, watches without emotion. After the opening credits, a man and woman are seen in the desert, helpless and alone. Their wagon is broken and the woman, Lorna Keyes (Lyn Loring), is burning with fever. Her husband, Reverend John Keyes (Roy Thinnes), is trying but he cannot help her. They are doomed to broil under the relentless sun. Then a wagon happens by with two men and a woman: Caleb Hobbs (Ray Milland), his friend Joseph (Hank Worden) and Caleb's mute

daughter Deliverance (Mimieux). They take the Keyeses into their town.

San Melas is an odd town to find in the western desert: Much of its construction style is Eastern and many of its residents dress in an Eastern manner. The town's leader, Caleb, ex-plains to John that it reminds the residents of the towns they left behind in Connecticut when they moved out west. There is no church, how-ever; it burned down recently, and its pastor died. John's tour is cut short by the arrival of Moon (Henry Silva), a black-garbed gunslinger who demands gold from Caleb (and receives it), leers at Deliverance and ropes elderly Joseph and drags him through the street just to remind everyone who has power. Trying to intercede, John gets the same treatment. John is later told that the town's gold mine has run dry and that nobody will stand up to Moon's bullying. John is encouraged to wait while Lorna recovers and asked to prepare a sermon for Sunday.

Lorna shows signs of improvement under

the care of Bethia (Gloria Grahame), Caleb Hobbs' housekeeper, but is still not well enough to travel. Lorna sees that Deliverance has made a favorable impression on her husband and is uncomfortable with that. Deliverance makes candles and is sculpting one with Lorna's likeness. John gives an energetic sermon outdoors for the townspeople; a crippled boy named Ethan (Buddy Foster) is inspired to walk a few steps. Caleb is thrilled that the reverend has had such a positive impact and asks him to consider staying, but John and Lorna are expected in another western town and are anxious to get going. Even so, John is tempted. Lorna is happy for John's success, but insists that they leave soon.

John has a dream of a man, shirtless and bloody, chasing him. He escapes the man and finds comfort in Deliverance's arms. He awakens. Lorna comforts him, then rises when she hears chanting in the yard. She sees children in masks performing a ritual; she goes outside and finds a dead owl where they were standing. She screams and collapses. John and Caleb find her in the morning but there is no evidence of a ritual. Lorna is put back to bed as Deliverance finishes detail on the candle with Lorna's likeness. The next day Caleb dismisses John's worries. John asks about Deliverance and is told that she has been mute since childhood. Joseph rides into town yelling that the mine has had a cave-in and a new vein of gold has been found. Now the town's fortunes will be reversed.

Lorna writes a letter and asks Bethia to send it for her. Somehow Deliverance receives the letter and she burns it. The church is being rebuilt, led by John. Then Moon arrives and everything stops. Caleb tells him about the gold and assures him that he will get his regular share. Moon doesn't care; he wants Deliverance. He kisses her roughly and announces that he's taking her with him. Nobody tries to stop him, even when he throws one of his guns in the dirt and dares them to. As Moon starts to ride away with Deliverance, John lifts the gun and shoots him in the back. The townspeople cannot believe it. Deliverance approaches him and utters the first words she has spoken since childhood: "Thank you."

John is in torment, having killed a man. The church reconstruction goes forward. Caleb consoles John and asks him to stay for another Sunday sermon, the first in the new church.

Lorna is not getting better. Bethia cares for her but one afternoon cuts off some of Lorna's hair while she is sleeping. The candle doll now has Lorna's hair and features. Deliverance presses the doll's head with her fingers and Lorna suddenly suffers splitting headaches. Lorna demands they leave but John is reluctant to do so. He has more dreams about the bloody man chasing him, and now the dream ends with him embracing Deliverance, with Moon watching. Unsure of his own mind, John finds Moon's grave. Deliverance interrupts him there and they kiss for the first time. Moon watches from behind a nearby tree. As much as John wants to stay, however, he knows he has to take Lorna and leave.

The next day, as the Keyeses are preparing to leave, Deliverance squeezes the candle doll and Lorna collapses. She is returned to bed. John tries to deliver the first sermon in the new church but cannot. He has broken the Commandments about which he was going to preach. As he tries to gather himself, the townspeople begin to laugh. Their laughter fills his ears and he cannot stand it. He runs to Lorna; the townspeople follow. Caleb explains to the befuddled, broken man of God that they changed the signposts in the desert to lure him to San Melas in time for the solar eclipse, occurring that very day. Moon laughs as Caleb relates how they needed a man who has fallen from grace. Deliverance, now calling herself Lilith (after a demon who forsook Adam in the Garden of Eden), drops the candle doll, thus killing Lorna. John finds himself hung upside down inside the burning church and realizes that the bloody man in his dreams was the former pastor, trying to warn him away from these devil worshippers and their ritual of immortalization. All of the townspeople crowd around outside as the sun is eclipsed. Chanting and cheering, some of them wear animal masks as the church, with John trapped inside, burns down to the ground yet again.

A station wagon breaks down in the desert; a man, woman and young boy don't know what to do. A passing pick-up truck stops and its three inhabitants—Caleb, Joseph and Deliverance—offer assistance. As the pick-up truck drives toward San Melas, the man sees a road sign for the town in the rear view mirror. The lower line reads "SALEM."

It's the twist ending that viewers remember about *Black Noon*. There are plenty of clues along the way, from the moment when Deliverance scares away a rattlesnake just by staring to the Eastern style of the town's construction; from the town's unusual name to the too-good-to-be-true healing at John's first sermon; from the half-seen children's ritual with the owl to Bethia's odd cutting of Lorna's hair. Anybody who doesn't expect something wild at the climax simply isn't paying enough attention; yet, even knowing a revelation is coming, the climactic sequence in the new church is still quite potent. Its wholesale, delighted blasphemy is unnerving and chilling, especially in a made-for-television production!

One reason the ruse works so effectively is the odd juxtaposition of occult and western elements. *Black Noon* is a fairly traditional western in many respects, with an atypical focus on a religious lead figure. That is uncommon enough to distract viewers from the story's real destination. The last thing one expects is *greater* emphasis on religious aspects, or, in this case, anti-religious aspects. But the early 1970s featured quite a few movies where the devil made somebody do it, in blockbusters such as *The Exorcist* and *The Omen* to lesser-known films with story structures and/or downbeat, shock endings similar to that of *Black Noon*. Films such as *The Devil's Rain* and *Race with the Devil* are comparable in tone, unsuspected conspiracy and/or dark, nihilistic conclusions. And, of course, *Rosemary's Baby* began the cycle, and remains the touchstone of the "devil worship" genre. Yet *Black Noon*, because so few people have seen it since its original telecast, because it predates many of the more notorious films, and because it is elegantly and efficiently staged, has grown in reputation while many of the later films have been forgotten.

Another asset is the town's strong cast of characters. Ray Milland is terrific as Caleb, a seemingly kind-hearted, caring and generous man who is utterly duplicitous. He makes all of the oddball elements of the town seem natural and insignificant. As Joseph, Hank Worden calls upon his long association with John Ford Westerns to establish his credibility. He's quite spry for his age, too; he's a delight to watch. And rarely has the radiant luminosity of Yvette Mimieux been so well presented. With her long hair flowing behind her, Mimieux's ethereal beauty is perfect for the role. There is absolutely no question that she can and eventually will steal John's affections from Lorna, especially if she doesn't try to do so. And Henry Silva is properly dastardly as Moon. He's a bit over the top, but that's what the role demands and Silva is a method actor.

Although she is present in most of the town scenes, Gloria has almost nothing to do. She is Bethia, evidently Caleb's housekeeper, and her only job is to tend to Lorna — and, by extension, all of the "guests" brought back to the town. While Caleb is extremely verbose, Bethia's longest line is "Excuse me, sir. It's your wife. She's asking for you." It's a thankless role, one that any actress could play without undue strain. But Gloria was trying to re-establish herself in Hollywood, and horror projects were hot at the time. It seemed like a smart move; even if her part were slight, it was a project sure to be noticed. Gloria was recruited by writer-producer Andrew J. Fenady, who had utilized her in a western role five years earlier in *Ride Beyond Vengeance*. Fenady remembered her when he cast *Black Noon* and was happy to add her prestigious name to the cast list. Star Roy Thinnes recalls that Gloria was rather stand-offish on the set, not the outgoing person he expected to find.

The film would have been even stronger with a better performance from Thinnes. A TV-movie veteran (most of them after *Black Noon*), Thinnes is fine as Reverend John Keyes in most scenes, but is somewhat lacking during one crucial sequence, the first sermon. As he faces the townspeople outdoors delivering his first sermon, Thinnes adopts some very distracting mannerisms. He uses a sing-song voice when reciting the "Blessed be the..." verses and actually hops up and down several times while making his moral points. As this is the sequence when young Ethan takes his first, faltering steps forward, evidently inspired by the pastor's oratory, Thinnes' physical antics undercut the believability of this scene. Following this, however, Thinnes hits his acting stride. His self-loathing after shooting Moon in the back is very believable and his utter disbelief at the climax is quite effective.

Another problem: the dream sequences that reveal to John a man, shirtless and bloody, who chases him into the embrace of Deliverance. Although the sequences are effective in that they are usually interpreted by the viewer incorrectly (that the man is trying to capture or harm John), they are also obviously cheaply made and ridiculous looking, staged on boring sets with lots of mist. And all of them are filmed in slow motion, which makes them even sillier. Dream sequences are always tough to stage inventively, but the look of these dreams seriously undermines their importance and significance to the story.

Despite the film's religion-related storyline it does not rely on Biblical history nor the history of the Salem witch trials to which it obviously refers, but rather invents its own. Fenady's script is quite clever in its use of the backwards town name and its obfuscation of the solar eclipse/church burning as its destination. The film's power lies in its consistency of concept and the malevolence of its conclusion. And if anyone had any questions about the effectiveness of the ritual, the film's modern-day coda reveals that Caleb, Joseph and Deliverance haven't aged at all over the following decades. Evidently San Melas is still operational, and it is not somewhere that a pious man should ever visit — especially during a solar eclipse event.

Black Noon premiered on CBS on November 5, 1971, almost a week after Halloween. CBS barely promoted the telecast, which was scheduled against the premiere of another horror-themed TV-movie, NBC's *A Howling in the Woods* with television favorite Barbara Eden. Neither program finished in the top 20 of that week. In the years since its initial telecast, however, *Black Noon*'s reputation has steadily grown. *TV Guide*'s listing refers to it as a "suspenseful Western allegory," but it was otherwise not widely reviewed. *Variety*'s critic didn't care for it, referring to the program and its ilk as "spooky, hokey escapism." In his book *Television Fright Films of the 1970s*, David Deal disagrees: "*Black Noon* was television's first occult western. It was also notable for its high level of entertainment value and for the fact that it is one of the few telefilms where Satanic evil comes out on top." Deal also calls the project a "highly recommended gem." The Internet Movie Database (*imdb.com*) also offers testimonials of several people who viewed the telefilm in 1971 and still recall its vivid atmosphere and shock ending. Some refer to it as the scariest movie they ever witnessed, noting that they were very young and impressionable when they saw it. Even so, it is remarkable that a little-seen TV-movie could retain such an impact nearly four decades after its original broadcast. Such is the power of a well-written and unexpected movie conclusion.

Gloria's participation in *Black Noon* is minimal, yet for the fans of her late-career horror work it remains a key title. It isn't sleazy or gory like *Blood and Lace* or *Mansion of the Doomed*, yet it is, in the eyes of many people, a great deal more effective than either of those exploitation pictures. While pedestrian in some respects, *Black Noon* is a first-rate demonstration that made-for-television entertainment need not be conventional and predictable. Its ending is wonderfully, disturbingly subversive; indeed, it is a wonder that network executives actually greenlighted such a project. Making it proved to Gloria that horror films did not have to be demeaning or disreputable; it helped her accept the significance that the horror genre would have during the remainder of her career.

The Girl on the Late, Late Show (1974)

CREDITS David Gerber Productions/Screen Gems Television/Columbia Pictures. *Originally Telecast on* NBC-TV. *Directed by* Gary Nelson. *Produced by* Christopher Morgan. *Executive Producer*: David Gerber. *Associate Producer-Writer*: Mark Rodgers. *Director of Photography*: Robert Morrison. *Film Editor*: Richard C. Meyer. *Music by* Richard Markowitz. *Art Directors*: Ross Bellah and Robert Purcell. *Casting*: Al Onorato. *Set Decorators*: Audrey Blasdel and John Franco, Jr. *Makeup Supervision*: Ben Lane. *Unit Production Manager*: Malcolm Harding. *Assistant Director*: John Anderson. *Casting Executive*: Renée Valente. *Music and Sound Effects*: Sunset Editorial. *Production Coordinator*: Louis H. Goldstein. *Filmed at the* Burbank Studios. Color. Flat (1.33:1). 73 minutes. Initially telecast on April 1, 1974. Not currently available on commercial home video.

CAST *William Martin*, Don Murray; *Frank J. Allen*, Bert Convy; *Lorraine*, Yvonne De Carlo; *Carolyn Parker*, Gloria Grahame; *Johnny Leverett*, Van Johnson; *Inspector De Biese*, Ralph Meeker; *Norman Wilder*, Cameron Mitchell; *The Librarian*, Mary Ann Mobley; *Lieutenant Scott*, Joe Santos; *Paula*, Laraine Stephens; *Bruno Walters*, John Ireland; *John Pahl-*

man, Walter Pidgeon; *Inspector Feldman*, Felice Orlandi; *Patricia Clauson*, Sherry Jackson; *Cat Psychiatrist*, George Fischbeck; *Galatin*, Dan Tobin; *Studio Guard*, Frankie Darro; *Personnel Director*, Lew Horn; *Page in Hotel*, William Benedict; *Butler*, Karl Bruck; *Prideaux*, Burr Smidt; *Janet*, Candice Rialson; *Priest*, Julio Medina; *Jack*, Peter Colt.

Gloria's third and final made-for-television movie may be the best of the trio, and is one that prominently features highlights of Gloria's past career at Columbia Studios. Not only does Gloria portray the title character, but excerpts from three of her better films, *In a Lonely Place, The Big Heat* and *Human Desire*, are used to illustrate her character's former stardom. Gloria couldn't have wished for a better recitation of her career at a time when she was trying to reestablish herself. Besides providing visual reminders of Gloria's former glory, the telefilm also describes her character in glowing terms that accurately apply to Gloria in her heyday and easily transfer from that character to the actress enacting her. Because Columbia helped finance the project, Gloria's past triumphs were made available for dramatic impact. It's as if the character were written just for her, which, once they signed Gloria for the part, is exactly the case.

TV producer William Martin (Don Murray) is always looking for a new subject to feature on his early morning talk show. He notes that three of the five movies being shown the following week on his network's late, late show happen to feature actress Carolyn Parker, who disappeared at the height of her fame in 1954. He determines to fly to California, find Carolyn and interview her on his show the same week her movies are showing.

Martin starts at Pacific General studios, where Carolyn made the seven movies that comprised her career. He is welcomed by studio boss Norman Wilder (Cameron Mitchell) and given free run of the place. The talent file for Carolyn is missing and no leads are forthcoming. Martin calls her agent, Tom Prideaux (Burr Smidt), who mysteriously says, "For God's sake!" and hangs up. When Martin visits the agent's office that night, he is assaulted by a man rushing out, and discovers that Prideaux has been murdered. Martin describes the killer to Lt. Scott (Joe Santos) of the Los Angeles police. Next he visits former producer John Pahl-

man (Walter Pidgeon), who confirms that he cancelled Carolyn's final film, *Bright Memory*, in the midst of production because of clashes with its director, Norman Wilder. The only remaining footage is in a bank vault; Pahlman agrees to arrange for Martin to see it. Driving up the coast after the meeting, Martin is followed by a blue pick-up truck that tries to force him off the road. Now he has proof that someone is trying to kill him, and he believes it has something to do with inquiries into the whereabouts of Carolyn Parker.

Martin arranges to screen the footage from *Bright Memory* with Lt. Scott. It reveals nothing about Carolyn, but in footage of the other actors, Martin spies her agent's killer, and Lt. Scott sets about identifying the man. Next, Martin interviews Johnny Leverett (Van Johnson), the actor who co-starred in *Bright Memory*. Leverett recalls Carolyn with nostalgia. "She was a girl you'd see in a polo coat at a football game. Talk to her for five minutes and lose her in the crowd, but remember for the rest of your life." Leverett admits that he accompanied Carolyn to San Francisco for a weekend, but is adamant that no hanky panky took place. Lt. Scott identifies the agent's killer as a former stuntman named Bruno Walters (John Ireland). Martin visits Carolyn's former mansion, which is large, somewhat decrepit—and empty. Martin learns that the daughter of Carolyn's former roommate is in the area, dancing at a topless bar called "The Action." Martin's interview with Patricia Clauson (Sherry Jackson) lasts late into the night, at her place. The next morning he discovers that Patricia was thrown off of her balcony soon after he left her.

Martin now believes a murder occurred in 1954 that was never discovered, and that Bruno Walters is trying to keep the mystery covered. He flies to San Francisco where he learns that Carolyn spent two weekends there before she and her roommate Sandra Clauson disappeared. Further research reveals that a Mary Williams sought treatment for assault at a local hospital during the second weekend; Mary Williams was Carolyn Parker's real name. Martin finds Sandra Clauson's grave and arranges for the body to be exhumed, figuring that Carolyn is actually in the grave. There *is* no corpse in the casket. An anonymous call to Martin demands $5000 for information about

Carolyn. He agrees, and a stakeout is established. The caller is aware of it, and demands that Martin lose the police tail. He does, only to find Walters waiting for him. Walters chases Martin up a circular tower ramp to the top, where they fight. Walters goes over the guard rail and plunges to the ground below.

In the hospital receiving his last rites, Walters confesses that in 1954 Carolyn was romantically pursued by Norman Wilder, all the way to San Francisco and back. When she tried to sneak away from him at her home, Wilder went berserk and ran her down with his car. Only it wasn't Carolyn he killed; it was her roommate Sandra. Carolyn was hiding from Wilder in the bushes nearby, and she witnessed her friend's death. Wilder had Bruno Walters and Tom Prideaux dump the body in the ocean, and then placed the distraught Carolyn in a Mexican hospital for two years; that was followed by years of institutionalization for Carolyn, who has never quite recovered. After confessing, Walters dies and Lt. Scott arrests Wilder.

Having solved most of the mystery, Martin returns to Carolyn's mansion and finds a woman (Gloria Grahame) sitting alone in a room, watching a small portable television. She is silently crying, watching herself on the late show when she was twenty years younger. She looks up at Martin and very sadly asks, "Who were you expecting to find? Carolyn Parker?" She turns back to the television, no longer aware of the visitor. Martin walks away without saying a word and the end credits roll.

The Girl on the Late, Late Show is a nostalgic but convoluted mystery. As long as it remains in Hollywood, the mystery is on firm ground, offering an engrossing glimpse of Tinseltown from the inside. Its character types are familiar but as played by such veterans as Cameron Mitchell, Yvonne De Carlo, Walter Pidgeon and Van Johnson they are perfectly convincing. The police angles, too, are solid, although the investigating officer Lt. Scott (Joe Santos) rather foolishly confides every scrap of information to Martin, who ought to be his lead suspect. Where the story veers into some confusion is in San Francisco, when Martin connects the disappearance of Carolyn to the similar disappearance of her roommate Sandra. Only a few lines of dialogue are provided to prove the connection and it seems an awfully

long jump, especially given that the dates in question are twenty years old. Clearer extrapolation of these matters would have benefitted the story. The telefilm's other fault, which is a familiar one to mysteries densely packed with information and suspects, is the too-convenient confession. This one occurs when ex-stuntman Walters falls from the circular tower and miraculously survives until he can explain what really happened to Carolyn. Even though he's been given his last rites, Walters is chipper enough to spell everything out for Martin and the cops, even mimicking his high-pitched "old woman" voice that fooled Martin into losing his police tail during the stakeout. It is not until after he confesses everything that he suddenly dies.

Two other elements deserve mention, partly because they are thematically related — and diametrically opposed. The first is ex-producer John Pahlman's (Walter Pidgeon) attitude regarding the "new" Hollywood. When Martin first meets Pahlman at the producer's palatial estate, the elderly former executive forcefully denounces modern Hollywood, and specifically the practice of having actresses disrobe onscreen. Pahlman's disgust for the screen's new permissiveness is palpable, undoubtedly reflecting similar feelings held by older, conservative viewers who still yearn for the type of old-fashioned entertainment represented by stars such as Pidgeon and Van Johnson. Pahlman's feelings also reflect the nostalgic tone of the story, as Martin tries to recapture some of the screen's former glory in the person of the missing Carolyn.

The second element flies right in the face of such nostalgia. Sandra's daughter Patricia (Sherry Jackson) is a dancer at a topless bar and Martin interviews her there. Pat is shown dancing in all her glory, with just her arms covering her bare breasts, sometimes turning her back to the audience at opportune moments so her arms can swing freely. Not only does Martin interview her, he takes her home even though he has a serious girlfriend, Paula (Laraine Stephens), worrying about him in New York. This is a very risqué scene for television in 1974, with Patricia very attractively representing the new permissiveness that Pahlman deplores. The film is showing both aspects of Hollywood: the old-style glamour and good taste symbolized by Pahlman and his ethos, and the modern, let-

The Girl on the Late, Late Show. This publicity shot presents the cast: back row, left to right: Ralph Meeker, Don Murray; middle row: Joe Santos, Van Johnson, Cameron Mitchell; front row: Yvonne de Carlo, Gloria Grahame, Laraine Stephens.

it-all-hang-out honesty of Patricia, who is not at all ashamed of dancing topless at "The Action." Both elements exist and thrive side by side in the cultural chaos that is Hollywood, and the film embraces that dichotomy.

The murders that follow Martin as he searches for Carolyn are important to the structure of the mystery but not integral to the real story being told. Carolyn's disappearance is the literal mystery and a symbolic one as well. When Martin begins his search for her, he isn't aware that she is missing, and has been for the past two decades. What could have happened to her? How can a big star simply disappear at the height of her fame and then gradually be forgotten? How did Norman Wilder get away with killing Sandra and ruining Carolyn's life for so long? The film indirectly indicts Hollywood for these transgressions, for Carolyn's film career is directly involved in her fate. But the film also presents Martin's search for the truth as a noble enterprise, and indicates that whether or not she is found, Carolyn will always exist: through her films, Carolyn's radiance will always glow brightly.

Gloria Grahame is perfectly cast as Carolyn Palmer, the famous film actress whose career ended quite abruptly. The parallels between Gloria and Carolyn are significant, yet not precise. Carolyn suddenly disappears amidst the cancellation of her latest movie and, in due time, is forgotten. Gloria's film career stalled after 1956, partly because she wanted to spend time with her newborn daughter Marianna (Paulette). Unlike Carolyn, Gloria's name publicly resurfaced a few years later when she notoriously married the son of a former husband (her stepson Tony Ray). Also, Gloria had made the effort to remain somewhat familiar to audiences through TV guest shots and stage plays. Despite those efforts, however, it is certain that Gloria's appearance in this telefilm was regarded by many viewers as a comeback endeavor with more than a spooky resemblance to that of the character she was portraying. Even if the parallels were not exact, Gloria's casting fit the parameters of the character to a tee.

Columbia produced *The Girl on the Late, Late Show* and therefore was able to dip into its vaults to provide footage from Gloria's earlier movies to showcase the acting prowess of Carolyn Parker. Strangely, the brief clips chosen from *The Big Heat* and *Human Desire* are unexceptional in highlighting Gloria's brilliance in those films. What those clips do establish is that Carolyn was a big star of her time, sharing the screen with legends like Broderick Crawford, Glenn Ford, and, in the *Bright Memory* clip invented for this telefilm, Johnny Leverett (Van Johnson). Columbia's other pictures with Gloria, *Prisoners of the Casbah* and *The Glass Wall*, were not utilized. However, two clips are shown from *In a Lonely Place* and they high-

light Gloria's acting opposite Humphrey Bogart. As Norman Wilder is being arrested, he tells Martin that that film, which is being shown on television that very night, is "the best movie I ever made."

Carolyn Parker is notable because she is the lynchpin to the film's mystery. Gloria had not been a film's centerpiece character since *Prisoners of the Casbah* in 1953, and, with the possible exception of 1974's *Mama's Dirty Girls*, she never would be again. Carolyn is not the main character in this telefilm but she is its key. Everything revolves around Carolyn's film career, her disappearance, her suspected murder and her eventual reappearance. It was, indeed, a perfect part for Gloria, who reveled in the high regard she received from the veteran cast. (She had worked with several of them in the past: Walter Pidgeon, Cameron Mitchell, and old friend John Ireland.) Moreover, it was a part that was designed to draw attention to her. In its synopsis of the telefilm's first airing, *TV Guide* noted, "Gloria Grahame is featured in this 1974 TV-movie as the young star who vanished mysteriously at the height of her career." Finally, the job paid very well, and Gloria didn't actually have to do much at all. Apart from the vintage footage that Columbia provided, Gloria filmed a brief flashback scene for *Bright Memory* with Van Johnson, a couple of even briefer flashback shots with Cameron Mitchell and the memorable final scene with Don Murray. The only quibble she had was that her character's name was misidentified in the opening credits as "Carolyn Porter."

The Girl on the Late, Late Show was more than an ordinary telefilm; it was also a pilot, the second in which Gloria had appeared, for a proposed series centering on TV show producer William Martin, played by Don Murray. Despite a lack of limitations on the subjects that could be covered by a show about a television producer, the pilot was considered to be to flimsy — and too expensive — to work as a series. *Variety* opined that it "wasn't much of a movie and was even less as a pilot." Sensing that the format each week would involve big name guest stars that it would have to pay in accordance with their stature in the industry, NBC passed on the project. The pilot was then unceremoniously broadcast on April Fool's Day without advertising as the first half of a double feature; the second half was *Honky Tonk*, a lighthearted reimagining of the 1941 Clark Gable–Lana Turner western with Richard Crenna and Margot Kidder as their replacements.

Unsurprisingly, the film was largely ignored. Despite the way in which it was so offhandedly presented to the public, and the fact that it has never been commercially released on home video, it has never slipped into oblivion. In their book *Hollywood on Hollywood*, James Robert Parish, Michael R. Pitts and Gregory William Mank describe it thusly: "It received little notice, which is a shame since the film has an outstanding cast of veterans and a rather captivating story premise." Assuming the film finally finds its way onto DVD, other viewers will undoubtedly agree with that assessment. Besides its other rewards, it offers glimpses of Gloria Grahame in her prime and serves as a fictional recap of the aftereffect of a star such as Gloria passing brightly, dazzlingly overhead before disappearing into the ethereal cosmos.

Rich Man, Poor Man (1976)

(aka *Rich Man, Poor Man Book I*)

CREDITS Harve Bennett Productions/Universal Television. *Originally Telecast on* ABC-TV. *Directed by* David Greene (four parts) and Boris Sagal (four parts). *Produced by* Jon Epstein. *Executive Producer*: Harve Bennett. *Teleplay by* Dean Reisner. *Based on the Novel by* Irwin Shaw. *Directors of Photography*: Howard Schwartz and Russell L. Metty. *Film Editors*: Douglas Stewart and Richard Bracken. *Music Score*: Alex North. *Art Directors*: John E. Chilberg II and William M. Hiney. *Sound*: James F. Rogers. *Set Decorations*: Joseph J. Stone. *Titles and Optical Effects*: Universal Title. *Main Title Design by* Wayne Fitzgerald. *Unit Manager*: Ben Bishop. *Assistant Directors*: Ralph Sariego, Thomas Blank and Hap Weyman. *Costumes by* Charles Waldo. *Editorial Supervision*: Richard Belding. *Music Supervision*: Hal Mooney. *Excerpts from One Note of Triumph used through the courtesy of* Norman Corwin. Technicolor. Flat (1.33:1). Monaural Sound. Approximately 540 minutes. Initially telecast on February 1, 2, 9, 16, 23 and March 1, 8 and 15 of 1976. Currently available on DVD. Previously available on VHS.

CAST *Rudy Jordache*, Peter Strauss; *Tom Jordache*, Nick Nolte; *Julie Prescott*, Susan Blakely; *Bayard Nichols*, Steve Allen; *Axel Jordache*, Edward Asner; *Willie Abbott*, Bill Bixby; *Al Fanducci*, Dick Butkus; *Virginia Calderwood*, Kim Darby; *Colonel Deiner*, Andrew Duggan; *Arnold Simms*, Mike Evans; *Smitty*, Norman Fell; *Clothilde*, Fionnuala Flanagan; *Linda Quales*, Lynda Day George; *Sue Prescott*, Gloria Grahame; *Sid Gossett*, Murray Hamilton; *Roy Dwyer*, Herbert Jefferson, Jr.; *Marsh Goodwin*, Van Johnson; *Kate*, Kay Lenz; *Joey Quales*, George Maharis; *Irene Goodwin*, Dorothy Malone; *Mary Jordache*, Dorothy McGuire; *Brad Knight*, Tim McIntire; *Duncan Calderwood*, Ray Milland; *Bill Denton*, Lawrence Pressman; *Teddy Boylan*, Robert Reed; *Teresa Santoro*, Talia Shire; *Richards*, Dick Sargent; *Arthur Falconetti*, William Smith; *Asher Berg*, Craig Stevens; *Claude Tinker*, Dennis Dugan; *Mr. Tinker*, Frank Aletter; *Walters*, Nicholas Hammond; *Miss Lenaut*, Josette Banzet; *Miss Erdlatz*, Aneta Corsaut; *Buddy Westerlake*, Mike Baird; *Talbott Hughes*, James Ingersoll; *May*, Elisabeth Brooks; *Martin*, Martin Ash; *Postman*, Bernie Kuby; *Augie Meadows*, Julius Harris; *Harold Jordache*, Bo Brundin; *Elsa Jordache*, Lieux Dressler; *Jay Ledbetter*, Ben Archibek; *Calderwood's Butler*, Bryan O'Byrne; *Jack*, John Finnegan; *Mary Jane*, Taaffe O'Connell; *Nichols' Secretary*, Mary Angela; *Joe Kuntz*, Sandy Ward; *Dave*, Arthur Bernard; *Gloria Bartley*, Jo Ann Harris; *Gym Announcer*, Cliff Emmich; *Mr. McKinley*, Walter Lott; *Red Webster*, Morgan Jones; *Senator Mickelwaite*, Richard Eastham; *Mrs. Jardino*, Angela Clarke; *Porter*, Ernest Anderson; *Quentin McKinley*, Darnell Williams; *Fight Official*, Tony Ballen; *Alec Lister*, David Knapp; *Miss Budnick*, Caryn Matchinga; *Doctor*, Milt Kogan; *Intern*, Sterling Calder; *Walter*, Stephen Coit; *Ring Announcer*, Jimmy Lennon; *Barone*, John Larroquette; *Nurse*, Marcia Lewis; *Lou (Frank) Martin*, Antony Carbone; *Alsie*, Nate Esformes; *Jerry Matusik*, Charles Tyner; *Fresco Murphy*, Paul Sorensen; *Waitress*, Carol Ann Susi; *Kevin MacInness*, Gene Tyburn; *Manager*, Joan Crosby; *Vegas Tourist*, Herb Armstrong; *Martha*, Helen Craig; *"Pappy" Papadakis*, Ed Barth; *Pete Tierney*, Roy Jenson; *Young Billy*, Allen Price; *Chemist*, Thomas Bellin; *Pinky*, Harvey Jason; *Dr. Jerry Fetterman*, George Wyner; *Wayne*, Anthony James; *Barry*, George Brenlin; *O'Hara*, Terrence Locke; *Third Mate*, W. T. Zacha; *Minister*, John Carlyle; *Monsignor*, Bill Quinn; *Captain*, Peter Mamakos; *Bell Captain*, Stuart Nisbet; *Photographer*, Warren Munson; *Dr. Simms*, Gordon Jump; *Phil McGee*, Gavan O'Herlihy; *Older Billy*, Leigh McCloskey; *Karen Hugasian*, Smith Evans; *Wesley Jordache*, Michael Morgan; *Bartender*, David Mauro; *Mayor of Antibes*, Berry Kroeger; *Frenchman*, Todd Martin; *Student*, Fred Karger; *French Waiter*, Jan Arvan; *Police Chief Ottman*, Ed Ness; *Policeman*, Ed Cross; *Theater Manager*, William Bronder; *Dr. Tinker*, John Furlong; *Richard*, Bob Purvey.

Gloria had appeared in some large, important productions in her day, from *It's a*

Wonderful Life and *The Greatest Show on Earth* to *Not as a Stranger* and *Oklahoma!* But perhaps the biggest of all was the eight-night ABC-TV miniseries *Rich Man, Poor Man* which, over the month and a half that it aired in 1976, truly became "event" television. *Rich Man, Poor Man* was not television's first miniseries (that distinction belongs to *The Blue Knight* with William Holden, a four-hour telefilm shown over four consecutive evenings in 1973), but its overwhelming success jump-started the format of long-form novels on television, made stars of its leading players and altered the landscape of television. Gloria's part in this historical event is small — she appears in just the first two of twelve hourly chapters — but along with most of the other big stars who played cameo roles, her name and character sketch opens each of the chapters as if she were present for the entire program. In fact, as Julie Prescott's mother, Gloria has more screen time than fellow "guest stars" Steve Allen, Dick Butkus, Dorothy Malone and Dick Sargent. It is also a vignette of some range, as Sue Prescott observes her daughter transform from a polite, virginal girl to a confused and compromised young woman.

On V-E (Victory in Europe) Night, 1945, the townspeople of Port Phillip, New York, are celebrating in the streets. Joining them is Rudy Jordache (Peter Strauss), a high school senior who plays his trumpet at a bonfire, leading the folks in "America the Beautiful." Mocking Rudy's patriotism is his brother Tom (Nick Nolte), who would rather see some action. Tom and pal Claude Tinker (Dennis Dugan) sneak into the movie *Wake Island*, where Tom starts a fight with a soldier, knocking him senseless in the alley next to the cinema. Julie Prescott (Susan Blakely) volunteers as a Candy Striper at a hospital; Rudy escorts her home. They've been seeing each other for a while, and Julie wants to get married, but Rudy wants to go to college. Tom teases Rudy about Julie and their subsequent fight ends quickly when their father Axel (Ed Asner) belts Tom in the mouth. While Rudy worries about being able to pay for college, Axel is called to the high school to get Tom out of trouble with his French teacher. Axel insults the teacher and slaps her across the face, threatening to do worse if Tom's grades slip any lower. A black soldier recovering from

war wounds likes Julie and offers her his back pay of $800 if she wants it; Julie starts to think seriously about going to New York City.

Instead, Julie meets rich Teddy Boylan (Robert Reed), who plies her with liquor and takes her home to his empty mansion. They have sex and afterwards Julie finds that he has given her $800. Julie begins to see Teddy often, not for money but for sexual thrills. One night Tom and Claude follow them to the mansion, where Tom starts a fire in the greenhouse. Claude is temporarily trapped and his arm is burned; Julie sees Tom clearly from the window, and he sees her. Julie's mother (Gloria Grahame) finds the $800 that Julie has hidden, assumes the worst and suggests that Julie leave town before her reputation is compromised. Julie agrees. Rudy does not receive the college scholarship for which he was hoping; he will just have to continue to work at the family bakery. On Rudy's birthday, Claude's father tells Axel that Tom caused the fire and needs to be sent away before Teddy's lawyers come after him. Axel agrees and clobbers Tom. For the first time Tom hits back, sending his father into a glass bakery case. As punishment for setting the fire, Tom is sent away to his uncle Harold's home in Ohio; Tom tells Rudy he set the fire, but does not mention seeing Julie there. With Tom gone, Axel reconsiders and provides Rudy with the money to go to college, happily surprising his miserable wife Mary (Dorothy McGuire), who has always favored Rudy over Tom.

In 1947 Tom is working as a mechanic for his uncle Harold (Bo Brundin). One of the other mechanics is teaching Tom how to box properly, and Tom is learning to control his temper. When Harold and his family take a vacation, Tom stays at the house and has a passionate affair with the Irish servant girl, Clothilde (Fionnuala Flanagan). She teaches Tom all about love and gentleness. For the first time in his life Tom is happy. When the family returns, Tom tries to keep the affair secret, but Harold learns about it and demands that it stop. Meanwhile, Teddy Boylan befriends Rudy and recommends him for a job at a department store in Whitby, where Rudy is going to college. Julie is in New York City trying to find a job as an actress. She lands a one-line gig in a play, and meets an exuberant ex-soldier, Willie Abbott (Bill Bixby), with whom she begins a love affair. Tom's affair with Clothilde comes to an end when, to his disgust, she rejects Tom in favor of keeping her menial job, even though it means sleeping with Harold, who has been trying to bed her since he hired her.

Tom's bad luck continues when he meets another girl, Teresa Santoro (Talia Shire), and approaches her at a party while he is drunk. Tom is pummeled by Teresa's date and dumped in a river; Teresa fishes him out. Rudy gets the job at the Calderwood department store. Rudy and his college roommate, Brad Knight (Tim McIntire), go skiing and have a brainstorm to open a ski rental business; after much deliberation, Axel and Mary agree to fund the operation. Mary views it as the only hope they have to make any real money. Rudy sees Julie in her New York play but also watches Julie greet her lover Willie Abbott and accompany him to his hotel. Then one day at Harold's service station, Tom is arrested for statutory rape. Teresa is pregnant, and she is only seventeen. Harold calls Axel, who comes to the rescue with $3000 to pay off Teresa's father and keep Tom out of jail. Axel tells Tom he never wants to see him again. As Tom is leaving town in disgrace, Teresa joins him, for her father has kicked her out, too. They hitch a ride on a truck heading east. The $3000 had been earmarked for Rudy's ski rental business; now Rudy has to find a new source, and he turns to Duncan Calderwood (Ray Milland), the owner of the store where he works. But their meeting is cut short when Rudy's mother Mary calls with the news that Axel has disappeared, and is presumed to be dead.

In 1950 Tom returns to Port Phillip with $3000 to repay his father. However, everything has changed; the bakery no longer exists, his father has died and no one knows where his mother is, so he holds onto the money. Tom is now a prizefighter on his way to New York City for a bout, married to Teresa, who is pregnant again after losing their first child. His manager is Smitty (Norman Fell). Meanwhile, Rudy graduates from college with Brad; they are also going to New York to celebrate. Rudy is offered an assistant manager's job by Calderwood, and encouraged to date his daughter Virginia, better known as Ginny (Kim Darby). Rudy takes a pass on the date with the daughter but accepts

the job. Rudy locates Julie in the city, meeting her husband Willie Abbott and their new baby. Willie is trying to make it as a writer, and Julie tries photography as a hobby. Rudy is disheartened because he was finally ready to marry Julie, but it's too late. He returns to Port Phillip and his new job. Julie finishes an article of Willie's that was due, and is offered a job on a magazine. Tom wins his bout while Teresa is being taken to the hospital; afterwards Tom learns he has a baby boy, to be named Wesley.

In 1954 Rudy prepares a business plan to expand Calderwood's empire, which has greatly increased under Rudy's management. The plan includes building a shopping mall near Lake Whitby and making Rudy president of the company. Calderwood balks, so Rudy threatens to take the idea elsewhere. Julie, a successful magazine writer and photographer, is offered an assignment covering a controversial shopping mall being built away from any town center, near a lake. She declines, until she learns who is behind it. Julie is happy to see Rudy again at the construction site and invites him to her place to see her photos later in the week. The mall is having zoning problems, which Rudy addresses, with helpful political advice from Teddy Boylan. At Julie's place Rudy sees her son Billy, now six, and learns that Julie is considering a divorce. He pledges his love to her again, and offers to arrange a divorce for her, when they hear Tom's name on the radio. Rudy and Julie attend Tom's bout at Madison Square Garden; Rudy visits his brother in the dressing room after Tom wins the fight. Their reunion is uneasy but cordial. Rudy escorts Julie home, only to find Billy being taken to the hospital with illness. At the hospital, Julie reconsiders her position with Willie. The next day Tom gives the $3000 to Rudy — despite Teresa's anger the night before upon learning that Tom had such money and wanted to give it away — and Rudy reluctantly accepts it. Rudy offers Tom a partnership with him, but Tom tells him to "shove it." Tom returns to his hotel to find that Teresa has left him, and taken baby Wesley. Desperate to find his son, Tom leaves town, abandoning a chance to fight for a title. Julie tells Rudy she cannot proceed with a divorce, meaning that their romance is dead, again. The mall's zoning problems disappear after a political payoff, prompting Brad Knight,

Rudy's business partner, to collect the distraught Rudy and congratulate him on another successful business venture.

In 1958 Tom arrives in Los Angeles and reacquaints himself with Smitty, who is still angry that Tom left him in the lurch four years earlier. Even so, Smitty hires Tom as a sparring partner for his new fighter, Joey Quales (George Maharis). Tom dislikes Quales but assuages his distaste for him by bedding Quales' wife Linda (Lynda Day George). Rudy is managing the Calderwood business empire and trying to fend off the boss's daughter Ginny, who is intent upon having Rudy for herself. Rudy is heartened when he learns that Julie is finally divorced. He immediately asks her to marry him, again, but she puts him off yet again. In Las Vegas, Joey Quales trains for a big fight, but his suspicions about Linda result in someone trailing her. Quales finally gathers proof that Tom has been sleeping with his (Quales') wife, leading to her brutal beating. Linda calls Tom to warn him to get out of town, quickly. Quales is severely injured when he attacks Tom in his motel room. Smitty arrives too late to prevent the fight, but tells Tom that the mob will be after him because their investment, Quales, can no longer fight. Tom takes to the road yet again.

Rudy romances Julie, still pressing for her hand in marriage. She is stunned to find Willie back at home one evening, begging to return to the family he misses. She sends him away. On the run from the mob, Tom arrives by bus in New York, checking into a cheap hotel. Tom makes arrangements to leave the country as a merchant marine, but has a quiet, tearful reunion with his mother Mary before he goes. Mary gives Tom the money she has in the house and wishes him well. Calderwood calls in Rudy for a showdown; he wants Rudy to stop seducing his daughter and marry her. Aghast, Rudy tells his boss the truth about Ginny and resigns. Calderwood backs down, refuses the resignation and makes peace with his best employee. Since Willie won't leave Julie alone, Rudy proposes to hire Willie as a public relations manager for Calderwood's hotel — in California. Willie is offended by the idea but negotiates an even better deal, along with a new car. Tom contacts a cop about finding Teresa and Wesley but is ambushed by mob goons. He escapes

into the night, finding his way to his assigned ship. Rudy and Julie are talking marriage yet again when they learn that Willie has died in California, rolling the expensive Corvette that he had so sagely negotiated from Rudy. Julie leaves to tell, and console, her son Billy.

In 1962, Rudy decides to dissolve the partnership he has had with Calderwood. Now free of business, Rudy is being considered as a prime political candidate. He asks Julie to marry him, again, and this time she accepts, and the wedding takes place. Tom is in South America, changing ships. He joins the crew of the *Westgate*, only to learn that a fellow crewmate, Falconetti (William Smith), is a bully. After trying to dissuade Brad from marrying Ginny Calderwood, Rudy decides to run for a New York Senate seat. Julie is pregnant, but one morning she doesn't feel well and suddenly loses the child, as well as the ability to have any others. Another man joins the *Westgate* crew, Roy Dwyer (Herb Jefferson, Jr.); Falconetti attacks him and Tom does nothing to stop it. Tom later explains to the black sailor why he could not reveal himself. Roy and Tom bond, with Roy teaching Tom how to navigate and work toward a higher sailor's rating. On shore leave, they find a small yacht available for sale and Tom convinces himself and Roy that they can buy it, live on it and make it profitable. At the wedding of Brad and Ginny, Duncan Calderwood asks Rudy if Brad should be made the president of the company in Rudy's absence ... and Rudy says no. Before he can elaborate, Rudy is surrounded by the people who want to make him New York's next Senator. Julie watches the hubbub and becomes depressed.

Tom and Roy return from shore leave only to be mocked by Falconetti and his hangers-on. Later, Falconetti rapes Roy, finally spurring Tom to challenge him. Their fight takes place in an empty cargo hold, where Tom beats the snot out of the bully. After the fight is over, Falconetti stabs Tom in the leg, so Tom pulverizes him, causing Falconetti to lose his right eye. The ship leaves port before Tom can be arrested, but the captain tells Tom to leave the crew once the ship reaches New York. Rudy's campaign is tightly contested. Rudy's principal advisor is Marsh Goodwin (Van Johnson); Goodwin's wife pushes Julie into drinking even more frequently. Then Mary Jordache has a heart attack. Tom arrives in New York and is surprised to find that Rudy has been looking for him. They journey to the hospital at Whitby just in time for Tom to say goodbye to his mother, who dies in his arms. At the funeral they greet Teddy Boylan, and Tom learns that his old pal, Claude Tinker, died in Korea a decade earlier. Tom is stunned to discover that he has $48,000 — the result of the $3000 that Tom had given Rudy, and which Rudy had invested in his name. Tom returns to Europe to buy the boat with Roy and start a new life. Rudy is to find Tom's boy Wesley, and let him know where he is. Rudy wins the election, becoming a senator. Julie laughs until she cries.

In 1965 Tom and Roy have repaired their boat, named *Clothilde*, but are having a tough time making money with it. That is, until Rudy persuades the Goodwins to use it. Needing a cook at the last moment, Tom and Roy hire Kate (Kay Lenz), who proves to be a welcome addition to the crew. The Goodwins are troublesome passengers when drunk, but they make amends, ask to return the following year, and promise to recommend the *Clothilde* to their friends. Rudy arranges to donate a photographic enlarger to the Whitby campus newspaper. Then he gets a line on Wesley and arranges for Tom to come back to get his son. Wesley (Michael Morgan) is at a military academy; Tom has trouble with the chief administrator until he provides proof that his ex-wife Teresa has an arrest record for prostitution. He is granted custody of the young teenager and immediately takes him back to France. In California, Julie's son Billy is doing poorly in college; when Julie and Rudy confront him, he tells them to forget all about him. Julie is devastated and drinks ever more heavily. In Cannes, France, six months later, Wesley is having a blast learning how to drive and maintain the boat. One day the grown-ups leave him in charge while they go ashore; Wesley foolishly takes a couple of teenage girls out for a cruise, and somehow damages the boat's propeller. Tom walks the streets of Cannes searching for his son, finally finding him in an alley. Their meeting is tense, but Tom recalls how his father always beat him; instead, he puts his arm around the boy and tells him he will now be learning how to fix a propeller. From the shadows, one-eyed Falconetti watches them walk away.

Roy tells Tom he's seen Falconetti in town. Kate agrees to marry Tom, happily surprising him with the news that she is pregnant. The Whitby campus is the scene of a student protest against policies that Rudy supports. Rudy orders Julie to stop drinking, which only makes her drink more. Rudy travels to Washington D.C. but is immediately sent back by Marsh Goodwin because the student protest spread to Rudy's house, where rocks were thrown and Julie was photographed outside, drunk and nude. The embarrassing photograph is spread all around the campus, and the town. Rudy storms into the student newspaper office and darkroom, where he destroys the photo enlarger he had donated. He knocks down a female staffer, and a shelf of chemicals falls on her, disfiguring and scarring her face. Rudy knows his political career is over. He apologizes to Julie and describes to her how he had apologized to the girl, who will be partially blinded. They agree to make whatever sacrifices they must to salvage their relationship. Tom marries Kate in France, with Rudy and Julie in attendance. Tom has never been so happy, especially when Rudy presents him with a ship's radar for a wedding present. Stressed, Julie goes for a drink in the middle of the night, and runs into Falconetti. Someone tells Tom about it, so he goes to rescue her and gets into a brutal fight with his nemesis. Tom emerges with a broken arm and injured leg; he admits to Julie that he is proud he didn't kill Falconetti. The next morning, Tom is ambushed on the dock by two men and stabbed as Falconetti watches. At the hospital, Tom tells Rudy to "get the bad guys," and dies. Kate is stoic as she, Roy, Rudy, Julie and Wesley take Tom's ashes and spread them at sea. Tom's death brings Rudy and Julie closer again as they contemplate the past and the future.

Rich Man, Poor Man is a mammoth story, as evidenced by that laborious plot description — each paragraph represents one of its twelve chapters — yet entire subplots and minor characters are barely covered or not even mentioned, such as Professor Bill Denton (Lawrence Pressman), the politically liberal economics professor who teaches Rudy about business but then falls prey to a conservative backlash when his tenure is being considered. Or the young black soldier Arnold Simms (Mike

Evans), who amorously tries to befriend Julie Prescott only to lose her to poor timing and Teddy Boylan's fancy convertible. Or Teresa Santoro's friend Jay Ledbetter (Ben Archibek), the young punk who beats up drunken Tom but who gets his butt kicked in return. Or the seductive Gloria Hartley (Jo Ann Harris), Julie's friend who beds Rudy on his graduation night, then screams at him when he refuses to stick around — but, unaccountably, is delighted to see him a few years later. Or Phil McGee (Gavan O'Herlihy), the editor of the college newspaper who is openly hostile to Rudy. Or Talbott Hughes (James Ingersoll), the severely injured soldier for whom Julie reads while he is in the hospital, and who dies while she cavorts with Teddy Boylan.

Even with twelve hour-long chapters (minus commercial time) with which to work, the story sometimes hops rather clumsily, leaving dangling loose plot threads. Rudy and Brad's ski rental business, for instance, is never mentioned again after Mary calls Rudy to tell him that Axel has disappeared. Julie's son Billy becomes desperately ill one night, yet his illness is never defined. Rudy eventually decides to dissolve his partnership with Duncan Calderwood, yet cogent, concise reasons for his departure are not forthcoming. In addition, minor, plot-directional and extraneous characters pop in and wander out of the story constantly. Some, such as Falconetti's three hangers-on (Wayne, Barry and O'Hara), provide a bit more depth and detail in Tom's shipboard sequences. Likewise, other characters in the Calderwood business scenes and Rudy's political campaign function as intermediaries, sounding boards and, sometimes, simply space fillers.

Other characters are more daunting. A few, like businessman Richards (Dick Sargent), Irene Goodwin (Dorothy Malone) and publisher Asher Berg (Craig Stevens), are little more than space fillers, advancing the plot in tiny pieces with a piece of dialogue or a bit of action. A few, like soldier Al Fanducci (Dick Butkus), talent agent Bayard Nichols (Steve Allen) and military academy head Colonel Deiner (Andrew Duggan), are simply glorified one-scene cameos that do not justify inclusion on the all-star "guest star" list. And a few, like Virginia Calderwood (Kim Darby), Teresa Santoro (Talia Shire) and Joey Quales (George Ma-

haris), are tough to take because their characters are so downright sick, selfish or contemptible. Even Axel Jordache (Ed Asner, who won an Emmy for his work) falls prey to this problem, which originates with Irwin Shaw's immensely popular sprawling novel. Published in 1969, it is filled with conniving, nasty, troubled characters. Shaw's vision of the world in the book is bleak and yet hopeful, because no matter how insensitive, deceitful, diabolic, pathetic, bullying, self-delusional, unlucky, disgraceful, stupid or murderous his characters become, they always manage to press ahead with their unhappy lives. Happy times and good intentions are attendant but usually short-lived; betrayal, avariciousness and brutality are far more common.

Shaw's massive chronicle of the Jordache family is eminently readable but is not a very pleasant experience. Miniseries writer Dean Reisner had the sense (or was directed) to tone down the book's sexual candor and frequent brutality, broadening its appeal. Shaw's novel chronicles the lives of three Jordache family characters: Tom, Rudy and their sister Gretchen. Many of the miniseries events and characters are directly taken from the book, but some are merged, condensed or omitted to pare and streamline the narrative. Rudy's sister Gretchen, for instance, moves from the book to the movie as Julie Prescott, Rudy's girlfriend. In the book it is Gretchen who is seduced by Teddy Boylan; who moves to New York to act; who marries Willie Abbott; who bears the child Billy; and who becomes a successful film editor. Screenwriter Reisner transformed Gretchen into Julie Prescott, keeping most of Gretchen's characteristics intact (except that Julie is a writer and photographer instead of a film editor), and adds the characteristic that Julie is Rudy's lifelong love. The result is that while the two male leads remain consistent with their literary counterparts, the character of Julie becomes their equal, as Gretchen rarely was in the book. Having Julie form the apex of its triangle of primary characters helps balance the story. And Reisner was smart to prevent Julie from becoming romantically involved with both brothers, which had to have been tempting.

The miniseries shifts its focus between the three characters fairly equitably, telling Shaw's tale while toning down its harsher elements.

Thus, Tom remains a physical brute but at times he tries to do the right thing by his brother; by the end of the program he is its best-loved character. Julie is a slut but she evolves into an independent woman before her dreams begin to suffocate when she finally marries Rudy. The father, Axel, is an unrepentant racist who beats Tom black and blue, but at least he doesn't try to poison anybody before he rows down the river into oblivion. Rudy is the upstanding boy whose business acumen is astounding, but who turns bitter and unfeeling as a politician. All in all, Rudy's story is rather boring, as he gradually moves up the business ladder while continually pining for the girl he was not ready to marry when he was young. Tom's story is far more exciting, changing locales all around the country, bouncing from one scrape into another. Tom's various dilemmas keep the story moving forward; Rudy's machinations sometimes threaten to stall the drama. Julie's story is like Tom's, in that viewers recognize right away that she is making mistakes that will have long-term consequences. Unlike Tom's problems, which are partly external, involving people and situations he cannot control, the situations that Julie is forced to face are almost all domestic in nature. Julie's character transforms to the greatest degree, yet aspects of those changes are rapid and sometimes seem capricious.

It is undeniable, however, that the program is dramatically effective. This project simply would not have worked as a two- or even three-hour movie; there is just too much ground to cover. It might have worked as a regular television series, though expanding it from the present twelve chapters into twenty-two to twenty-six episodes, as was in 1976 the norm, would have proven daunting. As it was, Reisner and the producers first planned *Rich Man, Poor Man* as a series of two-hour, stand-alone television movies that would be shown in sequence over a period of time. When ABC's new chief of programming Fred Silverman decided in late 1975 that the twelve one-hour chapter format seemed the best fit, nobody was happy. Nick Nolte complained, "I can't say I was angry. Just damned displeased. I didn't have enough clout to be angry." Executive producer Harve Bennett was angrier. "This is like a man who says, 'This roast beef is magnificent! Let's make sandwiches out of it!'" Eventually Silverman capitulated somewhat, agreeing to telecast the first two chapters the first night, then the next two chapters on the next night before reverting to the one-hour format. To ensure a big finish, the network doubled up the chapters during the final two telecasts as well, thus condensing the twelve chapters into eight evenings of dramatic entertainment.

No other American television project of this magnitude had ever been telecast, let alone imagined. After *The Blue Knight*, several other projects experimented with length. Ambitious single night TV-movies sometimes lengthened to three hours, while two-part TV-movies of three- or four-hour duration were not uncommon, and both formats were usually well received. *QB VII* was a six-and-a-half-hour program telecast over two evenings in April of 1974. *Moses the Lawgiver* ran six hours spread over six nights in 1975. And then came *Rich Man, Poor Man*. It bested the perennial comedy favorite *All in the Family* in the ratings on most Monday evenings, something no regular series had been able to do. By the time of its finale in mid–March of 1976, *Rich Man, Poor Man* was setting ratings records; it was so popular that ABC, which had been terrified of failure, immediately ordered a sequel. Six months after the show's initial telecast, *Rich Man, Poor Man, Book II* made its debut as a regular hour-long dramatic series, spanning twenty-one episodes. Peter Strauss returned as Rudy for the duration, while Susan Blakely made a token appearance in the first episode as Julie.

Rich Man, Poor Man debuted in February 1976 and undeniably altered the face of television. NBC jumped on the bandwagon in the fall of 1976 with *Best Sellers*, a collection of four separate miniseries run consecutively; the third one, *Seventh Avenue*, also featured Gloria Grahame. Suddenly long-form programming was all the rage, and every network was developing its own. Within one year of its telecast the original *Rich Man, Poor Man* was eclipsed by another twelve-part miniseries, *Roots*, a project that shattered everyone's expectations about what television could and should be. The miniseries was here to stay, lasting nearly twenty years in full flower on America's television networks. *Washington: Behind Closed Doors* ran for twelve-and-a-half hours in 1977. *Holocaust* followed with a nine-and-a-half hour run in 1978. *Wheels* motored for ten hours that same year, and then *Centennial* expanded the concept exponentially with twenty-six-and-a-half hours of drama featuring a cast of hundreds. Over time, the miniseries format peaked and gradually diminished, partly because standard television series seasons continued to shrink, but mostly due to the proliferation of non-network programming options as cable television became popular. The miniseries format continues to thrive on cable, particularly on HBO, which once or twice a year presents long-form shows that have directly descended from *Rich Man, Poor Man* and its ilk.

Rich Man, Poor Man leads Peter Strauss, Nick Nolte and Susan Blakely became stars due to the show. Strauss and Blakely each made feature films but had their greatest subsequent successes on television. Nolte, on the other hand, made the jump to movie stardom with 1978's *Who'll Stop the Rain* and was a major movie star for years. Nolte plays Tom Jordache with a rough-and-tumble physicality that defines his character. Clean-cut but occasionally scraggly and battered, Tom is just rough enough to intimidate viewers but handsome enough to enthrall them, too. Nolte's best scenes are gentle ones with Dorothy McGuire, who played Tom's mother Mary. The reunion scene when Tom returns home before shipping out to sea is a gem that belies Tom's usual bravado. And it is Tom, not Rudy, who says goodbye to their mother Mary in the hospital. Again, Nolte plays the scene quietly, displaying an acting maturity that serves the character perfectly in that situation.

Peter Strauss is solid as Rudy, although he never looks as young as Rudy is supposed to be in the early chapters, no matter how much he cracks his voice. Strauss nearly underplays the role to a fault, for it seems that at one time or another, everybody else is more interesting than Rudy Jordache. He has his moments, certainly, but Rudy is staid rather than exciting. On the DVD commentary, Strauss comments that American audiences find Tom's character more appealing of the two, but that the situation is reversed in Europe, where Rudy is more appreciated. Strauss attributes this to the European predilection for those characters who use their brains and ambitiousness rather than

physical force to become self-sufficient. He may be right, yet of the brothers it seems clear that the rich man (Rudy) is simply not as endearing or popular as the poor man (Tom).

Susan Blakely was an Army brat who traveled and lived around the world and then became famous as a model in the 1960s. She made movies before *Rich Man, Poor Man*, but it was this miniseries that made her a household name. She is very likable and attractive as Julie Prescott in the show's early scenes. As her marriage to Willie Abbott deteriorates and Julie gains her independence, she should become even more accessible. Yet that does not happen. Even as Julie becomes a successful writer and photographer, the script saddles her with emotional problems and guilt that are exacerbated with Willie's untimely death and Rudy's Senate run. Julie becomes a raving drunk, which threatens to ruin Rudy's political career. Her unrelenting unhappiness threatens to swamp the drama at times, and for no cogent reason other than scripted guilt. Dean Reisner spent more than two years of his life constructing the script and then expanding it when the project's duration was lengthened. But he did not spend enough time on allowing Julie to enjoy parts of her life, particularly as she becomes successful. Her turns from naïve girl to dutiful wife to polished writer to guilt-ridden mother to sorrowful widow to Rudy's alcoholic political wife are jarring rather than smooth, and that is the fault of the script.

Of the "guest stars," the finest performances are delivered by Ed Asner as Axel and Fionnuala Flanagan as Clothilde; both won Emmy awards for their work. It cannot be coincidence that these are the characters who provide Tom with his worst and best life experiences, respectively. Also Emmy-nominated were Robert Reed (as Teddy Boylan), Dorothy McGuire (as Mary Jordache), Ray Milland (as Duncan Calderwood), Bill Bixby (as Willie Abbott), Norman Fell (as Smitty), Van Johnson (as Marsh Goodwin), Kim Darby (as Virginia "Ginny" Calderwood) and Kay Lenz (as Kate). Nolte and Strauss were nominated for Emmys and Golden Globe awards, while Susan Blakely, Ed Asner and Josette Banzet (as Miss Lenaut, the French teacher) won them. The bottom line is that the all-star cast proved to be worth its weight in gold, or at least awards and award nominations. Universal insisted on hiring big names for the small roles to ensure that viewers tuned in to the show, just in case the three leads proved incapable of carrying the load. For the most part that strategy proves sound, as long as the guest stars have parts that they can dig into. In only a few cases— Steve Allen, Dorothy Malone, Dick Sargent come to mind — is the strategy questionable, as their parts are neither large nor meaty enough to justify their casting (or billing). The unsung performers are Herb Jefferson Jr., whose portrait of Roy Dwyer is expert, and William Smith, whose embodiment of bigoted bully Arthur Falconetti is indelible. These are characters who interact with Tom, not Rudy. Tom's story is simply more interesting and powerful, due as much to the excellent characters and performers that surround Tom as to Tom's globe-hopping personal story.

Gloria Grahame essays the small role of Julie's watchful mother, Sue Prescott. Sue is worried that her teenage daughter needs to find a job now that she is graduating high school. She is also worried about Julie hanging around with Rudy, yet she still leaves Julie alone for a night while she visits her sister. Sue is right to worry about Julie, for soon Julie has bedded not Rudy, but an older man, Teddy Boylan, and "earned" $800 by doing so. Upon finding the money, Sue thinks the worst of her daughter and urges her to leave town before either of their reputations are ruined. It is a brief but effective portrayal, with Sue preoccupied just enough not to notice the changes occurring in her daughter, or to prevent their consequences. What's missing is a parting scene between mother and daughter; as it is, Julie simply leaves one day to try her hand at acting in New York City and her mother is never seen or mentioned again. Gloria is well-dressed and flowery in the role; she looks the very picture of middle-class domesticity. Hers is a solid, understated, perfectly appropriate performance.

In the DVD commentary, Peter Strauss states, "This was a perfect story for America at this time." His statement seems sincere but is difficult to understand. What is it about *Rich Man, Poor Man* that is so profound? The story takes place over a twenty-one year period, from 1945 to 1965. It encompasses events from the conclusion of World War II to the anti-establishment student protests of the mid–1960s, yet it barely touches on any social impact outside of its inner circle of characters. The Korean War, the assassination of John F. Kennedy, the space race and civil rights protests were major societal events during this era, yet the miniseries hardly acknowledges them. Neither Tom nor Rudy serves in the military. Rudy is so successful a businessman that he is drafted to become a politician, yet his political affiliation is never revealed! Events fly past these characters without notice because the script is incredibly insular; Rudy, Tom and Julie live in a world almost entirely self-contained. The closest that *Rich Man, Poor Man* comes to social commentary is the sequence in which Rudy finally throws a temper tantrum at the college newspaper office. Students protesting his position on R.O.T.C. recruiters on campus shatter windows at the newspaper office (because Rudy's name and title are prominently displayed) and then take their protest to his house, where someone photographs Julie drunk and naked. Rudy storms into the office and destroys its darkroom, including the photo enlarger that he had generously donated earlier. But he also knocks down a cute newspaper reporter, and a shelf of photographic chemicals falls on top of her, permanently disfiguring and scarring her. As photographers snap pictures of the distressed girl, Rudy realizes his political career is finished. Even here, the script's target is not the protest and its larger meaning, but the consequences to Rudy's future in politics. There is no world view to *Rich Man, Poor Man*, only the tight, narrowly focused, apolitical personal views of its primary characters.

The overriding theme of the piece revolves around a phrase that Axel Jordache uses a time or two, "the sins of the fathers." Axel asks Rudy if sons are responsible for their fathers "sins" and Rudy says no. Evidence to the contrary is supplied to both sons throughout the story but, to their credit, both Rudy and Tom overcome their father's brutal parenting to become honorable men. The key moment for Tom occurs after his son Wesley stupidly takes the boat *Clothilde* out to sea and damages the propeller. When Tom later finds the boy hiding in a Cannes alleyway, he has the anger and the opportunity to inflict some physical punishment. Visions of Axel clobbering him crowd Tom's mind (seen as flashbacks), however, and as he looks at the boy cowering before him, Tom's anger subsides. He puts his arm around his son and begins to discuss how the propeller is to be fixed. In this instance, meant also to symbolize Tom's future dealings with Wesley, Tom discards the past; Axel's sins are not his own. This change in Tom, who formerly was known to sucker punch anybody who looked at him cross-eyed, is the miniseries' most profound and satisfying moment. Tom's change is not immediate; several earlier instances show that Tom was willing to swallow his pride to avoid trouble, and yet every one of those instances still led to Tom punching someone. This time it is different, and the result is perfectly enacted.

Other than the "sins of the fathers" theme, profundity seems lacking in *Rich Man, Poor Man*. Rather, it is a clichéd story that resonates with the satisfaction of overcoming adversity. The Jordache boys are not rich and powerful. They struggle, each in their own fashion, to make their ways in the world. Tom uses physical prowess to fight his way to manhood — gradually learning to control the anger that flows through his fists and to act like a man. This is hastened, of course, by his taste of pure love from Clothilde (and later, Kate), by becoming a father, and by the support, which he never expects to receive, from his brother and Roy Dwyer. Rudy uses his education and business sense to rise from poverty to a position of financial power. And he does so without cheating people out of their own money and possessions. He simply provides people with what they want. When Rudy reaches the pinnacle of success, he forgoes further business dealings in favor of a life of public service. It is interesting that it is only as a Senator, when Rudy has the best of intentions, that his personality turns hard, cold and unforgiving. Rudy's most difficult challenge occurs near the conclusion of the story, as his political career goes down in flames. He re-dedicates himself to Julie ... although it may be too late to prevent his marriage from following the same route as his political career. Julie is a difficult case to judge. She overcomes several types of adversity both personally and professionally, yet at the end of the story she is as vulnerable as she has ever been. Her future with Rudy is not necessarily a bright one.

Despite the inherent flaws, superficiality and cold brutality of Shaw's tale, its filmization was incredibly popular. People responded to its aura, its characters, its new way of telling a story. *Rich Man, Poor Man* became a television rarity, a bona fide phenomenon, something that everybody in the country seemed to watch and discuss. Peter Strauss goes so far as to suggest that the Monday telecasts of the show were the reason that many restaurants and other businesses decided to close on Monday evenings. That may or may not be true, but the popularity of the show was undeniable. It is still regarded as a highlight of 1970s television history, a trailblazing show that inspired even more ambitious programming to follow. Its faithful fans are ecstatic that it has been recently made available on DVD for the first time.

Part of its trailblazing history is Gloria Grahame. As one of its twenty-six guest stars, Gloria enjoyed the sensation of being seen by millions of viewers for the first time in twenty years. She is shown to advantage in her few scenes, a gentle, understated reminder to everyone that she was still around and was well prepared to do her part in whatever project she was hired to make. Gloria makes a strong impression though the part is not particularly penetrating. She does her thing without upstaging co-star Susan Blakely and contributes emotional nuances that the script barely intimates. It was just a job for Gloria and, as with most of her jobs, she delivers a professional performance.

Seventh Avenue (1977)

CREDITS Universal Television. *Originally Telecast on* NBC-TV. *Directed by* Richard Irving (parts 1 and 2) and Russ Mayberry (part 3). *Produced by* Richard Irving. *Executive Producer*: Franklin Barton. *Written for Television by* Laurence Heath. *Based on the novel Seventh Avenue by* Norman Bogner. *Director of Photography*: Jack Priestley. *Film Editors*: Robert F. Shugrue and Larry Lester. *Music Score*: Nelson Riddle. NBC Best Sellers *Theme by* Elmer Bernstein. *Art Directors*: Loyd S. Papez and Philip Rosenberg. *Set Decorations*: Ed Stewart. *Assistant Director*: Kurt Baker. *Unit Manager*: Robert J. Anderson. *Sound*: Les Lararowitz. *Titles and Optical Effects*: Universal Title. *Sound Effects Editor*: Marvin Walowitz. *Music Editor*: Charles Paley. *Costume Designer*: Celia Bryant. *Casting by* Geri Windsor and Cis Corman. *Pro-*

duction Manager: David Golden. *Sound Editor*: Roger Sword. *First Assistant Camera*: Gary Muller. Technicolor. Flat (1.33:1). Monaural Sound. Approximately 270 minutes. Initially telecast on February 10, 17 and 24, 1977. Not currently available on commercial home video.

CAST *Jay Blackman*, Steven Keats; *Rhoda Gold Blackman*, Dori Brenner; *Eva Meyers*, Jane Seymour; *Myrna Gold*, Anne Archer; *Al Blackman*, Kristoffer Tabori; *Joe Vitelli*, Herschel Bernardi; *Frank Topo*, Richard Dimitri; *Finklestein*, Jack Gilford; *Morris Blackman*, Mike Kellin; *Harry Lee*, Alan King; *Douglas Fredericks*, Ray Milland; *Dave Shaw*, Paul Sorvino; *Gus Farber*, Eli Wallach; *John Meyers*, William Windom; *Marty Cass*, John Pleshette; *Edward Gold*, Robert Symonds; *Paula Cass*, Ellen Greene; *Celia "Ma" Blackman*, Anna Berger; *Barney Green*, Josh Mostel; *Mrs. Gold*, Leora Dana; *Mrs. Farber*, Madeline Lee; *Howie "Howard" Horton*, Richard Kline; *Creedan*, Louis Criscuolo; *Neal Blackman*, Joshua Freund; *Moll*, Gloria Grahame; *Sergeant Rollins*, Brock Peters; *Ray Boone*, Ron Max; *Detective Cleaver*, Graham Beckel.

Gloria's second television miniseries was part of a larger NBC anthology series, titled *Best Sellers*, comprised of four serialized novels. The first, *Captains and the Kings*, lasting nine hours spread over six evenings, was the only one to fare well in the ratings. The second was *Once an Eagle*, also a nine-hour program, with a seven-night duration. *Seventh Avenue*, a six-hour drama shown in three parts, was the third *Best Seller*, and *The Rhinemann Exchange*, a five-hour show also in three parts, concluded the series run. While *Seventh Avenue* failed to attract large numbers of viewers, it did receive some critical attention; its leads Steven Keats and Dori Brenner received Emmy nominations. It was based on a 1966 novel of the garment industry by Norman Bogner, first published as *Divorce* in England, then published a year later in America with the more evocative title *Seventh Avenue*. Bogner's novel is sleazy, overtly sexual and filled to the brim with savage emotional fury; even at a six-hour length it was necessary for NBC to tone down the novel's content and eliminate several of its characters and subplots. Yet the resulting miniseries is surprisingly watchable and occasionally powerful.

Seventh Avenue begins north of that New York City thoroughfare in December of 1938 as young Jay Blackman (Steven Keats) walks the streets, broke and hungry. He persuades a friend to get him into a Jewish wedding, where he works as a waiter and then bartender, snacking and drinking between serving the guests. Jay is noticed by Rhoda Gold (Dori Brenner) and they strike up a friendship. Jay's brother Al (Kristoffer Tabori) loses his trucking job and is beaten when he refuses to drive across a picket line. Then Jay loses his longshoreman job in a spat with his penny-pinching boss. Jay senses an opportunity with Rhoda, whose family has some wealth. Jay ingratiates his way into Rhoda's heart, although her sister Myrna (Anne Archer) takes an instant dislike to him. By New Year's Eve, Jay has met Rhoda's parents and charmed his way into Rhoda's bed.

Now fully committed to Jay, Rhoda hires him to work at the dress shop she manages. Jay learns quickly and has a way with the female customers. Quite rapidly he becomes the store's best salesman. Rhoda learns she is pregnant, but refuses to tell Jay or her family. Jay pressures Rhoda to bring in a line of dresses that they can receive on credit and sell at the store without having to cut the store's owner, Mr. Finkleman (Jack Gilford), in on the profit. While looking for the right dresses, Jay meets designer Eva Meyers (Jane Seymour) and is instantly smitten. Rhoda senses that she is losing Jay and still refuses to tell him about her pregnancy. Jay finds a location for a dress shop he can open with Rhoda. As he is showing it to her, Rhoda mentions an idea for marketing a rack of dresses at one price. Jay has a brainstorm: He will open the store with all dresses at $2! Rhoda takes his euphoria as an opportunity to tell him that she is pregnant; he responds by laughing. She runs away, upset, but he follows and apologizes. With no cash to his name, and facing a future of hard work, he advises Rhoda to get an abortion. A friend of Jay's arranges it, but at the last moment Rhoda cannot go through with the operation.

Jay sadly informs Rhoda's father (Robert Symonds) that he cannot marry Rhoda because he has no money and no future. But with $2000 they would be able to open a nice dress shop and keep all the profits for themselves. Jay's flattery works and Mr. Gold lends them the money to open the store. In the meantime, they must be married. A Jewish wedding takes place, but Jay is not happy. He realizes that he is sacrificing his freedom for security and is now tied to a woman he does not love. At the reception, Myrna corners him and calls him a rat. Jay responds by kissing her. Myrna slaps him. Jay tells her that someday she will beg him for sex. Myrna denies it, but not as forcefully as she might. Their exchange is overheard by Rhoda. This ends the first chapter.

The wedding night is awkward when Rhoda confronts Jay about his argument with Myrna. Jay tells the truth and apologizes. He makes up with Rhoda in bed before surprising her with the news that he doesn't want a honeymoon, he wants to work on their new store. They negotiate a lease with businessman Douglas Fredericks (Ray Milland) and then inform Finklestein that they are leaving his employ. Finklestein is rightfully angry. Jay and Rhoda's new store on 14th Street is an immediate success, and Rhoda works until just before the baby is to be born. In the meantime, Jay renews his acquaintance with Eva Meyers. Eva is married to a traveling salesman who is rarely home, and she is lonely. Jay begins to fill her lonely hours as they begin a torrid affair.

Jay's business is threatened by garment magnate Harry Lee (Alan King) and his right-hand enforcer Frank Topo (Richard Dimitri), but Jay warns them off for the time being. One Sunday afternoon, Jay angrily leaves Rhoda behind to visit Eva. Hours later, Rhoda has a baby boy. Jay returns from Eva's arms to discover he is a father. He is ecstatic, but his brother Al reprimands him for leaving Rhoda at the time when she most needed him. Jay recommits himself to being a family man, although he still spends time with Eva when he can. Jay's relative happiness is spoiled when Harry Lee sends some of his goons to burn a truck full of Jay's dresses. Jay confronts Harry afterward and is warned to pay Harry the proper kickbacks, or else. Always calculating, Jay counters by offering to go into business with Harry directly, having Harry's people actually make the dresses Jay wants to sell. After some considerable thought, Harry agrees, but demands that Jay put up half the cash for the deal, $150,000.

Jay reignites his affair with Eva, which leads to a confrontation with Eva's husband John (William Windom). John tells Jay, "Nobody's going to get hurt. I'm used to being the victim," then goes into another room and shoots himself. John's suicide pushes Eva into

drinking herself into oblivion whenever Jay is not around. Rhoda is taking seven or eight Benzedrine capsules per day to cope with her low self-esteem. Myrna gives Jay a hard time about Rhoda, then goes home to her lesbian lover. Jay mortgages himself to the hilt and makes the deal with Harry, then pressures Douglas Fredericks to lease them space in the new shopping malls that Fredericks is financing around the country. Fredericks refuses, but Harry allows Frank Topo to use dynamite on a few mall locations to make their case for them. Fredericks concedes.

In 1945 the war ends and Al comes home and finds Rhoda ready to divorce Jay. But Jay doesn't want a divorce; he wants his family. Jay finally tells Eva that he will not divorce Rhoda, and Eva calmly ends their five-year affair. On V-J (Victory in Japan) Day, Harry Lee announces that he has sold his share of the business to Jay and is retiring. This news is balanced by the threat of Frank Topo bringing the mob into the garment industry by interfering with the union and organizing a strike. The new union chief steward is Joe Vitelli (Herschel Bernardi), an old friend and confidante of Jay's, who refuses to bow to Topo's demands and is confident that he can avert a strike. Frank Topo takes Jay's place as Eva's lover, and he enjoys controlling her every move.

Jay returns home one day and finds Rhoda has moved out. Myrna is there to collect some of Rhoda's clothing. To Jay's surprise, Myrna is now friendly to him for the first time. They spend hours talking and she confesses that she has been a lesbian for years, but her lover recently left her. Now she doesn't know who, or how, to love. She asks Jay to make love to her; he is so surprised he hesitates. Myrna, thinking she has made a complete fool of herself, leaves quickly. She walks along the riverfront, and then very calmly and purposefully jumps into the river. This ends the second chapter.

Al visits Rhoda and her son Neal in Maine, where they are staying. As they play in the snow, it is obvious that Al has feelings for Rhoda. Jay hears of Myrna's suicide attempt and immediately calls Rhoda to come to the hospital where Myrna is recovering. Myrna awakens and begs the attendants to let her die. Rhoda arrives to see Jay talking gently to Myrna and, recalling what she had heard on her wedding night, assumes the worst. She leaves and refuses to even see her sister when Myrna is committed to a sanitarium. Meanwhile, the union is in turmoil, as the mob is pushing for a strike. They have an inside man, Dave Shaw (Paul Sorvino), who is ostensibly working with Joe Vitelli but actually undermining Joe's efforts at every turn. When Joe again refuses to bow to Frank Topo's demands, Topo arranges for his right-hand man, Ray Boone (Ron Max), to persuade Joe, permanently. Dave Shaw protests but changes his mind when Topo offers to have Ray Boone persuade him, too.

Jay visits Myrna in the sanitarium and is happy that Myrna is making positive strides in her recovery. Eva finds Frank Topo's gun and tries to break away from his control but she cannot resort to violence to do so. Topo retaliates by savagely raping her. Eva finds comfort and solace with Jay, who enthusiastically hires her as a designer for his dress company. Al and Rhoda come close to kissing but instead reach an understanding that they can never be anything other than best friends. Ray Boone beats Joe Vitelli and sets fire to his office, causing his death. Jay arrives just in time to see Boone leaving, and later identifies him for the police. Boone is ordered to hide out in an apartment run by Moll (Gloria Grahame) until the heat blows over. The strike goes forward.

Jay's company is pressured as he is forced to cancel orders and creditors begin to call for payment. Eva provides new designs for Jay, but they cannot be made in the current situation. Topo visits Jay to settle the strike and gain the mob a percentage of every garment sale, but Jay throws him out of the office. Mob guys go after Neal in Maine but Jay is there to rescue him. Al, now the New York district attorney, turns all his attention to finding Ray Boone and connecting him to Frank Topo and the mob. Rhoda finds Myrna with Jay and again thinks the worst, but they explain to her that Myrna was a lesbian and Jay was not having an affair with her. Rhoda and Myrna reconcile, but Rhoda is still not interested in being with Jay, although their divorce was never finalized. Jay is back with Eva, and Neal wants to meet her for the first time. Rhoda objects, but eventually relents. The garment strike intensifies.

Ray Boone finally loses his patience being cooped up in an apartment with Moll and has a loud fight with her. An informant leads the cops to Moll's apartment and they grab Boone without a struggle. Jay and Eva spend time outside the city and are happy. They return late at night, planning to finalize Jay's divorce from Rhoda and then marry, when a car drives past and one of Topo's hoods fires at them, hitting Eva. Cops just arriving to put Jay under protection shoot back, causing the car to crash and killing the attacker. Eva is taken to the hospital where she dies in Jay's arms. Al arrives to tell Jay that Ray Boone confessed, followed by Dave Shaw, so the garment strike will finally end.

After a four-month trial, Frank Topo is convicted of murder and will go to the gas chamber. Neal has his sixth birthday party surrounded by family and friends. Jay is essentially broke but is determined to keep the business alive. Posthumously, Eva's designs are featured in a *Style* magazine. Al has a girlfriend. Myrna has recovered and is going to Paris to study art. Rhoda's dress shop is doing well and she is happy. She and Jay, still technically married, meet at her shop and walk the city streets just as they did a decade earlier. This ends the third chapter, and the miniseries.

Seventh Avenue quite necessarily condenses, alters and tones down the original Norman Bogner novel for mainstream television broadcast. The book is harsh and savage, presenting Jay Blackman as a predatory opportunist, rarely compassionate about anyone but himself and his son Neal, whom he adores. The miniseries allows Jay to be as personable as he is ruthless, strengthens his ties to Rhoda (whom he grows to despise in the book) and eliminates a great deal of his womanizing. The miniseries keeps Jay tied to just two women, Rhoda and Eva Meyers, while the book introduced a third important lover, Terry Fredericks, the young, rebellious daughter of Douglas Fredericks, who bears Jay a child with tragic consequences.

The biggest change that writer Laurence Heath brought to Bogner's book is a change in tone. Bogner's novel, which the *Portland Sunday Telegram* praised as a "scorching success," is a tawdry, relentlessly grim tale of a selfish man whose turbulent path through life disrupts or destroys those of the people closest to him. The novel's Jay has passionate relationships with three different women and yet finds himself alone and miserable at story's end. The miniseries alters that pessimism by substituting glimmers of hopeful optimism at key moments, dispensing with the tragic Terry Fredericks storyline, softening the harsh corners of most of the characters and providing a conclusion that hints at Jay's possible reconciliation with Rhoda. The book's fans may be disappointed by Heath's condensations but the spirit of the book and its major plot details and characterizations are left intact while its excesses and general unpleasantness are sacrificed for the sake of entertainment. Bogner was not happy with the changes forced upon his material, yet felt it was handled as well as could be expected: "Given the righteousness of [the network's] Standards and Practices [division] at the time, a good deal of the novel was omitted in the event that it might corrupt and offend sensitive viewers. I think Heath did a reasonable job of it."

The miniseries is generally compelling because it comprises a great deal of narrative action over the course of several years. A number of the secondary characters (Gus Farber, Mr. Finklestein, John Meyers, Douglas Fredericks, even Jay's son Neal) are given short shrift in Heath's teleplay, yet that seems inevitable in the translation. The focus on a possible labor strike, the friendship of Joe Vitelli and the involvement of mob hit man Ray Boone are all Heath inventions, added to bring the focus of the piece back to its unique setting, the garment industry. Heath also fine-tuned the parts of the three leading female characters, focusing upon the Jay-Rhoda-Eva romantic triangle and the relationship between Rhoda and her sister Myrna, realizing that more than half of *Seventh Avenue*'s viewership was bound to be female. Heath also completely rewrote the character of Jay's brother Al, making him an integral part of the story at several junctions, although Al is rarely a realistic character (evolving from a truck driver to New York City's assistant district attorney).

Astute viewers may also notice parallels between *Seventh Avenue* and *Rich Man, Poor Man* (similar themes, situations, tone and even casting). *Seventh Avenue* was made, of course, in the wake of *Rich Man, Poor Man*'s thunderous success; it seems obvious that the networks were actively searching for literary properties that would remind viewers of that earlier tri-

umph. It must be noted, however, that Bogner's book was published three years before Irwin Shaw published his tome, so perhaps Shaw was actually following Bogner's lead when it came to writing about disparate brothers overcoming long odds to rise to power or business success in New York City following the end of World War II. Both books chronicle one brother's rapid rise through the business world (and both resultant telefilms cast Ray Milland as business tycoons who ultimately partner with that brother). Both books detail largely unhappy and tragic romantic entanglements, and both books are sometimes soaked in savagery and sexual sensationalism. It is no wonder that *Seventh Avenue* was chosen for the *Best Sellers* series.

Of the three separate chapters (shown on successive Thursday evenings), the third is the most problematic. That third chapter is directed by Russ Mayberry rather than Richard Irving, who helmed the first two parts and also produced the show, and it is severely slowed by four separate, lengthy flashbacks shown without almost no editing to them at all. The fourth flashback, coming near the end of the chapter, is actually from early in the same chapter! Nevertheless, the third chapter eventually resolves all of Jay's conflicts and relationships, albeit brusquely in many cases, bringing the chronicle of Jay Blackman to a close.

Its setting is nicely defined in visual terms, though barely explored in anything more than a cursory manner. The garment district of pre–World War II New York City looks appropriately hustling and bustling, with several sequences in garment manufacturing facilities and distribution centers that deftly reinforce the environment that these characters populate. The time period is less effectively wrought, although the abortion sequence is very powerfully handled and other moments firmly place the miniseries in its intended era. However, its language, acting style and noticeable lack of formality mark *Seventh Avenue* as perhaps more contemporary than it should have been. This doesn't necessarily detract from its quality or effectiveness, it simply places the then forty-year-old past in a more recognizable, modern context.

The result is that the miniseries has a greater connection to the audience than the original book. It isn't nearly as shocking — or as vile — yet the central story and its many tangents are suitably dramatic and generally compelling. As a chronicle of a man rising to power from humble beginnings, losing connection with the people closest to him as he climbs over others to reach his goal, and finally finding himself alone and unfulfilled, the story is familiar even if its setting is unusual. There is no great profound truth to be discovered (another parallel with *Rich Man, Poor Man*), but rather several key moments when Jay or one of the women learns and conveys something valuable about themselves. Connection to the characters is inevitably strengthened because of the length and depth of the miniseries, which is three times longer than a feature film. This connection to the characters makes the project memorable for viewers; Heath went to these lengths to make Jay in particular at least somewhat likable.

The other aspect that makes Jay likable is Steven Keats' performance. Keats isn't afraid to present Jay as the cad that he is, but he also works hard to provide for his family (first his parents and brother, later his wife and child) during the waning days of the Great Depression. Jay isn't afraid of confrontation because he's got the smarts to survive in the big city and the fists to hold on to what he can grab. Keats is able to turn on the charm with the ladies, too, which brings realism to his many romantic clutches. *Variety* noted, "Steven Keats gives a personable performance in the role," and others undoubtedly agreed, because Keats was nominated for an Emmy. Norman Bogner felt that Keats was "badly miscast," and noted that Michael Douglas had been considered for the part but that the producers felt that Douglas "didn't look Jewish enough." Steven Keats worked steadily, mainly in television, for almost twenty years before apparently killing himself in 1994.

Dori Brenner, the earthy actress who portrays Rhoda Gold, was also Emmy-nominated. Rhoda is a rather thankless character who finds surprising romance with Jay, then heartbreak as he cheats on her with Eva Meyers for the majority of the miniseries thereafter. Brenner certainly handles the dramatic fireworks as her character finds, then loses love, fights an addiction to Benzedrine, raises a son pretty much

all by herself, deals with a suicidal sister and eventually successfully re-enters the world of business. Brenner is really the heart and soul of *Seventh Avenue*, as Rhoda's fine, decent character is its one constant, even as she is wronged time and time again. Her warm, forgiving, nostalgic countenance at the conclusion hits just the right notes to end this miniseries on a hopeful, positive track.

Seventh Avenue was the second *Best Sellers* miniseries for Jane Seymour; she had also appeared in the very successful *The Captains and the Kings*. Seymour is *Seventh Avenue*'s sex interest: Eva Meyers allows herself to be seduced by Jay, endures the suicide of her husband John, loves and loses Jay, is tightly controlled and finally raped by Frank Topo, and briefly finds happiness back with Jay before being shot by mistake as the miniseries winds down. Seymour is suitably beautiful and seductive as Eva, and completely believable as a prospective fashion designer. She isn't quite as convincing as a lush, but regains her poise in Eva's later scenes, rediscovering happiness with Jay.

The third important female role is essayed by Anne Archer, portraying Rhoda's troubled sister Myrna Gold. It is, at least at first, a poorly written role, as Myrna's haughty persona and artistic pretentions are unconvincing and transparent, as Myrna's boyfriend Howard Horton (Richard Kline) soon discovers for himself. Myrna's clinch with Jay at the end of the first chapter, overheard by Rhoda, is soap opera melodrama at its most exploitative, a move which will have unconvincing ramifications for the rest of the story. It is only when Myrna finally opens herself to Jay just before her attempted suicide that Archer shines. Her later scenes are fine. Most of the other actors, including Ray Milland, Alan King, Herschel Bernardi, Richard Dimitri and John Pleshette, acquit themselves admirably. Others, like Eli Wallach, William Windom, Jack Gilford and Gloria Grahame, barely have the opportunity to create their characters, much less enliven them.

Gloria's role is that of Moll, the sluttish woman charged with keeping mob hit man Ray Boone out of sight. Moll is evidently an apartment building superintendent, for she introduces Boone to his room, flirtatiously noting, "*everything* is paid for." She is later confronted by the police and pressured to indicate the apartment in which Boone is hiding. Moll works for the mob, as she willingly consents to shopping for Boone, keeping him provisioned, comfortable and out of sight while the police are hunting for him for the killing of Joe Vitelli. Boone seems amenable to the arrangement, and to Moll's presence, seeing that he'll have lots of time on his hands. This changes, however, in Gloria's second scene. Boone gets up from bed to get himself a beer, leaving Moll behind him. Moll, in a flimsy negligee, coos to him to come back to bed. But Boone has had enough of Moll. He moves next to the bed, insults Moll, then holds his bottle of beer over her and pours it onto her as she screams with outrage. As it empties, Moll jumps up, still screaming, and storms from the room, with him yelling right back at her until she's gone. "Like being in jail," Boone mutters to himself. It is just moments later (in film time) that the police arrive.

Combining her three quick scenes, Gloria's screen time totals about one minute. She looks appropriately haggard and slatternly in a silk robe in her first scene, showing Boone around the apartment. Her second scene, the bed scene, finds her in a low-cut negligee. In the shot where Boone pours the beer onto Moll, Gloria has her right arm covering her left breast, lest the beer make the negligee quickly transparent. Gloria quickly jumps up and storms out of the room in quite natural outrage. Moments later Moll is arguing with the police about Boone until Sergeant Rollins (Brock Peters) warns her that she could face obstruction charges for hiding him. Still angry with Boone and seeing that there is nothing to be done, Moll points at his apartment door.

Gloria doesn't appear until about halfway through the third and final chapter, and receives no billing until the opening credits for that chapter. Her role is so minor that she is not mentioned in most of the press information regarding the production, and is not included in any of its advertising. It was probably a surprise for many of the telecast's viewers to suddenly see her pop up as Moll. Today it is hard to find because *Seventh Avenue* was never released commercially and has not been telecast in ages. It is available for viewing at the Library of Congress Moving Image Section and the UCLA Film and Television Archives.

Moll seems like a natural extension of some of Gloria's earlier floozy roles; if Debby Marsh (*The Big Heat*) had survived and was still supported by the mob, one could see her, still scarred, running a safe house for them. Gloria plays it cool, as if hiding a vicious fugitive was the most natural thing in the world. She is the perfect embodiment of a well-worn, perhaps ruined woman still trying to squeeze some pleasure out of her otherwise mundane life. While she had reservations about the size of the role, Gloria had seen that exposure in a major miniseries resulted in welcome exposure and was entirely positive for her paycheck. And Gloria was able to really cut loose when Boone pours the beer on her and create a real spectacle, which she enjoyed as an acting exercise. Other than Jay's outdoor fight with his boss in the first chapter, her beer scene is probably the miniseries' wildest moment.

But Gloria didn't reap any benefit from *Seventh Avenue*. At just three parts, it did not really qualify as a major miniseries, it failed to recruit large numbers of viewers, and her part was so minor that she gained no discernable benefits from being in it. *Seventh Avenue* failed to fulfill the expectations that *Rich Man, Poor Man* had engendered. For the most part the project could not be considered a raging success for anyone except the two Emmy nominees, Keats and Brenner.

Seventh Avenue was to be Gloria's last conventional made-for-television project; afterward she again concentrated on making her mark in feature films, appearing in three more before her death in 1981. She did eventually return to television, too, in three very unique projects that defied the usual definition of what made-for-television projects could entail.

The Dancing Princesses
(March 18, 1979)

CREDITS ATV Network/ITC Entertainment Group. *Produced and Directed by* Jon Scoffield. *Executive Producer:* Terence Baker. *Written by* Derek Marlowe. *Based on a story by* The Brothers Grimm. *Vision Mixer:* Carole Legg. *Vision Control:* Gerry Taylor. *VTR Editor:* John Hawkins. *Music Composed by* Laurie Holloway. *Choreography by* Norman Maen. *Music Played by* Jack Parnell and his Orchestra. *Musical Associate*: Conn Bernard. *Casting*: Joan Brown and Alec Fyne. *Format by* Terence Baker and Polly Broxup. *Makeup Supervisor*: Sheila Mann. *Wardrobe Supervisor*: Stuart Currell. *Floor Manager*: David McDonald. *Stage Manager*: Jane Cotton. *Production Assistant*: Paula Burdon. *Camera Operator*: Bill Brown. *Sound*: Ted Scott. *Lighting*: John Rook. *Designer*: David Chandler. Color. Flat (1.33:1). Monaural Sound. 52 minutes. Broadcast on British television on March 18, 1979. Broadcast on American television on December 29, 1981. Currently unavailable on DVD. Previously available on VHS.

CAST *The Soldier*, Jim Dale; *The King*, Freddie Jones; *The Chamberlain*, Peter Butterworth; *The Witch*, Gloria Grahame; *A Shoemaker*, Peter Benson; *A Soldier*, John Vine; *A Distraught Prince*, Fred Evans; *An Executioner*, Reuben Martin; *Princesses*, Lesley Collier, Jane Darling, Lavinia Lang, Lorna Nathan, Maureen Willsher and Jane Winchester; *Princes*, Lance Aston, Nicholas Chagrin, Wayne Eagling, Vince Logan, Ludovic Romano and Barrie Young.

While in Britain during the summer of 1978 performing the W. Somerset Maugham play *Rain*, Gloria also participated in a British television project based on the Brothers Grimm fairy tale #133, *The Twelve Dancing Princesses*. It mixed classical music with contemporary music to tell of the six (not twelve, as in the original tale) princesses who wear out their slippers each evening after having gone to bed. Gloria was hired to play the lovely witch who guides a soldier through the normally fatal process of attempting to decipher the riddle.

On a battlefield in an alien land, a soldier (Jim Dale) wanders around; he is the only survivor, and he has a bullet wound in his arm. A beautiful witch (Gloria Grahame) appears, indicating to him that Death is nearby. The witch tells the soldier that the king of this land has six daughters, and that he can have one of them if he accepts and succeeds in a challenge. The soldier dresses his wound and considers the matter, speaking directly (and narrating the story) to the camera. The witch tells him that each night the princesses are locked in their room, but every following morning their slippers are worn out, which is costing the king a fortune in replacements! The witch also advises him not to drink any wine he is offered, and she gives him an invisible cloak with which to hide himself from the princesses. Reluctantly

the soldier agrees to the challenge and goes to the dark palace. Death follows.

The king (Freddie Jones) agrees to see the soldier and offers him three chances to discover his daughters' secret. He is given castoff clothing from earlier attempters who have failed to meet the challenge. Taking a room next to that of the princesses, he is able to spy on them through a hole in the wall. The princesses enter his room and offer him wine; remembering the witch's warning, he spits it out. At 3 A.M. the princesses check to see if he is asleep and, convinced that he is, they leave their room through a special door under one of the beds. Using his invisibility cloak, the soldier follows them outside, then across a misty lake, hiding in their boat. He grabs gold and silver branches off strange trees he passes just to prove to himself that he is not dreaming. The princesses enter a beautiful ball and dance waltzes with six handsome princes. The soldier follows and drinks, becoming drunk, throwing away the branches he had collected. He barely makes it back to the palace before the girls, goes to bed and awakens with a bad headache and no proof of the night's adventure. The king is unhappy, and doesn't believe any of his story, especially when they cannot locate the door beneath the bed.

The following night the soldier vows not to drink. He sees one of the princesses clap to make the bed lift and the door open, and he again follows them. This time the destination is a 1920s style jazz club, with the six princesses donning flapper costumes and jitterbugging with the princes. Also present is the witch, in period costume, keeping an eye on the proceedings. This time, the soldier stays sober and takes a teapot to prove his story. But alas, the king is not convinced, even though the teapot contains gin. Angry, the soldier insults the king and prepares to leave. The witch visits the soldier, tells him she has kept him alive through two battles specifically to accept this challenge, and demands that he follow through. She also reveals that she is Death's mistress. "Now you know, even Death has his mistress, and for favors granted, we all have our debts to pay."

That night the soldier has a brainstorm, giving the king his invisibility cloak and opening the secret passage with the special clap. He leads the king outside, shows him the gold and silver branches, and they cross the lake. This time the princesses are dancing in a disco bar, jiving with the barely dressed princes. The king can hardly believe his eyes. The following morning the six sisters are lectured by their father, and the soldier is given the opportunity to choose his bride from among them. The soldier circles them but averts his eyes. None of them will do. He berates them because their secret has destroyed so many men who accepted, but failed, the challenge. The king begs him to stay, but the soldier leaves in disgust. He finds another soldier and joins him in the quest to find an honest battle to fight. The witch interrupts, calling him a fool. The soldier relinquishes his invisibility cloak and walks off into the mist with honor.

Many versions of this Grimm fairy tale have been produced over the years, including one by the British Broadcasting Corporation that had an unexpected impact on this one. The BBC produced a 1978 special, also featuring just six princesses, for broadcast during the Christmas season. Because of the BBC production, this ATV network production, originally scheduled to be telecast on December 17, 1978, was delayed until Sunday, March 18, 1979, when it was shown at 4:15 in the afternoon. As an off-season program, its ratings and popularity were negligible. The program did not receive an American broadcast for two years, finally being chosen as a PBS special for telecast on December 29, 1981, two and a half months after Gloria's untimely death.

Both British versions reduced the number of princesses from a dozen to a half-dozen, but it makes sense both economically (cutting the dancer payroll in half) and artistically (six couples dancing is easier to watch and appreciate than twelve). The stylistic conceit that sets this ATV version apart from all others is the mix of dancing styles it encompasses. The first dancing sequence is a traditional waltz, exactly what one would expect in a fairy tale. The second sequence, the jazz club dance, is jarring because of its modernity. The third sequence, the disco dance, is outlandish, with the princes dressed in briefs and jangling chains, and the princesses cavorting outrageously. Disco music was at its height then, so this sequence was obviously designed to conform to the most popular style of the era. Today it seems perfectly gauche, a se-

rious misstep that dispels the fairy tale's timeless quality.

The other alteration from the Grimm Brothers' original occurs at story's end, when the soldier refuses the king's offer and rebukes the daughters for their uncaring thoughtlessness. The soldier in this modern ending is a man of honor who would rather face death on a battlefield than live a privileged, empty existence as husband to any of them. The Grimm Brothers' ending has the soldier marrying the eldest daughter and living happily ever after! It might offend Grimm purists that writer Derek Marlowe altered the original ending, yet it would be difficult to dispute that Marlowe's new ending changes the tone of the story. Indeed, it rings truer and clearer than does the original fairy tale, and if the Brothers Grimm were alive to contemplate the matter, they might well agree that it is an improvement upon their story for its unexpected, vividly stated humanism.

This show exists mostly to spotlight the dancers, two of whom — Lesley Collier and Wayne Eagling — are noted as guest stars from the Royal Ballet. The framework of the story is important, but fully half of the running time takes place as the dancers waltz, jive and boogie to the music of Jack Parnell and his orchestra. The Grimm Brothers' story could not do justice to such dancing, and does not try, but this visual medium allows the princesses' nightly merrymaking to take center stage. Surrounded by atmospheric smoke and expressionistic sets, and filmed by high-set cameras, the dancing princesses twirl, bounce, glide and bound about the sets with frenetic passion, determined to enjoy every evening as it might be their last chance to revel with unbridled joy.

The actors fill their roles well. Jim Dale seems uncomfortable as the initially disconcerted soldier, but as the story warms, so does his wit and he becomes quite chatty. Dale makes the soldier's uncommon ingenuity convincingly real and is at his best when he rebuffs the witch in the middle of the story and confronts the king at its conclusion. Freddie Jones portrays the king as an irascible yet frustrated father, wanting to love his daughters but realizing that they have drifted away from him. In smaller roles, Peter Butterworth and Peter Benson make the most of their comic opportunities.

Gloria Grahame is luminous as the witch, who is ultimately revealed to be Death's consort. She has only three speaking scenes but they are key in moving the story forward. She also appears in at least two of the dancing sequences, usually appearing near their conclusions, there just to keep an eye on the soldier. In soft light, soft focus and with iridescent tinsel weaved through her flowing hair, Gloria is quite the apparition. She seems to float or glide into her scenes and carries herself with just the right amount of mystery. Her accent doesn't quite blend with those of the others, but she never seems out of place or miscast. Her presence is, pun intended, bewitching.

Because of its postponement, this version of *The Dancing Princesses* received little notice or fanfare in England, and was barely noted when it finally aired in America. It received a good review from Britain's *The Stage and Television Today*: "There was something for everyone in Derek Marlowe's translation of an old fable into a modern idiom and his dialogue blended simplicity and sophistication — though never at the expense of the story." In *Suicide Blonde*, Vincent Curcio wrote, "Both amusing and cool, there is an elegiacal quality about the proceedings, especially surrounding Gloria, that sticks in the mind."

This was a small-scale project for Gloria, one that she wanted to do because it was British — she loved everything British — and because the witch was so glamourous. The soft focus and soft lighting were a welcome change from the harshly lit, unflattering set conditions that she had been experiencing during the '70s, and she liked being the character of mystery in the piece. Furthermore, she was not expected to carry the story, so she could relax and enjoy the experience, which she did. Nearing the end of her career, this type of part was just what she needed.

The Merry Wives of Windsor
(1979)

CREDITS Bard Productions Ltd. *Staged at the* Globe Playhouse for the Shakespeare Society of America. *Production Conceived and Directed by* Jack Manning. *Produced by* R. Thad Taylor. *Executive Producer:* Bard Productions Ltd. *Associate Executive Producer:* William Bushnell, Jr. *Associate Producers:* Susan P. Marrone and Walter Scholz. *Written by* William Shakespeare. *Literary Consultant:* Stephen Booth. *Video Producer:* Felix Girard. *Video Director:* Bill Howell. *Assistant Directors:* Jeffrey G. Forward and Lillian Wilds. *Stage Manager:* Anthony Dinovi. *Choreographer:* Deborah Zall. *Costume Designers:* Terry Troutt and Neal San Teguns. *Lighting and Scenic Director:* Michael M. Berfgeld. *Technical Director–Set Constructor:* Mark Klopfenstein. *Production Stage Manager:* John D. Uhley. *Fencing Choreographer:* Lanny Broyles. *Property Mistress:* Laurelyn Palo. *Wardrobe Mistress:* Mary Michele. *Costume Assistants:* Oliver King, Shannon Eubanks and Janice Viera. *Musical Directors:* Arne Markussen and Virgilius Kasper. *Production Assistants:* Robert W. Amos and Renee Edge. *Lighting Technician:* Kristin Ringess. *Hair:* Renate Leuschner. *Makeup:* Sheryl Leigh Shulman, Jack Bricker and Art Harding. *Publicist:* Harriet Held. *Lighting Director:* Bob Dickenson. *Technical Director:* Les Nelson. *Audio:* Tim Pinch. *Cameras:* Jaimie Wing, Paul Challacombe and James Seligman. *Video Services:* MediaCom. *Shakespeare Society of America Legal Counsel:* Paul Augustine, Jr. *Globe Playhouse Composite Replica Built by* R. Thad Taylor. *Special Thanks to* AFTRA. Color. Flat (1.33:1). Monaural Sound. 150 minutes. Filmed in December, 1979. Currently available on DVD. Previously available on VHS.

CAST *Mistress Page*, Gloria Grahame; *Sir John Falstaff*, Leon Charles; *Mistress Ford*, Valerie Seelie-Snyder; *Master George Page*, Bert Hinchman; *Dr. Caius*, Joel Asher; *Master Frank Ford*, Lyle Stephen; *Mistress Quickly*, Dixie Neyland Tymitz; *Abraham Slender*, Eugene Brezany; *Justice Robert Shallow*, Philip Persons; *Sir Hugh Evans*, Richard Cordery; *Pistol*, Lee Fishel; *Bardolph*, Lanny Broyles; *Nym*, Paul Aron Scott; *Anne Page*, Lisa Barnes; *Fenton*, Addison Randall; *Robin*, Lucinda Dooling; *Host*, William Nye; *Bar Ladies*, Renee Mandel and Stephanie Seebold; *John*, David Brooks; *Robert*, Matt W. Wills; *Rugby*, David Stifel; *Man*, Brian Sullivan; *Old Man*, Keith Blackmer; *Simple*, Richie Levene; *Spirit of Herne's Oak*, Harve Von Lambach; *Queen Elizabeth*, Diane Cameron; *Sir Walter Raleigh*, Jeffrey G. Forward; *Lord Essex*, Les Sula; *Program Host*, John Houseman.

Since essaying the role of Robin in a Pasadena Playhouse version of *The Merry Wives of Windsor* as a high school student, one of Gloria's fondest ambitions was to tackle a Shakespeare play as an adult. She finally received her opportunity in 1979 at the Globe Theatre in Los Angeles, in the same play! This time she would portray Mistress Page, one of the two titular Merry Wives who bedevil Sir John Falstaff.

Although her part is noticeably the smallest of the three leads, Gloria was given top billing as she represented the only "name" in the cast. The play ran during September 1979; the cast was reassembled in December of that year to record their effort on videotape as part of a series intended to preserve every Shakespeare play on tape. Alas, the funding company ran out of money after taping just nine productions, but *The Merry Wives of Windsor* happens to be one of them, faithfully preserved for posterity.

The Merry Wives of Windsor is introduced by host John Houseman, who describes how wives in England differed from those in Spain in 1575, and how this production at Los Angeles' Globe Theatre replicates how Shakespeare's audience would have seen the play performed. It is somewhat odd that Houseman would mention 1575, for the play was first published in 1602 and later republished in a longer version in 1623, after Shakespeare's death. Houseman also notes the two romantic subplots that parallel the main story, and recounts the (probably inaccurate) history that Queen Elizabeth requested that the Falstaff character receive his own romance, which is how *The Merry Wives of Windsor* is alleged to have come into being.

Justice Robert Shallow (Philip Persons) accuses Sir John Falstaff and his servants of wronging him, as Shallow's nephew, Abraham Slender (Eugene Brezany), claims to have been pickpocketed by Falstaff's men while drinking with them. They deny it, and Falstaff (Leon Charles) considers the matter closed. The clownish Slender declares his love for Miss Anne Page, but his uncle and a Welsh parson, Sir Hugh Evans (Richard Cordery), wonder if Slender would be able to consummate such a marriage, were they able to arrange it. Meanwhile, Falstaff dismisses his pickpocketing servant Bardolph (Lanny Broyles) and hatches a plot to woo two wealthy Windsor wives, hoping that one or both will respond to his charms and provide him with money. But Falstaff's other two servants rebel against the plan, causing him to dismiss them as well, and prompting them to seek revenge against their former employer.

Mistress Page (Gloria Grahame) receives a love letter from Falstaff and cannot believe he

has the gall to offer himself to her. When her best friend Mistress Ford (Valerie Seelie-Snyder) receives the same letter, the two women compare them and immediately decide to humiliate the larger-than-life Falstaff by beating him at his own game. Falstaff's former servants pointedly tell Master Page (Bert Hinchman) and Master Ford (Lyle Stephen) about Falstaff's plan. Page laughs about the situation, while Ford permits his innate jealousy to surface. Ford disguises himself as a different man, Master Brook, someone who also has an interest in Mistress Ford. As Brook, he pays Falstaff to try to recruit her into adultery. Brook/Ford is shocked to discover that Falstaff already has a rendezvous with Mistress Ford arranged.

Pastor Evans and the French Dr. Caius (Joel Asher) are to have a duel, which is thwarted by an innkeeper who doesn't want to lose either of his friends. Falstaff visits Mistress Ford and is about to make his romantic move when Mistress Page arrives and warns that Master Ford is coming. She suggests Falstaff hide in a basket of clothing, which the women have arranged to have carried to the Thames and dumped. Ford enters, having been told (as Brook) by Falstaff that he will be there, but Ford fails to notice the large heavy basket being carried out of his home. The women maintain their innocence, laughing with glee as the men make fools of themselves.

Dr. Caius' servant, Mistress Quickly (Dixie Neyland Tymitz), promises to help him win the hand of young, buxom Anne Page (Lisa Barnes). But she also promises the same help to (and takes payment from) Slender and another young man, Fenton (Addison Randall), who really loves Anne for who she is and is not just after her dowry. Ford again disguises himself as Brook and visits Falstaff, who surprises him with the story of his humiliation, insisting he was at Ford's home, and then shocks him with the news that Mistress Ford has again invited him to visit while her husband is away. This time Brook/Ford is determined to catch Falstaff in the act of seducing his wife. Falstaff arrives at the appointed time and is wooing Mistress Ford when Mistress Page again enters with a warning that her husband is on his way. At Mistress Page's suggestion, Falstaff disguises himself as an old woman. Ford enters and, not recognizing the disguised Falstaff as a local witch whom he cannot bear, he beats the old hag until she leaves his home.

The two merry wives tell their husbands about Falstaff, his love letters to them, and their plan to humiliate him. The husbands are thrilled and advance the idea to give Sir John Falstaff one last lesson. Mistress Ford invites Falstaff to a midnight rendezvous at Herne's Oak, and he cannot prevent himself from accepting. Meanwhile, plans are made, separately, by Slender and Dr. Caius to use the occasion to rush away with Anne Page and be married. At midnight, Falstaff, who is dressed as a bull at her request, finds Mistress Ford waiting for him. Suddenly Mistress Page arrives and great cries erupt around them. The women run away as Falstaff surrenders himself to his unlucky fate. He is surrounded by hobgoblins, elves and fairies who chant and pinch him in some kind of ceremony. Then they reveal themselves to be local children. Other Windsor citizens laugh and laugh at Falstaff's distress.

Slender stomps back into the picture complaining that the girl he took away to marry isn't Anne Page; it's one of the servant boys. Then Dr. Caius storms into the proceedings dragging the servant Robin (Lucinda Dooling) behind him, decrying the fact that Robin isn't Anne Page. Finally, Anne is revealed to be with Fenton, who once again proclaims his love for her. This time, instead of rejecting him as a suitor, the elder Pages welcome him into the family. The play ends with the cast, still at the midnight ceremony, singing a song as the credits roll and Houseman delivers a brief epilogue.

The Merry Wives of Windsor is not one of Shakespeare's major plays, yet because it is a light, very accessible comedy, it is dramatized frequently by groups both professional and amateur. This particular production was staged at the Globe Theatre, a replica of the type of theater used in Shakespeare's era. Operated by the Shakespeare Society of America from 1972 to 2007, the Globe was a one-half-scale replica of the famous theater in England where Shakespeare presented the majority of his productions. For thirty-five years, R. Thad Taylor, the director of the Shakespeare Society, operated the theater, thus providing the only consistent source of Shakespearean theater in the Los Angeles area; the Society became the first organization in the world to stage all of Shakespeare's

plays in succession. Following Taylor's 2006 passing, the Society lost its lease and the Globe Theatre closed, ending a rich, if not profitable, chapter of Los Angeles theater history.

In the late 1970s Taylor was approached by Bard Productions Limited, a company that intended to create a videotape series of Shakespeare plays and market them to schools, universities and libraries around the country. Taylor agreed to allow the company to record various productions at the Globe Theatre, the fifth of which is *The Merry Wives of Windsor*. Only nine productions were recorded before Bard Productions Limited ran out of funding, but those nine shows were duly archived and eventually released on VHS and, later, DVD. Those nine productions, all filmed at the Globe Theatre, showcase an eclectic mix of actors from stage, screen and television. From Gloria Grahame and Bob Hoskins to Darryl Hickman and Efrem Zimbalist, Jr., they made a serious effort to bring classical Shakespeare to the masses in a manner as educational as it is entertaining. For the record, the other entries in this series were, alphabetically, *Antony and Cleopatra, King Lear, King Richard II, Macbeth, Othello, Romeo and Juliet, The Taming of the Shrew* and *The Tempest*.

The Merry Wives of Windsor was staged in September 1979, and was scheduled to be taped at the end of its stage run, but it was another two months before it was recorded. Late in the year the video company notified Thad Taylor that, for tax shelter reasons, the play needed to be recorded before the end of the year, so Taylor reunited his cast during the week between Christmas and New Year's Eve to do so, in a theater without an audience. Gloria had to fly from London, where she had just finished a three-week run in *The Glass Menagerie*. Adding further intrigue, the video equipment failed at times, lighting the stage for video recording was troublesome, the video director had no previous experience with Shakespeare and the warehouse housing the Globe Theatre was not exactly soundproof, to which the videotape bears ample evidence. But it was done, and exists today as the only filmed record of Gloria acting on stage.

The production reflects some of these difficulties. The first half in particular is rather dull and clumsy, dealing in greater detail with secondary concerns than with the main story-line. Staging the play at the Globe Theatre certainly resonates with proper historical context, designed to present the dramatics as closely as seventeenth-century audiences saw them as possible, yet that very conceit diminishes the artistry with which the play can be exhibited. The complete lack of modern flourishes or imaginative settings or mood music translates to a very basic, fundamental presentation. This more accurately reflects the actual theater experience of the 1600s but today is probably too dull for many viewers. Probably the biggest fault of the production is that — especially early — the performers seem unsure of themselves, or perhaps of the validity of playing to an empty house. After the Merry Wives appear on stage at about the thirty-eight-minute mark, the play gathers steam and begins to propel forward with purpose.

Shakespeare's play is a comedy of forgiveness despite various subjects and themes that could easily form the basis of darker, dramatic dramas. It is unconditionally cheerful and exuberant, even when Sir Hugh Evans and Dr. Caius (pronounced "Keys" in this production) are preparing to duel, and when Sir John Falstaff is trying to recover from two close escapes from the outraged Master Ford. About the worst thing that happens is that the Host of the Garter Inn falls prey to some German thieves, losing some of his horses ... but that does not happen in this production. That subplot, instigated by the two duelers (Pastor Evans and Dr. Caius) foiled by the Host's machinations to keep them apart, was cut from this version. Various other line trimmings occur throughout the text, and scenes are occasionally performed out of order. Yet the tone remains relatively constant in a pastoral sort of fashion, as Falstaff's scheming results in nothing more than minor inconvenience for anyone, including himself. Such mildness from Shakespeare, no matter how cleverly presented, is hardly representative of his magnificent tragedies: *Hamlet, King Lear, Macbeth, Othello.* Surely *The Merry Wives of Windsor* is escapist Shakespeare, real enough to engage and please audiences, yet not overbearingly thought-provoking.

The Bard had a great deal to say in the play, however, starting and ending with the realization that women are just as smart, cunning and capable of hijinks as any man. His Merry Wives understand immediately what tomfoolery Falstaff is attempting, and their attempt to teach him a lesson by using his own methods against him is at once moral, logical and mirthful. Mistresses Ford and Page are unequivocal; they know exactly where they stand with their husbands and are unafraid to risk their social standing to defend themselves. They are not weak-willed girls who run to their male protectors to solve problems for them; they are smart, independent women offended by Falstaff's immoral intentions, and devilish enough to teach Falstaff proper humility.

Mythological and historical allusions are sprinkled liberally throughout the text, and the wordplay is occasionally remarkable, reinforcing the notion that Shakespeare's plays — even his lighter ones — are filled with meaning, style and wisdom. *The Merry Wives of Windsor* is the only one of Shakespeare's plays to be written almost entirely in prose, which perhaps makes it more accessible than most for modern audiences. While at least some of its political sharpness has been lost to time (consult a reference text or curriculum guide for a better understanding of some of Shakespeare's more pointed quips), the play gently explores Britain's class differences, demonstrates what was expected of women of the time, dramatizes what people would do to obtain a modicum of wealth and also turns many of the era's conventions inside out. For instance, conventional stage wives of the early 1600s were usually portrayed as either "proper," humorless paragons of virtue; or "merry," lustful lovers of life who often fell prey to the predations of knights looking for a little fun in the towns they visited. Shakespeare's take is much more interesting and meaningful. He combines the two, allowing his Merry Wives to enjoy life and laugh about its foibles while still remaining solidly upstanding. Mistresses Ford and Page are capable, trustworthy, intelligent and quite colorful in their expressions and personalities. Moreover they are good friends with one another without any pretext or subtext, which was also unusual for stage wives of the era. In every way the Merry Wives are uncommon and extraordinary, which is exactly how Shakespeare wished to present them. As Mistress Page says in an aside to the audience in Act IV, Scene II, "Hang him [referring to Falstaff], dishonest varlet! We cannot misuse [him] enough. We'll leave a proof, by that which we will do, Wives may be merry and yet honest too."

Shakespeare has fun reversing expectations in this manner, and he does the same with Falstaff, taking a seemingly powerful and crafty masculine figure and making him the butt of the play's humor. Even more surprising is that the vain Falstaff endures his shame without rancor. Falstaff is not happy about the travails he experiences but he is able to put them in perspective, and there is at least the hint that he understands that his less-than-honorable impulses have led inexorably to his humiliations. Sir John Falstaff is given great theatricality by Leon Charles, a stage actor who died less than two years after this production completed (and less than two months before Gloria Grahame passed away). Charles (who worked in an off-screen capacity on many films as a dialogue coach) portrays Falstaff as a lecherous, larger-than-life rogue scheming to insure his future by any means possible. However, as he becomes aware that he is being played for a fool by the women he is attempting to swindle, he acquiesces to his fate with good humor. It is a winning performance with a great deal of *bonhomie*.

The men are more populous than the women on stage but with the exception of Falstaff, they are not nearly as interesting. Lyle Stephen is believable as the jealous Master Ford but has more fun dressing up as Master Brook and discovering his wife's seeming infidelity. Joel Asher is a caricature of a nervous, vain Frenchman as Dr. Caius and it is a wonder that Eugene Brezany didn't permanently break his voice, cracking it as often as he does as witless Abraham Slender. The other male performers are unremarkable in their parts.

Mistress Ford, portrayed by Valerie Seelie-Snyder, is the larger of the two "mistress" parts because she is the one who responds to Falstaff's romantic entreaties. Seelie-Snyder is vivacious and spirited in the part, enlivening the play the minute she steps on stage. Mistress Ford finds great enjoyment in being able to turn the tables on the men in her life and Seelie-Snyder expertly demonstrates her character's cleverness and joy. Seelie-Snyder also has a

stronger presence because of the production's lighting; her hair doesn't shadow her face as frequently or irritatingly as Gloria Grahame's hair does. The third main female part is Mistress Quickly, played zestfully by Dixie Neyland Tymitz. Mistress Quickly is Dr. Caius' servant, yet she accepts money from Slender and Fenton as well as her master to help sway Anne Page's affections. Tymitz is a dynamo on the stage, percolating with energy, constantly strategizing even when she herself is unsure of the goals she wishes to achieve. Lisa Barnes radiates warmth, sincerity and youthful vitality as beautiful Anne Page, the romantic target of several male characters (yet Anne Page is not even close to being at the center of the play). And Lucinda Dooling is long-legged and sprightly as Robin, the male servant character played forty years earlier by Gloria Grahame in a Pasadena Playhouse staging of the play.

Gloria shines as Mistress Page, a woman who relishes the prospect of humbling and humiliating a man with the temerity of Sir John Falstaff after he offends her. Like the other performers, Gloria received next to nothing for the privilege of performing at the Globe, but she didn't care. She joined the troupe, learned her lines and delivered them to the best of her ability. The only complaints made about Gloria were that she insisted on doing her own hairstyling and makeup, and that she removed the standard petticoats from under her dress. Costume designer Neal San Teguns was unimpressed: "As far as I was concerned, she looked like a wrinkled old sofa."

Nevertheless, Gloria gave it her all. Her approach to the role was play Mistress Page as a youthful woman of high moral character. Gloria's energy level could not be higher as she darts around the stage, scheming with Mistress Ford to punish Falstaff, refusing to take sides either for or against young Fenton when he pledges his love for her daughter, exhorting Mistress Ford to kick Falstaff out of the house before he is caught and she loses her good reputation. Gloria understood the rhythm of bygone English, even when the meaning may not have been concretely clear to her, and there are few examples of her just saying the words. She builds a nice conviviality with Seelie-Snyder, which brings a modern feel to the piece, as if they were suburban neighbors discussing uninvited love letters over coffee. Gloria has a strong stage presence, but also knows when to stand still and allow the other performers the spotlight. She is quite natural and certainly believable as Mistress Page; she probably wished she could have transferred Shakespeare's lessons about love to one or more of her ex-husbands.

After the play had run its course in Los Angeles, Gloria went to England to prepare for and star in a three-week run of *The Glass Menagerie*, flying back before the end of the year to make this recording. It was a hectic time and Gloria was not feeling particularly well, but she happily honored the commitment she had made. She was afraid that it would be the only time she would ever perform Shakespeare on stage, and she wanted to do it well. Plus, she realized full well that her name was the most recognizable one connected with the project, so she felt some responsibility to the other participants to be able to promote it. She didn't know that in just a few months another opportunity to play Shakespeare would arise, on a stage in DeKalb, Illinois, and in a part she had long dreamed of playing. The play was *Macbeth* and Gloria would appear as Lady Macbeth.

Bard Productions Limited ran out of funding after recording nine such theatrical productions; they are available on DVD. This bold experiment headed by the Shakespeare Society of America failed to fulfill its stated mission of recording every Shakespeare play at the Globe Theatre, but most people of an artistic bent would argue that some Shakespeare is better than none. Despite technical issues and a setting that tended to inhibit creative staging, *The Merry Wives of Windsor* is a singular program in many ways, including its place as an oddity in Gloria Grahame's oeuvre. It is certainly worth seeing as the only extant example of Gloria on stage, as well as its purely historical aspects. It isn't a great production but Gloria felt very privileged to participate.

Mr. Griffin and Me (1981)

CREDITS Liberty Mutual Insurance Company. *Directed by* Patrick O'Neal. *Produced by* Robert Halmi, Jr. *Teleplay by* Robert Sand. *Story by* John Bell and Rona Merrill. *Director of Photography*: John Lindley.

Film Editor: Murray Solomon. *Music Composed by* Jonathan Meredith. *First Assistant Director*: George Manasse. *Second Assistant Director*: Marc Nerlinger. *Art Director*: Norman Bielowicz. *Costume Designer*: Clifford Capone. *Makeup Artist–Hair Stylist*: David Forrest. *Production Supervisor*: Stratton Leopold. *Script Supervisor*: Mary Bailey. *Unit Manager*: Robert Altman. *Sound Mixer*: Jack Cooley. *Assistant Cameraman*: Ken Ferris. *Gaffer*: Denver Collins. *Key Grip*: Anthony Kupersmith. *Sound Recorder*: David Terry. *Property Master*: Dennis Shaw. *Sound Editors*: Randy Tung and Ron Kalish. *Assistant Film Editor*: Chip Cronkite. *Assistant Art Director*: Ann Bielowicz. *Assistant Sound Editor*: Linda Shawest. *Second Assistant Cameraman*: Joe Thomas. *Boom Man*: Thomas Valenti. *First Grip*: Mike Clayton. *Assistant Grip*: Eddie Edams. *Best Boy*: Marty Newborn. *Third Electric*: Dennis Moonadian and Billy Sherill. *Auditor*: Selma Weitz. *Production Secretary*: Beth Crutchfield. *Secretary to the Director*: Debbie Pace. *Casting Assistant*: Gogi Sargeant. *Wardrobe*: Bonnie Shaw. *Assistant Makeup*: Jimmie Delcach. *Payroll Service*: Pumpkin Payroll Services, Inc. *Production Assistants*: Bea Thomas, Peter Vongal, Jeffrey Lloyd Lynn, Mark Moore, Del Moore, Todd Alston, Rhetta Halmi and Max O'Neal. *Camera and Lenses by* Panavision. *Optical Effects by* EPX Unlimited. *Titles and Stills by* Cinema Television Design. *Special Thanks to* E. G. Sherrill.

MUSIC "Best of All," *Words by* Burgess Meredith, *Music by* Jonathan Meredith; "There You Were Again," by Joe Salvo and Irwin Fisch; "I'll Be Seeing You," by Sammy Fain and Irving Kahal, sung by Lynn Roberts. *Music Arranged and Directed by* Walt Levinsky. *Music Editor*: Thomas Gulino. Movielab Color. Flat (1.33:1). Magno Sound (monaural). 52 minutes. Originally telecast January 11, 1981. Not currently available on commercial home video.

CAST *Kenneth Griffin*, Burgess Meredith; *Mara Emerson*, Gloria Grahame; *Murphy*, Charles "Honi" Coles; *Jane Barlow*, Rosemary Murphy; *Country Girl*, Gail Kight; *Chuck*, Raymond C. Wilkes; *Bubba*, William Ralph Pace, Jr.; *TV Announcer*, Edwin Brant Frost; *Clarence*, E. G. Sherrill; *Doorman at Hotel*, Chester Davis; *Young Woman in Opera House*, Kathleen Joanne Roberts; *Man in Opera House*, Daniel G. Albright; *Mr. Harold*, Bernard Webb.

Gloria's final TV project was a one-hour comedy program titled *Mr. Griffin and Me*. It is a whimsical tale reuniting a famous couple — an Oscar-winning actress and her director husband who deserted her twenty-four years ago, at the pinnacle of their fame together — requiring all the star power its leads can muster. It was set, and filmed, in rural Georgia, a locale that greatly contributes to its old-fashioned flavor, even though the story is contemporary.

Gloria was quite sick, delaying the production for two days because of illness, but she was determined to finish what she began. She did, although the finished product offers evidence that her increasingly poor health was becoming a real concern.

A narrator provides a summation of the show business career of Kenneth Griffin (Burgess Meredith), a good actor who became a great director. Griffin weds his star, Mara Emerson (Gloria Grahame), and makes several hit movies with her. Then Griffin turned his talent to making musicals, and only musicals, and when these proved unprofitable, he suddenly disappeared — leaving his wife behind without even a word of explanation, and taking the most valuable paintings that they had collected together. The program's credits roll, and then Mara is seen on the big screen, in scenes from *The Big Heat.*

Mara describes some of her Hollywood adventures to an attentive college-age audience as slides from some of her movies flicker behind her. She is also seen winning an Academy Award, for which the audience applauds. A couple of questions from the audience confirm that, yes, her husband absconded with valuable paintings twenty-four years previously, and, no, she has no idea what ever happened to him, or them.

Meanwhile, an elderly, bearded, penniless Kenneth Griffin drinks in a bar, and sings whatever comes into his gin-soaked head. He's obviously very comfortable and cozy, known by everyone in the local bar, but not recognized as Kenneth Griffin the famous director by anybody. That changes when the regional television news program shows footage of a local foot race, and one of the contestants is Kenneth Griffin. When Kenneth sees that he is being filmed while running, he quits the race, but not before the footage has been shot. The news program airs Kenneth's abrupt departure from the race, and Mara's long-time secretary Jane Barlow (Rosemary Murphy), instantly recognizes him. Without telling Mara why, Jane quickly adjusts Mara's lecture schedule so that Macon, Georgia, is the very next stop.

Kenneth has a long-time assistant, an elderly black man named Murphy (Charles "Honi" Coles), who left California when Kenneth did, and who has kept an eye on him ever since.

Murphy tells Kenneth that Mara is coming to Macon; Kenneth's first instinct is to run. Second thoughts prompt him to ask Murphy to contact her. Murphy tells Mara that Kenneth died in 1963, but Mara doesn't believe him. Jane happens to mention that Mara "owns half of Malibu," which Murphy promptly repeats to Kenneth. So, at Mara's lecture, just as she is singing her signature tune "I'll Be Seeing You," her song is interrupted by a clean-shaven Kenneth Griffin. Mara calmly introduces him to the crowd to long, heartfelt applause.

Backstage, Kenneth tries to charm Mara, but Jane continually reminds him about the stolen paintings. Kenneth avoids the question, joining Mara in her fancy Packard Phaeton auto for a drive through the country. Kenneth dismisses the chauffeur, but then runs out of gas driving on a country road. He and Mara walk to a deserted riverfront amusement park, reminiscing about their past all the while. They board a Ferris wheel, but get off when it begins to rattle furiously. Looking back at it from a distance, they see the wheel spinning furiously. Then they hop into a paddleboat and paddle out into the river, but abruptly discover that it is still tethered to the dock. Kenneth and Mara arrange to have dinner in a dockside building, but their long-delayed talk is interrupted, this time by a Dixieland band. Kenneth sings "Best of All" to Mara before Murphy arrives with dinner, which accidentally crashes to the floor. Mara has had enough; she tells Kenneth that her lawyers will be in touch about the missing paintings.

Kenneth admits that they are in his "Heart of Darkness," a nearby mansion where he stays. So they go there, to a bedroom, where Kenneth confesses that he sold the paintings long ago. Then he throws Mara onto the bed, and she fights back ferociously. Outside, Murphy pulls up a chair to wait until the lights in the room turn off. The next morning both awaken with smiles and Murphy makes breakfast. Jane arrives and serves the couple breakfast in bed, reminding Mara that her next lecture begins in twenty minutes— twenty miles away. Mara and Kenneth have a brief spat and she pours a cup of milk over his head. He suggests they live together in Malibu, and Mara admits that she is broke. Then he pours a cup of milk over her head. They laugh together at their shared financial and romantic misfortunes and lost opportunities.

The next lecture has Mara talking about her career, then introducing Murphy, who tap dances across the stage. Kenneth sings "There's No Business Like Show Business" while Murphy taps around, and the program's end credits roll. There is one final shot of Kenneth, Mara, Jane and Murphy dancing on stage together, doing a simple routine led by Murphy, before the final fadeout.

Mr. Griffin and Me is gossamer thin, barely able to fill fifty-two minutes of running time. What could have and should have been a ninety-minute character study spotlighting two underrated actors delivering knockout performances is, due to a shamefully meager and meandering script, never properly developed or presented. Despite some interesting touches, dazzling views of a Packard Phaeton roadster and a cast that seems up for just about anything, the overall effect of this pastiche is formless and mushy.

To begin with, the central mystery is posited but never addressed. Kenneth left everything behind twenty-four years earlier: his wife, his career, his legacy. The only clues to his psyche revolve around music; the musicals he made fell out of favor and whenever Kenneth is onscreen in the present he is humming or singing, inventing songs on the fly and moving to a rhythm only he can hear. Okay, but does Kenneth's obvious love of music justify his disappearing act? He left Mara without a word of explanation, taking with him valuable paintings that belonged to her as well as himself. For what? To live as a hermit in rural Georgia, singing his made-up songs in bars for drinks? Mara asks him directly why he left her and the life they shared, and he does not, or cannot, answer. The script intimates that Kenneth is merely a harmless rascal who cannot resist his lazy impulses; that he never meant to harm Mara or defraud her, but that he just could not go on as he was living in Hollywood. The script also wants viewers to believe that there is something noble in Kenneth's rejection of his career. Perhaps there is, but this

Mr. Griffin and Me. Reunited after twenty-four years, actress Mara Emerson (Gloria) still feels her long-lost husband Kenneth Griffin (Burgess Meredith) is quite a rascal.

telefilm never makes its case that Kenneth was suffering or losing his soul in any way, and without evidence of Hollywood's evil influence, Kenneth's rejection is hollow and unconvincing. Kenneth comes across not as the charming rapscallion that the deficient script presents, but as a selfish, foolish old codger who sold his soul for drink and is more than willing to bilk his wife a second time if she allows him the opportunity.

The script also foolishly uses the missing paintings as an axis to pivot around, forcing the story to concentrate on what is essentially an insignificant issue and deflecting attention away from the characters, where it should be focused. The missing paintings also serve as a metaphor for the love Mara had for Kenneth, and which he took with him and dissipated until there was nothing left. But Mara still has feelings for her absent husband, which are rekindled despite Kenneth's clumsy and even rude behavior toward her. The reuniting bedroom scene is meant to be light and funny, with Mara initially put off by his awkward seduction and eventually rediscovering ecstasy with her true love, but the only element preventing this scene from becoming ugly is Murphy's presence outside, relaxing and keeping a watchful eye on the couple he obviously believes belongs together.

Mr. Griffin and Me is directed by actor Patrick O'Neal with an oppressive touch. He tries painfully hard to keep the atmosphere light and airy but his insistence on turning every sequence into wide-eyed whimsy is aggravating, as this approach undermines the performances and renders the story meaningless. A good example is the jaunt that Kenneth and Mara take in the beautiful Packard Phaeton. Kenneth leaves the chauffeur behind, only to run out of gas. So they walk to a deserted amusement park area, where Murphy is preparing their dinners. They board a Ferris wheel for a ride, but exit quickly when the thing starts to rattle and shake. As they look back at it from a distance, it spins madly (the film is obviously accelerated for comic effect). A paddlewheel jaunt on the lake follows; this ends suddenly when the paddlewheel reaches the end of its tether. Dinner is next, and Murphy lightly sets a tray of food on a folding stool. Naturally the stool folds and the food crashes to the floor. Is any of this funny? No.

None of this tomfoolery advances the story, develops the characters or amuses the audience. Director O'Neal continually downplays the story's serious aspects in favor of Kenneth's whimsical "come what may" attitude about life, interpreting Kenneth's sloth, penchant for drunkenness and seeming lack of concern regarding anybody but himself as merely various shades of Kenneth's sunny personality. Meanwhile, Mara Emerson has had to withstand public scrutiny of her husband's selfish desertion for almost a quarter of a century. It is an unbalanced portrait that necessarily builds pity for Mara and enmity against Kenneth. The balancing factors are supposed to be the actor portrayals, and Mara's everlasting love for Kenneth, but neither factor is as convincing as it is intended to be.

Burgess Meredith, to his credit, never attempts to make Kenneth a likable rogue. Charming, yes, but not particularly likable. Meredith sings a few songs, and even helped write one of the songs with his son Jonathan Meredith, who composed the telefilm's score. Meredith creates a singular character in Kenneth Griffin; it is unlike anyone else the versatile actor has ever played. And while Meredith was never a big movie star, he is familiar enough to movie fans in projects ranging from *Of Mice and Men* and *The Story of G.I. Joe* (where he portrayed Ernie Pyle) to *Rocky* and his several appearances on the *Batman* television series as the Penguin, to be recognized as a quasi-legendary performer in his own right, thus reinforcing the aura that surrounds Kenneth's disappearance. Furthermore, Meredith is a natural scene-stealer and he is provided a great deal of latitude regarding the boundaries of his fanciful portrayal. The problem with all of Meredith's muttering, talking to himself and singing is that it is difficult to take the character seriously, to believe that the man was actually a highly talented director way back when. Meredith's loosey-goosey style of acting actively undermines his character's credibility.

That is not the case with Gloria, who plays Mara. The film benefits from its early use of scenes from *The Big Heat* that quickly, powerfully establish Mara's credentials as a legendary Hollywood actress. Gloria also provides the proper gravity for her role when discussing her career with the audience. But most of the

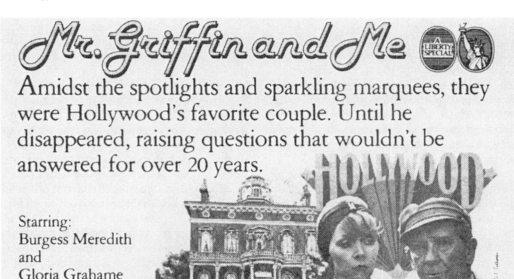

Mr. Griffin and Me. **This syndicated television special was sponsored by the Liberty Mutual Insurance Company.**

telefilm is comedic, and Mara is often the "straight man" to the shenanigans of the other cast members. Gloria seems attuned to this arrangement, and visibly enjoys herself when she is permitted to yuk it up, too, as in the scene where she pours milk onto Meredith in bed.

Both stars seem to be having a good time, and that fact goes a long way toward making *Mr. Griffin and Me* as palatable as it is. It also helps that the two main supporting players, Rosemary Murphy and Charles "Honi" Coles, also have fun with their roles. Murphy, a Broadway veteran who never quite reached movie stardom in the early 1970s and segued into TV, has a funny scene where she spots Kenneth running the televised marathon and nearly falls out of the bed in shock. Coles is a tap dancer, part of the tap-dancing group the Copasetics; he later popped up in small roles in *The Cotton Club* and *Dirty Dancing*. In this program he functions as the intermediary between his long-time employer and the wife Kenneth left behind. Coles is charming, good-

natured and calm during even the wildest and loudest moments that his friends create. And he has two brief tap dancing moments where he can display his hoofing talent.

All of this should have comprised a wonderfully nostalgic, humorous and beguiling program, but the Robert Sand teleplay is woefully slight and O'Neal's direction does not improve matters. Perhaps that explains why no traditional network bothered to buy it; *Mr. Griffin and Me* was a syndicated program sponsored by the Liberty Mutual Insurance Company. It aired once, on January 11, 1981, and promptly disappeared into the oblivion that awaited so much television programming before the popularity of home video. The *New York Times* television critic called the program "an hourlong drama with the texture of a slight but charming short story," but he also credited *The Big Heat* to Raoul Walsh instead of Fritz Lang. He also failed to recognize that *Mr. Griffin and Me* is quite distinctly a comedy, even if it isn't very funny.

Apart from a *Tales of the Unexpected* episode that would not air until 1984, this would be the final television appearance for Gloria Grahame. She had learned in 1980 that the breast cancer that she went into remission five years earlier had returned, stronger than ever. This time around, Gloria did not fight back very hard. She continued to follow specific diet parameters but refused to undergo radiation or chemotherapy treatments. She told her sister Joy that she preferred to work and ignore the cancer; she felt this was a battle she could not win. Publicly she didn't say a word about her illness, even when she felt so sick that she missed two days of filming in Georgia. As soon as *Mr. Griffin and Me* wrapped, Gloria went back to the stage in upstage New York, where she starred in the Noël Coward play *Private Lives*. Gloria spent most of the following year performing on stage in America and in Britain. In London, rehearsing for another run of *The Glass Menagerie*, Gloria finally became too ill to perform any longer.

Gloria never admitted publicly that the cancer had recurred. She blamed her deteriorating condition on things she had eaten and bad reactions to vitamin shots. She exerted almost superhuman effort to ward off the pain, refusing to let it dictate how she could live her life. But Gloria was, indeed, a very ill woman. During treatment from a London doctor, excess fluid was incorrectly drained from Gloria's abdomen and her bowel was punctured, leading to peritonitis (bacteria entering her bloodstream). Two of Gloria's children were notified and flew over from the States, saw the terrible condition she was in, and immediately flew Gloria back to New York. She was taken to St. Vincent's Hospital where she died peacefully a few hours later, with her children Tim and Paulette by her side.

Gloria Grahame was fifty-seven when she died, though most newspaper obituaries printed her birth year as 1925 rather than the correct 1923. Gloria did not care for the idea of growing old and, whenever asked about her age, either lied about it or deflected the question. She never stopped hoping to play Shakespeare's Juliet, arguing that it was traditional for established performers to play young roles, even past middle age. Gloria always tried to think young, to feel young, to be able to play with her kids without embarrassment, to tackle movie and stage roles that required the zest and energy of youth. She hated the betrayal of her own body as it aged; she often dressed in clothes and wore makeup that would be considered appropriate for a woman half her age. She maintained her exquisite attractiveness for a long time, but thwarting death was a battle she could not win. And at the end, Gloria accepted her fate, made peace with her inevitable fate and her mercurial past, and calmly passed away with honest dignity.

Television Series Appearances

After her film career slowed in the late 1950s and family responsibilities became paramount in her life, Gloria increasingly turned to live theater and network television for acting opportunities. She had begun her career on the stage and was eager to return to short engagements of good plays, especially as she was no longer being offered film roles of quality. This love of theater would remain with Gloria for the next two decades. In terms of television, Gloria had no intention of tying herself down to a weekly commitment — nor was she offered anything — but she did see the logic in appearing on dramatic and comedic series from time to time, to stay in the public eye. In between having her second, third and fourth kids and raising them outside of the glaring Hollywood spotlights, television appearances were easier to handle than movie shoots; they were usually filmed on nearby studio soundstages and paid fairly well. Yet it was only often at the instigation of old friends like writer-producer Stanley Rubin and ex-husband Cy Howard that Gloria agreed to such acting jobs.

Gloria certainly had opportunities to appear on television earlier in her career but always preferred the rigors of the big screen, especially during television's wild, *live* early years. For instance, one news clipping indicates that she had arranged to appear on the January 28, 1954, live broadcast of "A Place in the Sun," as staged on CBS's *Lux Video Theatre*, but there is no evidence that she actually fulfilled that commitment. Gloria had been asked to star in the 1951 movie version but was unable to convince Howard Hughes at RKO to loan her to Paramount for the role. Instead, she was pressured to make *Macao* and Shelley Winters triumphed in the part that was meant to have been hers. For reasons unknown, very possibly including nervousness about acting live on television, she evidently lost the plum part a second time.

Gloria's first television appearance was just five days after she won her Supporting Actress Academy Award for *The Bad and the Beautiful*, when she spent a few minutes in a "Maxie the Taxi" skit on the *Eddie Cantor Colgate Comedy Hour* clutching her Oscar while Cantor made jokes. It was a casting coup for Cantor, but did not present Gloria at her best. Following that experience, Gloria endeavored to keep her television appearances tightly scripted and well planned in advance. The following is a descriptive listing of her seventeen network and syndicated television appearances, all but three of which have been screened for this book.

G.E. Theater (CBS; 1961): "Don't Let It Throw You"

CAST AND CREDITS January 1, 1961 (Episode 9.12). *Host*: Ronald Reagan. *Guest Stars*: Dick Shawn, Gloria Grahame, Joey Forman, Jerome Cowan, John Fiedler, Paul Bradley *and* Walter Conrad. *Written by* Arnold and Lois Peyser. *Directed by* Herschel Daugherty. 30 minutes.

G.E. Theater was a lauded and popular ten-year anthology series that staged half-hour stories with many big-name guest stars culled from filmdom. It was the invitation of former beau Stanley Rubin, one of the show's producers, which persuaded Gloria to first appear on network television. This episode appeared near the middle of the ninth season, soon after she married her fourth husband, Tony Ray.

Song salesman Felix Franklin (Dick Shawn) wins big money at the crap tables in Las Vegas, thanks in part to a woman, Elena (Gloria Grahame), he considers his good luck charm. The money turns Felix's head; he quits his job and plans big moves. But before he can even leave town the IRS takes its cut and the casino owner makes every effort to get Felix back to the tables. That includes using Elena, who reluctantly confesses her part in luring him back to lose the money he had collected. Although he is angry at her deception, they ultimately discover they have a great deal in common.

Gloria is Elena Carlisle, a casino "shill" hired to get bettors to the tables and keep them happy once they get there. When Elena proves altogether too successful with Felix, she is sent away by the casino owner to end Felix's winning streak. Elena is squarely in line with Gloria's tradition of good-bad roles; her job is to get suckers to the tables, but in this case she likes Felix and genuinely wants him to win and get out of town while he can. Gloria looks fantastic in a dark cocktail dress and, later in the episode, quite alluring in lingerie. Elena is also a singer, although she is not given the opportunity to prove it (Dick Shawn's singing of the title song is clearly dubbed), making this yet another role depicting the decidedly non-musical Gloria posing as a talented singer.

Harrigan and Son (ABC; 1961): "My Fair Lawyer"

CAST AND CREDITS January 27, 1961 (Episode 1.15). *Star-*

ring: Pat O'Brien, Roger Perry, Georgine Darcy and Helen Kleeb. *Guest Stars*: Gloria Grahame, Forrest Lewis, Eloise Taylor, Barry Brooks *and* David Huddleston. 30 minutes.

Harrigan and Son, a half-hour comedy series featuring father-and-son lawyers, lasted just one season. This episode was in the middle of that season, and has a neighbor (Forrest Lewis) suing Harrigan Sr. (Pat O'Brien) for damages because smoke from the Harrigan fireplace irritated his eyes, nose and throat. Gloria's role is that of Lee Ann Fondan, a lawyer trying her first case on behalf of the neighbor. No copy of the episode could be located to view for this book.

Harrigan and Son. Lawyer Lee Ann Fondan (Gloria) tries her first court case in the episode "My Fair Lawyer," with the plaintiff (Forrest Lewis) still suffering the effects of the fireplace smoke about which he is suing.

The New Breed (ABC; 1961):

"Blood Money"

CAST AND CREDITS December 19, 1961 (Episode 1.12). *Starring*: Leslie Nielsen, John Beradino, Byron Morrow, John Clarke and Greg Roman. *Guest Stars*: Gloria Grahame, Charles McGraw, Ralph Taeger, Sandra Warner *and* Diana Millay. 60 minutes.

The New Breed was an hour-long crime drama that provided Leslie Nielsen with his first recurring dramatic series role. This episode occurred about halfway through the show's lone season. Lt. Price Adams (Nielsen) is the leader of Los Angeles' Metro Squad, which investigate highly unusual cases. A woman (Diana Millay) has an especially bad week: She loses her job, discovers she is suffering from a terminal illness and then fails to commit suicide, shooting her roommate instead. Gloria's role is that of a nurse, Nora Springer, involved in the case. No copy of the episode could be located to view for this book.

Sam Benedict (NBC; 1962):

"Too Many Strangers"

CAST AND CREDITS December 8, 1962 (Episode 1.13). *Starring*: Edmond O'Brien, Richard Rust and Joan Tompkins. *Guest Stars*: Marsha Hunt, Gloria Grahame, Judi Meredith, Michael Parks, Robert J. Wilke, Ross Elliott, Bernard Fein, Harriet MacGibbon, John Duke, Robert Bailey *and* Arthur Hanson. *Written by* Ellis Marcus. *Directed by* Lawrence Dobkin. 60 minutes.

Sam Benedict was a legal drama starring Edmond O'Brien as a defense attorney (based on the real-life exploits of attorney Jake Ehrlich), and set in San Francisco. This episode, which aired about one-third of the way through the show's only season, boasts two separate and very distinct cases. One involves a young man (Michael Parks) who has killed an older man to keep him away from the girl he loves; the other involves a mink coat given to Rita Bain (Gloria Grahame); the furrier demands its return because her rich (and now estranged) boyfriend never bothered to pay for it.

The murder case is highly dramatic, but the "Rita Bain" plotline is played for laughs, with Benedict assigning his young associate Hank Tabor (Richard Rust) to retrieve the coat

for the furrier. Gloria is hilarious (and gorgeous) as blonde Rita, unwilling to return the mink she believes she earned, and guarded by a perky Doberman pinscher named Rupert. Tabor fails at least twice to persuade Rita to return the coat, even though she is quite obviously taken by the young man. Gloria finally relents and brings it to Benedict's office, all the time jawing about how men treat women as property and have no right to do so. Benedict's secretary vehemently agrees with her. Gloria has obvious fun with the role and is delightful to watch; it's her all-time best appearance on television. It can be seen on videotape at the Library of Congress.

Burke's Law (ABC; 1964):

"Who Killed April?"

CAST AND CREDITS January 31, 1964 (Episode 1.19). *Starring*: Gene Barry, Gary Conway, Regis Toomey and Leon Lontoc. *Guest Stars*: Eddie Bracken, Jack Carter, Hans Conried, Gloria Grahame, Martha Hyer, Irene Hervey, Francine York, Eileen O'Neill, Michael Fox, Jean Paul King, Buddy Lewis, Mako, Danielle Aubry, Mark Goddard *and* Rue McClanahan. *Written by* Albert Beich. *Directed by* Lewis Allen. 60 minutes.

Burke's Law was a popular crime drama adventure series that ran for two seasons before evolving into *Amos Burke, Secret Agent* in 1965 for one final season; it returned to the air for two more seasons in 1994 and 1995 as *Burke's Law* again, still with Gene Barry as the dapper star. This episode aired near the middle of its first season of its first run. Los Angeles Chief of Detectives Amos Burke (Gene Barry) is not your run-of-the-mill police captain; he's a millionaire, driven from headquarters to crime scenes and other locations in a Rolls Royce. He's also a bachelor playboy, solving crimes between romantic rendezvous.

On his day off, Burke is called to the scene of the murder of a young woman in a junkyard. She was a car-hop at a popular drive-in restaurant, and dealt heroin on the side. The suspects include her boss (Eddie Bracken), her brother (Mark Goddard), her best friend (Martha Hyer), a popular hockey player (Jack Carter) and the hockey player's junkie wife (Gloria

Grahame). Hans Conried also appears in an amusing role as the therapist who questions why Burke finds his Rolls Royce so important.

Gloria has one scene as Helen Dekker, the wife of the hockey player, and she gives it her all. Helen cannot sit still, pacing around the room waiting for a fix, horrified that the police have arrived instead of her husband. Gloria is fairly convincing as a heroin junkie, though she has more intelligent dialogue than a real addict would probably be able to communicate under the same circumstances. Her desperation is the most dramatic element in an episode that nicely balances comedy, drama and the tragedy of homicide.

Grindl (NBC; 1964):
"Dial G for Grindl"

CAST AND CREDITS February 9, 1964 (Episode 1.20). *Starring*: Imogene Coca and James Millhollin. *Guest Stars*: Gloria Grahame, Tod Andrews, Gregory Morton *and* Douglas Henderson. 30 minutes.

Grindl was a half-hour situation comedy revolving around the adventures of Grindl (Imogene Coca), a housemaid employed by a domestic service. The series lasted just one season and this episode, which aired near its end, found the naïve housekeeper mistaken for a professional killer! Gloria's character is Olive York, somehow involved in the mistaken identity plot. No copy of the episode could be located to view for this book.

The Outer Limits (ABC; 1964):
"The Guests"

CAST AND CREDITS March 23, 1964 (Episode 1.26). *Control Voice*: Vic Perrin. *Guest Stars*: Gloria Grahame, Geoffrey Horne, Nellie Burt, Vaughn Taylor, Luana Anders, Burt Mustin and the voice of Robert C. Johnson. *Written by* Donald S. Sanford. *Directed by* Paul Stanley. 60 minutes.

The Outer Limits was an imaginative science fiction-horror hybrid series, and this episode was broadcast toward the conclusion of its first season (it lasted two seasons, and then the cable network Showtime revived it for another season in 1995). Like its predecessor *The Twilight Zone*, *The Outer Limits* was an anthology series that successfully mixed thrills, chills, imagination and stories of humanity, although the producers took care to make its stories especially symbolic or metaphorical.

An alien brain (laughably imagined as vibrating goo draped over a lampshade) traps a young drifter (Geoffrey Horne) in an old mansion, determined to discover in his mind the missing element in the equation of humankind's existence. Four other people are already present in the mansion: a shady businessman (Vaughn Taylor), his catty wife (Nellie Burt), a silent screen actress (Gloria Grahame) and a young woman (Luana Anders) with whom the drifter falls in love. The drifter escapes, but there is no happy ending for anyone else.

Gloria is Florinda Patten, an actress who dreams of returning to the screen even after being trapped in the mansion for some thirty years. She still considers herself a movie queen, and treats the drifter with indifference. Gloria is well cast and very attractive, although her eyebrows are incredibly thin. Atmospheric cinematography adds to the ambience, but the script is weak and the episode drags; it might have worked better at half the length.

The Fugitive (ABC; 1964):
"The Homecoming"

CAST AND CREDITS April 7, 1964 (Episode 1.28). *Starring* David Janssen and Barry Morse. *Narration by* William Conrad. *Guest Stars*: Shirley Knight, Richard Carlson, Gloria Grahame, Warren Vanders, James Griffith, Eddie Rosson, Mary Jackson and Walter Woolf King. *Written by* Peter Germano and Roy Huggins. *Directed by* Jerry Hopper. 60 minutes.

The Fugitive was a popular adventure series that lasted four seasons; this episode aired near the end of its first season. Dr. Richard Kimble (David Janssen), on the run from authorities who wrongly believe he killed his wife, finds refuge in rural Georgia as the lab assistant to a widowed scientist (Richard Carlson). Complications ensue when the scientist's daughter (Shirley Knight) returns from a year's stay at a sanitarium, and is astonished to find that her father has married another woman (Gloria

Grahame). Kimble befriends the daughter, but realizes that her new stepmother has little room in her future plans for the troubled girl.

As the shifty Dorina Pruitt, Gloria gets to affect the Southern accent she used so charmingly in *The Bad and the Beautiful*. Dorina's humble origins, just a dozen miles from her husband's new home, are highlighted twice by Dorina, as explanation for her efforts to completely monopolize her husband's attentions. After she tells Kimble the second time how she has had to crawl out of the dirt of her past and wipe it away, he remarks, "Not all of it." Dorina manipulates everyone in her world to achieve and maintain the luxuriant lifestyle she believes she deserves, even when her selfish desires threaten the sanity of an innocent young woman. It's a sly, underhanded role for Gloria, whose best moment may occur at the end, when her plans have been foiled. She glances around the nice house and at the handsome man she married, shrugs with disappointment, and then with resignation walks away.

Burke's Law (ABC; 1965): "Who Killed the Rabbit's Husband?"

CAST AND CREDITS April 14, 1965 (Episode 2.29). *Starring* Gene Barry, Gary Conway, Regis Toomey, Leon Lontoc and Eileen O'Neill. *Guest Stars*: Gloria Grahame, John Ireland, Una Merkel, Sal Mineo, Paul Richards, Francine York, Joanne Ludden, Lou Krugman, Stafford Repp, Bill McLean, Phil Arnold, David Fresco, Lyle Bettger, Lennie Weinrib, Vaughn Taylor, Jimmy Garrett, David Alan Bailey and Robert Bice. *Written by* Tony Barrett. *Directed by* Jerry Hopper. 60 minutes.

In this second-season episode of the popular adventure series, Los Angeles homicide chief Amos Burke (Gene Barry) and his team of detectives search for the missing wife of a murdered doctor. As they dig into her past it becomes clear that she is suffering from severe psychological strain. Her sister (Gloria Grahame) and former lovers (John Ireland, Sal Mineo, Paul Richards) disclose clues and secrets about her, most of which lead to more questions than answers. Finally, Burke and company find the woman and solve the crime.

Gloria is Doris Landers, the sister of the dead doctor's wife. Doris works as a concessionaire at Ocean Park, unable to repeat the social success of her beautiful sister. Dressed plainly and with little makeup, Gloria attempts to deglamorize herself for the role, but when Doris complains that men pay no attention to her when her sister is around, anyone who ever saw Gloria's early movies is bound to snort with derision. Gloria's acting is fine, but the role seems more suited to a less attractive actress.

Iron Horse (ABC; 1967): "Appointment with an Epitaph"

CAST AND CREDITS February 13, 1967 (Episode 1.23). *Starring*: Dale Robertson, Gary Collins, Robert Random, Roger Torrey and Ellen McRae [Ellen Burstyn]. *Guest Stars*: Bill Bixby, Robert Emhardt, Lew Gallo, Gloria Grahame, Susan Howard, John Ireland, Ron Hagerthy, Martin Ashe and Austin Roberts. *Written by* Harold Livingston. *Directed by* Herbert Herschman. 60 minutes.

Iron Horse, a western drama series that lasted two seasons, was set on and around a railroad line owned by Ben Calhoun (Dale

Iron Horse. Tarot card reader Rita Talbot (Gloria) has an eventful ride upon the title train as a killer stalks one of six passengers, each of whom believes him to be hunting them specifically, in the episode "Appointment with an Epitaph."

Robertson), who won it in a poker game. In this episode, six people are riding the line from Buffalo Pass to Scalplock, followed by a notorious killer (John Ireland). Each of the six people, for varied reasons, believes the killer is after him or her (he refuses to identify his intended victim); the killer, whose nickname is "the Executioner," is summarily deciding who will live and who will die.

Gloria is Rita Talbot, a tarot card–reading gambler on the way to Denver to open a saloon with her partner Frank Mason (Lew Gallo). She plays the 34-year-old shady lady (Gloria was then 44, and looked only 40) with natural confidence and a sly Southern accent that appears and disappears like a soft breeze. Rita is tart-tongued, blunt and brutally honest — traits that Gloria was not really known for. Gloria's character also acts as the harbinger of events through her reading of the cards. It's an interesting role that certainly adds depth and vigor to the dialogue-heavy episode.

Then Came Bronson (NBC; 1969):
"The 3:13 Arrives at Noon"

CAST AND CREDITS October 29, 1969 (Episode 1.7). *Starring*: Michael Parks. *Guest Stars*: Gloria Grahame, Larry Gates, Royal Dano, Garry Walberg, Bob Steele, Jonathan Kidd, John Hubbard, Kenneth MacDonald, Queenie Smith, Bill Benedict and Steve Raines. *Written by* Lee Cronin. *Directed by* Michael O'Herlihy. 60 minutes.

This drama-adventure series chronicled the wanderings of Bronson (Michael Parks), who drifts across America on his motorcycle, searching for the meaning to his life. This episode occurred about halfway during its first and only season, as Bronson rides his motorcycle into a small town and almost immediately has an accident. His bike needs work so he is forced to stay, during which time he learns that the town's most famous resident, a bank robber sent to prison thirty-five years previously, is to return the very next day.

Bronson meets each of the key players in the unfolding drama: the friend who betrayed the bank robber's trust, profited by turning him in and now owns most of the town (Larry Gates); the woman the bank robber loved (Glo-

ria Grahame), now married to a local official (Garry Walberg); the sheriff (Royal Dano) trying to keep the peace but clearly nervous about the immediate future. And despite his best efforts to vamoose before the paroled bank robber (Bob Steele) arrives on the bus, Bronson is there to witness his homecoming.

Gloria is cast as Charlene Braden, the bank robber's former girlfriend. Her first scene is a drunk scene, as she relates her sad story to Bronson, lamenting the fact that she was considered the prettiest girl in town and is now married to a man who won't, or can't, risk his life for her. Later, when he does just that by confronting the bank robber, Charlene is so proud of him she reiterates it to the crowd of waiting people. The drunk scene is overdone, but Gloria is excellent in her later shots, walking resolutely toward an uncertain, and possibly fatal, future.

Daniel Boone (NBC; 1970):
"Perilous Passage"

CAST AND CREDITS January 15, 1970 (Episode 6.14). *Starring*: Fess Parker, Patricia Blair, Darby Hinton, Dallas McKennon and Roosevelt (Rosie) Grier. *Guest Stars*: John Davidson, Liam Sullivan, Gloria Grahame, James Doohan, Alan Caillou and Ted Gehring. *Written by* Lee Karson. *Directed by* Nathan Juran. 60 minutes.

Daniel Boone was a family adventure show that fictionalized most of the elements of the outdoorsman's life and moved him all over the map. In this episode, broadcast near the end of its sixth and final season, Boone (Fess Parker) and his companion Gabe Cooper (Rosie Greer) destroy a bridge in 1770s Pennsylvania so that British soldiers are inconvenienced, whereupon the two are captured and sentenced to hang. Another patriot, Sam Weaver (John Davidson), is to share their fate but the trio manages to escape and make their way back to safety thanks to the help of an "underground" network of patriots residing in that Tory territory. One of those agents is tavern owner Molly Oakum (Gloria Grahame).

Gloria is given the opportunity to put her British accent to work as Molly, a single woman who admits she'd like to land a husband. Molly is intelligent and self-sufficient, qualities that Gloria conveys with ease. She also delivers a couple of funny lines. Gloria looks trim and fit and has her best moment when Molly admits that she is spooked by the idea that the British are closing in, since they may conclude that she is a spy. It's a nice, vivid performance that adds flavor to a rather mediocre adventure episode.

The Name of the Game (NBC; 1970): "The Takeover"

CAST AND CREDITS January 23, 1970 (Episode 2.17). *Starring*: Gene Barry. *Guest Stars*: Anne Baxter, David Sheiner, Michael Ansara, Warren Stevens, H. M. Wynant, David Opatoshu, Gloria Grahame, Anna Novarro, *and* Robert Carricart. *Teleplay by* John McGreevey *and* Ernestine Barton. *Directed by* Herbert Kenwith. 90 minutes.

This episode of the investigative crime drama series features Gene Barry as publisher Glenn Howard, who is pushed into service by the U.S. State Department. Howard is sent to the Asian country of Bhasa, where a military coup has just taken place. He is to determine if the provisional government is stable enough — and honest enough — to receive political and monetary support from America. Howard is chosen because he knows the overthrown president Ben Kaliman (Michael Ansara), whom Howard does not believe to be dead, as the new government has claimed.

In his investigations, Howard contacts several people close to the situation. One of them is Madame Noh (Gloria Grahame), the wife of Bhasa's finance minister (the only person killed in the otherwise bloodless coup). Madame Noh, for a price, confirms that her husband was implicated in money laundering that is being blamed on Ben Kaliman, and that he was having an affair with the wife of a high-ranking colonel, one of the men currently in power. For telling Howard the truth, Madame Noh is suspiciously run over by a car the following day.

Gloria has one brief scene with Barry and then is seen on the street the next day before her character's "accident." She is quietly effective in her scene, with a distinct lack of theatrics — as opposed to Anne Baxter, who chews

the scenery as if she is starving in the rest of the episode. Gloria looks resplendent in a silk kimono but her guest appearance is too brief to make much of an impression in the episode.

Mannix (CBS; 1970): "Duet for Three"

CAST AND CREDITS December 19, 1970 (Episode 4.13). *Starring* Mike Connors *and* Gail Fisher. *Guest Stars*: Katherine Justice, Robert Colbert, Robert Reed, Gloria Grahame, John Considine, Johnny Silver, Harold Fong, Terence Pushman, Liam Dunn *and* Sarah Lord. *Written by* Alfred Brenner. *Directed by* John Llewellyn Moxey. 60 minutes.

Private eye Joe Mannix (Mike Connors) is hired by a recent widow (Katherine Justice) when mysterious men begin to follow and threaten her. As Mannix digs into the case, the mysterious men are found dead, one by one, shot by a masked killer. Mannix's probe leads to the dead husband's past, which he had kept hidden from his wife. Now suddenly the past is violently catching up with the widow and she doesn't know why. A surprise conclusion involving her husband's true motive solves the case.

Gloria has a small role as Mae Darling, a talent agent and one of the people who, along with the dead husband, had been involved in black market commerce. Although Mae declines to give Mannix any pertinent information, she is shot by the masked gunman, and she dies before she can reveal the killer's identity. It's only a two-minute part, with the last half of it spent lying on her stomach in a hospital bed pretending to slowly expire. Gloria looks nice with long, flowing blonde hair, but there is nothing special in this particular television appearance.

Kojak (CBS; 1977): "Sister Maria"

CAST AND CREDITS March 15, 1977 (Episode 4.24). *Starring* Telly Savalas, Dan Frazer, Kevin Dobson *and* George Savalas. *Guest Stars*: Season Hubley, Ted Beniades, Harold Gary, Gloria Grahame, John Kellogg *and* Murray Hamilton. *Written by* Ross Teel. *Directed by* Ernest Pintoff. 60 minutes.

Detective Lieutenant Theo Kojak (Telly Savalas) and his men investigate a triple murder involving a shady airline owner (Murray Hamilton). The sister of one of the victims is a nun (Season Hubley) whose insistence on catching her sister's killer places her in distinct peril. The case is further complicated when one of the two hit men involved permanently silences the other (John Kellogg) and his wife (Gloria Grahame).

Gloria's part lasts less than a minute and a half but it is quite intense. Helen Rubicoff is feisty and greedy, insisting on more money for her husband's part in the original hit. Gloria plays Helen as a real bitch, carelessly insulting both her husband and the hit man from whom she tries to extract more money. She looks great and has a nice scream at the end, as Helen realizes that she has demanded too much.

Roald Dahl's Tales of the Unexpected (Syndicated; 1980): "Depart in Peace"

CAST AND CREDITS May 3, 1980 (Episode 2.10). *Host*: Roald Dahl. *Guest Stars*: Joseph Cotten, Gloria Grahame, Maureen O'Brien, John Bennett and Peter Cellier. *Written by* Ronald Harwood *based upon a story by* Roald Dahl. *Directed by* Alan Gibson. 30 minutes.

This British-based anthology mystery series—shot on videotape—lasted nine seasons. In "Depart in Peace," fine art collector Lionel (Joseph Cotten) has learned to clean and restore paintings. He is dating society woman Janet (Maureen O'Brien), who doesn't seem too interested in his hobby. When another society woman, Gladys (Gloria Grahame), tells Lionel that Janet thinks he's a bore, he decides to use his expertise to publicly embarrass her. The stunt backfires and makes him miserable, costing him more than he ever would have imagined.

Gloria is Gladys Ponsonby, a platinum blonde social butterfly with designs on Lionel. Filled with rapid-fire, often overlapping dialogue, Gladys' exchanges with Lionel are quite theatrical, yet real and convincing. Gladys has one extended scene in which she tries to seduce him, and when that fails, she badmouths the woman for whom he obviously cares. At the end of that scene, after Lionel leaves, Gladys laughs to herself and exclaims, "You *are* a bitch, Gladys dear." Gloria looks marvelous in a very low cut, slinky dress and her dyed, manicured coif. She's energetic and as radiant as ever, proving that she hadn't lost any of her charm or sex appeal.

Roald Dahl's Tales of the Unexpected (Syndicated; 1984): "Sauce for the Goose"

CAST AND CREDITS July 21, 1984 (Episode 7.9) *Guest Stars*: Gloria Grahame, Robert Morse, Lisa Dunsheath and Peter Murphy. *Written by* Bert Salzman, *based upon a story by* Patricia Highsmith. *Directed by* Bert Salzman. 30 minutes.

Gloria's final television appearance was aired three years after her death. She filmed a second episode of the half-hour mystery anthology series *Roald Dahl's Tales of the Unexpected* in the late summer of 1980, but it was not telecast until early in the seventh season. Although she does not look well throughout the episode, Gloria demonstrates her customary energy and wit. Loren (Peter Murphy) is rich but his wife Olivia (Gloria Grahame) is in love with a younger man. She finds a way to kill her husband, then spends most of the episode chasing the younger Stephen (Robert Morse), marrying him, and trying to kill him, while he is also trying to permanently silence her. Eventually they find common ground ... in their walk-in freezer. Yes, this television episode boasts startling parallels to Gloria's 1970s exploitation classics *Mama's Dirty Girls* and *Blood and Lace*.

Played almost entirely for laughs, the episode provides Gloria with a lot to do, and a wide range of emotions to play. At one point she is to slap Robert Morse, so she hauls off and wallops him for the sake of reality. She's still trim and lithe, but some might call her gaunt at this stage. Her hair is frizzy and she hardly looks like the wife of a rich man. Yet her comic timing remains solid, and she screams quite enthusiastically at several moments. This was Gloria's final appearance as a performer.

Gloria Grahame's television work is generally not as vivid, affecting or striking as her film work, but that is probably more a reflection of the material than what she was able to do with it. She is quite good in a few episodes and completely insignificant in others. She did not enjoy the lickety-split pace of television work, nor the diminution of the parts she was being offered, which was mostly due to her age. Once Gloria reached forty, she experienced what so many other actresses have suddenly learned: that studios and producers prefer to award their leading roles to women younger and more attractive. And that those studios and producers often don't realize that women over forty can be and often are stronger, sexier and more interesting than their younger counterparts. That fight is still being fought today

... but with somewhat better results for the women.

For Gloria, television was better than nothing during the 1960s, as long as it didn't require extensive commitment or time away from her family. Performing on television did not produce the artistic rewards of stage work, but it paid a whole lot better. And her appearances on network shows kept Gloria in front of the public often enough that she would not be forgotten. Between her series appearances and her made-for-television movies and miniseries, Gloria did more television than film in the second half of her forty-year career. All are worth seeing because Gloria appeared in them. She was like nobody else in film or television; Gloria Grahame was, truly, one of a kind.

· *Appendix A* ·
The Films Listed by Studio and Distributor

The following is a listing of Gloria's thirty-nine theatrical features and her eight made-for-television projects sorted by their respective studios, production companies, theatrical distributors and television networks. The production and distribution entities are listed alphabetically. Each entity's films are then listed chronologically. Films produced and distributed by more than one entity are listed under each entity.

ABC-TV
Escape, 1971; *Rich Man, Poor Man*, 1976.

American International Pictures (AIP)
Blood and Lace, 1971.

Andrew J. Fenady Productions (*see also* Fenady Associates)
Black Noon, 1971.

ATV Network
The Dancing Princesses, 1979.

Bard Productions, Ltd.
The Merry Wives of Windsor, 1979.

Bryna Productions
Ride Out for Revenge, 1957.

The Carlin Company
Blood and Lace, 1971; *Mama's Dirty Girls*, 1974.

CBS-TV
Black Noon, 1971.

Charles Band Productions
Mansion of the Doomed, 1976.

Columbia Pictures
In a Lonely Place, 1950; *The Glass Wall*, 1953; *The Big Heat*, 1953; *Prisoners of the Casbah*, 1953; *Human Desire*, 1954; *Ride Beyond Vengeance*, 1966; *The Girl on the Late, Late Show*, 1974.

Comptoir Française du Films Productions
Tarot, 1973.

Contemporary Filmmakers
Blood and Lace, 1971.

David Gerber Productions, Inc.
The Girl on the Late, Late Show, 1974.

Eric Biedermann
Tarot, 1973.

Fanfare Films
The Loners, 1972.

Feature Films
The Nesting, 1981.

Fenady Associates (*see also* Andrew J. Fenady Productions)
Ride Beyond Vengeance, 1966.

Four-Leaf Productions
The Loners, 1972.

Group 1 International Distribution Organization, Ltd.
Mansion of the Doomed, 1976.

HarBel Productions
Odds Against Tomorrow, 1959.

Harve Bennett Productions
Rich Man, Poor Man, 1976.

Independent Film Distributors, Ltd.
The Good Die Young, 1954.

ITC Entertainment Group
The Dancing Princesses, 1979.

Joseph Kaufman Productions
Sudden Fear, 1952.

The Katzman Corporation
Prisoners of the Casbah, 1953.

Liberty Films
It's a Wonderful Life, 1946.

Liberty Mutual Insurance Company
Mr. Griffin and Me, 1981.

Magna Productions
Oklahoma!, 1955.

Mark Goodson–Bill Todman Productions
Ride Beyond Vengeance, 1966.

MGM
Blonde Fever, 1944; *Without Love*, 1945; *It Happened in Brooklyn*, 1947; *Song of the Thin Man*, 1947; *Merton of the Movies*, 1947; *The Bad and the Beautiful*, 1952; *The Cobweb*, 1955; *Chandler*, 1971.

National General Pictures
The Todd Killings, 1971.

NBC-TV
The Girl on the Late, Late Show, 1974; *Seventh Avenue*, 1977.

The Nesting Company
The Nesting, 1981.

Orfeo Film Productions
Tarot, 1973.

Paramount Pictures
The Greatest Show on Earth, 1952.

Paramount Television
Escape, 1971.

Premiere Releasing Organization
Mama's Dirty Girls, 1974.

Remus
The Good Die Young, 1954.

RKO Radio Pictures
It's a Wonderful Life, 1946; *Crossfire*, 1947; *A Woman's Secret*, 1949; *Roughshod*, 1949; *Macao*, 1952; *Sudden Fear*, 1952; *Oklahoma!*, 1955.

Rodgers and Hammerstein Productions
Oklahoma!, 1955.

Romulus Films
The Good Die Young, 1954.

S. Benjamin Fisz Productions
A Nightingale Sang in Berkeley Square, 1979.

Santana Productions
In a Lonely Place, 1950.

Screen Gems Television
Black Noon, 1971; *The Girl on the Late, Late Show*, 1974.

Sentinel Productions
Ride Beyond Vengeance, 1966.

Stanley Kramer Pictures Corporation
Not as a Stranger, 1955.

Sumar Productions
The Man Who Never Was, 1956.

The Tiger Company
Ride Beyond Vengeance, 1966.

Triple Play Productions
Chilly Scenes of Winter, 1979.

20th Century–Fox
Man on a Tightrope, 1953; *Oklahoma!*, 1955; *The Man Who Never Was*, 1956.

United Artists
The Good Die Young, 1954; *Not as a Stranger*, 1955; *Ride Out for Revenge*, 1957; *Odds Against Tomorrow*, 1959; *Chilly Scenes of Winter*, 1979.

Universal Pictures
Naked Alibi, 1954; *Melvin and Howard*, 1980.

Universal Television
Rich Man, Poor Man, 1976; *Seventh Avenue*, 1977.

Vagar Films
Tarot, 1973.

William Mishkin Pictures
The Nesting, 1981

· *Appendix B* ·
The Stage Plays

Gloria Grahame began her show business career on the stage under her birth name, Gloria Hallward. It was only after she was signed to a movie contract with MGM that her moniker became Gloria Grahame. Due to the love of theater she developed at an early age (her mother Jean McDougall was an accomplished stage actress and director, and would become Gloria's personal, lifelong acting coach), Gloria began acting while still a child. Her formative years were spent on stage at the Pasadena Playhouse, where her mother acted and directed, and at Hollywood High School. Her professional stage career began when she joined a show tour a couple of months before her high school graduation; her mother tagged along as chaperone and coach. Gloria finished her courses by mail. Touring led Gloria first to San Francisco, then Chicago, and finally New York, where she appeared on Broadway within a year. Gloria's plans for domination of the Broadway stage was set aside when she reluctantly accepted a contract with MGM and moved back to California, but she always retained her love of the stage and the electricity of performing live. After her film career foundered in the late 1950s, Gloria returned to the stage, in America and in Britain. Most of her later career, in fact, took place on stage rather than in front of cameras.

After *The Nesting* finished production, Gloria went back to the stage, devoting her remaining time to an acting process she could truly appreciate. She loved learning different parts so much that she would often memorize the entire scripts of the plays in which she appeared. She loved the audience response when she off-handedly made a choice quip or a flashy entrance. She loved the camaraderie of each acting troupe she joined, whether it was professional or amateur, and watching young performers get their first taste of success. Gloria enjoyed the process of moviemaking, too, but it was much harder work for her than simply becoming a stage character for two or three hours each night. Films required precise manipulation, exact timing and a great deal of repetition. Gloria learned to excel at film acting, yet she loved cutting loose on the stage even more.

The following is a list (not comprehensive, unfortunately) of Gloria's stage work, from her earliest days as a child at the Pasadena Playhouse to her one-woman shows and classical play appearances made shortly before she died in 1981.

The Bluebird (1932, Pasadena Playhouse)
Role: A Fairy

The Toymaker of Nuremberg (?, Pasadena Playhouse)
Role: A Child

Ladies in Waiting (?)
Role: Cockney Maid

The Merry Wives of Windsor (?, Pasadena Playhouse)
Role: Robin

Killed Monday Night (?, Pasadena Playhouse)
Role: ?

Maid in the Ozarks (1940, Grand Playhouse, Los Angeles)
Role: Daisy Belle

Ever Since Eve (1942, Hollywood High School, Hollywood)
Role: ?

Good Night, Ladies (1942, San Francisco)
Role: understudy for ten female roles

(4/12/1942–?, Blackstone Theatre, Chicago)
Role: Dodie Tarleton

The Skin of Our Teeth (1942?, 1943, The Plymouth Theatre, New York)
Role: Drum Majorette; understudy for Sabina.

Macbeth. In the New Globe Theatre's production of *Macbeth*, staged at Northern Illinois University in May 1980, Gloria finally fulfilled her ambition of playing Lady Macbeth on the stage (courtesy of the Regional History Center, Northern Illinois University, DeKalb).

Stardust (1943, tour)
Role: ?

The World's Full of Girls (12/6/1943, Royale Theatre, New York)
Role: Florie

A Highland Fling (4/28–5/20, 1944, Plymouth Theatre, New York)
Role: Alicetrina MacLean

The Three Sisters (1960, The Theatre Group, University of California, Los Angeles)
Role: Natasha

The Marriage-Go-Round (2/1960, Fred Miller Theatre, Milwaukee)
Role: ?

Laura (7/1960, Cherry County Playhouse, Traverse City, Michigan)
Role: Laura Hunt

The Country Girl (6/1962, Lydia Mendelssohn Theatre, Ann Arbor, Michigan)
Role: Georgie Elgin

The Marriage-Go-Round (1962, Berkshire Playhouse, Stockbridge, Massachusetts)
Role: ?

The Little Hut (1963, Alexander White's LA Summer Playhouse, Los Angeles)
Role: Susan

The Time of Your Life (1972, national tour)
Role: Mary L.

The Price (3/1977, Theater East, Milwaukee)
Role: Esther Franz

Bell, Book and Candle (7/1977, Spring Lake Summer Theater, New Jersey)
Role: Gillian Holroyd

The Man Who Came to Dinner (12/6/1977–1/15/1978, Darien Dinner Theater, Darien, Connecticut)
Role: Lorraine Sheldon

Rain (6/7–7/1, 1978, Watford Palace Theater, England)
Role: Sadie Thompson

A Tribute to Lili Lamont (1978, New End Theatre, London)
Role: Lili Lamont

The Merry Wives of Windsor (9/1979, Globe Playhouse, Los Angeles)
Role: Mistress Page

The Glass Menagerie (11/20–12/8, 1979, Crucible Theatre, Sheffield, England)
Role: Amanda Wingfield

How the Other Half Loves (1980, Richmond Civic Theater, Richmond, Indiana)
Role: Fiona Foster

Private Lives (7/1980, Geneva Theater Guild, Geneva, New York)
Role: Amanda

Macbeth (4/7–4/12, 1980, Northern Illinois University, DeKalb)
Role: Lady Macbeth

Who's Afraid of Virginia Woolf? (1981, Duke's Playhouse, Lancaster, England)
Role: Martha

Light Up the Sky (8/1981, John Drew Theater, East Hampton, New York)
Role: Irene Livingston

Joy Hallward: The Older Sister's Film Appearances

Joy Hallward was born twelve years earlier than Gloria, on December 31, 1911, and lived well past Gloria, until February 23, 2003. She and their mother, Jean Grahame, were almost constant companions on Gloria's wild ride through Hollywood. Because of Gloria's four marriages, Joy was, at one time or another, sister-in law to Stanley Clements, Nicholas Ray, Cy Howard, and Tony Ray; and because of her own marriage to John Mitchum, she was also sister-in-law to Robert Mitchum, Dorothy Mitchum and Julie Mitchum — all of whom were involved in the movie industry, either in front of or behind the camera. That list also includes Joy herself, because she eventually made fifteen — and possibly more — movie appearances. That number could very well be higher because Joy was a bit player who found work populating scenes behind and around her films' central characters. All but two of Joy's fifteen known appearances were uncredited, indicating the size of her roles. Indeed, some of her employers never knew that Joy was Gloria's sister, and only one of her fifteen films is a Gloria Grahame movie.

Joy's tenure in films paralleled Gloria's rise to prominence in the industry. And a handful of the titles in which she appeared are major productions: *Knock on Any Door, In a Lonely Place, The Blue Veil, Magnificent Obsession*. It seems natural that director Nicholas Ray, who was romancing and then married Gloria, would find a way to fit Joy into the films he was making at the time. But after that, Joy was on her own. Her film list follows, along with her character name.

An Act of Murder (1948)
Role: Nurse

Knock on Any Door (1949)
Role: Jury member

In a Lonely Place (1950)
Role: Bit part

Born to Be Bad (1950)
Role: Mrs. Porter

Apache Drums (1951)
Role: Townswoman

You Never Can Tell (1951)
Role: Bit part

Iron Man (1951)
Role: Bit part

The Blue Veil (1951)
Role: Miss Golub

Has Anybody Seen My Gal? (1952)
Role: Bit part

Thunder in the East (1952)
Role: Englishwoman

Affair with a Stranger (1953)
Role: Bit part

So Big (1953)
Role: Maid

She Couldn't Say No (1954)
Role: Bit part

Witness to Murder (1954)
Role: Cheryl's co-worker

Magnificent Obsession (1954)
Role: Maid

Notes on Sources

These notes on sources used are designed to help readers locate specific sources pertaining to Gloria Grahame's life and career, and to the individual films discussed. The "Biographical Background and General Sources" section lists books, articles, interviews and profiles pertaining to Gloria personally, and general sources for film information. Each of Gloria's films is then listed separately, in chronological order of release, with relevant sources listed alphabetically within each film's listing. Following the film listings are two final, brief sections: Obituaries and Post-Death Profiles, and Magazine Product Advertisements and Beauty Features. By including such material, this bibliography is intended to provide a wealth of source information regarding its subject.

Types of Bibliographical Entries

Book (Year, Publisher), page listing. author. source type.

Periodical. date of publication. volume, issue #, page listing. author. source type.

Internet Source Name URL. author. source type.

The final notation for each entry is the type of source: **review** indicates that an evaluation of a film is made, even if that evaluation is a simple star rating; **analysis** indicates a deeper, lengthier evaluation of a film than can be made in a standard movie review; **profile** indicates biographical information about a film's participants, usually Gloria; **remembrance** indicates a participant's recollection of, or brief quotes about, a film's production or of its original source; **interview** indicates an interview with one or more participants in a film, or, in the Biographical Background section, of Gloria; **pictorial** indicates a photographic preview of a film, usually accompanied by a brief text; **article** indicates a wider range of subjects to which a film is related in some way; **history** indicates information regarding a film's production and popular or critical reception, or, a film's contextual place in cinema lore; **film listings** indicates an information focus on a specific studio's or genre's films; **TV listing** indicates telecast information, and sometimes brief descriptions or reviews of mostly made-for-television material; and **source** indicates a published origination of a film, usually a novel, play or short story.

Some sources were used for almost all of the films. General references include the Internet Movie Database, *The Motion Picture Guide* by Jay Robert Nash and Stanley Ralph Ross, and the annual *Screen World* series of books, overseen by Daniel Blum and John Willis. Essential to this study is Vincent Curcio's 1989 biography of Gloria Grahame, *Suicide Blonde*. The author appreciates these sources and recommends them.

Biographical Background and General Sources

American Movie Classics Magazine. September 1989 2:9, 12. Robert Moses. profile.

American National Biography (1999, Oxford University), 393–95. Diana Moore. profile.

The Columbia Checklist (1991, McFarland). Len D. Martin. film listings.

The Columbia Story (1989, Crown). Clive Hirschhorn. film listings.

Cult Movie Stars (1991, Fireside), 224–226. Danny Peary. profile.

Dark City: The Lost World of Film Noir (1998, St. Martin's Griffin), 52–54. Eddie Muller. profile.

The Encyclopedia of Hollywood Film Actors (2003, Applause), 286–87. Barry Monush. profile.

Encyclopedia of Television Series, Pilots and Specials: 1937–1973 (1986, New York Zoetrope). Vincent Terrace. TV listings.

Femme Noir: Bad Girls of Film (1998, McFarland), 174–91. Karen Burroughs Hannsberry. profile.

Film Comment. September, 1997. 33:5, 50–56, 58. Donald Chase. profile.

Film Noir: A Comprehensive Illustrated Reference to Movies, Terms and Persons (1995, McFarland), 162–63. Michael L. Stephens. profile.

Film Stars Don't Die in Liverpool (1986, Grove Press). Peter Turner. remembrance.

Filmbobbery. Autumn, 1999. 1:2, 4–7. Robert J. Lentz. profile.

Films and Filming. January 1980. 26:4, 6–7. Eric Braun. profile.

Films in Review. December 1989. 40:12, 578–88. Michael Buckley. profile, part 1.

Films in Review. January-February 1990. 41: 1, 2, 2–15. Michael Buckley. profile, part 2.

Films of the Golden Age. Winter, 1996. #3, 20–24. Dean Goodman. profile.

The Films of 20th Century–Fox (1979, Citadel Press). Tony Thomas and Aubrey Solomon. film listings.

Gangster Films (1996, McFarland), 125. Michael L. Stephens. profile.

Gods and Goddesses of the Movies (1974, Crescent Books), 89–91. John Kobal. profile.

The Great Movie Stars 2: The International Years (1995, Little, Brown), 216–18. David Shipman. profile.

Hollywood Studio Magazine. date ?, 20–21. Patrick Agan. profile.

I Was Interrupted (1995, University of California Press), 159, 173–74. Nicholas Ray. remembrance.

The Illustrated Directory of Film Stars (1981, B. T. Batsford), 191. David Quinlan. profile.

The Illustrated Encyclopedia of the World's Great Movie Stars and Their Films (1979, Harmony Books), 89. Ken Wlaschin. profile.

The Illustrated Who's Who of the Cinema (1983, Macmillan), 177. profile.

International Dictionary of Films and Filmmakers-3 (1997, St. James Press, 3rd Edition), 489–91. Jeff Stafford. profile.

InternetMovieDatabase.com. profile-filmography.

Interview. September, 2000. 30:9, 144. Graham Fuller. profile.

Killer Tomatoes (2004, McFarland), 65–78. Ray Hagen and Laura Wagner. profile.

Leading Ladies (1986, St. Martin's Press), 158. Don Macpherson. profile.

Leonard Maltin's Movie Encyclopedia (1994, Plume), 348–49. Leonard Maltin. profile.

Live Fast, Die Young (2005, Touchstone), 1–8. Lawrence Frascella and Al Weisel. history.

The MGM Stock Company: The Golden Era (1973, Arlington House), 284–88. James Robert Parish and Ronald L. Bowers. profile.

The MGM Story (1977, Crown). John Douglas Eames. film listings.

Motion Picture. September 1947, 78–79. Kate Holliday. profile.

Motion Picture. June 1953, 44–45, 66. Mark Benton. profile.

The Motion Picture Guide (1986, Cinebooks). Stanley Ralph Ross and Jay Robert Nash. reviews.

Movies Made for Television (1980, Da Capo). Alvin H. Marill. TV listings.

The New Biographical Dictionary of Film (2002, Alfred A. Knopf), 349–50. David Thomson. profile.

The Paramount Story (1985, Crown). John Douglas Eames. film listings.

People Are Crazy Here (1974, Dell), 215–19. Rex Reed. profile.

People Today. May 20, 1953. 6:10, cover, 30–33. profile.

Photoplay. July 1952, 29. Beverly Linet. profile.

Rating the Movie Stars (1983, Beekman House), 164–65. Joel Hirschhorn. profile.

RKO: The Biggest Little Major of Them All (1984, Prentice-Hall). Betty Lasky. history.

The RKO Story (1982, Arlington House). Richard B. Jewell and Vernon Harbin. film listings.

Screen Facts. 1964. 1:6, 38–51. Ray Hagen. profile.

Silver Screen. May 1953, 35, 58–60. Paul Marsh. profile.

SilverScreenActresses.com Denny Jackson. profile.

Suicide Blonde (1989, William Morrow). Vincent Curcio. biography.

TurnerClassicMovies.com. profile.

The United Artists Story (1986, Crown). Ronald Bergan. film listings.

Universal Pictures (1977, Arlington House). Michael G. Fitzgerald. film listings.

The Universal Story (1983, Octopus). Clive Hirschhorn. film listings.

Unsold Television Pilots (1991, Citadel Press). Lee Goldberg. TV listings.

Unsold Television Pilots Vol. 1: 1955–1976 (2001, iUniverse). Lee Goldberg. TV listings.

The Village Voice. October 29, 1979. 24:44, 1, 36–37. Arthur Bell. profile.

Who's Who in Hollywood 1900–1976 (1977, Arlington House), 166. David Ragan. profile.

Wicked Women of the Screen (1987, St. Martin's Press), 24–26, David Quinlan. profile.

Soundies

The Soundies Distributing Corporation of America (1991, McFarland), vii–24, 121, 125, 126, 133. Maurice Terenzio, Scott MacGillivray and Ted Okuda. history-filmography.

Blonde Fever (1944)

Delila (aka *Blue Danube*), publisher unknown. Ferenc Molnár. source play.

A Life on Film (1971, Delacorte Press), 179. Mary Astor. remembrance.

The London Times. February 19, 1945. review.

The Motion Picture Guide, A–B, 235. Nash-Ross. review.

RadioTimes.com. review.

Variety. November 22, 1944. Wear. review.

Without Love (1945)

Commonweal. April 13, 1945. 41:26, 649. Philip T. Hartung. review.

The Films of Spencer Tracy (1979, Citadel Press), 189–90. Donald Deschner. history-review.

Kate: The Life of Katharine Hepburn (1975, W.W. Norton), 126–27. Charles Higham. history-review.

Katharine Hepburn (1973, Galahad Books), 72–75. Alvin H. Marill. review.

Love, Lucy (1996, Berkley Boulevard), 139–40. Lucille Ball. remembrance.

The Motion Picture Guide, W–Z, 3886. Nash-Ross. review.

Nation. April 7, 1945. 160:14, 395–96. James Agee. review.

New Republic. May 7, 1945. 112:19, 645. Manny Farber. review.

New York Times. March 23, 1945. Bosley Crowther. review.

New Yorker. March 31, 1945. 21:7, 50. Walcott Gibbs. review.

Newsweek. April 9, 1945. 25:15, 91. review.

Spencer Tracy (1992, Crescent Books), 46–47. Alison King. history.

Time April 9, 1945. 45:15, 94. review.

Variety March 23, 1945. Abel. review.

It's a Wonderful Life (1946)

America. December 20, 1997. 177:20, 22. James Martin. review.

American Film. March, 1982. 7:5, 51. Jeanine Basinger. review.

American Heritage. February-March, 1991. 42:1, 62–63. Bruce Fretts. review.

American Heritage. October 2005. 56:5, 69–70. Aljean Harmetz. review.

American Movie Classics' Great Christmas Movies (1998, Taylor Publishing), 146–50. John Andrew Gallagher. history.

American Vision: The Films of Frank Capra (1986, Cambridge), 377–435. Raymond Carney. analysis.

Bob Dorian's Classic Movies (1990, Bob Adams), 96–97. Bob Dorian and Dorothy Curley. review.

The Cinema of Frank Capra (1975, A.S. Barnes), 205–17. Leland A. Poague. analysis.

Commonweal January 3, 1947. 45:12, 305. Philip T. Hartung. review.

The Complete Films of Frank Capra (1992, Citadel Press), 222–31. Victor Scherle and William Turner Levy. history-review.

Cult Movies (1989, Delta), 162–66. Danny Peary. analysis.

Cult Movies (2000, Billboard), 119–21. Karl French and Philip French. review.

The Entertainment Weekly Guide to the Greatest Movies Ever Made (1994, Warner Books), 17. review.

The Essential It's a Wonderful Life *Film Guidebook* (2004, Kerpluggo Books). Michael Willian. analysis.

Film: The Critics' Choice (2001, Billboard Books), 72–73. review.

Film Comment. November-December, 1986. 22:6, 9–13, 16–17. Richard Corliss. review.

Film Daily. December 19, 1946, 5. review.

The Films of Frank Capra (1974, Scarecrow Press), 58–86. Donald C. Willis. analysis.

The Films of James Stewart (1970, Castle Books), 103–06. Arthur F. McClure, Ted D. Jones and Alfred E. Twomey. history.

The 500 Best American Films to Buy, Rent or Videotape (1985, Pocket Books), 184. review.

Forties Film Talk (1992, McFarland), 174–75, 312–13. James Stewart and Donna Reed. remembrances.

Frank Capra (1980, Plume), 130–52. Charles L. Maland. analysis.

Frank Capra: Authorship and the Studio System (1998, Temple University Press), 64–94. Vito Zagarrio. analysis.

Frank Capra: The Catastrophe of Success (1992, Simon & Schuster), 510–30. Joseph McBride. analysis.

Hollywood Talks Turkey: The Screen's Greatest Flops (1990, Faber & Faber), 81, 86, 220–21. Donna Reed and James Stewart. remembrances.

International Dictionary of Films and Filmmakers — 1, 477–78. Charles Affron. review.

It's a Wonderful Life: A Holiday Classic (1992, Smithmark). Marie Cahill. history.

It's a Wonderful Life: *A Memory Book* (2003, Cumberland House). Stephen Cox. analysis.

It's a Wonderful Life: *The Fiftieth Anniversary Scrapbook* (1996, Courage Books). Jimmy Hawkins. remembrance-history.

The It's a Wonderful Life *Book* (1986, Alfred A. Knopf). Jeanine Basinger. analysis.

The It's a Wonderful Life *Trivia Book* (1992, Crown Trade Paperbacks). Jimmy Hawkins and Paul Petersen. remembrance-trivia quizzes.

James Stewart (1974, Pyramid Communications), 58–60. Howard Thompson. history.

James Stewart (1984, Stein and Day), 79–82. Allen Eyles. history.

James Stewart (1992, Crescent Books), 40–42. Helene McGowan. history.

James Stewart: A Biography (1996, Turner Publishing), 262–71. Donald Dewey. history.

James Stewart: Behind the Scenes of a Wonderful Life (1997, Applause), 153–59. Lawrence J. Quirk. history.

Jimmy Stewart: A Biography (2006, Harmony Books), 199–209. Marc Eliot. history.

Jimmy Stewart: A Life on Film (1993, St. Martin's Press), 64–73. Roy Pickard. history.

Magill's Survey of Cinema, First Series, Volume 2, Eas-Lon (1980, Salem Press), 856–59. DeWitt Bodeen. review.

Modern Maturity. December 1989–January 1990, cover, 38–43. Nancy Dillon. history.

The Motion Picture Guide, H–K, 1430–32. Nash-Ross. review.

The Name Above the Title (1972, Bantam), 417–26. Frank Capra. remembrance.

Nation. February 15, 1947. 164:?, 193–94. James Agee. review.

New Movies: The National Board of Review Magazine. February-March, 1947. #22, 5–8. Richard Griffiths. review.

New Republic. January 6, 1947. 116:1, 44. Manny Farber. review.

New York Times. December 23, 1946, 19. Bosley Crowther. review.

New York Times. December 2, 2001, 20. David L. Goodrich. history.

New Yorker. December 21, 1946. 22:45, 87–88. John McCarten. review.

New Yorker. January 12, 1981. 56:47, 29–31. article.

Newsweek. December 30, 1946. 28:27, 72–73. review.

The One Hundred Greatest Movies of All Time (1999, Entertainment Weekly Books), 96–97. review.

Photoplay. March 1947, 4. review.

Photoplay. April 1947, 48–49. pictorial.

Pieces of Time: The Life of James Stewart (1997, Scribner), 185–90. Gary Fishgall. history.

Rating the Movies (1982, Beekman House), 176. review.

Reader's Digest. December 1991. 139:836, 81–85. James Stewart. remembrance.

The Real Nick and Nora (2001, Southern Illinois University Press), 160–63. David L. Goodrich. history.

Retakes (1989, Ballantine Books), 164–65. John Eastman. history.

Screen Guide January 1947, 18–20. pictorial.

Theatre Arts. February, 1947. 31:2, 36–37. Hermine Rich Isaacs. review.

Time. December 23, 1946. 48:26, 54. review.

Time. December 10, 2007. 170:24, 90. James Poniewozik. review.

Variety. December 25, 1946. Bert. review.

Washington Post. December 25, 1983, H1. Gary Arnold. review.

Washington Star. February 6, 1947. Jay Carmody. review.

A Wonderful Life: The Films and Career of James Stewart (1988, Citadel Press), 101–05. Tony Thomas. history.

Zuzu Bailey's It's a Wonderful Life *Cookbook* (1996, Citadel Press), 3–11. Karolyn Grimes remembrance and Franklin Dohanyos history.

It Happened in Brooklyn (1947)

Commonweal. March 28, 1947 45:24, 594. Philip T. Hartung. review.

The Hollywood Musical (1981, Crown), 281. Clive Hirschhorn. review.

Jimmy Durante: His Show Business Career (1995, McFarland), 89. David Bakish. history.

The Motion Picture Guide, H–K, 1420. Nash-Ross. review.

New Republic. March 31, 1947. 116:13, 39. Shirley O'Hara. review.

New York Herald Tribune. March 14, 1947. Otis L. Guernsey. review.

New York Times. March 14, 1947, 28. Bosley Crowther. review.

New Yorker. March 22, 1947. 23:5, 88–89. John McCarten. review.

Newsweek. March 24, 1947. 29:12, 94. review.

The Peter Lawford Story (1988, Carroll & Graf), 99–100. Patricia Seaton Lawford. profile.

Time. April 7, 1947. 49:14, 99–100. review.

Variety. February 28, 1947. Stal. review.

Washington Star. March 15, 1947. Jay Carmody. review.

Crossfire (1947)

The Baltimore Sun. September 10, 1947. Donald Kirkley. review.

The BFI Companion to Crime (1997, University of California), 97. Edward Buscombe. review.

Bob Dorian's Classic Movies (1990, Bob Adams), 40–41. Dorian-Curley. review.

The Brick Foxhole (1946, Sun Dial Press). Richard Brooks. source novel.

Commonweal. August 1, 1947. 46:16, 386. Philip T. Hartung. review.

Dictionary of Films (1972, University of California Press), 73. Georges Sadoul. review.

Film History. 1989. 3:?, 29–37. Darryl Fox. analysis.

Film Reader. February 1978. #3, 106–27. Keith Kelly and Clay Steinman. analysis.

Filmbobbery. Autumn, 1999. 1:2, 16–17. Robert J. Lentz. history.

The Films of the Forties (1975, Citadel), 210–11. Tony Thomas. review.

Forties Film Talk (1992, McFarland), 46–47. Myrna Dell. remembrance.

The Great Cop Pictures (1990, Scarecrow Press), 155–57. James Robert Parish. history.

Heyday (1979, Little, Brown), 156–57. Dore Schary. remembrance.

International Dictionary of Films and Filmmakers-1 (Year, Co.), 238–39. Daniel Leab. review.

It's a Hell of a Life but Not a Bad Living (1978, Times Books), 88–93. Edward Dmytryk. remembrance.

Literature/Film Quarterly. 1984 12:3, 171–79. Leonard J. Leff and Jerold L. Simmons. analysis.

The London Times. January 5, 1948. review.

Magill's Survey of Cinema, Second Series, Volume 2, Cob-Hal (1981, Salem Press), 548–50. Larry S. Rudner. review.

More Than Night: Film Noir in Its Contexts (1998, University of California Press), 114–23. James Naremore. analysis.

The Motion Picture Guide, C–D (Year, Co.), 526. Nash-Ross. review.

Movies We Love (1996, Turner Publishing), 71–73. Frank Miller. history.

Nation. August 2, 1947. 165:5, 129–30. James Agee. review.

New Republic. August 11, 1947. 117:?, 34. Shirley O'Hara. review.

New York Herald Tribune. July 23, 1947. Otis L. Guernsey. review.

New York Journal-American. July 23, 1947. Rose Pelswick. review.

New York Times. July 23, 1947, 19. Bosley Crowther. review.

New Yorker. July 19, 1947. 23:22, 46. John McCarten. review.

Newsweek. July 28, 1947. 30:4, 84. review.

101 Greatest Films of Mystery and Suspense (2000, ibooks), 125–27. Otto Penzler. history.

Oscar A to Z (1995, Main Street Books), 195. #467 Charles Matthews. history.

PM. July 23, 1947. Cecelia Ager. review.

RKO: The Biggest Little Major of Them All (1984, Prentice Hall), 195–98, 202. Betty Lasky. history.

Robert Mitchum on the Screen (1978, A. S. Barnes), 93–95. Alvin H. Marill. history.

Robert Ryan (1997, McFarland), 189–91. Franklin Jarlett. profile-review.

Running Time: Films of the Cold War (1982, Dial Press), 36–37. Nora Sayre. history.

Saturday Review. December 6, 1947 30:49, 68–71. John Mason Brown. analysis.

Screen Writer. October 1947, 1–5. Adrian Scott. remembrance.

Somewhere in the Night (1997, Owl Books), 76. Nicholas Christopher. history.

Time. August 4, 1947. 50:5, 76. review.
Variety. June 25, 1947. Abel. review.

Song of the Thin Man (1947)

The Complete Films of William Powell (1986, Citadel Press), 231–34. Lawrence J. Quirk. review.
The Films of Myrna Loy (1980, Citadel Press), 231–33. Lawrence J. Quirk. review.
Forties Film Talk (1992, McFarland), 319. Leon Ames. remembrance.
Gentleman: The William Powell Story (1985, St. Martin's Press), 217–18, 225. Charles Francisco. history.
The Great Detective Pictures (1990, Scarecrow Press), 506–08. James Robert Parish and Michael R. Pitts. history-review.
The Motion Picture Guide, S (Year, Co.), 3036. Nash-Ross. review.
Myrna Loy: Being and Becoming (1987, Alfred A. Knopf), 208. James Kotsilibas-Davis. history.
New York Herald Tribune. August 29, 1947. Howard Barnes. review.
New York Times. August 29, 1947. Thomas M. Pryor. review.
New Yorker. September 6, 1947. 23:29, 68. John McNulty. review.
Newsweek. September 8, 1947. 30:10, 78. review.
Variety. July ?, 1947. Wear. review.

Merton of the Movies (1947)

Hollywood on Hollywood (1978, Scarecrow Press), 249–51. James Robert Parish, Michael R. Pitts and Gregory William Mank. history.
Hollywood's Hollywood (1975, Citadel Press), 102–07. Rudy Behlmer and Tony Thomas. history.
The Motion Picture Guide, L–M, 1937. Nash-Ross. review.
New York Herald Tribune. November 7, 1947. Otis L. Guernsey. review.
New York Times. November 7, 1947, 20. Thomas M. Pryor. review.
Newsweek. November 24, 1947. 30:21, 92, 94. review.
Red Skelton. (1979, E. P. Dutton), 135. Arthur Marx. history.
Red Skelton: The Mask Behind the Mask (2008, Indiana Historical Society Press), 170–71. Wes D. Gehring. history.
Seeing Red: The Skelton in Hollywood's Closet (2001, Robin Vincent), 143, 145–46. Wes D. Gehring. history.
Variety. July 12, 1947. Brog. review.

A Woman's Secret (1949)

Commonweal. March 4, 1949. 49:21, 521–22. Philip T. Hartung. review.
The Films of Nicholas Ray (2004, BFI Publishing), 32–34. Geoff Andrew. history.
Mortgage on Life (1948, Triangle Books). Vicki Baum. source novel.
The Motion Picture Guide W–Z (Year, Co.), 3913. Nash-Ross. review.
Nicholas Ray: An American Journey (1996, Faber & Faber), 105–10. Bernard Eisenschitz. analysis.

Newsweek. February 21, 1949. 33:8, 87. review.
See You at the Movies: The Autobiography of Melvyn Douglas (1986, University Press of America), 162. Melvyn Douglas. remembrance.
Time. February 28, 1949. 53:9, 90, 93. review.
'Tis Herself (2005, Simon & Schuster), 125–26. Maureen O'Hara. remembrance.
Variety. February 9, 1949. Brog. review.

Roughshod (1949)

BFI Monthly Film Bulletin. January 1951. 18:204, 206. review.
Commonweal. July 22, 1949. 50:15, 368. Philip T. Hartung. review.
Cue. June 18, 1949. review.
Finding My Way (1990, Harper San Francisco), 27–29. Martha Hyer Wallis. remembrance.
Forties Film Talk (1992, McFarland), 47. Myrna Dell. remembrance.
The Motion Picture Guide, N–R (Year, Co.), 2678. Nash-Ross. review.
New York Herald Tribune. June 17, 1949. Howard Barnes. review.
New York Times. June 17, 1949, 27. Bosley Crowther. review.
Newsweek. June 27, 1949. 33:26, 88. review.
Time. July 4, 1949. 54:1, 66–67. review.
Variety. May 11, 1949. Gilb. review.
The Western (1983, William Morrow), 183. Phil Hardy. review.
Western Films (1982, Da Capo), 282. Brian Garfield. review.

In a Lonely Place (1950)

Bogart (1997, William Morrow), 433–35. A. M. Sperber and Eric Lax. history.
Bogey: The Films of Humphrey Bogart (1979, Citadel), 154–56. Clifford McCarty. review.
The Book of Film Noir (1993, Continuum), 222–31. V. F. Perkins. analysis.
Commonweal. June 9, 1950. 52:?, 221. Philip T. Hartung. review.
Cult Movies 3 (1988, Fireside), 113–16. Danny Peary. review.
Dark City: The Film Noir (1984, McFarland), 93–96. Spencer Selby. analysis.
Dark City: The Lost World of Film Noir (1998, St. Martin's Griffin), 193–95. Eddie Muller. review.
The Entertainment Weekly Guide to the Greatest Movies Ever Made, 26. #54. review.
Film: The Critics' Choice 74–75. review.
Film Noir (2005, Virgin Books), 149, 161. Eddie Robson. review.
The Films of Nicholas Ray (2004, BFI Publishing), 46–52. Geoff Andrew. analysis.
The Films of the Fifties (1976, Citadel Press), 29–31. Douglas Brode. review.
Forgotten Films to Remember (1980, Citadel Press), 174–75. John Springer. review.
Hollywood on Hollywood (1978, Scarecrow), 189–91. Parish-Pitts-Mank. history.
Hollywood's Hollywood (1978, Scarecrow), 240, 242. Behlmer-Thomas. history.

Humphrey Bogart (1975, Star Books), 115–16. Alan G. Barbour. review.

Humphrey Bogart: Take It and Like It (1991, Grove Weidenfeld), 141–44. Jonathan Coe. history.

In a Lonely Place (1993, BFI Publishing), Dana Polan. analysis.

In a Lonely Place (2003, The Feminist Press), Dorothy B. Hughes. source novel.

Library Journal. June 1, 1950. 75:11, 992. Earle F. Walbridge. review.

Magill's Survey of Cinema, Second Series, Volume 3, Han-Luc (1981, Salem Press), 1135–37. Michael Shepler. review.

More Than Night: Film Noir in Its Contexts (2008, University of California Press), 127–28. James Naremore. review.

The Motion Picture Guide, H–K (1986, Cinebooks), 1366–67. Nash-Ross. review.

Movie Love in the Fifties (2001, Alfred A. Knopf), 148–63. James Harvey. analysis.

Movies on Movies (1978, Drake), 33. Richard Meyers. review.

New York Times. May 18, 1950, 37. Thomas M. Pryor. review.

New Yorker. May 27, 1950. 26:74, 63. John McCarten. review.

Newsweek. June 5, 1950. 35:23, 85–86. review.

Nicholas Ray: An American Journey (1996, Faber & Faber), 133–46. Bernard Eisenschitz. analysis.

Redbook. July, 1950, 17. review.

Thriller Movies (1974, Octopus Books), 93–95. Lawrence Hammond. review.

Time. June 5, 1950. 55:23, 91. review.

Variety. May 17, 1950. Wear. review.

The Greatest Show on Earth (1952)

The American Circus (1990, Henry Holt), 261. John Culhane. history.

American Movie Classics Magazine. May, 1994. 7:5, 7. history.

The Autobiography of Cecil B. DeMille (1959, Prentice Hall), 403–07. Cecil B. DeMille. remembrance.

Bad Movies We Love (1993, Plume), 283–84. Edward Margulies and Stephen Rebello. review.

BFI Monthly Film Bulletin. March, 1952. 19:218, 29–30. G. L. review.

Box Office Champs (1990, Portland House), 56–59. Eddie Dorman Kay. history.

Boxoffice. January 12, 1952. 60:11, 1334. review.

Catholic World. February, 1952. 174:1043, 384–85. Robert Kass. review.

Cecil B. DeMille (1973, Da Capo Press), 290–97. Charles Higham. history.

Cecil B. DeMille: A Life in Art (2008, Thomas Dunne Books), 395–98, 402–03. Simon Louvish. history.

Charlton Heston (1976, Pyramid Communications), 30–34, 36. Michael B. Druxman. history.

Charlton Heston (1986, St. Martin's Press), 15–19. Michael Munn. history.

Charlton Heston's Hollywood (1998, GT Publishing), 37–45. Charlton Heston. remembrance.

Christian Century. May 28, 1952. 69:22, 655. review.

The Circus Kings (1960, Doubleday), 355–59. Henry Ringling North. remembrance.

Commonweal. January 25, 1952. 55:16, 399–400. Philip T. Hartung. review.

The Complete Films of Cecil B. DeMille (1969, Citadel Press), 350–54. Gene Ringgold and DeWitt Bodeen. history.

DeMille: The Man and His Pictures (1970, Castle Books), 202–09. Gabe Essoe and Raymond Lee. history.

Films in Review. February, 1952. 3:2, 89. review.

The Films of Charlton Heston (1977, Citadel Press), 28–31. Jeff Rovin. history.

The Films of James Stewart (1970, A.S. Barnes), 145–49. Arthur F. McClure, Ken D. Jones and Alfred E. Twomey. history.

The Films of the Fifties (1976, Citadel Press), 78–80. Douglas Brode. review.

In the Arena (1995, Simon & Schuster), 102–13. Charlton Heston. remembrance.

James Stewart (1974, Pyramid Communications), 84, 86. Howard Thompson. history.

James Stewart (1984, Stein and Day), 107–08. Allen Eyles. history.

James Stewart: A Biography (1996, Turner), 326–28. Donald Dewey. history.

James Stewart: Behind the Scenes of A Wonderful Life 209–11. Lawrence J. Quirk. history.

Jimmy Stewart: A Biography 258–60. Marc Eliot. history.

Jimmy Stewart: A Life in Film (1993, St. Martin's Press), 99–106. Roy Pickard. history.

Magill's Survey of Cinema, First Series, Volume 2, Eas-Lon (1980, Salem Press), 697–99. Mike Vanderlan. review.

Motion Picture. March 1952. 56. article.

The Motion Picture Guide, E–G (1986, Cinebooks), 1107–08. Nash-Ross. review.

My Side of the Road (1980, Prentice Hall), 182–88. Dorothy Lamour. remembrance.

New Republic. February 11, 1952. 126:6 22. Robert Hatch. review.

New York Times. March 18, 1951. article.

New York Times. May 27, 1951. Thomas M. Pryor. article.

New York Times. January 11, 1952, 17. Bosley Crowther. review.

New York Times. January 20, 1952, Section 2, X. Bosley Crowther. review.

New Yorker. January 19, 1952. 27:49, 83–84. John McCarten. review.

Newsweek. January 21, 1952. 39:3, 90. review.

Oscar A to Z (1995, Main Street Books) 356–57. #832 Charles Matthews. history.

Pieces of Time: The Life of James Stewart (1997, Scribner) 225–29. Gary Fishgall. history.

Rocking Horse: A Personal Biography of Betty Hutton (2009, Bear Manor Media), 83–88. Gene Arceri. history.

Saturday Review. January 12, 1952. 35:2, 27. Arthur Knight. review.

Silver Screen. April 1952, 50. pictorial.

Theatre Arts. February 1952. 36:2, 32–33. Arthur Knight. review.

Time. January 14, 1952. 59:2 90–91. review.

Variety. January 2, 1952. Herb. review.

A Wonderful Life: The Films and Career of James Stewart (1988, Citadel Press), 141–42. Tony Thomas. history.

Macao (1952)

BFI Monthly Film Bulletin. July 1952. 19:222, 91. review.
Boxoffice. March 29, 1952. 60:22, 1358. review.
The Cinema of Josef von Sternberg (1971, A. S. Barnes), 166–69. John Baxter. analysis.
The Entertainment Weekly Guide to the Greatest Movies Ever Made (1994, Warner Books), 256. review.
Film Noir: A Comprehensive Illustrated Reference to Movies, Terms and Persons (1995, McFarland), 236–37. Michael L. Stephens. review.
The Films of Josef von Sternberg (1966, Museum of Modern Art), 52–53. Andrew Sarris. analysis.
Fun in a Chinese Laundry (1988, Mercury House), 283. Josef von Sternberg. remembrance.
Howard Hughes in Hollywood (1985, Citadel), 130. Tony Thomas. review.
Jane Russell: An Autobiography (1986, Jove), 118. Jane Russell. remembrance.
Macao (1984, Frederick Ungar). Bernard C. Schoenfeld and Stanley Rubin. screenplay.
Mitchum: In His Own Words (2000, Limelight), 90–92. Robert Mitchum. remembrance.
The Motion Picture Guide, L–M (1986, Cinebooks), 1784. Nash-Ross. review.
New York Times. May 1, 1952, 34. Bosley Crowther. review.
Newsweek. May 5, 1952. 39:18, 102. review.
Nicholas Ray: An American Journey 165–73. Bernard Eisenstein. analysis.
Robert Mitchum on the Screen. 120–21. Alvin H. Marill. review.
Time. May 12, 1952. 59:19, 106–07. review.
Variety. March 19, 1952. Holt. review.

Sudden Fear (1952)

Bad Movies We Love (1993, Plume), 289–91. Margulies-Rebello. review.
BFI Monthly Film Bulletin. October 1952. 19:225, 146. review.
Boxoffice. August 2, 1952. 61:14, 1395. review.
Christian Century. October 15, 1952. 69:42, 1207. review.
Commonweal. August 15, 1952. 56:19, 462. Philip T. Hartung. review.
The Complete Films of Joan Crawford (1988, Citadel Press), 182–84. Lawrence J. Quirk. history.
Joan Crawford (1974, Pyramid Communications), 114–17. Stephen Harvey. history.
Joan Crawford (1978, Simon & Schuster), 176–80. Bob Thomas. history.
Joan Crawford: The Essential Biography (2002, University of Kentucky Press), 161–65. Lawrence J. Quirk and William Schoell. history.
Joan Crawford: The Last Word (1995, Birch Lane Press), 156–59. Fred Lawrence Guiles. history.
London Times. September 22, 1952. review.
The Motion Picture Guide, S (1986, Cinebooks), 3192–93. Nash-Ross. review.
Nation. September 27, 1952. 175:13, 282–83. Manny Farber. review.
New York Times. August 8, 1952, 9. A. H. Weiler. review.
New Yorker. August 16, 1952. 28:26, 82. Philip Hamburger. review.
Newsweek. August 8, 1952. 40:7, 83. review.

Not the Girl Next Door (2008, Simon & Schuster), 223–24 Charlotte Chandler. history.
Oscar A to Z (1995, Doubleday), 834 #1955 Charles Matthews. history.
Saturday Review. October 18, 1952. 35:42, 31. Arthur Knight. review.
Sudden Fear (1948, Dell Publishing). Edna Sherry. source novel.
Theatre Arts. October, 1952. 36:10, 73. Robert Hatch. review.
Time. August 11, 1952. 60:6, 90, 92. review.
Variety. July 23, 1952. Holl. review.

The Bad and the Beautiful (1952)

BFI Monthly Film Bulletin. February, 1953. 20:229, 18. review.
The Best of MGM: The Golden Years, 1928–1959 (1981, Arlington House), 15–17. James Robert Parish and Gregory William Mank. review.
Boxoffice. November 22, 1952. 62:4, 1428. review.
Catholic World. January, 1953. 176:1054, 302. Robert Kass. review.
Christian Century. March 11, 1953. 70:10, 303. review.
Commonweal. February 6, 1953. 57:18, 450–51. Philip T. Hartung. review.
Cosmopolitan. February 1948. 124:2, 33–35, 154–56, 159–62. George Bradshaw. source story "Of Good and Evil."
The Dick Powell Story (1993, Riverwood Press), 141–43. Tony Thomas. history.
Directed by Vincente Minnelli (1989, Museum of Modern Art–Harper & Row), 209–16. Stephen Harvey. analysis.
The Entertainment Weekly Guide to the Greatest Movies Ever Made, 39. #96. review.
50 from the 50s (1979, Arlington House), 27–35. David Zinman. history.
The Films of Kirk Douglas (1972, Citadel Press), 92–97. Tony Thomas. review.
The Films of Lana Turner (1976, Citadel Press), 178–83. Lou Valentino. review.
The Films of the Fifties (1976, Citadel Press), 75–77. Douglas Brode. review.
The Films of Vincente Minnelli (1993, Cambridge University Press), 112–34. James Naremore. analysis.
500 Best American Films to Buy, Rent or Videotape (1985, Pocket Books), 32. review.
The Great Movies (1973, Ridge), 172–75. William Bayer. review.
Hollywood on Hollywood (Year, Co.), 30–32. Parish-Pitts-Mank. history.
Hollywood's Hollywood (Year, Co.), 322–28. Behlmer-Thomas. history.
A Hundred or More Hidden Things (2010, Da Capo Press), 152–58. Mark Griffin. analysis.
I Remember It Well (1975, Angus & Robertson), 252–60. Vincente Minnelli. remembrance.
Kirk Douglas (1976, Pyramid Communications), 66–71. Joseph McBride. history.
Kirk Douglas (1985, St. Martin's Press), 43–45. Michael Munn. history.
Ladies' Home Journal. February 1951. 68:2, 36–37, 134–35, 137, 139. George Bradshaw. source story "Memorial to a Bad Man."

Lana: The Lady, the Legend, the Truth (1982, E. P. Dutton), 136–39. Lana Turner. remembrance.

Lana: The Life and Loves of Lana Turner (1995, St. Martin's Press), 92–93. Jane Ellen Wayne. history.

Lana: The Memories, the Myths, the Movies (2008, Running Press), 311–13. Cheryl Crane remembrance (with Cindy De La Hoz).

Lana: The Public and Private Lives of Miss Turner (1971, Citadel Press), 132–34. Joe Morella and Edward Z. Epstein. history.

Lana Turner (1976, Pyramid Communications), 87–88. Jeanine Basinger. history.

Magill's Survey of Cinema, First Series, Volume 1, A–Eas (1980, Salem Press), 112–15. Joan Cohen. review.

The Motion Picture Guide, A–B (1986, Cinebooks), 123–24. Nash-Ross. review.

Movies on Movies 132–34. Richard Meyers. review.

New York Times. January 16, 1953, 19. Bosley Crowther. review.

New Yorker. January 17, 1953. 28:48, 89–90. John McCarten. review.

Newsweek. January 26, 1953. 41:4, 100–01. review.

Oscar A to Z, 56–57, #130 Charles Matthews. history.

The Ragman's Son (1988, Simon & Schuster), 192–93. Kirk Douglas. remembrance.

Rating the Movies (1982, Beekman House), 27–28. review.

Retakes 27–28. John Eastman. history.

Saturday Review. January 3, 1953. 36:1, 54–55. Hollis Alpert. review.

The Star Machine (2007, Alfred A. Knopf), 214. Jeanine Basinger. profile.

Theatre Arts. February 1953. 37:2, 80–81. Parker Tyler. review.

Time January 12, 1953. 61:2, 94. review.

Unfinished Business (1989, Applause Books), 318–21. John Houseman. remembrance.

Variety. November 19, 1952. Brog. review.

Vincente Minnelli: Hollywood's Dark Dreamer (2009, St. Martin's Press), 223–30. Emanuel Levy. history and analysis.

The Glass Wall (1953)

BFI Monthly Film Bulletin. July, 1953. 20:234, 107. review.

Boxoffice. March 7, 1953. 62:19, 1455. review.

Holiday. July 1953. review.

The Motion Picture Guide, E–G (1986, Cinebooks), 1036. Nash-Ross. review.

Movie Time. February 1953, 20–23, 76. review.

Newsweek. April 20, 1953. 41:16, 106–07. review.

Time. April 27, 1953. 61:17, 112. review.

Variety. March 4, 1953. Brog. review.

Man on a Tightrope (1953)

America. June 6, 1953. 89:?, 287. Moira Walsh. review.

BFI Monthly Film Bulletin. June 1953. 20:233, 86. K. R. review.

Catholic World. May, 1953. 177:1058, 145. Robert Kass. review.

Commonweal. June 26, 1953. 58:12, 298. Philip T. Hartung. review.

Elia Kazan (2005, HarperCollins), 274–78. Richard Schickel. history.

The Films of Fredric March (1971, Citadel), 206–08. Lawrence J. Quirk. review.

Forgotten Films to Remember (1980, Citadel Press), 204, 206. John Springer. review.

The Great Spy Pictures (1974, Scarecrow), 282–83. James Robert Parish and Michael R. Pitts. history.

Kazan (1999, Newmarket), 109–14. Jeff Young. history-review.

Library Journal May 15, 1953 78:10, 897. Earle F. Walbridge. review.

A Life (1988, Alfred A. Knopf), 476–85, 488–92. Elia Kazan. remembrance.

Man on the Tightrope (1952, Avon). Neil Paterson. source novel.

The Motion Picture Guide, L–M (1986, Cinebooks), 1847–48. Nash-Ross. review.

New York Times. September 7, 1952. Section 2, 5. Jack Raymond. history.

New York Times. June 5, 1953. 19. A. H. Weiler. review.

New York Times. June 21, 1953. Section 2, 1. Bosley Crowther. review.

New Yorker. June 13, 1953. 29:17, 66. John McCarten. review.

Newsweek. May 11, 1953. 41:19, 102, 104. review.

Saturday Review. May 30, 1953. 36:22, 30. Arthur Knight. review.

Time. April 27, 1953. 61:17, 108–09. review.

Variety. April 1, 1953. Abel. review.

The Big Heat (1953)

Alternate Oscars (1993, Delta), 121–22. Danny Peary. analysis.

America. November 7, 1953. 90:?, 159. Moira Walsh. review.

Best Video Films (1984, Warner), 183. review.

BFI Monthly Film Bulletin. April 1954. 21:243, 51. review.

The Big Heat (1992, BFI Publishing). Colin McArthur. analysis.

The Big Heat (2002, iBooks). William P. McGivern. source novel.

Boxoffice. September 26, 1953. 63:22, 1518. review.

Bullets Over Hollywood (2004, Da Capo Press), 172–73. John McCarty. review.

Catholic World. October 1953. 17:?, 63. Robert Kass. review.

ChicagoReader.com. Don Druker. review.

The Cinema of Fritz Lang (1969, A. S. Barnes), 182–86. Paul M. Jensen. analysis.

Crime Movies (1980, W.W. Norton), 237–40. Carlos Clarens. review.

Cult Movies 2 (1983, Delta), 22–25. Danny Peary. review.

Dark City: The Lost World of Film Noir, 43–45. Eddie Muller. review.

The Entertainment Weekly Guide to the Greatest Movies Ever Made, 91. #13. review.

Film Noir (2005, Virgin), 163–72. Eddie Robson. analysis.

Film Noir: A Comprehensive Illustrated Reference to Movies, Terms and Persons (1995, McFarland), 41–42. Michael L. Stephens. review.

The Films of Fritz Lang (1979, Citadel Press), 245–49. Frederick W. Ott. review.

The Films of the Fifties (1976, Citadel Press), 88–90. Douglas Brode. review.

500 Best American Films to Buy, Rent or Videotape (1985, Pocket Books), 46. review.

Forgotten Films to Remember (1980, Citadel Press), 203, 205. John Springer. review.

Fritz Lang (1976, Da Capo), 329–37. Lotte Eisner. history and review.

Fritz Lang (1978, Twayne), 148, 159–62. Robert A. Armour. review.

Fritz Lang in America (1969, Praeger), 84–91. Fritz Lang. interview.

Fritz Lang: The Nature of the Beast (1997, St. Martin's), 403–07. Patrick McGilligan. review.

Gangster Films (1996, McFarland), 30. Michael L. Stephens. review.

The Great Cop Pictures (1990, Scarecrow), 44–47. James Robert Parish. history.

The Great Gangster Pictures (1976, Scarecrow), 35–36. James Robert Parish and Michael R. Pitts. history.

The Guide for the Film Fanatic (1986, Fireside), 52. Danny Peary. review.

Lee Marvin: His Films and Career (2000, McFarland), 32–36. Robert J. Lentz. history-review.

Library Journal. October 1, 1953. 78:?, 1677. Herbert Cahoon. review.

London Times. February 11, 1984. Peter Waymark. review.

Magill's Survey of Cinema, Second Series, Volume 1, A-Clu (1981, Salem Press), 216–19. Charles M. Berg. review.

Marvin (1980, St. Martin's Press), 63–64. Donald Zec. history.

The Motion Picture Guide, A–B (1986, Cinebooks), 195. Nash-Ross. review.

Movie Love in the Fifties (2001, A. Knopf), 104–16. James Harvey. analysis.

Nation. November 21, 1953. 177:?, 434. Manny Farber. review.

New York Times. October 15, 1953, 43. Bosley Crowther. review.

Newsweek. November 2, 1953. 42:?, 90–91. review.

Public Enemies, Public Heroes (1999, University of Chicago Press), 186–220. Jonathan Munby. analysis.

Seeing Is Believing (2000, Owl Books), 189–94. Peter Biskind. review.

Sight and Sound. July-September, 1954. 24:1, 36. Lindsay Anderson. review.

Thriller Movies (1974, Octopus), 146. Lawrence Hammond. review.

Time. November 2, 1953. 62:?, 112. review.

Prisoners of the Casbah (1953)

BFI Monthly Film Bulletin. January 1954. 21:240, 11. review.

Boxoffice. October 31, 1953. 64:1, 1528. review.

Hollywood Talks Turkey: The Screen's Greatest Flops (Year, Co.), 55–56. Turhan Bey. remembrance.

The Motion Picture Guide, N–R (1986, Cinebooks), 2465. Nash-Ross. review.

Variety. October 28, 1953. Brog. review.

The Good Die Young (1954)

BFI Monthly Film Bulletin. April 1954. 21:243, 52–53. review.

Boxoffice. February 5, 1955. 66:15, 1704. review.

London Times. March 8, 1954. review.

The Motion Picture Guide, E–G (1986, Cinebooks), 1068. Nash-Ross. review.

Time. March 15, 1955. 65:11, 106. review.

Human Desire (1954)

BFI Monthly Film Bulletin. January 1955. 22:252, 9. review.

Boxoffice. August 14, 1954. 65:16, 1606. review.

The Cinema of Fritz Lang (1969, A.S. Barnes), 186–89. Paul M. Jensen. analysis.

Dictionary of Films (1972, University of California Press), 152–53. Georges Sadoul. review.

The Encyclopedia of Novels Into Film (2nd Edition) (2005, Facts on File), 30–31. Walter Metz. analysis.

Film Noir: A Comprehensive Illustrated Reference to Movies, Terms and Persons (1995, McFarland), 188–90. Michael L. Stephens. review.

The Films of Fritz Lang (1979, Citadel Press), 250–53. Frederick W. Ott. review.

Fritz Lang (1976, Oxford University Press), 338–43. Lotte Eisner. review.

Fritz Lang (1978, Twayne), 162–64. Robert A. Armour. review.

Fritz Lang in America (1969, Praeger), 92–97. Fritz Lang. interview.

Fritz Lang: The Nature of the Beast (1997, St. Martin's Press), 407–10. Patrick McGilligan. review.

The Motion Picture Guide, H–K (1986, Cinebooks), 1310–11. Nash-Ross. review.

New York Times. August 7, 1954, 7. Bosley Crowther. review.

Variety. August 11, 1954. Gene. review.

Naked Alibi (1954)

America. October 9, 1954. 92:2, 55. Moira Walsh. review.

BFI Monthly Film Bulletin. October 1954. 21:249, 148. review.

Boxoffice. August 28, 1954. 65:18, 1609. review.

Catholic World. October 1954. 180:1075, 64–65. Robert Kass. review.

Chuck Connors: The Man Behind the Rifle (1997, Artist's Press), 93–94. David Fury. review.

Film Noir: A Comprehensive Illustrated Reference to Movies, Terms and Persons (1995, McFarland), 261–62. Michael L. Stephens. review.

The Great Cop Pictures (1990, Scarecrow), 379–81. James Robert Parish. history.

The Motion Picture Guide, N–R (1986, Cinebooks), 2099. Nash-Ross. review.

New York Times. October 2, 1954, 21. Bosley Crowther. review.

Variety. August 25, 1954. Brog. review.

The Cobweb (1955)

America. August 20, 1955. 93:21, 493. Moira Walsh. review.

Bad Movies We Love (1993, Plume), 280–81. Margulies-Rebello. review.

BFI Monthly Film Bulletin. February 1956. 23:265, 14. review.

Boxoffice. June 11, 1955. 67:7, 1787. review.

Catholic World. June, 1955. 181:1083, 221. Robert Kass. review.

Celluloid Couches, Cinematic Clients (2004, State University of New York), 108–13. Janet Walker. analysis.

The Cobweb (1954, Alfred A. Knopf). William Gibson. source novel.

Commonweal. August 19, 1955. 62:20, 495–96. Philip T. Hartung. review.

Directed by Vincente Minnelli (1989, Harper & Row), 216–20. Stephen Harvey. analysis.

A Hundred or More Hidden Things (2010, Da Capo), 176–81. Mark Griffin. history and analysis.

I Remember It Well (1974, Doubleday), 283–85. Vincente Minnelli. remembrance.

Library Journal. July 1955. 80:13, 1576. Marilla Waite Freeman. review.

The Motion Picture Guide, C–D (1986, Cinebooks), 449. Nash-Ross. review.

New York Times. August 6, 1955, 13. Howard H. Thompson. review.

New Yorker. August 13, 1955. 31:26, 49. John McCarten. review.

Newsweek. July 20, 1955. 45:25, 94. review.

Psychiatry and the Cinema (1987, University of Chicago Press), 77–80. Krin Gabbard and Glen O. Gabbard. analysis.

Saturday Review. July 16, 1955. 38:29, 36. Lee Rogow. review.

Time. July 25, 1955. 66:4, 88. review.

Variety. June 8, 1955. Brog. review.

Vincente Minnelli: Hollywood's Dark Dreamer (2009, St. Martin's Press), 258–65. Emanuel Levy. history and analysis.

Vincente Minnelli: The Art of Entertainment (2009, Wayne State University Press), 169–71. Serge Daney. review.

Not as a Stranger (1955)

America. July 16, 1955. 93:16, 399. Moira Walsh. review.

Bad Movies We Love (1993, Plume), 232–33. Margulies-Rebello. review.

BFI Monthly Film Bulletin. September 1955. 22:260, 137. review.

Boxoffice. June 18, 1955. 67:8, 1790. review.

Catholic World. June 1955. 181:1083, 221–22. Robert Kass. review.

Commonweal. July 15, 1955. 62:15, 371. review.

Doctors in the Movies (2000, Medi-Ed Press), 10–15. Peter E. Dans. review.

Film Culture. Winter, 1955. 1:5, 35. Martin Dworkin. review.

The Films of Olivia de Havilland (1983, Citadel Press), 227–28. Tony Thomas. history.

Lee Marvin: His Films and Career (2000, McFarland), 55–58. Robert J. Lentz. history-review.

Library Journal. June 15, 1955. 80:12, 1487. Gerald D. McDonald. review.

Life. June 27, 1955. 38:?, 77–78, 81. pictorial.

Look. May 31, 1955. 19:?, 87–88. pictorial.

A Mad, Mad, Mad, Mad World (1997, Harcourt Brace), 121–33. Stanley Kramer. remembrance.

The Motion Picture Guide, N–R (1986, Cinebooks), 2199. Nash-Ross. review.

Nation. June 25, 1955. 180:26, 591. Robert Hatch. review.

New York Times. June 12, 1955. Section II, 5. Oscar Godbout. review.

New York Times. June 29, 1955, 24. Bosley Crowther. review.

New York Times. July 10, 1955. Section II, 1. A. H. Weiler. article.

New Yorker. July 9, 1955. 31:21, 66–67. John McCarten. review.

Newsweek. July 4, 1955. 46:1, 77. review.

Not as a Stranger (1954, Scribner), Morton Thompson. source novel.

Oscar A to Z (1995, Doubleday), 604–05. Charles Matthews. history.

Robert Mitchum (1984, Robson), 181–82. George Eells. history.

Robert Mitchum on the Screen (1978, A.S. Barnes), 138–39. Alvin H. Marill. history.

Saturday Review. June 25, 1955. 38:26, 24. Arthur Knight. review.

Stanley Kramer: Film Maker (1978, Samuel French), 177–85. Donald Spoto. history-review.

Time. July 4, 1955. 66:1, 70–71. review.

Variety. June 15, 1955. Land. review.

Oklahoma! (1955)

America. October 29, 1955. 94:5, 138, 140. Moira Walsh. review.

The Best, Worst and Most Unusual: Hollywood Musicals (1983, Beekman House), 62–63. review.

BFI Monthly Film Bulletin. October 1956. 23:273, 126–27. review.

Boxoffice. October 15, 1955. 67:25, 1858. review.

Catholic World. December, 1955. 182:1089, 217. Robert Kass. review.

Charlotte Greenwood (2007, McFarland), 211–21. Grant Hayter-Menzies. history-analysis.

Commonweal. October 28, 1955. 63:4, 90–91. Philip T. Hartung. review.

Encyclopedia of the Musical Film (1981, Oxford University Press), 210–11. Stanley Green. history.

Entertainment Weekly. December 23, 1994, 77. Steve Daly. article.

The Entertainment Weekly Guide to the Greatest Movies Ever Made 144. #56. review.

Fred Zinnemann: Films of Character and Conscience (2003, McFarland), 105–10. Neil Sinyard. history-analysis.

Getting to Know Him (1977, Random House), 314–21. Hugh Fordin. history.

The Great Movie Musicals (2010, McFarland), 219–21. Don Tyler. history.

Green Grow the Lilacs (2010, Samuel French), Lynn Riggs. source play.

A History of Movie Musicals: Gotta Sing Gotta Dance (1983, Exeter Books), 268. John Kobal. review.

Hollywood Mother of the Year (1992, Birch Lane Press), 44–58. Sheila MacRae. remembrance.

The Hollywood Musical (1981, Crown), 351. Clive Hirschhorn. review.

The Hollywood Musical (1981, St. Martin's Press), 194. Ethan Mordden. history.

Hollywood Musicals Year by Year (1999, Hal Leonard Corporation), 198–99. Stanley Green. history.

Library Journal. November 1, 1955. 80:19, 2478. Earle F. Walbridge. review.

A Life in the Movies (1992, Scribner), 134–47. Fred Zinnemann. remembrance.

London Times. September 10, 1956. review.

London Times. December 23, 1959. review.

Magill's Survey of Cinema, First Series, Volume 3, Lon-Sca (1980, Salem Press), 1246–48. Leslie Donaldson. review.

The Melody Lingers On (1986, Newmarket Press), 233–35. Roy Hemming. history.

Motion Picture Daily. Charles S. Aaronson. review.

The Motion Picture Guide, N–R (1986, Cinebooks), 2231. Nash-Ross. review.

The Movie Musical (1974, Pyramid Communications), 133. Lee Edward Stern. review.

Musical Stages (2002, Da Capo Press), 283–85. Richard Rodgers. remembrance.

Nation. October 29, 1955. 181:18, 369. Robert Hatch. review.

New York Times. October 11, 1955, 49. Bosley Crowther. review.

New Yorker. October 22, 1955. 31:36, 171–72. John McCarten. review.

Newsweek. October 24, 1955. 46:17, 106. review.

Richard Rodgers (1998, Yale University Press), 224–27. William G. Hyland. history.

Rod Steiger (2000, Fromm International), 91–97. Tom Hitchinson. history.

Rodgers and Hammerstein (1992, Harry N. Abrams), 48–49. Ethan Mordden. history.

Saturday Review. November 5, 1955. 38:45, 27–28. Arthur Knight. review.

Time. October 24, 1955. 66:17, 104, 106. review.

Variety. October 12, 1955. Hift. review.

The Western. 241. Phil Hardy. review.

The Man Who Never Was (1956)

The Age. January 28, 2003. article on identity of title character.

America. February 25, 1956. 94:22, 599–600. Moira Walsh. review.

BFI Monthly Film Bulletin. March 1956. 23:266, 29. review.

Boxoffice. February 11, 1956. 68:16, 1928. review.

Catholic World. April, 1956. 183:1093, 59. Robert Kass. review.

Commonweal. March 30, 1956. 63:26, 663–64. Philip T. Hartung. review.

The Great Spy Pictures (1974, Scarecrow), 287–88. Parish-Pitts. review.

Library Journal. March 1, 1956. 81:5, 627. Earle F. Walbridge. review.

London Times. March 12, 1956. review.

The Motion Picture Guide, L–M (1986, Cinebooks), 1856–57. Nash-Ross. review.

Nation. April 21, 1956. 182:16, 349–50. Robert Hatch. review.

New York Times. April 4, 1956, 24. Bosley Crowther. review.

New Yorker. April 14, 1956. 32:8, 77–78. John McCarten. review.

Newsweek. February 27, 1956. 47:9, 94–95. review.

100 Greatest Spy Movies (2009, Weider History Group), 23. #18 Gene Seymour. review.

Saturday Review. March 17, 1956. 39:11, 27. Hollis Alpert. review.

The Scotsman. October 13, 2004. Mike Theodoulou. article on identity of title character.

Straight From the Horse's Mouth: Ronald Neame, An Autobiography (2003, Scarecrow Press), 146–51. Ronald Neame. remembrance.

Time. March 26, 1956. 67:9, 106, 108. review.

Variety. February 15, 1956. Hift. review.

Ride Out for Revenge (1957)

BFI Monthly Film Bulletin. April 1959. 26:303, 48. review.

Boxoffice. November 23, 1957. 72:5, 2165. review.

The Motion Picture Guide, N–R (Year, Co.), 2609. Nash-Ross review.

Variety. October 23, 1957. Kove. review.

The Western (1983, W. Morrow), 258. Phil Hardy. review.

Western Films (1982, Rawson), 271. Brian Garfield. review.

Western Movies (1986, McFarland), 341. #2789 Michael R. Pitts. review.

Odds Against Tomorrow (1959)

America. October 24, 1959. 102:?, 110–11. Moira Walsh. review.

BFI Monthly Film Bulletin. February 1960. 27:313, 20–21. review.

Blacks in American Film and Television (1988, Garland), 158. Donald Bogle. review.

Boxoffice. October 12, 1959. 75:25, 2368. review.

Commonweal. November 13, 1959. 71:7, 209–10. Philip T. Hartung. review.

Dark City: The Lost World of Film Noir, 146–57. Eddie Muller. review.

Film Noir (2005, Virgin), 237. Eddie Robson. review.

Film Noir: A Comprehensive Illustrated Reference to Movies, Terms and Persons (1995, McFarland), 277. Michael L. Stephens. review.

The Films of Robert Wise (2007, Scarecrow Press), 106–10. Richard C. Keenan. analysis.

Forgotten Films to Remember (1980, Citadel Press), 250. John Springer. review.

Gangster Films (2008, McFarland), 229. Michael L. Stephens. review.

Inside Hollywood. May, 1960. 1:1, 10. article.

London Times. December 23, 1959. review.

More Than Night: Film Noir in Its Contexts (2008, University of California Press), 241–43. James Naremore. review.

Nation. November 28, 1959. 189:18, 408. Robert Hatch. review.

New York Times. October 16, 1959, 27. Bosley Crowther. review.

New Yorker. October 24, 1959. 35:36, 185–86. John McCarten. review.

Newsweek. October 19, 1959. 54:16, 108. review.
Odds Against Tomorrow (1958, Collins). William P. Mc-
Givern. source novel.
Odds Against Tomorrow: The Critical Edition (1999, The
Center for Telecommunication Studies). Abraham
Polonsky screenplay. John Schultheiss. analysis.
Robert Wise on His Films (1995, Silman-James Press),
155–57. Robert Wise. remembrance.
Saturday Review. October 3, 1959 .42:40, 29. Hollis Al-
pert. review.
Shelley II (1990, Pocket Books), 297–99. Shelley Win-
ters. remembrance.
Time. October 29, 1959. 74:17, 59. review.
*A Very Dangerous Citizen: Abraham Lincoln Polonsky
and the Hollywood Left* (2001, University of California
Press), 179–86. Paul Buhle and Dave Wagner. analy-
sis.

Ride Beyond Vengeance (1966) (aka Night of the Tiger)

Chuck Connors: The Man Behind the Rifle (1997, Artist's
Press), 185–92. David Fury. history.
London Times. April 14, 1966. review.
The Motion Picture Guide, N–R (1986, Cinebooks),
2608. Nash-Ross. review.
New York Daily News. September 29, 1966. Ann Guar-
ino. review.
New York Post. September 29, 1966, 65. review.
New York Times. September 29, 1966, 60. Howard
Thompson. review.
New York World Journal Tribune. September 29, 1966.
Judith Crist. review.
The Night of the Tiger (1956, McGraw-Hill). Al Dewlen.
source novel.
Variety. April 27, 1966. Murf. review.
The Western (1983, W. Morrow), 298. Phil Hardy. re-
view.
Western Films (1982, Rawson), 270–71. Brian Garfield.
review.
Western Movies (1986, McFarland), 340. #2779 Michael
R. Pitts. review.

Blood and Lace (1971)

The Motion Picture Guide, A–B (1986, Cinebooks), 239.
Nash-Ross. review.
New York Daily News. March 18, 1971. Ann Guarino. re-
view.
New York Post. March 18, 1971, 42. review.
New York Times. March 18, 1971, 48. A.H. Weiler. re-
view.
Psycho. November 1973, 55. pictorial.
Variety. March 11, 1971. Tone. review.

The Todd Killings (1971)

Cold-Blooded (1996, Feral House). John Gilmore. his-
tory of Charles Schmid.
Cue. October 23, 1971, 74. William Wolf. review.
Life. March 4, 1966. 60:9. Don Moser. article about
Charles Schmid.
The Motion Picture Guide, T–V (1986, Cinebooks),
3476–77. Nash-Ross. review.

New York. October 25, 1971, 73. Judith Crist. review.
New York Daily Mirror. October 22, 1971, 11. Newton
North. review.
New York Daily News. October 21, 1971, 92. Ann Guar-
ino. review.
New York Daily News. October 22, 1971, 72. Rex Reed.
review.
New York Post. October 21, 1971, 46. Frances Herridge.
review.
New York Times. October 21, 1971, 56. Howard H.
Thompson. review.
Variety. August 18, 1971, 15. Robe. review.
Village Voice. November 4, 1971. William Paul. review.
Women's Wear Daily. October 20, 1971, 16. Allan G. Mot-
tus. review.

Chandler (1971)

Cue. March 11, 1972, 4. Donald J. Mayerson. review.
The Great Detective Pictures, 86–87. James Robert Parish
and Michael R. Pitts. review.
The Motion Picture Guide, C–D (1986, Cinebooks), 393.
Nash-Ross. review.
New York Post. March 2, 1972, 24. review.
New York Times. March 2, 1972, 34. Roger Greenspun.
review.
Time. December 27, 1971. 98:26, 49. article.
Variety. December 8, 1971, 20. Murf. review.

The Loners (1972)

The Motion Picture Guide, L–M (1986, Cinebooks),
1715–16. Nash-Ross. review.
Variety. April 26, 1972. Whit. review.

Mansion of the Doomed (1976)

BadMoviePlanet.com. review.
Cult Horror Films (1993, Citadel Press), 159–62. Welch
Everman. analysis.
The Motion Picture Guide, L–M (1986, Cinebooks),
1872–73. Nash-Ross. review.

A Nightingale Sang in Berkeley Square (1979)

Blaggers, Inc. (2008, Pennant Books), 45–99. Terry
Smith history of 1974 bank robbery.
London Times. April 28, 1975, September 23, 1975, June
15, 1976, June 16, 1976, June 18, 1976, November 11,
1976, November 13, 1976, November 17, 1976, June
24, 1977, July 19, 1977, April 26, 1978, November 2,
1981. history of 1974 bank robbery.
London Times. January 23, 1981, August 18, 1982, December 12, 1983. TV listings.
New York Times. April 24, 1975, October 21, 1975. history of 1974 bank robbery.

Chilly Scenes of Winter (1979) (aka Head Over Heels)

Chilly Scenes of Winter (1976, Doubleday). Ann Beattie.
source novel.

Christian Science Monitor. October 29, 1979, 19. David Sterritt. review.

Cult Movies 3 (1988, Fireside), 57–61. Danny Peary. review.

East Side Express. October 25, 1979, 7. Martin A. Jackson. review.

The Entertainment Weekly Guide to the Greatest Movies Ever Made 247. review.

The Films of the Seventies (1984, McFarland), 131–32. #377. Marc Sigoloff. review.

Macleans. November 19, 1979. 92:47, 64, 66. Lawrence O'Toole. review.

The Motion Picture Guide, C–D (1986, Cinebooks), 415. Nash-Ross. review.

Nation. November 6, 1982. 235:15, 474, 476. Robert Hatch. review.

New Leader. November 19, 1979. 62:22, 23–24. Robert Asahina. review.

New West. November 19, 1979, 146–47. Stephen Farber. review.

New York. October 29, 1979. 12:42, 50–52. Mary A. Fischer. history.

New York. November 5, 1979. 12:43, 85–86. David Denby. review.

New York Daily News. October 19, 1979. Rex Reed. review.

New York Post. October 19, 1979, 35. Archer Winsten. review.

New York Post. August 13, 1982. Archer Winsten. review.

New York Times. October 19, 1979, C-12. Vincent Canby. review.

New Yorker. November 26, 1979. 55:41, 172, 174. Renata Adler. review.

Progressive. November, 1982. 46:11, 54. Michael H. Seitz. review.

Rolling Stone. September 30, 1982. #379 60, 63. Michael Sragow. review.

Soho Weekly News. October 25, 1979, 23–24. Stephen Saban. review.

Time. November 5, 1979. 114:19, 98. John Skow. review.

Variety. October 24, 1979, 17. Cart. review.

Village Voice. October 29, 1979, 45. Andrew Sarris. review.

Melvin and Howard (1980)

Christian Century. July 15–22, 1981. 98:23, 746. Gerald E. Forshey. review.

Christian Science Monitor. October 2, 1980, 19. David Skerritt. review.

East Side Express. November 13, 1980, 15. John Azzopardi. review.

Film Comment. September-October, 1980. 16:5, 56–59. Jonathan Demme. interview.

Film Quarterly. Fall, 1982 36:1, 32–40. Lucy Fischer. analysis.

Hollywood Talks Turkey: The Screen's Greatest Flops (1989, Faber & Faber), 109. Mary Steenburgen. remembrance.

Horizon. December, 1980. 23:12, 70, 72. Diane Jacobs. review.

Ladies' Home Journal. February 1981. 98:2, 18. Gene Shalit. review.

London Observer. May 17, 1981, 30. Philip French. review.

London Times. May 15, 1981. David Robinson. review.

Magill's Survey of Cinema, 1982 Annual (1982, Salem Press), 453–57. Frederick Travers. review.

The Motion Picture Guide, L–M (1986, Cinebooks), 1926. Nash-Ross. review.

Nation. November 15, 1980. 231:16, 524. Robert Hatch. review.

National Review. June 12, 1981. 33:11, 680–82. John Simon. review.

New Republic. November 8, 1980. 183:19, 22. Stanley Kauffmann. review.

New York. November 3, 1980. 13:43, 80–81. David Denby. review.

New York Daily News. September 26, 1980, 3. Rex Reed. review.

New York Daily News. October 17, 1980, 5. Kathleen Carroll. review.

New York Post. September 26, 1980, 39. Archer Winsten. review.

New York Times. September 26, 1980, C-32. Vincent Canby. review.

New York Times. October 24, 1980. Judy Klemesrud. article.

New Yorker. October 13, 1980. 56:34, 174, 178, 180, 183–84. Pauline Kael. review.

Newsweek. September 29, 1980. 96:13, 78. Charles Michener. review.

Oscar A to Z (1995, Doubleday), 546. #1300 Charles Matthews. history.

Playboy. February, 1981. 28:2, 36. Bruce Williamson. review.

Progressive. January, 1981. 45:1, 48–49. Michael H. Seitz. review.

Rolling Stone. March 19, 1981. #339, 43, 45. Michael Sragow. review.

Soho Weekly News. October 1, 1980, 17. Veronica Geng. review.

Soho Weekly News. October 22, 1980, 41–42. Seth Cagin. review.

Time. October 20, 1980. 116:16, 90. Richard Schickel. review.

Variety. September 10, 1980, 30. Cart. review.

Village Voice. September 24, 1980, 47. Andrew Sarris. review.

Village Voice. October 15, 1980, 56. Stuart Byron. review.

The Nesting (1981)

The Motion Picture Guide, N–R (1986, Cinebooks), 2120. Nash-Ross. review.

Tesco.net. review.

Variety. April 29, 1981. Lor. review.

Escape (1971, TV Movie)

The ABC Movie of the Week Companion (2005, iUniverse), 31. Michael Karol. review.

TV Guide. April 3–9, 1971. 19:14, A-49. TV listing.

Black Noon (1971, TV Movie)

Television Fright Films of the 1970s (2007, McFarland), 13–15. David Deal. review.

TV Guide. October 30–November 5, 1971. 19:44, A-64–A-65. TV listing.
Variety. November 10, 1971. Bok. review.

The Girl on the Late, Late Show (1974, TV Movie)

Hollywood on Hollywood (1978, Scarecrow), 121–22. Parish-Pitts-Mank. review.
TV Guide. March 30–April 5, 1974. 22:13, #1096 A-46. TV listing.
Variety. April 10, 1974. Mick. review.

Rich Man, Poor Man (1976, TV Miniseries)

Rich Man, Poor Man (1976, Dell), Irwin Shaw. source novel.
Total Television (1996, Penguin), 695. 4th Edition Alex McNeil. history.
TV Guide. January 31–March 13, 1976. 24:5–11 #1192–98. TV listings.

Seventh Avenue (1977, TV Miniseries)

Total Television 88. Alex McNeil. history.
TV Guide. February 5–19, 1977. 25:6–8. TV listings.
Variety. February 10, 1977. Fob. review.

The Dancing Princesses (1979)

The Stage and Television Today. March 22, 1979, 20. review.
TV Times. March 17–23, 1979, 20–21. TV listings.

The Merry Wives of Windsor (1979)

Shakespeare on Screen (1990, Neal-Schuman Publishers) 186. #383 Kenneth S. Rothwell–Annabelle Henkin Melzer. review.

Shakespeare on Television (1988, University Press of New England), 270. J. C. Bulman–H. R. Coursen. review.
ShakespeareSocietyofAmerica.org. history.

Mr. Griffin and Me (1981, TV Special)

TV Guide. January 10–16, 1981. TV listing.

Obituaries and Post-Death Profiles

London Times. October 8, 1981.
Macleans. October 19, 1981. 94:?, 4.
Magill's Survey of Cinema, 1982 Annual (1982, Salem Press), 488.
New York Times. October 8, 1981, B-10.
New York Times Biography Service October 1981, 1356.
Newsweek. October 19, 1981. 98:?, 111.
Reading Eagle. October 18, 1981, 16. Jim George. profile.
Screen World 1982 Annual (1982, Crown), V.33 234.
Time. October 19, 1981. 118:?, 95.

Magazine Product Advertisements and Beauty Features

Motion Picture. November 1952, 57. Feature "Festive Fashions."
Screenland. June 1945, 16, 60. Josephine Felts feature "Makeup for Career Girls."
Screenland. February 1946, 16. Josephine Felts feature "Your Lovely Hair."

Bibliography

Books

Andrew, Geoff. *The Films of Nicholas Ray*. London: BFI, 2004.

Curcio, Vincent. *Suicide Blonde*. New York: William Morrow, 1989.

Eisenschitz, Bernard. *Nicholas Ray: An American Journey*. London: Faber & Faber, 1996.

Frascella, Lawrence, and Al Weisel. *Live Fast, Die Young*. New York: Touchstone, 2005.

Hagen, Ray. *Killer Tomatoes*. Jefferson, NC: McFarland, 2004.

Hannsberry, Karen Burroughs. *Femme Noir: Bad Girls of Film*. Jefferson, NC: McFarland, 1998.

Kobal, John. *Gods and Goddesses of the Movies*. New York: Crescent, 1974.

Marill, Alvin H. *Movies Made for Television*. New York: Da Capo, 1980.

Monush, Barry. *The Encyclopedia of Hollywood Film Actors*. New York: Applause, 2003.

Moore, Diana. *American National Biography*. New York: Oxford University Press, 1999.

Naremore, James. *More Than Night: Film Noir in Its Contexts*. Berkeley: University of California Press, 1998.

Nash, Jay Robert, and Stanley Ralph Ross. *The Motion Picture Guide*. New York: Cinebooks, 1986.

Parish, James Robert, and Ronald L. Bowers. *The MGM Stock Company: The Golden Era*. New Rochelle, NY: Arlington House, 1973.

Peary, Danny. *Cult Movie Stars*. New York: Fireside, 1991.

Quinlan, David. *Wicked Women of the Screen*. New York: St. Martin's Press, 1987.

Ray, Nicholas. *I Was Interrupted*. Berkeley: University of California Press, 1995.

Reed, Rex. *People Are Crazy Here*. New York: Dell, 1974.

Shipman, David. *The Great Movie Stars 2: The International Years*. Boston: Little, 1995.

Stephens, Michael L. *Film Noir: A Comprehensive Illustrated Reference to Movies, Terms and Persons*. Jefferson, NC: McFarland, 1995.

Terenzio, Maurice, Scott MacGillivray, and Ted Okuda. *The Soundies Distributing Corporation of America*. Jefferson, NC: McFarland, 1991.

Thomson, David. *The New Biographical Dictionary of Film*. New York: Alfred A. Knopf, 2002.

Turner, Peter. *Film Stars Don't Die in Liverpool*. New York: Grove Press, 1986.

Periodicals and Newspapers

The Age, America, American Film, American Heritage, American Movie Classics Magazine, Baltimore Sun, Boxoffice, British Film Institute's Monthly Film Bulletin, Catholic World, Christian Century, Christian Science Monitor, Commonweal, Cosmopolitan, Cue, East Side Express, Entertainment Weekly, Estimates, Film Comment, Film Culture, Film Daily, Film History, Film Quarterly, Film Reader, Filmbobbery, Films and Filming, Films in Review, Films of the Golden Age, Holiday, Hollywood Studio Magazine, Horizon, Inside Hollywood, Interview, Ladies' Home Journal, Library Journal, Life, Literature / Film Quarterly, London Observer, London Times, Look, Macleans, Modern Maturity, Motion Picture, Motion Picture Daily, Movie Time, Nation, National Review, New Leader, New Republic, New Statesman, New West, New York, New York Daily Mirror, New York Daily News, New York Herald Tribune, New York Journal American, New York Post, New York Times, New York World Journal Tribune, New Yorker, Newsweek, People, Photoplay, Playboy, PM, Progressive, Psycho, Reader's Digest, Reading Eagle, Redbook, Rolling Stone, Saturday Review, The Scotsman, Screen Facts, Screen Guide, Screen Writer, Screenland, Sight and Sound, Silver Screen, Soho Weekly News, The Stage and Television Today, Theatre Arts, Time, TV Guide, TV Times, Variety, Village Voice, Washington Post, Washington Star, Women's Wear Daily.

Internet Sources

Internet Movie Database, www.imdb.com.

Silver Screen Actresses, www.silverscreenactresses.com.

Turner Classic Movies, www.turnerclassicmovies.com.

Index

Titles in **bold italics** are Gloria Grahame's films, telefilms and short films.
Page numbers in **bold italics** indicate photographs or artwork.